Brief Contents

Detailed Contents

Companion Website

Want to know more? Review what you have been learning by visiting: **https://study.sagepub.com/harding**

For Students:

SAGE Videos – Watch two videos which have been selected from the SAGE Video collection to assist you with your learning.

Podcasts – Discover the realities of policing through this series of podcasts where Neil, of Northumbria Police and London's Metropolitan Police Service, shares his experiences and insights.

Essay Questions – Use the five essay questions in each chapter to prepare for exams and essays.

Multiple Choice Quiz – Take this quiz to test your understanding of the key concepts covered in each chapter.

Acknowledgements

This book has involved a number of people who have worked hard to enable it to become reality rather than a gleam in the eye of Sage.

First, we are, of course, very grateful to our contributors. They have kept to the deadlines we have imposed and responded to our queries with patience and goodhumour. It may be a cliché, but without them there would have been no book.

Second, the support and encouragement from Sage has been everything we could have wished for. Natalie Aguilera, Amy Jarrold and George Knowles have been a wonderful editorial team in every way.

Last, there are our long-suffering families who have put up with the demands of our working on the book with considerable patience; how many weekends have been ruined by the claim 'I can't really spare the time as I have to do some work on the book'? Jamie would like to thank all of his family, particularly Allison for her constant support and invaluable advice, and Callan and Corryn for all the reminders of what matters most, e.g. the 'Who stole the food?' game. Pam says sorry to Damian for getting the answerphone, to Rory and Callum for lag on the Xbox and thank you to Jonny – two heads are better than one – proofreading by reading out loud (rol) can be fun! George wishes to thank Carmel for her unfailing love, and Ruth, Ethan, Sophie and Thomas for having grown up into relatively normal human beings.

Contributors

Tim Bateman is Reader in Youth Justice at the University of Bedfordshire.

Charlotte Bilby is Reader in Criminology in the Department of Social Sciences at Northumbria University.

Hannah Bows is a Senior Lecturer in Criminology and Sociology in the School of Social Sciences, Business and Law at Teesside University.

Joanne Clough is a Senior Lecturer in the School of Law at Northumbria University and is a practising Solicitor-Advocate.

Bankole Cole is Reader in Criminology and Human Rights in the Department of Law and Criminology, Sheffield Hallam University.

Ian R. Cook is a Senior Lecturer in Social Sciences, in the Department of Social Sciences at Northumbria University.

Pamela Davies is Associate Professor in the Department of Social Sciences at Northumbria University.

Matthew Hall is Professor of Law and Criminal Justice, School of Law, University of Lincoln.

Jamie Harding is a Senior Lecturer in Research Methods in the Department of Social Sciences at Northumbria University.

Mike Hough is a Visiting Professor at the School of Law, Birkbeck, University of London, and was previously Director of the Institute for Criminal Policy Research.

Alison Howey is a Senior Lecturer on the Bar Professional Training Course (BPTC) in the Faculty of Business and Law at Northumbria University and a practising Barrister.

Matt Jones is a Lecturer in Criminology in the Department of Social Sciences at Northumbria University.

Mary Laing is a Senior Lecturer in Criminology in the Department of Social Sciences at Northumbria University.

Ian Mahoney is a Lecturer in Criminology in the Department of Social Science at Liverpool Hope University.

George Mair is Professor of Criminal Justice and Head of the Department of Social Science at Liverpool Hope University.

Ian Marsh is a Principal Lecturer in Criminology in the Department of Social Science at Liverpool Hope University.

Tim Newburn is Professor of Criminology and Social Policy in the Department of Social Policy and Mannheim Centre for the Study of Criminology and Criminal Justice, London School of Economics and Political Science.

Timi Osidipe is a Lecturer in Criminology at the University of Bedfordshire.

Harriet Pierpoint is Reader in Criminology at the Criminal Justice Centre for Criminology, University of South Wales.

Mike Rowe is Professor of Criminology in the Department of Social Sciences at Northumbria University.

Kelly Stockdale is a Lecturer in Criminology in the Department of Social Sciences at Northumbria University.

Esther F.J.C. van Ginneken is an Assistant Professor in Criminology at Leiden University in the Netherlands.

Colin Webster is Professor of Criminology in the School of Social Sciences at Leeds Beckett University.

Tanya Wyatt is Reader in Criminology in the Department of Social Sciences at Northumbria University.

List of Abbreviations

ACPS	Advisory Council on the Penal System
ACTO	Advisory Council on the Treatment of Offenders
AG	Attorney General
ASBOs	Anti-Social Behaviour Orders
BME	Black and Minority Ethnic
CACD	Court of Appeal (Criminal Division)
CCRC	Criminal Cases Review Commission
CCTV	Closed Circuit Television
CDA	Crime and Disorder Act
CICB	Criminal Injuries Compensation Board
CICS	Criminal Injuries Compensation Scheme
CJA	Criminal Justice Act
CNA	Certified Normal Accommodation (the figure that each prison was originally designated to hold)
CO	Community Order
COP	Community Orientated Policing
CPS	Crown Prosecution Service
CPTED	Crime Prevention Through Environmental Design
CRC	Community Rehabilitation Company
CRP	Crime Reduction Programme
CSP	Community Safety Partnership
CSR	Comprehensive Spending Review
CYPA	Children and Young Persons Act
DPP	Director of Public Prosecutions
DTO	Detention and Training Order
EU	European Union
FDR	Fast Delivery Report
FMI	Financial Management Initiative
FTEs	First-time Entrants
HMIC	Her Majesty's Inspectorate of Constabulary
HMIP	Her Majesty's Inspectorate of Prisons
HMP	Her Majesty's Prison

IEP	Incentives and Earned Privileges Scheme
IPCC	Independent Police Complaints Commission
IPP	Imprisonment for Public Protection
ISVA	Independent Sexual Violence Advisor
KPIs	Key Performance Indicators
LACS	League Against Cruel Sports
MAPPA	Multi-agency Public Protection Arrangements
MCA	Member Case Assessment
MoJ	Ministry of Justice
NDPB	Non-departmental Public Body
NGO	Non-governmental Organisation
NPS	National Probation Service
NOMS	National Offender Management Service
NUM	National Ugly Mugs
NWCU	National Wildlife Crime Unit
ONS	Office of National Statistics
PACE	Police and Criminal Evidence Act (1984)
PAW UK	Partnership for Action Against Wildlife Crime in the UK
PbR	Payment by Results
PCA	Police Complaints Authority
PCB	Police Complaints Board
PCCs	Police and Crime Commissioners
PCSO	Police Community Support Officer
PFI	Private Finance Initiative (PFI)
POP	Problem Orientated Policing
PPO	Prisons and Probation Ombudsman
PRC	Police Recorded Crime
PRT	Prison Reform Trust
PSD	Professional Standards Department
PSR	Pre-sentence Report
RSPB	Royal Society for the Protection of Birds
SCH	Secure Children's Home
SOCA	Serious Organised Crime Agency
SNOP	Statement of National Objectives and Priorities
SSO	Suspended Sentence Order
STC	Secure Training Centre
TIP	Trafficking in Persons
TR	Transforming Rehabilitation
UN	United Nations
UNCRC	UN Convention on the Rights of the Child
VAC	Voluntary Aftercare
VCSE	Voluntary, Community and Social Enterprise
VPS	Victim Personal Statement
YJB	Youth Justice Board

YJCEA	Youth Justice and Criminal Evidence Act (1999)
YOI	Young Offender Institution
YOP	Youth Offender Panel
YOT	Youth Offending Team
YRO	Youth Rehabilitation Order

1 Introduction

Pamela Davies, George Mair, Jamie Harding

One of the very first serious points for consideration in putting together our ideas for this book from the outset was the title. We unanimously agreed on *An Introduction to Criminal Justice* and are proud to have this on the front cover. However, behind this title, and as evident in the competitor titles from other publishers, sit a range of other potential and similar titles, including variations on the themes of '*The Criminal Process*', '*Criminal Justice*' and '*The Criminal Justice System*'. We felt it important not to wed ourselves to a label that foregrounded the contents as driven by considerations of criminal justice as a 'system' or as a 'process'. There are problems with both formulations. A system implies a group of closely related parts that work together efficiently with little outside interference; a process is a series of actions that flow towards a planned outcome with a clear beginning and end. Neither term quite captures what criminal justice is and does, though process is probably the more accurate. Both terms will be used in this chapter and later by our contributors.

Another serious consideration, admittedly towards the end of our editorial journey in compiling this book, was the front cover. In considering images we were anxious to ensure that the cover design fitted with the title of the book and that both give a true reflection of the book's content and do not convey a false impression of the text to would-be readers. We rejected one of the first mock-ups which superimposed our title on a background picture of a lawyer's/judge's wig. For us this was a non-starter. The book is not about the legal system, nor is it a law textbook. We settled on a more abstract and, as Natalie Aguilera from Sage put it, 'Hitchcock-inspired' cover.

We make these introductory points as a segue for illustrating the distinctiveness of this publication. Under this title and within the pages between the covers, what we have engineered is a book that is more than the sum of its parts. *An Introduction to Criminal Justice* contains within it a set of chapters that outline and reflect upon policy, practice, research and theoretical developments in the field of criminal justice. Each of these chapters is brought alive by their authors who draw on their research-rich biographies. In compiling this book, and in bringing these contributions together, we have produced a comprehensive text that is infused with wisdoms drawn from scholars adopting various combinations of historical, socio-legal and politico-economic analyses. The remainder of this introductory chapter continues to enlighten the reader about the rationale for the book. We elaborate on the above and convey our aims and ambitions in devising a text aimed at undergraduate students of criminology, criminal justice studies and related programmes. The chapter provides an overview of the content and outlines how we have chosen to organise the contents of the book into three constitutive parts.

Finally, one of the most important elements of this introduction is the inclusion of an overarching timeline of criminal justice since 1945 to date. This overview of the key developments in criminal justice in England and Wales since the end of the Second World War highlights a lengthy list of landmark developments or events that have been significant in respect of criminal justice as we move from the twentieth to the twenty-first century. As Mair notes in Chapter 2, the pace of change accelerates rapidly from the early 1990s and each of the chapters in the volume discusses developments that feature on this timeline.

An Introduction to Criminal Justice

As we have begun to establish above, the book is focused on criminal justice rather than criminology and the rationale for this book is to bring together a wealth of contemporary knowledge and thinking about matters concerning criminal justice in England and Wales. We do so with the aim of exposing undergraduates of criminology and/or criminal justice studies degrees to a range of scholarship that is research rich yet eminently accessible. Our ambition is to captivate new generations of students early in their studies, to enthuse them to be inquisitive and questioning in their journey towards independent criminological thought and in our ambitions for them to become collegiate forward-thinking practitioners as well as imaginative scholars and researchers. Criminology as an academic field of study has expanded enormously in the last 30 years, but we would contend that at its heart lies criminal justice – the agencies, institutions, processes and procedures that deal with victims, offenders and offending. If criminology were to lose touch with this central focus it would lose its way and while we are in no way trying to delimit criminology's field, we make no apologies for making criminal justice the centre of our attention. Students studying criminology (or criminal justice, or police studies, etc.) need to have a thorough grounding in how the criminal justice process operates and this book aims to deliver this knowledge.

In claiming the book is 'more than the sum of its parts' – i.e. more than a collection of separate and discrete individual chapters, which a cursory glance at the contents pages may indicate – we take the opportunity early in this book to persuade the reader to visit these chapters as part of a package, assembled coherently. When the book is used in this way, we hope it will be evident that the book gathers a momentum in establishing that a comprehensive criminological understanding of criminal justice begins with an understanding as signposted by this text as a whole. In this way we anticipate the book will be a unique teaching resource. We now commence the job we have set ourselves, to tackle practical and normative issues in the Criminal Justice System. That system is to be imagined in the widest possible sense – to include an increasing plethora of agencies and institutions (the book incorporates chapters that focus on the police and multi-agency partners, prosecution and the courts, prisons and parole) that are subsumed under the umbrella 'Criminal Justice System'. The 21 substantive chapters sandwiched between this introduction and the concluding chapter variously explore criminal processes and procedures and how 'the system' deals with those who are channelled into it. It thus examines criminal justice *agencies* and *institutions* as well as 'agency' in the criminal justice process. Thus our examination of criminal justice goes beyond mere description of what a state system of justice is, and what its constitutive components traditionally have been and contemporarily are. The text provides the basic overviews of these agencies and institutions, past and present and, in our final chapter we also ponder their futures. However, we have required our contributors to address the main points of debate and contention in matters of criminal justice. These issues and debates might sometimes be rooted in philosophical thought or epistemological differences of opinion, in different political or ethical values. They may be contemplated from different standpoints or through different lenses from which the system and processes of justice are viewed. Such perspectives may be legal, moral or criminological and, at other times, the starting point for the assessment might be victimological. This has given rise to a rich, varied and sometimes partisan analysis, but always a contribution that is thorough, authoritative, and imbued with the most up-to-date examples and references.

The above has guaranteed that a number of major themes run throughout the pages of the book. One example is the place of the victim in matters of criminal justice. The victim has slowly emerged as an increasingly important feature in criminal justice policy making and as a driver for change. As with other incremental developments and shifts in criminal justice focus however, some have questioned whose interests are being served (Duggan and Heap, 2014). Such questions are criminologically and victimologically important and a range of chapters, particularly in Part 2 of the book consider inequalities in criminal justice. In these chapters we find that the distinctions between victims and offenders often become blurred when justice, fairness and equality are the lens through which we consider the effectiveness of criminal justice practices and procedures. Questions of bias, prejudice, inequality, and injustice begin to emerge in Chapters 5 and 6 raising further questions that some of the later contributions take into consideration, especially in Part 3 where crime and harm, deprivations and human rights (see Chapter 22) enter the analysis of criminal justice. The latter set of concerns sees another recurring feature within the book – the connections between criminal justice within and between sovereign states and the interconnections between the global and the supra-national, the European, national, regional and local. These are big criminal justice questions that the book, though pitched at level 4 undergraduates, taps into in an accessible yet scholarly way. The book encourages the novice scholar to be aware of the importance and significance of the temporal and the episodic, of pendulum swings (for example welfare v. justice, see Chapter 18), of moments of crisis and the signal or trigger events (e.g. the murder of two-year-old James Bulger in Liverpool in 1993, which opened the way for a more punitive approach to criminal justice; see Chapters 2 and 18). At the start of several of the chapters we have provided shorter timelines of key developments in recognition of the importance of some key landmark points in time which are sometimes represented by dates when legislation was enacted and sometimes when key reports or inquiries were published following major inquiries or reviews.

While we have encouraged these big themes to emerge, we have maintained a consistency of approach within each of the chapters. There are common features that help readers engage more swiftly with what may seem challenging content. Each chapter has:

- an introduction that clearly sets out the chapter's purpose and scope;
- a summary reminding the reader of the key points;
- a case study/studies and/or summary of recent research;
- an annotated list of further reading, both academic and web sources where appropriate, for readers who wish to explore further the topics covered in each chapter;
- discussion questions/suggested exercises.

We have also encouraged contributors to include where appropriate, a critical commentary arising from different perspectives on the criminal justice process, an outline of the historical background to the element of the process that is foregrounded and a discussion of the key current issues. Inequalities are thus often a feature of the discussion and we have ensured that the challenges and disadvantages faced by people with mental health problems are also represented (see Chapter 5).

How the Book is Organised

As noted above, the book is organised into three parts – Part One: The Criminal Justice Process in Context; Part Two: The Criminal Justice Process; and Part Three: Key Issues in Criminal Justice. The first part sets a context for the discussion of processes and experiences that are examined in some detail in Part Two. Criminal justice, as already flagged, is identified as a contested terrain and this is illustrated by exploring different models and perspectives that have been preferred, popularised and politically championed at various points in history and contemporarily. The adversarial nature of the criminal justice process of England and Wales is explained, together with key historical developments and milestones that have shaped the contemporary nature of this process in England and Wales.

Historical developments and milestones are a logical place to commence discussing criminal justice. Looking back in time at key landmark developments and simultaneously pointing out the ways in which criminal justice has traditionally been defined and conceptualised is a useful exercise in which to engage students at the start of an introductory module on criminal justice. These are foundational matters in the study of criminal justice. Knowing these contexts informs the ways in which policy, practice, research and theorising will continue to develop into the twenty-first century. Historical understandings are crucial if we are to fully appreciate the present. Future trajectories of criminal justice including its significance and relevance for government and the general public are in part shaped by past experiences. Emerging patterns and key themes such as the expanding criminal justice process, modernisation, penetration of the voluntary and private sectors in matters of criminal justice, risk and accountability are all made sense of through having a comprehensive appreciation of criminal justice and the criminal justice process in context.

Those who work within and those who come into contact with the Criminal Justice System have been the subject of much criminological, and more recently victimological, work. Much criminological research has focused on the clientele that are processed through the Criminal Justice System. No criminal justice textbook would be complete without a significant focus on those who experience the Criminal Justice System – whether as alleged perpetrators, offenders, victims and/or witnesses. In a run of eight chapters this first part of the book thus provides a comprehensive foundation for the study of the criminal justice process.

This book deals with criminal justice in England and Wales, rather than all of the United Kingdom. As McAra (2008: 481) notes, it is inappropriate to subsume Scotland in a United Kingdom-wide discussion, because Scotland has a separate justice and penal system from that of England and Wales, and also a distinctive history in terms of crime control. We recommend reading about criminal justice in Scotland elsewhere (e.g. Croall et al., 2016). The political history of Northern Ireland has had major impacts on many aspects of criminal justice, with the change from the Royal Ulster Constabulary to the Police Service of Northern Ireland being a major element of the peace process. The unique role of the Maze prison (see, for example, McKittrick and McVea, 2012) is also a distinctive feature of Northern Ireland's historical legacy and community safety presents particular challenges in a society that has seen such radical changes (Brunger, 2012). It is for these reasons, in addition to the powers of the Northern Ireland Executive over criminal justice policy, that the situation in Northern Ireland is not covered in this book. Instead, the focus is on placing criminal justice in England and Wales into its unique historical and socio-legal context. We trust that you will find it a helpful and illuminating discussion.

Criminal Justice Since 1945: A timeline

1945 **Labour win general election (5 July)**

1946 Police Act

Dogs introduced experimentally by the Metropolitan Police

1948 Criminal Justice Act

Arrival at Tilbury docks of the *Empire Windrush* from Jamaica

Opening of National Police College

1949 Royal Commission on Capital Punishment set up

Legal Aid and Advice Act

1950 **Labour win general election (23 February)**

Timothy Evans hanged (10 Rillington Place)

1951 **Conservatives win general election (25 October)**

1953 Derek Bentley hanged

John Christie hanged (10 Rillington Place)

1955 **Conservatives win general election (26 May)**

First episode of *Dixon of Dock Green* (last episode 1976)

Ruth Ellis hanged

1956 Suez crisis

1957 Homicide Act

Home Office Research Unit formed

ACTO report 'Alternatives to Short Terms of Imprisonment'

1958 Street disturbances involving racial violence in Notting Hill and Nottingham

1959 **Conservatives win general election (8 October)**

Mental Health Act

Obscene Publications Act

White Paper 'Penal Practice in a Changing Society'

ACTO report 'The Treatment of Young Offenders'

Royal Commission on the Police set up

1960 ACTO report 'Corporal Punishment'

Cornish Committee on the Prevention and Detection of Crime established (reported 1965)

Royal Commission on the Police (reported 1962)

1961   Criminal Justice Act

Suicide Act

Special Patrol Group Unit formed in Metropolitan Police

1962   Royal Commission on the Police

ACTO report 'Non-Residential Treatment of Offenders'

1963   Prison Commission (1877 Prison Act) abolished and replaced by the Prison Department

Children and Young Persons Act (CYPA)

Great Train Robbery

National Crime Prevention Centre set up

1964   **Labour win general election (15 October)**

Mary Whitehouse begins her clean-up TV campaign (mutates into the National Viewers' and Listeners' Association)

White Paper 'The War Against Crime in England and Wales'

'The Sentence of the Court' (1st edn)

The Longford report 'Crime: A challenge to us all'

Kilbrandon report (Scotland)

Criminal Procedure (Insanity) Act

Police Act

Drugs (Prevention of Misuse) Act

Royal Commission on the Penal System set up (never reported)

Last executions in the UK

Criminal Injuries Compensation Board (CICB) set up to administer the Criminal Injuries Compensation Scheme (CICS) for victims of violent crime

Legal Aid extended to criminal cases

1965   Murder (Abolition of Death Penalty) Act

White Paper 'The Child, the Family and the Young Offender'

1966   **Labour win general election (31 March)**

Mountbatten Report

Race Relations Act

1967   Criminal Justice Act

Abortion Act

Sexual Offences Act

Dangerous Drugs Act

1968   Firearms Act

Theatres Act – abolition of theatrical censorship

Criminal Appeal Act

White Paper 'Children in Trouble'

Enoch Powell's 'rivers of blood' speech

1969   Children and Young Persons Act

Divorce Reform Act

1970   **Conservatives win general election (18 June)**

Equal Pay Act

ACPS report 'Detention Centres'

ACPS report 'Non-Custodial and Semi-Custodial Penalties' (the Wootton report)

1971   Misuse of Drugs Act

Courts Act

1972   Road Traffic Act

Criminal Justice Act

Erin Pizzey opens the first refuge for victims of domestic violence in Chiswick

1973   Community service orders introduced on a pilot basis

1974   Three-day week

Labour win general election (28 February – minority government)

Labour win general election (10 October)

IRA bombings in the UK (Birmingham, Guildford, Woolwich)

Robert Martinson 'What Works: Questions and answers about prison reform'

Juries Act

Prevention of Terrorism Act

Control of Pollution Act

Rehabilitation of Offenders Act

Introduction of the Police National Computer (project approved in 1969)

ACPS report 'Young Adult Offenders' (the Younger report)

First Victim Support project set up in Bristol

1976   Bail Act

Police Act

First UK Rape Crisis Centre opened in London

1977   Criminal Law Act

Police Complaints Board created

1978   Inner Urban Areas Act

Consumer Safety Act

Expenditure Committee report 'Reduction of Pressure on the Prison System'

1979   Winter of discontent

Conservatives win general election (3 May)

May Committee report

1980   Magistrates' Courts Act

Prison Inspectorate established

1981   Scarman report on the Brixton riots

Contempt of Court Act

Royal Commission on Criminal Procedure

Home Affairs Committee report 'The Prison Service'

1982   Criminal Justice Act

First British Crime Survey

First Neighbourhood Watch scheme introduced

1983   **Conservatives win general election (9 June)**

Mental Health Act

Home Office Crime Prevention Unit formed

HO Circular 114/83 'Manpower, Effectiveness and Efficiency in the Police Service' (FMI principles imposed on the police)

1984   Police and Criminal Evidence Act (PACE)

HO Circular 8/84 'Crime Prevention'

1985   Prosecution of Offences Act

Police Complaints Authority replaced the Police Complaints Board

1986   Public Order Act

Crown Prosecution Service begins work

Drug Trafficking Offences Act

Childline established

The Islington Crime Survey

1987   **Conservatives win general election (11 June)**

First Domestic Violence Unit established in London (Tottenham)

1988	Criminal Justice Act
	Legal Aid Act
	Road Traffic Act
	Green Paper 'Punishment, Custody and the Community'
	Safer Cities programme launched
1989	Children Act
1990	White Paper 'Crime, Justice and Protecting the Public'
	Strangeways riot (and in 25 other prisons)
	Criminal Justice (International Cooperation) Act
	Victims' Charter
1991	Criminal Justice Act
	Woolf Report on the Strangeways riot
	Criminal Procedure (Insanity and Unfitness to Plead) Act
	Home Office Standing Conference on Crime Prevention report published (Morgan report)
	Launch of the Citizen's Charter
	The UK became a signatory to the UN Convention on the Rights of the Child (UNCRC)
1992	**Conservatives win general election (9 April)**
	Formation of the National Criminal Intelligence Service (NCIS)
	National Standards for the Probation Service
	Wolds Remand Prison opened – the first private prison in Britain
1993	James Bulger murdered
	Stephen Lawrence murdered
	Michael Howard becomes Home Secretary
	Royal Commission on Criminal Justice
	Bail (Amendment) Act
	Criminal Justice Act
	Sheehy report on the police service
	Prison Service becomes an executive agency of the Home Office
1994	Sexual Offences Act
	Criminal Justice and Public Order Act
	Police and Magistrates' Courts Act
	First Prisons Ombudsman appointed

1995   Criminal Appeal Act created the Criminal Cases Review Commission

Learmont report on prison security

Posen report on the police

Incentives and Earned Privileges Scheme introduced in prisons

1996   Criminal Procedure and Investigations Act

Security Services Act

Audit Commission report 'Misspent Youth'

1997   **Labour win general election (1 May)**

Firearms (Amendment) Act

Protection from Harassment Act

Sex Offenders Act

Crime (Sentences) Act

White Paper 'No More Excuses'

Police Act

Social Exclusion Unit established

1998   White Paper 'Modernising Justice'

Consultation paper 'Joining Forces to Protect the Public'

Crime and Disorder Act

Human Rights Act (came into force October 2000)

1999   Access to Justice Act

Criminal Cases Review (Insanity) Act

Youth Justice and Criminal Evidence Act

Greater London Authority Act

Local Government Act

Publication of the Macpherson report into the Stephen Lawrence investigation

Launch of the 'Equal Treatment Bench Book' by the Lord Chancellor and Lord Chief Justice

Replacement of the Police Disciplinary Code with the Code of Conduct

Launch of Working Families Tax Credit

2000   Criminal Justice and Court Services Act

Powers of Criminal Courts (Sentencing) Act

Race Relations (Amendment) Act

2001   **Labour win general election (7 June)**

'Review of the Criminal Courts in England and Wales' (the Auld report)

'Making Punishments Work' (the Halliday review of the sentencing framework)

National Probation Service begins work

Anti-terrorism, Crime and Security Act

Criminal Justice and Police Act

Criminal Defence Service (Advice and Assistance) Act

International Criminal Court Act

Private Security Industry Act (established the Security Industry Authority)

White Paper 'Policing a New Century: A blueprint for reform'

Establishment of the Commission for Judicial Appointments

Victim Personal Statements (VPS) introduced

2002   Police Reform Act

Proceeds of Crime Act

White Paper 'Justice for All'

ACPO introduce the National Crime Recording Standard

2003   White Paper 'Respect and Responsibility – Taking a stand against anti-social behaviour'

Courts Act

Crime (International Cooperation) Act

Anti-social Behaviour Act

Sexual Offences Act

Criminal Justice Act

European Union (Accessions) Act (15 new countries join the EU in May 2004)

The (first) Carter report 'Managing Offenders, Reducing Crime'

'Securing the Attendance of Witnesses in Court', consultation paper

Victim Support provides a Witness Service in all criminal courts

Conditional cautions introduced

2004   Home Office response to the Carter report 'Reducing Crime – Changing Lives'

Domestic Violence, Crime and Victims Act

Appointment of the first female Law Lord

National Offender Management Service (NOMS) introduced

Independent Police Complaints Commission replaces the Police Complaints Authority

2005   **Labour win general election (5 May)**

       Constitutional Reform Act

       Prevention of Terrorism Act

       Mental Capacity Act

       Serious Organised Crime and Police Act

       'The Code of Practice for Victims of Crime' published

2006   Criminal Defence Service Act

       Police and Justice Act

       Identity Card Act

       Terrorism Act

2007   Offender Management Act

       UK Borders Act

       Mental Capacity Act

       End of Custody licence introduced (June)

       Serious Crimes Act

       The Corston Report on vulnerable female offenders

       Creation of the Ministry of Justice

       The (second) Carter report 'Securing the Future: Proposals for the efficient and sustainable use of custody in England and Wales'

       The Witness Charter published

2008   Criminal Evidence (Witness Anonymous) Act

       Criminal Justice and Immigration Act (introduces the youth rehabilitation order)

       Sentencing Guidelines Council issues comprehensive guidelines for magistrates' courts

       'Youth Crime Action Plan'

       NOMS restructured to bring Prison and Probation Services together under a single HQ

       'Engaging Communities in Fighting Crime' (the Casey review)

       'Punishment and Reform: Our approach to managing offenders' (Ministry of Justice)

2009   Green Paper 'Engaging Communities in Criminal Justice'

       Members of the public in England and Wales allowed to vote online to choose Community Payback projects

       Government plans five new private prisons holding 1,500 inmates each

Coroners and Justice Act introduces a new Sentencing Council for England and Wales

Policing and Crime Act

House of Commons Justice Committee 'Cutting Crime: The case for justice reinvestment'

Sarah Payne appointed first Victims' Champion

2010 **General election (6 May) results in a hung parliament. Coalition government (Conservatives/Liberal Democrats) formed**

End of Custody licence terminated (April – just before the election)

Coalition plans to abolish the Youth Justice Board and replace it with a Youth Justice Division in the Ministry of Justice (not taken forward due to opposition)

Green Paper 'Breaking the Cycle: Effective punishment, rehabilitation and sentencing of offenders'. Proposes Payment by Results (PbR)

Sentencing Council begins work

Louise Casey appointed as first Victims' Commissioner

Jonathan Djanogly MP appointed Victims Minister

Gillick v. *United Kingdom* (2010)

2011 White Paper 'Breaking the Cycle: Government response'

Birmingham prison becomes the first ever prison to pass from state to private control

House of Commons Justice Committee 'The Role of the Probation Service'

Riots in London, Birmingham, Manchester, and a number of other English cities (August)

Review of Imprisonment for Public Protection (IPP) sentences

Police Reform and Social Responsibility Act

Legal Aid, Sentencing and Punishment of Offenders Bill

9 September – prison population stands at 86,842 – highest ever recorded

Government response to the Justice Committee's report: 'The Role of the Probation Service' (October)

Terrorism Prevention and Investigation Measures Act

2012 Legal Aid, Sentencing and Punishment of Offenders Act

Consultation Paper 'Punishment and Reform: Effective Probation services'

Consultation Paper 'Punishment and Reform: Effective community sentences'

Proposals to replace ASBOs

July 'Swift and Sure Justice'

September – Chris Grayling replaces Ken Clarke as Justice Secretary

November – elections for Police and Crime Commissioners

November – Restorative Justice Action Plan

College of Policing due to be established by the end of the year

2013   1 January – prison population lower by almost 3,000 since 1 January 2012

Coalition Mid-Term Review

January – 'Transforming Rehabilitation' consultation paper

Consultation on the implementation of direct entry in the police (January)

Criminal Justice Board meets for the first time (February)

1 March – prison population has increased by almost 1,000 since January

'Transforming Youth Custody' consultation paper

'Transforming Legal Aid' consultation paper (April)

'Transforming Rehabilitation: A strategy for reform' government response to the January consultation paper signals the end for the probation service

October – National Crime Agency launched

31 October – Cameras allowed into courtrooms for the first time

Crime and Courts Act – all community sentences for adults to have a punitive element

A revised 'Code of Practice for Victims of Crime' published

'The Witness Charter: Standards of care for witnesses in the Criminal Justice System' published

Victims' Right to Review introduced

House of Commons Justice Select Committee inquiry into the needs of older prisoners

2014   Offender Rehabilitation Act

Anti-social Behaviour Crime and Policing Act

Domestic Violence Disclosure Scheme – Clare's Law

Pilot launched of scrutiny panel for cautions

2015   **Conservatives win general election (7 May)**

Michael Gove becomes Justice Secretary; Theresa May remains as Home Secretary

Counter-Terrorism and Security Act

Revised 'Code of Practice for Victims of Crime' published

2016   The 2016 Police and Crime Bill

2016   Theresa May becomes Prime Minister and Liz Truss Justice Secretary

——————— ## References ——————————————————————

Brunger, M. (2012) 'Dispatches from the Field: Developing community safety in Northern Ireland', *Crime Prevention and Community Safety*, 14 (2): 140–64.

Croall, H., Mooney, G. and Munro, M. (eds) (2016) *Crime, Justice and Society in Scotland*. Abingdon: Routledge.

Duggan, M. and Heap, V. (2014) *Administrating Victimisation: The politics of anti-social behaviour and hate crime policy*. Basingstoke: Palgrave Macmillan.

McAra, L. (2008) 'Crime, criminology and criminal justice in Scotland', *European Journal of Criminology*, 5 (4): 481–504.

McKittrick, D. and McVea, D. (2012) *Making Sense of the Troubles*. London: Viking.

Check out the Companion Website

Want to know more about this chapter? Review what you have been learning by visiting: **https://study.sagepub.com/harding**

- Practice with essay questions
- Test yourself with multiple-choice questions
- Listen to a series of podcasts featuring Neil of Northumbria Police and London's Metropolitan Police Service
- Watch videos selected from the SAGE Video collection

Part One

The Criminal Justice Process in Context

George Mair, Jamie Harding,
Pamela Davies

The criminal justice process does not exist in a vacuum and in this first part of the book we seek to provide a context for criminal justice. The chapters in this part cover a range of topics but all of them provide a frame of some kind within which criminal justice can be understood more fully; they discuss issues which are relevant to criminal justice as a whole.

Part One opens with a chapter that attempts to provide a history of the key developments which have taken place in criminal justice since 1945. It may be a truism to claim that we cannot fully understand the present without an appreciation of the past, but that does not mean that it is wrong. Criminal justice has changed in many ways over the last 70 years – some for the better, some for the worse – but all too often we focus on what is going on now, without seeing how this is a result of what has gone on in the past. This brief historical overview is followed by an exploration of how crime is defined and how it is counted (Chapter 3). Crime is an artefact and this chapter demonstrates how this is the case, and discusses the two main methods used to count crime – police-recorded crime and the Crime Survey for England and Wales – showing the strengths and limitations of each. Chapter 4 looks at the various purposes of the criminal justice process. Any overarching aim for the process as a whole – such as to catch and deal with offenders – is so vague as to be meaningless. All of the main agencies have specific objectives of their own and whether these 'fit' with the objectives of other agencies is a moot point. The picture is complicated further now by the introduction of payment by results and increasing privatisation – the implications of which have yet to be fully felt. The idea that one of the purposes of any criminal justice agency is to make a profit is something that strikes a false note where public service has been the norm for so long.

In Chapter 5 Hannah Bows discusses the characteristics of offenders. Who are these individuals who commit crime, who are dealt with by the courts and are fined, given a community penalty or sentenced to imprisonment? Not surprisingly, they are young men, very often with a mental health problem. But gender, ethnicity and socio-economic status are also key factors – although it is important that our knowledge is limited to those offenders who are caught up in the criminal justice process. What about those who offend but are never caught? Chapter 6 builds on this analysis by exploring how diversity and criminal justice are related. The obvious issues are discussed – are women and ethnic minority offenders dealt with differently from white males? – but so too is the way in which criminal justice deals with the rich, those of high socio-economic status. Do such offenders avoid involvement in the criminal justice process and are they dealt with leniently if they are arrested and charged? If certain types of offenders are dealt with differently, what does this say about a process that is all about justice? The issues examined in Chapters 5 and 6 are – to a considerable degree – shaped for the general public by the way the media represent the criminal justice process. Chapter 7 explores media representations of the police, the courts and prisons showing how these distort the 'real' picture. And it is these distortions that drive public perceptions, so that the public do not have an accurate understanding of what the police do and how they work; or of what prisons are actually like. Perhaps most worrying is how far such distorted perceptions might feed into policy making.

The last two chapters in this part of the book cover governance and research respectively. In Chapter 8 Tim Newburn begins to unravel the knotty question of who actually is in charge of criminal justice. Given the increasing demands for accountability, this is an important question, but there is no simple answer. A range of bodies have governance concerns but how far these can hold a fragmented system to account is hard to discern. As we write, the Hillsborough inquest has just been completed with a verdict of unlawful killing, but serious questions of accountability remain with suggestions that governance has failed in its remit. Finally, Mike Hough looks at research. Carrying out social research is by no means a simple task, and researching the criminal justice process carries its own specific difficulties. Hough is uniquely placed to discuss these issues as he has spent half of his career working in government (as a member of the Home Office Research and Planning Unit) and half running a university-based criminological research unit. Only by carefully designed and rigorously executed research can we begin to understand how the criminal justice process works, although all too often politics, policy and research do not relate to each other as well as might be desired.

These eight chapters have been designed as stand-alone contributions, but they have many links between them and, taken together, they provide a strong foundation to explore the criminal justice process in Part Two.

Check out the Companion Website

Want to know more about this chapter? Review what you have been learning by visiting: **https://study.sagepub.com/harding**

- Practice with essay questions
- Test yourself with multiple-choice questions
- Listen to a series of podcasts featuring Neil of Northumbria Police and London's Metropolitan Police Service
- Watch videos selected from the SAGE Video collection

2 Criminal Justice Since 1945: A Brief History

George Mair

Introduction

In the 70 years since the end of the Second World War there have been many major developments in criminal justice – new agencies have been introduced, new sentences have been created, new organisational structures have been implemented, new ideas have emerged and become received wisdom. These developments have been introduced partly because of the ingrained perception of governments that they have to be seen to be doing something, and partly as a response to what are seen as problems that require action. This chapter will provide an overview of the most important of these major developments since 1945, and it is vital to bear this in mind in what follows; it would require a lengthy book to set out and explain what has been going on in criminal justice since 1945 (see the timeline in Chapter 1) in detail with some consideration of the context and background of developments, and some analysis of their significance, consequences and implications. Criminology in general has been a somewhat myopic discipline; it tends to focus on the contemporary and while this is laudable it can lead to a short-term approach that ignores more rounded historical analyses.

It would be possible to organise the chapter in several ways. It could be done thematically, exploring some of the various trends that have characterised the period; it could be done by discussing each of the main criminal justice agencies separately; or – and this is the approach followed here – a simple chronological approach might be taken. Each of these structures has its advantages, but the chronological permits exploration of developments in criminal justice as a whole to be examined and trends will be picked up as we progress. The chapter is divided into five main parts. The first explores the period from 1945 to 1960 – a period that began with considerable optimism that something could be done about crime. Next, the sixties and the seventies will be discussed when, arguably, things started to go wrong. Third, the 1979–97 period when successive Conservative governments began to break with the past. Following this, the 13 years of Labour government from 1997 to 2010 will be examined. And finally, from 2010 to the present day – a period that has been dominated by austerity. A brief conclusion will draw together the main themes that characterise the 70 years as a whole.

Criminal justice is deeply embedded in the social, political, cultural and economic conditions within which it operates, and an awareness of this wider context is necessary to appreciate fully how criminal justice has developed. Due to limitations of space, this chapter is unable to provide very much of this background but there are a number of excellent books that explore the history of the postwar period generally and offer vital contextual and background material for this chapter (for the first half of the period covered by this chapter, see, for example, Hennessy, 2006, 2007; Sandbrook, 2006, 2007, 2010, 2012; Kynaston, 2007, 2009, 2015).

1945–60

Terence Morris (1989: 13) has claimed that Britain in 1945, at the end of the Second World War, was 'both exhausted and exhilarated' and it would be difficult to disagree with this judgement. Exhausted because of the six years of war and exhilarated because the war was now over, and with the election of a reforming Labour government in 1945 there was the promise of a new dawn. Crime had risen considerably between 1938 and 1945 (particularly amongst males under the age of 21), but it was generally agreed that this was a result of the conditions of wartime: the blackout, fathers in the armed forces, mothers in employment, evacuation, the black market, etc. With the end of the war, normal conditions would return and thus crime would fall. In addition, with the introduction by the new government of the various measures that became known collectively as the welfare state, it was expected that the conditions that led to crime – poverty, unemployment, poor housing, lack of education and the like – would be diminished if not eradicated and this too would lead to a decrease in offending. Rehabilitation, which had grown along with the probation service in the years before the war, was still unquestioned as an acceptable way of dealing with offenders. At this time – and until 1979 – there was generally a consensus between the two main political parties on criminal justice. This is not to say that Conservatives and Labour did not disagree on specific issues, but on the whole criminal justice was not a significant party political matter.

The 1948 Criminal Justice Act (which to a great extent replicated a Bill that had been abandoned in 1939 due to the imminence of war) reflected, to a certain extent, the optimism of the time. The Act abolished corporal punishment as a sentence of the courts (although it continued to be used as a punishment in prisons for some years); partly as a quid pro quo gesture and partly in an effort to keep young offenders out of prison, detention centres were introduced for offenders between 12 and 21; attendance centres were also introduced for this age group (again, partly to provide an alternative to a custodial sentence); penal servitude and hard labour were abolished; and the use of borstal was extended (again with the aim of keeping young offenders out of prison). Hidden away in the Act was a clause permitting the government to fund research into crime; this small gesture resulted in 1957 in the formation of the Home Office Research Unit, which was to play a large part in the growth of criminology for the remainder of the century.

Perhaps the most significant aspect of the 1948 Act was what it failed to do. Despite considerable pressure, there was nothing in the Act that addressed what was the most contentious post-war criminal justice issue for the next 20 years – the abolition of capital punishment. Sidney Silverman, a backbench Labour MP, tabled an amendment to the Bill when it was going through the report stage to suspend the death penalty for five years and this was passed by the House of Commons. The House of Lords defeated the amendment and the government set up a Royal Commission to examine the issue – but not to consider abolition. The Royal Commission reported in 1953 recommending a defence of mental deficiency whereby the accused could not be held responsible for murder; it suggested that juries might be given the power to decide on whether the death penalty or life imprisonment should apply; and it was opposed to the idea of introducing categories of murder with only the most serious attracting the death penalty. Nothing came of the Royal Commission's report.

Three controversial cases in the mid-fifties, however, came to the rescue of the abolitionists, although as Rawlings (1999: 140) notes 'it is arguable that the controversy surrounding these cases reflected not so much a revulsion against hanging as a feeling that too many mistakes were being made'. The cases of Timothy Evans, Derek Bentley and Ruth Ellis all raised serious misgiving about the use of the death penalty and the Homicide Act of 1957 introduced two categories of murder – capital and non-capital – and new defences of provocation and of diminished responsibility. The battle to abolish the death penalty was not over and it took another eight years before the 1965 Murder (Abolition of Death Penalty) Act.

The other key theme from the mid-fifties onwards was the rise in crime. Despite the belief (or hope) that crime would fall after the war and remain low with the introduction of the welfare state, from 1955 crime began to rise – and especially amongst the 17–20-year-old age group (young adults). Table 2.1 shows the figures for males.

Table 2.1 Male offenders found guilty of indictable offences 1950–65 (%)

Age group	1950	1955	1960	1965	Percentage increase
10–13	21.1	17.9	17.4	11.9	9.6
14–16	15.1	14.9	17.6	17.5	124.4
17–20	11.3	12.5	17.8	21.6	270.1
21–24	10.5	11.2	12.5	13.5	148.7
25–29	12.1	11.2	10.3	11.7	86.7
30–49	24.1	26.0	19.9	19.5	56.3
50+	5.8	6.3	4.5	4.3	44.1
Total no.	96,839	90,467	140,668	187,424	93.5

The number of males found guilty of indictable offences more than doubled between 1955 and 1965, but the increase amongst young adults was almost 300 per cent; indeed, between 1954 and 1958 the number of young adult males found guilty of an indictable offence more than doubled. At the same time, prison numbers began to cause concern and the Advisory Council on the Treatment of Offenders (ACTO) was asked by the Home Secretary to look into the matter. In 1957, the ACTO report *Alternatives to Short Terms of Imprisonment* was published and the twin topics of crime amongst 17–20 year olds and efforts to devise alternatives to custody began their rise to prominence. Claims could be made for either to be the most significant criminal justice issue for the next 50 years.

The rising importance of crime and law and order was emphasised by the publication at the end of the decade of the White Paper *Penal Practice in a Changing Society*, which acknowledged that crime was a problem, that 17–20 year olds were especially involved, that prisons were overcrowded and that a 'fundamental re-examination of penal methods' (Home Office, 1959: 7) was necessary – but then drew back from acting upon this immediately. There were demands for the re-introduction of corporal punishment which the Home Secretary took seriously enough to ask ACTO to consider whether there were any grounds for bringing it back; the ACTO report firmly concluded there were not (ACTO, 1960).

Despite claims that the 1950s were a golden age for policing (Reiner, 2010) and possibly also for probation (Mair and Burke, 2012) because there seems to have been considerable public trust and confidence in these two agencies, such claims do not withstand detailed scrutiny. Along with the ever-rising crime rate, the explosive emergence of the teenager (symbolised by Teddy Boys) and rock 'n' roll, and street disturbances in 1958 involving racial violence in Notting Hill and Nottingham, it might well be argued that the optimism that had characterised the end of the war had completely dissipated by the end of the 1950s (for a useful view of the 1945–70 period, see Bottoms and Stevenson, 1992).

1960–79

In 1960 the average prison population was 27,000 – almost double the 1945 figure of 14,700 – and by 1970 it was 39,000. In 1964 the number of indictable offences recorded by the police hit the 1 million mark for the first time – a hugely symbolic moment. These were troubling figures and also meant increasing pressure on the police, courts, probation and the prison service. Partly in response to such pressure two major inquiries were set up to examine the police and probation respectively.

The Royal Commission on the Police was appointed in January 1960 and reported in two parts: first on pay in November of that year recommending an increase and regular reviews of pay in relation to other occupations; the second report in May 1962 proposed a new system of investigating complaints, recommended further force amalgamations and the appointment of a Chief Inspector of Constabulary, and suggested that the Home Office should have greater power over the provincial forces (something it already had for the Metropolitan Police). The 1964 Police Act incorporated these recommendations. The probation service (although strictly speaking it was *not* a single service but a collection of more than 100 individual services covering England and Wales) was perhaps not considered worthy of a Royal Commission but a Departmental Committee was appointed by the Home Secretary in 1959 to carry out a full-scale review of the service. The Morison Report was a substantial piece of work and also published two separate reports (Home Office, 1962a, 1962b). Most of the recommendations in the two reports were uncontentious and accepted by government; they covered recruitment, pay, what the tasks of the service should be, the amalgamation of areas, and interestingly argued against the idea of a national service. However, the Committee has been accused of 'complacency as it never looked at probation with a critical eye' (Mair and Burke, 2012: 126) and thereby missed the opportunity to build a probation service for the future.

By 1964 the problem of crime and how to deal with it had become such a pressing matter that a White Paper was published by the Conservative government just before they lost the election of that year to Labour. *The War Against Crime in England and Wales* (Home Office, 1964) lets one know just by the use of the word 'war' that things are serious. Essentially, the document was a tacit admission of failure as the fundamental reassessment of the penal system that had been mentioned in the 1959 White Paper was now deemed to be necessary. A Royal Commission on the Penal System was set up and holds the dubious honour of being the only Royal Commission never to report. There were serious disagreements among the members with several resignations (led by Professor Leon Radzinowice from the Institute of Criminology at the University of Cambridge), but the terms of reference for the Royal Commission were far too extensive and it is difficult to see how it could possibly have managed its task (it did leave behind five volumes of published evidence). One of the side effects of the dissolution of the Royal Commission was the replacement of ACTO by the Advisory Council on the Penal System (ACPS), which continued its role of offering advice to government until the arrival of Margaret Thatcher as Prime Minister in 1979 when it was abolished.

The last executions in the UK took place in 1964 with two individuals being hanged at the same time on 13 August – one in Manchester prison and the other in Liverpool. Besides the problem of numbers, another crisis hit the prison service in the mid-sixties – escapes of high-profile prisoners. In 1964 Charles Wilson, one of the Great Train Robbers escaped from Birmingham prison; the following year another member of the gang, Ronnie Biggs, escaped from Wandsworth; in 1966, the spy George Blake escaped from Wormwood Scrubs; and in the same year, Frank Mitchell – 'the Mad Axeman' – escaped from Dartmoor. These escapes were a severe embarrassment to the government and an inquiry was quickly set up under Lord Mountbatten to look into prison security; it reported in 1966 (Home Office, 1966).

The Mountbatten inquiry made two major recommendations, both of which continue to influence prison practice – one directly and the other indirectly – today (he also recommended the appointment of an Inspector General of Prisons). First, Mountbatten recommended a fourfold classification of prisoners to reflect their security level and dangerousness. Category A prisoners were the most serious and should be held in top-security prisons where escape should be impossible, followed by categories B, C and D – the last being suitable for open prisons. The second recommendation was that all category A prisoners should be held in a single top-security prison to be called Vectis and situated in the Isle of Wight. The rationale for this was that it would be cost-effective and the tightest security would only be needed in a single prison (which would be located on an island to make escape even more difficult). ACPS was asked to consider the Mountbatten recommendations and concluded that while the classification scheme should proceed, Vectis should not and category A prisoners should be dispersed throughout the prison system (ACPS, 1968). The Home Office followed ACPS advice – a decision which continues to be significant almost 50 years later.

The consequences were that costs increased as security was tightened up at many prisons; there was an over-emphasis on security that did nothing to aid rehabilitative work; and staff (and inmate) tensions developed with the strains of having to cope with dangerous prisoners in a number of prisons. Add to this over-crowding: in 1969 a total of 2,886 inmates were two-to-a-cell while 10 years later this figure was 11,752. Throw in appalling sanitary conditions whereby inmates – even in shared cells – had to use a chamber pot in their cell. And it is no wonder that there were a number of serious prison disturbances beginning with Parkhurst in 1969 and 1979, followed by Albany in 1971 and 1972, Gartree in 1972 and 1978, Hull in 1976 and 1979 and Wormwood Scrubs in 1979. Clearly prisons were in crisis and two major inquiries explored the issues of overcrowding, poor conditions and staff unrest: the House of Commons Expenditure Committee (1978) followed by a Home Office Departmental Committee chaired by Mr Justice May (Home Office, 1979).

Policing changed significantly during the 1960s with the introduction of unit beat policing and the widespread introduction of Panda cars that took police officers away from face-to-face contact with the general public. As a result of the increased ownership of cars and the concomitant rise in motoring offences, the police lost a significant amount of public goodwill; and they also began to be seen very negatively by young people as the sixties went on; it was during this period that the term 'the pigs' became commonplace. Drug use and other acts associated with youthful hedonism led to increased police intervention, as did the need to control large-scale political demonstrations and industrial disputes. It is difficult to be clear about the overall impact of these developments upon the police, but their (at times) heavy-handed tactics certainly did not make them more popular with the working class or young people. And the gulf between the police and those policed would grow greater.

It was during the sixties that the alternatives to custody theme really began to take off as a result of prison overcrowding. The 1967 Criminal Justice Act was focused around trying to keep people out of prison and introduced parole and the suspended sentence of imprisonment. But prison numbers continued to grow and an ACPS report (1970) suggested several possible new approaches that might be tried in order to cut prison numbers, such as deferral of sentence, the use of intermittent custody and – most notably – the introduction of a community service order. The Criminal Justice Act of 1972 introduced community service along with the suspended sentence supervision order and day training centres, all of these providing more business for the probation services which had recently suffered the loss of juveniles. Community service proved to be a highly popular sentence although with it came an emphasis on reparation and punishment and a probation workforce who were not trained social workers, thereby changing the nature and focus of probation work.

In 1974 Robert Martinson's article 'What Works? Questions and answers about prison reform' was published in a little-known journal, but despite this it has become one of the most influential articles in criminology. Martinson did *not* claim that Nothing Works; his argument was much more complex and nuanced than that, but for a variety of reasons Nothing Works was the message that emerged and which has been associated with him ever since. And although there is no evidence that this message had any direct influence upon the practice of probation officers, it has been generally seen as heralding the death knell of the rehabilitative ideal. Along with the introduction of community service and prison overcrowding, Nothing Works helped to push probation's aim from the rehabilitation of offenders to providing an alternative to custody, which became its rationale for the next 20 years or so.

As noted earlier, juvenile crime became a significant issue from the mid-fifties onwards. During the 1960s the welfare/punishment debate about how to deal with juvenile offenders began to build. The age of criminal responsibility was raised to 10 in the Children and Young Persons Act 1963 (the Ingleby Committee, set up in 1956 to inquire into juvenile courts, methods of dealing with juvenile offenders, and the prevention of cruelty to children, had proposed raising it to 12 in 1960) and following the Labour election win in 1964 a White Paper (Home Office, 1965) proposed abolishing juvenile courts and replacing them with family councils and family courts. These proposals were dropped because of the scale of the opposition they aroused and eventually in 1969 another Children and Young Persons Act was passed. This legislated to raise the age of criminal responsibility to 14, to prefer care to criminal proceedings, and to phase out detention centres and borstals for juveniles and introduce a new approach for juveniles – intermediate treatment. Unfortunately, most of this rather welfare-oriented approach was never implemented as the Conservatives won the 1970 general election and decided not to proceed. The 1970s saw the number of custodial sentences for juveniles double.

The sixties and the seventies are generally perceived as being very different decades. The sixties are associated with increasing freedom, a growing youth culture, an explosion of popular music, sexual permissiveness, drug taking, a period when exciting changes that changed the UK for the better took place. A considerable amount of liberalising legislation was passed (see Box 2.1 below). Others would see it as a time when everything began to go wrong and the problems of the seventies originated. The seventies brought the three-day week, increasing industrial unrest, the spread of IRA activity to mainland Britain, an oil crisis, a financial crisis that was only resolved by a desperate, last-minute loan from the International Monetary Fund, and the so-called 'winter of discontent'. 'Who governs Britain?' was a common question during the second half of the seventies. In 1970 1.5 million indictable offences were recorded by the police; by 1979 this number had increased by almost 1 million. In November of 1979, the prison population hit 43,036 – the highest recorded. It is little wonder that one of the key issues of the election of 1979 was law and order (Downes and Morgan, 1994).

Box 2.1

Key Labour social reforms during 1965–70

1966 – Race Relations Act

1967 – Abortion Act

1967 – Sexual Offences Act

1967 – National Health Service (Family Planning) Act

1968 – Theatre Act

1969 – Divorce Reform Act

1970 – Matrimonial Property Act

1970 – Equal Pay Act

1979–97

Just how far there had been a post-war consensus on law and order between the main political parties is a matter for debate, but there is little doubt that following their 1979 election win the Conservatives saw themselves as breaking emphatically with the past. New Right thinking emphasised personal responsibility, a free market economy, privatisation of public services, de-emphasising the welfare state and thereby rolling back the boundaries of the state, and managerialism. The three Es (economy, efficiency and effectiveness) was the rallying cry for Conservative policy under Margaret Thatcher and this was expected to be applied to criminal justice policy too. There was a tension throughout the Thatcher years between taking a hard line on crime (which meant spending money) and the desire to cut government spending. But despite the rhetoric and political posturing, criminal justice got off relatively lightly during the Thatcher governments (1979–90). This is probably because the main concern of the new government was the economy and the need to curb trade union power. The Falklands War too was an important issue in the early eighties. In addition, pragmatism was almost as important as rhetoric so, for example, despite the need to save money, police pay was increased substantially shortly after the election; and short sharp shock detention centres were set up for young offenders. For the most part, Home Secretaries during the eighties were a relatively liberal bunch (William Whitelaw during 1979–83 and Douglas Hurd 1985–9 especially) and Mrs Thatcher did not seem to take a great deal of interest in criminal justice matters.

The new government's response to the May report on prisons (see above) was to emphasise that cutting prison numbers was desirable and various means should be explored to achieve this. The 1982 Criminal Justice Act introduced youth custody, encouraged the use of senior attendance centres for young adults and of supervision orders for juveniles, and introduced the day centre and specified activity requirements to the probation order in an effort to make the order more demanding and thus encourage its use as an alternative to a custodial sentence. Prison numbers, however, continued to grow during the decade, apart from a brief few years at the end of the eighties which may have been due to sentencers anticipating the implementation of the 1991 Criminal Justice Act.

But if prison numbers for adults did not fall during the 1980s, this was not the case for young offenders where there was a sustained fall in the use of custody. In 1982 a total of 29,200 14–20-year-old males were sentenced to custody; in 1989 this figure had almost halved to 15,700. The decline in custody for this age group was only partly to do with policy. Demography played a key role as the numbers in this age group had fallen; a 'systems approach' to the sentencing of young offenders whereby academics (led by Norman Tutt and Henri Giller) worked with individual local authorities to analyse in detail patterns of offending and sentencing in their areas, then to offer constructive plans for diversion from custody, all based upon labelling theory, also played a part. In terms of policy, police cautioning was encouraged and Intermediate Treatment was introduced in 1983; both of these also led to a decline in the use of custody for 14–20 year olds.

The police were in the front line for much of the decade. Rioting in Brixton and in a number of other places in 1981; the 1984–5 miners' strike; further rioting in Handsworth, Brixton and on the Broadwater Farm estate in Tottenham in 1985 (with a police officer killed in the latter); and the lengthy demonstrations around Rupert Murdoch moving the operation of News International to Wapping in 1986–7 all led to questions about the role and legitimacy of the police and how policing should be carried out. The 1984 Police and Criminal Evidence Act (PACE) extended police powers of arrest and detention but balanced this by introducing codes of practice for the questioning of suspects. The report by Lord Scarman

(1982) into the Brixton disturbances had called for more police accountability and PACE made statutory provision for this. The Act also replaced the old Police Complaints Board with a full-time Police Complaints Authority. The following year, the police role in prosecuting arrestees was removed with the introduction of the Crown Prosecution Service. By this time there were 43 police forces in England and Wales following a number of amalgamations since 1945.

The probation service seemed to be too small or too innocuous to be noticed by the government but in 1984 the Home Office published a Statement of National Objectives and Priorities (SNOP – Home Office, 1984) that shook the service badly. Like other criminal justice agencies it also had to contend with 'the three Es', a Financial Management Initiative (FMI), and pressure for greater accountability, all of which were alien to its culture and traditions. In 1989 the first of a series of National Standards were introduced and, with hindsight, like SNOP the key term here was 'National'. For a brief moment, probation looked as if it might come in from the cold. The 1988 Green Paper held out a promising future for the service – but only if they grasped the nettle of community punishment (Home Office, 1988). The Criminal Justice Act of 1991 – which set out a carefully planned and coherent approach to sentencing focused around a just deserts framework – introduced the combination order (which combined probation supervision and community service) and made probation a sentence of the court for the first time since its introduction in 1967. Community sentences became sentences in their own right. But a curfew order was also included in the Act (although this was not implemented until 1994) following trials of electronic monitoring as a condition of bail in 1989–90 (Mair and Nee, 1990) and this was not something that probation was comfortable with. The unit fine was introduced following a successful trial (Moxon et al., 1990) and the Youth Court replaced the Juvenile Court. Around the same time, partnership work began to be encouraged among the criminal justice agencies, and crime prevention too began to be pushed. While both have undoubted advantages, partnership work led to competition and, ultimately, privatisation (the first private prison opened in 1992); while crime prevention could easily be seen as an admission of failure that we could not rely on the police to contain crime.

The riot at Manchester prison (Strangeways) in April 1990 (followed by a number of disturbances at other prisons in the same month) was the worst in British prison history. The report into the disturbances by Lord Justice Woolf (1991) made recommendations covering organisational issues, improved sanitation, a greater role for prison officers, better links between prisoners and their families and the like. The recommendation to end overcrowding by introducing a new prison rule was, however, rejected by government partly because at the time prison numbers were decreasing. Kenneth Clarke, Home Secretary from 1992 to 1993, was not committed to the 1991 Act and following complaints about its operation by some sentencers decided to change two of its key elements. The Criminal Justice Act 1993 scrapped unit fines and reintroduced the admissibility of previous convictions (which had been severely limited in the 1991 Act). In May 1993 he was replaced by Michael Howard as Home Secretary at a time when the Conservatives were behind Labour in opinion polls. A decision was taken to play the criminal justice card (notoriously, Howard proclaimed 'Prison Works' at the party conference in 1993) in the belief that the Labour Party would not be able to match hard-line Conservative policies. But the Labour Party's Shadow Home Secretary at the time, Tony Blair, not only matched Conservative rhetoric in the ensuing four years but also outdid it (Blair became Party Leader in 1994). The law and order cat was out of the bag and more than 20 years later shows no sign of being put back in.

The murder of James Bulger in Liverpool in 1993 opened the way for a more punitive approach to criminal justice. The Criminal Justice and Public Order Act 1994 was an incoherent mixture of provisions but was clearly a punitive measure introducing secure training centres for 12–14 year olds, and doubling the maximum sentence in a young offenders institution for 15–17 year olds; as was the Crime (Sentences) Act 1997 which introduced mandatory 'three strikes' sentences modelled on those in California. The Police and Magistrates' Courts Act 1994 gave the government greater power over the direction and funding of the police. Probation training programmes were suspended from 1996 and it was now being 100 per cent funded by central government. The impact upon sentencing was noticeable quickly as Table 2.2 shows. The prison population began what seemed to be an unstoppable rise; in 1993 it was 44,566 while four years later in 1997 it stood at 61,467, an increase of 38 per cent.

Table 2.2 Offenders sentenced for indictable offences 1979–97 (%)

	Discharge	Fine	Probation	Community service	Combination order	Prison
1979	11	50	6	3	–	14
1981	12	45	7	5	–	15
1983	13	43	7	7	–	16
1985	13	40	8	8	–	18
1987	14	38	9	8	–	18
1989	16	40	10	7	–	16
1991	19	35	10	9	–	15
1993	22	34	10	11	2	15
1995	19	30	11	10	3	20
1997	18	28	11	9	4	22

1997–2010

If anyone was naïve enough to think that the new Labour government elected in 1997 would reverse Conservative criminal justice policies then they were in for a rude awakening. Themes that had originated with the Conservative administrations of 1979–97 – partnership, competition, privatisation, accountability, performance measurement – were all carried on by the new government. Labour had made it clear in 1996 that they would be focusing on youth crime if elected and they published six papers on this topic within months of taking office. They adopted a zero tolerance rhetoric and appointed a Drugs Czar, both copied from the USA (although neither lasted very long). In 1998 the Crime and Disorder Act appeared, a huge piece of legislation covering a range of issues, many of them focused on young people (see Box 2.2). It is little wonder that the phrase 'the Nanny State' began to be bandied around.

Box 2.2

Key initiatives in the Crime and Disorder Act 1998

- Youth Justice Board
- Youth Offending Teams (YOTs)
- Abolition of *doli incapax*
- Age of child silence dropped from 14 to 10
- Child safety order (under 10)
- Child curfew order (under 10)
- Reparation orders
- Action plan orders
- Parenting orders
- Referral orders
- Removal of truants
- Reprimands and warnings to replace cautions for juveniles
- Detention and training orders
- Statutory time limits for young offenders
- Racially aggravated offences
- Sex offender orders
- Local authorities to share responsibility for crime with the police (Crime and Disorder Reduction Partnerships)
- Drug treatment and testing orders
- Anti-social behaviour orders

One of the new government's big ideas was modernisation and a White Paper with the title 'Modernising Justice' was published the year after the election (Home Office, 1998a). In the same year – and as part of the modernisation project – a discussion paper proposing much closer working between the prison and probation services was also published (Home Office, 1998b). Even more controversial (as far as the probation service was concerned) was the proposal that a unified probation service should be established with staff becoming civil servants. Suggestions were made for new names for this service and for the various community sentences. An Effective Practice Initiative was rolled out in June 1998 in an effort to make proba-tion work more successful (Home Office, 1998c). And in 2000 the Criminal Justice and Courts Services Act created a National Probation Service, under direct Home Office control, which came into operation in April 2001; probation became a fully-fledged criminal justice agency as it lost responsibility for family court welfare work; and the names of the three main orders were changed in a somewhat heavy-handed way (the probation order became the community rehabilitation order, the commu-nity service order became the community punishment order, and the combination order became the community punishment and rehabilitation order).

Despite considerable government rhetoric about devolving services, probation – which had always been a local service – was now a centralised one. And there were moves in the same direction with regard to the police. In the mid-sixties, Regional Crime Squads had been established, in 1992 a National Crime Intelligence Service began work, and the 1997 Police Act created a National Crime Squad. A Police Standards Unit was set up in 2001. Stephen Lawrence's murder in 1993 had led to a major inquiry into the Metropolitan Police's handling of it and when the report was published in 1999 it accused the Met of 'institutional racism' and made 70 recommendations (Macpherson, 1999) most of which were agreed by the gov-ernment. The Police Reform Act of 2002 introduced an Annual Policing Plan, power to make forces improve if found to be deficient by the Inspectorate, statutory codes of practice to promote consistency across forces, and gave police authorities greater powers to suspend/terminate Chief Constables' contracts. As Newburn (2003: 99) concludes 'the police reform programme has further centralised control over British policing'. Another national law enforcement agency was created in 2006 when the Serious Organised Crime Agency (SOCA) was established.

The government's determination to tackle criminal justice issues is shown clearly by the Crime Reduction Programme (CRP, 1999–2002) and its much-vaunted com-mitment to evidence-based policy and practice – a commitment that was always more rhetorical than real. The CRP had a planned spend of £400 million with £25 million for evaluation, which pleased academics considerably. Unfortunately, the programme was much too ambitious, was poorly designed, implemented too quickly, and created expectations that were never going to be met. A great deal of interesting research was carried out, but overall little was achieved (for a series of articles discussing the CRP see the special edition of *Criminal Justice* edited by Mike Hough in 2004).

Criminal justice had to be modernised and a discussion document *Criminal Justice: The way ahead* was published in 2001 (Home Office, 2001), as was a major report on the sentencing framework (Halliday, 2001). The end result was the Criminal Justice Act 2003, which set out the purposes of sentencing that should be considered when passing sentence: punishment, crime reduction, reform and rehabilitation, protection of the public, and reparation. The Act also introduced: imprisonment for public protection (IPP), an indeterminate sentence intended to protect the public against criminals who were seen as posing a serious risk but whose offences did not lead to a life sentence (IPPs led to increases in the custodial population); a new sentence of custody plus (deferred indefinitely due to lack of resources); two new sentences – the community order (CO) and the suspended sentence order (SSO); and a Sentencing Guidelines Council and a Sentencing Advisory Panel. The introduction of the two new sentences meant that all of the penalties associated with the probation service were scrapped and replaced by the CO and the SSO, which became available to the courts in April 2005 (see Chapter 15).

These were significant changes but more were to come following the publication of a paper entitled *Managing Offenders, Reducing Crime* by the businessman Patrick Carter (2003; now Lord Carter). Carter argued that sentences were poorly targeted, that too many low-risk offenders were imprisoned and should be diverted from custody. He urged greater use of electronic monitoring and of fines, and the need for closer liaison between the prison and probation services – indeed that a National Offender Management Service (NOMS) bringing the two together should be introduced. And NOMS was created in 2004. If that was not controversial enough, he also pressed the case for more competition from private and voluntary sector providers for probation work (contestability). The government response to Carter was suspiciously quick (within two months) and it was very positive. The 2007 Offender Management Act made it possible for probation services to be commissioned from providers in the public, private and voluntary sectors – paving the way for the privatisation of the probation service.

While it can be unclear just who runs the Criminal Justice System (see Chapter 8), oversight until 2007 lay with the Home Office, but in that year a separate Ministry of Justice was created. The split was partly a response to a number of examples of Home Office inefficiency (with the Home Secretary at the time – John Reid – branding it not fit for purpose); partly because the department was a dustbin for issues that belonged nowhere else in Whitehall; partly in response to the increased terrorism threat following 9/11; and partly because it made sense to keep issues of control and justice apart. So the Home Office remained in overall control of the police, security services and immigration while the new Ministry of Justice took responsibility for the courts, prisons and the probation service. Perhaps, too, the new structure can be seen as yet another example of New Labour's obsession with modernisation.

The sentences available for those aged under 18 were radically overhauled by the Criminal Justice and Immigration Act 2008. In a move which paralleled what had been done with community sentences in the 2003 Act, the new sentences that had been introduced in the 1998 Crime and Disorder Act (see above) were rationalised. The Youth Rehabilitation Order (YRO) replaced nine existing sentences and came into operation at the end of November 2009. Like the community order and the suspended sentence order, the YRO has a number of requirements (18) that can be used, individually or in combination, to address the risk posed and the needs associated with the offender (for details see Youth Justice Board, 2010).

Prison numbers continued to increase, despite the downward trend in crime. Both police-recorded crime data and Crime Survey for England and Wales figures showed that crime had been falling for around a decade, yet because of the perceived need to be tough on crime more people were being sent to prison and for longer periods. A second report by Patrick Carter (2007) argued that there would be a need for 6,500 new prison places by the end of 2012 and he suggested a prison-building programme with three Titan prisons holding around 2,500 prisoners each. When Labour came to power in 1997 the prison population had been just over 61,000; when they left office in spring 2010 it was 85,500. At the other end of the spectrum, another of Labour's obsessions – the Respect agenda (launched in 2005 and aimed at tackling antisocial behaviour) – continued to resonate, as did a wish to engage communities in the fight against crime. A Green Paper *Engaging Communities in Criminal Justice* (Ministry of Justice/Home Office, 2009) discussed stronger community-focused partnerships, developing the visibility of community service (now community payback or unpaid work) so that offenders would be recognised; involving the public in choosing projects for work by offenders, and keeping the public better informed about crime and justice.

When Labour lost the election in 2010 they left behind the largest prison population since records began, decreasing crime over more than 10 years, a blurring of the boundaries between custody and community and between crime and incivility, and a probation service that was reeling from continuous change. Was this progress or not?

2010 to Present Day

The defining feature of criminal justice since 2010 has been something that happened in 2008 – the financial recession. In the short term, the impact of this was mitigated by the Labour government, but when the Conservatives and Liberal Democrats joined to form a Coalition government (dominated by the Conservatives), the full effects of austerity began to be felt. In his first budget in June 2010 following the election, George Osborne announced that all government departments (apart from the Health Service and overseas development aid budgets) would have to reduce their budgets by an average of 25 per cent over the next five years. Both the Home Office and the Ministry of Justice were hit hard. The figures in Tables 2.3 and 2.4 show very plainly the impact of cuts on the police and prison services during this period.

The police have tried to soften the impact of the cuts by protecting front-line staff – constables have had the lowest percentage decrease in numbers. And they have also been helped by the continuing drop in crime. The drop in operational prison staff has, however, had serious consequences: suicides in prisons have increased by 38 per cent between September 2010 and September 2015, having fallen over the preceding three years; between June 2010 and June 2015, self-harm incidents amongst male inmates increased by 54 per cent, compared to a 15 per cent increase in the previous three years (for female prisoners there was a decrease of almost 40 per cent); prisoner-on-prisoner assaults increased by 14.5 per cent in the same period, having been stable for the preceding three, while serious assaults increased by 69 per cent (compared to 5 per cent in the preceding three years); and

Table 2.3 Police service strength, England and Wales, 2010–15

Rank	31.3.10	31.3.15	Decrease	% decrease
Chief Officers	223	201	22	9.9
Chief Superintendents	472	337	135	28.6
Superintendents	1,023	820	203	19.8
Chief Inspectors	1,966	1,657	309	15.7
Inspectors	7,222	5,701	1,521	21.1
Sergeants	22,852	19,148	3,704	16.2
Constables	107,873	98,954	8,919	8.3
Total police ranks	**141,631**	**126,818**	**14,813**	**10.4**
Police community support officers	16,685	12,331	4,354	26.1
Other staff	82,116	67,991	14,125	17.2
Total police workforce	**240,432**	**207,140**	**33,292**	**13.8**

Table 2.4 Prison staff (operational) in post, England and Wales, 2010–15

Grade	31.3.10	31.3.15	Decrease	% decrease
Senior managers	320	180	140	43.8
Managers	1,110	770	340	30.6
Custodial managers	980	1,360	+380	
Supervising officers	3,940	1,950	1,990	50.5
Prison officers	19,910	14,910	5,000	25.1
Operational support	7,700	4,580	3,120	40.5
Total operational staff	**33,960**	**23,750**	**10,210**	**30.1**

assaults on staff increased by 40 per cent having decreased for three years, while serious assaults on staff increased by 99 per cent, compared to an increase of less than 5 per cent in the previous three years (Ministry of Justice, 2015).

In June 2010, a matter of weeks after the formation of the new government, the new Justice Secretary (Ken Clarke) made a speech spelling out his priorities: saving money, rationalising the system (usually another way of saving money), another review of sentencing policy, increased use of the private and voluntary sectors in working with offenders, and the introduction of payment by results. Clarke burnished his liberal credentials by stating that there were too many in custody (it was expensive, unproductive and ineffective), but perhaps the most interesting point about the speech was what he did not say – there was not a single mention of the probation service.

The idea of diverting offenders from custody was killed off in a Green Paper at the end of the year (Ministry of Justice, 2010: 2):

We will not end short sentences … We will certainly not be saving robbers, burglars and those who use knives from prison sentences. We will not allow our jails to run out of capacity and we will not introduce any early release scheme.

Punishment had to be more robust and credible. Despite the rhetoric, Clarke became perceived as being too liberal – perhaps as a result of his desire to tackle drug problems, mental illness and poor education among prisoners, perhaps because of his support of a 50 per cent discount for early guilty pleas. The August 2011 riots that took place in various parts of London and several other cities resulted in more than 3,000 arrests and demands for punitive measures. By September 2011 the prison population stood at 86,842, the highest ever recorded.

The Police Reform and Social Responsibility Act 2011 changed the governance of the police by introducing Police and Crime Commissioners (PCCs) who were to be responsible for the efficiency and effectiveness of forces and to hold the Chief Constable to account. The PCCs are elected officials and the first elections were held in November 2012 with very low turnouts. So far, the PCCs do not seem to have made much difference, but their potential is considerable, especially if they become responsible for overseeing the provision of prison and probation services, in addition to commissioning victim services. Yet another Act concerned with criminal justice received royal assent in 2012. The Legal Aid, Sentencing and Punishment of Offenders Act introduced cuts in legal aid, increased curfew requirements, deductions from prisoners' pay to support victims of crime, a minimum of six months custody for threatening with a knife, made squatting an offence and toughened up the Youth Rehabilitation Order (it also abolished the IPP sentence). Several months after the Act became law, Clarke was replaced by Chris Grayling as Justice Secretary and things got worse.

Grayling seemed to be determined to demonstrate his toughness with regard to crime and banned books being sent to prisoners. He also introduced the Criminal Courts charge which meant that if an offender pleaded not guilty, even to a relatively minor offence, and was subsequently found guilty and fined, say £200, he/she could end up paying between £150 and £1,200 for the Courts charge. The charge caused obvious problems for offenders who were not well off and a number of magistrates resigned because of its draconian nature. It was abolished shortly after Michael Gove replaced Grayling as Justice Secretary following the 2015 election.

In 2013, the Crime and Courts Act scrapped SOCA and replaced it with the National Crime Agency. Around the same time, police forces began to be faced with more pressure from government to find cuts to meet the decreased funding they were receiving, and one of the ways they were encouraged to consider was greater collaboration or even the merging of forces (in Scotland, the forces had merged to become Police Scotland in April 2013). How far this might go – regionalisation, nationalisation – is an interesting question for the future. Following the terrorist attacks in Paris in December 2015, it looks as if cuts to the police may have been halted, although this might be a temporary measure.

The probation service lost its fight against privatisation in February 2015 when 21 Community Rehabilitation Companies (CRCs) took responsibility for the supervision of all low- and medium-risk offenders sentenced to community orders and suspended sentence orders, leaving high-risk offenders, the preparation of court reports and risk assessment in the hands of the NPS. This gave CRCs around 70–75 per cent of probation work, leaving the rest to a much shrunken NPS. Two CRCs – Sodexo and Purple Futures – run 11 areas between them, and Sodexo has already begun to cut staff before a year into its contract. The fragmentation of probation would seem to be a much more worrying prospect than its privatisation.

After becoming Justice Secretary, Michael Gove gave strong hints that he was keen to try to improve prisons. On 8 January 2016 David Cameron delivered a speech which he claimed was the first time for more than 20 years that a Prime Minister had made a speech devoted to prisons. It was, to say the least, somewhat surprising:

> ... simply warehousing ever more prisoners is not financially sustainable, nor is it the most cost-effective way of cutting crime.
>
> Worse than that, it lets other parts of the criminal justice system that are failing off the hook. It distracts us from the job of making prisons work better.
>
> And it fuels prison overcrowding, which hampers efforts to rehabilitate offenders – and that just makes us all less safe. (Cameron, 2016)

He went on to promise: greater autonomy for prison governors with six 'reform prisons' to be created in 2016; the development of 'meaningful metrics' on prison performance and prison league tables; more and better education for inmates, and more help for those with mental health and drug problems; and more use of electronic monitoring, particularly tracking tags, for prisoners on licence (and for community sentences). Exactly how this is going to be achieved, where the resources will come from, how it can be managed with the prison population as high as it is (85,500), are all pertinent questions. But for the first time in more than 20 years is there a glimmer of hope for the prison system?

Summary

This chapter has attempted to provide a meaningful overview of the key developments in criminal justice since the end of the Second World War. It has not addressed several topics that might have been included, for example the (re)introduction of victims into the criminal justice process that has been underway since the Criminal Injuries Compensation Scheme began in 1964, and the impact of terrorism on criminal justice since the 9/11 attacks on the USA. However, it is hoped that the chapter does give a flavour of the immense amount of changes that have taken place in criminal justice over 70 years – with the pace of change accelerating rapidly from the early nineties when criminal justice legislation seemed to be appearing annually.

What have been the key themes that could be identified? Can they be said to add up to the modernisation of the criminal justice process? In no particular order one might note:

- the increasing size and scope of the 'system';
- partnership, competition and privatisation;

- greater accountability;

- fragmentation;

- local/central tensions;

- increasing punitiveness;

- blurring the boundaries between crime and incivilities;

- blurring the boundaries between community sentences and custody;

- the arrival of new technologies (electronic monitoring, virtual remand hearings).

What about the rise in crime for the first 50 years of the period and the fall over the past two decades? Have we any idea why crime is falling? And what about the seemingly inexorable rise in the prison population since 1955? And the persistent debates about how to deal with young offenders?

The Royal Commission on the Penal System set up in the mid-sixties was the only Royal Commission never to report. Perhaps it is time for a fundamental examination of the criminal justice process, what it does, how it does it, and how far it is effective. This would be an incredibly ambitious project but the time seems more appropriate than ever for such a task. Criminal justice is too important to be left to the uncoordinated whims of politicians.

Discussion Questions

1. What evidence is there for continuities and discontinuities in criminal justice policy since 1945?

2. What do you think is the single most significant criminal justice issue in the past 50 years?

3. What have been the key changes that have taken place with regard to (1) the police, (2) prisons, (3) probation, (4) the courts?

4. How possible is it to formulate a coherent approach to criminal justice?

Further Reading

There are no books that cover the period fully. Perhaps the best in terms of its coverage is Terence Morris, *Crime and Criminal Justice since 1945* (Oxford: Basil Blackwell) but this was published in 1989 and so is now outdated. The last few chapters of Philip Rawlings *Crime and Power* (Harlow: Longman) are useful, but stop at 1998. David Downes, Tim Newburn and Paul Rock are currently working on an official history of post-1945 criminal justice and this is likely to be the definitive work for some time.

References

Advisory Council on the Penal System (1968) *The Regime for Long-Term Prisoners in Conditions of Maximum Security*. London: HMSO.

Advisory Council on the Penal System (1970) *Non-Custodial and Semi-Custodial Penalties*. London: HMSO.

Advisory Council on the Treatment of Offenders (1957) *Alternatives to Short Terms of Imprisonment*. London: HMSO.

Advisory Council on the Treatment of Offenders (1960) *Corporal Punishment*. London: HMSO.

Bottoms, A.E. and Stevenson, S. (1992) 'What went wrong? Criminal justice policy in England and Wales, 1945–70', in D. Downes (ed.), *Unravelling Criminal Justice*. London: Macmillan.

Cameron, D. (2016) 'Prison reform'. Prime Minister's speech to the Policy Exchange, 8 February 2016. Available at: www.gov.uk/government/speeches/prison-reform-prime-ministers-speech

Carter, P. (2003) *Managing Offenders, Reducing Crime*. London: Strategy Unit.

Carter, P. (2007) *Securing the Future: Proposals for the efficient and sustainable use of custody in England Wales*. London: Cabinet Office.

Downes, D. and Morgan, R. (1994) '"Hostages to fortune?" The politics of law and order in post-war Britain', in M. Maguire, R. Morgan and R. Reiner (eds), *The Oxford Handbook of Criminology*, 1st edn. Oxford: Clarendon Press.

Halliday, J. (2001) *Making Punishments Work: Report of a Review of the Sentencing Framework for England and Wales*. London: Home Office.

Hennessy, P. (2006) *Never Again: Britain 1945–1951*. London: Penguin.

Hennessy, P. (2007) *Having It So Good: Britain in the fifties*. London: Penguin.

Home Office (1959) *Penal Practice in a Changing Society*. London: HMSO.

Home Office (1960) *Report of the Committee on Children and Young Persons* (The Ingleby Report). London: HMSO.

Home Office (1962a) *Report of the Departmental Committee on the Probation Service* (The Morison Report). London: HMSO.

Home Office (1962b) *Second Report of the Departmental Committee on the Probation Service*. London: HMSO.

Home Office (1964) *The War Against Crime in England and Wales 1959–1964*. London: HMSO.

Home Office (1965) *The Child, the Family and the Young Offender*. London: HMSO.

Home Office (1966) *Committee of Enquiry into Prison Escapes and Security* (The Mountbatten Report). London: HMSO.

Home Office (1979) *Report of the Inquiry into the United Kingdom Prison Services* (The May Report). London: HMSO.

Home Office (1984) *Probation Service in England and Wales: Statement of national objectives and priorities*. London: Home Office.

Home Office (1988) *Punishment, Custody and the Community*. London: HMSO.

Home Office (1998a) *Modernising Justice*. London: HMSO.

Home Office (1998b) *Joining Forces to Protect the Public: Prisons–probation. A consultation document*. London: Home Office.

Home Office (1998c) *Effective Practice Initiative: National implementation plan for the supervision of offenders*. Probation Circular 35/1998. London: Home Office.

Home Office (2001) *Criminal Justice: The way ahead*. London: The Stationery Office.

Hough, M. (ed.) (2004) 'Evaluating the crime reduction programme in England and Wales', *Criminal Justice* (Special Issue), 4 (3): 211–325.

House of Commons (1978) *Fifteenth Report from the Expenditure Committee: Session 1977–78, the reduction of pressure on the prison system*. London: HMSO.

Kynaston, D. (2007) *Austerity Britain 1945–51*. London: Bloomsbury.

55555555

555

Kynaston, D. (2009) *Family Britain 1951–1957*. London Bloomsbury.

Kynaston, D. (2015) *Modernity Britain 1957–1962*. London: Bloomsbury.

Macpherson, W. (1999) *The Stephen Lawrence Inquiry: Report of an inquiry by Sir William Macpherson*. London: The Stationery Office.

Mair, G. and Burke, L. (2012) *Redemption, Rehabilitation and Risk Management: A history of probation*. London: Routledge.

Mair, G. and Nee, C. (1990) *Electronic Monitoring: The trials and their results*. Home Office Research Study 120. London: HMSO.

Martinson, R. (1974) 'What works? Questions and answers about prison reform', *The Public Interest*, 35: 22–54.

Ministry of Justice/Home Office (2009) *Engaging Communities in Criminal Justice*. London: The Stationery Office.

Ministry of Justice (2010) *Breaking the Cycle: Effective punishment, rehabilitation and sentencing of offenders*. London: The Stationery Office.

Ministry of Justice (2015) *Safety in Custody Statistics England and Wales: Deaths in prison custody to June 2015, Assaults and self-harm to March 2015*. London: Ministry of Justice.

Morris, T. (1989) *Crime and Criminal Justice since 1945*. Oxford: Basil Blackwell.

Moxon, D., Sutton, M. and Hedderman, C. (1990) *Unit Fines: Experiments in four courts*. Research and Planning Unit Paper 59. London: Home Office.

Newburn, T. (2003) *Crime and Criminal Justice Policy*, 2nd edn. Harlow: Longman.

Rawlings, P. (1999) *Crime and Power: A history of criminal justice 1688–1998*. Harlow: Longman.

Reiner, R. (2010) *The Politics of the Police*, 4th edn. Oxford: Oxford University Press.

Sandbrook, D. (2006) *Never Had It So Good: A History of Britain from Suez to the Beatles*. London: Abacus.

Sandbrook, D. (2007) *White Heat: A history of Britain in the swinging sixties*. London: Abacus.

Sandbrook, D. (2010) *State of Emergency: The way we were – Britain 1970–1974*. London: Allen Lane.

Sandbrook, D. (2012) *Seasons in the Sun: The Battle for Britain, 1974–1979*. London: Allen Lane.

Scarman, Lord (1982) *The Brixton Disorders 10–12 April 1981: Report of an inquiry by the Rt. Hon. The Lord Scarman, OBE*. London: HMSO.

Woolf, H. and Tumim, S. (1991) *Prison Disturbances April 1990*. London: HMSO.

Youth Justice Board (2010) *The Youth Rehabilitation Order and Other Youth Justice Provisions of the Criminal Justice and Immigration Act 2008: Practice guidance for youth offending teams*. London: Youth Justice Board.

Check out the Companion Website

Want to know more about this chapter? Review what you have been learning by visiting: **https://study.sagepub.com/harding**

- Practice with essay questions
- Test yourself with multiple-choice questions
- Listen to a series of podcasts featuring Neil of Northumbria Police and London's Metropolitan Police Service
- Watch videos selected from the SAGE Video collection

3 Definitions and the Counting of Crime

Ian Mahoney

Introduction

This chapter will argue that there are no universally agreed definitions of crime and that, even in the case of crimes such as murder, there is often disagreement as to which acts should be categorised as such. It will show how debates about the definition of crime influence its measurement, highlighting the different methodologies used in compiling police crime figures, the Crime Survey for England and Wales (CSEW) and other measures. Weaknesses in the methodologies of each of these forms of data collection will be used to demonstrate the impossibility of determining the true 'crime rate' with particular reference to current concerns over the validity of figures compiled by police forces. The extent to which changing levels of crime since the 1950s can be mapped through statistics will be discussed.

Defining Crime

Crime is notoriously difficult to define. Definitions change over time and are subject to prevailing political, social, cultural, economic and popular discourses and as Clive Elmsley argued a 'definition of crime that embraces all of its different perspectives and satisfies every generalisation and nuance is probably impossible' (2013: 2). Acts that many may believe should be criminalised are often not, whilst acts that may be deemed to be relatively trivial and low level are. Definitions of crime vary internationally and culturally. An act that is deemed illegal in one culture may be seen as perfectly acceptable in another and our own experiences in relation to many actions will influence our understanding and interpretation of such an act. Consider, for example, the act of taking someone's life. Think for a moment about the death penalty in one of the many states (for example, the USA, China, Iran, Iraq and Japan) that retain it; or the act of killing during war; or mercy killings and euthanasia. All of these acts involve the deliberate taking of life, and yet are not ordinarily treated as murder. Given that an act is in itself not inherently criminal and considering the vast and varying definitions of crime then, how should we define the concept? How do we constitute an act as illegal, or criminal?

We shall see that attitudes towards certain acts change over time, or technology evolves and definitions of crime become out of date and require updating, or new definitions are created. The continual changes in the construction and definition of crime also have a significant influence upon understandings of crime trends. Our recent experience suggests that crime is falling following the most dramatic rise in our history; yet looking further back we see that the picture is not as simple as this. Recording methods and practices change and new survey methods highlight problems with pre-existing studies and statistics.

The Construction of Crime

According to the *Oxford English Dictionary* a crime is an 'act or omission which constitutes an offence and is punishable by law; illegal activities; and an action or activity considered to be evil, shameful or wrong. It is a wicked or sinful act' (*OED*, 2011). Given that the dictionary has multiple definitions, we immediately begin to see then that defining crime is problematic. Consider speeding; it fits with the first two parts of the definition, but many people would consider it not as evil, shameful, wrong, wicked or sinful by virtue of everyone else doing it. The dictionary definition also underlines the historic nature of crime and the manner in which it is defined. A 'wicked or sinful act' carries with it a range of connotations that can be traced back to perceptions of morality and sin, echoing the religious basis for many early forms of discipline, morality and maintenance of the social order.

Other definitions of crime are equally problematic. For Edwin Sutherland, crime is a 'legal description of an act as socially injurious and legal provision of a penalty for the act' (Sutherland, 1940: 7). There are many socially injurious acts that we may feel are immoral and deserve punishment, but which are not illegal. The banking crisis of 2008 which led to a deep, global recession was caused predominantly by weak banking regulation and irresponsible and risky lending practices by banks (this is discussed further in Chapter 6). This has had a profound impact upon many millions of people with significant rises in unemployment, the repossession of homes and a consequent rise in homelessness and partial nationalisation of several banks in the UK. Significant social harm was done and yet there have been only minimal attempts to increase banking regulation to reduce subsequent harm and those responsible for causing the crisis have gone largely unpunished throughout much of the Western world – with the exception of Iceland, which has seen a number of bankers, including senior executives, imprisoned for up to five years (*BBC News*, 2013). What emerges is that we are talking about specific elements of the definition and that, as such, an act is not inherently criminal. There is no universal acceptance as to what acts should, or should not, be classified as criminal.

Crime and the Law

> There is no crime without declaration. That is, some person or body of persons through established procedure creates the concept of crime. This means, first, that the concept of crime originates in the formulations of criminal law and, second, that the concept is imposed on persons and their alleged behaviours. The crime phenomenon thus exists because of the creation of the concept of crime by means of the criminal law, its enforcement, and its administration. (Quinney, 2000: 1)

Examining the rule of law and whether an act has been deemed illegal or not is one way of understanding crime. Richard Quinney (2000) draws our attention to the idea that crime is not an objective reality but rather something formulated through criminal law. Laws surrounding crime and deviance tend to be formulated via one of two means – via statute or case law. Statutes are laws made by legislative bodies, such as parliament, following debate and consideration. In England and Wales laws formulated via these means are considered multiple times – as Green Papers, White Papers, and then eventually as a parliamentary Bill. They are considered by both houses of parliament and, if passed, are signed into being by royal assent, at which point they become law (although it may be some months before they are implemented). Case law (or common law) on the other hand is formulated through the courts and is based around judgments that have resulted from the outcome of a case or trial. Judgments are either seen as binding (i.e. must be adhered to) or can be used to inform and guide subsequent judgments made by other judges in similar cases.

New legislation regularly updates the statutes and therefore definitions of crime, helping to reform and reinforce the legal and moral boundaries within society; however, the amount of criminal justice-related legislation in recent years has been unprecedented. *Halsbury's Statutes of England and Wales* documents the creation of legislation in England and Wales and lists more offences created via both primary (debated in parliament) and secondary (through the use of other methods including statutory instruments) legislation in the 19 years from 1989 to 2008 than were created in the preceding 637 years! The Law Commission (2010: 5) estimates in excess of 3,000 new offences created by New Labour between 1997 and 2010 although this number is disputed (see Morgan, 2011: 18); and over 1,750 new offences created between 2009/10 and 2014/15 (Ministry of Justice, 2014: 8). The myriad of new offences and recodification of existing offences creates a mine-field for anyone engaged in the study of crime whether that be from a historical, legal, criminological, sociological or other perspective and it is important to remain aware of the fluidity of the concept of 'crime'.

The common sense approach of relying upon acts defined as criminal through the law draws upon clearly outlined facts in order to formulate understandings of crime and deviance and as such is relatively straightforward. There is a great deal of criticism of such an approach due in no small part to the argument that as it is the most powerful in society who create laws and thereby construct crime, it is the most powerful who are best placed to influence understandings of crime, deviance and punishment (see for example Quinney, 1970; Matthews and Young, 1992; Young and Matthews, 1992; Muncie, 2001; Lea, 2002; Matthews, 2014). Such arguments draw attention to the manner in which criminal justice policies and definitions of criminality are disproportionately focused upon the poorest and most vulnerable in society, while more 'respectable' elements of society, such as the middle and managerial classes, are faced with relatively minor sanctions for their own socially injurious acts. Edwin Sutherland was among the first to seek to develop this critique in the 1940s when he argued that criminologists and sociologists should expand definitions of crime so that they encompass not just the actions of the poorest and lowest echelons of society (Sutherland, 1940, 1949). Sutherland contended that attention should not be limited to the activities of the working classes but should also incorporate White Collar Crime and the deviant, shadowy and often illegal enterprises undertaken by the middle and managerial classes:

> The crimes of the lower class are handled by policemen, prosecutors, and judges, with penal sanctions in the form of fines, imprisonment, and death. The crimes of the upper class either result in no official action at all, or result in suits for damages in civil courts, or are handled by inspectors, and by administrative boards or commissions, with penal sanctions in the form of warnings, orders to cease and desist, occasionally the loss of a license, and only in extreme cases by fines or prison sentences. Thus, the white-collar criminals are segregated administratively from other criminals, and largely as a consequence of this are not regarded as real criminals by themselves, the general public, or the criminologists. (Sutherland, 1940: 7–8)

Sutherland's argument retains its relevance today and reveals another problem that arises from focusing on the rule of law and legal constructions of crime: there are many forms of social and civil wrongs, as well as environmental harms, which go relatively unchecked. Indeed, significant environmental harm is regularly caused by humanity. The emissions scandal that rocked the Volkswagen Group in 2015 (Hotten, 2015) had the potential to cause significant harm to the environment and national governments' attempts to meet climate change objectives but at the time of writing it was unclear as to what, if any, sanctions were to be put in place following this. In addition to this there are regular, often high profile, oil and chemical spills and leaks around the world (e.g. Exxon Valdez in 1989, Bhopal in 1984 and Deepwater Horizon in 2010) which have severe repercussions for local communities and the environment but which rarely attract significant legal sanctions.

It therefore becomes evident that whilst the law informs us which acts have been criminalised by nation states, and which sanctions these offences will attract, it has a very narrow focus and fails to encompass a significant number of acts that involve significant harm but are rarely, or ineffectively, policed. As such it fails to satisfy criminological curiosity (Lacey and Zedner, 2012: 163).

Crime as a Social Construction

An alternative manner in which we can view crime is to look at the manner in which acts are constructed as criminal within society. The law is one way of constructing crime; however, it fails to address wider harms and other, more problematic definitions. As already noted, many acts that have been criminalised are seen as socially acceptable, particularly when it comes to speeding! If a criminalised act becomes socially acceptable, then an alternative way of defining crime may be to examine the social and cultural context in which the act is constituted as criminal and the idea that it is socially constructed and formed through culturally bound interactions. This certainly helps us to understand the way in which the same act may be criminalised in one culture, while not in another, or the way in which the legal status of acts changes over time.

The role that various institutions play in society also helps to influence the manner in which an act may or may not be defined as criminal. Paul Chevigny (2001) examined the social construction of crime in relation to Dante's *Inferno* and the way in which violent crime is treated most seriously in society compared to the *Inferno*, where acts of betrayal and breaches of trust are treated with the greatest severity due to being seen as the most deliberate, calculated and socially harmful (2001: 790). In contrasting the focus on different forms of harm Chevigny points us towards the fact that there are alternative approaches which can be undertaken to examine the constitution of acts as harmful or criminal, and that there is no clear and objective truth in relation to crime.

More recently, Ray Surette (2015) examines in detail the formation of the concept of 'copycat crimes' as well as touching upon how drink driving, serial killers and road rage became constituted as criminal acts. He highlights the influence that social expectations, pressure groups and the media play in influencing the criminalisation (or indeed decriminalisation) of an act and the corresponding political and criminal justice responses. In doing so Surette draws further attention to the influence of shared understandings of what is or is not an acceptable form of action and in turn demonstrates how wider social condemnation and pressure can play a pivotal role in the definition and treatment of crime.

As Surette outlines, social attitudes towards acts change over time, so the status of that act also changes. Consider the case of homosexuality. Homosexuality was illegal from the mediaeval period until the mid-twentieth century due in part to the prominent role which religion played in medieval and early modern society, and the way in which it was classed as sodomy and so viewed as an unnatural and immoral act. It was as a result of pressure groups and increasingly liberal attitudes in the post-war West that homosexuality was legalised, initially for consenting men over the age of 21 *in private* (so as to not offend moral sensibilities among the wider population) in the 1967 Sexual Offences Act. It was not until 1994 that the age of consent was lowered to 18 however, and 2001 that it was lowered to 16 to match the age of consent for heterosexual relations; it has been a long process. The changing attitudes towards homosexuality also reveal the levels of influence that religion and the church have over ideas about morality and deviance. Ideas surrounding crime being 'wicked' or 'a sin' carry with them undertones of religiosity (as noted earlier) and enable us to trace the historical roots of perceptions of crime and punishment accordingly.

The second example that we will examine here is the classification of certain substances as illegal. Consider the elementary case of the crime-fighting sleuth, Sherlock Holmes:

> Sherlock Holmes took his bottle from the corner of the mantelpiece and his hypodermic syringe from its neat morocco case. With his long, white, nervous fingers he adjusted the delicate needle and rolled back his left shirt-cuff. For some little time his eyes rested thoughtfully upon the sinewy forearm and wrist, all dotted and scarred with innumerable puncture-marks. Finally he thrust the sharp point home, pressed down the tiny piston, and sank back into the velvet-lined armchair with a long sigh of satisfaction. (Conan Doyle, 2007: 97).

Arthur Conan Doyle's creation could be found regularly consuming various combinations of cocaine and opiates (e.g. morphine) to escape 'the dull routine of existence' (Conan Doyle, 2007: 98) which he so readily abhors. This may appear relatively shocking in contemporary society, but at the time opium, cocaine and morphine were all legal substances and it was not until the Dangerous Drugs Act 1920 that they were first defined as illegal in England and Wales. More recently, cannabis has seen its status as an illegal substance vary considerably. Some countries, such as the Netherlands, have considerably more lax controls than others, with the country famous for its 'coffee shops'. In the USA, a number of states including Alaska, Colorado and Oregon have legalised cannabis use with many others having decriminalised its use to varying extents. Meanwhile, in the UK, despite its status as a Class B substance which carries with it a sentence of up to five years if someone is caught in possession, in reality someone in possession is likely to receive a spot fine of up to £90 or a police warning (gov.uk, 2015). So we see how attitudes to drugs vary considerably over time.

Lastly, the construction of an act such as murder has also had an interesting path to the present day. Not all acts that involve the taking of someone's life are classed as murder. In England and Wales the crime of murder is committed, where a person:

of sound mind and discretion (i.e. sane);

unlawfully kills (i.e. not self-defence or other justified killing);

any reasonable creature (human being);

in being (born alive and breathing through its own lungs);

under the Queen's Peace (i.e. not during times of war);

with intent to kill or cause grievous bodily harm (GBH).

(Crown Prosecution Service, 2015)

Each of these elements must be proven for an act to be classified as murder. In contrast, there are multiple forms of manslaughter broadly covered by the terms 'voluntary manslaughter' and 'involuntary manslaughter' (Crown Prosecution Service, 2015). The definition and treatment of murder has, moreover, been subject to change over time. Prior to 1965, a person could be tried for manslaughter, murder or capital murder, the last of which could lead to a death sentence. After the abolition of the death penalty in mainland Britain (Northern Ireland followed suit in 1971), the death sentence was commuted to life imprisonment. More recently, in early 2010 shortly before they lost the general election, the Labour government was exploring the possibility of introducing categories of murder (first and second degree as used in the USA). If this had been introduced, first-degree murder (i.e. murder with intent to kill) would probably have carried a mandatory life sentence (as murder currently does), while second-degree murder, with intent to cause grievous bodily harm, would have carried a discretionary life sentence, as would manslaughter. We therefore begin to see the fluidity of meanings surrounding what, on the face of it, appears to be a relatively straightforward offence to define and the challenges facing criminologists and policy makers when it comes to formulating and critiquing legal constructs.

It emerges then that the concept of 'crime' is not only ambiguous and arguably not fit for purpose in many cases, but also that it is continually evolving. Changing technology, perceptions and understandings of morality and legality, and tolerances towards certain acts, whether that be homosexuality or consumption of banned substances, change and so the law has to change to reflect this. Nicola Lacey and Lucia Zedner have sought to transcend these difficulties by examining the process of criminalisation firstly as practice (i.e. through examining the activities of legislators, judges, the police and the public) and secondly criminalisation as a result of changes in criminal justice policy and practice (2012: 161). This approach helps to avoid getting stuck in the continual quandary of distinguishing between legal and social constructions of crime because 'Thinking about criminalization as an outcome and as practice cuts across the distinction between legal and social constructions of crime: both outcomes and practices are shaped by law and broader social dynamics' (Lacey and Zedner, 2012: 161). However, it is still important to note the fact that criminalisation is in itself a process and is subject to continual change and renewal.

One of the knock-on effects of the way in which acts are criminalised is the influence that such definitions have upon the recording of crime and it is to this which we will now turn.

The Recording of Crime

Crime records have received a great deal of scrutiny since their inception and particularly in recent years (see for example Hough et al., 2007; Young, 2011). On the one hand, they provide us with a great deal of information about what types of criminal acts are being committed, where, and by whom. On the other hand, they rely on criminal acts being recorded or reported in the first instance and not every crime or type of crime will have the same levels of reporting. This part of the chapter examines some of the debates surrounding the recording of crime and whether or not we can ever truly know crime levels with any real degree of accuracy.

Prior to 1857, there was little in the way of effective or meaningful crime statistics. They were collected by the Home Office from 1805 onwards; however, these figures related only to court-based proceedings and convictions and so did not cover other crimes recorded by and reported to the police. Police-recorded crime began to be collected in 1857 and it was finally possible to start piecing together a picture of crime in communities (Elmsley, 2013: 21–3).

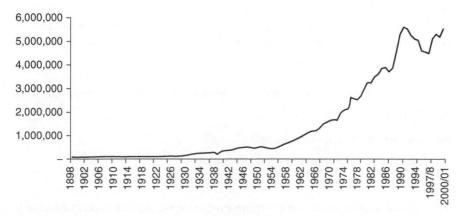

Figure 3.1   Total recorded crime by year 1898–2001

Source: gov.uk, undated

N.B. New recording practices were introduced in 2001/2 which meant that outcomes were no longer comparable.

Figure 3.1 shows that, by today's standards, crime remained comparatively low until after the Second World War, when it began to increase rapidly. These changes are relative – total recorded crime levels have increased by more than 10 per cent year-on-year 19 times between 1898 and 2000/1, and by nearly 50 per cent between 1940 and 1941 following the outbreak of the Second World War (gov.uk, undated); a dramatic and highly significant increase when considering overall trends and this highlights the historical amnesia of commentators who argue that we are living in a time of unprecedented changes in crime levels.

There are multiple and often conflicting explanations put forward to explain the changing nature of crime in society and in particular the significant rise since the 1950s. Some of these include:

- the liberation of women from the home, providing them with an increase in offending opportunities (Adler, 1975; Simon, 1975);
- an increase in properties left empty during the day, thereby providing more opportunities for would-be burglars (Field, 1990);
- a significant rise in the levels of lead in the atmosphere, which resulted in neural underdevelopment among children and a higher propensity to violence (Nevin, 2000);
- a breakdown in traditional nuclear families and the lack of a stable father figure to provide a positive role model for children (Murray, 1990);
- high levels of unemployment leading to a rise in violent and property crime (Field, 1999; Carmichael and Ward, 2001);
- violence in the media and video games leading to an increase in violent behaviour (Anderson et al., 2003: 81).

Since the mid 1990s however, the Crime Survey for England and Wales (CSEW, formerly the British Crime Survey) has reported a sustained fall in crime levels. Again, there are many ideas about why this is; these have been summarised by Rawnsley (2013) and include:

- the removal of lead from petrol and paint resulting in a reduction in violence;
- the proliferation of CCTV;
- improvement in car and home security;
- the steep decline in the cost of consumer goods;
- the larger size of consumer goods such as televisions;
- more liberal abortion laws (the controversial theory argues that making it easier to get an abortion has diminished the number of children born into the 'underclass');
- an ageing population (most crime is committed by young men and most of their victims are other young men);
- rising numbers of women (they are less likely to commit crime than men);

- a more feminised society;

- a more middle-class society;

- more immigrants (immigrants are less likely to commit crime despite popular discourses suggesting otherwise);

- home computer games (give young men an alternative to vandalising, robbing and fighting);

- easy access to hardcore porn on the internet;

- cheap gyms;

- the civilising role of social media;

- a rise in police levels under New Labour between 1997 and 2010;

- a decline in the consumption of alcohol among the young;

- reductions in the use of illegal drugs and a rise in prescriptions of psychiatric drugs;

- austerity;

- some crime is not actually falling; it is changing in ways we have yet properly to discern (for example credit card fraud and other forms of digital crime are under-recorded because people don't report them and the banks don't want to admit to their scale).

The key point from this is that there is no simple answer as to why crime rates have fallen in such a sustained manner. The theories outlined above draw upon correlations – they look at social changes and their coincidence with crime rates, drawing conclusions based on the correlation shown. However, simplistic cause and effect models or ideas do not work when examining crime rates and crime trends. While correlation may imply causation, it does not mean that such an assumption is accurate and we need to move away from these simple assumptions that underpin many theories underpinning understandings of crime trends. There may be some truth in these trends, however a single study alone cannot confirm it and it is likely that there are overlapping factors and these changes reflect important shifts in public behaviour and standards. While it may be true for instance that CCTV has led to changes in behaviour, particularly in relation to car theft in and around public car parks, this does not explain why people still engage in violence, especially in well-policed town centres. Likewise, a reduction in atmospheric lead may have helped the decline in violence but doesn't help us to explain why fraud and cybercrime trends have risen dramatically.

Uses of and for Crime Statistics

The uses of police-recorded crime statistics are considerable and varied, they:

- help to indicate overall crime trends (particularly when used in conjunction with the CSEW);

- cover offences and victims that fall outside the scope of the CSEW (e.g. offences relating to the possession of weapons or drugs, and apparent 'victimless crimes');

- enable detailed analysis of local crime trends;

- provide detail on the incidence of individual offences and types of offence;

- provide information on detection rates and criminal justice outcomes;

- underpin the data on crime detection rates and criminal justice outcomes which can help to provide indicators on the size and distribution of police workloads and inform policing priorities and resource distribution.

(House of Commons Public Administration Select Committee, 2014: 7–8)

They are also used by a multitude of other people and agencies ranging from governments seeking to implement crime and harm reduction strategies, to risk-based agencies (e.g. insurance companies) seeking to assess the chances of a person or piece of property becoming a victim of crime, individuals assessing the risk of harm to themselves, and the police seeking to deter and detect crime. Crime data are also highly politically salient, with politicians and the media regularly reporting changing trends. Their focus on short-term changes in crime trends, however, frequently ignores the longer term trends and this is one of the reasons for perceptions among the wider public that crime has been rising continually despite widespread evidence to the contrary.

Police-recorded Crime

Until the 1980s, most of the data available on crime levels in England and Wales came from police-recorded crime statistics. These statistics draw upon the information supplied by the police and are based on crimes detected, reported and recorded by the police. The manner in which crimes are reported and recorded changes over time and this can have a significant impact upon crime figures. At the time of writing (March 2016), the All Party Parliamentary Group for Children (APPGC) had recently proposed diverting children involved in crime, deviance and delinquency away from the criminal justice agencies and towards welfare agencies in order to reduce instances of criminalising young people and preventing them from carrying a criminal record with them from an early age (APPGC, 2015: 7). If this were to be acted upon there would be a significant influence upon recorded crime rates through removing a number of offences from the records as a result of a change in practices; however, this would be significantly outweighed by the benefits to the young people who would be less likely to be criminalised, and to wider society by ensuring that they are better placed to engage as active members of society.

There are a number of steps that must occur for an act to be recorded as such for the purposes of Police Recorded Crime (PRC) statistics which are detailed below using information from Her Majesty's Inspectorate of Constabulary (HMIC, undated) and each of these steps carries with it a number of problems which can lead to significant inconsistencies between the number of actual offences and the number and type recorded by the police:

1. Detection of an incident by a victim or by the police: some events may be 'victimless' or simply go undetected. Alternatively an individual may not feel that the act was a crime in the first place. As such, many offences will never reach the police and so are not included in PRC figures.

2. Reporting of an incident to the police: not every offence is reported to the police. Some incidents may be deemed too trivial by the victim or not recognised as being potentially illegal in the first instance, whilst others may feel ashamed by the event, scared of any future repercussions or feel that others, including the police, will not believe them.

3. Deciding whether a crime should be recorded: the police must decide whether it is appropriate for an incident to be categorised as an offence based upon the circumstances of the act and whether there is any evidence to the contrary. As such there are many opportunities for an incident to remain just that and not be recorded as a crime.

4. Closing incident records: if an incident is not deemed to be a crime, the case will be closed and no crime will be recorded.

5. Recording crime(s): if an incident is deemed to be a crime, the police will then have to decide how many offences have been committed. This can vary considerably based on the circumstances of an offence and can lead to considerable variation in the number of crimes recorded, as well as variations in how the offence is categorised which can have a direct impact upon recorded crime figures. Consider, for instance, a case whereby someone has been assaulted and threatened on three occasions. According to Home Office Counting Rules (HOCR), if the victim reports the assaults and threats after each incident, then three crimes are recorded; if, on the other hand they report all three occurrences at once, only one crime is recorded (Home Office, 2015: 19). As such, depending on the reporting practices of the individual, the number of crimes recorded can vary considerably despite the same person being victimised repeatedly.

6. Closing crime records: cases are closed when a crime has been solved, i.e. when someone has been cautioned, charged or summonsed to appear in front of a court or, alternatively, evidence may indicate that the crime never actually occurred; e.g. a missing item is located after being mislaid.

7. Checking records are correct: a crime registrar is tasked with overseeing compliance with recording practices. They may detect discrepancies in crime records that require amending. Moreover, having a different registrar in each force means that there is a degree of subjectivity right the way through the system and therefore no guarantee that two similar offences will always be recorded identically.

As we can see above, there are a significant number of variables that come into play when it comes to detecting, reporting and recording incidents as crimes and all of these influence PRC statistics and trends. The crime most widely reported by the public has traditionally been theft because of the need for an incident number when reporting theft or damage to the insurance company. A household in a deprived neighbourhood is less likely to have insurance and therefore less likely to report such incidents to the police (Sparks, 1981; Young, 2011), thereby skewing the results considerably. Richard Sparks (1981) has noted a similar skewing resulting from early US crime survey findings which suggested that educated, white middle-class men were proportionately more likely to be victims of violent crime than black men despite wider evidence to the contrary. Sparks has argued that this is because of a lower tolerance of violence among white and middle-class individuals and also due to the fact that they are better suited to understanding and responding to surveys of that nature (Sparks, 1981: 34). This anomalous finding – that a middle-class white man was more likely to be a victim of violent crime than a black man from a deprived neighbourhood – in turn informed policing strategies and is therefore indicative of the influence which crime statistics and trends can have upon policy and practice.

As the discussion above suggests, debates surrounding the ability of police-recorded crime statistics to track changes in crime levels rather than police recording practices are well documented and were an integral part of the introduction of the British Crime Survey in 1982 (Hough et al., 2007). More recently, evidence has emerged of a continuing practice of the manipulation of police-recorded crime figures. Evidence for this can be found in testimonies from whistle-blowers presented to the House of Commons Public Administration Select Committee (PASC) (2014) whereby it was found that, among other problems, the use of numerical 'targets' in some police forces 'drive perverse incentives to misrecord crime, tend to affect attitudes and erode data quality' (PASC, 2014: 3). Such discrepancies and (mis)recording practices carry with them serious ramifications, not least the undermining of public trust. Cases such as this also help to emphasise the risks associated with relying upon official data when examining changing crime trends. This has been noted as being particularly troubling in relation to sexual assaults and rapes, which, in some instances, have either been 'no-crimed' (and not recorded) or classed as a 'crime related incident' (and therefore not recorded as a crime per se) in up to 30 per cent of some jurisdictions (PASC, 2014: 15). The recording of rape and sexual assaults provides a clear and extreme example of the way in which recording practices can influence crime rates and police-recorded crime and shines a light on the constructed nature of such statistics, and emphasising the dangers of relying solely on official records.

Victim Surveys

As already noted, PRC statistics rely on crimes being reported to, or detected by the police. This has obvious limitations in that it fails to record or account for crimes which are not reported to the police in the first instance and so we are left with a considerable 'dark figure' of crime – acts that have not been reported or detected, and which therefore remain unrecorded. The growing critique of the police and official crime statistics challenged the accepted orthodoxy that the police were able to fulfil their traditional role effectively and that official figures were accurate (see Hough et al. (2007) for more detailed discussions on the origins of the British Crime Survey). Victim surveys were designed to provide more accurate representations of the impacts of crime and helped to support the aforementioned arguments. The latest critiques and concerns arising from further investigations (e.g. the PASC report) further underline these criticisms.

Modern victim surveys trace their roots back to those commissioned by the US President's Commission in 1967 (Sparks, 1981). The National Crime Victimization Survey conducted in the USA in 1973 was the first national survey of its kind and provided the foundations and impetus for a nationally funded United Kingdom Crime Survey – the British Crime Survey (BCS) (now known as the Crime Survey for England and Wales (CSEW)) which was first conducted in 1982 and published in 1983 (Hough and Mayhew, 1983). The survey is currently conducted annually and in 2015, 33,500 households were sampled having been selected from the national Postcode Address Finder database. Approximately 650 extra households were included to provide a booster sample for under-represented groups (predominantly along the lines of ethnicity) and there is a separate survey, introduced in 2009, which covers experiences of victimisation among 10–15 year olds. It is worth noting that the number of households, while significant, was reduced from 50,000 in 2011/12 in the midst of the then Coalition government austerity drive, reflecting the wider challenges facing police and victim related services under the continuing narrative of austerity in England and Wales.

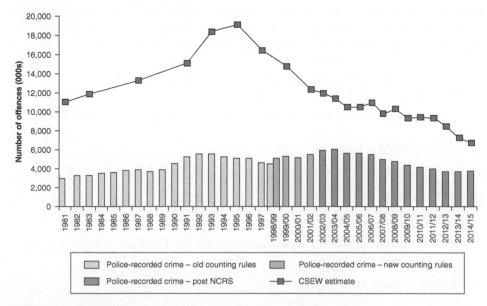

Figure 3.2 BCS/CSEW and police-recorded crime 1981–2014/15

Source: ONS, 2015

Figure 3.2 highlights the substantial variation between police-recorded crime figures and CSEW findings. We can see that self-reported crime rates have been consistently higher than those recorded by the police, thereby helping to underscore one of the key problems with police-recorded crime. However, what we are also able to see is that both data sets indicate that the number of offences committed each year have been falling since 2002/3, with CSEW findings showing a much longer drop dating back to the mid 1990s. Victim surveys and the BCS/CSEW heralded a dramatic shift in understandings of crime and its impacts, particularly upon victims, and such surveys have helped to inform and shape public opinion, policing and political strategies since.

Victim surveys provide a critical insight into the reporting and recording of crime and go a significant way towards addressing the dark figure of crime. The significant gap, even now when reported and recorded crime appears to be narrowing, underlines the dramatic failure of the police to be able to record or detect all forms of crime, or for people to report the offences to them in the first instance. Such information is crucial when seeking to understand the real impact of crime on society and communities and provides a more accurate depiction of what is going on. Alongside the BCS, the Liverpool Crime Survey (1984) and Islington Crime Survey (1986) (amongst others) sought to expand critical local knowledge of crime and underlined the fact that there was a significant difference between how effectively the police viewed their work, and perceptions among the public (Jones et al., 1986). As a result victim surveys have had some impact on police practice, and police forces are now expected to engage in more locally focused practices in order to address local crime issues rather than simply assuming that national strategies are the most effective. Moreover, national victim surveys help us to understand anxieties surrounding crime and to develop a more accurate understanding of the true figures for crime (although they are still far from accurate), particularly underreported offences such as rape and sexual assaults of which it is estimated only 15 per cent are currently reported and only 1–2 per cent of incidents result in a conviction (based on figures from Ministry of Justice et al., 2013: 6).

Victim surveys, and in particular the CSEW, are not without their critics, however, and Richard Sparks identified six key problems with early victim surveys:

1. Under-reporting of incidents;

2. Response biases;

3. Time-in-sample bias;

4. Methods of data collection;

5. Movers and Stayers (although Sparks acknowledges that such a problem is uniquely limited to longitudinal surveys);

6. Missing variables. (Sparks, 1981)

It is thus evident that there are a number of key elements which needed to be addressed in early surveys, some of which, particularly the under-reporting of incidents, response biases and missing variables, continue to haunt today's victim surveys. An example of this can be seen in the fact that a large number of crimes are not covered by the survey – it is not, for instance, possible to include someone who was killed during that period! Likewise, because the survey contacts households and looks at individual experiences of victimisation it does not look at so-called 'victimless crimes' such as shoplifting, or crimes committed by businesses including corporate espionage and fraud. Vulnerable groups are also under-represented. The survey contacts households and many of the most vulnerable in society do not have a stable or fixed abode. Anyone unfortunate enough to find themselves homeless may be sofa-surfing, living in a hostel, or on the streets (to name but a few locations) and such individuals have been consistently identified as being at much greater risk of victimisation than the average person.

Attempts have been made to rectify some of the survey's limitations with sub-samples being taken for 10–15 year olds since 2009 for example, to examine their experiences of victimisation. In 2014/15 fraud and cybercrime were included in the survey for the first time. The results of this indicate that there were 3.6 million fraud and 2 million computer misuse offences in the twelve months to June 2016 which had not previously been recorded by the survey (ONS, 2016), indicating a significant change in offending behaviour and a large number of offences still going unrecorded. At present, these data are not incorporated into the main CSEW reports as there is less than twelve months of data available (hence why, in Figure 3.2, there is no significant increase in CSEW recorded crime), however it is expected to be included in the primary outputs as of 2017. The impact that this could have on future crime trends is sizeable, and it could nearly double the number of offences recorded in the crime survey. This thereby outlines the manner in which crime statistics and trends, as well as our understandings and definitions of crime, go through substantial revision and reconstruction on a regular basis.

Self Report – Offenders

Victim surveys and much of the information contained within police-recorded crime figures rely heavily on the self-reporting of crime by victims. We know, however, that many offences are not detected by anybody and we are therefore limited in our ability to detect or understand the influence of such 'hidden' crimes. Self-reported surveys conducted with offenders have been developed to seek to address this gap, providing insights into the motivations, justifications and neutralisations which can shed further light onto crime and criminal behaviour as well as towards the propensity for some offenders to commit a considerable number of offences (see Bermasco, 2010 for a detailed discussion on the benefits and challenges of working with offenders to understand criminal behaviour). Yet there are some glaring limitations, not least the fact that offenders are, in many cases hard to find and either unwilling or unable to share their narratives; and there are often concerns raised over the veracity of their narratives (Bermasco, 2010: 3–5). As such samples are often limited to those already caught up in the Criminal Justice System (in prison or on probation for example) this in turn provides skewed data on the propensity for individuals to commit crime as well as the likelihood of such a captive population to continue on their existing trajectory. What has emerged as a result of engaging offenders in self-report studies, however, is an understanding of people's propensity to crime and more in-depth information surrounding motivations towards such activities and this information can in turn be drawn upon to better understand crime trends as a result.

Identifying the Real Crime Rate

It is unlikely that we will ever know 'true' crime rates. The shifting and ever-evolving definitions of crime are one of the reasons for this. These constant shifts are a result of changes in people's perceptions of crime and which acts should be branded as criminal and deviant or acceptable. While the law provides us with a working definition of what is and is not illegal, and therefore what is likely to be included in crime statistics, it is evident that these definitions are problematic and fail to address many crimes which cause considerable social harm. Moreover, the addition of new legal definitions of crime make overall comparison over time almost impossible despite regular efforts to make crime and victim surveys more encompassing. These factors, combined with under-reporting, under-recording and misinterpretation of acts as criminal or not by both the criminal justice agencies and individuals, mean that society will never have a 100 per cent accurate picture of crime, and perhaps the best that we can do is seek to understand which crimes are more prevalent and which are liable to cause the most harm and distress on an individual, societal and international level.

Summary

In this chapter we have examined the complex and often conflicting pathways used to determine and define crime, as well as the challenges arising from the use of crime trends and criminal statistics. As Elmsley (2013) has argued, it is unlikely that there will ever be a perfect definition of crime and its constituent elements. The definitions that do exist provide us with a working framework upon which we are able to delineate which acts are seen as legal and acceptable in society and which are not; and thereby act as a barometer for public sentiment towards those acts. Like other potential definitions, legal definitions are problematic and reflect the influence of power and authority in their formulation. They often fail to account for some of the most harmful acts in society, whether that be irresponsibility and the manipulation of key rates by bankers, which played a pivotal role in the global economic collapse, or significant environmental damage such as has potentially been caused by the recent (2015) Volkswagen emissions scandal. The socially constructed nature of crime, which varies based on the cultural context in which it is constituted, is clear to see.

This in turn has a significant and pronounced effect on crime statistics and trends, themselves constructed through recording, reporting and detection practices. Whilst attempts have been made, such as with the introduction of victim surveys and self-report surveys, to address the dark figure of crime, it is improbable that we will ever be able to claim that we have a full and accurate measure of crime. Yet the picture need not be entirely bleak for either criminology or crime trends. We can see the way in which recording practices have changed; the impact of crime upon individuals, communities and wider perceptions of criminality; the effectiveness of political and policing interventions and strategies; and potentially the influence of wider changes in society, whether that be the rise in consumption and its impact upon theft and burglary, or the influence of biosocial elements such as levels of lead in the environment and atmosphere. We have a good understanding of the limitations of the measures which we do have and so changes continue to be made to improve them and we are able to glean a great deal of information from the trends, whilst remaining careful to avoid drawing cause and effect explanations from overly simplistic correlations.

Discussion Questions

1. Re-read the section on 'Defining Crime' in this chapter. How would you define crime?

2. After reading about 'crime as a social construction', would you define yourself as a criminal?

   o Yes?

   o No?

   o Abstain?

Let us think about this question another way.

3. Have you ever done any of the following?

   a. Used a phone whilst driving (since 2008)?

   b. Driven faster than the legal speed limit?

   c. Bought a drink underage/for someone underage?

   d. Illegally downloaded or streamed a song or film?

4. Did your answer change when moving from the first question to the second? If so, why do you think this is?

5. In addition to the examples given in this chapter, what other activities can you think of that have been decriminalised over time?

6. What other activities can you think of that have been criminalised over time?

7. What do you think are the most appropriate ways to measure crime? Can we ever know the true crime rate?

——— **Further Reading** ———

Coomber, R., Donnermeyer, J.F., McElrath, K. and Scott, J. (2013) *Key Concepts in Crime and Society*. London: Sage.

Curra, J. (2016) *The Relativity of Deviance*. 4th edn. London: Sage.

Hughes, G., McLaughlin, E. and Muncie, J. (eds) (2013) *Criminological Perspectives*. 3rd edn. London: Sage.

McLaughlin, E. and Muncie, J. (2013) *The SAGE Dictionary of Criminology*. 3rd edn. London: Sage.

Muncie, J. and McLaughlin, E. (2001) *The Problem of Crime*. 2nd edn. London: Sage.

Payne, B.K., Oliver, W.M. and Marion, N.E. (2015) *Introduction to Criminal Justice: A balanced approach*. London: Sage.

The latest statistics and bulletins on crime in England and Wales, drawing upon data from Police Recorded Crime figures and the Crime Survey for England and Wales can be found here: www.ons.gov.uk/peoplepopulationandcommunity/crimeandjustice

The following will take you to official Home Office guidance detailing the differences between PRC and the CSEW including differences in scope, methodology, recording practices, measures and revisions policies: www.ons.gov.uk/ons/guide-method/method-quality/specific/crime-statistics-methodology/user-guide-to-crime-statistics.pdf

——— **References** ———

Adler, F. (1975) *Sisters in Crime: The rise of the new female criminal*. New York: McGraw-Hill.

All Party Parliamentary Group for Children (2015) *Building Trust: One year on – Progress in improving relationships between children and the police*. National Children's Bureau. Available at: www.ncb.org.uk/media/1237461/one_year_on_report_-final_copy.pdf [accessed 15 December 2015].

Anderson, C.A., Berkowitz, L., Donnerstein, E., Huesmann, L.R., Johnson, J.D., Linz, D., Mallmuth, N.M. and Wartella, E. (2003) 'The influence of media violence on youth', *Psychological Science in the Public Interest*, 4: 81–110.

BBC News (2013) 'Iceland jails former Kaupthing bank bosses', 12 December. Available at: www.bbc.co.uk/news/business-25349240 [accessed 17 December 2015].

Bermasco, W. (2010) *Offenders on Offending: Learning about crime from criminals*. Cullompton: Willan.

Carmichael, F. and Ward, R. (2001) 'Male unemployment and crime in England and Wales', *Economic Letters*, 73 (1): 111–15.

Chevigny, P.G. (2001) 'From betrayal to violence: Dante's Inferno and the social construction of crime', *Law and Social Inquiry*, 26 (4): 787–818.

Conan Doyle, A. (2007) *The Complete Stories of Sherlock Holmes*. Hertfordshire: Wordsworth.

Crown Prosecution Service (2015) *Homicide; Murder and Manslaughter: Legal guidance* [Online]. Available at: www.cps.gov.uk/legal/h_to_k/homicide_murder_and_manslaughter/ [accessed 10 December 2015].

Elmsley, C. (2013) *Crime and Society in England*. 4th edn. Abingdon: Routledge.

Field, S. (1990) *Trends in Crime and their Interpretation: A study of recorded crime in post-war England and Wales. Home Office Research Study 119*. London: HMSO.

Field, S. (1999) *Trends in Crime Revisited. Home Office Research Study 195*. London: HMSO.

gov.uk (undated) *Recorded Crime Statistics for England and Wales 1898–2001/2*. Available at: www.gov.uk/government/uploads/system/uploads/attachment_data/file/116649/rec-crime-1898-2002.xls [accessed 17 December 2015].

gov.uk (2015) *Drug Penalties* [Online]. Available at: www.gov.uk/penalties-drug-possession-dealing [accessed 11 December 2015].

Her Majesty's Inspectorate of Constabulary (undated) 'The crime recording process'. Available at: www.justiceinspectorates.gov.uk/hmic/our-work/crime-data-integrity/crime-recording-process/ [accessed 17 March 2016].

Home Office (2015) *Home Office Counting Rules for the Recording of Crime*. Available at: www.gov.uk/government/uploads/system/uploads/attachment_data/file/489732/count-general-january-2016.pdf [accessed 22 March 2016].

Hotten, R. (2015) 'Volkswagen: The scandal explained', *BBC News* [Online] 10 Dec. Available at: www.bbc.co.uk/news/business-34324772 [accessed 5 February 2016].

Hough, M. and Mayhew, P. (1983) *The British Crime Survey: First report*. London: HMSO.

Hough, M., Maxfield, M., Morris, B. and Simmons, J. (2007) 'The British crime survey after 25 years: Progress, problems and prospects', in M. Hough and D. Maxfield (eds), *Surveying Crime in the 21st Century, Crime Prevention Studies Vol. 22*. Cullompton: Willan.

House of Commons Public Administration Select Committee (2014) *Caught Red-Handed: Why we can't count on police recorded crime statistics*. London: TSO. Available at: www.publications.parliament.uk/pa/cm201314/cmselect/cmpubadm/760/760.pdf [accessed 15 December 2015].

Jones, T., Maclean, B. and Young, J. (1986) *The Islington Crime Survey*. Aldershot: Gower.

Lacey, N. and Zedner, L. (2012) 'Legal constructions of crime', in M. Maguire, R. Morgan and R. Reiner (eds), *The Oxford Handbook of Criminology*. 5th edn. Oxford: Oxford University Press.

Law Commission (2010) *Criminal Liability in Regulatory Contexts. Consultation Paper No 195*. London: Law Commission.

Lea, J. (2002) *Crime and Modernity: Continuities in left realist criminology*. London: Sage.

Matthews, R. (2014) *Realist Criminology*. Basingstoke: Palgrave MacMillan.

Matthews, R. and Young, J. (1992) *Issues in Realist Criminology*. London: Sage.

Ministry of Justice (2014) *New Criminal Offences England and Wales 1st June 2009–31st May 2014* [Online]. Available at: www.gov.uk/government/uploads/system/uploads/attachment_data/file/385537/new-criminal-offences-june-2009-may-2014.pdf [accessed 11 December 2015].

Ministry of Justice, Home Office and the Office for National Statistics (2013) *An Overview of Sexual Offending in England and Wales*. Available at: www.gov.uk/government/uploads/system/uploads/attachment_data/file/214970/sexual-offending-overview-jan-2013.pdf [accessed 5 February 2016].

Morgan, R. (2011) 'Austerity, subsidiarity and parsimony: Offending behaviour and criminalisation', in A. Silvestri (ed.), *Lessons for the Coalition: An end of term report on New Labour and criminal justice*. London: Centre for Crime and Justice Studies.

Muncie, J. (2001) *The Problem of Crime*. 2nd edn. London: Sage.

Murray, C. (1990) *The Emerging British Underclass*. London: Institute of Economic Affairs.

Nevin, R. (2000) 'How lead exposure relates to temporal changes in IQ, violent crime and unwed pregnancy', *Environmental Research*, 83 (1): 1–22.

Office for National Statistics (2015) *Crime in England and Wales, Year Ending March 2015*. Available at: www.ons.gov.uk/ons/dcp171778_411032.pdf [accessed 5 February 2016].

Office for National Statistics (2016) Crime in England and Wales, Year Ending June 2016. Available at: www.ons.gov.uk/peoplepopulationandcommunity/crimeandjustice/bulletins/crimeinenglandandwales/yearendingjune2016/pdf [accessed 17 October 2016].

Oxford English Dictionary (2011) 12th rev. edn. Oxford: Clarendon Press.

Quinney, R. (1970) The Social Reality of Crime. Boston, MA: Little, Brown.

Quinney, R. (2000) Bearing Witness to Crime and Social Justice. Albany: State University of New York Press.

Rawnsley, A. (2013) 'A crime mystery. It's going down, but no one really knows why', The Guardian [Online] 28 April. Available at: http://www.theguardian.com/commentisfree/2013/apr/28/crime-is-down-what-a-mystery [accessed 14 March 2016].

Simon, R. (1975) Women and Crime. Lexington, MA: D.C. Heath.

Sparks, R. (1981) 'Surveys of victimization – An optimistic assessment', Crime and Justice, 3: 1–60.

Surette, R. (2015) 'Thought bite: A case study of the social construction of a crime and justice concept', Crime, Media, Culture, 11 (2): 105–35.

Sutherland, E. (1940) 'White collar criminality', American Sociological Association, 5 (1): 1–12.

Sutherland, E. (1949) White Collar Crime. New York: The Dryden Press.

Young, J. (2011) The Criminological Imagination. Cambridge: Polity.

Young, J. and Matthews, R. (1992) Rethinking Criminology – The realist debate. London: Sage.

Check out the Companion Website

Want to know more about this chapter? Review what you have been learning by visiting: **https://study.sagepub.com/harding**

- Practice with essay questions
- Test yourself with multiple-choice questions
- Listen to a series of podcasts featuring Neil of Northumbria Police and London's Metropolitan Police Service
- Watch videos selected from the SAGE Video collection

4   Purposes of the Criminal Justice Process

Joanne Clough

Introduction

The Criminal Justice System in England and Wales is the process of collecting evidence, establishing guilt (or innocence) of an accused person through the trial process, punishing those who are convicted and managing the sentencing orders of the court. This system operates through the efforts of a myriad of different agencies including the police, prosecution and defence lawyers, court staff, the judiciary, probation officers and prison staff. All of these agencies undertake very different roles, with differing responsibilities and therefore have a range of differing aims and purposes, as will be discussed further in Part Two. Some agencies have been partially privatised, e.g. the probation service and some prison establishments, which adds an additional layer of complication as aims within the one agency can also be competing. Nevertheless, the success of the system as a whole relies on their mutual interdependence.

Bearing in mind the multi-functional interplay between all the agencies within the Criminal Justice System, it is fair to say that the aim of the system at one stage of the criminal justice process is not the same as at a later stage of the process. Thus, it is the purpose of the police to take responsibility for detecting crime, collecting evidence and presenting criminals to be prosecuted. The prosecution's aim is to determine whether to charge and with which offence; they are responsible for presenting the evidence of the police at court. The courts carry out an adjudication role to determine whether an accused person is innocent or guilty and make decisions about the punishment of those who are convicted, ensuring that sentences are passed fairly and without prejudice. The probation service and prisons carry out the wishes of the courts by ensuring that sentences are completed and offenders are rehabilitated.

Despite these varied roles and differing aims within the process, it can be said that the main purpose of the Criminal Justice System is to deliver justice, although this may sound rather general and trite. If this is managed successfully, criminals are convicted, punished and rehabilitated, which, in turn, ensures that the general public are safeguarded from future harm. It should be borne in mind that the government, who through parliament create the legislative framework for the Criminal Justice System, has targets and strategies which inform the shape of the criminal justice process, so the focus of the system can shift according to differing governmental aims and objectives. The then Lord Chancellor and Justice Minister, the Rt Hon Michael Gove MP, operating within a Conservative government, stated in his inaugural speech that he intended to implement 'one nation justice' which focuses on the importance of the rule of law and the streamlining of criminal justice processes for the benefit of the victims of crime (Gove, 2015).

This chapter will explore the range of differing purposes that dominate the various stages of the process with consideration of the theories behind each aim. Within the overarching aim of achieving justice, it is suggested that the purposes of the system are:

- to act as a form of social control;
- to prevent crime;

- to investigate breaches of the criminal law;
- to prosecute offenders;
- to formally identify offenders through the trial process;
- to punish offenders.

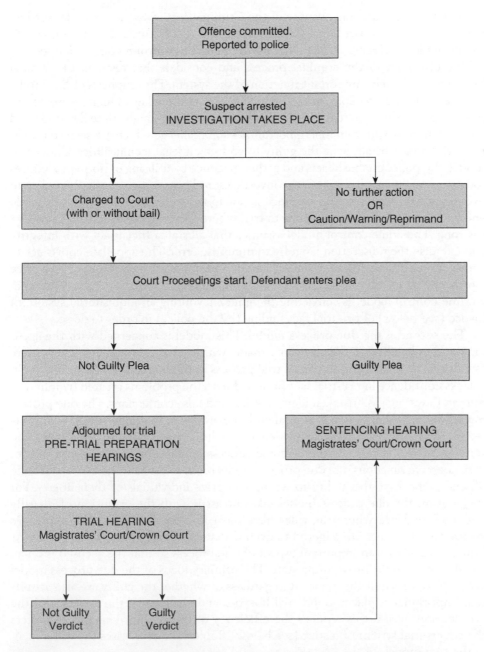

Figure 4.1 An overview of the Criminal Justice System in England and Wales

Before looking at these aims individually, it is important to first consider the key theories that underpin the system.

Theories of Criminal Justice

As noted, the overarching purpose of the Criminal Justice System is to deliver justice and there are two differing theoretical models that are used to explain how this can be achieved (Packer, 1968). The first is the **crime control model**, which focuses on the efficiency of the criminal process and considers that restraint of criminal behaviour is the most important function of the system. The emphasis of this model is to uphold social freedom, to ensure individuals hold the law in high regard and to prevent people living in fear. This ideal is achieved through high crime detection and conviction rates, with minimal opportunities for challenge which are seen to undermine the model by allowing the guilty to go free on legal technicalities. Under this model, the police establish facts and gather evidence by utilising uniform procedures to ensure quality control within the investigation. This practice allows the police to exonerate anyone where the evidence is not found to be suggestive of guilt while encouraging more guilty pleas prior to trial where the evidence against the assailant is strong. The crime control model assumes that all state officials act with integrity and exercise their discretion lawfully to minimise error. The appellate courts act to correct any mistakes made by the police; such mistakes are considered to be a price worth paying for the successful repression of criminal activity. The priority within a crime control model is convicting the guilty, favouring an inquisitorial system of justice (see below) of pre-trial fact finding (by the police) in order to do so.

The second is the **due process model**. This model is concerned with the accuracy and reliability of the decisions made within the Criminal Justice System, favouring the formal and impartial trial process as the means of determining guilt. It lacks confidence in pre-trial fact finding due to the problems created by inherent human flaws such as mistaken identities, lies and false confessions. The due process model distinguishes between factual guilt, i.e. evidence that a person has committed a crime, and legal guilt, i.e. evidence which has been obtained legally for the state to prove its case. As the criminal process stigmatises criminals and utilises very coercive sanctions, the due process model seeks to restrain the powers of state officials, who have the ability to wrongly deprive individuals of their liberty. For this reason, the due process model takes no issue with the exclusion of illegally obtained evidence where the rules have been flouted; such harsh consequences ensure that the rules are adhered to even if that means a guilty person walks free. Equality of arms is an important aspect of due process so that the accused is on an equal footing to the prosecuting state. The primary focus of the due process model is therefore to acquit the innocent, regardless of whether the guilty are also acquitted. Importance is placed upon civil liberties and challenging the accuracy of the prosecution even if this reduces the efficiency of the system. This model prefers the adversarial system of justice (see below). Table 4.1 summarises the differences in the two models.

Table 4.1 The differences between the crime control and due process models of criminal justice

Crime control	Due process
Primary function of the CJS:	**Primary function of the CJS:**
To control crime by arresting and convicting those who commit offences	To control crime lawfully and respect citizens' civil liberties
Primary value: Efficiency	**Primary value:** Reliability
Operation:	**Operation:**
Based on speed and efficiency, which relies upon informality and uniform approaches. Reduction in legal challenges to ensure speed and finality. Early stages of the process are most important with investigators' and prosecutors' decision making relied upon.	Importance of reliable and accurate fact finding, evidence gathering and decision making. Requires formal processes and legal challenges to ensure accuracy. Accuracy is more important than speed. Later stages of formal fact finding through defence lawyers and judiciary decision making relied upon.
Priority:	**Priority:**
Quantity of factually guilty offenders caught and convicted	Quality of procedures, which ensures factually and legally guilty offenders are convicted.

Of course, there is no definitive answer as to which of the two models is more likely to explain more satisfactorily how justice is achieved (and they are both, of course, models so unlikely to be clearly identifiable in practice). Both models share the belief that law enforcement is desirable and that a certain level of scrutiny exists to regulate that process (Duff, 1998). Some suggest that the crime control model is an underlying purpose that falls within the due process model (Ashworth and Redmayne, 2005) while others argue that due process is not a goal in itself, but rather a way of setting limits on the pursuit of justice (Smith, 1997). This chapter highlights that in England and Wales the system appears to be an amalgamation of the two models with priorities from each of them prevailing at differing stages of the process.

Social Control

The Wolfenden Committee (1957: paras 13–14), commissioned in 1954 to report on the criminality of homosexual activity and prostitution, declared that the function of criminal law is, 'to preserve public order and decency, to protect the citizen from what is offensive or injurious and to provide sufficient safeguards against exploitation or corruption of others, particularly those who are especially vulnerable ...'. The law has developed over many centuries as a means of setting a code of conduct within which civilised society operates. There are literally thousands of criminal offences currently in force in England and Wales which together indicate the limits of citizens' legitimate activity and set out the consequences of infractions. Criminal convictions represent public condemnation of the prohibited conduct, and give permission for the state to inflict a punishment of some kind. Consequently, the limits set by the criminal law allow an individual to make rational choices about what behaviour he or she wishes to engage in.

The Criminal Justice System operates within the parameters set by the criminal law. It is the means by which breaches of the criminal code are identified and punished. For Durkheim (1884: 63), the real function of the Criminal Justice System is 'to maintain inviolate the cohesion of society by sustaining the common consciousness in all its vigour'. In other words, the Criminal Justice System is there to manage disorder and breaches of the rules. In theory, it creates and maintains a well-ordered society where crime is minimised.

The Criminal Justice System sits at the most powerful end of the spectrum of measures that maintain order in society. At the other end of the continuum are institutions such as schools, religious orders and even the family environment which all encourage us to operate within a commonly accepted structure of practices and behaviour. For example, the requirement to attend school is one of the state's methods of maintaining a civilised society by educating its citizens to a minimum standard. The Criminal Justice System falls at the opposite end of the scale, adopting the most coercive method of control. Hence, the ability of the police to stop and search, to arrest individuals and to investigate a crime while holding that person against their will, are much more obvious forms of state power which begin to infringe on personal freedoms. The Criminal Justice System is therefore an instrument of social control which represents the accumulation of powers, processes and sanctions surrounding the criminal law, and provides a method by which the state can interfere in personal autonomy in order to regulate the behaviour of its citizens.

But the Criminal Justice System is not only there to deal with those who violate the rules. The legislative system has been utilised to maintain order and avoid disorder; for example, to control the perceived threat of those who advocate and lead lifestyles that differ from the norm. For example, the Public Order Act 1986 was an Act designed to control public processions and assemblies as well as to create new criminal offences relating to public order. Siegel (2015: 485) defines a public order crime as 'crime which involves acts that interfere with the operations of society and the ability of people to function efficiently'. This behaviour has been labelled as such because it is contrary to shared values and social customs. This legislation allows the state to impose control over those who 'threaten' civilised society by adopting practices such as protesting or raving.

Crime Prevention and Investigation

Enforcement of the criminal law is largely the responsibility of the police, supported by other investigative agencies that have responsibility for particular aspects of the law, for example, the Department for Work and Pensions investigate low-level benefit fraud. The primary legislation that governs criminal investigations, irrespective of the investigating agency, is the Police and Criminal Evidence Act 1984 (PACE) and related Codes of Practice; this legislation is regularly reviewed and updated. The law confers powers upon the police to stop, search, arrest and detain individuals whom they know or suspect to have committed a crime. The Codes of Practice provide rules on the conduct and procedure for investigations, searches, detention and treatment of suspects, police interviews, and identification procedures. The central purpose of all investigative agencies, including the police, is to deliver justice through crime prevention and investigation, with an overarching aim to protect the public.

Crime Prevention

Crime prevention is undertaken by proactive policing whereby law enforcement agencies take active measures to prevent crime from happening. Such policing methods provide a check on those who make a living from criminal activity and send a message that such activity is not acceptable to society. For example, police powers to stop and search persons and vehicles, allow officers to identify potential criminal activity such as the movement of weapons or drugs, and prevent it from continuing as well as preventing future linked offences from happening at all. The police have powers to obtain search warrants on properties that they suspect are being used for criminal activity and they rely on intelligence to intercept criminal activity, such as drug dealing, before it happens. Furthermore, the police power of arrest can be utilised to prevent a crime from taking place. For example, section 16 of the Crime and Disorder Act 1998 permits the police to remove school children of a certain age and take them to school or other appropriate place in order to prevent truancy and potential antisocial behaviour. This style of policing fits neatly within the crime control model of criminal justice as it can involve arresting people known to the police to determine if a crime has been committed and to prevent further crimes from occurring. A due process model would insist upon hard evidence that a crime has been committed before an arrest takes place.

There are, of course, concerns that proactive policing powers have the scope to be abused and thus to undermine the aim of delivering justice. One study demonstrated that only 11 per cent of police stop and searches led to an arrest and only half of these arrests finally resulted in a caution or conviction (Miller et al., 2000). These figures suggest that police officers were conducting unfounded searches where no criminal activity was likely to result. While the conducting of these searches could be entirely legitimate, to avoid further speculation about the motives of police officers, a range of measures were introduced to put constraints on the exercise of police discretion. Officers are now required to provide certain information to suspects before a search can take place, including the purpose and grounds for the search and they must make a written record of the search (PACE 1984: ss.2–3). As the police can now be held to account for the potential misuse of their powers, it means that our investigatory system can be viewed as an amalgamation of both due process and crime control models.

There are a number of specific policing initiatives that reflect the crime prevention efforts of police forces. 'Hot Spots Policing' was developed in the USA in the mid 1990s and was based on the criminological assumption that crime tends to be clustered within particular places (Block, 1995). By targeting police resources to the specific times and places where crime occurs more frequently, crime and disorder were effectively reduced in those areas. While there were concerns that this method might displace criminal activity to areas where the police presence was not so obvious, this was found not to be the case (Weisburd and Braga, 2006). Critics suggest that the hot spots are identified on unreliable statistical identification of offenders and crime-prone areas, resulting in racial profiling and socially unjust outcomes (Tonry, 2011). Others suggest that focusing on particular areas risks ethical and privacy breaches, particularly if areas were being targeted on the basis of unreliable data (Ratcliffe, 2002).

Another form of proactive policing is 'Intelligence-led' policing, which tackles crime through the use of data relating to crime trends and offender profiles so that a small number of high volume recidivists can be proactively targeted in order to prevent crime (Ratcliffe, 2008). This approach focuses on the small number of offenders who comprise the main bulk of criminal activity and monitors the places and circumstances within which they operate. Intelligence-led policing requires high levels of resourcing to enable analysis and evaluation of statistics through mapping and information technology which is generally done by specialised police officers and their support teams (Cope, 2004).

Criminal Investigations

While the police have a plethora of duties, including dispute management, traffic control and finding missing people, their role as investigators of criminal offences reflects their central function as enforcers of the criminal law. The role of investigating crime tends to be a more reactive method of policing. While police officers often investigate and gather evidence resulting from the proactive methods already mentioned, much investigatory police work arises from complaints being made by members of the public about specific crimes that have already taken place or are in progress. The purpose of investigating crime and gathering evidence is to prove that an accused person committed the alleged offence. It is the responsibility of the police to present a case for the prosecution to prove the offence against the accused in court.

Investigations of routine matters are carried out by police constables but the more serious crimes are investigated by plain-clothed CID (Criminal Investigation Department) officers. Under PACE, police officers have the power to arrest anyone whom they reasonably suspect to be committing an offence, or who has committed an offence (PACE 1984: s.24). Once in custody at the police station, the suspect may only be detained if there are reasonable grounds to believe that it is 'necessary' to do so in order to secure or preserve evidence, or to obtain evidence by questioning (PACE 1984: s.38). Suspects must be informed of their rights to speak to a solicitor, to inform someone that they have been arrested and to consult a copy of PACE and the Codes. As a starting point, a suspect can be held without charge for a maximum of 24 hours (there are provisions to extend this), with regular reviews throughout that period to ensure that detention remains 'necessary'. While detained, the suspect will be interviewed about his suspected involvement in the offence. The suspect has a right to silence when being questioned although inferences can be drawn from that silence if they choose not to say something to the police during the interview that they later rely on in their defence at trial (Criminal Justice & Public Order Act 1986: ss.34–37).

The UK's adversarial system of justice (see below) requires the prosecution to prove their case and this relies upon legally admissible evidence being obtained by the police. The test of success for the police is commonly whether an investigation leads to a prosecution and ultimately a finding of guilt. This can put pressure on the police to obtain evidence in breach of the rules where they know an offender is guilty. Although breach of the procedural rules is not an offence in itself, this behaviour can give rise to complaint and the possibility that evidence obtained as a result of the breach might be excluded from the criminal trial. Consequently, it is vital that police officers follow the rules and that offenders are aware of the rules in order that due process can be achieved.

Methods of Investigation

The simplest form of evidence gathering is witness tracing and interviewing. Although witnesses can be imprecise and sometimes untruthful, witness testimony provides compelling evidence about the crime in terms of what has been seen or heard. Eye witnesses can take part in procedures to assist the police with identifying a suspect. In addition, anything that the suspect says in his police interview can be used in evidence against him. Consequently the police interview is a crucial way of obtaining evidence and even when a suspect is denying involvement in a crime, by providing an account to the police, his evidence often fills gaps in the police case.

Over the years, policing has stimulated the development of technical and expert services to assist in the investigation of crime. As a starting point, the police can refer to the Police National Computer database which holds information on people, vehicles and places. Forensic science techniques such as fingerprinting and DNA profiling have opened up the ability of police to identify those who were present at the scene of a crime through the ridges on a person's fingers or the strands of their DNA in a suspect's bodily fluids; both very useful techniques where there is no eye witness to make an identification. Mobile phones can be tracked through the triangulation of global positioning satellites and phone call and text message records can be obtained from a suspect's network provider. The increased use of CCTV cameras in public places has helped officers to identify suspects at the scenes of crimes and visual enhancing techniques allow investigators to zoom in on an image where it is blurred or distant. The use of intelligence is also crucial to building up a bank of evidence against a suspect.

Community Engagement

Prevention and investigation of crime cannot be undertaken by the police alone. They rely heavily upon the cooperation of the communities they serve in order to assist in the fight against crime. Consequently, good community relations are extremely important for this purpose, so proactive policing or 'reassurance' policing is a key aspect of the wider public relations agenda within local police forces. As well as serving as a visible reminder that the police are on hand to enforce the law and to act as a deterrent from engaging in criminal activity, proactive crime prevention makes the wider population feel safe and instils confidence that the police are doing their duty. Research has suggested that where police are not seen to be on the streets, there is a risk of breakdown in law and order (Ashworth and Redmayne, 2005). This in turn, helps to encourage members of the public to come forward and assist police in their investigative duties, for example by providing witness statements or responding to requests for information through media broadcasts such as *Crimestoppers* or *Crimewatch*. The role of members of the public, and agencies other than the police, in preventing crime is discussed further in Chapter 10.

On the other hand, proactive police work has the unintended consequence of redirecting police resources away from crime that is actually taking place. This can have the effect of reducing public confidence in police activity. Where the relationship between police authorities and the public breaks down, crime can ensue and there is no greater example of this than the London riots in August 2011, which were partly fuelled by the public's perception of institutional racism within the police force (Banakar, 2014). Equally, where the public perceive police to be abusing their powers, mistrust can follow. For example, the recent example of the *News of the World* phone-hacking scandal illustrates events that do little to reassure the public that the police are utilising their powers lawfully to protect the public. As a result, the police have to conduct a careful balancing act between crime prevention, public safety and crime investigation when utilising their police powers to achieve the aim of delivering justice.

The Prosecution of Offenders

After an investigation has taken place and the police have gathered evidence suggesting that a particular suspect has committed a criminal offence, that suspect can be charged and prosecuted in the criminal courts. The decision to charge a suspect is taken by the Crown Prosecution Service (CPS), the independent agency responsible for prosecuting criminal offences in England and Wales. The work of the CPS is discussed extensively in Chapter 13.

Acting on behalf of the accused person, and representing their interests in the police station and at court, are the defence solicitors and advocates. Unlike the CPS, defence solicitors work for private firms undertaking defence work either through state-managed legal aid funding or by their private paying clients. There is also a state-controlled Criminal Defence Service which operates in a similar manner to the CPS but acting on behalf of criminal defendants in the same manner as private solicitors. The Criminal Defence Service is currently available in four areas of England and Wales and was set up with a view to being rolled out across the country so that those who are accused of committing crimes could have access to free legal advice and representation from a state-funded solicitor. The role of the defence is to safeguard the accused's rights and ensure that processes are followed according to the law. For this reason, defence solicitors tend to be viewed as providing a legal challenge to the police and prosecution, thus creating an element of due process within the system.

Adversarial v. Inquisitorial Justice

There are two linked aims of the prosecution process, namely to convict the guilty and acquit the innocent. These aims are achieved within a criminal justice process which is either adversarial in nature or inquisitorial in nature, the choice being dependent on the particular country's system.

The Criminal Justice System in the England and Wales and other common law jurisdictions operates within an adversarial context. An adversarial system requires the prosecution to prove the guilt of the accused with the prosecution and defence seen as the 'adversaries' in the trial process. Prosecution and defence will prepare and present their side of the case to the court, and it is the judge who listens to the evidence, ensures procedures are followed correctly and makes ultimate decisions. By contrast, most of continental Europe operates within an inquisitorial system of criminal justice. In this system, the courts play a central role by taking control of proceedings and utilising investigatory powers to make decisions in criminal cases. The judge questions witnesses and decides what evidence should be called at trial, thus rendering the prosecution and defence as secondary parties to the process. The state therefore plays a much larger role in inquisitorial systems and must be trusted to operate impartially.

The Criminal Trial

The purpose of the criminal courts is to formally identify who has committed an offence, attribute responsibility to the wrongdoer and impose penalties based on an assessment of the harm caused. This is achieved through the trial process, and in their role as adjudicator of disputes, the purpose of the courts is to do justice and encourage social order by working fairly and consistently within the boundaries set by law and procedure. The less serious matters are tried in the magistrates' courts before lay magistrates (sometimes district judges) who are the triers of both fact and law. The serious cases are dealt with at the Crown Court before a legally qualified judge who determines legal matters and a jury who determines guilt or innocence. For more detail on the operation of the individual courts, see Chapter 14.

An Adversarial Form of Justice?

Within the adversarial system, the criminal courts act as an adjudicator of disputes between the prosecution and the defence where the 'truth' is determined after a factual contest between the parties. In a criminal trial, both parties attempt to reconstruct events encompassing the criminal action, constructing a narrative of events and using the evidence collected by the police to present their version in a manner that convinces either the magistrates or the jury that their version of the facts is correct. The judge is the neutral intermediary in the contest who is present to ensure that both parties abide by the laws of procedure and evidence in their presentation of the case so as to ensure a fair trial for the accused. It is the role of the judge to determine how the law applies in a particular case and to advise the jury of how it applies. The jury decides which version of the facts they find to be correct and then apply the law, as outlined by the judge, to the facts to determine a verdict.

One obvious criticism of this system is the strategic manipulation of evidence by the parties in the criminal trial who have a vested interest in the outcome and who use the evidence in a way that suits their narrative of the case (Kirchengast, 2010). It can be argued that this distorts the reality of events so that the triers of fact (jury or magistrates) are not getting an accurate picture of what actually took place. Instead, the jury must determine what their preferred version of this distorted reality is, and give a verdict based on that determination, which may be very different from the 'truth'.

Nevertheless, the adversarial trial system is, in theory, a good example of due process in action. In order to ensure equality of arms (a fair contest between the parties), a number of important safeguards have been put in place over the years to assist the defendant. First, the burden of proof is placed upon the prosecution to prove the criminal offence charged and to disprove any defences raised (*DPP v. Woolmington* [1935] AC 462). This means that there is no legal requirement for the accused to prove anything (although tactically he may choose to do so in order to strengthen his version of the case) except in a handful of specified exceptions to the rule. The accused is afforded a right to silence and has the benefit of dispensation from self-incrimination so he is under no obligation to assist in prosecuting the case against him. The prosecution is required to prove its case 'beyond reasonable doubt' so the court can only convict if it is sure of the accused's guilt. This high standard is appropriate in the criminal courts where both liberty and personal reputation are at stake. The state also sets aside a budget within the treasury for legal aid which provides funded representation for any defendant of limited means and whose case warrants legal representation in the interests of justice (Legal Aid, Sentencing and Punishment of Offenders Act 2012: s.17). This means that no accused person should have to represent themselves against a legally qualified prosecutor in a court presided over by a legally qualified judge.

In reality, however, the criminal trial process in England and Wales shows many features common to the crime control model of justice. In the first instance, the mechanisms in place to ensure equality of arms are slowly being eroded through policies and procedures implemented by the past three consecutive governments. Although the accused has a right to silence, this is not an absolute right. Should the accused choose to exercise his right to silence, in specified circumstances, the jury may draw an adverse inference, the most obvious inference being that the accused has elected not to put forward an account either because he has no account to give or none that would stand up to questioning (Criminal Justice and Public Order Act 1994: ss.34–37). The accused's right to legal advice at the police station can be achieved by a telephone call to a representative from the Criminal Defence Service but, as the advice is via a call-centre, this advisor will have no knowledge of the accused person and will be unable to assist the accused in the pressurised environment of the police interview. It could be argued that the notion of equality of arms in the courtroom is diminished by the continual cost-cutting exercises being undertaken by the treasury, whereby legal aid solicitors are reducing in number as they find it more difficult to run cases thoroughly due to a reducing legal aid budget. All of these issues, amongst others, have brought about a diminution of the system to sit squarely within a due process model.

Secondly, a fundamental feature of the due process model is the requirement that the prosecution prove their case within a trial setting. The jury trial system is lauded as a means of securing community participation and common sense within a legal environment (Darbyshire, 1991). Judgment by one's peers ensures that the law is applied in line with popular opinion thus commanding public confidence and ensuring justice for the lay person (Auld, 2001). However, the reality of the system is that most cases are dealt with in the magistrates' courts where a jury trial is not possible (Ministry of Justice, 2015). Furthermore, most criminal cases result in a guilty plea which means that the trial process is largely redundant for the majority of criminal prosecutions. In the fourth quarter of 2012, for example, 67 per cent of criminal cases in the Crown Court resulted in a guilty plea; this figure has remained steady at approximately 70 per cent since 2008 (Ministry of Justice, 2012). This means that the prosecution are relieved of their duty to prove the case beyond reasonable doubt and a trial does not need to take place at all. On the one hand, the large number of guilty pleas could be due to the police doing an effective job by uncovering evidence that clearly points to the guilt of the accused. Consequently, the strength of the evidence would influence a wavering defendant to plead guilty rather than attempt to convince a jury that they did not commit the offence (Hedderman and Moxon, 1992).

On the other hand, it is possible that the pressures placed on the accused by the system have resulted in a high level of guilty pleas (McConville et al., 1994). For one, the system provides a one-third discount in sentence if a guilty plea is entered at the 'earliest possible opportunity', with a staged reduction in this discount the later in the process the guilty plea is entered (Sentencing Guidelines Council, 2007). In addition, it is possible to get an indication from the court as to the possible sentence that an offender might receive. For example, at the allocation hearing in the magistrates' courts, where the case has been deemed suitable for summary trial, the magistrates, upon request, may give an indication to the offender of whether he might receive a custodial or non-custodial sentence should he change his plea to guilty (Magistrates' Courts Act 1980: s.20). Similarly in the Crown Court, and usually on the day of trial, it is possible, with the written consent of the offender, to seek an indication from the trial judge as to the likely sentence in the event of either a guilty plea or a finding of guilt post trial (*R v. Goodyear* [2005] EWCA Crim 888). However, research has indicated that the discount available for a guilty plea is not really a consideration in cases where defendants felt there was a sufficient chance of being found not guilty (Dawes et al., 2011); hence these pressures may not be operating in a counter-productive manner at all.

The Punishment of Offenders

Sentencing is the process of imposing punishment on an offender after a finding of guilt, whether that is following a guilty plea or a finding of guilt after trial. It is probably the most high-profile stage of the criminal justice process as it is the stage in which all convicted persons face the consequences of their criminal actions and it is the most emotive stage in the process for all those affected by the criminal activity. The determination of sentence is the responsibility of either lay magistrates (or district judges) in the magistrates' courts or the judge in the Crown Court. Regardless of which court the offender falls to be sentenced in, section 125 of the Coroners and Justice Act 2009 dictates that the court must follow any available sentencing guidelines when dealing with a convicted offender unless it is contrary to the interests of justice to do so. The sentencing guidelines are produced and issued by the Sentencing Council whose role is to promote consistency and transparency in sentencing.

Under the current sentencing regime, the sentencing process starts with a determination of the seriousness of the offence, based on an assessment of the culpability of the offender and harm caused from the facts of the case (Sentencing Guidelines Council, 2004). This provides the court with a starting point for the sentence and a range of higher and lower sentences that could legitimately be imposed for the offence. The court then considers any offence-related aggravating factors (matters that make the offence more serious, e.g. vulnerable victim or high-value crime) which could bring the sentence to the higher end of the range, as well as mitigating factors (matters that reduce the seriousness of the offence, e.g. opportunistic offence) which may bring the offence back to the lower end of the range. Finally, the court must reduce the sentence according to the effect of any offender-related mitigation (for example, age of the accused or problematic personal circumstances) and any discount available for a guilty plea (if appropriate) in order to reach a final sentence for the case that falls within the range identified. Research has shown that in 2014, 97 per cent of sentences imposed in the Crown Court fell within the given range (Sentencing Guidelines Council, 2015) so the courts largely follow their duties in this regard. Starting from the least onerous, the penalties that a court may impose on an offender, where they have the power to do so, are discharge, fine, community order, and imprisonment (suspended or immediate). These can be imposed alongside a range of ancillary, or additional, sentencing orders, such as disqualification, orders for compensation, forfeiture and restraining orders (see Chapters 15 and 16 for more detail).

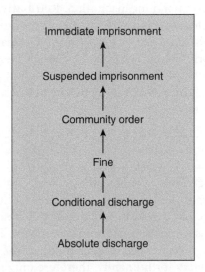

Figure 4.2 Range of sentencing options in ascending hierarchical order

Sentencing is a very political issue, largely due to the high level of media scrutiny and the significance of victim impact within this aspect of the Criminal Justice System. Although various governments have implemented differing policies indicating their stance on the fight against crime, it was not until the Criminal Justice Act 2003, that a statutory statement of the aims of punishment was set out in law. Section 142 of the Act provides that a court dealing with an adult offender must have regard to the five statutory purposes of sentencing:

- punishment of offenders;
- the reduction of crime (including reduction by deterrence);
- the reform and rehabilitation of offenders;
- the protection of the public; and
- the making of reparation by offenders to persons affected by their offences.

In practice, it is a matter for the sentencing court to decide how these apply and which take precedence in a particular circumstance.

Theories of Punishment

Behind this statutory statement lie two key theoretical justifications for imposing punishment, namely utilitarianism and retributivism. Both theories concede that punishment must be inflicted on those who commit crimes but they differ in their views of what constitutes justice in punishment. Utilitarian philosophies, based on the works of philosophers Cesare Beccaria, Jeremy Bentham and John Stuart Mill, justify punishment as a means of preventing future offending through the use of deterrence, social protection and incapacitation. Retributive theories, which were influential in the late eighteenth and early nineteenth centuries, and revived in the UK in the 1970s and 1980s, are associated with the German tradition of idealism, and in particular the work of Georg Wilhelm Friedrich Hegel and his predecessor, Immanuel Kant. The focus of retributivism is responding proportionately to any offence committed so that offenders receive what they deserve for their actions as a just response to wrongdoing.

Utilitarianism

Utilitarianism seeks the greatest overall welfare for society and promotes the most effective and efficient means of achieving such ends. Within utilitarianism, the 'greatest happiness principle' prevails; i.e. morality is based upon the extent to which an action maximises pleasure and minimises pain. To maximise the greatest good for the greatest number, utilitarianism judges the effects of punishment upon its wider consequences for humanity, therefore only punishments that serve to improve human existence should actually occur. One of the key advocates of utilitarianism, Jeremy Bentham, suggested that the greater good could be served by either disabling the physical abilities that allow a criminal to offend, by removing the desire for offending, or by making the offender afraid of committing further offences (Bentham, 1830). It can be said therefore that utilitarian principles are based upon incapacitation, rehabilitation and deterrence.

Incapacitation

This element of utilitarian theory aims to identify particular groups of offenders who do serious harm to society and remove them from society for periods of time to protect society from further harm they might cause. Under the current sentencing regime, incapacitation is echoed within the statutory aim of protection of the public (Criminal Justice Act 2003: s.142(1)(d)).

The most obvious form of incapacitation is a custodial sentence which completely removes the offender from society, thereby eliminating the offender's ability to commit crimes that might harm the public. A court can only impose a custodial sentence if 'the offence … was so serious that neither a fine alone nor a community sentence can be justified' (Criminal Justice Act 2003: s.152 (2)). The use of incapacitation is therefore reserved for the most serious of crimes as well as for recidivists, dangerous offenders and career criminals. Incapacitation can also take the form of orders beyond custodial sentences. An order disqualifying an offender from driving as a result of driving with excess alcohol, for example, is designed to prevent any future driving transgressions for a set period of time.

There are two forms of incapacitation. Collective incapacitation aims to prevent the occurrence of specific offences so the deprivation of freedom is determined by the type of crime committed. For example, section 51A of the Firearms Act 1968 imposes a minimum term of five years' imprisonment for offenders aged 18 years or over who have committed a single offence of possession, purchasing or acquiring a specified prohibited firearm. The purpose of such provisions is to remove such offenders from the community so as to protect the public from harm from firearms. These are particularly attractive political strategies as they send a message of zero tolerance on crime; however, the efficacy of this type of punishment is questionable. It has been argued that the removal of offenders for a few years has a minimal effect on public safety and eventually these people are replaced by younger people who commit the crimes in any event (Golash, 2005).

Selective incapacitation focuses on offenders who are deemed a high risk of committing future crimes and sentences these offenders to disproportionately harsh sentences to prevent future offending. The current regime of incapacitating 'dangerous offenders' for extended periods of time based on a prediction that there is a 'significant risk' to members of the public of serious harm by the offender committing further serious offences (Criminal Justice Act 2003: ss.224 et seq.) is a good example of a selective incapacitation sentencing strategy. The problem with this form of sentencing is that we do not have the ability to predict accurately who will commit serious crimes in the future (Mathiesen, 2006) with some research indicating that predictions of future risk are incorrect eight times out of nine (Golash, 2005). The regime of extended sentences therefore has the ability to trigger undeservedly harsh punishments for people who are erroneously predicted as likely to reoffend.

Incapacitative strategies may only serve to delay future wrongdoing. Offenders in prison are housed amongst other like-minded individuals and there is a risk that upon release, the offender can continue to offend either in line with their existing criminal activity or within new criminal ventures through their new contacts (Honderich, 2006). Equally, those involved in organised crime can often continue to control criminal activity from 'the inside'. This is known as the 'capacitating effect' which gives rise to opportunity and desire to commit offences (Honderich, 2006). Incapacitation has the added consequence of causing harm to the family of the offender. For example, offenders with young children lose contact with their offspring and this has been found to create a risk of offending behaviour in the child (Muftić et al., 2015).

Rehabilitation

Rehabilitation involves attempting to change an offender's attitude to offending behaviour to promote a future crime-free life. It is generally believed that an offender will need professional support to be successfully rehabilitated, therefore staff within the probation service, the Youth Offending Team, and prison psychology teams (to name but a few) are typically involved in implementing this aspect of a sentence.

Reform and rehabilitation is a specific statutory aim of sentencing as set out in s.142 of the Criminal Justice Act 2003 and sentences with a rehabilitative focus tend to be non-custodial ones. An offender can be made subject to a requirement to participate in a rehabilitation activity as part of a community order or a suspended sentence order. The National Probation Service and Community Rehabilitation Companies run a range of programmes that help offenders think before they act, stop acting violently, and behave appropriately within relationships. It is also possible to deal with particular offending-related issues so courts can impose drug, alcohol or mental-health treatment requirements as appropriate for an offender's circumstances (Criminal Justice Act 2003: s.177). Prisons also claim to engage in rehabilitative work with inmates but many consider prison to 'dehabilitate' rather than rehabilitate (Mathiesen, 2006: 53).

While the aim of rehabilitation is to prevent future offending, some studies have found it to be ineffective (Martinson, 1974). Critics also suggest that rehabilitation disregards human agency and decision-making by assuming that offenders wish to change (Golash, 2005). Bearing in mind that for most sentences, the offender's suitability is assessed before imposing the penalty, the success of such programmes is likely to directly correlate with the desire of the offender to effect personal change and their personal circumstances being susceptible to such change (Halleck and Witte, 1977). Sentences with a focus on rehabilitation can also be criticised as being disproportionately long when compared to their custodial counterparts (Hudson, 1998). A community penalty can run for up to three years (Criminal Justice Act 2003: s.177 (5)) depending upon the seriousness of the offence and the rehabilitative requirements to be completed. Offenders must complete the programme of treatment requirements before the sentence will end. An offender convicted of a sophisticated one-off shoplifting offence (value £200–£1,000) could receive a community penalty of up to two years with a weekly programme requirement lasting 26 weeks, depending upon his personal circumstances and attitude to offending. Some offenders may prefer to undertake a relatively short prison sentence rather than submit to the more onerous routine of weekly rehabilitative meetings and assessment (Lewis, 2005).

Deterrence

Deterrence operates as a penal practice where offending is reduced by encouraging the public to abide by the rules of the state or face harsh punishment. The success of this form of punishment depends upon the pain of punishment for committing a crime being substantially higher than the pleasure of committing the crime. Deterrent sentences tend to be disproportionate to the harm of the crime committed but this is justified on the basis that a deterrent sentence will prevent greater harm to society. Reduction of offending by deterrence features as one of the statutory aims of sentencing outlined in the Criminal Justice Act 2003.

General deterrence aims to deter all people from committing a particular type of offence. Bentham (1748–1832) contended that people are rational beings who will adjust their behaviour in order to avoid the encumbrance of punishment, particularly if sentences are precisely calculated to be sufficiently harsh to deter people from particular offending behaviour. An example of this in current sentencing practice is the guideline for carrying a bladed article in public where an offender faces up to four years' imprisonment (starting point of 12 weeks' imprisonment). The rationale behind this harsh sentencing guideline is to deter people from carrying knives and therefore to prevent knife-related violence.

Individual deterrence aims at deterring a particular offender from reoffending. If a court sentences with this in mind, it is the propensity to reoffend, rather than the seriousness of the offence, which becomes the determining factor in setting the severity of the sentence. Recidivists are therefore subjected to a steadily increasing level of sentence if the lower level of penalty fails to prevent reoffending. This approach is evidenced in the current legislation on sentencing persistent offenders (Criminal Justice Act 2003: s.143 (2)).

The principle of marginal deterrence assumes that increasing the level of sentence for a crime will decrease offending rates (Posner, 1985). However, empirical evidence of the success of marginal deterrence is hard to find (see for example von Hirsch et al., 1999). One obvious criticism of deterrence is that the offender must know the severity of the punishment that awaits him, consider this when deciding whether to commit the offence, consider it certain that he will be caught and convicted, and believe that the harsh penalty will be imposed before refraining from offending behaviour (Bottoms, 2004). Although a link has been found between the perception of a high risk of detection with reduced offending (von Hirsch et al., 1999), human beings do not always operate on the basis of such rational thinking so the deterrent sentence is very much dependent upon the motivations of the offender being susceptible to influence.

Retribution and just deserts

According to retributivism, or just deserts theory, an illegal action should be sanctioned with a punishment that is deserved by the offender. Punishment is correlated with the harm done by the crime rather than the moral guilt of the criminal so that the punishment fits the crime.

Proportionality is the central principle for retributivism. Kant (1996) referred to this as 'like for like', such that the form and gravity of punishment should be based on matching the evil inflicted by the offender with the infliction of a similar evil on the offender in return. While some offences may be difficult to match, it is clear that imposing the death penalty for murder and requiring castration for rape, are punishments that match the crime both qualitatively and quantitatively. The approach is grounded in morals and ethics rather than the usefulness to society as a whole. The concept of 'an eye for an eye' taken from the Old Testament, is one example which demonstrates the morality-based principles of ensuring the punishment fits the crime.

A punishment is considered unjust if it is excessive or inappropriate, if it fails to respect the dignity of the offender or if it is imposed for reasons other than just deserts. Georg Hegel rejected the utilitarian view of humans as beings who were purely in pursuit of pleasure and happiness. He believed that a criminal is a rational being with the freedom to choose his actions and he gives implicit consent to be punished should he choose to commit a crime. To decide a punishment based on threats and coercion (e.g. a deterrent sentence) is, for Hegel, akin to treating a man like a dog, instead of treating him with the respect and freedom of choice he deserves as a man. Therefore, while retributivists disagree with the use of prisoners to test drugs as this is disrespectful to personal dignity; utilitarian theorists see the utility of sacrificing one person's welfare for the benefit of the many. Similarly, where a punishment could contain elements of reparation to return the community to how it was before the crime was committed, or elements designed to reform the criminal, these are the outcomes of a successful punishment rather the operational reasons for imposing the punishment in the first instance.

The Criminal Justice Act 1991 was a good example of a retributivist sentencing framework as the underlying aim of this legislation was to ensure that offenders received their just deserts in sentencing (although it was not a pure justice model). It was made clear from the provisions of this Act that the main sentencing focus was the assessment of seriousness and the setting of sentences which were proportionate to the harm created by the offence. Matters such as rehabilitation were only of significance where the appropriate level of sentence was a community penalty. The Criminal Justice Act 2003 sentencing framework has since overturned some of the rules introduced by the 1991 Act; however, offence seriousness remains a key aspect in determining an appropriate sentence.

Restorative Justice

The focus of restorative justice is the victim of crime and the desire for an offender to make good to the victim for any harm or injury caused. It places both victim and offender at the centre of the sentencing process so these parties may determine a mutually agreeable resolution to the conflict created by the criminal offence. Restorative justice is not widely used in the UK but the current government continues to actively promote its use by introducing pre-sentence measures within the provisions of the Crime and Courts Act 2013. The nature of restorative justice is discussed further in Part Three, particularly in Chapter 21.

Critics of restorative justice suggest that it is a disguised form of pain for the offender (Daly, 2003), particularly where the penalty was imposed without the offender going through the trial process. Nevertheless, it appears to be the case that restorative justice can constitute a form of rehabilitation (Duff, 2003) as the message to the offender is one of putting right the harm caused and avoiding future offending. Although some critics consider that restorative justice could be viewed by victims as second rate justice (Hudson, 2003), the reality is that a victim must consent to this form of punishment for it to be effective. Some also consider that the principles of restorative justice threaten the model of due process and the inherent safeguards contained within such a system. For example, the right against self-incrimination, the notion of confidentiality, and the right to representation are all at risk within a sentencing structure which involves such an open acknowledgement of personal responsibility for criminal behaviour (Ikpa, 2007).

Summary

The focus of this chapter has been a consideration of the purposes of the Criminal Justice System. While the overarching aim of the system is to secure justice for all, it is clear that this is achieved in different ways at differing stages of the system. The Criminal Justice System can be seen as a method of ensuring citizens conform to social behavioural norms and this is achieved through policing criminal activity, and convicting and punishing the guilty. Of utmost importance is ensuring that the system is fair and just, as a finding of guilt is a symbolic indicator that the accused differs from the rest of the law-abiding community. It marks the power of the courts and the criminal process to identify a citizen as a rule breaker, justification for the infliction of punishment upon that person and some closure for the victim of the crime.

Discussion Questions

1. Amongst the various aims of the Criminal Justice System, does any one particular purpose stand out as the most important?

2. Which of the agencies within the Criminal Justice System carries the heaviest burden in achieving the aim of delivering justice?

3. Which model of criminal justice provides a more effective Criminal Justice System: the due process or the crime control model?

4. Which of the theories of sentencing does the sentencing system in England and Wales predominantly follow?

Further Reading

There are very few scholarly articles dealing exclusively with the purposes of the Criminal Justice System. As well as the reading identified above, the following may be of interest to a reader who wishes to find out more.

A detailed theoretical reflection of the purposes of the Criminal Justice System can be found in the first few chapters of Lucia Zedner's book:

Zedner, L. (2004) *Criminal Justice*. Oxford: Oxford University Press.

For a general overview of sentencing within the Criminal Justice System:

Ashworth, A. (2015) *Sentencing and Criminal Justice*. 6th edn. Cambridge: Cambridge University Press.

Easton, S. and Piper, C. (2016) *Sentencing and Punishment: The quest for justice*. 4th edn. Oxford: Oxford University Press.

For a comparative study of the system of prosecutions:

Fionda, J. (1995) *Public Prosecutors and Discretion: A comparative study*. Oxford: Oxford University Press.

Crime and court statistics are available from the Home Office and Ministry of Justice websites. Sentencing Guidelines can be downloaded from the Sentencing Council website.

References

Ashworth, A. and Redmayne, M. (2005) *The Criminal Process*. 3rd edn. Oxford: OUP.

Auld, L.J. (2001) *Review of the Criminal Courts of England and Wales*. London: HMSO.

Banakar, R. (2014) 'Law, community and the 2011 London riots', in R. Nobles and D. Schiff (eds), *Law, Society and Community*. Farnham: Ashgate.

Bentham, J. (1830) *The Rationale of Punishment*. London: R. Heward.

Block, C. (1995) 'STAC hot-spot areas: A statistical tool for law enforcement decisions', in *Crime Analysis through Computer Mapping*. Washington, DC: Police Executive Research Forum.

Bottoms, A.E. (2004) 'Empirical research relevant to sentencing frameworks', in A. Bottoms, S. Rex and G. Robinson (eds), *Alternatives to Prison: Options for an insecure society*. Cullompton: Willan.

Cope, N. (2004) 'Intelligence led policing or policing led intelligence? Integrating volume crime analysis into policing', *British Journal of Criminology*, 44: 188–203.

Daly, K. (2003) 'Restorative justice: the real story', in G. Johnstone (ed.), *A Restorative Justice Reader*. Devon: Willan.

Darbyshire, P. (1991) 'The lamp that shows that freedom lives: Is it worth the candle?', *Criminal Law Review*, Oct: 740–52.

Dawes, W., Harvey, P., McIntosh, B., Nunney, F. and Phillips, A. (2011) *Attitudes to Guilty Plea Sentence Reductions*. London: Sentencing Council.

Duff, P. (1998) 'Crime control, due process and "the case for the prosecution"', *British Journal of Criminology*, 38: 611–15.

Duff, R. (2003) 'Restorative punishment and punitive restoration', in G. Johnstone (ed.), *A Restorative Justice Reader*. Devon: Willan.

Durkheim, E. (1884) *Division of Labour in Society*. New York: The Free Press.

Golash, D. (2005) *The Problem of Punishment*. New York: Cambridge University Press.

Gove, M. (June 2015) 'What does a one nation justice policy look like?' [Online]. Available at: www.gov.uk/government/speeches/what-does-a-one-nation-justice-policy-look-like [accessed 24 April 2016].

Halleck, S.L. and Witte, A.D. (1977) 'Is rehabilitation dead?', *Crime & Delinquency*, 23 (4): 372–82.

Hedderman, C. and Moxon, D. (1992) *Magistrates' Court or Crown Court: Mode of trial decisions and sentencing*. Home Office Research Study No. 125. London: HMSO.

Honderich, T. (2006) *Punishment: The supposed justifications revisited*. London: Pluto Press.

Hudson, B. (1998) 'Doing justice to difference', in A. Ashworth and M. Wasik (eds), *Crime, Law and Social Change*. Oxford: Oxford University Press.

Hudson, B. (2003) 'Restorative justice: The challenge of sexual and racial violence', in G. Johnstone (ed.), *A Restorative Justice Reader*. Devon: Willan.

Ikpa, T. (2007) 'Balancing restorative justice principles and due process rights in order to reform the criminal justice system', *Washington University Journal of Law & Policy*, 24: 301.

Kant, I. (1996) *Kant: The metaphysics of morals*. Cambridge: Cambridge University Press.

Kirchengast, T. (2010) *The Criminal Trial in Law and Discourse*. Basingstoke: Palgrave Macmillan.

Lewis, S. (2005) 'Rehabilitation: Headline or footnote in the new penal policy?' *Probation Journal*, 52 (2): 119–35.

Martinson, R. (1974) 'What works? Questions and answers about prison reform', *The Public Interest*, 35: 22–54.

Mathiesen, T. (2006) *Prison on Trial*. 3rd edn. Winchester: Waterside Press.

McConville, M., Hodgson, J., Bridges, L. and Pavlovic, A. (1994) *Standing Accused: The organisation and practices of criminal defence lawyers in Britain*. Oxford: Clarendon Press.

Miller, J., Bland, N. and Quinton, P. (2000) *The Impact of Stops and Searches on Crime and the Community* (Police Research Series Paper 127). London: Home Office.

Ministry of Justice (2012) *Court Statistics Quarterly October to December 2012* [pdf]. Available at: www.gov.uk/government/uploads/system/uploads/attachment_data/file/198246/court-stats-quarterly-q4-2012.pdf [accessed 24 April 2016].

Ministry of Justice (2015) *Criminal Court Statistics Quarterly, England and Wales* [pdf]. Available at: www.gov.uk/government/uploads/system/uploads/attachment_data/file/437672/ccsq-bulletin-january-march-2015.pdf [accessed 24 April 2016].

Muftić, L., Bouffard, L. and Armstrong, G. (2015) 'Impact of maternal incarceration on the criminal justice involvement of adult offspring: A research note', *Journal of Research in Crime and Delinquency*, 53 (1): 93–111.

Packer, H. (1968) *The Limits of the Criminal Sanction*. Stanford: Stanford University Press.

Posner, R. (1985) 'An economic theory of the criminal law', *Columbia Law Review*, 85 (6): 1193–231.

Ratcliffe, J. (2002) 'Damned if you don't, damned if you do: Crime mapping and its implications in the real world', *Policing and Society*, 12 (3): 211–25.

Ratcliffe, J. (2008) *Intelligence-led Policing*. Cullompton: Willan.

Sentencing Guidelines Council (2004) *Overarching Principles – Seriousness: Definitive guideline*. London: Sentencing Guidelines Council.

Sentencing Guidelines Council (2007) *Reduction in Sentence for a Guilty Plea: Definitive guideline*. London: Sentencing Guidelines Council.

Sentencing Guidelines Council (2015) *Crown Court Sentencing Survey 2014*. London: Sentencing Guidelines Council.

Siegel, L. (2015) *Criminology: Theories, patterns, & typologies*. 12th edn. Boston: Cengage Learning.

Smith, D. (1997) 'Case construction and the goals of the criminal process', *British Journal of Criminology*, 37: 319–46.

Tonry, M. (2011) 'Less imprisonment is no doubt a good thing – More policing is not', *Criminology and Public Policy*, 10: 137–52.

von Hirsch, A., Bottoms, A., Burney, E. and Wikstrom, P. (1999) *Criminal Deterrence and Sentence Severity: An analysis of recent research*. Oxford: Hart.

Weisburd, D. and Braga, A. (2006) 'Hot spots policing as a model for police innovation', in D. Weisburd and A. Braga (eds), *Police Innovation – Contrasting perspectives*. Cambridge: Cambridge University Press.

Wolfenden Committee (1957) *Report of the Committee on Homosexual Offences and Prostitution*. Cmnd 247. London: HMSO.

Check out the Companion Website

Want to know more about this chapter? Review what you have been learning by visiting: **https://study.sagepub.com/harding**

- Practice with essay questions
- Test yourself with multiple-choice questions
- Listen to a series of podcasts featuring Neil of Northumbria Police and London's Metropolitan Police Service
- Watch videos selected from the SAGE Video collection

5   Characteristics of Offenders

Hannah Bows

Introduction

Understanding who commits crime and why is a core area of criminological research and teaching. Criminology has always been concerned with understanding patterns and predictors of offending and exploring the reasons why some people offend and others do not, and much of the existing criminal justice policy and practice has been influenced by criminological research into offending. A number of common characteristics are observed in relation to offenders; offenders tend to be young, white men who come from deprived backgrounds with low socio-economic status and have significantly poorer mental health than their contemporaries. However, although many offenders share a number of common characteristics, one of the undisputable facts is that people who commit criminal acts are not a homogenous group and this chapter will highlight both the similarities and differences within each of the characteristics.

The structure of the chapter is as follows. It begins by considering and defining the term 'offender' and briefly outlining how crime is measured and how we gather data on offenders, building on Chapter 3. The chapter then moves on to consider why it is important to analyse the characteristics of offenders and how this influences crime prevention and rehabilitation programmes. The key social characteristics of offenders: age; gender; ethnicity; class; and mental health are then explored in turn before a discussion of the overlaps and distinctions across and within each characteristic. The chapter concludes by summarising the key themes in relation to offender characteristics and provides suggestions for further reading.

Context

Crime can be broadly divided into 'violent' and 'non-violent' categories. Violent offences include sexual offences, homicide, assaults, wounding and grievous bodily harm, while non-violent offences include property offences such as theft, fraud, and drug offences. Criminological research has been particularly interested in analysing offenders of the former category; offenders who commit murder, assault, rape and other violent offences have always been of particular interest to criminologists. However, despite the amount of research attention on these offences, the majority of offenders commit less-serious crimes. For example, in the UK there were 573 homicides in 2015 compared to 3,812,000 theft offences (ONS, 2016). This is similar internationally: for example, theft accounts for 76.5 per cent of all known crime cases in Japan (National Police Agency, 2010 cited in Haginoya, 2014) and in the USA, in 2011, an estimated 14,610 persons were victims of homicide (Smith and Cooper, 2013), compared to 16.6 million victims of identity theft in 2012 (Harrell and Langton, 2013).

An 'offender' is typically considered to be someone who commits a criminal offence. However, not all those who commit offences become known as offenders; it is estimated that only a small proportion of crime is detected and reported. A recent report by Her Majesty's Inspectorate of Constabulary (HMIC, 2014) found one in five crimes go unreported. Furthermore, certain criminal acts are thought to be disproportionately underreported – for example, it is estimated that 85 per cent of rapes and sexual assaults go unreported to the police (Home Office, 2013). While the statistics inform us who has convictions for offences, they fail to enlighten us on who commits crime in a broader sense (Teague, 2005). Consequently, the characteristics of offenders discussed in this chapter relate to known offenders and therefore may not be representative of the characteristics of all offenders.

Measurements of crime and information on both victims and offenders are largely drawn from data collected by criminal justice organisations (such as the police, Crown Prosecution Service, Prisons and Probation) and national crime surveys such as the Crime Survey for England and Wales (CSEW, formerly the British Crime Survey) and other similar surveys internationally (such as the National Crime Victimization Survey in the USA). Other smaller studies by researchers and academics also contribute to our understanding of offending. Generally, both the police and the Crime Survey for England and Wales have produced consistent findings in relation to trends in crime and offending over the last 20 years. While both data sources are useful in providing estimates on the levels of crime and victimisation, both the CSEW and police-recorded data suffer from a number of limitations (see Chapter 3). In addition, while these statistics give us some idea of the prevalence of different crimes, they do not give us much information on the people committing them.

Therefore, in order to understand more about those who commit offences, we need to look across the offending literature. The primary focus of this chapter is on data available in England and Wales, however material from other, international sources will be utilised where relevant to highlight the ubiquitous nature of these key characteristics. A number of common themes are observed in relation to the age, gender, ethnicity, class and mental health of offenders.

Age

One of the ubiquitous findings across criminological research internationally is the age of offenders. It is a well-established and widely cited criminological fact that perpetrating crime and being a victim of crime decreases with age, often referred to as the age–crime curve/distribution. The high prevalence of criminal and deviant behaviour in teenage years is well documented and much of the criminological literature has agreed that offending peaks in the mid to late teens and decreases thereafter (Farrington et al., 2006).

Throughout the history of criminology, researchers have demonstrated this link – for example, in the nineteenth century Adolphe Quetelet found the proportion of the criminal population peaked in adolescence and then declined with age (see Ulmer and Steffensmeier, 2015), although this may be argued to in part reflect the life expectancy at the time! However, modern research has repeatedly found a relationship between age and crime across both violent and non-violent offences.

In England and Wales, official statistics attest to the age–crime distribution. Across all types of crime, young men are the most common offenders. Figure 5.1 shows the age distribution of offenders in England and Wales. The 2012/13 CSEW data reveal:

- 35% of property offences involved an offender aged under 16, and 41% involved an offender aged 16–24.

- 90% of known or suspected homicide offenders were males aged 16–24.

- Those aged 10–17 accounted for 11.8% of arrests in 2012/13, a 24% decrease since 2011/12 (ONS, 2015). However, it is important to remember this represents a reduction in arrests, not necessarily offending.

Meanwhile, official statistics for the prison population reveal prisoners are most likely to be found in a slightly older age group (25–39). On 30 June 2013 there

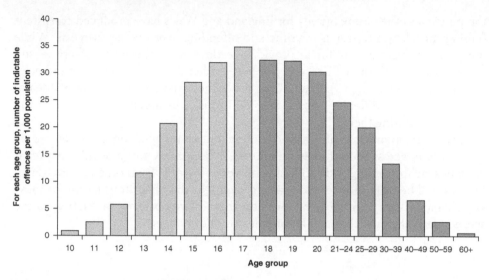

Figure 5.1   The peak rate for offending is at age 17

Source: Criminal Statistics, Ministry of Justice; the data is for 2009; England & Wales; updated Dec 2010

were 83,842 prisoners in prison establishments in England and Wales and almost one-half of these were aged 25 to 39 (House of Commons, 2013).

While the peak age of offenders tends to be in the younger age groups globally, the average age of offenders varies internationally and by crime type.

Box 5.1

Peak Age of Offending – International data

Australia

Official statistics show the most common age group in 2013/14 was 15–19, however the median age of offenders varied by crime type (Australian Bureau of Statistics, 2014). The median age was lowest for the principal offences of: unlawful entry with intent (20 years of age); robbery and extortion (21 years of age); theft (24 years of age); and property damage (24 years of age). However, for violent offences, the median age was considerably higher: sexual assault (32 years of age); homicide (31 years of age); abduction and harassment (31 years of age); and offences against justice (31 years of age).

USA

Greenfield (1997) reports that 40 per cent of sex offenders are aged 30 or older while only 8 per cent are aged 18–20 according to Bureau of Justice statistics.

> **UK**
>
> Findings from the Crime Survey for England and Wales report that those convicted of sexual crime were most likely to be aged 20–39. Similarly, an analysis conducted by the Home Office (2003) found domestic violence offenders had an average age of 35.

Thus, while it would appear offending does decrease with age, the earlier claims made by criminologists that offending peaks in late adolescence may not be accurate for all kinds of offenders.

It has generally been assumed that offenders 'grow out' of crime as they age. For example, Hoffman and Beck (1984: 617) identified what they term an age-related offending 'burnout' after which recidivism rates diminish. The effects of age have been found to be both direct and indirect; Shover and Thompson (1992) reanalysed data from the Rand Inmate Survey (USA) in a study of age, differential expectations, and desistance. They found a direct, positive relationship between aging and desistance, as well as indirect effects of age on desistance, whereby age interacts with past experiences to alter the assessment of risks and rewards of crime which then leads to desistance. However, some researchers have found other explanations for higher offending rates in younger groups. Brown and Males (2011) conducted an analysis of aggregate arrest, poverty and population data from California and concluded that the adolescent peak in rates of offending is not a consequence of developmental factors, but rather an artifact of age differences in economic status; young people offend at higher rates than adults because they are poorer than adults. However, Shulman et al. (2013) challenged these findings by analysing data from the National Longitudinal Study of Youth and found that criminal offending peaks in adolescence, even after controlling for variation in economic status.

Recently, there has been increased attention paid to offenders at the other end of the spectrum. Over the last decade, the number of 'older' offenders (those aged 50 and over) has rapidly increased. Although offenders aged 50 and over present the lowest overall crime rate of all adult age groups, the number of arrests among individuals in this age category is rapidly increasing (Aday and Krabill, 2012). In England and Wales, the number of male prisoners aged 60 and over more than trebled in the 10 years from 1994 to 2004, making them the fastest growing age group in the custodial population. The number of sentenced prisoners aged 60 and over rose 119 per cent between 1999 and 2009 (Age UK, 2011), and the number aged between 50 and 59 has doubled. Clinks (2013) reported that 12 per cent of the prison population, or nearly 10,000 inmates, are aged 50+. As this population continues to age (along with the general population), research reports that older offenders have a range of complex and physical and mental health needs (Clinks, 2013), with significantly poorer health than their non-incarcerated contemporaries (Aday and Krabill, 2012) and these issues are likely to increase in the future. This point is discussed further in Chapter 16.

Research into older offenders has found around half have committed sex offences (Fazel et al., 2001). However, studies elsewhere have observed older offenders committing other crimes, for example a recent study in Japan found 22 per cent of burglary offenders were aged 50 and over. This was not significantly lower than the 28 per cent of those offenders aged 15–29 (Haginoya, 2014). There remain significant gaps in the international research in relation to older offenders, in particular around prevalence, types of offending and theories relating to offending in later life.

Gender

'Most of the time when we read about, hear about and talk about "crime" and "criminals", we are actually reading, hearing and talking about men and men's behavior' (Wykes and Welsh, 2009: 1).

The second most consistent finding across criminological literature is the gender of offenders. Regardless of the type of crime (whether violent or non-violent) the vast majority is committed by (young) men with comparatively few crimes committed by women, commonly referred to as the 'gender gap' (Felson, 2002; Heimer, 2000; Laub and McDermott, 1985), although research has found this gap narrows when self-reported studies are also included (Stroh et al., 2016)

The gender gap holds particularly true for violent offences where men are disproportionately the offenders, however this pattern is also observed in non-violent offences; a recent study by Haginoya (2014) exploring burglary in Japan found 97 per cent of offenders were men. In England and Wales, less than one in five arrests recorded by the police in 2010/11 and in the preceding four years involved females (Ministry of Justice (MoJ), 2013a). Heidensohn and Silvestri (2012) point out that women account for a very small proportion of all known offenders, and as a consequence relatively little attention has been given to them.

Data from the CSEW for 2012/13 indicates:

- 83% of property offences were committed by men and 90% of homicide offences involved a male offender.
- For other violent crimes, 81% were male.

This pattern is observed internationally, for example Australian statistics from 2009–10 reveal a total of 186,244 alleged offenders across Victoria, Queensland and South Australia were processed of whom 140,152 (75 per cent) were male and 46,092 were female (AIC, 2011). In Canada, 78 per cent of those accused of Criminal Code offences in 2009 were male (Mahony, 2011).

The gender gap in offending has become one of the key themes of modern feminist criminology and gender studies of crime (Heidensohn and Silvestri, 2012).

The gap has been present since crime recording began, although female rates of offending have increased over time, and thus there have been claims over recent years that the gender gap is narrowing. This is reflected to a certain extent in the increasing female prison population; although there are fewer than 4,000 female prisoners in England and Wales compared to around 82,000 males (MoJ, 2015) the rise has been much greater among female offenders – an increase of 115 per cent between 1995 and 2010, compared to 50 per cent for men (Prison Reform Trust, 2013). There are conflicting explanations for this increase; some scholars argue that rather than committing more crime, women are being sentenced more punitively than in the past leading to an increase in the prison population (Gelsthorpe, 2007; McIvor, 2007), whereas others argue the increase can be explained by the development of women's rights and equality (Adler, 1975).

The increase in female offending and the rapidly growing female prison population has been of significant concern for researchers and policy makers over the last decade. The reasons for female offending are argued to be different from those for men; the official data show that women are more likely to commit less serious, economically driven offences (MoJ, 2013a) and these arise from complex needs and systemic disadvantage (Home Office, 2007). Female prisoners are more likely than males to have a history of child and/or adult abuse (physical and/or sexual). They also are more likely than men to have a psychiatric diagnosis and are more likely to self-harm. According to the Prison Reform Trust (2013) the rate of attempted suicide for women was more than twice that of males in 2012 with 46 per cent of women having attempted suicide at some point while incarcerated.

Ministry of Justice statistics (House of Commons Justice Committee, 2013) gathered from women's community projects show that almost half of the women referred to the projects have needs in more than four areas:

- 48% with drug or alcohol problems;
- 40% having experienced domestic violence, sexual abuse or rape;
- 8% involved in prostitution;
- 52% having children.

There is also research that demonstrates the overlaps between gender and class. Several researchers have argued that the 'feminisation of poverty' (Glendinning and Millar, 1992), which may be linked to lone parenthood, wage inequality and increasing divorce rates, is responsible for increased female crime (Carlen, 1998). However, other more recent research has found no differences between the genders; Hoeve et al. (2014) in their six-year study involving 1,258 adolescents and young adults found that financial problems increase the risk of delinquency (and vice versa) but that gender and age did not moderate the delinquency link.

In 2006 Baroness Corston was commissioned by the Home Office to examine what could be done to avoid women with particular vulnerabilities ending up in prison. Her report (Home Office, 2007) identified three categories of vulnerabilities for women: domestic circumstances and problems such as domestic violence, childcare issues, and being a single parent; personal circumstances such as mental illness, low self-esteem, eating disorders and substance misuse; and socio-economic factors such as poverty, isolation and employment. The report recommended that the only women who should be in custody were those very few who commit serious and violent crimes and who present a threat to the public. For the vast majority of women in the Criminal Justice System, solutions in the community would be more appropriate.

Ethnicity and Nationality

The relationship between race, ethnicity and crime is characterised by conflict and debate. Since the beginning of the twentieth century, racial and ethnic differences in the rates of offending have been consistently observed across the globe (Hawkins et al., 1998). Official figures from the CSEW shed light on the number of BME (Black and Minority Ethnic) offenders at each stage in the criminal justice process in England and Wales:

- Overall, in 2011/12 per 1,000 population aged 10 or older, a person from a Black ethnic group was six times more likely to be stopped and searched than a person from a White ethnic group, while someone from an Asian ethnic group was approximately twice as likely to be stopped and searched compared to a White person.

- In addition, per 1,000 population aged 10 or older, a Black person was nearly three times more likely to be arrested than a White person, and an individual from the Mixed ethnic group was twice as likely. However, it is interesting to note there were no differences in the rate of arrests between Asians and Whites. (MoJ, 2013b)

In terms of the prison population, a recent report (MoJ, 2013b) found 26.1 per cent of prisoners and 15.4 per cent under supervision from the Probation Services on Court Orders declared themselves to be BME, which is disproportionately high compared to the overall BME population in England and Wales – just 14 per cent in the 2011 census. Furthermore, the proportion of Muslim prisoners has risen from 7.7 per cent in 2002 to 13.4 per cent in 2012 compared to 4.2 per cent of the general population according to the 2011 census (MoJ, 2013b). There was a decrease in the foreign national population (who may or may not be from BME backgrounds) in custody, which was down 3 per cent on the previous year to 10,512 on 30 June 2015 (representing 12 per cent of the prison population). Looking at the longer trend, the foreign national prison population increased from the year 2002 to its highest value of 11,498 at the end of June 2008 when it accounted for 14 per cent of the population. There was then a small decrease until March 2011 when it fell to 10,745. Since then the foreign national population has remained stable, representing around 12–13 per cent of the prison population.

Criminologists have been concerned with understanding the links between race, ethnicity and criminality and explaining the disproportionate numbers of black and ethnic minority offenders throughout the criminal justice process; that is, the number of BME offenders is larger proportionately than the number of BME citizens in the wider community in England and Wales. At every stage of the Criminal Justice System, BME individuals (typically men) are disproportionately represented; they are disproportionately more likely to be stopped and searched, arrested, convicted and imprisoned (Runnymede, 2012). Criminologists have thus focused on the wider structural, cultural and political contexts when seeking to understand the reasons for the over-representation of those from BME backgrounds. And considerable effort has been devoted to exploring how far discrimination is responsible for this disproportionate involvement (Webster, 2012; Bowling and Phillips, 2002; Phillips and Bowling, 2003).

In terms of the types of crimes offenders are committing, official figures reveal there are similarities and differences across ethnic groups. Violence against the person is one of the most common offences across all ethnic groups. The two most common offences for white and black people are 'other offences' and 'theft and handling', whereas for Asian people they are 'drug offences' and 'violence against the person'.

There are two primary explanations for the race disparities seen across offending groups. The first has been termed the 'differential involvement hypothesis' (Piquero and Brame, 2008) and postulates that black people simply commit more crime, in particular serious crime, which leads to Criminal Justice System processing. This explanation also suggests that black people continue to commit crime into adulthood whereas white offending appears to decrease with age. The second hypothesis termed the 'differential Criminal Justice System selection hypothesis' presupposes that the disparity can be explained by differential police presence and patrolling coupled with discrimination in other areas of the Criminal Justice System (namely courts and prisons) leading to higher rates of arrest, conviction and incarceration of black individuals (Piquero and Brame, 2008). This 'ethnic penalty' (Roberts and McMahon, 2008) results in minority ethnic groups, in particular black people, being disproportionately disadvantaged in the Criminal Justice System. This is linked to what has been referred to as 'institutional racism' in the Criminal Justice System, particularly in the police force but also the courts and prison system. As a result of racist stereotypes and prejudices, black and other ethnic minority groups are more likely to be arrested, prosecuted and convicted than their white contemporaries.

Box 5.2

Institutional Racism in the Police

'Institutional racism' was most famously used in the Macpherson Report in 1999, which was conducted to investigate the process and outcomes of the police investigation into the murder of a black teenager, Stephen Lawrence on 22 April 1993. The report concluded the flaws and failings of the murder investigation resulted from 'professional incompetence, institutional racism and a failure of leadership by senior officers' (Macpherson, 1999: 137).

As yet, there remains disagreement about which of these hypotheses more accurately explains the disparities; however, research over the last decade has leaned more towards the latter, with studies finding institutional racism is still prevalent across the Criminal Justice System (Miller, 2010). However, despite the many claims about discrimination against BME groups, it is very difficult to prove, as there are many factors involved (for example offending patterns, age, socio-economic status) making it difficult to establish definitively that there is discrimination based on ethnicity.

Class/Poverty

Official statistics show a link between socio-economic status and crime. For example, criminal justice data reveal just under a third of all working-age offenders (aged 18–62) who were convicted/cautioned or released from prison in 2010/2011 were claiming out-of-work benefits two years before (MoJ, 2014). Furthermore, offenders released from prison are more likely to be claiming benefits after conviction/caution or release, than other offenders – over half (54 per cent) of those released from prison were claiming out-of-work benefits one month after, gradually decreasing to 42 per cent after two years (MoJ, 2014: 3). The median gross income of offenders one year after conviction/caution or release from prison in 2003/04 was £8,600. This means that in 2004/2005, half of the offenders had income under £8,600 (MoJ, 2014). It is not clear whether this is a result of imprisonment or a characteristic of offenders prior to imprisonment.

A significant focus of the existing research has been on linking class and poverty in adolescence with the risk of offending, which is unsurprising given the overlaps between age (youth), gender (male) and class (lower) across the offending population. For example, in their study of youth offending and poverty, Hay and Forrest (2009) report that persistent offending between the ages of 10 and 14 was significantly affected by both recent experience of poverty and long-term patterns of poverty experienced during the first decade of life. They calculated that the chances of being a persistent offender were increased by approximately 45 per cent for those experiencing poverty at age nine and by approximately 80 per cent for those experiencing poverty during the first decade of life. A study by Hällsten and colleagues (2013) of the children of immigrants and native Swedes living in Stockholm up to their thirties, explained the difference in crime between the two groups was accounted for by parental socio-economic resources and neighbourhood segregation (itself an expression of economic disadvantage) rather than ethnicity or culture.

Links between homelessness and offending have also been noted by many studies. For example, *The Hidden Truth about Homelessness* (Reeve and Batty, 2011), a survey of 400 rough sleepers by Sheffield Hallam University, found that 20 per cent of respondents had committed imprisonable offences with the primary aim of spending a night in police cells. Moreover, nearly 30 per cent admitted to committing a minor crime such as shoplifting or antisocial behaviour. Research by Niven and Stewart (2005) showed that 30 per cent of those released from prison had nowhere to live and that those who were homeless prior to custody had a one-year reconviction rate of 79 per cent compared to 47 per cent for those with accommodation.

An obvious offending link would be between those from low socio-economic backgrounds and economically motivated offences. However, research has found the relationship between poverty and crime is consistently observed in relation to violent offences (homicide, assault and domestic violence) (Pridemore, 2011). As Hay et al. (2007) point out, the effects of poverty on delinquency are especially evident in studies that measure crime in terms of involvement in serious rather than trivial offending. This relationship holds across many different settings – among developed and developing countries, and both between and within countries.

Although the relationship between class and economic status and crime has been well established, some research has argued they are not the primary causes of offending. For example, Sampson and Laub (1994) in their long-term study of poor criminal men in Boston found poverty was only an indirect cause of criminality. They argue that the key factors strongly and directly related to delinquency are low parental supervision, erratic, threatening and harsh discipline and weak parental attachment; however, it is worth noting that these variables are associated with poverty.

Several criminological theories of offending are based on the link between poverty and criminal activity (see Box 5.3).

Box 5.3

Criminological theories relating to poverty

Social disorganisation

Rather than focusing on individual factors causing crime, social disorganisation theory is interested in place and space and tries to explain why certain communities experience high levels of crime while others do not. Shaw and McKay (1942) argued that crime was concentrated in particular zones, linked to high transition in inner cities, which became progressively lower as

(Continued)

(Continued)

one moved further away from these spaces to outer zones. These areas are characterised by high levels of transition, with people moving in and out, as well as poverty. The lack of community cohesion and poor environmental conditions can explain high levels of crime in these areas.

Strain

Associated with the work of Merton (1938) and Agnew (1985), strain theories link crime to widespread conformity to cultural norms and values that prioritise economic success and associated material goods. Societal structures operate to increase the chances of some attaining such successes while making it disproportionately difficult for others; for example, high levels of education increase the chances of economic success although many do not have access to such education. As a result, those who cannot achieve this mainstream success experience 'strain' and may seek alternative illegitimate opportunities to achieve these goals. Thus, those who are poor and do not have the legitimate means of achieving material goods may instead turn to crime as a way of gaining them.

Subculture

Cohen's subculture theory (1955) argues that young men, saddled with a common problem (namely poverty and deprivation) find a common solution in embracing values that provide them with the means of attaining material goods and status which otherwise lie beyond their reach (Lilly et al., 2002).

However, these theories fail to explain why the majority of people in poverty or deprivation do not offend (a key limitation of most criminological theories). Hay and Forrest (2009) suggest that in fact the existing statistics may indicate that poor people are more likely to be persistent offenders or, alternatively, they may be more likely to be caught and severely sanctioned.

Several scholars have criticised the alleged links between poverty and crime, for example arguing that the studies that support a causal link between poverty and crime are narrowly based on cross-sectional analyses of the relationship between family poverty and a single point in time and adolescent involvement in crime reported at that sample single point in time (Hay and Forrest, 2009), and some have gone as far as to suggest the relationship between the two is more of a myth than reality (Dunaway et al., 2000). Despite these criticisms, overall there appears to be a clear link between poverty, class and offending, although this may not be a simple and direct relationship.

Mental Health

The vast majority of prisoners have some mental health problem or condition (Fazel and Danesh, 2002; HMIP, 2008; Senior et al., 2013). The first full survey in England and Wales conducted by the Office for National Statistics found that only one prisoner in 10 had no mental disorder (Singleton et al., 1998). The link between mental illness and violent offending in particular is well-established: a significant body of research suggests that those with mental illness or impairments have an increased risk of committing violent offences (e.g. Sirotich, 2008; Silver et al., 2008; Khanom et al., 2009; Flynn et al., 2014). Those who carry out less-serious offences are also more likely than the general population to suffer from mental disorders or conditions. Khanom et al. (2009) found that 40 per cent of offenders who receive Community Orders are suffering from at least one diagnosable mental disorder.

A range of mental health conditions have been linked to offending. Several studies have found schizophrenia to be particularly prevalent in homicide offenders. For example, Eronen et al. (1996) calculated that the risk of male homicidal behaviour for schizophrenia is eight times higher than that of the general population in Finland. They conclude that comorbidity of alcoholism and mental disorder elevates the risk to commit a homicide even further. Rickford (2003) found that two-thirds of women in prison showed symptoms of at least one neurotic disorder such as depression, anxiety and phobias. Even more alarming, however, was Rickford's finding that 14 per cent of women in prison suffered from a severe mental disorder such as schizophrenia or delusional disorders, which compares with less than 1 per cent of the general population (Wilson, 2005: 56). Other mental health conditions have also been observed consistently in the existing research. Silver et al. (2008) report that, controlling for respondents' past violent behaviour and other relevant factors, a history of mental health treatment is more strongly associated with assaultive violence and sexual offences than with other types of crimes.

Specific research attention has been paid to the proportion of young offenders with mental health problems within juvenile facilities as these rates are vastly disproportionate compared with youth in the general population (Abram et al., 2003; Schubert et al., 2011; Campbell et al., 2014). Lader et al. (2000) found 95 per cent of young offenders suffer at least one mental health problem and 80 per cent suffer two or more. Research has found links between young people, mental health problems and an increased risk of offending (Copeland et al., 2007) and, in particular, an increased risk of engagement in serious offending (Hoeve et al., 2014).

There have also been strong links observed between substance or alcohol misuse, mental health and offending. Brooke et al. (1996) conducted a study of 750 unconvicted remand prisoners and reported:

- psychiatric disorder was diagnosed in 469 inmates (63%);
- the main diagnoses were: substance misuse, 285 (38%); neurotic illness, 192 (26%); and personality disorder, 84 (11%).

According to a study by the Prison Reform Trust (2004), nearly two-thirds of sentenced male prisoners (63 per cent) and two-fifths of female sentenced prisoners (39 per cent) admitted to hazardous drinking prior to imprisonment, which carries the risk of physical or mental harm. Of these, about half were judged to have a severe alcohol dependency. In addition, it is not uncommon for prisoners who have alcohol problems also to have drug problems. According to the PRT study, just over a quarter of male prisoners and about a fifth of female prisoners who are hazardous drinkers are dependent on at least one type of illicit drug. A report by the Ministry of Justice has found that 69 per cent of prisoners had used illicit drugs in the year before custody, and that 31 per cent had used heroin; four weeks prior to sentence 36 per cent of prisoners (both genders) reported heavy alcohol use (MoJ, 2008).

The risks of self-harm and suicide are particularly high among offenders. A study by Hawton et al. (2014) reports that 20–24 per cent of female prisoners self-harmed each year compared to 5–6 per cent of male inmates. This compares to figures of around 0.6 per cent of the general female population of the UK (Hawton et al., 2014). MoJ statistics show that there were more than 30,700 self-harm incidents in the 12 months to September 2015 – an increase of over 7,000 from the previous three years. In both sexes, self-harm was associated with younger age, white ethnic origin, prison type, and a life sentence or being on remand. In addition, increasing numbers of prisoners are committing suicide: in 2015/16 a total of 100 deaths in custody were classed as self-inflicted while in 2014/15 the figure was 79 – an increase of 27 per cent (MoJ, 2016). In terms of post-release, Pratt et al. (2010) found markedly higher rates of suicide (8 times higher for men and 36 times higher for women) for post-release offenders compared to non-offenders within a year of release. Being aged under 25, released from a local prison, with a history of alcohol misuse or self-harm, a psychiatric diagnosis, and requiring Community Mental Health Services (CMHS) follow-up after release exacerbated the risk. It is not clear whether these issues are a direct result of prison. As the World Health Organization (2007) acknowledges, the causes of suicide in prison are complex. However, poor mental health or psychiatric conditions have been observed among prisoners who have attempted or completed suicide (Kerkhof and Bernasco, 1990; Green et al., 1993; Daniel and Flemming, 2006).

As a result of the plethora of research linking mental health with offending, and the numerous reports and official figures that demonstrate elevated risk levels for self-harm and suicide among offending populations, particularly those incarcerated, there have been several calls for reform of how such offenders are dealt with. In particular, it has been argued that mental health units or hospitals should be used to treat offenders rather than prisons. Her Majesty's Chief Inspector of Prisons (HMCIP) reported in 2002 that 41 per cent of inmates in dispersal prisons should be in secure hospitals or psychiatric wards due to the level of their mental health problems or illnesses (HMCIP, 2002). Similarly, Cavadino's evaluation of three prisons in England concluded that they were all 'totally unsuitable places in terms of regime and physical conditions' for mentally ill people (Cavadino, 1999: 58). Mental health problems among prisoners are discussed further in Chapter 16.

The Intersections

As has already been noted several times in this chapter, there are substantial overlaps between the different offender characteristics. While each characteristic has been discussed separately here, in reality offenders typically embody a number of these. For example, the majority of offenders are not only young but also male and from a low socio-economic background. Furthermore, there is little argument that, independently, race and mental health are two of the most important issues in the juvenile justice system (Desai et al., 2012); however, there are differences observed across ethnic groups. Some studies, for example, find a difference in mental health problems between white and black offenders, with white offenders having higher rates of mental health problems than black offenders (Coid et al., 2002). Vaughn et al. (2008) found that black offenders are less likely to be diagnosed with a mental health problem compared with white, but are more likely to report delinquency. Sayed et al. (2015: 3) argue that:

> these findings indicate that there may be variance in mental health problems between Whites and Blacks, and furthermore, that the different life experiences of each group can create altered paths to criminal activity. It may not be the presence of mental health illnesses alone that influence offending but other risk factors that are also present with the disorders, such as substance-related disorders.

Gender also intersects with other characteristics, including age. For example, research has found that female offenders are more likely than male offenders to self-harm in prison and some research suggests those at the youngest and eldest ends of the spectrum of offenders have worse mental health than other age groups (Fazel et al., 2001).

Thus the intersections between age, gender, ethnicity, class and mental health must be appreciated in order to understand the characteristics of offenders and research must be sensitive to these overlaps.

Summary

This chapter has outlined and explained the most common characteristics of (known) offenders observed in the international data and research; as such these characteristics are limited to offenders who are, or have been, in the Criminal Justice System and self-report studies. The most common themes across the literature relate to age, gender, ethnicity, class and mental health, with substantial overlaps across and within these categories. Offenders are typically young white men from poor backgrounds with a higher rate of mental health problems than the general population. However, increasing numbers of female offenders and older offenders are being processed through the Criminal Justice System internationally, while those from BME backgrounds continue to be disproportionately represented at all stages, particularly in England and Wales. These characteristics help us to build a picture of who offenders are, which can inform theory, policy and practice.

Discussion Questions

1. What might be the causes of the disproportionate involvement of young people in crime?

2. Which criminological theories best explain the age–crime curve?

3. How does mental health and gender impact on offending?

4. Why are young black men disproportionately represented in the Criminal Justice System?

5. Do young black men commit more crime than men from other ethnicities?

Further Reading

DeLisi, M. and Conis, P.J (2012) *Violent Offenders: Theory, research, policy, and practice*. 2nd edn. Burlington, MA: Jones and Bartlett Learning.

Ulmer, J.T. and Steffensmeier, D. (2014) 'The age and crime relationship: Social variation, social explanations', in K.M. Beaver, J.C. Barnes and B.B. Boutwell (eds), *The Nurture Versus Biosocial Debate in Criminology: On the origins of criminal behavior and criminality*. Thousand Oaks, CA: Sage.

References

Abram, K., Teplin, L., McClelland, G. and Dulcan, M. (2003) 'Comorbid psychiatric disorders in youth in juvenile detention', *Archives of General Psychiatry*, 60: 1097–108.

Aday, R.H. and Krabill, J.J. (2012) 'Older and Geriatric Offenders: Critical issues for the 21st century' in L. Gideon (ed.), *Special Needs of Offenders in Correctional Institutions*. Thousand Oaks, CA: Sage.

Adler, F. (1975) *Sisters in Crime*. New York: McGraw Hill.

Age UK (2011) *Supporting Older People in Prison: Ideas for practice* [Online]. Available at: http://www.ageuk.org.uk/documents/en-gb/for-professionals/government-and-society/older%20prisoners%20guide_pro.pdf?dtrk=true

Agnew, R. (1985) 'A revised strain theory of delinquency', *Social Forces*, 64 (1): 151–67.

Australian Bureau of Statistics (2014) *Recorded Crime – Offenders, 2013–14*. Canberra: ABS. Available at: www.abs.gov.au/ausstats/abs@.nsf/Lookup/by%20Subject/4519.0~2013-14~Main%20Features~Introduction~2

Australian Institute of Criminology (AIC) (2011) *Australian Crime: Facts and figures*. Canberra: AIC. Available at: http://www.aic.gov.au/publications/current%20series/facts.html

Bowling, B. and Phillips, C. (2002) *Racism, Crime and Justice*. Harlow: Pearson Education.

Brooke, D., Taylor, C., Gunn, J. and Maden, A. (1996) 'Point prevalence of mental disorder in unconvicted male prisoners in England and Wales', *British Medical Journal*, 313: 1524–7.

Brown, E. and Males, M. (2011) 'Does age or poverty level best predict criminal arrest and homicide rates? A preliminary investigation', *Justice Policy Journal*, 8 (1): 1–30.

Campbell, A., Abbott, S. and Simpson, A. (2014) 'Young offenders with mental health problems in transition', *Journal of Mental Health Training, Education and Practice*, 9 (4): 232–43.

Carlen, P. (1988) *Women, Crime and Poverty*. Milton Keynes: Open University Press.

Cavadino, P. (1999) 'Diverting mentally disordered offenders from custody', in D. Webb and R. Harris (eds), *Mentally Disordered Offenders: Managing people nobody owns*. London: Routledge.

Clinks (2013) *Working with older offenders: A resource for voluntary, community and social enterprise organisations* [Online]. London: Clinks. Available at: www.clinks.org/sites/default/files/basic/files-downloads/Working%20With%20Older%20Offenders%20-%20 January%202014.pdf

Cohen, A.K. (1955) *Delinquent Boys*. New York: Free Press.

Coid, J., Petruckevitch, A., Bebbington, P., Brugha, T., Bhugra, D., Jenkins, R. and Singleton, N. (2002) 'Ethnic differences in prisoners 1: Criminality and psychiatric morbidity', *The British Journal of Psychiatry*, 181 (6): 473–80.

Copeland, W.E., Keeler, G., Angold, A. and Costello, E.J. (2007) 'Traumatic events and posttraumatic stress in childhood', *Archives of General Psychiatry*, 64: 577–84.

Daniel, A.E. and Flemming, J. (2006) 'Suicides in a state correctional system 1992–2002', *Journal of Correctional Health Care*, 12: 24–35.

Desai, R.A., Falzer, P.R., Chapman, J. and Borum, R. (2012) 'Mental illness, violence risk, and race in juvenile detention: Implications for disproportionate minority contact', *American Journal of Orthopsychiatry*, 82 (1): 32–40.

Dunaway, R.G., Cullen, F.T., Burton, V.S. and Evans, T.D. (2000) 'The myth of social class and crime revisited. An examination of class and adult criminality', *Criminology*, 38 (2): 589–632.

Eronen, M., Hakola, P. and Tiihonen, J. (1996) 'Mental disorders and homicidal behavior in Finland', *Archives of General Psychiatry*, 53 (6): 497–501.

Farrington, D.P., Coid, J.W., Harnett, L.M., Jolliffe, D., Soteriou, N., Turner, R.E. and West, D.J. (2006) *Criminal Careers up to Age 50 and Life success up to Age 48: New findings from the Cambridge Study in Delinquent Development*. London: Home Office. Available at: http://www.crim.cam.ac.uk/people/academic_research/david_farrington/hors299.pdf

Fazel, S. and Danesh, J. (2002) 'Serious mental disorder in 23,000 prisoners: A systematic review of 62 surveys', *Lancet*, 359: 545–50.

Fazel, S., Hope, T., O'Donnell, I. and Jacoby, R. (2001) 'Hidden psychiatric morbidity in elderly prisoners', *The British Journal of Psychiatry*, 179 (6): 535–9.

Felson, R.B. (2002) 'Violence and gender reexamined', *American Journal of Psychiatry*, 160 (9): 1711–12.

Flynn, S., Rodway, C., Appleby, L. and Shaw, J. (2014) 'Serious violence by people with mental illness: National clinical survey', *Journal of Interpersonal Violence*, 29 (8): 1438–58.

Gelsthorpe, L. (2007) 'Sentencing and gender', in R. Sheehan, G. McIvor and C. Trotter (eds), *What Works with Women Offenders*. Cullompton: Willan.

Glendinning, C. and Millar, J. (1992) *Women and Poverty in Britain: The 1990s*. Hemel Hempstead: Harvester Wheatsheaf.

Green, C., Kendall, K., Andre, G., Loman, T and Polvi, N. (1993) 'A study of 133 suicides among Canadian federal prisoners', *Med. Sci. Law*, 33: 121–7.

Greenfield, L.A. (1997) *Sex Offenses and Offenders: An analysis of data on rape and sexual assault*. Washington: Bureau of Justice Statistics.

Haginoya, S. (2014) 'Offender demographics and geographical characteristics by offender means of transportation in serial residential burglaries', *Psychology, Crime and Law*, 20 (6): 515–34.

Hällsten, M., Szulkin, R. and Sarnecki, J. (2013) 'Crime as a price of inequality? The gap in registered crime between childhood immigrants, children of immigrants and children of native Swedes', *British Journal of Criminology*, 53(3): 456–81.

Harrell, E. and Langton, L. (2013) *Victims of Identity Theft, 2012* [Online]. Washington: US Department of Justice. Available at: www.bjs.gov/index.cfm?ty=pbdetail&iid=4911

Hawkins, D., Laub, J.H. and Lauritsen, J.L. (1998) 'Race, ethnicity and serious juvenile offenders', in R. Loeber and D. Farrington (eds), *Serious and Violent Juvenile Offenders: Risk factors and successful interventions*. Thousand Oaks, CA: Sage. pp. 30–46.

Hawton, K., Linsell, L., Adeniji, T., Sariaslan, A. and Fazel, S. (2014) 'Self-harm in prisons in England and Wales: An epidemiological study of prevalence, risk factors, clustering, and subsequent suicide', *The Lancet*, 383 (9923): 1147–54.

Hay, C. and Forrest, W. (2009) 'The implications of family poverty for a pattern of persistent offending', in J. Savage (ed.), *The Development of Persistent Criminality*. Oxford: Oxford University Press.

Hay, C., Fortson, E.N., Hollist, D.R., Altheimer, I. and Schaible, L.M. (2007) 'Compounded risk: The implications for delinquency of coming from a poor family that lives in a poor community', *Journal of Youth and Adolescence*, 36(5): 593–605.

Heidensohn, F. and Silvestri, M. (2012) 'Gender and crime', in M. Maguire, R. Morgan and R. Reiner (eds), *The Oxford Handbook of Criminology*. 5th edn. Oxford: Oxford University Press.

Heimer, K. (2000) 'Changes in the gender gap in crime and women's economic marginalization', *Criminal Justice*, 1: 427–83.

Her Majesty's Chief Inspector of Prisons (HMCIP) (2002) *Annual Report by HMCIP for England and Wales 2001–2002*. London: The Stationery Office.

Her Majesty's Chief Inspector of Prisons for Scotland (HMIP) (2008) *Out of Sight: Severe and enduring mental health problems in Scotland's prisons*. Edinburgh: HMIP.

Her Majesty's Inspectorate of Constabulary (HMIC) (2014) *Crime-Recording: Making the victim count: The final report of an inspection of crime data integrity in police forces in England and Wales*. London: HMIC. Available at: https://www.justiceinspectorates.gov.uk/hmic/wp-content/uploads/crime-recording-making-the-victim-count.pdf

Hoeve, M., Jak, S., Stams, G.J.J. and Meeus, W.H. (2014) 'Financial problems and delinquency in adolescents and young adults: A 6-year three-wave study', *Crime and Delinquency*, 1–22.

Hoffman, P.B. and Beck, J.L. (1984) 'Burnout – Age at release from prison and recidivism', *Journal of Criminal Justice*, 12 (6): 617–23.

Home Office (2003) *Domestic Violence Offenders: Characteristics and offending related needs*. London: Home Office. Available at: http://webarchive.nationalarchives.gov.uk/20110218135832/http:/rds.homeoffice.gov.uk/rds/pdfs2/r217.pdf

Home Office (2007) *The Corston Report*. London: Home Office. Available at: www.justice.gov.uk/publications/docs/corston-report-march-2007.pdf

Home Office (2013) *Overview of Sexual Offending*. London: Home Office. Available at: www.gov.uk/government/uploads/system/uploads/attachment_data/file/214970/sexual-offending-overview-jan-2013.pdf

House of Commons (2013) *Prison Population Statistics*. London: House of Commons. Available at: http://researchbriefings.parliament.uk/ResearchBriefing/Summary/SN04334#fullreport

House of Commons Justice Committee (2013) *Women Offenders: After the Corston Report. Second report of session 2013–14*. London: House of Commons. Available at: www.parliament.uk/documents/commons-committees/Justice/Women-offenders.pdf

Kerkhof, A.J. and Bernasco, W. (1990) 'Suicidal behavior in jails and prisons in the Netherlands: Incidence, characteristics and prevention', *Suicide Life Threat. Behavior*, 20: 123–37.

Khanom, H., Samele, C. and Rutherford, M. (2009) *Community Sentences and the Mental Health Treatment Requirement*. London: Sainsbury Centre for Mental Health.

Lader, D., Singleton, N. and Meltzer, H. (2000) *Psychiatric Morbidity among Prisoners in England and Wales*. London: Office for National Statistics.

Laub, J.H. and McDermott, M. (1985) 'An analysis of serious crime by young black women', *Criminology*, 23 (1): 81–98.

Lilly, R.J., Cullen, F.T. and Ball, R.A. (2002) *Criminological Theory: Context and consequences*. 3rd edn. Thousand Oaks, CA: Sage.

Macpherson, W. (1999) *The Stephen Lawrence Inquiry.* Report of an Inquiry by Sir William Macpherson of Cluny (Cm 4262-1). London: HMSO.

Mahony, T.H. (2011) *Women and the Criminal Justice System: A gender-based statistical report*. Ottawa-Gatineau: Statistics Canada.

McIvor, G. (2007) 'The nature of female offending', in R. Sheehan, G. McIvor and C. Trotter (eds), *What Works with Women Offenders*. Cullompton: Willan.

Merton, R. (1938) 'Social structure and anomie', *American Sociological Review*, 3: 672–82.

Miller, J. (2010) 'Stop and search in England: A reformed tactic or business as usual?' *British Journal of Criminology*, 50 (5): 954–74.

Ministry of Justice (2008) *The Problems and Needs of Newly Sentenced Prisoners: Results from a national survey*. London: MoJ. Available at: http://webarchive.nationalarchives.gov.uk/20100505212400/http:/www.justice.gov.uk/publications/docs/research-problems-needs-prisoners.pdf

Ministry of Justice (2012) *National Offender Management Service Offender Equalities Annual Report 2012/13*. London: MoJ. Available at: www.gov.uk/government/uploads/system/uploads/attachment_data/file/256911/noms-offender-equalities-annual-report.pdf

Ministry of Justice (2013a) *Statistics on Women and the Criminal Justice System, 2013*. London: MoJ. Available at: www.gov.uk/government/uploads/system/uploads/attachment_data/file/380090/women-cjs-2013.pdf

Ministry of Justice (2013b) *Statistics on Race and the Criminal Justice System 2012*. London: MoJ. Available at: www.gov.uk/government/uploads/system/uploads/attachment_data/file/269399/Race-and-cjs-2012.pdf

Ministry of Justice (2014) *Experimental Statistics from the 2013 MoJ /DWP /HMRC Data Share: Linking data on offenders with benefit, employment and income data. Joint statistical report from the Ministry of Justice and the Department for Work and Pensions*. London: MoJ. Available at: www.gov.uk/government/uploads/system/uploads/attachment_data/file/304411/experimental-statistics.pdf

Ministry of Justice (2015) *Official Statistics. Prison population figures: 2015*. London: MoJ.

Ministry of Justice (2016) *Safety in Custody Statistics England and Wales – Deaths in prison custody to March 2016. Assaults and self-harm to December 2015 quarterly update to December 2015*. London: MoJ. Available at: www.gov.uk/government/uploads/system/uploads/attachment_data/file/519425/safety-in-custody-march-2016.pdf

National Police Agency (2010) *Crime Statistics: Crimes in Heisei 22*. Available at: www.npa.go.jp/toukei/index.htm

Niven, S. and Stewart, D. (2005) *Resettlement Outcomes on Release from Prison in 2003, Home Office Findings 248*. London: Home Office. Available at: www.homeoffice.gov.uk/rds/pdfs05/r248.pdf

Office of National Statistics (2015) *Youth Justice Statistics 2013/14*. London: ONS. Available at: www.gov.uk/government/uploads/system/uploads/attachment_data/file/399379/youth-justice-annual-stats-13-14.pdf

Office of National Statistics (2016) *Crime in England and Wales: Year ending December 2015*. London: ONS. Available at: www.ons.gov.uk/peoplepopulationandcommunity/crimeandjustice/bulletins/crimeinenglandandwales/yearendingdecember2015

Phillips, C. and Bowling, B. (2003) 'Racism, ethnicity and criminology. Developing minority perspectives', *British Journal of Criminology*, 43 (2): 269–90.

Piquero, A.R. and Brame, R.W. (2008) 'Assessing the race–crime and ethnicity–crime relationship in a sample of serious adolescent delinquents', *Crime and Delinquency*, 54 (3): 390–422.

Pratt, D., Appleby, L., Piper, M., Webb, R. and Shaw, J. (2010) 'Suicide in recently released prisoners: A case control study', *Psychological Medicine*, 40: 827–35.

Pridemore, W.A. (2011) 'Poverty matters: A reassessment of the inequality–homicide relationship in cross-national studies', *British Journal of Criminology*, 51 (5): 739–72.

Prison Reform Trust (2004) *Alcohol and Re-offending – Who cares?* London: Prison Reform Trust. Available at: www.prisonreformtrust.org.uk/Portals/0/Documents/Alcohol%20briefing.pdf

Prison Reform Trust (2013) *Prison: The facts – Bromley briefings Summer 2013.* London: Prison Reform Trust. Available at: www.prisonreformtrust.org.uk/Portals/0/Documents/Prisonthefacts.pdf

Reeve, K. and Batty, E. (2011) *The Hidden Truth about Homelessness. Experiences of single homelessness in England.* University of Sheffield: Centre for Regional Economic and Social Research.

Rickford, D. (2003) *Troubled Inside: Responding to the mental health needs of women in prison.* London: Prison Reform Trust.

Roberts, R. and McMahon, W. (2008) *Ethnicity, Harm and Crime: A discussion paper.* London: Centre for Crime and Justice Studies.

Runnymede (2012) *Criminal Justice v. Racial Justice. Minority ethnic overrepresentation in the criminal justice system* [Online]. London: Runnymede. Available at: www.runnymedetrust.org/uploads/publications/pdfs/CriminalJusticeVRacialJustice-2012.pdf

Sampson, R.J. and Laub, J.H. (1994) 'Urban poverty and the family context of delinquency: A new look at structure and process in a classic study', *Child Development*, 65: 523–40.

Sayed, S., Piquero, A.R., Schubert, C.A., Mulvey, E.P., Pitzer, L. and Piquero, N.L. (2015) 'Assessing the mental health/offending relationship across race/ethnicity in a sample of serious adolescent offenders', *Criminal Justice Policy Review*, 1–37.

Schubert, C.A., Mulvey, E.P. and Glasheen, C. (2011) 'Influence of mental health and substance use problems and criminogenic risk on outcomes in serious juvenile offenders', *Journal of the American Academy of Child & Adolescent Psychiatry*, 50 (9): 925–37.

Senior, J., Birmingham, L., Harty, M.A., Hassan, L., Hayes, A.J., Kendall, K., Webb, R. et al. (2013) 'Identification and management of prisoners with severe psychiatric illness by specialist mental health services', *Psychological Medicine*, 43 (07), 1511–20.

Shaw, C.R. and McKay, H.D. (1942) *Juvenile Delinquency and Urban Areas: A study of rates of delinquents in relation to differential characteristics of local communities in American cities.* Chicago: University of Chicago Press.

Shover, N. and Thompson, C.Y. (1992) 'Age, differential expectations and crime desistance', *Criminology*, 30 (1): 89–104.

Shulman, E.P., Steinberg, L. and Piquero, A.R. (2013) 'A mistaken account of the age–crime curve: Response to Males and Brown', *Journal of Adolescent Research*, 29 (1): 25–34.

Silver, E., Felson, R.B. and Vaneseltine, M. (2008) 'The relationship between mental health problems and violence among criminal offenders', *Criminal Justice and Behavior*, 35 (4), 405–26.

Singleton, N., Meltzer, H., Gatward, R., Coid, J. and Deasy, D. (1998) *Psychiatric Morbidity among Prisoners in England and Wales.* London: ONS.

Sirotich, F. (2008) 'Correlates of crime and violence among persons with mental disorder: An evidence-based review', *Brief Treatment and Crisis Intervention*, 8 (2), 171–94.

Smith, E.L. and Cooper, A. (2013) *Homicide in the U.S. Known to Law Enforcement, 2011*. Washington D.C.: U.S. Department of Justice, Bureau of Justice Statistics.

Stroh, M., Eichinger, M., Giza, A., Hirschmann, N., Bögelein, N., Pitsela, A. and Neubacher, F. (2016) 'Are female offenders underreported compared to male offenders? A German-Greek comparison of crime reporting, rating of offence seriousness and personal experiences of victimisation', *European Journal on Criminal Policy and Research*, 1–19.

Teague, M. (2005) 'Statistics may ignore hidden crime', *Probation Journal*, 52 (1): 76–7.

Ulmer, J.T and Steffensmeier, D. (2015) 'The age and crime relationship: Social variation, social explanations', in K.M. Beaver, J.C. Barnes and B.B. Boutwell (eds), *The Nurture Versus Biosocial Debate in Criminology: On the origins of criminal behavior and criminality*. Thousand Oaks, CA: Sage.

Vaughn, M.G., Wallace, J.M., Davis, L.E., Fernandes, G.T. and Howard, M.O. (2008) 'Variations in mental health problems, substance use, and delinquency between African American and Caucasian juvenile offenders: Implications for reentry services', *International Journal of Offender Therapy and Comparative Criminology*, 52: 311–29.

Webster, C.S. (2012) 'Different forms of discrimination in the criminal justice system', in The Runnymede Trust *Criminal Justice v. Racial Justice: Minority ethnic overrepresentation in the criminal justice system*. London: The Runnymede Trust.

Wilson, D. (2005) *Death at the Hands of the State*. London: The Howard League for Penal Reform.

World Health Organization (2007) *Preventing Suicide in Jails and Prisons*. Geneva: WHO.

Wykes, M. and Welsh, K. (2009) *Violence, Gender and Justice*. London: Sage.

Check out the Companion Website

Want to know more about this chapter? Review what you have been learning by visiting: **https://study.sagepub.com/harding**

- Practice with essay questions
- Test yourself with multiple-choice questions
- Listen to a series of podcasts featuring Neil of Northumbria Police and London's Metropolitan Police Service
- Watch videos selected from the SAGE Video collection

6 Diversity and the Criminal Justice Process

Colin Webster

Introduction

According to Ashworth and Redmayne (2010: 424) 'The principle of equality before the law, or non-discrimination, ought to be respected as a fundamental element in the administration of justice'. It is far from clear that this is actually the case. As Chapter 5 began to explore, members of ethnic minorities, women and girls, young people and groups having low social and economic status may experience disadvantage or discrimination at the hands of the police and criminal justice agencies. Discrimination can also sometimes work positively in the sense of protecting vulnerable children and young people from abuse and exploitation, and protecting child and youth offenders from punishment that is too harsh. Similarly, girls and women can be protected or treated leniently as well as harshly because of stereotyping and discrimination. Contrastingly, discrimination or bias in favour of powerful groups having high social and economic status can advantage them further.

The meaning of diversity in decisions to stop and search, arrest, prosecute or caution, sentence and imprison is, however, most often associated with different or discriminatory treatment by the Criminal Justice System. The police and the courts struggle to accommodate diversity and pressures to reform policing and criminal justice are meant to ensure, as far as is possible, equality before the law. While not denying the importance of efforts to remove discrimination from the criminal justice process through recognising diversity, the chapter emphasises that the criminal justice process should not be regarded as separate from the ways in which society is arranged and structured. Discrimination and bias in criminal justice may well reflect the power and advantage of some groups over others in wider society. Discrimination and diversity in policing and the Criminal Justice System cannot be considered in isolation.

Finally, by way of introduction, it is the view of this author that policing diversity and the recognition of diversity by the law and the courts is double edged. Not only must the law and criminal justice process recognise and adapt to an increasingly diverse society in terms of ethnicity, gender, sexuality and social class background, the criminal justice process must also recognise its own part in replicating unequal and biased treatment and resisting reforms and pressures for more equality. As the chapter will show, this is a particular problem with regard to treating the social status of victims and suspects equally.

Purpose and Scope of the Chapter

- From the outset, it is important to stress that the approach taken in this chapter is to provide an overview of the topic, not detailed data on the different treatment of groups in criminal justice, as befits the task of putting the operation of criminal justice into its wider context of societal diversity.

- Case studies and illustrations are used throughout so that, for example, social class bias is shown comparing the criminal justice treatment of tax dodgers and benefit cheats; and how financial and corporate crime mostly goes unpunished.

- Indeed, perhaps unusually for a chapter about criminal justice and diversity, social status or social class is foregrounded as an important dimension of bias and unequal treatment by the law, the police and the courts, showing how some social groups go unpunished for wrong-doing and other groups disproportionately go to prison.

- The chapter begins with policing and criminal justice processes, which are first positioned amid a debate about the growing demands for, and ascendency of, human rights, tolerance of diversity and equality in modern western societies.

- The focus then turns to policing ethnic and social diversity in a changing world whereby the police struggle to reform and adapt to these changes, and in some cases resist them, before turning to the issue of race, ethnicity and the criminal justice process.

- In examining diversity and the criminal justice process the chapter asks where, to the extent that bias and discrimination exists, it may be found, and through what mechanisms it operates. Is bias mostly found at earlier police stages, or at later stages of the criminal justice process, in the court?

- Not to be left out, the outcomes of criminal justice processes found in prisons are examined, not so much in terms of the well-established over-representation of visible minority prisoners and prisoners from socially marginalised, low status groups, but in terms of race relations and discrimination in prisons.

- Here the chapter summarises a rare prison study showing how diversity in a prison paradoxically led to an uneasy interethnic solidarity and cohesion among the men there, reminding readers how little of prison life is known, while prison is the cornerstone of the whole Criminal Justice System.

- How criminal justice processes treat girls and women is considered next, particularly when they are victims of alleged domestic violence, sexual assault and rape. Such an examination reveals rather complicated differences in treatment by the police and the courts, which can sometimes favour and protect girls and women, in other instances disadvantage them creating adverse (and perverse) outcomes for them due to discrimination.

- Throughout, the ways often-powerless victims are subject to abuse and exploitation by often-powerful criminal actors – whether this be through property and violent offences against them; because of their gender, age or sexuality; or through sexual abuse and exploitation – are linked to the issue of the abuse of power by individuals and groups, including sometimes the inadequate (or worse) responses of the police and Criminal Justice System to such abuses.

- The final part of the chapter examines the crimes of the powerful explicitly, implicating narrower policing and Criminal Justice System processes in wider societal processes based on different treatment according to an individual's social status or class or an organisation's wealth and political influence. Evidence is presented supporting the adage that the rich do indeed get richer while the poor get prison (Reiman and Leighton, 2010).

Diversity, Freedom and Human Rights

Deep changes in the social structure and dominant attitude of contemporary market democracies are everywhere putting pressure on the values that have sustained the ideals of equality before the law. And yet, these structural pressures towards *more* inequality, are countervailed by popular attitudes and values that in many ways demand *more* equality and fairness. Increasing ethnic diversity, rising immigration, evolving family structures and growing inequality are just some of the economic and demographic changes in Britain today. These changes are accompanied by shifts in cultural and political values too. More likely to be tolerant towards difference, more open to diversity, equal rights, fairness and individual freedom (particularly for men and women), public expectations placed on institutions such as the police and the courts have grown accordingly. A general decline in deference towards powerful elites, while not significantly challenging the power of those elites, does nevertheless place an obligation on elites to be accountable. The implications of change for the law, policing and criminal justice have seen significant reforms and adaptations towards human rights and the accommodation of diversity.

Normally, we think of the law and criminal justice as above everyday bias or prejudice, unsullied by corruption or undue influence. After all, the story goes, as individuals we are equal before the law. We fully expect to be treated equally without prejudice and that our civil and human rights are protected. The government cannot be seen to discriminate with respect to its own citizens. Due process demands that every civil or criminal case be investigated and decided, prosecuted and tried in court, according to principles of fairness and equal treatment, so that every case is judged on its merits (see also Chapter 4). On this basis the justice system is perceived as the lynchpin of a system framed by the human rights of its citizens.

The idea of equal rights gained more general acceptance following the Second World War. The United Nations Charter the 'Universal Declaration of Human Rights' was internationally adopted in 1948:

- Article 1 declared: 'All human beings are born free and equal in dignity and rights.'

- Article 2 stated that the rights the Charter set forth were enjoyed by all 'without distinction of any kind, such as race, colour, language, religion, political or other opinion, national or social origin, property, birth or other status.'

Today, for the UK, human rights law derives from the European Convention on Human Rights (ECHR) (see also Chapter 22). Of course, the implementation of this human rights doctrine within and across nation states is only possible with legal and judicial structures in place to override recalcitrant governments and powerful interests. The declaration of human rights must have the force of law to be effective. It is notable that although the USA became a signatory, it did so only on the understanding that the declaration would not have the force of law. The consequences were the continuation of deep and widespread racial discrimination in the USA.

As this chapter will set out to show, ideals of freedom, equality and rights as intrinsic features of criminal justice have been sorely tested by the practical realities of bias, prejudice, discrimination, social status and economic self-interest. That the law and criminal justice are not above political, cultural and economic influence and pressure in society, means that policing and criminal justice constantly struggle to accommodate diversity and change. The police and the courts have attempted to adapt to change to be effective and relevant, while continuing to protect individual human rights, property and freedoms in ways accepted as fair, just and equal.

In offering remedies or redress to the abuse of power by the police and the courts against *individuals* – abuses such as bias or wrongful conviction – the ECHR may not be appropriate where abuses of power are taking place against a relatively powerless and marginalised *group* as a whole (Sanders et al., 2010). The Convention does not in its present form recognise the case for special treatment or protection of certain groups. Recent reforms in the criminal law, in policing, and in criminal procedure, have nevertheless gone some way to recognising diversity and the existence of special groups. For example, racially motivated victimisation has been recognised in law and that such offences have a basis in hostility to the victim's membership of a group (see also Chapters 13, 14 and 20). These legal reforms reflect wider changes in Britain's cultural values and a shift to a more diverse society. In this context of wider changes, it is worth asking the question 'How fair is Britain?' across domains beyond the legal and criminal justice to include such areas as physical security, health, education, employment and standard of living (EHRC, 2010).

In the context of laws and a criminal justice process, failure to adapt means they are likely to become increasingly inconsistent and confused, and less fair. Equality before the law, after the specific characteristics of an individual's case have been taken into account, is clearly inconsistent with the disproportionate attention given to the arrest, prosecution and punishment of one social or ethnic group more than another (Hudson, 1993). A criminal justice tradition that concentrates on securing fairness for the individual also needs to recognise and seek fairness for groups. As Smith (1997: 1045) has argued, equal treatment does not mean the same treatment. Hence there is room for different treatment of groups according to their specific needs: for example, for the police and other agencies to take special action to meet the needs of ethnic minorities as victims of racial attacks.

To conclude this section, although policing diversity and administering justice in diverse settings in a way defines contemporary policing and justice, there are areas where the very existence of diversity narrows rather than expands the scope and imagination of policing and criminal justice processes, worsening social division and polarisation. That is why policing, the law and the administration of justice must be put in the context of contrasting ways crimes by the powerful and powerless are dealt with, considered in the concluding section of this chapter.

Ethnic Diversity, Policing and Criminal Justice

Any examination of diversity in the Criminal Justice System requires an examination of policing processes. It is after all the police who through their enforcement of the law supply the system with those they believe have committed an offence. Law enforcement and policing approaches become important sources of the profile of the offender population.

Table 6.1 summarises the most recent available information about the proportion of individuals from each ethnic group found at different stages of the criminal justice process (Ministry of Justice, 2013). These findings have been consistent over many years and the police statistics are broadly consistent with the *Crime Survey for England and Wales*, based on individuals telling the survey what has happened to them.

Table 6.1 Proportion of individuals in policing and criminal justice processes by ethnic group, compared to the general population (%), 2011–12

	White	Black	Asian	Mixed
Stops and searches	67	14	10	3
Arrests	80	8	6	3
Disorder	69	2	5.5	0.5
Cautions	84	7	5	–
Court proceedings	71	8	5	2
Convictions	73	7.5	4.5	2
Sentenced to custody	71	9	5.5	2
Prison population	73	14.5	7	3.5
Population (aged 10 and over, 2011)	87	3	6.5	2

Of immediate note are the proportions of Asian and particularly black people who are stopped and searched by the police on foot or in a vehicle compared to their numbers in the general population. In contrast, white people are distinctly underrepresented in police stops and searches compared to their numbers in the population as a whole. Looking further, it can be seen how black people are over-represented at every stage of the Criminal Justice System from stops and searches to imprisonment compared to their numbers in the general population. Furthermore, the evidence suggests that black and Asian people are more frequently stopped, more often repeatedly stopped and more subject to more-intrusive searches (Phillips, 2012).

The problem appears to be the application of officers' discretion to act towards an individual – that the officer believes the person may have, may be in the course of, or may be about to commit a crime – according to their membership of an ethnic group. Deriving 'suspicion' about individuals on this basis faces a further problem; that actual rates of offending between ethnic groups are very similar, the frequency with which an offence is discovered to have actually occurred is very similar, and in any case little more than a tenth of stop and searches uncover criminality across all ethnicities.

Despite all this – and in particular that black people are nearly seven times more likely to be searched than whites, and Asians twice as likely – police stop and search powers have greatly expanded through the Terrorism Acts from 2000, which having been used disproportionately against black and Asian people, have had virtually no effect in themselves uncovering or apprehending actual terrorists. For example, in 2009/10, of the 101,248 people stopped and searched under these powers, *none* of them was arrested for terrorism-related offences and only 0.5 per cent were arrested for *any* offence, compared with a 10 per cent arrest rate for street searches under normal police powers (EHRC, 2010; Dodd, 2012).

The following series of case studies further illustrate how issues of ethnic diversity are reflected in different areas of criminal justice. The idea is that readers will learn more at this stage by immersing themselves more fully in some of the best direct studies of this nature.

Case Study: Policing Diversity in a Changing World (Loftus, 2009)

Criminological accounts of policing have tended to portray the police negatively as possessing values and attitudes generally hostile to ideals of diversity and equal treatment. In this account the police are said to be resistant to being challenged and reformed as to how police officers behave towards visible minorities, young people and women victimised by men. It is often said that police officers belong to a closed, like-minded 'police culture' that reinforces stereotypes and unequal treatment. More recently the focus has shifted to a recognition of diverse cultures within the police itself, to police reform resulting from policing diversity, and more generally the positive aspects of police values and attitudes (Cockcroft, 2012; Loftus, 2009).

If policing, as is conventionally thought, is primarily about catching thieves, then this emphasis can ignore its core function, which is the control of public places. Young men in public places might be policed differently according to officers' perception of their social status (Choongh, 1998). The presence of different social groups in, and their use of, public space varies according to class, age, gender and ethnicity, and this will be reflected in their contact and conflict with the police.

Bethan Loftus' (2009) study of policing and police culture sees as its greatest challenge and development today the emergence of respect for, and recognition of, diversity. Developments that have transformed the nature of society, with which this chapter began, have seen the greater political recognition of minority groups, women's rights and the burgeoning economic exclusion of some groups. It is this changed landscape in which the police operate that for Loftus is the defining feature of policing, police culture and police processes. As Loftus points out, police conduct has come under considerable scrutiny in recent years in respect of police involvement in miscarriages of justice; abuses of power and corruption; lack of accountability; and erosion of civil liberties (see Chapter 19 in this volume with respect to miscarriages of justice). These scandals and pressures have focused criticism on police processes of interrogation, patrolling, stop and search and detaining individual members of the public.

The Police and Criminal Evidence Act (PACE) 1984 has been a key framework of rules governing police powers to achieve a balance between competing rights and interests of the suspect and the police. Yet many studies over many years have found that the police circumvent these rules; there is evidence of stop and search being used to gather intelligence on certain populations and that such encounters are driven by police stereotypes on the basis of appearance. The remainder of this case study briefly summarises the implications for policing a diverse society of these sorts of abuses of police powers.

Earlier critical reports about police powers such as Lord Scarman's in 1981 following the violent disorder between the police and black young people in South London, and the report by Sir William Macpherson in 1999, following the racist murder of Stephen Lawrence and the failed police investigation, both condemned the influence of racism on policing. The Race Relations (Amendment) Act 2000 brought a comprehensive reform programme to British policing specifically aimed at eradicating racism and other forms of stereotyping and discrimination, including the long-standing failure of the police to adequately protect the rights of women, notably in their approach to those who are victims of domestic violence, sexual assault or rape. Perhaps still, the area of greatest controversy or disagreement among criminological critics of police culture and processes, while mostly ignored by policy makers, is that of policing the growing numbers of the economically impoverished, who some have designated 'police property'. The term indicates the power of the police to control and discriminate against those the police judge – through their appearance and demeanour – to be of low social status or worth (Reiner, 2010).

Loftus' close-up, in-depth study across Local Policing Units found contrasting responses among police officers towards policies aimed at recognising demands of greater diversity and accordingly improving fairness and equality within policing. There was plentiful evidence that overt verbal and physical discrimination were routinely experienced by women and minority officers. Reforms aimed at tackling discrimination among police colleagues and the ways the police treated the public, victims and suspects met considerable resistance, especially among an older generation of white, male, heterosexual officers. The beginnings of an opposing standpoint emphasising fairness and equality among young, minority, female and lesbian and gay officers was also apparent and had the effect of moderating, but not fundamentally changing, the views of older officers. Rather, older officers became more covert in their views – expressing private resentment, anxiety and resistance towards reform – while attempting to preserve their power and privileges.

Attitudes and behaviour nevertheless changed among many officers. Overt racist language disappeared. Officers arrested perpetrators of domestic violence. Many officers began to rethink the way they policed minority ethnic communities. Because of these changes Loftus was able to conclude that British policing had transformed and that the police realised they have to change their behaviour. Although not fully dismantling discrimination and stereotypes towards low-status victims and women victims of domestic violence, reforms have succeeded in bringing attention to equality and fairness, particularly in respect of ethnicity and gender. While efforts at changing police processes and culture focusing on diversity have had real if sometimes modest effects on officers and the police organisation, few such improvements are found in the police use of discretionary powers and authority towards the (especially white) poor – whether in police perceptions of the poor or their treatment.

Case Study: Difference or Discrimination in the Treatment of Young People by the Police and Youth Justice System (May et al., 2010)

Tiggey May and her colleagues' (2010) large study of the youth justice system focused on discretion in the decisions made by the police, criminal justice practitioners and the courts at different stages in the criminal justice process. In particular, they explored whether officers' and officials' judgements and decisions contributed to the over-representation of individuals from black and minority ethnic backgrounds found in the youth justice process. To do this the researchers examined policing processes such as stop and search in three police force areas; interviewed police officers and young people; and analysed 18,083 cases processed by the local youth justice systems.

The supply of individuals that are dealt with by youth justice depends on their referral by the police so an important question is whether there is different or discriminatory treatment by ethnicity and whether this occurs at the policing stage of the criminal justice process or later, for example in the way individuals are treated by Youth Offending Teams (YOTs) or the courts.

On the contribution of police processes and activity in providing suspects to the youth justice system the study found:

- When the police are reacting to reports from the public that a crime has taken place there is less room for police officers to use their own discretion. When police officers have the opportunity to use their own discretion – to be proactive, for example with drugs and road traffic offences – then this is when scope for discrimination is enabled.

(Continued)

(Continued)

- When proactive arrests are given priority and there are systematic differences in the type of offence the police focus on, then this can influence which young people end up in the youth justice system.

- There were large differences between the areas studied in the ways young people were entering, and the sorts of young people drawn into, the youth justice system.

- Although this reflected differences between areas in the nature of crime and disorder, it also reflected the markedly different styles of policing adopted by different policing areas.

- In some areas, encounters with the public could be characterised as following a professional 'rule of law' style of policing. Other areas employed a more confrontational and more personalised policing style, which placed less priority on respectful and fair treatment.

- However, confrontational policing often occurred in situations which genuinely required robust police action, and sometimes individuals – police and suspects – brought their own stereotypes and prejudices to the encounter, reflecting long histories of difficult relations between police and public.

The role of police activity in supplying suspects for the youth justice system should be understood in the context of officers sometimes having to deal with high levels of crime and disorder, and high levels of antagonism and conflict between police and public. This conflict often involved racial stereotyping and discrimination by police *and* public, whereas in some situations, adversarial or confrontational tactics seemed inevitable. The study was struck, though, by the contrasts in policing styles between different areas that shared similar problems and histories.

As regards the role of youth justice processes and decisions, once the police proceeded and referred individuals, the study found:

- Some evidence that at some stages of the youth justice system there may be discrimination against ethnic minority young people, because differences between ethnic groups in treatment and sentences could not be accounted for by features of the offence or criminal history of the suspects or defendants.

- In general, differences between YOT and court areas in the way in which suspects and defendants were treated – regardless of ethnicity – were greater than differences between ethnic groups in the treatment they received.

An overall conclusion from this study might be that contact and conflict between the police and young people may be more significant than their subsequent treatment by the youth justice system in relation to different or discriminatory treatment. The youth justice system, however, might be accused of operating a system of fair treatment and justice according to area.

Case Study: The Multicultural Prison and Diversity (Phillips, 2012)

This case study takes a somewhat different approach to that usually taken. The usual approach is to explain the disproportionate presence of visible minorities in the prison population as an outcome of discrimination in policing and criminal justice processes, such as the harsher treatment of black and Asian people, or by factors such as minority defendants electing to be tried in the Crown Court hoping to receive a fairer hearing but risking receiving longer sentences than handed down by the magistrates' court. Rather, this case study considers the ethnic and racial relations that evolve in the prison once defendants arrive and attempt to negotiate their place in the prisoner society they meet.

Coretta Phillips' (2012) in-depth study of the complex relationship between mainly white and black prisoners in two south-east English prisons provides, among other things, a more general up-to-date overview of ethnicity and prisons in relation to the globally diverse prison population of England and Wales. Some of the features of this overview can be summarised as follows:

- Prisons largely contain a population permanently positioned at the bottom of the social structure.

- The mechanisms by which these populations are in prison are primarily economic as they are controlled and disciplined as an economically surplus and expendable group.

- Their pre-prison lives are often 'marked by family disruption, economic disadvantage, and social and political marginalization. To these experiences are then added the pains of imprisonment.' (pp. 22–3)

- Race relations in UK prisons are defined by the disproportionality of black and minority prisoners compared to their numbers in the population, and failing attempts by the prison service to accommodate diversity.

- Prisons, nevertheless, can be places where prisoners from different ethnicities, cultures and backgrounds get on with one another. While racist hostility does arise in situations of tension and stress, overall, serious black–white opposition or conflict is relatively rare, paradoxically rarer than in the more segregated society outside the prison gates.

- It is not that relationships between prisoners are not sometimes volatile or violent; it is that these conflicts are less about race and more about masculine assertion based on loyalty to the areas prisoners come to prison from.

- Where racism is more likely to occur is in the hidden racism of some prison officers expressed in the myriad of ways prison officers both control and favour individual prisoners and groups of prisoners.

Gender, Sex Crimes and Criminal Justice

The question of the gender of suspects and defendants in respect of policing diversity and whether the courts treat women differently from men is now considered.

The evidence suggests women are treated less harshly than men, are less likely to be arrested, more likely to be cautioned and less likely to be remanded in custody by the courts, more likely to receive a community sentence and less likely a custodial sentence, compared to men. This reflects their different offending patterns and profile. On the other hand, when women are sent to prison as a result of policing and criminal justice processing and judgments, this arguably leads to more serious consequences for them and their children in that they face not only discrimination as ex-prisoners but prejudice as 'criminal women'. This is particularly the case as the custody rate for women has been rising steeply.

Criminological studies over many years have emphasised the following peculiarities of administering criminal justice in respect of women defendants (Heidensohn, 1996):

- The courts make detrimental moral value judgements about girls' and women's supposed sexual behaviour which is absent in regard to male defendants.

- The Criminal Justice System tends to sexualise and thus exaggerate the seriousness of women's offences.

- Girls and women are easily stigmatised as deviant according to social norms rather than the criminal law, often leading to their harsher treatment.

For many years the criminal justice response to female victims of crime was lamentable. The police did not take abuse and violence by men towards women seriously, much as they did not take racist violence towards minorities seriously. Such crimes were considered minor disputes to be 'smoothed over'; treated as one-off 'fights' or occurrences rather than an aspect in a process of escalating violence; and where victims were blamed for their mistreatment as having 'provoked' abuse and attack; and so on. The ubiquity and seriousness of domestic violence began to be officially recognised by the Home Office from the late 1980s. Campaigns and lobbying by women activists had put pressure on the Home Office to act. The first Domestic Violence Units in which the police devised specialist responses to crime of this nature were set up in 1987. After a patchy beginning, further pressure was exerted on the police to 'act robustly' with regard to domestic violence by the 1998 Crime Reduction Programme and the Violence against Women Initiative (Joyce, 2013). Research was commissioned focusing on domestic violence, rape and sexual assault showing the scale of the problem and the effectiveness of police policies.

This attention and these policies made important changes and improved the effectiveness of the police response to domestic and sexual crimes against women (and men), not least a growing recognition of the imbalance of power in society, and police and criminal justice prejudices towards women and children. This had been shown in the attitudes of the courts towards prosecuting domestic and sexual violence, which more often than not took a sceptical or lenient view of sexual misconduct by men towards girls and women (Joyce, 2013). In cases of rape the courts denigrated women victims as a defence and downgraded the severity of rape by implying that the victim was a willing sexual partner or was sexually provocative (see Chapter 14 for further discussion).

Recent reforms to the police and the Criminal Justice System continue to come up against prejudice and bias against women. Yet here in relation to women's equality and rights, as elsewhere, the 2010 Equality Act based on previous legislation such as the 2003 Sexual Offences Act and 2004 Domestic Violence, Crime and Victims Act outlaws discrimination in the police and court treatment of female victims of crime. Updating the law so as to secure and extend human rights and end discrimination on grounds of gender does not always in itself bring realisation of these aims of justice in practice. So for example, in the case of successful prosecutions of rape, and the situation regarding the policing of domestic violence, progress has been slow or non-existent. It is, though, fair to say that changes in societal attitudes to female victims of crime, and a much greater concern that such behaviours are totally unacceptable and criminal, have occurred.

What is interesting is how little research there is about the social distribution of domestic and sex crimes; whether domestic violence, sexual assault or rape are randomly spread across all social classes or concentrated among men from specific sorts of social background, just as violence and homicide are concentrated among younger men living in poorer areas (Kingston and Webster, 2015).

Class, Policing and Criminal Justice

It is often assumed that the underlying purpose of the criminal justice process is to control crime efficiently *and* fairly. An alternative view, argued by Choongh (1998: 625), is that this underlying aim is sacrificed or discarded in practice by the police in favour of the subordination of sections of society viewed as 'anti-police and innately criminal'. In other words, rather than selecting individuals suspected of having actually committed a crime, the police believe that:

> an acceptable and efficient way to police society is to identify classes of people who in various ways reject prevailing norms because it is amongst these classes that the threat of crime is at its most intense ... the police are then justified in subjecting them to surveillance and subjugation, regardless of whether the individuals selected for this treatment are violating the criminal law at any given moment.
>
> (Choongh 1998: 627)

The ways 'diversity' in terms of social differences are policed refers to police beliefs about social status and class. The derogatory ways the police can treat victims of crime, as well as suspects, because of their perceived lower social status, was recently and strikingly demonstrated in Greater Manchester and Doncaster when the police were revealed to have not protected vulnerable girl victims of sexual exploitation because they did not believe the girls' stories (Coffey Report, 2014; Jay Report, 2014).

To understand this better, a brief detour into contemporary understandings of social class is necessary. The idea of 'social class' is a way of classifying differences in income, wealth, occupation, values and the social status that accrues from these advantages. However, according to Mike Savage and his colleagues' (BBC Science, 2013) *Great British Class Survey* many people do not see themselves as belonging to any kind of class. So how can we talk about the relevance of class for discussions of criminal justice and diversity? Part of the problem is we tend to limit discussions about class to differences between the middle and working classes when we should really be focusing on the growing extremes of wealth and poverty that polarise society (Dorling, 2014; Sayer, 2015). It is these extremes, too, that are of most interest when looking at bias and diversity in the Criminal Justice System.

Class distinctions are fundamentally tied up with wealth, income and inequality. But class distinctions carry moral and cultural characteristics as well as influence, so that individuals may feel 'entitled' or feel 'inferior'. Thus individuals labelled and stereotyped by others as 'Chavs' are seen as variously 'vulgar', 'rough', ostentatious, violent, unemployed and probably criminal (Jones, 2016). Today, an underlying social divide between a small, wealthy, elite class pitted against a 'precariat' of poor, insecure, often younger people at the bottom, lacking social networks and opportunity (Standing, 2014), seems most apposite when discussing class and criminality. 'Precariat' because this growing group is identified by its main characteristic, living consistently precariously compared to other groups. It has by far the lowest income, is likely to rent property, has few social ties, with few associates in higher-status occupations. Finally, the precariat tends to be segregated and stuck in the poorest places. This 'new dangerous class' is where the attentions of the police and the criminal law are most likely to be found, and from whence most police suspects and court defendants are drawn. At the same time, laws and regulations pay little attention to the law-breaking and wrongdoing of the elite who occupy the top rank of the class hierarchy. As it is these extremes that are the focus of this section, it is worth noting that Savage's (2015) estimates are that this elite is about 6 per cent of the population and the 'precariat' at the bottom consists of about 15 per cent of the population.

In direct contrast to the position of the precariat, the rich elite might be seen as both above the law and, not coincidentally, making the law to suit their own interests and maintain their privileges (Sayer, 2015). Rich elites engage in a whole range of dishonest practices from laundering drug money and tax evasion to mis-selling mortgages and insurance, but many of these harmful practices are not officially criminal nor subject to the criminal justice process.

These practices – many of which are protected by secrecy rules – might in other circumstances be regarded as criminal. The crimes of powerful companies and individuals go unpunished because of their capacity to shape the law or regulations to their advantage. When wrongdoing *is* discovered, notably in fraud cases, punishment is likely to be an out-of-court settlement that avoids the guilty admitting criminal liability. Even in the more punitive USA, only a tiny handful of former bankers who caused the 2008 Financial Crash have been criminally indicted, most eventually acquitted, on charges such as fraud and conspiracy relating to the crash (Harris, 2012).

In focusing on financial and corporate crime as an example of class bias in criminal justice the following case studies should speak for themselves.

Tax Crime and Criminal Justice

Any discussion of tax crime requires there be a crucial clarification. Tax avoidance is legal, but contrary to the spirit of taxation law, while tax evasion is always illegal, involving the non-disclosure of a source of income to an authority that has a legal right to know about it. Nevertheless, arguments about criminality versus formal legality can ignore harms and moral wrongs. Therefore we often hear in the news about perfectly legal 'offshore' tax havens used by individuals and corporations to take their money elsewhere, to another country, in order to escape the rules and laws of the society in which they operate. In doing so however, they rob their own society of cash for hospitals, schools and roads (Shaxson and Christensen, 2013)!

'Tax haven' locations are used by those wishing to avoid or evade their obligation to pay tax; to hide criminal activities from view such as tax evasion itself, money-laundering or crimes generating cash that needs to be laundered – theft, fraud, corruption, insider dealing, piracy, financing of terrorism, drug trafficking, human trafficking, counterfeiting, bribery and extortion. They are also used for perfectly legal – although secretive and often morally dubious – reasons, such as to hide their wealth from a spouse or to avoid the costly obligation to comply with regulations that would apply onshore.

'Onshore', in Britain the area in which bias in the administration of the law and criminal justice process is arguably greatest, is in respect of the treatment of tax and benefit fraud.

Box 6.1

Tax Dodgers and Benefit Cheats … 'Only the Little People Pay Taxes'

As this case study shows, contrasting treatments of dishonesty are not unusual. Theft and impunity in corporate financial services is routine and unpunished. Nowhere is this truer than in the contrasting treatment of tax dodgers and benefit cheats. While benefit fraud, although not insignificant, is greatly exaggerated in the popular press and by government, tax avoidance and evasion is hardly mentioned, never mind prosecuted. The UK government's announcement that £1.2 billion was lost to benefit fraud by job seekers in 2012/13 gave an impression that such fraud is widespread when it is not. A far greater scandal is the £120 billion annual revenue losses as a result of evasion, avoidance and failure to collect taxes (Christenson, 2015).

Taxes paid in the UK by US firms such as Apple, Coca Cola, eBay, Starbucks, Facebook and Amazon are only a fraction of what they owe. Starbucks had paid no tax whatsoever on its £398 million turnover in the UK and what Facebook said were its revenues of £20.4 million, was a fraction of the actual £175 million the firm made in the UK in 2011 (Rogers and Goodley, 2012). In effect these companies are paying tax as a percentage of their turnover in single figures or less. Other multinational companies too, such as Asda, Google, Ikea, Vodafone, avoid corporation tax by diverting profits earned in Britain to their parent companies, tax havens or lower-tax jurisdictions (Shaxson, 2010). For example, according to Goodley et al. (2012) it is estimated that:

(Continued)

(Continued)

- US companies Amazon, Facebook, Google and Starbucks paid just £30 million tax in the UK on sales of £3.1 billion over four years, which is 0.1 per cent.

- Apple avoided £550 million in tax on £2 billion worth of sales in Britain by channelling business through Ireland, while Starbucks paid no corporation tax in Britain over three years.

- Nineteen US-owned multinationals were paying an effective tax rate of 3 per cent on British profits, instead of the standard rate of 26 per cent (reduced to 20 per cent at the time of writing).

- HM Revenue & Customs estimate of the total tax gap between what is owed and collected is £35 billion but is widely recognised as a serious underestimate. Tax Research UK estimated the gap as £120 billion a year: £25 billion in legal tax avoidance, £70 billion in fraudulent tax evasion and £25 billion in late payments.

- The government's own Audit Commission Report (National Audit Office, 2015) found that tax fraud is costing the government a 'staggering' £16 billion every year but HM Revenue & Customs focus their efforts on easy, low-value prosecutions for evading income tax, VAT and tobacco duty instead of chasing down multinationals involved in evasion and aggressive tax avoidance and organised criminal activity.

- If criminal investigation of tax dodgers is aligned to 'chasing small fry while letting the big fish go', the Department for Work and Pensions prosecutes 10 times more benefit cheats, worth a fraction of the loss in tax, than tax dodgers (Toynbee, 2015), again making the priorities of the Criminal Justice System the crimes of the poor rather than the rich.

Financial Crime and Criminal Justice

Galbraith (2014: 156) has convincingly written about the 'criminal foundations of the financial crisis'. It is important to realise though that this sort of crime preceded the financial crash. Routine theft and fraud in financial services, for example, can be illustrated by several large-scale 'crime waves' over the last 30 years in which regulatory authorities – never mind the Criminal Justice System – have failed to examine (let alone act upon) their harmful and criminal risks.

Tombs (2015) points to firstly, the mis-selling of fraudulent personal pensions in the 1980s where more than 2 million victims lost their pensions after being persuaded to replace their secure occupational pension schemes with high-risk private schemes. Secondly, the mis-selling of particularly risky endowment mortgages in the 1990s, which could probably never buy the properties they were used to purchase, when there were as many as 5 million victims. Thirdly, the mis-selling of 'payment protection insurance' (PPI), which was supposed to protect borrowers from having to repay debt in the event of them being made redundant or becoming sick, which has affected almost 5 million people. If you took out PPI, you would, in the case of sickness or redundancy, have your mortgage and/or credit card debt taken care of by the insurance you had bought in advance. Across all these 'crime waves' though, the law, police and the courts failed to act, ultimately with the effect of ignoring the criminal behaviour of elites and protecting their interests.

Box 6.2

Are Banks Immune from Criminal Prosecution?

Perhaps the biggest scandal is PPI, precisely because what was sold seemed so benign. As John Lanchester (2013) has argued, the PPI scandal involved clear criminal fraud on an industry-wide scale, which under the Fraud Act of 2006, is 'fraud by failing to reveal information'. The complete silence on the issue of the criminal law and PPI is because the political and prosecutorial will is not there. PPI involved an industry-wide, systematic cheating of the banks' own customers. Even when criminality is overt such as laundering money for drug dealers, which was the case for the British bank HSBC, prosecution was deferred by a (admittedly very large) fine and the bank agreed to have an independent monitor inside the bank. The US Department of Justice said that the bank had laundered at least $881 million in money for Mexican and Colombian cartels. Drug dealers deposited hundreds of thousands of dollars in cash at HSBC in Mexico, facilitated by HSBC in Britain. And yet no criminal prosecution was ever sought.

The title of Charles Ferguson's (2012) study *Inside Job: The financiers who pulled off the heist of the century*, headlines the story of what has really been going on – widespread criminality rarely punished. Rarely are individual executives fined, much less criminally prosecuted. It is important to understand that much of the financial corporate behaviour mentioned here really is criminal. That is, deliberate concealment of financial transactions that aided criminality, and large-scale tax evasion; assisting in major financial frauds and in concealment of criminal assets. The 2008 financial crisis was the logical culmination of fraudulent financial criminality and tolerance of overtly criminal behaviour in the financial sector. None of this conduct was punished in any significant way, there having been very few prosecutions and no criminal convictions of large financial institutions or their senior executives. Eventually, over time, a sense of personal impunity and a lack of deterrence encourages even more criminality.

Box 6.3

One Rule for the Rich and Another for the Poor ...

Fred Goodwin, former boss of the Royal Bank of Scotland, bankrupted and bailed out by UK taxpayers at a cost of £45 billion, merely lost his knighthood and had his pension cut from £703,000 to £342,500 per year.

Nicholas Robinson, an electrical engineering student with no criminal record, was jailed for six months for stealing bottles of water worth £3.50 during the riots in London in August 2011. While the UK government has yet to prosecute any bankers for deceitfully mis-selling worthless insurance said to have reached £16 billion in 2013, it immediately set up 24-hour courts to try those arrested in the riots.

(Sayer, 2015: 272)

When is Cheating and Serious Harm a Crime? The Case of Volkswagen

Worldwide, drivers were sold millions of vehicles that were far more polluting than claimed, after the carmaker installed illegal software to cheat emission tests that allowed its diesel cars to produce up to 40 times more pollution than allowed (Ruddick, 2015).

The switch to diesel resulted in the UK having one of the largest diesel car fleets in the world (Vidal, 2015). New research shows, however, that diesel fumes are worse than expected for health, triggering cancers, heart attacks and the stunting of children's growth. According to this new research there are 5,879 premature deaths in London each year from nitrogen dioxide pollution (NO_2) mostly from diesel engines (Vaughan, 2015). Most of the UK's largest cities have been in breach of EU safety limits on NO_2 for years, prompting legal action that led to a Supreme Court ruling that the government must publish a clean-up plan.

Although Volkswagen faces a barrage of legal claims from British car owners over the emissions tests, the company is unlikely to face criminal proceedings, or even fines in Britain, but is likely to face a fine of billions of dollars and criminal investigations in the USA (Topham and Wearden, 2015). Corporations not only go unpunished but perpetrators can receive large rewards for business failure and alleged criminality; former chief executive of Volkswagen Martin Winterkorn, who was paid a salary of €1.6 million boosted to nearly €16 million in 2014 with bonuses and loyalty payments, resigned as the extent of the emissions test-rigging scandal emerged (Topham, 2015). At the time of writing he is to net a €1 million (£740,000) annual pension and was in line for a €3.2 million payoff after quitting.

Steve Tombs and David Whyte (2015) argue that corporate harm and crime has a significant class dimension because it has the effect of redistributing wealth, income, health and quality of life from the poor to the rich. Rarely criminalised, corporate criminals are 'below the radar' of the police and the courts and often their wrongdoing is not even considered *a crime*. As we saw in the case of Volkswagen, corporate crimes against the environment could be punished but are not, even though pollution-related deaths have occurred, because such crimes are neither criminalised nor subjected to investigation. As Ferguson (2012) showed, a range of serious financial frauds in the USA that caused the 2008 financial crash prompted little or no credible criminal justice response, and not in the UK either.

Sometimes the Police Commit Crimes Too

Routine illegality by the powerful is not of course limited to the activity of private corporations, it is found in public policing too, as is discussed further in Chapter 19. A catalogue of historical police corruption has recently come to light: falsifying evidence against striking miners in the 1980s; fabricating evidence against football supporters following the Hillsborough disaster; alleged covering up of systematic sexual abuse in the Jimmy Savile case from the 1970s; and corruption in the original investigation of the murder of Stephen Lawrence. Very little, though, seems to change because so little is done about police corruption and illegality as recent and current cases reveal. A recent case in point are the revelations that the Metropolitan Police spied on the late Stephen Lawrence's parents and their supporters as they struggled to seek justice for their son at the time of the Macpherson inquiry into the police investigation (Evans, 2015).

At the time of writing, the long-awaited result of the Hillsborough disaster inquest findings has revealed that 96 Liverpool football fans who died as a result of a crush at Sheffield Wednesday's ground in 1989 were unlawfully killed. South Yorkshire Police systematically lied about what had taken place, blaming and disparaging the fans in order to deflect blame from themselves, thereby causing untold anguish among the friends and relatives of the dead for 27 years. The officer in command at the time was 'responsible for manslaughter by gross negligence', according to the inquest findings. The Chief Constable of South Yorkshire Police has been suspended amidst a seeming widespread collapse in public trust. At the time of the disaster, police treatment of the victims and their families showed, and continued to show over many years, the contempt in which the police hold individuals they believe to be of low social status and worth.

Summary

In the context of growing diversity resulting from family, neighbourhood, demographic and social structural change, expectations that individual human rights and difference be respected and treated equally by the police and the courts have grown.

As a consequence, the police and criminal justice have undergone pressure to reform, adapt and adopt practices and legal measures to accommodate growing diversity. The extent to which these efforts have succeeded or been resisted and thwarted have been considered here.

The conclusions from this chapter are complicated because although some patchy improvements in the ways the police and courts handle diversity show a new awareness – especially towards women and minorities – class remains an unacknowledged aspect of criminal justice and diversity. In some important respects equal treatment has grown and bias and discrimination has receded. But only in some respects. The criminal justice process still reflects and replicates the inferior or biased treatment of social groups and individuals on grounds of social status, wealth and income, reflecting growing social inequality. It is, though, probably fair to say that progress has been made in regard to race and sex discrimination, although much less so in regards to younger people and age discrimination.

———————— **Discussion Questions** ————————

1. What evidence is there that tolerance of diversity has grown in Britain? Consider the adequacy of criminal justice responses to these changes in public attitudes and growing public expectations on the police and the courts.

2. To what extent have police reforms succeeded in improving the policing of diversity?

3. Is bias and discrimination more likely or less likely to be found in policing, the courts or the prisons?

4. Has, as is often claimed, criminal justice treatment of women victims of domestic violence been a story of improvement?

5. Despite public support for, and legal and institutional adoption of anti-discrimination approaches in respect of gender and race, why is class bias and discrimination ignored by the police and the courts?

6. Why do some go unpunished but others do not while both are involved in serious crime and harms?

———————— **Further Reading** ————————

Comprehensive policing, criminal justice and victimisation data on race and the Criminal Justice System is published annually and can be found in Ministry of Justice (2013) *Statistics on Race and the Criminal Justice System 2012*. London. Available at: www.gov.uk/government/statistics/statistics-on-race-and-the-criminal-justice-system-2012

A useful collection is found in Bhui, H.S. (ed.) (2009) *Race and Criminal Justice*. London: Sage.

Broader consideration of criminal justice and diversity is found in Sanders, A., Young, R. and Burton, M. (2010) *Criminal Justice*. Oxford: Oxford University Press (chapter 2); and Ashworth, A. and Redmayne, M. (2010) *The Criminal Process*. 4th edn. Oxford: Oxford University Press (chapter 14).

Reiman, J. and Leighton, P. (2010) *The Rich Get Richer and the Poor Get Prison: Ideology, class, and criminal justice*. 9th edn. Boston: Pearson.

———————— **References** ————————

Ashworth, A. and Redmayne, M. (2010) *The Criminal Process*. 4th edn. Oxford: Oxford University Press.

BBC Science (2013) *The Great British Class Survey – Results*. Available at: http://www.bbc.co.uk/science/0/21970879

Choongh, S. (1998) 'Policing the dross: A social disciplinary model of policing', *British Journal of Criminology*, 38 (4): 623–35.

Christenson, J. (2015) 'On Her Majesty's Secrecy Service', in D. Whyte (ed.), *How Corrupt is Britain?* London: Pluto Press.

Cockcroft, T. (2012) *Police Culture: Themes and concepts*. London: Routledge.

Coffey Report (2014) *Real Voices: Child sexual exploitation in Greater Manchester*. An independent report by Ann Coffey, Greater Manchester Police and Crime Commissioner.

Dodd, V. (2012) 'Police up to 28 times more likely to stop and search black people – study', *The Guardian*, 12 June.

Dorling, D. (2014) *Inequality and the 1%*. London: Verso.

Equality and Human Rights Commission (2010) *How Fair is Britain? Equality, human rights and good relations in 2010, the first triennial review*. London: House of Commons. Available at: www.official-documents.gov.uk/ and www.equalityhumanrights.com/key-projects/how-fair-is-britain/

Evans, R. (2015) 'Police facing claims that senior officers knew about spying on Stephen Lawrence family', *The Guardian*, 12 June.

Ferguson, C. (2012) *Inside Job: The financiers who pulled off the heist of the century*. Oxford: One World.

Galbraith, J.K. (2014) *The End of Normal: The great crisis and the future of growth*. New York: Simon and Schuster.

Goodley, S., Bowers, S. and Rogers, S. (2012) 'UK urged to reform tax rules over profit moving by global firms', *The Guardian*, 16 October. Available at: www.guardian.co.uk/uk/2012/oct/16/uk-tax-rules-profit-global-flrm

Harris, J. (2012) 'Credit crunch: Elusive ghosts of the financial feast lurk in the shadows', *The Guardian*, 6 August. Available at: www.guardian.co.uk/business/2012/aug/06/credit-crunch-elusive-ghosts-shadows

Heidensohn, F. (1996) *Women and Crime*. 2nd edn. Basingstoke: Palgrave.

Hudson, B. (1993) *Penal Policy and Social Justice*. London: Palgrave.

Jay Report (2014) *Independent Inquiry into Child Sexual Exploitation in Rotherham*, Rotherham Metropolitan Borough Council.

Jones, O. (2016) *Chavs: The demonization of the working class*. 2nd edn. London: Verso.

Joyce, P. (2013) *Criminal Justice: An introduction*. 2nd edn. London: Routledge.

Kingston, S. and Webster, C. (2015) 'The most "undeserving" of all? How poverty drives young men to victimisation and crime', *Journal of Poverty and Social Justice*, 23 (3): 215–27.

Lanchester, J. (2013) 'Are we having fun yet?' *London Review of Books*, 35 (13), 4 July: 3–8.

Loftus, B. (2009) *Policing Culture in a Changing World*. Oxford: Oxford University Press.

May, T., Gyateng, T. and Hough, M. (2010) *Differential Treatment in the Youth Justice System*. Research Report 50. London: Equality and Human Rights Commission. Available at: www.equalityhumanrights.com/uploaded_files/research/differential_treatment_in_the_youth_justice_system_final.pdf

Ministry of Justice (2013) *Statistics on Race and the Criminal Justice System 2012*. London: MoJ.

National Audit Office (2015) *Tackling Tax Fraud: How HMRC responds to tax evasion, the hidden economy and criminal attacks*. Available at: www.nao.org.uk/wp-content/uploads/2015/12/Tackling-tax-fraud-how-HMRC-responds-to-tax-evasion-the-hidden-economy-and-criminal-attacks-Summary.pdf

Phillips, C. (2012) *The Multicultural Prison: Ethnicity, masculinity, and social relations among prisoners*. Clarendon Studies in Criminology. Oxford: Oxford University Press.

Reiman, J. and Leighton, P. (2010) *The Rich Get Richer and the Poor Get Prison: Ideology, class, and criminal justice*. 9th edn. Boston: Pearson.

Reiner, R. (2010) *The Politics of the Police*. 4th edn. Oxford: Oxford University Press.

Rogers, S. and Goodley, S. (2012) 'How much tax do Starbucks, Facebook and the biggest US companies pay in the UK', *The Guardian*, 16 October.

Ruddick, G. (2015) 'Volkswagen scandal: US chief says carmaker "totally screwed up"', *The Guardian*, 22 September.

Sanders, A., Young, R. and Burton, M. (2010) *Criminal Justice*. Oxford: Oxford University Press.

Savage, M. (2015) *Social Class in the 21st Century*. Milton Keynes: Pelican Books.

Sayer, A. (2015) *Why We Can't Afford the Rich*. Bristol: Policy Press.

Shaxson, N. (2010) *Treasure Islands: Tax havens and the men who stole the world*. London: Bodley Head.

Shaxson, N. and Christensen, J. (2013) *The Finance Curse: How oversized finance sectors attack democracy and corrupt economics*. Kindle edn.

Smith, D.J. (1997) 'Race, crime, and criminal justice', in M. Maguire, R. Morgan and R. Reiner (eds), *The Oxford Handbook of Criminology*. 2nd edn. Oxford: Clarendon Press.

Standing, G. (2014) *The Precariat: The new dangerous class*. London: Bloomsbury.

Tombs, S. (2015) 'Corporate theft and impunity in financial services', in D. Whyte (ed.), *How Corrupt is Britain?* London: Pluto.

Tombs, S. and Whyte, D. (2015) *The Corporate Criminal: Why corporations must be abolished*. London: Routledge.

Topham, G. (2015) 'VW scandal: Outgoing boss's €28m pension pot to pay out €1m a year', *The Guardian*, 24 September.

Topham, G. and Wearden, G. (2015) 'VW faces deluge of UK legal claims over emissions tests', *The Guardian*, 24 September.

Toynbee, P. (2015) 'Is Osborne serious about catching tax cheats – or just the little guys?' *The Guardian*, 17 December.

Vaughan, A. (2015) 'Nearly 9,500 people die each year in London because of air pollution – study', *The Guardian*, 15 July.

Vidal, J. (2015) 'The rise of diesel in Europe: The impact on health and pollution', *The Guardian*, 22 September.

Check out the Companion Website

Want to know more about this chapter? Review what you have been learning by visiting: **https://study.sagepub.com/harding**

- Practice with essay questions
- Test yourself with multiple-choice questions
- Listen to a series of podcasts featuring Neil of Northumbria Police and London's Metropolitan Police Service
- Watch videos selected from the SAGE Video collection

7   Media Representations of Criminal Justice

Ian Marsh

Introduction

Crime, criminals and how they are dealt with are topics that excite a massive media interest. A glance at the television schedules, or the film listings for your local cinema, or the headlines in national or local newspapers, will quickly indicate both the vast and seemingly insatiable interest the general population has in crime and criminals, and the key role the media play in portraying and describing all aspects of criminal behaviour. We could ask why there is so much interest in this area, after all, most people are not involved in spectacular criminality yet we seem to love to watch and read about it. Some of this crime will be fictional, other 'real life', and our appetite for reading and watching about both appears to be enormous – popular television programmes such as soap operas invariably include criminality in their story lines; television documentaries, news programmes and our newspapers highlight and discuss crime and criminal justice issues on a daily basis. And the knowledge and understanding the public have about crime and criminals is largely based on what they have seen or heard through the various media forms. In a study looking at crime news in the USA, Dorfman (2001) found that over three-quarters (76 per cent) of the public said they formed their opinions about crime from what they saw or read in the news, more than three times the number of those who said they got their primary information on crime from personal experience (22 per cent).

Box 7.1

The Spread of the Media

In general terms, it is clear that the media, and particularly the visual media, play an ever larger part in the lives of more and more people. A report from the 'Childwise' market researcher for instance, showed that in 2015 children aged 5–16 had on average 6.5 hours of 'screen time' a day – that might be watching TV, playing on games consoles, or using a mobile phone or tablet. Teenage boys had the highest usage, an average of 8 hours a day, while for 5 to 10 year-olds it was 4.5 hours.

More generally, British TV viewers watched an average of 225 minutes of TV every day in 2010, although this was behind the US figure of 280 minutes a day. This includes the finding from Ofcom that just under a quarter of UK consumers also watch the TV over the internet (www.digitalspy.co.uk). With the spread of new media, and particularly social media, it becomes even more difficult to track the extent of media usage. However, with around 2 billion people connected to the internet worldwide, with YouTube generating 92 billion page views per month and with Wikipedia hosting 17 million articles, the influence and extent of the media is clearly enormous.

As well as the massive interest the general public have in crime and criminals, there is also a deep fascination with how these crimes and criminals are discovered and dealt with by the Criminal Justice System – with how the police go about catching and charging offenders, with how the courts and judiciary sentence them and with what happens to those offenders who enter the penal system.

In this chapter, the focus is on the way that the media represent the Criminal Justice System, and in particular how the major criminal justice agencies are presented in our mass media. The discussion will consider the three major areas or stages of the criminal justice process and the enforcement of the law. First, the police and how they have been represented in the media, then the courts and sentencing and, finally, prisons and punishment. In each case, we will look at real life or factual representations and also at how these different areas of our Criminal Justice System and process are presented in fictional accounts. It is not always easy to separate out what is fact from fiction – and fictional programmes such as dramas and soap operas will usually try and make their 'fiction' as realistic as possible. As Mason (2003: 5) puts it: 'Audiences "commuting" between the realms of factual news and entertainment programming has implications for public perceptions of law enforcement agencies, the courts and prisons as well as offenders and victims.'

Of course, the Criminal Justice System in England and Wales, and elsewhere too, is a massive operation. Data from the Ministry of Justice showed that 1.44 million defendants were proceeded against in magistrates' courts in 2014, and

86.8 thousand in the Crown Court (Ministry of Justice, 2015). With regard to jury service, over 400,000 people were summoned to serve as jury members in 2008 (Jury Central Summoning Board). In terms of police procedures, Home Office data show that in the 12 months to March 2015, the police in England and Wales arrested almost 1 million people (950,000), carried out 541,000 stop and searches, issued 1.02 million fixed penalty notices for motoring offences and breath tested 607,000 people (Home Office, 2015).

Nonetheless, and in spite of the massive numbers involved, most people still only have a fairly limited experience of the Criminal Justice System and its workings. As with our knowledge and understanding of criminal behaviour, so our understanding of the Criminal Justice System is derived largely from the mass media we consume. The reporting of crime is a staple part in most forms of our media; and media reports of crime tend to focus on crimes that have reached the stage of getting to court. There is a tremendous interest in 'who gets what' from within our Criminal Justice System. Furthermore, because the media will almost inevitably focus on the more spectacular crimes and those that lead to the most severe punishments, the picture portrayed by the media about law enforcement and punishment is liable to be distorted in a similar way. For instance, much of the media coverage of punishment focuses on prisons, the most severe form of punishment available in our Criminal Justice System, even though the great majority of offenders who are sentenced do not receive prison sentences. After all, offenders being fined are not likely to make such interesting reading or viewing in comparison to stories and films about imprisonment.

While it is understandable that the media focuses on solved crimes, through covering the trials and courtroom drama, Leishman and Mason (2003) point out that this coverage can give the wider public the impression that most crime is solved and that the police are pretty effective in detecting crime – impressions which information on the actual clear-up rates of all crimes committed demonstrates to be way off the mark. The crimes covered by the media are the more solvable sorts of crime because, as mentioned above, they are the more serious sorts of crime, such as murder and sexual offences. And these are the crimes that the police will usually solve – because they will spend considerable resources on high profile and serious crimes and because such crimes are often relatively easy to solve as the offender (in the case of murder) will more often than not have had some previous association (and often a close association through marriage or family ties) with the victim. This sort of media coverage might reassure the public that the police are effective at catching criminals, but can also lead to criticism when they fail to solve crimes.

The British Crime Survey (Kershaw et al., 2000) found that television or radio news was cited by most people (nearly three-quarters of the population) as their major source of information about the Criminal Justice System, with newspapers also having a significant impact. So it would seem fair to suggest that how the media portray the police, the courts and judiciary and our penal system will have a major influence on public knowledge and public opinion. It is also worth pointing out that the main criminal justice agencies themselves can have some influence on both what is reported in the media and how it is reported. This can be illustrated by the sometimes collaborative nature of the relationship between the media and the police looked at in the next section.

Media Portrayal of the Police

Robert Reiner, one of the foremost academic writers on the media and policing, highlights the collaborative nature of the relationship between the police and journalists and broadcasters. He cites the comment of Sir Robert Mark, Commissioner of the Metropolitan Police in the early 1970s, that the police and media relationship could be compared to 'an enduring, if not ecstatically happy, marriage' (2007: 259). Reiner describes the relationship between the police and media as one of 'mutual dependence and reciprocal reinforcement'. As we have highlighted in introducing this chapter, the way that the Criminal Justice System, including and in particular the police, has dealt with offenders, has always been a significant part of the mass media content, in both factual and entertainment contexts. The police are concerned with how they are portrayed by the media and, more specifically, with creating and encouraging a positive police media image, as they are aware that public support and cooperation will help them in enforcing the law.

It is self-evident that in order to solve crimes the police need to collect relevant information; and the public are one of the most important sources of information for the police when investigating crime. This is notably the case with regard to some of the more serious crimes, such as murder investigations, when the police make use of the media as part of their investigation strategy – for instance, through using the media to appeal for information that might help them solve the crime. One of the earliest and longest running 'reality TV' programmes, *Crimewatch*, is based on this idea, but appeals to the public from victims and/or senior police officers can also be made via newspapers. These communications, whether through television or the press, are presented by the police in a way that they hope will persuade people to come forward with information – either as witnesses or perhaps through suspecting someone of an offence or being an acquaintance of an offender. However, police use of the media in this way can cause difficulties – such appeals can generate an enormous amount of information, much of which will be irrelevant to the particular enquiry; they can also lead to an expectation that the particular case should be solved by the police.

More seriously, there have been problems with media appeals where relatives of a victim have made a public appeal and later been found to have been involved in the offence itself. Examples of media appeals by family members who have later been found to be guilty and that have attracted widespread media attention include appeals given by Karen Matthews and Mick and Mairead Philpott. In 2008 Karen Matthews, the mother of missing nine-year-old Shannon, made a tearful appeal for anyone holding her daughter to come forward. She was later found guilty of kidnapping, false imprisonment and perverting the course of justice and sentenced to eight years imprisonment, along with Shannon's uncle. The case of the Philpotts again attracted massive publicity. In May 2012, Mick and Mairead Philpott appealed at a press conference for anyone with information about a fatal house fire that killed six of their children to contact the police. The couple were later arrested, found guilty and jailed (Mick for life and Mairead for 17 years) for causing the deaths of the children themselves.

The nature of the police–media relationship has inevitably been affected by recent changes in the media industry, particularly by the technological developments that have enabled a massive increase in media outlets. The 24-hour continuous news programmes on satellite television have increased the demand for news stories and the time available to delve into such stories; as the police are an important source of news stories this has increased the media demands on them. Technological advances have also impacted on the accountability of the police; the use of lightweight cameras, including on mobile phones, has increased the scrutiny that the police are subject to. For instance, amateur filming of the policing of demonstrations or police dealing with incidents can be used on news programmes and through the internet.

In his examination of media images of policing, Mawby (2003) considers why these images matter. He cites Reiner's (2007) categorisation of media representations of policing (and law and order more generally) under the headings of either 'hegemonic' or 'subversive'. The first sees the police as being in a dominant position with regard to the media in that they can choose and filter the information they provide, and the media treatment of the police can play an important role in fostering a positive and favourable image of the police. By contrast, the 'subversive' position suggests that the media can be a threat to authority and can undermine respect for the police; in the past it has done this by exposing police malpractice and corruption. Mawby suggests that these quite distinct headings and positions indicate the importance of examining media images.

In the final part of this section, we will provide a potted history of the way the police have been represented in the media, and particularly in television drama. Leishman and Mason (2003) argue that since the formation of the 'modern police' in the nineteenth century, the police have always been concerned with presenting a positive image to the general public. In the early days of organised policing, there was by no means universal public support for there even being a centralised, government-run police force. Histories of the origin and development of formal, modern policing in England and Wales illustrate the concerns about and opposition to the police. Emsley (1996) refers to police officers being regularly assaulted by the public and having to patrol with cutlasses in some of the 'rougher' working-class areas, with certain areas virtually left to themselves and unpoliced. In view of these reactions and worries, it is not surprising that the police were concerned from the start with promoting and maintaining a positive image of themselves and their role in society. To some extent the police did win the public over and became an accepted and acceptable part of British society; and the development of a sort of admiration for, and certainly acceptance of, the new police was in part at least due to the portrayal of them in both fiction and newspaper reporting of the time.

From these early days, the new police were represented in two main ways – as an approachable patrol officer helping to prevent crime through his (early police officers were invariably male) presence on the streets or as a skilled detective, working, almost Sherlock Holmes-like, to solve major crime. This combination, or division, of images has been continued through to the present day in media presentations of police and policing – a combination of a soft police service and hard law enforcement (Leishman and Mason, 2003).

Indeed, this dual approach in policing – of service against force, of soft against hard policing – has led to a tension that is still apparent in the police service today – the uniformed bobby on the beat against the more hidden work of the plain-clothed detective. In her discussion of the way the role of the police has been portrayed by the media, Jewkes (2015) considers two 'mediated ideals' of the police, representative of these two styles of policing. Here, we will consider these two ideals in a little more detail – on the one hand, illustrated by PC (later Sergeant) George Dixon in the *Dixon of Dock Green* series that ran from 1955 to 1976 on the BBC, who exemplified community policing at its best and, on the other, by Detective Inspector Regan and Detective Sergeant Carter, the no-nonsense crime fighters in *The Sweeney* (which ran for four series from 1975 to 1978 on ITV), whose style of and approach to investigating and arresting major criminals often skirted on the margins of legality.

Of course, there have been many more television and film representations of police and policing which we will not be able to consider in this brief overview. Police detective films, for instance, have been a popular staple of cinema films for years – and many of these films portray police officers kicking out against authority and the constraints placed on them in doing their job (a theme central to *The Sweeney* television drama). Films such as *A Touch of Evil* and *The Big Heat* in the 1950s, through to the glut of police and detective films in the 1960s and 1970s, including *Bullit, Klute, Serpico* and *The French Connection* portrayed the leading police officers as heroic crime fighters. Probably the seminal film of this kind was *Dirty Harry* (1971), starring Clint Eastwood, which focused on the conflict between crime-solving and following the rules, and was followed by other vigilante cop films such as *Lethal Weapon* and *Die Hard* in the 1980s and 1990s (Leishman and Mason, 2003). Here, though, our focus will be on British television representations and in that context *Dixon of Dock Green* and *The Sweeney* provide almost opposing stereotypical examples of the role of the police officer and of different styles of policing.

Jewkes (2015) and other commentators have highlighted and examined the key role that the *Dixon of Dock Green* series played in setting a benchmark for television portrayals of the police. The series and, particularly the character of Dixon, created a symbolic representation of the 'British bobby'. In his discussion of media images of the police, Mawby (2003) argues that, in the early days of the series, Dixon was viewed as a realistic portrayal of policing but that towards the end of its run it was widely viewed as irrelevant and outdated – with tougher police series such as *Z Cars* (1962–78), *Softly, Softly* (1966–76) and, as mentioned, *The Sweeney*, seen as providing a more modern and accurate picture of policing.

During the period when these early police television series were shown, there was a change in the construction of policing, reflecting changes in the police's relationship with the wider public. The last three series mentioned above, and especially *The Sweeney*, were made at a time when there was more questioning of (and dissatisfaction with) the police. Mawby (2003: 221) sees the central characters as 'symbolic of their respective times' – the late 1950s and the less settled mid 1970s – with the optimism of Dixon and his pride in his job replaced by the cynicism of Regan.

Leishman and Mason (2003: 69) describe *The Sweeney* as 'perhaps the ultimate celebration of the police breaking the rules in order to obtain a conviction'. It was the first police drama to acknowledge police corruption, or at least rule-bending, as part and parcel of everyday policing. As mentioned, it was clearly a product of its times and the late 1960s and early 1970s were a time when public confidence in the police was being undermined in a number of ways and in particular through concerns over police corruption. Robert Mark, Commissioner of the Metropolitan Police 1972–7, established a department to investigate complaints against police officers and during his five-year term in office 500 officers were dismissed or required to resign. Although scandals and corruption were not unique to this period, what was new was the revelation that they were systematic and widespread and went to the very top of the police force.

The publicity surrounding these and other high-profile cases affected the police's relationship with the wider public. In a similar vein, the publicity surrounding the way the police handled demonstrations and industrial disputes excited concern and widespread criticism. Perhaps most dramatic were the television and news pictures of the policing of the miners' strike of 1984/1985. The policing of this strike was very confrontational (indeed one 'event' is popularly referred to as the 'battle of Orgreave') and polarised the police from 'ordinary' working people. Also the inner-city riots and disorders of the early 1980s in Brixton, Toxteth, Moss Side and elsewhere reflected an increased alienation between the police and sections of the population.

All of these events were filmed and appeared in our living rooms almost as they occurred and they could be seen as signifying and encouraging a move away from traditional notions of policing, and the image of the local bobby, towards a more militaristic and reactive form of policing.

Before moving on to look at media representations of other areas of our Criminal Justice System, any review of police drama on British television would be incomplete without mentioning *The Bill*, which in terms of longevity has been Britain's most successful police programme. First broadcast in 1984 it continued until 2010 and finally outstripped *Dixon of Dock Green* in August 2005. Each episode attracted over 4 million viewers and it was broadcast in over 50 countries worldwide. *The Bill* recounted the goings on in and around a fictional Metropolitan police station,

Sun Hill, located in the East End of London (based on the 'real' London Borough of Tower Hamlets). It is unusual in police dramas in that it adopted a serial, soap opera format and did not focus on one aspect of police work only but rather on the lives and work of officers on one shift of the uniform division and on the work of detectives based there.

In terms of the division between 'soft' and 'hard' policing and the portrayal of these different police styles exemplified by *Dixon of Dock Green* and *The Sweeney* respectively, *The Bill* established a kind of mid-way position and balance between the two poles, as well as accommodating both the uniformed and detective sides of policing (Leishman and Mason, 2003). Indeed, Reiner (2007: 326) argues that *The Bill* can be interpreted as the 'synthesis of the dialectic' that was represented by the police portrayals in *Dixon* and *The Sweeney*. It shows a range of contrasting images of police work, from community constables to rule-bending detectives.

In similar vein to Reiner's argument, Leishman and Mason (2003) suggest that as *The Bill* developed in the 1990s and into the 2000s it became a new synthesis of police representations in the media. It began to highlight more disturbingly corrupt police characters, while the 'ordinary' police officers began to be portrayed with serious moral failings and personal flaws.

So far we have focused on fictional representations of the police and in concluding we will refer briefly to the police reality programmes of recent years – what might be termed 'factional representation'. Here we will focus on one major example of this genre – *Crimewatch*. It began on BBC1 in 1984 and is broadcast on a monthly basis; it uses dramatic reconstructions and surveillance film of crimes to try and gain information from the public that will help the police to solve particular crimes. It was developed from a popular German programme *Aktenzeichen XY*, which had been running since 1967. Our discussion will be based on the more in-depth analysis of the programme offered by Jewkes (2015), in which she examines some of the myths about crime that she argues it helps to perpetuate.

From its beginning until 2007 *Crimewatch* was presented by Nick Ross; however, and tragically, it became the subject of police and media attention in 1999 when Ross's co-presenter, Jill Dando, was the subject of a violent murder. As well as continuity of presenters, the format of the programme has remained virtually the same since 1984. There are reconstructions of a few (usually three or four an episode) serious crimes, plus appeals to the public for information about offenders and suspects from a range of crimes across the country. There are updates on crimes and offenders covered in previous programmes – particularly where some progress has been made in catching offenders. Jewkes (2015: 180) comments that this continuity and reference back to previous episodes and crimes serves the purpose of:

> congratulating the audience for helping to secure convictions, making them feel absolutely integral to the show, and further giving the (inaccurate) impression that *Crimewatch* is largely responsible for solving serious crime in the UK.

Jewkes goes on to emphasise the inherent tension between information and entertainment that lies at the heart of *Crimewatch* and, indeed, 'reality' television programming in general. While specific items might not be included just for entertainment value, programme editors are aware that there has to be some visual and journalistic impact so as to make 'good television'. This tension between entertainment and television's public service remit is illustrated by the sort of crimes that are represented on the show – basically the most uncommon (statistically) crimes such as murder and rape are those which are most often featured, while the more common but less spectacular property crimes and corporate crimes are rarely shown.

However, it is clear that *Crimewatch* has been important in helping the police improve their public relations through demonstrating the police and public working together to investigate and solve real crimes:

> The benefits to [the police] in terms of the warm feelings induced by watching the police and public working together to solve crimes arguably outweighs all other benefits of the programme. (Jewkes 2015: 187)

While very popular and clearly having some positive impact on the police relationship with the wider public and on solving particular crimes, *Crimewatch* has been criticised for contributing to the fear of crime through its emphasis on and dramatic reconstructions of violent and sexual crime. *Crimewatch* has also been criticised for its reliance on police information and for the fact that the police largely determine the content of the programme; indeed without police cooperation it would not exist.

Media Portrayal of the Courts

Although we have what is termed 'open justice' in the UK, with our courts open to the public, who are able to watch the proceedings in cases at both the magistrates' court and the Crown Court, television cameras or filming and photographing are not allowed in our courts. Indeed, the issue of whether to allow the televised recording of court proceedings has been widely debated for many years and raises the question as to what exactly does the phrase justice must be 'seen to be done' mean.

In his overview of the issues around this debate on public viewing of British justice, Stepniak (2003) considers the rationale for why cameras were initially banned from English courtrooms and why this ban has remained in force. It was the Criminal Justice Act of 1925 that banned the taking and publishing of photographs in courts in England and Wales, in part due to the publication of a photograph in *The Daily Mirror* in 1912 of Judge Bucknill passing the death sentence on Frederick Seddon. This photograph, which was taken secretively without the court's consent, caused a public outcry and was widely referred to in parliament in the years up to the 1925 Act. Although passed before television broadcasting had begun, the Act's provisions have since been extended to include television. More generally, the growing level of public interest in gruesome crimes and criminal trials helped persuade the authorities to ban cameras and keep them banned.

However, that was over 90 years ago, before the massive technological developments which enable filming and photographing to be done in a much more discreet manner and before the enormous increase in news and information, including films and pictures available through the internet as well as traditional media sources.

Those in favour of filming and photographing in courts can refer to a range of research that suggests cameras have virtually no effect on proceedings (Stepniak, 2003). A review by Mason (2001) looked at the filming of the International Criminal Tribunal for the former Yugoslavia in The Hague, which is an English-speaking court that has been using audio-visual equipment since 1996. There are six remote-controlled cameras in each of the three courtrooms, with the footage filmed live but broadcast after a 30-minute delay (in case participants mistakenly identify other protected parties). In research that involved interviewing judges, prosecutors, defence counsel and court staff, Mason found that the vast majority of respondents (92 per cent) said they were only 'occasionally' or 'rarely' aware of the cameras in court. Very few (4 per cent) felt that the judges were affected by the cameras, although a large majority (80 per cent) felt that counsel would be much more likely to be affected, and may tend to 'play acting' and 'dramatics'. As with other studies, this research offered strong support for cameras in court, on the grounds that they enabled justice to be seen to be done, that filming would enable the international community to have faith in the trials and that cameras might well enable relatives of those who died to see a trial that they would otherwise have been unable to.

It was in the 1990s that viewers in England and Wales were also able to see televised trials from other countries, largely due to the spread of satellite television. However, two trials from the USA that gained massive publicity in Britain had a major effect in turning public and political opinion against the idea of routinely allowing cameras in British courts – the O.J. Simpson case and the Louise Woodward case; as did the live broadcast from Italy of the appeal in 2011 of US citizen, Amanda Knox. The media coverage of these and other high-profile court cases in the USA, while being viewed by some commentators as showing justice being done, has also led to accusations of justice being reduced to 'an enterprise for the entertainment of the public' (Stepniak, 2003: 257). Brief details of two of these cases are set out below.

Box 7.2

Courts on TV?

Although the courtroom drama has long been a regular and popular element of films, TV dramas and soap operas, as we have seen in our discussion above, there has been a long-running debate as to whether television cameras should be allowed in British courts. Televised trials from the USA and Europe have been shown on satellite TV in Britain and have had a major impact on this debate – examples of some of these cases are highlighted below.

O.J. Simpson Murder Trial

American football star O.J. Simpson was tried for the 1994 murders of his ex-wife Nicole and her friend Ronald Goldman. Weekly reviews broadcast on the BBC were watched by an average of 1 million viewers and the live weekday coverage on Sky by an estimated 7 million viewers. Eventually Simpson was acquitted of the double murders. The televising of this high-profile and lengthy trial (from November 1994 to October 1995) raised the issue of cameras in court in the USA and elsewhere as well as highlighting issues around racism and prejudice in the Criminal Justice System ... In reflecting on the coverage given this trial, *The Mail on Sunday* described the damage the case had done to the US Criminal Justice System:

> We have watched an astonishing display of irrelevance for months on end, invented defence strategies, personal jury dramas, and a judge fighting back tears. It has been long, preposterous entertainment ... Part of the fault lies in the continuous television coverage, which has turned what used to be a solemn duty into a frivolous spectacle ... The root of the problem is the American appetite for publicity. (*The Mail on Sunday*, 1 October 1995)

(Of course, the O.J. Simpson case still attracts massive media interest over 20 years later as evidenced by the BBC2 drama *The People v OJ Simpson* broadcast in early 2016.)

Amanda Knox

In 2009 Amanda Knox was convicted of murdering Meredith Kercher, an English student, two years previously in Perugia, Italy. She was sentenced to 26 years imprisonment and served four years under what was termed 'cautionary detention', as under Italian law she would not be considered guilty until the verdict was confirmed by a higher court. During her appeal at the second-level trial in October 2011, the murder conviction was overturned and she was released. The media coverage of the murder, the initial trial, the appeal and release of Amanda demonstrated some quite divergent approaches – there was a good deal of strong criticism of Amanda but also, and especially after her conviction, there was some strong media support for her. Also the media reporting focused on Amanda's sexuality and her appearance and behaviour as much as on the case itself. Amanda's boyfriend Raffaele Sollecito, who was also convicted of the murder and then released, received far less media coverage and, presumably as a consequence, is a much less well-known figure than Amanda. As an illustration of the different ways in which this case was reported, the British tabloid press in particular christened her 'Foxy Knoxy', with headlines such as 'Foxy Knoxy: Inside the twisted world of flatmate suspected of Meredith's murder' (*Daily Mail*, 6 November 2007). However, in the USA in particular there was a good deal of media orchestrated support; Seattle (Amanda's home town)-based residents founded the 'Friends of Amanda' support group in 2008; and headlines such as 'Amanda is Innocent of Brutal Murder, Retired FBI Agent Claims' (*ABC News*, 2010) were commonplace. The ambivalent attitude towards Amanda Knox, is illustrated by the account given by CNN news after her release:

> Amanda Knox freed, but truth about student's slaying elusive.
>
> Who is Amanda Knox?

(Continued)

(Continued)

Is she a two-faced she-devil, angelic and compassionate to some but Satanic and Lucifer-like to others? Is she 'Foxy Knoxy', as the British tabloid press leered and sneered at her … or is she the fresh-faced girl from Seattle she still appears to be, even after spending nearly four years behind bars before her conviction was quashed? Is Knox simply the victim of character assassination, painted falsely as a 'femme fatale' by prosecutors and media the world over? (www.cnn.com, 4 October 2011)

Moving on from the 1990s, the debate over live broadcasting from court has continued into the twenty-first century. Although the issues are not exactly the same, for many years there was no televised broadcasting of the UK parliament, partly due to a concern it would encourage politicians to play up to the cameras and would bring parliament into disrepute. This ban was ended in November 1989 and television cameras in parliament are seen as part of the landscape. However, any recording of proceedings in a court in England and Wales is still seen as contempt of court. And it is also contempt to produce a drawing inside the court – the artists' pictures of trials that we do see are done from notes made in court but drawn from memory outside the courtroom itself.

In August 2004, the Lord Chancellor, Lord Falconer, announced that there would be 'wide-ranging consultation on the contentious issue' (of cameras being used in courts) and that judges had agreed to a pilot scheme whereby appeal court cases would be filmed in the next few months. As he put it: 'Technology and public attitudes have moved on since the legislation controlling the broadcasting of courts was passed in 1925' (*BBC News 24*, 15 November 2004).

Lord Falconer saw one of the key issues or problems as the danger that witnesses might be put off coming to court if they knew they were to be filmed; which is partly why the pilot was restricted to appeal cases, where witnesses rarely appear in person. The broadcasters were delighted with this move, which at least opened up the possibility of partial televising of trials in the UK. However, the resulting footage from the pilot scheme was never broadcast and there has been relatively slow progress since then.

In January 2013 the government announced that broadcasters would be allowed into the Court of Appeal from October 2013 and that this is likely to be extended to Crown Courts in due course. As before, this move has not been widely approved by the judiciary. The Lord Chief Justice at the time, Lord Judge, commented that the government plans to extend filming to Crown Courts would 'provoke disruption and deter witnesses from giving evidence'. Speaking before the House of Lords' constitution committee in January 2013 he commented: 'I'm perfectly happy with cameras coming into court, provided their presence doesn't increase the risk that justice won't be done … [but] I'm very troubled about having cameras just swanning around the court' (cited in *The Guardian*, 30 January 2013). He also referred to problems that had occurred in New Zealand where cameras have been allowed and where cheers and booing had accompanied sentences.

More recently, in March 2016, the Ministry of Justice proposed a pilot scheme to allow TV cameras into the Crown Courts in England and Wales. This would not involve the filming of entire trials but would allow the remarks made by judges when passing sentence to be filmed and thus would allow the wide public to see and hear judges passing sentences on serious criminals (ww.bbc.co.uk/news, 20 March 2016). It is worth noting that the proceedings of the Supreme Court (which began work in 2009) are filmed and streamed on the court's website www. supremecourt.uk.

Media Portrayal of Prisons

The modern prison was established in the later eighteenth and, particularly, the early parts of the nineteenth century – and imprisonment became a normal form of punishment. Indeed, with the decline in public, physical punishments and the end of transportation to America (in the later eighteenth century) and, eventually, to Australia (in the mid-nineteenth century) imprisonment soon became the main area for the disposal of offenders who had been found guilty of the more serious forms of criminal behaviour.

In terms of the more general issues concerning the emergence of the modern prison, the moving of punishment away from the public arena to behind the walls of the prison has given this form of punishment a secrecy that means the wider public are pretty poorly informed as to what prisons are like and how they function. It has meant that most people rely on the media for their information and understanding of prison and prison life. Mason (2003) points out that media representations of prison do not only affect the wider public but can and do influence those working in the Criminal Justice System. He refers to two Director Generals of the prison service acknowledging the role the media played in their own experience of prisons:

> In 1992, Derek Lewis confessed that prior to taking the post as head of the prison service, 'his knowledge of prison life came from the media and the BBC comedy programme *Porridge* … ' (and) more recently, the current Director General, Martin Narey, said that the BBC documentary *Strangeways* 'played a big role in my deciding to join the prison service'. (Mason, 2003: 279–80).

We have seen throughout this chapter that crime is a natural and major subject for the media to cover and that the most serious crimes receive the greatest coverage. This means that the media inevitably present a distorted picture of crime and punishment (as the more serious crimes naturally receive the most severe punishments). However, in spite of prison being the form of punishment that most usually springs to mind when punishment is considered, our knowledge of prisons is limited. As Levenson (2001: 14) puts it:

> Despite this familiarity [with prisons], few people are aware of even the basic facts about imprisonment, such as the number of prisoners or the number of prisons, let alone the realities and routines of prison life. Rather, the familiarity is based on the symbolism of the prison and is fed by media images and portrayals of the prison in television and film, from *Porridge* to *Prisoner Cell Block H*, *Escape from Alcatraz* to *Shawshank Redemption*.

There are obvious dangers with this reliance on media portrayals. Rather than emphasising punishment, prisons can be portrayed as easy-going and even privileged places. Unsurprisingly, the media coverage will almost inevitably highlight the more extreme aspects of prison life, such as riots or deaths in prison – the events they see as newsworthy. Indeed, these two contrasting aspects of the media representation of prisons – as easy-going 'holiday camps', as the popular press regularly put it, or as dangerous and violent places – are highlighted by Coyle (2005). On the one hand, prisons are portrayed as dangerous, where there is an ever-present threat of violence and brutality. On the other hand, the holiday camp portrayal suggests prisoners lie in bed all day if they choose to, eat well and have amenities and leisure activities that most people on the outside do not have access to (these two media pictures are explored in Box 7.3). In reality, Coyle (2005: 105) points out, daily life in prison is 'far removed from either of these extremes'. In similar vein, Levenson (2001) makes the point that giving people accurate information about the Criminal Justice System is vital to secure public confidence in it; as the public relies so heavily on the media any misrepresentation is very damaging.

In contrast to these media representations and images of prison life, the most overwhelming feature of prison life would seem to be the routine and boring nature of it. Large institutions necessarily follow a fairly strict timetable and routine, and the features that are common in institutions of many kinds are liable to be more important in custodial institutions that have to be focused on security. The prison day is dominated by routine – cells are unlocked and locked at given times, meals are served at the same time and the activities of the day follow a tightly scheduled pattern. Arguably, the major feature of day-to-day prison life is the monotony of it.

Box 7.3

Media Representations of Prison Life

Consider the extracts below, illustrating the contrasting extremes of the media picture of prison life – the holiday camp and the brutal and violent environment. They are taken from a number of different newspapers and the *BBC News* website. In reading these extracts it is important to consider how the both the content and style reflect the different media sources – some being from popular, more sensational papers and others from arguably more serious sources such as the BBC or *The Guardian*.

Time to get tough on holiday camp prisons

Plans to stop prisoners receiving perks including access to gym equipment, games and TV were welcomed yesterday. Justice Secretary Chris Grayling is finalizing a series of measures to toughen up jails amid concerns that life inside has become too soft. He has also vowed to put an end to 'holiday camp' prisons, with a ban on Sky TV, fewer television sets and less pocket money for inmates. Mr Grayling believes prisoners do not deserve the kind of lifestyle that is beyond the reach of many families on low wages.

(*Daily Express*, 16 April 2013)

Huntley's happy to die in jail: child killer's cushy life

Ian Huntley is happy – Britain's law chief wants him to die behind bars – because he has got such a cushy life in jail … The double child killer is so comfortable being a con he does not want to be let out.

Huntley is monitored round the clock in Wakefield Prison's healthcare wing – so he does not get vigilante attacks. He gets three meals a day in the West Yorkshire jail – plus extra dishes in cookery classes … He also gets regular letters from smitten sweetheart Maxine Carr, who was also jailed for giving him a false alibi for the 2002 murders of 10-year-old Soham schoolgirls Holly Wells and Jessica Chapman … and unlike other inmates he is allowed to see visitors in a private room. According to insiders the monster, who was ordered to serve at least 40 years, 'struts round as if he owns the place'.

(*Daily Star*, 26 March 2007)

Concerns over prison conditions

Conditions at Dartmoor Prison are putting staff, visitors and the public in 'real danger', a report has claimed. The Independent Monitoring Board says the jail has too many prisoners and that some cells are 'barely habitable' … Margaret Blake, vice chairman of the Independent Monitoring Board, formerly the Jail's Board of Visitors, said: 'We have been concerned for some time … that the condition of the prison is deteriorating … Shortages and resources mean that prisoners are left longer in their cells. Tensions can increase and frustrations can lead to a greater risk of attacks between prisoners or attacks on staff.'

(*BBC News*, 5 November 2009)

Chief Inspector of Prisons says conditions in young offender institutions are deteriorating

The Chief Inspector of Prisons, Nick Hardwick, says young people aged 15 to 18 are being held in deteriorating conditions in the Youth Offenders Institutions (YOI) network, with fewer feeling safe while they are locked up. The inspection showed that fewer young inmates felt they could tell someone they were being victimised or believed a member of staff would take them seriously.

(*The Guardian*, 26 October 2011)

As was suggested earlier, the images of prison from the media are a, if not the, major source of information on prison and prison life for the vast majority of the population. As we have seen, the media representation of prisons can be both fictional as well as factual and can be found in written forms and in film and television. Before looking at fictional representations of prison it is important to acknowledge the role of television documentaries in providing the public with information about prison life. In this context, various English prisons have featured in recent documentaries. Strangeways prison in Manchester, Britain's largest high-security prison, has been the subject of a series of fly-on-the-wall documentaries, firstly an eight-part series in 1980, then a follow-up to the infamous riots there in 1990 and then a three-part series in 2011. In commenting on the later of those series, the Governor of Strangeways, Richard Vince, said that he hoped the documentary would dispel some of the myths surrounding the Manchester jail. He commented, 'We are pleased to be able to show the high quality, important and at times difficult work that prison staff do' (*Manchester Evening News*, 10 May 2011). Other prisons that have been the focus of prime-time television documentaries have been Wormwood Scrubs (a two-part documentary in 2009), Holloway, Europe's largest female prison (a three-part documentary in 2009) and, most recently, Aylesbury prison, which houses some of the most dangerous young offenders in the country (a two-episode documentary in 2013).

However, as we have indicated, much of the public's knowledge of prison and prison life comes from fictional representations of prison in literature, film and television. Although perhaps not as much a feature of day-to-day television as the police, prison and prisoners are a common feature on a range of television programmes. In her review of this aspect of media coverage Jewkes (2006: 137) provides a number of examples:

> The world of prison and prisoners has now permeated most television genres: sitcom (*Porridge*), 'serious' drama (*Buried*, *Oz*), light entertainment drama (*Within these Walls*, *Bad Girls*, *The Governor*, *Prisoner*), documentary (*Strangeways*, *Life: Living with Murder*, *Jailbirds*, *Prison Weekly*, *Feltham Sings*) and reality TV (*The Experiment*, *Real Bad Girls*), to name but a few.

Here we will look at a television programme that is most generally cited as influencing people's views on and knowledge of prison – *Porridge*. This was a BBC television sitcom broadcast between 1974 and 1977, written by Dick Clement and Ian La Frenais and starring Ronnie Barker and Richard Beckinsale. It was set in a fictional prison 'HMP Slade' and led to various spin offs, including a film and a follow-up series *Going Straight*. While dramas and comedies are not always seen as bona fide sources of information, it is interesting that *Porridge* was popular with British prisoners, who recognised it had a high degree of authenticity. As ex-prisoner and, more recently, *Guardian* columnist Erwin James put it:

> What fans could never know, however, unless they had been subject to a stint of Her Majesty's Pleasure, was that the conflict between Fletcher and Officer Mackay was about the most authentic depiction ever of the true relationship that exists between prisoners and prison officers in British jails up and down the country … When I was inside, *Porridge* was a staple of our TV diet. In one high-security prison a video orderly would be dispatched to tape the programme each week. If they missed it, they were in trouble. (James, 2005)

In her examination of popular media and prisons, Jewkes (2006) considers the impact and importance of *Porridge*. A key element of this programme was its depiction of human relationships and particularly that between the old-time, persistent criminal, Norman Fletcher, and the naive, young first-time offender, Lennie Godber. The relationship between a street-wise, cunning mentor figure and an innocent, gullible friend is common to many British sitcoms (Jewkes cites *Only Fools and Horses* and *Blackadder*, among others, as examples). The series illustrates a period in British prison history when the 'justice' model was coming to the fore and the welfare/rehabilitation emphasis of the previous decade was being undermined. Jewkes (2006: 139–40) sees this 'dynamic … (as being) represented in the form of a "soft" screw and a "hard" screw; the benign and well-meaning Mr Barrowclough, who always saw in his charges the potential for reform, and officious disciplinarian, Mr MacKay, who ruled his wing with an iron will and military disposition.'

From a more critical angle, *Porridge* can also be interpreted as working against prisoners' interests and against penal reform by the rather cosy picture of prison life that might make the wider public less concerned about prison conditions and the reality of a prison system facing dangerous levels of overcrowding. From this perspective, *Porridge*, while giving the public some sense of what prison is like, could be seen as having ignored the humdrum, boring but often tense reality of prison life by showing it to be, basically, a 'bit of a laugh'. It does not encourage the viewing public to think critically about prisons.

Box 7.4

Probation and the Media

While television and films seem to be saturated with productions about the police, prisons and courts, the exception to the rule about media fascination with criminal justice is the lack of interest in probation. There have been some television series about probation, e.g. *Probation Officer* (1959–62), *Jack of Hearts* (1999) and *Public Enemies* (2012), but these have been few and far between. Documentaries about probation work are also rare. And as for films, the only recent effort has been the Steve Coogan film *The Parole Officer* (2001), a somewhat lame comedy set in England where we do not have parole officers, but obviously intended to appeal to the US market. So why the dearth of product?

Probation work does not have a high public profile like the police, prisons or courts; it is a small organisation; its members are not recognisable by their uniforms (cf. the police or prison officers); they work quietly in private; their work does not appear to be characterised by tension and implicit or explicit violence; and they do not work in recognisable surroundings (police stations, prisons and courts are all instantly recognisable). And if we list the main news values/news imperatives first articulated by Steve Chibnall (1977) and then refined by Yvonne Jewkes (2015) to explain what lies behind decisions about what constitutes 'the news', then it is difficult to see how probation fits well with them and therefore why probation is not deemed to be newsworthy.

(Continued)

(Continued)

- Predictability

- Simplification

- Risk

- Sex

- Celebrity

- Violence

- Children

- Individualism

- Spectacle

Only very rarely does probation work tick any of these boxes.

A number of murders in England and Wales in the last decade (John Monckton 2004, Robert Symons 2004, Mary-Ann Leneghan 2005, Naomi Bryant 2005 and Lauren Bonomo and Gabriel Ferez 2008) have brought media attention, but not for good reasons as officers have been – somewhat unfairly – blamed for these cases.

Because of this low media profile, the public have little idea about what probation work involves; whereas they *think* they know about the workings of the police, prisons and courts. It seems likely that this low profile for probation will continue, reflecting Meryl Aldridge's (1992) judgement some years ago about probation lacking in news values.

Summary

It would seem, then, that the media are a, if not the, major source of information about the Criminal Justice System for most of the population. However, it is important to be aware that there are different kinds of media that offer ever more various ways of providing this information, and that most of the media are under pressure to provide stories and news which are popular and in turn profitable. The brief points below highlight the main points covered in this chapter.

- Crime and criminal justice is a staple part of the media

- The vast majority of the public rely on the media for their knowledge of the Criminal Justice System

- Media representation of the police can be seen as either hegemonic or subversive according to Robert Reiner

- What happens to offenders when they come to court is a key element of media representation of crime and justice

- Media portrayal of prisons provides two distinct, contradictory pictures – as easy-going 'holiday camps' or as violent and brutal establishments

Discussion Questions

1. What role (if any) has the media played in developing your knowledge and understanding of the police, the court system and prison life?

2. What part has fictional media (in the form of film, television, magazines, books, etc.) played in this process?

3. Consider current portrayals of police officers in television programmes (both police drama and more general soap operas and dramas). How do they relate to Reiner's categorisation of 'hegemony' and 'subversive' representations of policing?

4. How are uniformed police officers represented in comparison to detectives?

5. What do you consider to be the main advantages of and potential difficulties and problems with the televising of criminal trials?

6. How would you describe the portrayal of prison life from the different media extracts on pp. 140–1 above? What reaction might these images produce from the wider public? How might politicians and policy makers use these images?

Further Reading

Jewkes, J. (2015) *Media and Crime*. 3rd edn. London: Sage. An excellent introduction to the complicated relationship between crime and the media.

Leishman, F. and Mason, P. (2003) *Policing and the Media: Facts, fictions and factions*, Cullompton: Willan Publishing. An examination of the nature and effects of media images of crime and policing. It looks at how the police promote themselves in the media and considers both fictional and documentary representations of police and policing.

Marsh, I. and Melville, G. (2014) *Crime, Justice and the Media*. 2nd edn. London: Routledge. Another good introductory text.

Mason, P. (ed.) (2006) *Captured by the Media: Prison discourse in popular culture*. Cullompton: Willan Publishing. This book explores media representations of and discourses on prison, again considering both fictional and factual representations. It includes articles looking at press, television and cinematic portrayals of prison and prison life.

For current research papers and findings the journal *Crime. Media, Culture* is a particularly relevant resource.

References

Aldridge, M. (1992) 'The probation service and the press: The curious incident of the dog in the night-time', *British Journal of Social Work*, 22 (6): 645–61.

Chibnall, S. (1977) *Law-And-Order News: An analysis of crime reporting in the British press*. London: Tavistock.

Coyle, A. (2005) *Understanding Prisons*. Milton Keynes: Open University Press.

Dorfman, L. (2001) 'Off balance: Youth, race and crime in the news', Building Blocks for Youth (www.buildingblocksforyouth.org).

Emsley, C. (1996) *Crime and Society in England 1750–1900*. Harlow: Longman.

Home Office (2015) *Police Powers and Procedures England and Wales, Year Ending 31 March 2015*. London: Home Office.

James, E. (2005) 'Doing time with porridge', *Guardian*, 5 October.

Jewkes, Y. (2006) 'Creating a stir? Prisons, popular media and the power to reform', in P. Mason (ed.), *Captured by the Media: Prison discourse in popular culture*, Cullompton: Willan.

Jewkes, Y. (2015) *Media and Crime*. 3rd edn. London: Sage.

Kershaw, C., Budd, T., Kinshott, G., Mattinson, J., Mayhew, P. and Myhill, A. (2000) *The British Crime Survey*. London: HMSO.

Leishman, F. and Mason, P. (2003) *Policing and the Media: Facts, fictions and factions*. Cullompton: Willan.

Levenson, J. (2001) 'Inside information: Prisons and the media', *Criminal Justice Matters*, 43:14–15.

Mason, P. (2001) 'Courts, cameras and genocide', *Criminal Justice Matters*, 43: 36–7.

Mason, P. (ed.) (2003) *Criminal Visions: Media representations of crime and justice*. Cullompton: Willan.

Mawby, R. (2003) 'Completing the "half-formed picture"? Media images of policing', in P. Mason (ed.), *Criminal Visions: Media representations of crime and justice*. Cullompton: Willan.

Ministry of Justice (2015) *Criminal Justice Statistics Quarterly, December 2014: Overview tables*. London: MoJ.

Reiner, R. (2007) 'Media-made criminality: The representation of crime in the mass media', in M. Maguire, R. Morgan and R. Reiner (eds), *The Oxford Handbook of Criminology*. 4th edn. Oxford: Oxford University Press.

Stepniak, D. (2003) 'British justice: Not suitable for public viewing', in P. Mason (ed.), *Criminal Visions: Media representations of crime and justice*. Cullompton: Willan.

Check out the Companion Website

Want to know more about this chapter? Review what you have been learning by visiting: **https://study.sagepub.com/harding**

- Practice with essay questions
- Test yourself with multiple-choice questions
- Listen to a series of podcasts featuring Neil of Northumbria Police and London's Metropolitan Police Service
- Watch videos selected from the SAGE Video collection

8 Government, Governance and Criminal Justice

Tim Newburn

Introduction

This chapter looks at the general shape of the Criminal Justice System and its relationship to government and to systems of governance and control. Which government departments have responsibilities in the broad field of criminal justice and penal policy and what is the split between them? What other bodies – governmental and non-governmental – are involved in what might broadly be termed the *governance* of the major institutions in the criminal justice and penal systems? Finally, and relatedly, what is the current and potential future role of the private sector in these domains?

The Emergence of Modern Criminal Justice

The last two centuries or so have seen the progressive rationalisation and bureaucratisation of criminal justice and penal processes. From localised, community-based systems of policing and punishment there have developed huge state-managed apparatuses, and vast bodies of laws, rules and regulations, aimed at controlling crime. Eighteenth-century England was characterised by increasing concerns about crime. By mid to late century crime and disorder were seen as a threat to social stability. It was around this time that what we now understand as 'the police' emerged, in 1829 in London and then across England and Wales during the middle of the nineteenth century. Indeed, the nineteenth and early twentieth centuries saw the creation of all the fundamental institutions of the modern Criminal Justice System: the police, the courts and related systems of criminal prosecution, the prison, probation and, in due course, an increasingly complex array of non-custodial penalties. By the end of the nineteenth century separate systems for dealing with juvenile offenders were also emerging, and the first half of the twentieth century, dominated by two world wars, saw the consolidation and reform of modern Criminal Justice Systems. This period began to draw to an end from the late 1960s and was the era in which the 'solidarity project' – in which the state was the guarantor of full citizenship and security for all – was increasingly eclipsed by market forces. Recent decades have seen the emergence of a rapidly expanding mixed economy in many areas of criminal justice and, crucially, what to many appears to be a decisive shift in what are believed to be the purposes and ambitions of our criminal justice and penal policies.

Current Government Responsibilities

Parliament, as the highest legislative authority, is the body responsible for the passage and repeal of law, including criminal law. In addition to its legislative function parliament also controls finance and is a forum for scrutinising government proposals and action. In addition to debates within the two main houses of parliament – the House of Commons and the House of Lords – discussion and debate of proposals and activity in relation to crime and justice takes place within a number of select committees. Select committees examine the work of government departments, generally in meetings that are open, resulting in reports that are publicly available. Because criminal justice and penal policy is linked to more than one government department, and there are also a number of cross-cutting Select Committees, there are quite a number of parliamentary forums which can or may consider such matters. The key ones are: the Home Affairs Select Committee; the Justice Committee; and the Public Accounts Committee.

The Home Affairs Select Committee describes its responsibilities as: 'examining the expenditure, policy and administration of the Home Office and its associated public bodies'. In recent years it has investigated matters as widely ranging as: the role of the Home Office; 'the migration crisis'; new psychoactive substances; and countering extremism. The Justice Committee examines the expenditure, administration and policy of the Ministry of Justice and associated public bodies, and in recent times has conducted inquiries into restorative justice, the role of the magistracy and young adult offenders. The Public Accounts Committee scrutinises the value for money – the economy, efficiency and effectiveness – of public spending and while this only occasionally touches on matters to do with the Home Office or Ministry of Justice, it has conducted important inquiries into specific areas such as probation as well as general overviews of the whole field of criminal justice.

Box 8.1

House of Commons Public Accounts Committee Report: *The Criminal Justice System* (2014)

Summary

The Criminal Justice System is complex and to operate effectively relies on numerous inter-dependencies between the different bodies involved. There are weaknesses in the system that have persisted for far too long and which cause delay and inefficiency, and serve to undermine public confidence.

Main conclusions

- Government departments need to demonstrate a clearer link between their actions and the recent reduction in crime (departments tend to suggest declines in crime are linked to wider social, technological and economic changes; unclear how their own actions have influenced crime levels);

- greater strategic alignment at top level is not matched at the front line (senior managers tend to cooperate, but collaboration at a local level is poor);

- collaboration between police forces undoubtedly improves efficiency (43 forces but collaboration should be the norm);

- the quality of police case files is poor and getting worse;

- the remarkably slow progress in improving IT systems over the last decade means there are still too many disparate systems, which fail to operate together;

- the Criminal Justice System is too reliant on a small number of large suppliers, and is missing the opportunity to fully exploit what markets can offer (more work is required to enable Small and Medium Enterprises (SMEs) to bid for, and win, government contracts).

In addition to specific committees established to investigate activities in Scotland, Wales and Northern Ireland there are a number of other parliamentary committees that are intended to monitor government activities in the general area of criminal justice and penal policy. They include:

- The Public Administration Select Committee – which in recent years has investigated and reported on matters including the reliability of crime statistics.

- The European Union Home Affairs Sub-committee – covering European Union
  legislation and activity.

- The Intelligence and Security Committee.

There are three main government departments relevant to matters of crime and justice. The first, and until recently the largest and most important, is the Home Office. For the bulk of its history, the Home Office had responsibility for police, prisons, probation and a number of other smaller bodies. In May 2007 a new Ministry of Justice was established which incorporated what was previously known as the Department for Constitutional Affairs (DCA). The Ministry of Justice has responsibility for all those areas of activity previously the responsibility of the DCA – the magistrates' courts, the Crown Court, the Appeal Courts and the Legal Services Commission – as well as incorporating a set of responsibilities which previously belonged to the Home Office – including prisons, probation (now jointly referred to as the National Offender Management Service) and sentencing. Finally, there is the Attorney General who is the chief legal adviser to the government and has governing oversight of the prosecuting authorities in England and Wales (including the Crown Prosecution Service (CPS) and the Serious Fraud Office). The Attorney General also has overall responsibility for the Treasury Solicitor's Department, the National Fraud Authority and Her Majesty's CPS Inspectorate.

The next step is to consider the two main Departments of State in a little more detail.

Home Office

The Home Office was established in the late eighteenth century when a distinction was first formally drawn between responsibility for Domestic Affairs and the Colonies and Foreign Affairs. Prior to this there had been two Secretaries of State but their responsibilities were divided geographically. The term 'Home Office' itself didn't become fully established until about the 1840s. The Home Office has had a rather odd history, traditionally having very varied responsibilities, with new ones often added on a sporadic and somewhat ad hoc basis. Sir Frank Newsam, Permanent Secretary in the Home Office in the 1950s commented that:

> The history of the Home Office ... consists first, of the *extension* of its jurisdiction to new subjects by a long series of Acts of Parliament, and secondly of the *removal* from its jurisdiction of certain subjects which have grown to such importance that new Departments had to be created to deal with them or were more appropriate to deal with them. (Newsam, 1955: 25)

Arguably, it was during the Second World War and the decade after that the Home Office grew into a major department of state, with a sizeable staff and all the accoutrements of a modern bureaucracy. In its review of its own history for its bicentenary in 1982 the Home Office confirmed that it was not until the late 1950s 'that the Office came to be recognisably different from its pre-war self' (Home Office, 1982: 15).

Historically, the Home Office's core function was to advise on the exercise of the Royal Prerogative of Mercy through Free Pardons, reprieves in capital cases and through the remission of sentence. For a great many Home Secretaries, until the abolition of capital punishment in the mid-1960s, this was undoubtedly their most onerous task. Out of this delegated duty came a more general responsibility for the criminal law and for policy on the management and treatment of offenders. For the bulk of the twentieth century these responsibilities included juvenile justice, probation, parole, the release and recall of life sentence prisoners and issues to do with mentally disordered offenders who had been before the courts. Since the early nineteenth century, from the time of Sir Robert Peel, perhaps the most famous of all Home Secretaries, a core component of the job has related to the maintenance of the Metropolitan Police and, subsequently, other local police forces. The word *maintenance* here, however, hides much complexity, and the relationship between the Home Secretary, local police forces and local government has been ever-changing and subject, at various times, to considerable dispute (we return to this below). Other major responsibilities held by the Home Office for much of the twentieth century included immigration and nationality, broadcasting, and civil defence. The role of Home Secretary continues to be thought of as one of the three most significant cabinet positions (alongside the Chancellor of the Exchequer and the Foreign Secretary), though in some respects this is more a reflection of the history of the position than its current range of responsibilities which are now very significantly reduced.

With the creation of the Ministry of Justice and the hiving off of one or two other, smaller policy areas the Home Office now has a much more focused set of responsibilities than for much of its history. It is currently responsible (using its own terminology) for:

- working on the problems caused by illegal drug use;
- shaping the alcohol strategy, policy and licensing conditions;
- keeping the UK safe from the threat of terrorism;
- reducing and preventing crime, and ensuring people feel safe in their homes and communities;
- securing the UK border and controlling immigration;
- considering applications to enter and stay in the UK;
- issuing passports and visas;
- supporting visible, responsible and accountable policing by empowering the public and freeing up the police to fight crime;
- fire prevention and rescue.

The Home Office encompasses the central government department itself and four Non-Departmental Public Bodies (NDPBs):

- The Independent Police Complaints Commission (whose statutory purpose is to secure and maintain public confidence in the police complaints system);
- The Gangmasters Licensing Authority (established to tackle exploitation of vulnerable workers in the agriculture sector);
- The Office of the Immigration Services Commissioner (which has responsibility for regulating immigration advisers and whose Commissioner has statutory regulatory and prosecutorial responsibilities); and
- The Security Industry Authority (responsible for regulating the private security industry).

The College of Policing, which is a quasi-NDPB, with responsibility for raising the professional status of police officers and police staff, also comes under the umbrella of the Home Office. The Passport Office, once a separate entity, became a division of the Home Office in 2014. Within its general structure the Home Office also has a number of:

- Advisory Non-Departmental Public Bodies – these offer expert advice and include the Advisory Council on the Misuse of Drugs, the Migration Advisory Committee; and the National DNA Database Ethics Group among others.
- Tribunal Non-Departmental Public Bodies – generally concerned with the rights and obligations of individuals in relation to a branch of government, and include the Investigatory Powers Tribunal and the Office of Surveillance Commissioners among others.
- Arm's Length Bodies sponsored by the Home Office – these are numerous and include the Anti-Slavery Commissioner, HM Inspectorate of Constabulary, the Independent Reviewer of Terrorism Legislation and others.

At the end of 2015 the Home Office had a total of a little over 29,000 staff, with a further 2,000 being employed in its four NDPBs, and had a budget of approximately £10.7 billion for the financial year 2015–16.

The Police Service

Of all the institutional responsibilities retained by the Home Office, by far the most significant in criminal justice is its relationship with the police service. There are currently 43 police constabularies in England and Wales, all of which are subject to very considerable control from the centre. The pre-2012 system for police governance was established by the Police Act 1964, amended subsequently by the Police and Magistrates' Courts Act 1994 and consolidated by the Police Act 1996.

Under the Police Act 1964, and as amended, there were intended to be three main parties involved in police governance: the Home Secretary; the chief constable; and the local police authority. The 1964 Act gave particular responsibilities to each of the parties in this tripartite structure. The main duty of a police authority was to 'secure the maintenance of an adequate and efficient police force for the area'. To this end, police authorities, subject to the secretary of state's agreement, were to have the power to appoint the chief constable, with the support of the secretary of state to call upon a chief constable to retire, and to determine the number of persons of each rank that would constitute the establishment of the force. Henceforward, police authorities were to consist of a mix of locally elected councillors (two-thirds) and magistrates (one-third). Chief constables were to be responsible for the 'direction and control' of their force and were to submit to the police authority an annual report on the policing of the area. Finally, the Act required a secretary of state to exercise their powers in a manner and to the extent 'best calculated to promote the efficiency of the police'. The Home Secretary could call on a chief constable to submit reports on the policing of the area and could require local police authorities under specific circumstances to use their power to call upon the chief constable to retire in the interests of efficiency. Although the broad conceit was that this was a system involving checks and balances in which the three components were held in some form of equilibrium, in reality police authorities were always the least powerful of the three (Jones and Newburn, 1997).

Radical reform of police governance has more recently been brought about by the Police Reform and Social Responsibility Act 2011. The Act contained provisions for the election of Police and Crime Commissioners (PCCs), one for each local area for a four-year term, apart from the Metropolitan and City of London forces, as a replacement for police authorities. The first elections took place in November 2012. In the Metropolitan area, where historically the Home Secretary was the police authority for the force, the Metropolitan Police Authority (MPA), which had only been established in 2000, was replaced by a Mayor's Office for Policing and Crime. The PCC responsibilities include securing the maintenance of the police force, ensuring that it is efficient and effective, as well as holding the chief constable to account for the exercise of a range of duties. The Commissioner is also responsible for appointing and dismissing the chief and for agreeing the appointments of deputy and assistant chief constables. They have a duty to issue Police and Crime Plans, setting out: local police and crime objectives (including the policing of the local area, crime and disorder reduction in that area, and the discharge by the relevant police force of its national or international functions); financial and other resources which the elected local policing body is to provide; and the means by which the chief officer of police's performance in providing policing will be measured. The most significant change, arguably, was that chief constables henceforward were to be appointed by the PCC and, under specific circumstances, the PCC could suspend the chief constable from duty and call upon them to resign or retire. This was one of a number of ways in which the new Act removed a small number of the Home Secretary's powers. The 2011 Police Reform and Social Responsibility Act allows the Secretary of State to give guidance about the matters to be dealt with in police and crime plans, to which the police and crime commissioner must have regard, but goes no further.

The other significant body in this field is Her Majesty's Inspectorate of Constabulary (HMIC). Established by the County and Borough Police Act 1856, its function from the outset was to inspect police forces so as to ensure 'efficiency'. Such inspections, if passed, meant that central government would meet its share of the cost of local policing. HMIC is independent of both government and the police service. Its statement of purpose is:

> Through inspecting, monitoring and advising, to promote and advance improvements in the efficiency and effectiveness of policing. We will do this independently, professionally and fairly, always championing the public interest, and we will explain what we do and why.

The Inspectorate assesses police forces and policing by activity (recent reports have included such subjects as police legitimacy, child protection and digital crime), publishing its reports and also reporting to parliament on its activities. HMIC has considerable discretion in deciding the nature of the inspection programme, though this is subject to approval by the Home Secretary. Inspectors are Crown appointments on the advice of the Home Secretary and the Prime Minister. Until 1993 all Inspectors were drawn from the police service, all having been serving police officers. In 1993 two full-time Inspectors of Constabulary were appointed from outside the police service, and in 2012 the first 'civilian' Chief Inspector of Constabulary, Sir Thomas Winsor, was appointed. HMIC inspects all 43 constabularies and a number of other bodies including British Transport Police, Civil Nuclear Constabulary, Her Majesty's Revenue and Customs (HMRC), the Ministry of Defence Police and the National Crime Agency. It has no authority to inspect the work of Police and Crime Commissioners.

The Independent Police Complaints Commission (IPCC) (see Chapter 19), which replaced the previously existing Police Complaints Authority in 2002, oversees the police complaints system and sets the standards by which the police should handle complaints. In addition to the police, the IPCC is also responsible for dealing with serious complaints and conduct matters relating to staff in the National Crime Agency, HMRC and Home Office immigration and enforcement staff.

The Ministry of Justice

Emerging, seemingly out of nowhere, in early 2007, the Ministry of Justice was created as a consequence of the then Home Secretary, Dr John Reid, announcing that the Home Office was no longer 'fit for purpose'. In some respects, by creating a Ministry of Justice England and Wales was simply catching up with what is already standard practice in many nations where a justice ministry or department is an established feature. When the Ministry was first created Lord Falconer, the then Justice Secretary, claimed that:

> The justice system is performing significantly better than in the past, but there is still considerable room for improvement ... By bringing together courts, prisons and probation services we will have a coherent system looking at the whole life of an offender from conviction to punishment to rehabilitation. (Quoted in Gibson, 2008: 17)

The Ministry of Justice (MoJ) has responsibility for the bulk of the Criminal Justice System beyond policing, which mainly covers the courts, prisons, and probation services. It employs approximately 76,000 people (if prisons and probation are included) and has a budget of around £9 billion. As such, it works directly with a range of other government agencies including:

- One non-ministerial department (the National Archives).
- Six Executive Agencies (Criminal Injuries Compensation Authority, HM Courts and Tribunals Service, HM Prison Service, the Legal Aid Agency, the National Offender Management Service (NOMS), and the Office of the Public Guardian).
- Six Executive NDPBs including the Children and Family Court Advisory and Support Service (CAFCASS), the Parole Board, the Criminal Cases Review Commission (CCRC) and the Youth Justice Board (YJB).
- A wide range of NDPBs such as the Law Commission, Sentencing Council for England and Wales, and the Victims' Advisory Panel.
- Numerous other agencies, including the Victims' Commissioner, HM Inspectorates of Prisons and of Probation, the Prisons and Probation Ombudsman and Independent Monitoring Boards of Prisons.

Space doesn't allow for a full discussion of all the major agencies forming part of, or linked to the MoJ and so we will focus on arguably the two of greatest interest to criminologists: NOMS (including HM Prison Service and probation), and the YJB (though clearly a case could also be made for others).

National Offender Management Service

Historically, the prison and probation services were separate entities. The prison service was always linked with the Home Office, though the relationship has varied from full integration to independence. The idea of 'executive agencies' was introduced in the 1980s, the intention being to separate organisations delivering specific services from the primary policy-making departments of government. The prison service became an Agency in 1993, with the Strangeways prison riot and the Woolf Report which followed (Woolf, 1991) being key influences on the decision to make some radical changes to the management and running of the prison system. This new status lasted a decade until the creation of the National Offender Management Service.

NOMS was established in 2004, largely as a consequence of criticisms of Home Office policy in the area of 'offender management' in the Carter Review (2003). The review, critical of the operation of both prison and probation services, argued for the creation of a new body that would ensure more effective end-to-end management of offenders. The outcome, though flagged some years previously by the Home Office (1998), was a radical one, and a new umbrella body, with a single chief executive, was created to incorporate the previously separate prison and probation services. NOMS now has overall responsibility for offender management, for the running of all public sector prisons in England and Wales (109 in all) and for overseeing the delivery of probation services via the National Probation Service and the new community rehabilitation companies.

NOMS has a regional organisation, with 10 Directors of Offender Management (DOMs) responsible for covering different regions of England and Wales. The DOMs are responsible for the delivery of prison and probation services, reporting directly to the NOMS board. So far as public prisons are concerned, they are managed by a governing governor (a director in private prisons). Such is the extent of contracting out of particular areas of activity within prisons that a recent Justice Select Committee Report (House of Commons Justice Committee, 2015) concluded that 'prison governors in public sector prisons and some private sector prisons are no longer responsible for the sum total of everything that happens within their prison walls'. Furthermore, decisions made by government ministers over such matters as the Incentives and Earned Privileges scheme (a system, introduced in 1995, which seeks to promote conforming behaviour by enabling people to earn benefits in exchange for responsible conduct) also meant that governors 'were constrained in their operational decisions'.

The first private sector prison (the Wolds) was introduced in 1992. Though the introduction of private prisons was initially quite controversial they are now an established part of the prison estate. In 2010 the Justice Secretary opened a competition for a number of prisons. In 2011 contracts were awarded for four with HMP Birmingham becoming the first public sector prison to be fully privatised the following year (with the private sector both running and owning the prison). There are 14 private prisons at the time of writing (out of a total of just over 120) holding about 17 per cent of the prison population and managed by three companies: G4S Justice Services, Serco Custodial Services and Sodexo Justice Services. The first four private prisons were contracted out on a management-only basis, with initial contracts lasting five years. In the past 20 years contracts have been far wider, encompassing design, construction, management and finance. The land on which such prisons are built remains in government hands, with contractors typically receiving a lease for a period in the region of 25 years (Genders, 2013). Contractually, private prisons are required to meet a variety of performance targets, with the threat of being handed over to the public sector within set periods of time. A report by the National Audit Office in 2003 was highly critical of elements of the terms of some of these contracts, and recommended that the system of performance measurement needed to be 'sharpened' (National Audit Office, 2003). In 2011 HMP Doncaster became the first prison to be run on a 'payment by results'

(PbR) basis, a pilot project which ran for three years, finishing one year earlier than its initial intended 2015 end date. The overall aim was to reduce reconviction rates within a year of discharge from custody, supported by a 'proactive delivery model facilitated by case management' within the prison (Pearce et al., 2015). The generally disappointing results achieved in the early years of PbR illustrate the complexity of cultural change in environments such as criminal justice.

Probation

With its origins in the Victorian temperance movement and the system of police court missionaries of the late nineteenth century, the probation service was formally established in 1907 as a result of the Probation of Offenders Act. With an original mission to 'advise, assist and befriend' those under supervision, the nature of probation and the role of the probation officer changed markedly during the twentieth century as criminal justice as a whole underwent a series of significant reforms. With growing scepticism about the rehabilitative impact of all criminal justice interventions, and the growing political desire to be seen as 'tough', non-custodial sanctions increasingly became described as 'punishments in the community', and the probation service itself gradually moved further and further from its social work traditions. In addition, what was originally a local service gradually became increasingly centrally governed, and eventually entirely centralised. As one observer put it some time ago, the probation service has 'moved from a theologically to a psychiatrically driven discourse and then to what has been termed a post-psychiatric paradigm based less on therapy than on system involvement and offender management' (Harris, 1994: 34).

In 2005 proposals were published in a consultation paper that would give the Secretary of State a statutory duty to make arrangements with others to provide probation services, together with the ability to create new bodies to replace probation boards with which new contractual relationships could be established. In effect this signalled the arrival of other agencies onto the scene. In 2007 the Offender Management Act was passed, ensuring in future those services could be provided by a mixture of public, private and voluntary agencies. Competition was the way forward (see Mair and Burke, 2012).

This emerging approach to criminal justice, initiated by a Labour administration, received a further iteration under the incoming Coalition government in a Green Paper in 2010 (MoJ, 2010). Finding that up to 50 per cent of offenders released from prison reoffended within a year, and that short sentences had reconviction rates closer to 60 per cent the Green Paper proposed a 'rehabilitation revolution'. The government subsequently introduced a range of 'Transforming Rehabilitation' (TR) reforms which focused on the achievement of specific outcomes (MoJ, 2013). As part of the process of reorientation, the market for rehabilitative services was opened up to a range of private and third sector providers, and new payment incentives were put in place to focus activity on the reduction of reoffending. As part of these reforms 21 Community Rehabilitation Companies (CRCs) were established to deliver rehabilitation services in England and Wales for low- and medium-risk offenders. Offenders assessed as posing a high risk and those released from prison who had committed the most serious offences were to be supervised by the newly created (as of June 2014) public sector National Probation Service, which had replaced the previously existing 35 individual Probation Trusts.

Prison and Probation: Complaints and External Oversight

As with policing, both prisons and probation are subject to scrutiny by external inspectorates. HM Inspectorate of Prisons was created by the Criminal Justice Act 1982, and consolidates under one person the prisons inspection function that had been in operation since 1815 when magistrates were first given powers to inspect prison establishments. HMI Prisons is responsible for inspecting private prisons in the same way as public sector prisons. Its establishment in its modern guise in the 1980s was in direct response to the report of the May Committee (Home Office, 1979) inquiry into the UK prison services. Its terms of reference include to:

- inspect or arrange for the inspection of prisons and young offender institutions in England and Wales;
- report on the treatment of prisoners and conditions in prisons;
- submit an annual report to be laid before parliament.

The Inspectorate's responsibilities have been extended in recent years to also include the inspection of immigration service detention centres, secure juvenile accommodation inside and outside the prison estate on behalf of the Youth Justice Board, police custody suites jointly with HM Inspectorate of Constabulary, court custody facilities, Border Force customs custody suites, and Secure Training Centres jointly with OFSTED. The Chief Inspector is independent of the prison service and has freedom to determine what to inspect, how inspections should be carried out, and whether inspections are announced or unannounced. They are required to inspect all prisons and other establishments that detain people, to publish the methodology for their inspections and, as the terms of reference state, to publish their findings and to report to parliament. Prisons in England and Wales also have Independent Monitoring Boards (IMBs). The Prison Act 1952 requires every prison to be monitored by an independent board appointed by the Secretary of State. Such boards, though similar to HMIP in some very general respects, are responsible for the day-to-day health of individual prison establishments. They are made up of local citizens who work on a voluntary basis.

There is also an independent Inspectorate for Probation. Its function is to report on the effectiveness of work with adults and children who have offended. Such assessments currently focus on the goals of reducing reoffending, protecting the public, and improving the well-being of children at risk of reoffending, irrespective of who undertakes such work. In 2014/15, for example, the work of HMI Probation included:

- six Full Joint Inspections and 31 shorter assessments of provision within the youth justice system;

- an audit of workloads held by Probation Trusts, followed by an audit of the way cases had been transferred to the National Probation Service (NPS), and which to the Community Rehabilitation Companies (CRCs);

- 14 inspections of Adult Offending Work; and

- 43 inspections of offender management in prisons (jointly with HMI Prisons);

- a series of thematic reviews on subjects as diverse as girls in the Criminal Justice System, and on people with learning difficulties in the Criminal Justice System.

Finally in relation to prisons and probation there is the Prisons and Probation Ombudsman (see Chapter 19). Again, the origins of this institution lie in the Strangeways disturbances in 1990. In the aftermath an independent adjudicator of prison complaints was established. In 1994 the office of the Prisons Ombudsman was established and in 2001 the remit was extended to include probation and was renamed the Prisons and Probation Ombudsman to reflect this. It was further extended in 2006 to include immigration detention. The ombudsman is independent of NOMS, the Border Agency and YJB as well as MoJ. The ombudsman's responsibility is to investigate a variety of categories of complaint that have not been satisfied by internal complaints systems and also, since 2004, to investigate all deaths in prisons, probation approved premises, immigration detention facilities and secure training centres.

Box 8.2

National Audit Office (2015) *Inspection: A comparative study*

In 2005, the National Audit Office studied HMI Constabulary, HMI Prisons, HMI Probation, HM Crown Prosecution Service Inspectorate, and the Independent Chief Inspector of Borders and Immigration.

Key findings

- The act of inspection has a direct cultural impact on sector performance (in short, prisons, police, etc, seek to comply with Inspectorate expectations);

- Poor inspection results can trigger intervention action by oversight bodies (but oversight bodies need considerable discretion in responding to inspections);

(Continued)

(Continued)

- The benefits of the knowledge and good practice identified by inspection findings and recommendations are not always maximised;

- Inspectorates' independence can be perceived as limited – although Chief Inspectors are statutory appointments, the fact of appointment by the Secretary of State and the fixed-term nature of the contracts, can be perceived as limiting independence;

- Despite developing their approaches to inspection, inspectorates' identification and sharing of how they could learn from each other has been limited; and

- Inspectorates and departments agree on the importance and potential of joint inspection work, but have struggled to make this work in practice.

Youth Justice Board (YJB)

Initially created by the Crime and Disorder Act 1998, the YJB was linked to a number of government departments, but primarily the Home Office. Its principal function was to monitor the operation of the youth justice system and the provision of youth justice services, together with monitoring national standards, and establishing appropriate performance measures (see Chapter 18). Prior to the 1998 Act, youth justice teams, comprised mainly of social workers, had primary responsibility for working with young offenders subject to non-custodial penalties, and for liaising with other agencies. Stimulated by a concern with efficiency and consistency – broadly in line with the managerialist changes affecting the bulk of criminal justice, new multi-agency bodies called Youth Offending Teams (YOTs) were introduced by the 1988 Act. YOTs are a partnership of organisations (including the police and local authority), which have a legal responsibility to prevent offending and reduce reoffending, and which are overseen by a management board usually chaired by a senior official within the local authority. It is the duty of every local authority, together with partner agencies, to establish one or more YOTs for their area, which are overseen by the YJB.

In the aftermath of the creation of the Ministry of Justice, the YJB became its joint responsibility alongside the Department of Children, Schools and Families. Following the 2010 general election it became the sole responsibility of the MoJ and it is currently responsible for:

- overseeing youth justice services;
- the placing of children and young people remanded or sentenced to custody;
- advising the Secretary of State for Justice on the operation of, and standards for, the youth justice system;

- providing a 'secure estate' for children and young people, with young offender institutions, secure training centres and secure children's homes;

- making grants to local authorities or other bodies for the development of plans that support its targets; and

- commissioning and publishing research on preventing youth offending.

The 'secure estate' for young offenders is mentioned above. As with the youth justice system more generally, custodial institutions for juveniles are separate from the adult system. There are currently five young offenders' institutions (run either by the prison service or by private providers), three privately run secure training centres and nine local authority secure children's homes.

Statutory Partnerships

Having considered the broad outline of the two main government departments with interests in criminal justice, and examined the main agencies linked with the Home Office and the Ministry of Justice, there remain three further points to consider briefly: two are statutory partnerships and the third a broad area of criminal justice concern – victims of crime.

The first of the statutory partnerships is what are generally referred to as *Community Safety Partnerships* (CSPs). Originally established by the Crime and Disorder Act 1998, there are around 300 of these multi-agency bodies in England and 22 in Wales. They are usually established at district or unitary authority level and are made up of representatives from police, probation, local authority, health, and fire and rescue authorities. They are now expected to work directly with Police and Crime Commissioners, both by exchanging reports and by attending PCC meetings. Their work is discussed further in Chapter 10.

The second set of statutory partnerships are referred to as *Multi-Agency Public Protection Arrangements* (MAPPA). Established by the Criminal Justice Act 2003, these bodies are designed to protect the public, including previous victims of crime, from serious harm by sexual and violent offenders. They operate in each of the 42 criminal justice areas in England and Wales and require the local criminal justice agencies and other bodies dealing with offenders to work together in partnership in dealing with these offenders. The MAPPA is not a statutory body, but simply a mechanism through which it is intended that other bodies will be able to discharge their responsibilities more effectively. The supervision of this work is carried out by the Strategic Management Board (SMB) in each area. It has a range of governance-related functions, including monitoring performance, ensuring anti-discriminatory practice, measuring compliance with the MAPPA Key Performance Indicators, and producing the annual MAPPA report. Each area also has two lay advisers, who are members of the public, intended to provide an independent perspective on the work of these groups.

Examples of non-statutory partnerships are considered in Chapter 12.

Victims

It is something of a cliché within criminology to observe that victims have traditionally been something of a forgotten party in formal criminal justice. A cliché it may be, but it reflects an important reality. Until relatively recently there was little official recognition given to victims of crime by the main criminal justice agencies, and within criminal justice processes (see Chapter 20). A number of significant changes have been introduced in the past decade or so, including the creation of the Witness Service, new protections for vulnerable and intimidated witnesses, and significant engagement with the idea – if not always the reality – of restorative justice.

The Domestic Violence, Crime and Victims Act 2004 sets out a number of responsibilities in relation to the victims of offenders sentenced to 12 months or more for a violent or sexual offence (together with the statutory Code of Practice for Victims of Crime – the 'Victims' Code'). Under these provisions, victims are entitled to be offered inter alia:

- an enhanced service if a victim of serious crime, a persistently targeted victim or a vulnerable or intimidated victim;

- a needs assessment to help work out what support is needed;

- information on what to expect from the Criminal Justice System;

- referral to organisations supporting victims of crime;

- information about police investigations including arrest, charge of a suspect and any bail conditions imposed;

- the opportunity to make a Victim Personal Statement (VPS) to explain the impact of the crime;

- information as to whether the suspect is to be prosecuted or not or given an out of court disposal; and

- the option to seek a review of the police or CPS's decision not to prosecute in accordance with the National Police Chiefs Council (NPCC) and CPS Victims' Right to Review schemes.

In 2012 the government appointed a Victims' Minister and also created the role of the Victims' Commissioner. The role of the latter is to promote the interests of victims and witnesses, encourage good practice in their treatment, and regularly review the Code of Practice for Victims, which sets out the services victims can expect to receive. This shift towards greater recognition of victims' needs and 'rights' is arguably the product of two separate, but sometimes overlapping, developments. On the one hand, it simply reflects the growing recognition of a victim perspective, something often absent in modern state-organised Criminal Justice Systems (Christie, 1977). Equally, however, it is also a reflection of the movement towards penal severity that has characterised the vast majority of liberal democracies in the last quarter century or more (Lacey, 2008).

Conclusion

Recent times have seen a number of important shifts in the organisation of government in relation to criminal justice, and in the governance of those institutions that make up the Criminal Justice System. In conclusion we might very briefly mention four. First, and radically so far as government itself is concerned, the past decade has seen the establishment of a Ministry of Justice separate from, and so far as criminal justice is concerned, far outstripping the government department traditionally charged with responsibility for this general field: the Home Office. The creation of the new Ministry has, to date at least, left relatively undisturbed the second general development: centralisation. The gradual accretion of power to the centre – there are, of course, countervailing movements – can be seen across the broad spectrum of the Criminal Justice System. The one-time local probation service is now a national service – though the increasing presence of the voluntary and private sectors complicates the picture – indeed is now only one part of a larger, overarching body: the National Offender Management Service. The police service, though still divided into an increasingly anachronistic 43 separate constabularies, has seen the consolidation of Home Office control in recent decades (though now somewhat offset by the introduction of PCCs). In addition, all areas of criminal justice – prisons, probation, policing and youth justice for example – have experienced much enhanced central scrutiny of performance.

Linked with this, the third general set of developments we might identify are those that are generally referred to under the rubric of 'managerialism', in which among the most prominent priorities in institutional governance have been concerns with economy, efficiency and effectiveness. Here, citizens are recast as 'customers', 'clients' and consumers of services, and the various professionals (probation officers and prison officers and governors for example) become providers of services, all too often with their professional autonomy and expertise diminished. Fourth, this managerialist mentality tends to be accompanied by faith in the 'market', and a desire to stimulate competition in the provision of services. It is here that some of the more dramatic changes have taken place. Initially, the growth of private sector involvement began with the privatisation of a small number of prisons. More recently and radically it has been followed by the privatisation of the forensic science service and the creation of a market for 'community rehabilitation companies', and the next frontier appears to be marketisation of ever-greater elements of policing. Can we expect further developments in this direction? If the previous Prime Minister's major speech on prisons in February 2016 is a guide, the answer would appear to be, at least in part, 'yes'. In his speech, David Cameron said:

> because we know that state monopolies are often very slow to change themselves, and because the involvement of the private and voluntary sectors in prisons has been one of the most important drivers of change in this system since the 1990s, we'll ensure there is a strong role for businesses and charities in the operation of these [new] reform prisons and the new prisons we will build ... And we'll adopt the same principle in youth justice too ...

> With freedom and autonomy must come accountability ... Any modern public service has to be able to demonstrate its value ... we will now develop meaningful metrics about prison performance ... And I can also announce that we will not only publish this data, we will develop new Prison League Tables ... Using this information, we can use other tools – like payment for performance – to drive further improvements. (Cameron, 2016)

The emerging trends in the governance of criminal justice are complex and predictions for the future must come heavily hedged with caveats. On the one hand, the general shift towards ever-greater central governmental control – or at least more or less direct governmental influence – over great swathes of the criminal justice and penal systems shows little sign of diminishing. On the other, the growing profile of the private sector, and the increasing marketisation of offender supervision and punishment, leaves much of criminal justice potentially subject to the desire for profit. Arguably, policing has been less affected by privatisation than both prisons and probation, and it seems likely that this may be the next frontier for such reforms.

Summary

There are now two government departments with primary responsibility for criminal justice matters: the Home Office and the Ministry of Justice. The former, the more long-standing of the two, now only has responsibility for policing, terrorism, drugs and alcohol and borders/immigration. The relatively newly created Ministry of Justice, by contrast, has responsibility for prisons, probation, courts and for youth justice. Processes of centralisation and managerialism have seen the replacement of localised probation services with a unified national service and, in turn, its incorporation along with the prison system into an overarching National Offender Management Service. The providers in this system, however, are now quite different from those of only a decade or two ago. Alongside private prisons, which are now well-established, the private and voluntary sectors now play a very significant role in the supervision of all but the most serious offenders serving community sentences. The future for criminal justice provision looks very much as if it will involve a mixed economy.

———————— **Discussion Questions** ————————

1. How would you characterise the recent changes made to the system for the governance of the police?

2. Give three examples – with a brief description of each – of centralising measures in criminal justice.

3. Why was the National Offender Management Service (NOMS) established?

4. What have been the main examples of privatisation in the Criminal Justice System?

————————— **Further Reading** ——————————————————————————

Gibson, B. (2008) *The New Home Office*. 2nd edn. Hook: Waterside Press.

Gibson, B. (2008) *The New Ministry of Justice*. 2nd edn. Hook: Waterside Press.

Though now slightly outdated, these two books give a basic outline of the two departments.

Shute, S. (2013) 'On the outside looking in: Reflections on the role of inspection in driving up quality in the criminal justice system', *Modern Law Review*, 76 (3): 494–528.

There is a good deal of useful information on the general public service website: www.gov.uk/browse/justice

Government department websites also contain a lot of information about the Criminal Justice System and process. Well worth a look are:

Home Office: www.gov.uk/government/organisations/home-office

Ministry of Justice: www.justice.gov.uk

——————— **References**—————————————————————————————————

Cameron, D. (2016) Speech on prison reform. Available at: www.gov.uk/government/speeches/prison-reform-prime-ministers-speech [accessed 16 February 2016].

Carter Review (2003) *Managing Offenders, Reducing Crime: A new approach*. London: The Stationery Office.

Christie, N. (1977) 'Conflicts as property', *British Journal of Criminology*, 17 (1): 1–15.

Genders, E. (2013) 'Prisons and privatisation: Policy, practice and evaluation', in A. Dockley and I. Loader (eds), *The Penal Landscape*. London: Routledge.

Gibson, B. (2008) *The New Ministry of Justice: An introduction*. Winchester: Waterside Press.

Harris, R. (1994) 'Continuity and change: Probation and politics in contemporary Britain', *International Journal of Offenders Therapy and Comparative Criminology*, 31 (1): 30–40.

Home Office (1979) *Committee of Inquiry into the United Kingdom Prison Services* (The May Inquiry), Cmnd 7673. London: HMSO.

Home Office (1982) *Home Office 1782–1982: To commemorate the bicentenary of the Home Office*. London: Home Office.

Home Office (1998) *Joining Forces to Protect the Public: Prisons–Probation. A consultation document*. London: Home Office.

House of Commons Justice Committee (2015) *Prisons: Planning and policies*, HC 309. London: The Stationery Office.

House of Commons Public Accounts Select Committee (2014) *The Criminal Justice System*, Session 2013–14, HC 1115. London: The Stationery Office.

Jones, T. and Newburn, T. (1997) *Policing After the Act*. London: Policy Studies Institute.

Lacey, N. (2008) *The Prisoners' Dilemma: The political economy of punishment in comparative perspective*. Cambridge: Cambridge University Press.

Mair, G. and Burke, L. (2012) *Redemption, Rehabilitation and Risk Management: A history of probation*. London: Routledge.

Ministry of Justice (2010) *Breaking the Cycle: Effective punishment, rehabilitation and sentencing of offenders*. London: Ministry of Justice

Ministry of Justice (2013) *Transforming Rehabilitation: A strategy for reform*. London: Ministry of Justice.

National Audit Office (2003) *The Operational Performance of PFI Prisons*. London: NAO.

National Audit Office (2015) *Inspection: A comparative study*. London: NAO.

Newsam, F. (1955) *The Home Office*. London: George Allen and Unwin.

Pearce, S., Murray, D. and Lane, M. (2015) *HMP Doncaster Payment by Results Pilot: Final process evaluation report*. London: Ministry of Justice.

Woolf, Lord Justice (1991) *Prison Disturbances April 1990: Report of an inquiry by the Rt. Hon. Lord Justice Woolf*, Cm 1456. London: HMSO.

Check out the Companion Website

Want to know more about this chapter? Review what you have been learning by visiting: **https://study.sagepub.com/harding**

- Practice with essay questions
- Test yourself with multiple-choice questions
- Listen to a series of podcasts featuring Neil of Northumbria Police and London's Metropolitan Police Service
- Watch videos selected from the SAGE Video collection

9   Researching Criminal Justice

Mike Hough

Introduction

This chapter is concerned with social scientific – or criminological – research into crime and justice. This sort of research is, of course, by no means the only source of systematic information about crime. The administrative statistics generated by the police and the justice system have provided insights into the topic for at least three centuries, and the contribution of the hard sciences is also important. However, this chapter is restricted to a discussion of criminological research grounded in sociology, psychology and the other human sciences. It has five further sections. I begin with an account of the – quite short – history of criminology and associated research. This is followed by a discussion of the inherently political nature of research into social control – which is, at heart, what criminology is about. The third section discusses the ethical and practical issues that criminological research presents, and the fourth examines the sensitive question whether we researchers actually achieve any significant impact on crime and justice. The final section speculates about the future of criminological research.

At the outset, I should say a little about my background. This isn't simply to 'present my credentials': the reader is also entitled to have some idea of the factors that have shaped my perspective and my prejudices about criminological research. I spent the first 20 years of my career working as a government researcher in the Home Office. I was a member of the small team that started the British Crime Survey (now the Crime Survey for England and Wales) and would have been labelled by many of my current academic colleagues as an 'administrative criminologist' at that time, if not now. (Administrative criminology is discussed below in the section on politics.) I left the Home Office in 1994 to set up a university-based policy research centre. This is now located at Birkbeck, University of London. The team has probably held around 250 research grants and contracts from research councils, government departments, the EU and charitable trusts, with a total value approaching £20 million. We like to think that we are genuinely independent of our funders, and hope that this can be seen in the quality and content of the very large number of publications that we have produced over the years[i]. But it would be disingenuous to suggest that doing policy research in a highly politicised – and economically precarious – environment is free of compromises, trade-offs and – occasionally – overt political interference. These ethical issues are familiar to anyone who aspires to 'speak truth to power'.

History

Before the Second World War there was very little empirical[ii] social research on crime and its control in Britain or elsewhere. The seeds of modern British criminology were sown in 1948, when the Criminal Justice Act 1948 empowered the Home Office to fund social research. It set up the Home Office Research Unit in 1957, and the Institute of Criminology at the University of Cambridge was established two years later. The Home Office Research Unit funded much of the Cambridge research programme, and also provided funding for a centre at the University of Oxford, initially the Penal Research Unit, later renamed the Centre for Criminological Research. Whether conducted within the Home Office or in universities, the focus of this early research was on ways of rehabilitating offenders and thus reducing recidivism, and researchers worked within the framework of liberal reform.

The Consensus Fractured: Positivists v. Radicals

The comfortable reformist consensus within the emerging discipline of criminology was broken in 1968, with the establishment of a series of National Deviancy

Conferences (NDC) by a breakaway group of politically radical criminologists[iii]. Reflecting the countercultural spirit of the time, and consistent with other trends such as the 'anti-psychiatry' movement[iv], the NDC group were critical of the a-theoretical empiricism of orthodox criminology, and the 'medical model' of rehabilitation, which was dubbed positivism. The emerging position of the NDC criminologists was later labelled by Jock Young (1986), a key NDC member, as 'left idealism' – with a theoretical orientation that was consistent with a Marxist perspective.

If the 1970s saw a sharp polarisation of criminology between critical criminologists and the 'positivist' old guard in Cambridge, Oxford and the Home Office, both sides began to adopt a deep pessimism from the mid 1970s into the 1980s about the scope for rehabilitating offenders, following an influential review by Martinson (1974) that was widely (and erroneously) believed to conclude that 'nothing works'. The Home Office Research Unit (relabelled in 1981 the Research and Planning Unit) advocated situational approaches to crime control, deploying physical and social design solutions to eliminate opportunities for crime. This was accompanied by what David Garland (1996) has called a process of 'responsibilisation' for crime control, placing greater obligations both on local authorities and on the individual citizen. At the same time, Jock Young and colleagues (e.g. Lea and Young, 1984) began to develop the 'left realist' approach to criminology. This stressed the extent to which crime had a disproportionate impact on the less affluent members of society; it had a very significant impact in encouraging politicians of the centre-left to take crime issues seriously, and to challenge the Conservatives' self-appointed role as the party of law and order. The Left Realists deployed some of the same empirical research methods as the Home Office, notably the use of crime surveys, but took care to brand themselves as distinctively different.

The basic thesis of Left Realism – that politicians of the left should take crime problems more seriously – was an important and long-overdue message. However, the messengers clearly needed to differentiate themselves from the work of the Home Office researchers, and they did this by attaching the label of 'administrative criminologists' to the government researchers and government-funded academics. Jock Young started using the term in the mid-1980s, at the same time that he and his colleagues were developing their 'Left Realist' position. He set out a definition of administrative criminology in his essay 'The failure of criminology' (Young, 1986), contrasting it with 'positivism and the social democratic ways of reforming crime' (p. 9). Administrative criminology, as he defined it, with its focus on situational measures, involved an antagonism to the idea that social circumstances cause crime, or at least a lack of interest in the social causes of crime, on the grounds that these were not readily amenable to political intervention. He identified J.Q. Wilson as the key US theorist (cf. Wilson, 1975), and Ron Clarke (cf. Clarke and Mayhew, 1980) in the Home Office as the key UK figure. However, Young's label of administrative criminologist has gradually lost this rather specific meaning, and has come to refer to anyone who does policy research for or within government – even though the majority of these now have little sympathy for the supposed Wilson/ Clarke position that the social causes of crime are irrelevant to criminal policy. The label has acquired other connotations, most of them unflattering: unimaginative, a-theoretical, politically suborned and corrupted by the pressures of grantsmanship (see Hough, 2014, for a fuller discussion).

Consensus Re-emerging

The 1990s saw rehabilitative aspirations themselves rehabilitated, with new and more sophisticated research demonstrating that some approaches, such as cognitive behavioural treatment (CBT)[v], could be effective both in prisons and probation settings. Local authorities were also given a statutory responsibility to set up crime-reduction partnerships. A greater pragmatism emerged both in criminal policy and in criminological research, with the sharp divisions between critical criminologists and reformists becoming blurred. And of course the most significant issue on the criminological landscape from the mid 1990s until the present day is that levels of crime began to fall sharply. Leaving aside emerging patterns of cybercrime, both property crimes (such as burglary and car crime) and violent crime have been in rapid decline[vi]. It is doubtful that new forms of cybercrime have fully offset this fall, which according to the Crime Survey for England and Wales, is from 19 million crimes in 1995 to around 7 million in 2015 (ONS, 2015). The debate over the counting of crime is discussed further in Chapter 3.

The Politics of Criminological Research

Criminology has as its focus forms of social harm that are – or should be – addressed by the institutions of justice. Even if the day-to-day operation of the judicial and policing systems are protected from direct political control, both the definition of crime and the structure and funding of the Criminal Justice System fall within the remit of politicians. The academic study of the system inherently has political dimensions to it. Some criminologists are avowedly a-political and are interested simply in describing and explaining how the system works. Even so, their work – if perceptive and robust – will certainly carry implications for policy. My personal view is that it is virtually impossible to research crime and justice without wishing to see some improvements resulting from the effort. What counts as an improvement, and whether the research was its cause, is something to which I shall return in the section on impact.

Much criminological research is funded by bodies independent of universities, as is the majority of empirical research. Significant funders of criminological research in universities are:

- the government research councils (such as the Economic and Social Research Council (ESRC), and the Arts and Humanities Research Council);
- government departments, mainly the Home Office and Ministry of Justice;

- other public bodies such as the Youth Justice Board, the College of Policing, the Sentencing Council and the government inspectorates;

- police forces and other criminal justice agencies and services;

- the European Commission;

- charitable foundations, such as the Nuffield Foundation, the Leverhulme Trust and the Joseph Rowntree Foundation.

Political Imperatives

All of these funders want *something* from their research investment. At best, they want the research to help create new insights about a policy area, or more instrumentally to solve specific policy problems by bringing new knowledge to bear on them. This motivation characterises the charitable trusts in particular, though they will usually have decided in advance to focus only on a specified set of issues. The same is generally true of the research councils, although these face increasing pressures to demonstrate the social utility of their investments, and will press researchers hard to ensure that their research is of value to policy debate and achieves an impact.

Closer to government, other motivations may also be at play, besides the straightforward ones of generating better understanding and improving policy or practice. Research can be used to support a pre-existing policy, or to demonstrate a commitment to action, or to buy time before anything actually needs to be done (cf. Nutley et al., 2007; Tarling, 2011). One would hope that politicians and their civil servants rarely commission research with a concern only for such short-term tactical considerations. Nevertheless research can end up serving these functions, even if there is rarely an audit trail to this effect. I can identify only one significant such documented example, when a Home Office minute from 1981 recorded the then Home Secretary's decision to go ahead with the British Crime Survey:

> The Home Secretary said that he was inclined to think the project should go ahead, despite the reservations that had been expressed (some of which he shared) since it would be desirable for the Home Office to show its willingness to contribute to the public debate about crime which would inevitably follow the recent urban disorders. (Hough and Maxfield, 2007: 15)

In hindsight, it is striking that what turned out to be a really significant criminological enterprise was approved on grounds (associated with the 1981 Brixton and Bristol riots) that bore no relation to the case we had made for the survey, focusing on the value of more accurate measurement of crime.

More often, political tactics of this sort emerge not when research is commissioned but at the point of publication. Findings are routinely incorporated into government departments' narratives of their activities, justifying courses of action, demonstrating openness of mind and commitment to evidence, buying a bit of time, and so on.

However, results sometimes challenge existing policy or practice and these are inevitably embarrassing to some degree, and especially so when the research has been commissioned by the government itself. In such circumstances the most desirable response – assuming that the research is genuinely reliable – is to acknowledge the findings and to announce plans to address them. But what often happens is that the methodological quality of the research is called into question, or the interpretation of results is challenged, or publication is delayed or reduced in visibility. The rationale for these tactics is rarely made explicit, and thus the underlying motivation may be opaque. I have only been told on one occasion that the content of a report of mine was simply too politically embarrassing – and too personally costly for the civil servants involved – to submit to the Home Secretary for publication. (We agreed to wait until the expected change in government occurred, and it was eventually published in a low-key way (Hough, 1998). I found this less frustrating than the delaying tactics on other projects that were hidden by a 'fig-leaf' explanation about the need for further or fuller analysis.)

For the most part, contract researchers and their 'minders' in government departments conduct a war of attrition when research findings are unpalatable, involving concessions and trade-offs on both sides until a mutually acceptable draft can be agreed. Clearly, for researchers who value their integrity there must be 'lines in the sand' that must not be crossed. On the other hand, quite a lot of concessions can be made before the overall edge of a critical report is blunted. If one really wants to achieve some influence over decisions made by people in a position of power, some things have to be said delicately, unabrasively and obliquely. Compromise is not always the same thing as *being compromised*.

I do not wish to sound overly cynical. Much of the contract research I have done for government departments or their satellite bodies has been a process of genuine co-production of knowledge, with open-minded and enthusiastic officials funding – and facilitating – projects because they really want to find things out, and to put this knowledge to good use.

Few other funders are quite so interventionist at the point of publication, although some of the best charitable trusts take great care to support the proper dissemination of research results – and in my experience, without any attempt to influence the content or tone of results[vii]. The same is usually true of research funded by the UK research councils and the European Commission, although the latter have sometimes proved remarkably uninvolved. There is considerable – and growing – enthusiasm to see the research exploited, without any desire to 'spin' the findings in any particular way. However, the scale of the activities of these funding bodies means that they do not generally get engaged in the process of transferring research into policy and practice in specific projects. This is left to the researchers themselves – who sometimes do this well, and sometimes are concerned only to ensure that the project has respectable academic outputs – as they were required to do in the past.

Evidence-based Policy

A potentially important development in policy formation, both within government departments and within criminal justice agencies is an explicit commitment to 'evidence-based policy' (EBP). The government set up in 2013 a network of 'What Works' centres, currently nine in number[viii], which are repositories of research evidence designed for use by practitioners. The prototype, and the best-known centre, is the National Institute for Health and Care Excellence (NICE), which maintains a very extensive database on the relative effectiveness of different treatments for a wide range of medical conditions. It is very widely used by the medical profession.

In 2013 the College of Policing, in partnership with the ESRC, established the What Works Centre for Crime Reduction (WWCCR), designed to serve the same function for police and other practitioners in the Criminal Justice System as NICE does for doctors. At the time of writing, the WWCCR is still at an early stage of development and it is fair to say that it has yet to become culturally embedded in the police service. However, if government retains its commitment to the professionalisation of the police, and to genuinely underpin their work with research evidence, this has considerable implications for the nature and volume of criminological research in universities.

In parallel with these developments, the government's system of distributing research funds to universities, the Research Excellence Framework, now rewards those university departments that can demonstrate that their research has a positive impact on the 'real world', creating an institutional incentive to contribute to the process of making policy evidence-based. Sceptics tend to suggest that the attachment to evidence-based policy is just a passing fad in the Westminster policy village, and one that risks promoting simplistic notions about crime reduction. Optimists see the development as a real game-changer. Whatever the case, it is clear that it will take time and considerable investment before the WWCCR develops anything like the capacity of NICE.

Practical and Ethical Issues

As mentioned above, the majority of empirical research projects require funding, because it is time-consuming, and thus expensive, to collect data. Once funding has been secured, there are several practical and ethical issues that need to be dealt with.

Practical Issues

Empirical criminological research usually requires access to at least one of three groups: people working in criminal justice agencies (or their datasets); people who have broken the law; and victims of crime. Getting access to criminal justice agency staff and their data can take time and effort, because researchers necessarily make demands on staff, who want to make sure that the investment of their time is worthwhile. Increasingly, the police, the prisons, the probation service and the courts have centralised 'gate-keeping' systems to which researchers must apply. These systems tend to be cautious and conservative, and without some sort of enthusiastic sponsorship within or outside the agency, ideally at senior level, the process may be extended, and the outcome uncertain. These gatekeeping systems also cover access to offenders who are under criminal justice supervision, such as prisoners who are potential candidates for interview; and similar controls may apply to the administrative data that relate to these offenders. In the past, local contacts could provide an alternative route to access, as prison governors or police superintendents or probation managers often had sufficient autonomy to permit local access to their workforce or clientele without reference to the central gate-keepers. However, the role of the latter is becoming increasingly important, and there is increasing emphasis on the costs of providing access.

A current 'unknown' in the research landscape is whether the new 'community rehabilitation companies', which have taken over some of the roles of the proba-tion service, will welcome research and encourage access to their staff and the people they supervise. They may turn out to be eager for research – but equally they may be unprepared for the demands and risks (both reputational and finan-cial) that research can present to their organisations. It is fair to say that private prisons now have a respectable history of allowing researchers access.

Research that involves interviews with, or observation of, people involved in crime can be fascinating and rewarding but, again, there are issues of access (even if the research has official support). People serving prison sentences may well be keen to take part in a research project, not least because it may relieve the boredom of prison life. Other people who have been in trouble with the law may be less moti-vated: giving an interview to a researcher may not be a priority, or they may feel concerned about confidentiality, or embarrassed or uncomfortable about reliving their experiences of crime and justice. We regularly offer these people incentive payments to take part in research – usually around £20, but sometimes more, if the demands on their time are great – though officials in criminal agencies are now very rarely prepared to permit such payments. Sometimes we have made contribu-tions not to individuals but to the running costs of the programme from which we recruited them – especially when interviewing young offenders.

Similar considerations may also apply when trying to engage with people who have been the victims of crime – although when approached with tact and cour-tesy, they are often keen to 'have their say'. Whilst we routinely offer payments to people serving community penalties or those who have left prison, in the case of victims we sometimes offer to make a donation to a charity of their choice, instead. Mounting sample surveys of the general public does not generally require incentives of this sort. For example, the Crime Survey for England and Wales still manages to secure agreement from three-quarters of the randomly selected sam-ple, even though interviews can last between 45 minutes and well over an hour. Increasingly, however, as people are bombarded with real or fake survey requests, 'survey fatigue' is becoming a significant problem, and new solutions to provide incentives for people to take part are becoming increasingly necessary. We have used not only cash payments in several surveys, but also incentives such as gift vouchers, lottery tickets and payments to charity.

Fieldwork can also be challenging simply because crime is not restricted to normal office hours, and key parts of the justice system, such as the police, face the heaviest demands on their time in the evenings and at weekends. If researchers want to see crime and justice in action, they often have to work unsocial hours.

Ethical Issues

The ethical issues that regularly surface in criminological research relate to securing *informed consent* and observing whatever pledges of *anonymity and confidentiality* have been made to respondents. Where research participants are members of the general public, this is rarely problematic, although it is important that researchers or interviewers do not browbeat potential respondents into participation, and even more important that anything disclosed in confidence is respected – with some qualifications, discussed below.

Ethical issues can become trickier when respondents are vulnerable in various ways, and may also disclose information that relates to serious crimes. When researching drug-dependent offenders, for example, we often make incentive payments, and we are sometimes fairly sure that the (untaxed) payment goes to the next illicit drug purchase. The value of the resultant research findings has to be traded against the fact that in a minor way we have supported an illegal drug habit and turned a blind eye to the risks of tax evasion – whilst arguably giving the local community some minor respite from acquisitive offending or sex work that would otherwise have happened. Our view – and the consensus amongst criminological academics – is that this is ethically acceptable, although government departments are increasingly refusing to support research that involves cash payments to offenders. Some researchers do, however, tend to style such payments as a contribution to cover incidental expenses – a fig leaf that might at least cover the indecency of tax evasion.

The most sensitive – and far more challenging – ethical issues that we have faced relate to disclosure of information about serious crimes. Respondents from time to time tell us things about their own undetected offending, or give us information that potentially identifies someone who has committed a serious crime. During one interview a sex worker revealed to the researcher that she was fearful that her partner would kill her on his release from prison. In the course of the interview, she also disclosed that, as a child, one of her parents made her regularly watch explicit pornography. All of these disclosures were given under conditions of confidentiality. By chance the researcher saw a poster shortly afterwards in a police station requesting information about the murder of the respondent, and quite reasonably assumed that the partner might have been responsible. After consultation with our university ethics committee and academics at the British Society of Criminology we decided to reveal her fears about her partner to the police, but to withhold the other compromising information about her family. When we told the police they (understandably) requested a full transcript of the interview, we explained that if the respondent was still alive she would certainly not have wanted the police to see some of the details in the transcript. The officers agreed and decided that it would be better for everyone if they came and read and took notes of the relevant parts of the transcript rather than read the whole document or took copies of it. As it happens, a client, rather than the partner, turned out to have killed the victim. However, this episode illustrates the tangled nature of some real-life ethical issues, which had to be solved not by reference to codes of conduct but from first principles. That particular case turned on the extent to which obligations of confidentiality survive beyond the grave. More often, the risk is that respondents will reveal information about their own serious offending, and we take care at the start of interviews to explain to respondents that our commitment to confidentiality is not absolute, and that if very serious offending is revealed we are obliged (both ethically and by law) to pass on the information.

One further set of ethical issues relates to the nature of the policies that research may be designed to support. Around the turn of the millennium we did a great deal of research into the impact of 'coerced treatment' for drug-dependent offenders (see for example Hough, 1996, 2001, 2002; Hough et al., 2003a). Our evaluations suggested that arrest referral schemes and other arrangements for encouraging this group to seek treatment were effective in reducing drug problems and offending, and we engaged not only in researching these programmes but also in advocacy of them. Over time, however, the Home Office introduced legislation that (I felt) crossed a line between deploying *reasonable coercion* into treatment and requiring *mandatory treatment*. The ethical problems in doing such research were largely solved for us when our criticisms of the new policies ended the supply of relevant research contracts for my centre.

Similar criticisms are sometimes made of our research that shows that if the police treat people according to the principles of 'procedural justice' they are more likely to comply with the law and cooperate with the authorities (e.g. Hough et al., 2013). In our view there is not much merit any more in the argument that treating people with decency and respect serves as an 'ideological cloak' that masks the real functions of the police in furthering the interests of the powerful – but some radical criminologists would disagree[ix]. The wider point here is that applied policy research inevitably has an ethical dimension to it – if one accepts that politics and ethics are unavoidably intertwined. An ethically responsible researcher needs to attend to the policy uses to which their research is put.

Impact – Making a Difference?

It is perennially hard for criminological researchers to know when their work has really made a difference. It is sometimes straightforward to point to publication of research at Time 1, followed by a policy change at Time 2 – a plausible amount of time later, neither much too soon or much too late. But even in such cases, establishing the causal chain can be problematic. Did the researcher catch the crest of the wave of fashion at just the right time? Did politicians and their advisors reach the same conclusions as the research, drawing on totally separate evidence? Did they ever actually read the research, or did their advisors and others in high places?

I can point to examples of our own work which – despite great expenditure and much publicity and attempts to link into policy – achieved at best a marginal impact. Our study, *Policing for London* (FitzGerald et al., 2002), fell into this category. Senior officers in the Metropolitan Police certainly drew on the research to some extent to justify (then) innovative policies of neighbourhood policing; and the study was one of the earliest to highlight the potential perverse effects of numerical targets. However, we failed to capture their imaginations, or to secure any real engagement from other police leaders or from Home Office politicians, and the report had less traction – and fewer citations – than we thought it deserved. On the other hand, our report on the growth in the prison population (Hough et al., 2003b) and our research into the unfairnesses of indeterminate prison sentences (Jacobson and Hough, 2010) undoubtedly hit home, with the senior judiciary and the Secretary of State for Justice requesting pre-publication copies. It is usually hard to provide an evidenced 'audit trail' of impact well after the event. One is over-reliant on the – sometimes faulty – recollections of conversations with government ministers, their advisors, senior judges and managers within the justice system. This is the stuff of anecdote, of course, and questionably reliable.

This may change, of course, with the requirement for university researchers to demonstrate 'impact'. When I submitted my work on procedural justice as a 'case study' on policy impact for HEFCE's 2013 Research Excellence Framework, to my considerable embarrassment an administrator in my department spent a considerable time assembling statements from, for example, HM Inspectorate of Constabulary, the College of Policing and the National Audit Office to support my claims about impact. Those who were approached responded positively, perhaps because of the novelty of the request – but one wonders what will happen when droves of academics are chasing their policy contacts for testimonials.

Too little is known within academic criminology about the 'craft' of policy research, and it is discussed (and written about) too little. Most academic criminologists are positioned institutionally some distance both from local criminal justice managers and from the machinery of central government. As a consequence they don't understand what is involved in making an impact. To achieve some leverage on policy as a 'public criminologist' (Loader and Sparks, 2010), one requires various skills that are only loosely linked to academic qualities.

Of course, there is a large element of luck and happenstance in determining when research achieves an impact, and when it sinks like a stone. Having something coherent and interesting to say is, of course, a precondition – and one that despite our best efforts our research sometimes fails to provide. To be able to say it with authority is also important. Where good and potentially useful studies have failed to secure traction, this is sometimes simply because the researchers do not have the credibility they need with key audiences[x]. This implies that policy researchers do not only have to do high-quality work, but also have to build networks among or around those who take policy decisions, to establish their credentials as people worth listening to. Timing is a critical factor[xi] and researchers often cannot predict whether their publications will become available at a critical moment in the policy cycle. Scale can be important, if only because large-scale studies with big budgets tend to be taken more seriously than small-scale ones, other things being equal. Having non-academic allies – or, at least, sympathetic listeners – is critically important, whether these are politicians and their advisers, civil servants, non-government organisations, criminal justice agencies, non-departmental public bodies or journalists. What is undeniably the case – and what is very obvious to anyone who has engaged with policy for any length of time – is that criminologists are indeed minor players with small voices in the policy arena, and that their research will achieve little if they fail to foster, in some way or other, forms of reach into the political process.

The Future

Does criminology face a healthy future? Criminologists have a poor track record as futurologists. We completely failed in the 1980s and early 1990s to anticipate the very large falls in conventional crime that began in the UK in 1995, and didn't do very well in predicting the rise of cybercrime. My predictions for the future of criminological research are, accordingly, heavily hedged.

A starting point is to ask what criminology has achieved in the last 40 or so years. The answer has to be, 'A lot'. We are hugely better informed about crime measurement and crime trends than we were in the 1970s, and we understand some of the factors that drive these trends. We also have a much better idea of what sorts of rehabilitative programmes help people stop breaking the law, and what styles of policing help to promote the rule of law. We are much better informed about trends and practices in other countries, which provides a better perspective than previously. The institutions of justice are also more open to research scrutiny than they were – notwithstanding ongoing problems in getting access to them – and this has helped the process of extending accountability and freedom from corruption and misconduct. An optimist would see this trajectory continuing, as there is surely plenty of headroom for improvement.

There are several other reasons for anticipating a continued growth in criminological research. Within central government, there is cross-party commitment to 'evidence-based policy' and there are starting to be institutional arrangements across a range of social policy areas to make sure that this becomes a reality – with nine 'What Works' centres live or in the process of development. There is also a well-established policy trend for the professionalisation of the criminal justice workforce, and the police in particular, which is unlikely to be challenged by a government of a different hue. Professions are – by definition – hungry for firm evidence about what constitutes best practice, and this should spur on the demand for criminological research. And as we have discussed, the system for funding university research, the Research Excellence Framework, now rewards institutions that conduct research which has practical 'real world' pay-offs.

There are countervailing trends, of course. At the time of writing, the era of austerity is far from over, and the government of the day shows a resolute commitment to 'small state' policies – which probably include containing expenditure on government research, whether funded directly, or through the university funding mechanisms. It also seems possible that the increasing trend towards privatising parts of the Criminal Justice System may work to reduce demand for, and funding of, research conducted for the public good. Organisations that are competing against each other may be reluctant to 'open their books' to independent researchers – although they may well do their own private research – and where their contracts include forms of payment by results in reducing crime, independent published research may be seen as a significant threat.

A further threat to research is that tendency in late-modernity (e.g. Giddens, 1998) for experts – including academic experts – to lose their privileged voice, and for politicians to attach more weight to public opinion than to 'self-styled experts'. And it is fairly clear that the public's anxieties about crime have been substantially calmed over the last two decades, pushing 'law and order' down the political agenda – even if particular forms of crime, such as historical and current child sexual abuse have received a great deal of media attention. Funding research into issues that are not of public concern may look like poor politics – though properly evidenced justice reform is easier to achieve in times when the public debate is no longer over-heated.

The way in which these opposing trends play out probably depends on whether the period of relative stability of the last two decades, with falling crime and lower levels of public disorder[xii], turn out to be the start of a long-run trend or not. The optimistic view is that social problems such as crime will become increasingly well-managed through technocratic processes. A more pessimistic view might see the last 20 years as a brief respite before a perfect storm of social instability triggered by factors such as the global economic downturn, mass migration triggered by armed conflict and the breakdown of the rule of law in failing states, and food shortages caused by global warming. A sensible criminologist might prefer the first scenario, even if the second promises to be better for business.

Summary

Criminological research in the UK has little more than a post-war history. Its main origins can be found in the University of Cambridge, the Home Office Research Unit and the University of Oxford, but there has been a very rapid expansion from the 1970s onwards. Criminological research was initially based firmly in this tradition, with a particular focus on the rehabilitation of offenders. The 1970s saw the emergence of a significant body of more critical research, which saw the state and its machinery of social control as equally or more problematic than the offenders who passed through the system. The considerable polarisation between 'establishment' criminology and radical criminology has lessened over time.

Criminological research is inherently political, because the object of study is the relationship between state institutions and citizens. Elected politicians and those

(Continued)

(Continued)

who manage the Criminal Justice System are the primary audiences for much criminological research. Given that these people are often also the commissioners of criminological research, there is an inherent risk that they may use (or abuse) their position as funders to ensure that findings create no political embarrassment.

Some funders fully embrace the value of independent research, and of using researchers who are committed to 'speaking truth to power', and publishing their findings without fear or favour. Others have a less impressive track record. Many research reports in our field take a long time to see the light of day, and often research is used for reasons other than simply to support policy or improve practice – for example simply to demonstrate that *something* is being done, or to buy time. A promising development is the establishment by the government of a network of What Works centres that serve as evidence warehouses for a range of social policy areas, including law and order. These may turn out to play a significant role in stimulating appetites for high-quality policy research.

Criminological research often faces a range of practical problems, in penetrating organisations that do not always welcome the spotlight of research, and in reaching people who are involved in illegal or otherwise risky behaviour. These are by no means insuperable, however. Behind these practical problems there are sometimes ethical problems to be found, such as whether to respect or break confidences about involvement in serious crime.

Once research has been completed, and reports or papers written, getting policy or practice to heed the results is itself a skill, and one that many academics do too little to foster. Good research doesn't speak for itself. Achieving an impact is a process of persuasion, where networks have to be built with politicians, their advisors and officials, senior people within the institutions of criminal justice and influential NGOs. One needs to establish credibility with the right people, and deliver the message in the right language and style, at the right time – all the while competing with other sorts of people – electors, pressure groups, industrial interest groups and so on – who are equally keen to secure the ear of the powerful.

The future of criminological research is hard to predict. To thrive, it certainly needs to earn its keep in the eyes of policy, whether through helping to solve specific problems, or by providing a broader and richer perspective on ways of securing and maintaining social order.

Box 9.1

A Case Study in Securing Policy Impact

This case describes research that the author and colleagues in 12 other institutions conducted into public trust in the police and courts across Europe. The research aimed to persuade policy makers that fairness is not simply a desirable feature of justice systems, but a precondition for effective justice; that institutional legitimacy is key to justice policy. It has influenced the operational strategies of the Metropolitan Police; and been disseminated by invitation to senior staff from the Cabinet Office, Home Office, Ministry of Justice (MoJ) and Office of National Statistics (ONS). It has also featured in the broadcast media and the national press.

The underpinning research

In 2009 a group of researchers collaborating an on EU project, EUROJUSTIS, had developed a set of survey items to measure trust in justice. Key members of the group at LSE, Oxford University and the Institute for Criminal Policy Research bid successfully to design a question-naire module within the fifth European Social Survey (ESS), to test various hypotheses relating to 'procedural justice theory'. (Overall funding for the ESS, from the EU and national research councils, includes provision for intermittent modules designed by academics who compete for space on the questionnaire. Our developmental work and analysis were part-funded by two EU grants.) Fieldwork was undertaken late 2010 and results were analysed by ICPR, LSE and Oxford from Autumn 2011 onwards.

This research has, more than any other criminological project, shifted police and judicial legitimacy to the centre of criminal policy preoccupations in the UK. Previously, there was no systematic UK – or indeed European – test of procedural justice theory, and it was unclear to what extent US evidence was applicable across the Atlantic. This research has both developed and extended procedural justice theory, and demonstrated that its basic ideas are applicable across Europe.

The research systematically explored concepts of public trust in justice, public perceptions of the legitimacy of the police and the courts, and public compliance and cooperation with the law. Analysis of the results led to benchmarking of countries on dimensions of trust in justice and perceived legitimacy. These 'league tables' show the UK falling into the middle quartiles on most measures: better than most ex-communist countries, but worse than Nordic countries and other European neighbours.

The significance of this research lies in its exploration of the relationships between different forms of trust, public perceptions of legitimacy and compliance and cooperation. For example, trust in police fairness is a better predictor of police legitimacy than trust in police competence. This has important implications for police forces in how they should manage their relations with those they police: the police can easily squander their legitimacy by high-handed, unfair or disrespectful treatment.

The research evidences the conclusion that if justice systems treat people fairly, legally and respectfully, they build their legitimacy, and secure compliance and cooperation.

Key UK consumers of this research have been:

- senior police, including the College of Policing;
- policy officials and researchers in government spending departments and the Cabinet Office;
- the National Audit Office;
- Her Majesty's Inspectorate of Constabulary; and
- various politicians.

———— **Discussion Questions** ————

1. Should academic criminologists always aim to be policy-relevant?

2. Who, if anyone, should hold academic criminologists to account for the quality of their advice to policy and practice?

3. Is it ethical to pay interviewees to talk about the crimes they have committed?

4. Is it ethical to break the confidentiality of a research interview when the respondent admits to a previously undetected and serious crime?

5. Should funders of research make sure that the work they commission is always published?

6. Should government-funded research always be made publicly available?

7. Will the government-sponsored What Works Centre for Crime Reduction make policy more disciplined in attending to proper evidence?

———— **Notes** ————

i. Throughout this chapter, the 'we' who are often mentioned are my colleagues and myself in the various incarnations of my research centre.

ii. Empirical research involves the collection and analysis of observable phenomena (or *data*) to develop theories. Hypothesis-testing using quantitative or qualitative data is a concept that is central to empirical research.

iii. The key people, all of whom went on to become very visible criminologists, were Kit Carson, Stan Cohen, David Downes, Mary McIntosh, Paul Rock, Ian Taylor and Jock Young.

iv. Key 'anti-psychiatrists' were Thomas Szasz, David Cooper and Ronald Laing.

v. See e.g. www.campbellcollaboration.org/lib/project/29/

vi. The reasons for the fall (and the scale of the fall) are contested, but reductions in opportunities for crime, better policing and surveillance, falls in the value of stolen property and even such things as elimination of leaded petrol have all been put forward as reasons.

vii. On one occasion, the joint-funder employed a PR company to stage-manage the launch of the project report (FitzGerald et al., 2002).

viii. See www.gov.uk/guidance/what-works-network (accessed 27 January 2016)

ix. One could perhaps make a more persuasive case that this was true in nineteenth- and early twentieth-century policing, when the Marxist analysis of false consciousness amongst the proletariat was more compelling, but it would be a brave person who argued that the police should not try to do their work in line with principles of procedural justice.

x. I would place our study *Policing for London* in this category.

xi. For example, our study of Imprisonment for Public Protection (Jacobson and Hough, 2010) was about to be published when the new Conservative administration came to power, and the then Secretary of State for Justice wanted to do something about this highly problematic sentence.

xii. Albeit with hiccups, notably the riots of 2011.

Further Reading

The following are all good edited volumes on many aspects of criminological research, with a wide range of chapters on methods, ethics, and politics of research.

Gadd, D., Karstedt, S. and Messner, S. (2012) *Sage Handbook of Criminological Research Methods*. London: Sage Publications.

Hoyle, C. and Bosworth, M. (2011) *What is Criminology?* Oxford: Oxford University Press.

King, R. and Wincup, E. (2007) *Doing Research on Crime and Justice*. Oxford: Oxford University Press.

Zedner, L and Ashworth, A. (eds) (2003) *The Criminological Foundations of Penal Policy: Essays in honour of Roger Hood*. Oxford: Oxford University Press.

References

Clarke, R.V.G and Mayhew, P.M. (eds) (1980) *Designing Out Crime*. London: HMSO.

FitzGerald, M., Hough, M., Joseph, I. and Qureshi, T. (2002) *Policing for London*. Cullompton: Willan Publishing.

Garland, D. (1996) 'The limits of the sovereign state: Strategies of crime control in contemporary society', *British Journal of Criminology*, 36 (4): 445–71.

Giddens, A. (1998) *The Third Way: The renewal of social democracy*. Cambridge: Polity Press.

Hough, M. (1996) *Problem Drug Use and Criminal Justice: A review of the literature*. Drugs Prevention Initiative paper No. 15. London: Home Office Central Drugs Prevention Unit.

Hough, M. (1998) *Attitudes to Punishment: Findings from the 1992 British Crime Survey*. Social Science Research Paper No 7. London: South Bank University.

Hough, M. (2001) 'Balancing public health and criminal justice interventions', *International Journal of Drug Policy*, 12: 429–33.

Hough, M. (2002) 'Drug user treatment within a criminal justice context', *Substance Use and Misuse*, 37 (8–10): 985–96.

Hough, M. (2014) 'Confessions of a recovering "administrative criminologist": Jock Young, quantitative research and policy research', *Crime Media Culture*, 10 (3): 21526.

Hough, M. and Maxfield, M. (eds) (2007) *Surveying Crime in the 21st Century*. Cullompton: Willan Publishing.

Hough, M., Clancy, A., Turnbull, P.J. and McSweeney, T. (2003a) *The Impact of Drug Treatment and Testing Orders on Offending: Two-year reconviction results*. Findings 184. London: Home Office.

Hough, M., Jacobson, J. and Millie, A. (2003b) *The Decision to Imprison: Sentencing and the prison population*. London: Prison Reform Trust.

Hough, M., Jackson, J. and Bradford, B. (2013) 'Trust in justice and the legitimacy of legal authorities: Topline findings from a European comparative study', in S. Body-Gendrot, M. Hough, R. Levy, K. Kerezsi and S. Snacken (eds), *European Handbook of Criminology*. London: Routledge.

Jacobson, J. and Hough, M. (2010) *Unjust Deserts: Imprisonment for public protection*. London: Prison Reform Trust.

Lea, J. and Young, J. (1984) *What is to be Done About Law and Order?* London: Penguin.

Loader, I. and Sparks, R. (2010) *Public Criminology?* London: Routledge.

Martinson, R. (1974) 'What works? Questions and answers about prison reform', *The Public Interest*, Spring: 22–54.

Nutley, S., Walter, I. and Davies, H.T.O. (2007) *Using Evidence: How research can inform public services*. Bristol: The Policy Press.

ONS (Office of National Statistics) (2015) *Crime in England and Wales, Year Ending June 2015*. Available at: www.ons.gov.uk/ons/rel/crime-stats/crime-statistics/year-ending-june-2015/stb-crime-ye-june-2015.html [accessed 14 January 2016].

Tarling, R. (2011) 'Relations between government researchers and academics', *The Howard Journal*, 50 (3): 307–13.

Wilson, J.Q. (1975) *Thinking About Crime*. New York: Basic Books.

Young, J. (1986) 'The failure of criminology: The need for a radical realism', in R. Matthews and J. Young (eds), *Confronting Crime*. London: Sage Publications.

Check out the Companion Website

Want to know more about this chapter? Review what you have been learning by visiting: **https://study.sagepub.com/harding**

- Practice with essay questions
- Test yourself with multiple-choice questions
- Listen to a series of podcasts featuring Neil of Northumbria Police and London's Metropolitan Police Service
- Watch videos selected from the SAGE Video collection

Part Two

The Criminal Justice Process

Jamie Harding, Pamela Davies, George Mair

As was noted in Chapter 1, there are different opinions among criminologists as to whether we can reasonably discuss a 'Criminal Justice System'. While some of our contributors have opted to use this term, we (the editors) question its helpfulness. The key reason is that agencies that are concerned with one or more aspects of criminal justice, whether or not this is their main function, do not necessarily work together in a harmonious manner to achieve common objectives. There are some examples of close working: for example, Chapter 13 describes how an initially difficult relationship between the police and the Crown Prosecution Service became much more harmonious with time. In contrast, Chapter 17 notes that one of the aims of the Transforming Rehabilitation programme is to ensure more continuity of services before and after an offender leaves prison: this is the latest of a long history of initiatives in this area, none of which have achieved their aim of creating 'seamless' services (Harding and Harding, 2006).

Indeed, as Chapter 12 demonstrates, criminal justice agencies often appear to form the most effective relationships with agencies whose main concerns lie outside criminal justice. Similarly, Chapter 18 discusses Youth Offending Teams bringing together agencies such as probation and the police with those that are not primarily concerned with offending, such as mental health services and housing. While there can be many positive effects of the blurring of boundaries between those agencies that do and do not work mainly in the area of criminal justice, one consequence can be fragmentation: Chapter 15 notes the many different agencies that can be involved in administering community punishment to just one offender – agencies with substantially different objectives, as is inevitable when some form part of the public sector, some are commercial and some from the third sector. Partial privatisations have occurred across a number of areas of criminal justice in the interests of greater efficiency, meaning that objectives of profit and public service often sit together in an uneasy and poorly defined relationship.

So if this part of the book does not discuss a unified system, what is it about? Although the title of this section describes it as a process, it could also be characterised as a set of processes that may or may not be linked to each other. For offenders, these processes typically begin with arrest by the police (see Chapter 11) and may then proceed through any number of the stages discussed in subsequent chapters: prosecution, conviction and punishment, and (in rare cases) the quashing of a conviction by the Court of Appeal (Criminal Division) (Chapter 19). Some processes, e.g. prosecution (Chapter 13) and the work of the courts (Chapter 14) are clearly very closely linked. However, services for young offenders (Chapter 18) take the offender down a distinct (if sometimes similar) pattern to that of adult offenders, and victims and witnesses (Chapter 20) naturally follow a quite different pathway after the crime from that of the offender. Services to prevent crime (Chapter 10) seek to stop these processes from beginning at all.

Despite the difficulties in defining what it is that brings the different chapters of this book – and particularly this section – together, there are several elements and concepts that are discussed in a number of chapters. For ease of reference for the reader, key areas of overlap are noted below, together with the chapter where the most detailed discussion occurs:

- The probation service has a role in community punishment, imprisonment and resettlement from prison. The main discussion of the recent history of the service appeared in Chapter 8.

- Restorative justice is a concept that can influence policing, community sentences, youth justice and services to victims. The main discussion is in Chapter 20.

- Different types of offences (summary only, either-way or indictable) are discussed in relation to prosecution and the alternatives, the courts and community penalties. The main discussion is in Chapter 14.

For some of the chapters in this part, there are a large number of important historical developments that are key to understanding how the process in question operates today, so these are presented in a timeline at the start of the chapter. In other cases, the historical context is of less significance, so no timeline is included because the focus is largely on the present situation.

This part of the book develops the broad context that was outlined in Part 1 and applies it to the practical concerns of criminal justice. Each process will be shown to draw more or less heavily on the topics discussed in Part 1. For example, Chapter 11 will show that, since the publication of the MacPherson report in 1999, diversity has become a hugely important issue for the police, while

Chapter 16 shows that the mental health problems of offenders become a matter of particular urgency when large numbers are grouped together in prisons. Reading this part of the book should provide a clear understanding of how factors such as history, media representation, diversity and the characteristics of offenders all have an impact on the day-to-day work of agencies that are involved in criminal justice.

Reference

Harding, A. and Harding, J. (2006) 'Inclusion and exclusion in the re-housing of former prisoners', *Probation Journal*, 53 (2): 139–55.

Check out the Companion Website

Want to know more about this chapter? Review what you have been learning by visiting: **https://study.sagepub.com/harding**

- Practice with essay questions
- Test yourself with multiple-choice questions
- Listen to a series of podcasts featuring Neil of Northumbria Police and London's Metropolitan Police Service
- Watch videos selected from the SAGE Video collection

10 Community Safety and Crime Prevention

Esther F.J.C. van Ginneken

Introduction

Historically, crime prevention has been seen as the task of the police and even conceived of as their primary function. Yet in the twentieth century policing in England and Wales developed into a function that was mostly focused on responding to crime, rather than proactively preventing it. The preventative function of the police was reduced to deterrence, through the prospect of apprehension and punishment. Since the 1970s, however, a shift has taken place from achieving justice in response to past actions, to a preoccupation with security (Johnston and Shearing, 2003). This is typical of society's current obsession with risk; especially how to predict and reduce it (see, for example, Chapter 15). On a micro level, offenders are subjected to risk assessments to determine the appropriate level of restrictions and suitable rehabilitation programmes. These procedures are intended to minimise the risk of reoffending. On the meso level, policing efforts are increasingly targeted at high-risk communities and crime 'hot spots' (see Braga et al., 2014, for a systematic review of hot-spots policing). On a macro level, there is a constant monitoring of the terrorist threat (discussed further in Chapter 22) and prevention measures are taken accordingly. This also signifies that the nature of crime prevention is changing; it is no longer just an individual, local or national affair, but increasingly a global one. Before addressing these contemporary issues in crime prevention, this chapter concentrates on the birth of 'community safety' in England and Wales, and on the more traditional understanding of crime prevention.

Timeline

1982   First British Crime Survey conducted

1982   First Neighbourhood Watch scheme introduced

1984   Home Office circular identified a role for the community in crime prevention

1986   Five Towns Initiative launched

1988   Safer Cities Programme launched

1991   Morgan Report published

1998   Crime and Disorder Act created Crime and Disorder Reduction Partnerships

The Policy Context

Until the late 1970s, the role of the Criminal Justice System was mainly to detect and punish crime. The prevention of crime was considered a positive side effect (for example through deterrence), but not the primary focus. However, since the early 1980s there has been an increase in support for the idea that it is better to prevent crime before it has occurred, which has resulted in various crime prevention policy initiatives. A variety of factors contributed to the growing concern with crime prevention.

First, the Criminal Justice System was considered ineffective at reducing crime. Throughout the 1970s and 1980s, research by the Home Office showed limitations of the Criminal Justice System generally, and the police in particular, in preventing crime. Statistics showed increasing crime rates and the British Crime Survey, first carried out in 1982, identified a large proportion of unreported crimes, as well as high levels of fear of crime. Traditional police detection methods were not considered well-suited for certain types of crime, particularly opportunistic property crimes. During this time, there was a booming market for mass-produced consumer goods, such as TVs and video-recorders. These commonplace goods were difficult to trace, easy to sell and could often be stolen without much effort or risk of getting caught.

There was also diminishing faith in the ability of offender rehabilitation to achieve crime reduction. Initial post-war optimism about rehabilitation, and the benefits of improved social and economic conditions, turned into pessimism when evidence failed to appear for the effectiveness of rehabilitation programmes, culminating in the sentiment that 'nothing works', which was voiced in Martinson's (1974) review of prison rehabilitation programmes (Cullen and Gendreau, 2001).

The weakening of welfare and rehabilitation ideals coincided with the increased popularity of rational theories of crime (closely associated with routine activity theory, which is discussed below) and 'new-right' politics. In the UK, the Conservative governments led by Margaret Thatcher emphasised the importance of individual responsibility and criticised the welfare state for creating a culture of dependency on state provision. These ideas fitted well with the message police were giving out, that the public were partly responsible for dealing with low-level property crime, such as household burglary.

The police's role in crime prevention was discussed in Chapter 4. However, from the 1980s onwards, an increasing variety of organisations were drawn into crime prevention. Local authorities in particular were given more and more responsibilities in order to deal with crime in the community. A circular sent around in 1984 by the Home Office stated:

> A primary objective of the police has always been the prevention of crime. However, since some of the factors affecting crime lie outside the control or direct influence of the police, crime prevention cannot be left to them alone. Every individual citizen and all those agencies whose policies and practices can influence the extent of crime should make their contribution. Preventing crime is a task for the whole community. (Home Office, 1984: 1)

Various community-level initiatives were supported for the purpose of crime prevention. The Five Towns Initiative (1986) was greatly expanded with the Safer Cities Programme (1988), which provided local communities with funding to target local crime problems. The objectives were threefold: reduce crime, reduce fear of crime and enhance local community spirit. In order to achieve this, many agencies and groups had to collaborate, including local authorities, police, probation, residents, social services, education and ex-offenders. A local steering committee with representatives from these groups had to set funding priorities and oversee the implementation of initiatives. A great diversity of activities was funded through the Safer Cities Programme, including over 500 domestic-burglary prevention schemes. A Home Office evaluation (Ekblom et al., 1996) concluded that, on the whole, these burglary schemes were successful at reducing crime; the more money invested per household, the more successful the scheme.

During the same period, the UK also saw a widespread implementation of Neighbourhood Watch schemes. Neighbourhood Watch began in the USA, with the first UK scheme starting in 1982. These schemes were intended to boost informal surveillance by neighbourhood groups, so that thieves would be deterred and the police could be alerted promptly if crime was detected. Initially, Neighbourhood Watch spread quickly, but its popularity has waned. According to the Neighbourhood and Home Watch website (www.ourwatch.org.uk/), approximately 3.8 million households (14 per cent of the UK total) are currently covered by schemes. The results of Neighbourhood Watch have been mixed. The necessary cooperation between public and police has not always been present, because many programmes have not been implemented fully. Moreover, the schemes have appeared especially attractive to communities that already have high levels of informal social control; the benefits for these areas may have been low, while police resources have been diverted from areas that needed them most.

From Crime Prevention to Community Safety

By the early 1990s, the term crime prevention was beginning to be replaced by community safety. While prevention was associated with physical measures, such as locks, bolts and street lighting, community safety was more associated with growing collaboration among different authorities and organisations. However, one difficulty with such an approach was identified by the Morgan Report in 1991, which stated:

> At present, crime prevention is a peripheral concern of all the agencies involved and a truly core activity for none of them. (Home Office, 1991: 3)

The report recommended the establishment of a local authority coordinator, better information exchange, and closer involvement of businesses as partners. It supported the replacement of the concept of crime prevention with community safety:

> The term crime prevention is often narrowly interpreted and this reinforces the view that it is solely the responsibility of the police. The term community safety is open to wider interpretation and could encourage greater participation from all sections of the

community ... We see community safety as having both social and situational aspects, as being concerned with people, communities and organisations including families, victims and at risk groups, as well as with attempting to reduce particular types of crime and the fear of crime. (Home Office, 1991:13)

Due to the unpopularity of Morgan's recommendations with the Conservative government, especially the emphasis on socio-economic causes of crime and the recommendation to increase powers of local authorities, its main recommendations were initially not implemented. However, the New Labour Government elected in 1997 implemented many of the report's recommendations through the 1998 Crime and Disorder Act. This Act granted statutory responsibility to chief police officers and local authorities – in partnership with probation and health authorities – for community safety, which involved the formulation and implementation of a strategy for the reduction of crime and disorder in the area. This led to the establishment of Community Safety Partnerships (CSPs; also variously known as Community Safety and Crime Reduction Partnerships and Crime and Disorder Reduction Partnerships). In 2015 there were about 300 CSPs in England and 22 in Wales (www.gov.uk/government/publications/2010-to-2015-government-policy-crime-prevention/2010-to-2015-government-policy-crime-prevention). A 2006 Home Office report reviewing the CSPs identified problems with communication among agencies, accountability, strategic direction and visibility in the community. On the basis of this review, changes were proposed and many were implemented through the Police and Justice Act 2006.

Limitations of Community Safety

So crime prevention – and later community safety – has become a much greater priority over the last few decades, with increasing community responsibilities and multi-agency collaboration. There are a few general criticisms that can be raised about the notion of community safety and how it has been implemented in England and Wales. Fundamentally, there is a problem with the term itself when used exclusively in a crime and disorder context. Safety should have a much wider reach, to include traffic, health, the environment, and so on (Pease, 2002). This criticism of the limited focus of government policy can be extended to the question of who benefits from the strategies. Arguably, community safety strategies have the interests of businesses at heart, rather than those of disadvantaged members of the community. In other words, they were intended to reduce the fear of the business community, so that enterprise could flourish – at the cost of marginalising and stigmatising groups in the community that were perceived as disorderly (Gilling, 1999). For example, the focus on antisocial behaviour and disorder has led to a host of government policies that have contributed to the demonisation of young people (see Chapter 18).

Difficulties in Evaluating Crime Prevention Initiatives

A central concern at all stages of policy has been to demonstrate that crime prevention and community safety initiatives have been effective in the prevention of crime. However, there are major difficulties in evaluation, linked particularly to the concepts of displacement and diffusion of benefits.

Displacement

It is recognised that crime and motivated offenders do not simply disappear with targeted crime prevention. In some instances, the offender may make some adjustments in order to get the benefits from the crime in a different way. Crime displacement, as this is called, can take a variety of forms (Hakim and Rengert, 1981):

- Spatial: the crime is committed elsewhere

- Temporal: the crime is committed at another time

- Tactical: the offender uses a different method

- Target: the offender selects a different target

- Functional: the offender commits a different type of crime.

The evaluation of burglary prevention schemes that were part of the Safer Cities Programme identified some evidence for spatial and functional displacement, but only when the financial investment per household was relatively low (Ekblom et al., 1996).

According to Cornish and Clarke (1987), whether and what kind of displacement occurs depends on the perceived benefits, risks and skills needed. In other words, displacement is determined by the correspondence between available opportunities and the offender's goals and capabilities. The success of a crime prevention effort is more complicated than its ability to achieve a net reduction in crime: crime displacement may result in more harm (malign displacement) or less harm (benign displacement) than the original target crime. For example, the introduction of steering-column locks in the UK initially led to a displacement of car theft to older cars (target displacement), because only new cars were outfitted with the locks. This meant that there was a shift in the victimised population from generally wealthier to poorer car owners.

Diffusion of Benefits

Conversely, a crime prevention initiative may reduce crime beyond the primary prevention target. While there was evidence of displacement resulting from low-cost burglary prevention schemes, the higher-cost schemes were associated with reductions in crime in adjacent areas and other property crimes (Ekblom et al., 1996).

This diffusion of benefits may in some instances be explained by the lack of potential offenders' knowledge about the specific scope of the intervention. For example, the exact location of CCTV or speeding cameras may not be known and as a result offences may be reduced in a wider area.

Theories Influencing Crime Prevention and Community Safety

Two theories that have been particularly influential in the development of crime prevention and community safety policies are routine activity theory and broken windows theory.

Routine Activity Theory

Routine activity theory attempts to explain when and where crime occurs by focusing on the manifestation of opportunities for crime (Cohen and Felson, 1979). These opportunities depend on the convergence of three elements:

1. A likely offender: anyone who might commit a crime

2. A suitable target: a victim or object (in the case of an object, the victim may be absent from the criminal event)

3. The absence of a capable guardian: anyone who may intervene if a crime is committed.

According to Felson (1998), there are four main elements (VIVA) that influence a target's risk of criminal attack:

• Value: Higher value is of more interest

• Inertia: Weight of an item – small goods are more likely to be stolen

• Visibility: Exposed items are more likely to become targets

• Access: Items that are easy to get to are more likely to become targets.

Changes in people's routine activities over time may help explain global trends in crime; for example, the increasing crime rate since the 1960s has been attributed to more empty homes (absence of capable guardians) and increased availability of suitable targets, particularly portable electronic goods. The increase in empty homes is related to the rise in single-person households and greater participation of women in the workforce. The recent decline in crime at the beginning of the twenty-first century, on the other hand, may be seen as the result of improved security, and changes to the market and characteristics of previously attractive targets. Instead, new types of crime such as credit card fraud have become more attractive, but these are often not represented by traditional crime statistics. Routine activity theory may thus help us understand how changes in society in relation to suitable targets or capable guardians can lead to more or less crime.

Broken Windows Theory

[I]f a window in a building is broken and is left unrepaired, all the rest of the windows will soon be broken. [...] [O]ne unrepaired broken window is a signal that no one cares, and so breaking more windows costs nothing. (Wilson and Kelling, 1982)

The main idea of broken windows theory is that disorder causes more serious crime, because people perceive disorder as a signal that there is a lack of social control in the area and that crime is a low-risk activity. In more detail, Wilson and Kelling (1982) argued that social and physical incivilities (e.g. loitering, litter, and abandoned buildings) leads to fear among residents and workers in an area. This then causes people to move out of the area and remaining residents to isolate themselves, which decreases informal social control. A resulting increase in urban decay and social disorder attracts potential offenders, who commit more serious crimes.

Wilson and Kelling were inspired by a small experiment by Zimbardo (1969) who left one abandoned car in the high-crime area the Bronx, New York, and another in the upscale area Palo Alto, California. The car in the Bronx was vandalised almost immediately and completely stripped of its parts in 24 hours, whereas the car in Palo Alto remained untouched until Zimbardo damaged the car himself; after that, the car was also quickly vandalised and stripped. This experiment cannot serve as more than an anecdote, but since then there have been many more studies examining the ideas behind broken windows theory, especially in relation to the effect of policing disorder.

The evidence about the relationship between disorder and crime is mixed, which may be partly explained by the different ways in which disorder is measured (e.g. surveys, observations, or police data). Some studies have found support for a relationship between disorder and crime, including the idea that disorder precedes more serious crime (Keizer et al., 2008; Skogan, 2015); however, this may vary for different types of disorder and crime (Taylor, 2001). A contrasting perspective offered by Sampson and Raudenbush (1999) is that disorder and crime are not causally related to each other, but have similar preceding conditions (e.g. collective efficacy and poverty).

Sampson and Raudenbush (2004) conducted a study to determine how *perceived* disorder relates to measurements of *actual* disorder. They used a variety of data sources, including a neighbourhood survey, census data on neighbourhood composition, police data on violent offences and systematic observation on disorder. Their results showed that neighbourhood composition was a stronger predictor of perceived disorder than objective measures of actual disorder; residents perceived more disorder in neighbourhoods with more poverty and a greater proportion of black and Latino residents, independent of actual violent crime and disorder.

Furthermore, this effect did not differ for white and black participants, implying that they hold the same implicit prejudices. This has important implications for policing disorder and addressing fear of crime.

In line with broken windows theory, it would be expected that an increase in policing of minor misdemeanours would result in a crime reduction. According to Wilson and Kelling, police patrol strengthens the informal social control in a neighbourhood, which minimises fear of residents. The police act as a deterrent, but they also give a sense of safety. A systematic review of disorder policing found that policing strategies that aim to improve social and physical disorder conditions are associated with a crime reduction effect, while aggressive, zero-tolerance policing is not effective (Braga et al., 2015).

Classification of Crime Prevention

Crime prevention activities can be classified in various manners: a broad distinction is made between situational and social crime prevention, while a more nuanced difference is between primary, second and tertiary crime prevention measures. This section discusses these distinctions and gives examples of approaches that fall into some of the categories. Much of the discussion focuses on situational and primary crime prevention, because these are the elements that are unique to crime prevention/community safety, while other chapters in this part of the book also discuss measures associated with social, secondary and tertiary crime prevention (see also the companion website for further discussion of secondary social crime prevention).

Situational Crime Prevention

Situational crime prevention is concerned with making changes to the environment in order to reduce or remove opportunities for crime. It is aimed at influencing the risk/rewards balance that potential offenders supposedly take into account, drawing heavily on routine activities theory.

Situational crime prevention has been criticised on a number of grounds. First, it may be seen as a Band-Aid solution: the blocking of opportunities can – to some extent – visibly reduce crime, but does not address why there are likely offenders in the first place. Its superficial success, however, makes situational crime prevention an attractive investment.

A second critique is the lack of an ethical dimension. Even when crime prevention efforts may contribute to a net crime reduction, they may erode societal values such as social trust and equality. Increasingly, situational crime prevention techniques are used as undesirable-behaviour prevention techniques. This criticism has been levelled particularly at measures associated with environmental design (see below).

A third criticism is related to the assumption of the rational actor, who takes account of the perceived risks and benefits from criminal acts. Situational crime prevention has limited value for non-opportunistic and expressive crimes, where emotions are dominant. Moreover, some offenders may engage in criminal behaviour for the appeal of risk and not be motivated to avoid it (Katz, 1988). However, even thrill-motivated crimes could be thwarted by blocking opportunities. Indeed, situational crime prevention may also be applied to violent crimes; for example, Felson and Clarke discuss how the replacement of glass with plastic cups can prevent harmful incidents in a bar setting.

Box 10.1

Situational Crime Prevention in Practice: Alley-gating in Liverpool

In Liverpool, gates were installed to control access to alleys running along the back of terraced houses. Only residents were given keys to the alley-gates protecting their property. A total of 3,178 gates were installed, protecting 106 blocks of houses. A quasi-experimental design was used to compare the change in burglary rates in the housing blocks with alley-gates and similar housing blocks without gates (Bowers et al., 2004). It was found that burglaries in the alley-gated areas were reduced by 37 per cent compared to the control areas. There was also evidence of diffusion to surrounding areas and the benefits greatly outweighed the displacement that was observed in some areas. It was calculated that £1.86 was saved for every pound spent.

Social Crime Prevention

Social crime prevention aims to address the social conditions and individual risk factors that increase the likelihood of offending. It seeks to reduce offending by increasing informal social control and changing people's attitudes. On the individual level, risk-focused prevention is aimed at individuals (often young people) who are considered at risk of offending. On the community level, crime prevention aims to change the potentially criminogenic features of residential communities.

Developmental Criminology research has influenced social crime prevention, identifying many factors that appear to put young people at a greater risk of involvement in crime. Among these factors are low income of parents, poor housing, living in dilapidated inner city areas, high degree of impulsiveness and hyperactivity, low intelligence and low school achievement, poor parental supervision and harsh discipline, and parental conflict (Farrington, 2002). Children with one or more risk factors have a greater likelihood of engaging in offending behaviour (and getting convicted) in later life than children who do not have any risk factors. Risk-focused prevention aims to counteract these factors, with the aim of reducing future crime; an approach that became especially popular in the 1990s.

Primary, Secondary and Tertiary Crime Prevention

Another way of distinguishing types of crime prevention is by looking at the target population, as shown by Figure 10.1

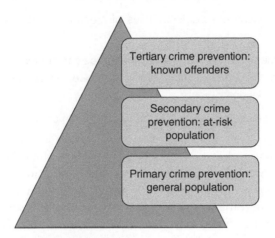

Figure 10.1 Types of crime prevention

- Primary crime prevention: targeted at the general population in order to prevent crime before it occurs (e.g. target hardening)

- Secondary crime prevention: targeted at an at-risk population (e.g. impoverished neighbourhoods, children with risk factors)

- Tertiary crime prevention: targeted at known offenders to reduce offending and/or harms associated with it (e.g. offending behaviour programmes in prison).

Situational and social crime prevention techniques may be used at each of these levels. However, situational crime prevention may be more useful at the primary level and social crime prevention at the secondary and tertiary levels.

Primary crime prevention through environmental design

Jeffery's (1977) ideas about Crime Prevention through Environmental Design (CPTED); and Newman's (1972) theory of Defensible Space were developed at roughly the same time, early in the 1970s. Newman offered design suggestions on reducing crime by organising the physical environment in such a way that it promotes a sense of community and responsibility for keeping the area safe. Jeffery's and Newman's ideas were not popular initially, but later evolved into a variety of adapted CPTED approaches. Building on Newman's theory of Defensible Space, Moffatt (1983) outlined the following six elements of environmental design that encourage social control:

- Territoriality: physical elements can be used to denote private and semi-private spaces, so that residents are more inclined to take responsibility

- Surveillance: the physical layout can enable observation (formal or informal)

- Access control: restricted access to targets can reduce crime

- Activity support: encourage particular uses of areas to increase surveillance and deter criminals

- Image management: certain environmental features can contribute to a safe image of an area (e.g. adequate lightning, well-maintained landscape). This is closely related to broken windows theory.

- Target hardening: increasing the effort that is needed to commit a crime.

The crime preventative function of defensible architectural design relies, in theory, on an increase in the perceived risk of criminal behaviour by introducing the potential for more guardianship. CPTED may be implemented in many different ways and is therefore difficult to evaluate. However, there is some support for the view that it can lead to reductions in crime and fear of crime (Casteel and Peek-Asa, 2000; Cozens and Love, 2015).

The use of environmental design to influence crime and disorder is popular in England and Wales. It has not only been used to increase social control, but also in a more hostile way to remove benefits of what is considered unwanted behaviour. For example, controversial 'anti-homeless spikes' and graffiti-resistant benches were introduced in London, although the spikes were removed after substantial criticism. (https://twitter.com/ethicalpioneer/status/474981723022049280/photo/1?ref_src=twsrc%5Etfw#)

Similarly, noise is used as a method to prevent loitering and entrances to private housing are separated from entrances to social housing (*Guardian*, 25 July 2014).

While these measures may remove visible 'disorder', they do not address the underlying causes, which are often related to poverty and social exclusion (Raymen, 2015).

Primary crime prevention through closed circuit television (CCTV) and the surveillance society

CCTV cameras are nearly a national symbol of the UK, with an estimated 5 million cameras installed; one for every 13 people (*Daily Telegraph*, 10 July 2013). It is difficult to reach an accurate estimate of numbers, because the majority of cameras are privately owned and operated. The installation of CCTVs took a growth spurt under the Conservative government in the 1990s, and it is estimated that during this time approximately 78 per cent of the Home Office's crime prevention budget was spent on CCTV (Koch, 1998). The crime preventative logic of CCTV is that it increases the risk of getting caught and therefore makes crime less attractive. In other words, it has a deterrent function. It also has a wider security function, of making people feel safe (in theory) and showing them that something is being done about crime. Furthermore, CCTV can assist with the detection of crime (or accidents), a prompt emergency response, and the apprehension of offenders.

The evidence of the extent to which CCTV fulfils these functions is perhaps not as convincing as would be expected from the financial commitment to it. Experimental evaluations of CCTV schemes show a reduction in crime in car parks and vehicle crime, but no significant effects for other types of crime or in other places (Gill and Spriggs, 2005; Welsh and Farrington, 2009). The CCTV schemes that were associated with reductions in crime were also accompanied by other interventions such as improved lighting and security guards. It is likely that the deterrent effect of CCTV cameras is quite minimal, because they do not lead to certain arrest frequently enough. Moreover, any benefits may be thwarted by inefficient implementation or an insufficient number of operatives (Piza et al., 2014a, 2014b). Available CCTV images also do not guarantee the apprehension or conviction of a suspect, because matching a person to video is highly susceptible to error (Davis and Valentine, 2009). The lack of convincing evidence that CCTV reduces crime led Groombridge (2008) to state that 'the Home Office, and therefore the Treasury, has wasted enormous sums of tax payer's money on the deployment of CCTV' (p. 74).

CCTV may also serve other functions, such as making the public feel safer. However, CCTV cameras are not clearly associated with a decrease in fear of crime or positive appraisals of its effects, and may even have the opposite effect, possibly because people are primed about crime and the cameras foster suspicion (Gill and Spriggs, 2005; Gill et al., 2007; Williams and Ahmed, 2009).

Secondary crime prevention through family and parent interventions

There is evidence that early family/parent training programmes are associated with a reduction in children's criminal behaviour at a later age (Piquero et al., 2009). A belief that this is the case, and a focus on some of the risk factors for young people which were discussed above, were factors that influenced the Sure Start Local Programmes, launched in 1998 by the Labour government. Similar to the Community Safety Partnerships, these programmes have a high level of local autonomy and are run through multi-agency cooperation. They were intended to benefit the development of children in deprived areas and offered, for example, parenting courses, home visits and early education programmes. The diversity in implementation across different areas complicates general conclusions about Sure Start's achievements. Evaluation results have been mixed: a small-scale evaluation in Wales found improvements in parenting and a reduction in children's problematic behaviour (Hutchings et al., 2007), while a larger evaluation in England found adverse effects for children from more socially deprived families (Belsky et al., 2006). On the companion website you can find further discussion on the potential benefits and harms of secondary social crime prevention.

Tertiary crime prevention through cognitive-behavioural interventions

Cognitive-behavioural programmes are intended to improve offenders' cognitive skills so that they are better able to consider the consequences of (criminal) actions. These programmes have been introduced in the UK on a large scale from the early 1990s. Prisoners are often expected to complete thinking skills courses as part of their sentence plans and they may also be included as a requirement of community orders. Popular programmes are the Thinking Skills Programme, the Sex Offender Treatment Programmes and Controlling Anger and Learning to Manage It (see the Ministry of Justice website for a list of accredited Offender Behaviour Programmes: www.justice.gov.uk/offenders/before-after-release/obp). Research evidence suggests that high-quality cognitive-behavioural treatment can significantly reduce the likelihood of recidivism among offenders (Lipsey et al., 2007). However, there is evidence of a 'completion effect', where programmes are only successful for those who are motivated to stop offending in the first place (Friendship et al., 2003; Hollin et al., 2008).

Cybercrime

In a broad sense, opportunity not only influences where and when crime takes place, but also what crime can exist at all. Changes in society have contributed to changes in the nature of crime, with the global nature of cybercrime presenting particularly difficult challenges in terms of crime prevention and community safety.

The advent of the internet in the late twentieth century brought about radical changes to society. Use of the internet grew exponentially and by the end of 2014 there were over 3 billion internet users (www.internetworldstats.com/stats.htm). The internet has created substantial new opportunities for crimes. In relation to cybercrime, we may be able to distinguish between 'computer-assisted crimes' and 'computer-focused crimes' (Furnell, 2002). Computer-assisted crimes existed before the internet, but have taken a new form online, for example: theft, fraud, child pornography, intellectual property violations and money laundering. Computer-focused crimes, on the other hand, could not exist without the internet, such as hacking, viral attacks and website defacement.

Cybercrime presents new challenges for criminological theories and crime prevention. Yar (2005) argues that we cannot simply transpose routine activity theory to cyberspace to understand patterns of crime, because the organisation of time and space that influences when and where terrestrial crime happens does not apply. Nonetheless, the concept of capable guardianship does apply, which has been used for the purpose of crime prevention. For example, firewalls and strong passwords can make internet crime more difficult to achieve.

Cybercrimes also present legislative challenges. In 2015, revenge porn became a criminal offence under the Criminal Justice and Courts Bill. Revenge porn is the sharing of sexual images (photos and videos) of another person without their consent and with the purpose of causing embarrassment or distress. Anyone found guilty of this offence could be sentenced to a maximum of two years in prison. In order to raise awareness of this new legislation – to alert potential offenders of the risks – the Ministry of Justice launched the campaign 'Be Aware B4 You Share' (see Figure 10.2), which is an example of a crime prevention initiative associated with cybercrime.

Policing has had to adapt to cybercrime, with different organisations having been created to deal with, for example, fraud, child pornography and hacking (see Wall, 2008/11 for details). However, there are concerns over an atmosphere of

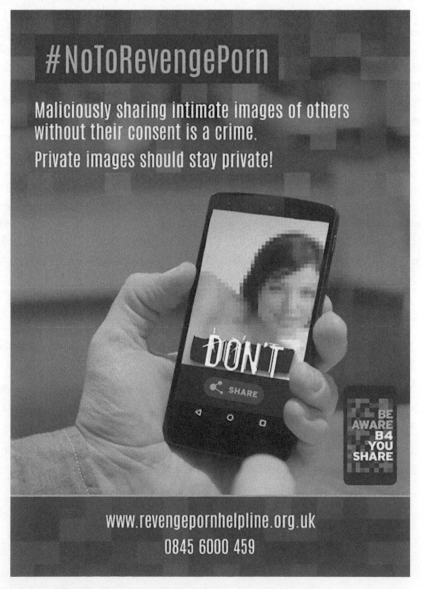

Figure 10.2 Image from the 'Be Aware B4 You Share' campaign

(image from the Ministry of Justice website, reproduced under the Open Government License, www.nationalarchives.gov.uk/doc/open-government-licence/version/3/)

continued 'fire fighting', with little attention and few resources being focused on effective prevention (Craven et al., 2007: 68).

Summary

A growing concern about crime in the late twentieth century led to substantial investments in crime prevention initiatives, which later evolved into community safety strategies. Local communities were given resources and responsibilities to coordinate these initiatives, which involved many different agencies and organisations. Ideas about situational crime prevention have been particularly influential. The rationale behind this is that crime can be reduced by increasing the efforts or risks associated with specific crimes. There is some research evidence to support the effectiveness of such an approach, although one of the most widely adopted crime prevention measures, CCTV, is not convincingly associated with reductions in crime. A strong criticism that has been levelled at many other implemented programmes and strategies is that they do not eliminate underlying causes of crime; in fact, there is a risk that vulnerable groups of the population are further marginalised. The same can be said of recent measures that aim to tackle disorder or undesirable behaviour in the community, which includes legal powers to sanction antisocial behaviour, as well as hostile urban design to prevent it. The growth of cybercrime has led to measures regulating activities that many would consider to be private, further highlighting the difficult balance between promoting safety and respecting personal freedoms.

Discussion Questions

1. Does the current government take an evidence-based approach to crime prevention? Has this changed over time?

2. To what extent should crime prevention be the responsibility of individuals? Give examples of situations where it should and should not be the individual's responsibility.

3. Is increased surveillance and access to personal data justifiable on the basis that those who have nothing to hide have nothing to fear?

Further Reading

The *Journal of Research in Crime and Delinquency* published a special issue (Volume 52, number 4) on broken windows theory: 'Reimagining broken windows: From theory to policy' (edited by Welsh, Braga and Bruinsma, 2015). In their introduction the issue's editors neatly summarise the development of the theory, as well as the key research studies.

Further reading on the notion of pre-crime can be found in: Zedner, L. (2007) 'Pre-crime and post-criminology?', *Theoretical Criminology*, 11 (2): 261–81.

For an even more comprehensive exploration of the notion of prevention in relation to legal issues, civil liberties, security and crime, see: Ashworth, A. and Zedner, L. (2014) *Preventive Justice*. Oxford: Oxford University Press.

Evans, K. (2011) *Crime Prevention: A critical introduction*. London: Sage, addresses the broader political context surrounding crime prevention policies, including the 'war on terror', human rights issues and immigration.

For more general reading on crime prevention, there are two handbooks:

Welsh, B.C. and Farrington, D.P. (eds.) (2012) *The Oxford Handbook of Crime Prevention*. Oxford: Oxford University Press. This is a collection of chapters from experts on developmental, community and situational crime prevention.

Tilley, N. (ed.) (2005) *Handbook on Crime Prevention and Community Safety*. Abingdon: Routledge. This offers a more detailed examination of prevention in relation to specific types of crimes.

References

Belsky, J., Melhuish, E., Barnes, J., Leyland, A.H. and Romaniuk, H. (2006) 'Effects of Sure Start local programmes on children and families: Early findings from a quasi-experimental, cross sectional study', *British Medical Journal*, 332 (7556): 1476.

Bowers, K.J., Johnson, S.D. and Hirschfield, A.F.G. (2004) 'Closing off opportunities for crime: An evaluation of alley-gating', *European Journal on Criminal Policy and Research*, 10 (4): 285–308.

Braga, A.A., Papachristos, A.V. and Hureau, D.M. (2014) 'The effects of hot spots policing on crime: An updated systematic review and meta-analysis', *Justice Quarterly*, 31 (4): 633–63.

Braga, A.A., Welsh, B.C. and Schnell, C. (2015) 'Can policing disorder reduce crime? A systematic review and meta-analysis', *Journal of Research in Crime and Delinquency*, 52 (4): 567–88.

Casteel, C. and Peek-Asa, C. (2000) 'Effectiveness of Crime Prevention through Environmental Design (CPTED) in reducing robberies', *American Journal of Preventive Medicine*, 18 (4): 99–115.

Cohen, L.E. and Felson, M. (1979) 'Social change and crime rate trends: A routine activity approach', *American Sociological Review*, 44 (4): 588–608.

Cornish, D.B. and Clarke, R.V. (1987) 'Understanding crime displacement: An application of rational choice theory', *Criminology*, 25: 933.

Cozens, P. and Love, T. (2015) 'A review and current status of Crime Prevention through Environmental Design (CPTED)', *Journal of Planning Literature*, 30 (4): 393–412.

Craven, S., Brown, S. and Gilchrist, E. (2007) 'Current responses to sexual grooming: Implications for prevention', *The Howard Journal of Criminal Justice*, 46 (1): 60–71.

Cullen, F.T. and Gendreau, P. (2001) 'From nothing works to what works: Changing professional ideology in the 21st century', *The Prison Journal*, 81 (3): 313–38.

Davis, J.P. and Valentine, T. (2009) 'CCTV on trial: Matching video images with the defendant in the dock', *Applied Cognitive Psychology*, 23 (4): 482–505.

Ekblom, P., Law, H., Sutton, M., Crisp, P. and Wiggins, R. (1996) *Safer Cities and Domestic Burglary*. London: Home Office, Research and Statistics Directorate.

Farrington, D.P. (2002) 'Developmental criminology and risk-focused prevention', in M. Maguire, R. Morgan and R. Reiner, R. (eds), *The Oxford Handbook of Criminology*. 3rd edn. Oxford: Oxford University Press. pp. 657–701.

Felson, M. (1998) *Crime and Everyday Life*. 2nd edn. Thousand Oaks, CA: Pine Forge Press.

Friendship, C., Blud, L., Erikson, M., Travers, R. and Thornton, D. (2003) 'Cognitive-behavioural treatment for imprisoned offenders: An evaluation of HM Prison Service's cognitive skills programmes', *Legal and Criminological Psychology*, 8 (1): 103–14.

Furnell, S. (2002) *Cybercrime: Vandalizing the information society*. London: Addison Wesley.

Gill, M. and Spriggs, A. (2005) *Assessing the Impact of CCTV*. London: Home Office Research, Development and Statistics Directorate.

Gill, M., Bryan, J. and Allen, J. (2007) 'Public perceptions of CCTV in residential areas "It is not as good as we thought it would be"', *International Criminal Justice Review*, 17 (4): 304–24.

Gilling, D. (1999) 'Community safety: a critique', in *The British Criminology Conferences: Selected Proceedings* (Vol. 2). Papers from the British Criminology Conference, Queens University, Belfast, 15–19 July 1997. This volume published March 1999. Editor: Mike Brogden.

Groombridge, N. (2008) 'Stars of CCTV? How the Home Office wasted millions – a radical "Treasury/Audit Commission" view', *Surveillance and Society*, 5 (1): 73–80.

Hakim, S. and Rengert, G.F. (eds) (1981) *Crime Spillover*. Beverly Hills, CA: Sage Publications.

Hollin, C.R., McGuire, J., Hounsome, J.C., Hatcher, R.M., Bilby, C.A. and Palmer, E.J. (2008) 'Cognitive skills behaviour programs for offenders in the community: A reconviction analysis', *Criminal Justice and Behaviour*, 35 (3): 269–83.

Home Office (1984) *Crime Prevention* (circular no. 8/1984). London: Home Office.

Home Office (1991) *Safer Communities: The local delivery of crime prevention through the partnership approach (Morgan Report)*. London: Home Office, Standing Conference of Crime Prevention, August.

Hutchings, J., Bywater, T., Daley, D., Gardner, F., Whitaker, C., Jones, K. and Edwards, R.T. (2007) 'Parenting intervention in Sure Start services for children at risk of developing conduct disorder: Pragmatic randomised controlled trial', *British Medical Journal*, 334 (7595): 678.

Jeffery, C.R. (1977) *Crime Prevention through Environmental Design*. London: Sage Publications.

Johnston, L. and Shearing, C. (2003) *Governing Security: Explorations in policing and justice*. Abingdon: Routledge.

Katz, J. (1988) *Seductions of Crime: Moral and sensual attractions in doing evil*. New York: Basic Books.

Keizer, K., Lindenberg, S. and Steg, L. (2008) 'The spreading of disorder', *Science*, 322 (5908): 1681–5.

Koch, B.C.M. (1998) *The Politics of Crime Prevention*. Aldershot: Ashgate.

Lipsey, M., Landenberger, N.A. and Wilson, S.J. (2007) 'Effects of cognitive-behavioural programs for criminal offenders: A systematic review', *Campbell Systematic Reviews*, 3 (6): 1–27.

Martinson, R. (1974) 'What works? Questions and answers about prison reform', *The Public Interest*, 35 (2): 22–54.

Moffatt, R.E. (1983) 'Crime prevention through environmental design: A management perspective', *Canadian Journal of Criminology*, 25, 19–31.

Newman, O. (1972) *Defensible Space*. New York: Macmillan.

Pease, K. (2002) 'Crime reduction', in M. Maguire, R. Morgan and R. Reiner (eds), *The Oxford Handbook of Criminology*. 3rd edn. Oxford: Oxford University Press.

Piquero, A.R., Farrington, D.P., Welsh, B.C., Tremblay, R. and Jennings, W.G. (2009) 'Effects of early family/parent training programs on antisocial behaviour and delinquency', *Journal of Experimental Criminology*, 5 (2): 83–120.

Piza, E.L., Caplan, J.M. and Kennedy, L.W. (2014a) 'Is the punishment more certain? An analysis of CCTV detections and enforcement', *Justice Quarterly*, 31 (6): 1015–43.

Piza, E.L., Caplan, J.M. and Kennedy, L.W. (2014b) 'CCTV as a tool for early police intervention: Preliminary lessons from nine case studies', *Security Journal* [advance online publication], doi: 10.1057/sj.2014.17.

Raymen, T. (2015) 'Designing-in crime by designing-out the social? Situational crime prevention and the intensification of harmful subjectivities', *British Journal of Criminology* [advance online publication].

Sampson, R.J. and Raudenbush, S.W. (1999) 'Systematic social observation of public spaces: A new look at disorder in urban neighbourhoods', *American Journal of Sociology*, 105 (3): 603–51.

Sampson, R.J. and Raudenbush, S.W. (2004) 'Seeing disorder: Neighbourhood stigma and the social construction of "broken windows"', *Social Psychology Quarterly*, 67 (4): 319–42.

Skogan, W. (2015) 'Disorder and decline: The state of research', *Journal of Research in Crime and Delinquency*, 52 (4): 464–85.

Taylor, R.B. (2001) *Breaking Away from Broken Windows: Baltimore neighborhoods and the nationwide fight against crime, grime, fear, and decline*. Boulder, CO: Westview Press.

Wall, D.S. (2008/2011) 'Cybercrime and the culture of fear: Social science fiction(s) and the production of knowledge about cybercrime', *Information, Communication and Society*, 11 (6): 861–84 (revised February 2011).

Welsh, B.C. and Farrington, D.P. (2009) 'Public area CCTV and crime prevention: An updated systematic review and meta-analysis', *Justice Quarterly*, 26 (4): 716–45.

Williams, D. and Ahmed, J. (2009) 'The relationship between antisocial stereotypes and public CCTV systems: Exploring fear of crime in the modern surveillance society', *Psychology, Crime and Law*, 15 (8): 743–58.

Wilson, J.Q. and Kelling, G.L. (1982) 'Broken windows', *Atlantic Monthly*, 249 (3): 29–38.

Yar, M. (2005) 'The novelty of "cybercrime": An assessment in light of routine activity theory', *European Journal of Criminology*, 2 (4): 407–27.

Zimbardo, P.G. (1969) 'The human choice: Individuation, reason, and order versus deindividuation, impulse, and chaos', *Nebraska Symposium on Motivation*, 17: 237–307.

Check out the Companion Website

Want to know more about this chapter? Review what you have been learning by visiting: **https://study.sagepub.com/harding**

- Practice with essay questions
- Test yourself with multiple-choice questions
- Listen to a series of podcasts featuring Neil of Northumbria Police and London's Metropolitan Police Service
- Watch videos selected from the SAGE Video collection

11 The Police

Matt Jones and Kelly Stockdale

Introduction

This focus of this chapter is on the public police in England and Wales. Often described as gatekeepers of the Criminal Justice System, the police play a central role in the regulation and response to crime and deviance within our society. However, with this responsibility comes intense scrutiny and criticism – more than any other criminal justice organisation. Therefore, the central aim of this chapter is to substantiate the view that an understanding of the police – their structure, composition and responsibilities – is immensely complex due to the competing demands placed on them by a myriad of stakeholders. As such, we argue that any discussion of the police must acknowledge these complexities and the malleability of the police mission, as it is continually shaped by changing social, political and economic demands placed on them.

The chapter begins by clarifying confusion between 'the police' and 'policing' before moving on to present four key stages in the public police's development that have influenced them today. This historical consideration is important, as the police celebrate their historical past and a lot of what they do and why they do it, is embedded in their historical traditions. We then go on to identify some of the key stakeholders in the police – the dominant figures who shape what the police do, their priorities and hold them to account. It is here, for example, where we introduce and outline the responsibilities of the latest police stake-holder – the Police and Crime Commissioner. We then go on to consider the role and function of the police, considering whether there are 'core' police respon-sibilities and whether or not they have exceeded these in recent years. Related to this, we then present some 'models' of policing that help to explain what the police do and how they do it. Throughout the chapter, we draw upon contem-porary policy and practice to help illustrate some of the academic debates of the police presented.

Timeline

1829   Metropolitan Police Act established the Metropolitan Police

1835   Municipal Corporations Act gave County and Borough authorities powers to set up a police force

1856   County and Borough Police Act created arrangements for uniformed polic-ing systems across England and Wales

1964   Police Act introduced 'tripartite' system of responsibility for police accountability

1981   Scarman report into the disorders in Brixton and elsewhere

1984   Police and Criminal Evidence Act provided a code in relation to police powers and the investigation of crime

1999   MacPherson report into the investigation of the murder of Stephen Lawrence

2002   Police Reform Act gave additional powers to groups such as security staff and neighbourhood wardens

2006   Policing and Justice Act gave volunteer specials the same powers as paid police officers

2010   Comprehensive Spending Review outlined 20 per cent cut in police funding grant

2012   Police and Crime Commissioners introduced

Differentiating Between the Public 'Police' and 'Policing'

It is a common mistake to reference 'the police' and 'policing' interchangeably – when in fact they refer to two different systems of social regulation and require differentiation. 'Policing' refers broadly to a complex matrix of organisations and practices that are concerned with the regulation of crime and social order. Whereas 'the police' are part of the matrix of 'policing', but are a prescribed social institution that is funded by the tax payer and operate as a result of the public consenting for them to maintain social order on their behalf.

The public police in England and Wales have a well-established structure – one that is embedded within its history. Based on a territorial system (in a geographical sense), it is made up of 43 organisations (see Figure 11.1), each of which has its own resources and senior management team to set local priorities, but are somewhat homogenised by the national policy steer of the Home Office and universal accountability structures. A distinguishing feature of the public police is their ability to use legitimate force when deemed necessary – a power enshrined in law but not afforded other organisations within the aforementioned 'policing' matrix.

A further distinguishing feature of the public police is the police constable – a symbolic and iconographic representative of crime fighting with their black and white uniform, hardhat and truncheon. As of 1 March 2015, there were 126,818 police officers in England and Wales – equating to approximately one police officer for every 445 members of the public (Woods, 2015). However, it should also be noted that these officers are supported by 63,719 police staff – all of whom play a valuable role in the mechanics of the public police.

Alternatively, policing and the aforementioned matrix of organisations concerned with maintaining social order, beyond the public police, is made up of a complex system of organisations – mainly within the private sector – that lack a coherent or unifying mandate or regulation/system of accountability. In recent years we have seen a dramatic increase in these organisations – due mainly to the reduction in size of the public police due to cuts in their public funding. As a consequence, private organisations and individuals have started to carry out roles that had historically been held by the public police. For example, our night-time economy (e.g. pubs and clubs) is now predominately regulated by licensed private security agents; similarly large sports and music events are now policed by private stewards and security staff that are funded by the venues' and events' organisers themselves. As of 15 February 2016, there are 15,049 licensed protection personnel in the UK, 204,006 licensed door supervisors, 47,670 Public Space Surveillance operatives and 94,193 licensed security guards (SIA, 2016) – a cumulative total of individuals engaged in activities allied to 'policing' that far outweighs the workforce strength of the public police.

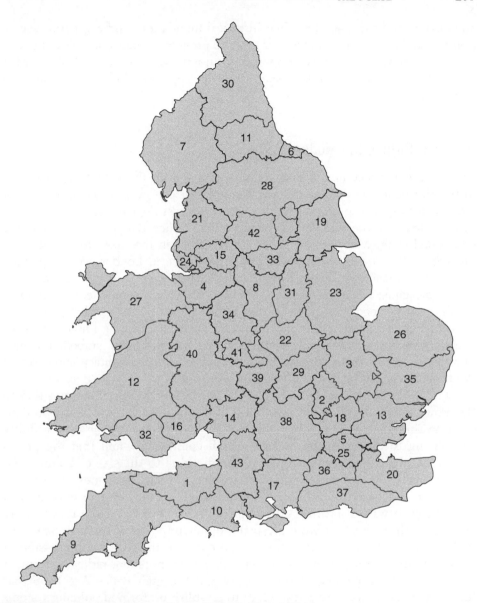

Figure 11.1 The 43 police territories in England and Wales

(webarchive.nationalarchives.gov.uk/), reproduced under the Open Government License, www.national archives.gov.uk/doc/open-government-licence/version/3/

Historical Developments in Policing

In order to understand the public police in a contemporary context we must first acknowledge the historical backdrop in which they are located, as the mission, structures and image of the public police are deeply embedded in these histories. In reality, the public police are part of an on-going system of continuity and change and are shaped by their historical foundations and competing social, political and economic climates over time. To provide a detailed account of police histories here would almost be impossible, but instead, in this part of the chapter, four influential periods that have shaped the development of the public police are identified and discussed:

Period 1: Birth of the Modern Police

There are many accounts of policing in history – from the volunteer 'constable' in the thirteenth century, to the first examples of private policing as a result of land ownership and developing industrialisation across England and Wales (Reiner, 2010). However, the foundations of the public police that we know today are embedded in the Metropolitan Police Act 1829 when the then Home Secretary, Sir Robert Peel, established the Metropolitan Police in London. Peel appointed two Commissioners – Charles Rowan and Richard Mayne – who were responsible for designing and implementing structures on which this modern police force would be developed. For example, they established the iconographic police uniform, designed a structured policy of recruitment and training for new recruits and set priorities that are still evident today: e.g. establishing a symbolic presence of officers on the streets; differentiating the police from the military; and ensuring the professional interaction of officers with the public.

Despite these efforts, initially there was considerable public opposition to this new system of policing. It was felt that it was more expensive and burdensome to the tax payer; that the Home Office had taken over the responsibility of policing to the exclusion of local watch committees; and that the promises made of a better system could not be met due to the size of London and the relatively low (often poor quality) number of recruits the new system was attracting. It should also be noted that initially, this new system only applied to London. It wasn't until the Municipal Corporations Act 1835 that County and Borough Authorities were given the opportunity to set up a police force if they wanted to, with many choosing to enhance their existing provision of nightwatchmen and parish constables rather than pursuing radical reform. It was not until the passing of the County and Borough Police Act 1856 that formal arrangements were put in place to establish uniformed policing systems across England and Wales – establishing a framework that underpinned policing until the 1960s.

Period 2: Conflict and Criticism

Social developments in the latter half of the twentieth century brought with them challenges for and criticisms of the police.

First, in the 1960s, technological change brought with it enhancements to the occupation of policing. The bobby on the beat was somewhat replaced by the police panda car – equipped with radio communication devices. Despite the efficiency benefits these developments brought, it led to a system of 'fire brigade policing', where the police car siren and blue flashing light became associated with the police amongst the public, rather than the patrolling police officer. It was this technological change that ignited a period of isolation between the police and the community.

However, in the 1980s the public police were subject to more severe criticism related to their culture and related practices. By the end of the 1970s, the socio-demographic composition of the UK population had changed – due mainly to post-war immigration and the subsequent expansion of the European Union – creating a multi-ethnic and culturally diverse Britain (Hall, 1993). This newfound heterogeneity within British communities proved antagonistic to the then homogeneous insularity of the predominantly white, male and heterosexual police occupational culture, initiating a period of diminishing public confidence and associated calls for reform to public policing that would continue for two decades. Particularly, between 1981 and 1999, there were two damning reports that proved instrumental in reshaping policing priorities and mind-sets – the Scarman Report (1981) and the Macpherson Report (1999).

The Scarman Report was commissioned by the government in the immediate aftermath of the Brixton Riots – two days of social unrest and conflict between the police and members of the community in Brixton. Scarman (1981) was critical of the police and their relationship with the Black and Minority Ethnic (BME) community in this report – recommending increased recruitment of BME officers; stricter accountability and discipline processes for those officers found to exhibit racist views and practices; and more proactive engagement with diverse communities. Unfortunately, the years following Scarman were dominated by the social and political unrest fuelled by Thatcherism, allowing for only a muted and sporadic attempt at implementing these recommendations (McLaughlin, 2007). Twelve years after the recommendations of Scarman (1981), Stephen Lawrence, a London schoolboy, was killed in a racist attack, launching a murder inquiry by the Metropolitan Police. In June 1997, the newly elected Labour government launched an investigation into 'the matters arising from the death of Stephen Lawrence' which culminated in a report by Lord Macpherson (1999). The case and the Macpherson Report subsequently became a 'public relations catastrophe' (McLaughlin, 2007: 148) for the police. Macpherson identified significant failures during the investigation of the schoolboy's murder, failures that he argued were fuelled by 'institutional racism' (p. 321) across all levels of the Metropolitan Police. Specifically, he highlighted how the recommendations of Scarman (1981) had been ignored, representing a failure by management to respond to changing policing priorities.

Period 3: Post-millennium Policing

After a period of institutional reflection, the new millennium saw the introduction of a fresh, centralised, policy direction in policing, one that placed diversity and its potential to bring about cultural reform and change at its core. This is not to say that this was the first time that the concept of diversity had been considered (McLaughlin, 2007), but rather the severity of Macpherson and its damage to police reputation provided the impetus for it to be taken seriously and made an operational priority – described by Loftus (2009: 35) as the start of a 'new politics of policing diversity'.

There were four noticeable policy tenets that shaped this new diversity-centred mindset all of which have been underpinned by what has been referred to as a 'new managerialism' in policing (Loader and Mulcahy, 2003):

1. Placing the 'public' and concept of 'community' at the centre of the policing mission;

2. Workforce modernisation;

3. Creating an 'ethical conscience'; and

4. Mechanisms of accountability.

Hall et al. (2009) identified three 'orders of change' concerning police reform that related to the nature and impact of the proposed initiatives. 'First order' reform represents a continuity of quantitative initiatives that have been utilised in the past (e.g. increasing police numbers in problematic areas); 'second order' reform refers to less common but still 'normal' reform initiatives (e.g. changing the way that an area of policing is delivered); 'third order' reform refers to more radical initiatives that represent a fundamental change in police direction. In this regard, the new diversity reform agenda was described by Hall et al. as a 'third order' programme representing 'a paradigm shift relating to fundamental … changes in the police mindset and in external expectations of what the police are there to deliver' (p. 5). Similarly, Reiner (2010), citing Shearing and Bayley (1996: 585), argued that 'future generations will look back on [this] era as a time when one system of policing ended and another took its place'.

Period 4: Austerity Policing

At the time of writing this chapter, the police in England and Wales are in a period of responding to significant cuts in their budgets – due in the main to the fiscal consequences of a wider trend of financial austerity that has been experienced internationally. Specifically, in 2010, a Comprehensive Spending Review (CSR) announced by the government outlined a 20 per cent cut in the central government police funding grant for all 43 forces in England and Wales by 2014/15 (see HMIC, 2011). As a consequence, the public police in England and Wales have been forced to reconsider their core responsibilities, local priorities and ways of working in order to accommodate this reduction in public funding for policing. Some of these considerations and consequences will be explored throughout this chapter.

Key Stakeholders

The Modern Police Family

Whereas traditional policing, as detailed above, concerns the role of serving police officers and their interactions with members of the public, there has been a rapid expansion in terms of demand for policing services, and policing itself has developed to encompass civilian staff, volunteers, partner agencies, and private firms operating as part of a wider 'policing family'.

In order to strengthen frontline policing, to provide a more 'visible' police force within communities, and to increase public confidence in policing the Labour government proposed a series of reforms. The 2001 Home Office White Paper 'Policing a New Century: A blueprint for reform' (www.gov.uk/government/publications/policing-a-new-century-a-blueprint-for-reform) set out the government's intentions to increase the capacity of police officers by enhancing the role of police staff, allowing them to carry out certain policing functions that at that time were traditionally carried out by police officers. It also proposed the introduction of 'Community Support Officers', employed as police staff but wearing a similar uniform to warranted officers they would be a visible presence in the community. With a remit based around community engagement, reassurance, and visibility they would also have basic powers in relation to dealing with minor offences and antisocial behaviour. These proposals, including the newly created post, renamed as Police Community Support Officers (PCSOs) were introduced as part of the Police Reform Act 2002. This Act therefore relinquished the need for warranted officers to perform traditional policing roles and extended some powers of policing activity to this new, wider 'policing family'.

In addition to the creation and widening of police staff roles to encompass tasks previously administered by police officers, a raft of voluntary positions are now available within police forces, including Police Support Volunteers and membership of Independent Advisory Boards, Neighbourhood Watch Networks, etc. (for the full range of voluntary roles, see www.police.uk/volunteering/). One of the key volunteer positions within police forces is that of Special Constable, or 'specials': a role that carries the same powers and similar uniform to regular police officers. Introduced through the Police and Justice Act 2006 an amendment was made to Section 30(2) of the Police Act 1996 allowing volunteer specials to have the same powers as their paid police officer counterparts. The use of volunteer community members to carry out a range of roles and services within a police force is seen as an effective way to forge links with the community and for citizens to be more involved with crime control. It is also a cost-effective way for police officers to supply a service, particularly in the current financial climate and ever-tightening pressure on police budgets, as 45 per cent of policing roles are performed by non-warranted staff and volunteers.

Staffing and volunteer numbers across the 43 police territories in England and Wales:

130,000 Police Officers

65,000 Police Staff,

14,000 Police Community Support Officers

18,000 Special Officers

9,000 Police Support Volunteers

(Home Office, 2013)

However, the use of volunteers is not without its problems, Bullock (2015: 6) argues there is a 'blurring of roles' between traditional police officer and police staff roles with those carried out by police support volunteers. This is problematic; police support volunteers can engage in roles that constitute 'frontline policing' activity yet they lack the same regulation and processes that hold paid employees to account. Furthermore as boundaries become more blurred then it is increasingly difficult for the public to keep abreast of all the different roles and responsibilities for each member of the modern policing family. Stenning makes an important point that the 'policing family is not always harmonious' (2009: 23): there is often scepticism about the roles, or sometimes even fear or anger that the creation of new volunteer roles might adversely affect pre-existing staff. It is therefore important to note that relationships within the modern policing family are shaped by political and economic factors (Bullock, 2015: 11).

It is also important to note that the extended police family did not stop with the expansion of public policing roles, extended duties for staff, and the provision of volunteers: the 2001 White Paper also recognised the role other organisations contribute to community safety and security, and built on previous powers given to private security provision, including the 1994 Police Act. Jones and Newburn (1998) argue this was necessitated by the substantial growth in the private ownership of property and possessions over the last 30 years, and the subsequent growth in the need for appropriate security in order to protect it. Furthermore the introduction of privately owned areas available for public use, such as shopping malls and leisure places, and the increasing use of private security carrying out work that was previously associated with the public police has blurred the boundaries between private and public (Jones and Newburn, 1998). The policing family expanded further to include neighbourhood wardens, security staff and street wardens. The legislation adopted in the Police Reform Act 2002 makes provisions for organisations to be accredited and given additional powers, similar to those of a PCSO.

Key to the extension of the police family in this way is visibility; accredited staffs are required to wear a badge or kite-mark on their uniform. Use of quasi police-attire is important due to the symbolic significance of the police uniform as a symbol of power and authority (Young, 1999). Cooke (2005) states that there has been little attempt to keep the public informed of the changes and raises concerns that the public may not fully understand the roles, functions, power, authority and accountability of these new agencies. The importance of these elements is discussed throughout the chapter and raises significant concerns.

Politics and the Police

An important element of policing is the social context within which it is situated; earlier sections of this chapter have outlined how politics have influenced the police, from the initial strategies to win over political opposition to their formation to landmark events including riots, protests, scandals, and subsequent reports into policing. Reiner (2010) argues that despite the claim from officers and police chiefs that policing is politically neutral, it cannot be such due to the power dimensions. Whilst there is an attempt for officers to impartially enforce the law, this ignores social divisions (such as class, gender, age, ethnicity, etc.) and the way in which laws and their enforcement replicate these divisions. The specific role of the police is to maintain order, they are key to the successful functioning of the state, and as such Reiner asserts 'policing is inherently and inescapably political' (2010: 32).

We can see the political elements to policing as we move through this chapter and it is useful to reflect on the areas of policing that are specifically linked to politics, i.e. police budgets predominantly based on government funding, the quadripartite model of police governance whereby the police are accountable to the Home Secretary, and the formation of Police and Crime Commissioners, which will be discussed later in this chapter. In addition to these elements it is important to consider other elements of policing with a critical eye. For example the Home Secretary in December 2011 created a new policing professional body: the College of Policing. Its purpose is to 'find the best ways to deliver policing in an age of austerity' (www.college.police.uk/About/). The College of Policing sets the standards for professional development, including codes of practice and regulations for all 43 police forces in England and Wales. The College is owned by and accountable to the Home Secretary: the Home Secretary has the power to veto regulations. There are plans to establish the College of Policing as a statutory body, independent of government when parliamentary time allows. However, this demonstrates some of the blurred boundaries between policing and politics in place today.

The Public – Legitimacy

The public's acceptance of being governed by the police is critical: in order for the police to fulfil their role of maintaining order they need the support and cooperation of the majority of the public for most of the time. Central to the public voluntarily cooperating with the police is how legitimate they perceive their actions to be (Tyler, 2004). Perceptions of police legitimacy are only in part based on police practice: someone who is in contact with the police may not necessarily go on to withdraw their support from policing as an institution (Reiner, 2010). Instead a greater extent of police legitimacy is based on whether the public views the police's actions as being procedurally fair (Tyler, 2004). Police legitimacy has since been defined as both an obligation to obey and a moral alignment with the police (Jackson et al., 2012).

The legitimacy of the police and the way in which policing by consent has been achieved and established in Britain is due to the way in which the initial policing policies were adopted. It is important to note that these policy choices were made when the public, particularly the working classes, were opposed to the existence of the police. Reiner (2010: 70–7) sets out eight of the original policies of policing that helped to establish police legitimacy and public acceptance of the police:

- Bureaucratic organisation: emphasis is on the organisation rather than the individual; there is a standardisation of skills and roles across the force, a professionalisation of the role and a clear chain of command.

- The rule of law: the way in which the police enforce the law is itself subject to legalistic procedures and constraints, the public may complain if they believe the police to be abusing their powers.

- The strategy of minimal force: police aim to use as little force as necessary, garnering public support rather than an over-reliance on weapons and violence.

- Non-partisanship: police should be impartial and operate without bias.

- Accountability: discussed in more detail below, the key concept in terms of legitimacy is that the police are identified as public and not state; 'the police are the public and the public are the police' (Reith, 1956: 287).

- The service role: this relates to the wider roles and services carried out by police, those that are beyond the core duties of law enforcement, providing a beneficial service to the public.

- Preventative policing: particularly in the early years the role of uniformed officers in preventing crime played an important part in achieving legitimacy for their function.

- Police effectiveness: public perception in relation to the effectiveness of the police with regards to preventing crime and preserving social order provides the final tenet on which police legitimacy was built.

Whilst the value of some of these policies has been questioned each has helped to play a part in securing police legitimation and demonstrates some of the ways by which the policing role was initiated in order to align with working class and middle class citizens, seek moral alliances and foster their obligation to obey directives from the policing institution.

Accountability

The accountability of the police, the way in which they are answerable to the public and the systems by which they are held to account for their actions, has also undergone significant change over time – particularly since the 1980s. Yet the basic principle of accountability is a fundamental part of democratic policing: the decisions made by police forces and by individual officers should reflect citizens' wishes (Jones, 2003: 694–5). One element of this is the recruitment of officers historically from working-class backgrounds to represent the masses.

A critical element of policing is the role of discretion: this includes street-level discretion whereby rank and file police officers have the freedom to decide what to do in a given situation, in addition to organisational policy making with all 43 police forces across England and Wales able to exercise a degree of freedom in relation to the implementation of some policies; the section later in this chapter on models of policing provides a good example of this. Reiner (2010) argues that there is an interdependent relationship between police powers and accountability: it is accountability that helps to control the actions of the police, allowing their discretion within a broader framework of communal values. This links the fundamental issues around police legitimacy as outlined above: the professionalisation of the role and the bureaucratic nature of the police force means that individual officers are held to account through a quasi-military chain of command. Yet as 'street-level bureaucrats' (Lipsky, 1980) individual police officers often represent citizens' direct encounters with the police force as a whole; both through their individual actions and when considered collectively, rank and file police officers not only play a critical role in delivering policy but also their actions add up to policy.

In order to maintain a consistent service across all 43 police forces and to ensure individual police officers deliver a standard of service, they are held to account by a series of policies and systems, key to which are:

- The Police and Criminal Evidence Act (PACE) 1984 provided a code in relation to police powers and the investigation of crime.

- The tripartite system, established under the 1964 Police Act, distributed responsibility for police accountability between the Home Office, the local police authority and chief constable of the force. This was later expanded in 2012 to the 'quadripartite' system that saw the abolishment of local police authorities in favour of publicly elected Police Crime and Commissioners (PCCs) and the addition of Police and Crime Panels. Police and Crime Panels are intended to scrutinise and support the work of the PCC and are mostly comprised of ten elected councillors with two co-opted independent members.

Furthermore, following Macpherson the development and implementation of the Independent Police Complaints Commission (IPCC), as detailed in Chapter 19, created a mechanism for the public to complain about individual officers and their actions. However, Reiner (2010) notes that there is still little opportunity for the public to complain at an organisational level in relation to police policy or tactics although, in theory, the public may now influence policing priorities as part of the PCC public consultation process. Further proposals in the Policing and Crime Bill 2016 will address this further with the launch of a new route whereby charities and pressure groups, acting on behalf of the public, will be able to lodge 'super complaints'. The aim of which is to capture any systemic issues, patterns or trends that undermine police legitimacy that are not covered by the current system, for example national or cross-force issues.

Police and Crime Commissioners

The introduction of Police and Crime Commissioners (PCCs) in 2012 marked a significant constitutional change in governance for policing in England and Wales. As discussed earlier this saw a move from the previous tripartite model to a new 'quadripartite' framework consisting of: Home Secretary, chief constables, elected commissioners (PCCs) and a representative Police and Crime Panel.

- The idea of Police and Crime Commissioners stemmed from US models of police governance.

- The introduction of PCCs formed part of the Conservative Party Election Manifesto in 2005 and 2010. The Coalition government went forward with the plans, save for the inclusion of Police and Crime Panels.

- PCCs are responsible for the force budget.

- It is also part of the PCC's role to set the police and crime objectives for the force, through a 'Police and Crime Plan'.

- PCCs were introduced through the Police Reform and Social Responsibility Act 2011 across 41 of the 43 police forces in England and Wales: the Metropolitan Police and City of London Police are overseen by the Mayor's Office for Policing and Crime by an equivalent governance arrangement.

The role of the PCC is to be the 'voice' of the people and to hold the police (and in particular the chief constable) to account. The implementation of PCCs raises fundamental questions in relation to the political nature of stakeholders in the police, the role that it has, and whether politics can be kept out of policing (Lister, 2013).

Box 11.1

Police and Crime Commissioner Elections

PCCs are publicly elected officials. Candidates for the office of PCC are eligible if they were British citizens, over the age of 18, and on the electoral register within the police area where they wish to stand. Criteria that disqualified a potential candidate from standing, included:

serving police officers, police employees, or employed by the local council; subject to a bankruptcy restrictions order; convicted of an imprisonable offence.

All candidates paid a non-refundable £5,000 deposit to stand.

Elections took place on 15 November 2012. Public participation was low with fewer than 15% of voters turning out across the 41 police force areas.

The majority of PCC candidates were affiliated with the main political parties. Of those elected 16 were Conservative, 13 Labour, and 12 were independent candidates.

Elected PCCs were in office by 22 November 2012. Under the Police Reform and Social Responsibility Act 2011 PCCs had a duty to prepare a Police and Crime Plan as soon as practicable after taking office, these needed to be in place by March 2013.

The most recent PCC elections took place on 5 May 2016, with many candidates standing for a second term in office.

The Role and Function of the Police Today

Defining the role and function of the police is surprisingly difficult – a testament to the complexity of what they do and what they are responsible for. There are several points of reference that are used to define their role – the 'Peelian Principles' (an unofficial police mission statement said to originate from Sir Robert Peel when he set up the modern police in 1829) makes reference to their responsibility to prevent crime and disorder; to secure and maintain public respect; to secure the willing cooperation of the public in the task of securing observance to the law; and to maintain the principle that the police are the public and the that the public are the police. Similarly, the police oath, sworn by every serving police officer, makes explicit reference to their responsibility to keep the peace and prevent offences against property and the person.

Box 11.2

The Police Oath

I do solemnly and sincerely declare and affirm that I will well and truly serve the Queen in the office of constable, with fairness, integrity, diligence and impartiality, upholding fundamental human rights and according equal respect to all people; and that I will, to the best of my power, cause the peace to be kept and preserved and prevent all offences against people and property; and that while I continue to hold the said office I will to the best of my skill and knowledge discharge all the duties thereof faithfully according to law. (www.durham.police.uk)

It is proportionate to argue that the 'core' role and function of the police relates to crime control within society – an expectation perpetuated by their prescribed legal status and ability to use reasonable force. There is a public expectation that when crime is being/has been committed, the police are the first point of call to respond. This is summed up by Bittner (1974) who argues that the public expect the police to intervene when 'something-is-happening-that-ought-not-to-be-happening-and-about-which-someone-had-better-do-something-now'.   The current political rhetoric supports this crime-fighting model of policing as recently stated in a speech by the then Home Secretary – 'the police's remit is simple – we need them to be the tough, no-nonsense crime fighters they signed up to become' (May, 2011).

However, in reality, the role and responsibility of the police has expanded beyond their core role in recent decades. In 2012/13 there were 19.6m incidents recorded by the police – just under two-fifths (38 per cent) of which received an emergency or priority response (College of Policing, 2015). The police now play a significant role in shaping the experiences of victims and have established specialist officers and teams to support victims of sexual offences, hate crime and domestic violence. Further, the nature of policing has become much more proactive (in comparison to the reactionary nature of their core role); as the police subscribe to the view that crime and social disorder can be predicted, planned for and prevented. For example, community/neighbourhood policing (to be discussed in more depth in the next section) is being increasingly used by the police as a risk management strategy – building up trust and confidence with communities through proactive engagement so that they then feel confident to communicate information about deviant groups and individuals to the police before an incident occurs (Ericson and Haggerty, 1997). The police also have a responsibility to respond to and invest resources in combatting new types of crime – recent examples of which include cybercrime, terrorism, and revenge porn.

Given the realities of austerity on policing – i.e. the 20 per cent cut to police budgets previously outlined – the growing role of the police is a contentious one as they are forced to do more but with less resources. This has forced many police constabularies to retreat to their core role and function and to consider where they are doing more than they are legally obligated. A growing area of contention in this regard has been the increased reliance on the police in the response to individuals with mental health difficulties – with police cells being increasingly used as a 'place of safety' under the Mental Health Act. It has been estimated that up to 20 per cent of incidents attended by the police relate to mental health – raising questions as to whether they are the most appropriate (in terms of resources and professional qualifications) public body to be responding. Other examples of contention are the policing of large public events and the policing of roads – where the question is whether the police should have a responsibility to provide resources for such events, or whether alternative public agencies and/or private security organisations should share in the burden of growing public demand for policing and security.

Modelling Police Work

The following section considers some of the ways policing is operationalised in England and Wales. In doing so it will consider three 'models' of policing: community orientated policing (COP), problem orientated policing (POP), and restorative policing. Various models of policing have been introduced since the 1990s in an attempt to provide a policing strategy for the twenty-first century and this section represents just a snapshot of these; further models of policing for example, intelligence-led policing, are also worth exploring. This chapter focuses on these three models due to their fundamental attempts to reform policing philosophies. Whilst these models are presented as separate it is important to recognise that they are not clear-cut concepts, each have numerous definitions and there is much overlap, both theoretically and in the way individual police forces adopt and adapt the different philosophies and processes.

Community Orientated Policing (COP)

Community orientated policing is a philosophy of policing embedded in notions of police forces pro-actively geared towards community involvement, partnership and co-production. COP is seen as both an organisational strategy and a philosophy (Trojanowicz and Bucqueroux, 1990; Tilley, 2003), it reflected a shift in power to neighbourhood groups, promoting the public's involvement in generic issues (for example, Police and Community Together (PACT), which was about the public setting police priorities at a local level) due to the belief that safer communities involved community and police working together to resolve issues (Goldstein, 1990). COP therefore was a challenge to police forces and requires a transformational shift both internally within the organisation and externally in relation to the way that the police interact with the public. It was also seen as a rejection of the technocratic professionalism; whilst improvements in technology were seen as successful in reducing crime, the removal of the 'bobbie on the beat' did little to reassure the public, hence an increase in the fear of crime despite falling crime rates (Waddington, 1999; Innes, 2004). COP was seen as a process not a product, and was based on citizen involvement, problem solving and decentralisation (Skogan, 2008: 28). In addition to these three areas Thurman et al. also argue for the inclusion of a fourth element: that COP aims to bring about a change in the internal organisation and culture of a police force where employee input is valued (2001: 8). However, there are issues both with the attempt at reform and with the COP model, particularly in relation to the ways in which the community were included and involved in policing: mostly at a low level and predominately it involved consultation rather than collaboration.

Problem Orientated Policing (POP)

Problem orientated policing proposes a whole new way of thinking about crime and police response to crime, at its root is the concept of applying scientific principles to issues of crime and disorder (Bullock et al., 2006). Its use in England and Wales was linked to a broader government strategy on effective reduction of crime and disorder, which built on the National Intelligence Model and a focus on intelligence-led policing and harnessed the concepts of best value using the deployment of officers and use of resources for maximum effect. Part of this targeting towards the root causes of crime and disorder was a recognition that police could not solve them on their own: it required 'joined up thinking' and partnership working with other agencies, the legislation for which was set out in the Crime and Disorder Act 1998. Chapters 10 and 12 provide further details with regards to multi-agency working.

The concept of problem orientated policing stems from attempts at police reform in the USA, particularly in relation to reform within the Chicago police department. Goldstein (1990) defines it as the identification of specific problems identified both through the systematic analysis of data and from engagement with the community to hear their concerns. The response to this involves tailor-made solutions that go beyond standard responses and are imaginative, make full use of police officers' skills and expertise, and are informed by good practice.

POP paved the way for the current drive towards Evidence-based Policy and Practice (Bullock et al., 2006) and also reinforced the message that the Criminal Justice System's response to crime and disorder is often limited: a wider partnership approach that includes the community to tackle the root cause of problems is crucial (Goldstein, 1990).

Restorative Policing

Restorative policing shares some of the same values and builds on COP, taking the idea further so that communities are not just involved generically, but they are actively involved and have a decision-making role at a case level (Bazemore and Griffiths, 2003: 303). Fundamentally, restorative policing prioritises conflict resolution and aims to promote community ownership over crime (Bazemore and Griffiths, 2003). The three core principles of restorative policing are to repair the harm caused by an offence, to promote stakeholder involvement in dealing with the offence and to transform the relationship between communities and police, and the Criminal Justice System as a whole (Bazemore and Griffiths, 2003: 336–7). Its goal is to develop restorative resolutions towards crime and harm to the 'greatest extent' across all police functions and to promote greater ownership of crime and conflict by the community (Bazemore and Griffiths, 2003: 345).

Restorative policing is seen as being the 'next step' to police reform, it builds on previous attempts at reform such as Community Orientated Policing (COP) and Problem Orientated Policing (POP), which aimed to create new relationships between the police and the community (Bazemore and Griffiths, 2003). Whilst COP failed to build community capital, restorative policing brings with it a set of 'tools' or 'levers': it is these additional tools that can help build social capital where other programmes such as POP and COP have failed (Bazemore and Griffiths, 2003: 337).

The levers offered by restorative policing go further than involving the public in determining police priorities: it allows citizens to be involved in informal sanctioning. Traditionally the preserve of courts and professionals, restorative policing engages with the public at a deeper level giving them a 'case-level decision-making role' in the justice process (Bazemore and Griffiths, 2003: 338). The techniques of restorative conferencing are key: the process itself involves the community, allowing them to take ownership of the issues. It is this community ownership that, although potentially problematic due to being set within traditional adversarial criminal justice processes, provides the largest opportunity for transformative change within policing (Bazemore and Griffiths, 2003: 343).

It is important to note that these three models of policing have been adopted, alongside other models, to different degrees and adapted in different ways by police forces. This adoption and adaption not only occurs across the 43 police forces in England and Wales but also within an individual force. Restorative ways of working, for example, are more likely to be adopted by neighbourhood policing teams than by departments with a more traditional crime and justice approach (i.e. major crime teams). Additionally models of policing are rarely adopted on their own, in practice various adaptations of models are in operation within each force. Furthermore, the adoption of each philosophy brings about organisational change that allows for the implementation of other models, hence restorative policing building on previous models of COP and POP. It can therefore be very difficult to separate out the different models in practice, yet the fundamental philosophies behind each model remain distinct.

Summary

In this chapter we have attempted to provide a foundation understanding of one of the central Criminal Justice System organisations in England and Wales: the police. The overarching argument that has shaped the discussion of this chapter is that understanding and critical consideration of the public police in England and Wales is inherently complex.

To substantiate this claim we first outlined and clarified how the public police are one of many organisations and actors within a wider matrix of 'policing'. On a daily basis, we witness and encounter many examples of 'policing', from the private security guards at supermarkets and sports events (an example of private policing) to the iconographic police constable patrolling our communities. However, what differentiates that police constable from other forms of policing, is his/her unprecedented and legally embedded power to use reasonable force in the course of their police duties.

We then went on to demonstrate how the police – in terms of what they do, why and how they do it – are deeply embedded in their historical past. Specifically we

(Continued)

(Continued)

outlined the introduction of the modern police in 1829 by Sir Robert Peel and the roll-out of a territorial system of multiple police constabularies across England and Wales. Throughout the chapter we highlighted several other key temporal points and events that we believe have shaped what the police do and represent today.

Linked to this discussion of history, we also argued in this chapter that the role, remit and understanding of the police is never static – it is continuously evolving in response to competing demands. For example, we have shown how demographic changes in society prioritised diversity and wider cultural reform; we highlighted how economic challenges shaped contemporary policing within a period of austerity; and we demonstrated how changing political agendas can bring new initiatives for the police to incorporate and respond to (e.g. the introduction of Police and Crime Commissioners).

As one of the most scrutinised criminal justice agencies, we have also shown how the police face an unprecedented level of scrutiny and review. Importantly, a key stakeholder in this regard is the public, who the police ultimately represent and act on behalf of. More formally, we have outlined the new quadripartite system of accountability that underpins the police – ensuring that they are legitimate and existing within their legal and ethical mandate.

However, if we look beyond the competing demands and resource tensions that shape police debates, the unifying and defining characteristic of the police is that they are – either reactively or proactively – predominately concerned with crime, which often affords them the title of 'crime fighters'. However, our discussion has illustrated how in recent years this core remit has broadened to include responsibility for victims and non-crime related social issues, e.g. mental health. Thus, at the time of writing this chapter the ultimate question facing the police is whether or not their role and responsibilities, in a climate of economic austerity, have become too broad.

What is certain is that our social and academic preoccupation with the police is fuelled by the mystique created by its continual change and as such we can guarantee that the core principles discussed in this chapter will be useful when attempting to understand the challenges and priorities shaping police debates in England and Wales in the months, years and decades ahead.

Discussion Questions

1. Why do we have a police force/service?

2. How and in what ways has the system of policing changed over time since the nineteenth century? Consider the new strategies and styles that have developed over the last 20 years: why have these come about? How do they differ from each other? Have they been implemented consistently across all 43 police forces?

3. What is the future of the police, policing and security?

Further Reading

The following books provide helpful further material on the police and policing:

Newburn, T. (ed.) (2008) *Handbook of Policing*. 2nd edn. Cullompton: Willan.
Reiner, R. (2010) *The Politics of the Police*. 4th edn. London: Open University Press.
Rowe, M. (2014) *Introduction to Policing*. 2nd edn. London: Sage

References

Bazemore, G. and Griffiths, C. (2003) 'Police reform, restorative justice and restorative policing', *Police Practice and Research*, 4 (4): 335–46.

Bittner, E. (1974) 'Florence Nightingale in pursuit of Willie Sutton: A theory of the police', in H. Jacob (ed.), *The Potential for Reform in Criminal Justice*. London: Sage.

Bullock, K. (2015) 'Shoring up the "home guard"? Reflections on the development and deployment of police support volunteer programmes in England and Wales', *Policing and Society*: 1–17. Available via advanced access at http://www.tandfonline.com/doi/pdf/10.1080/10439463.2015.1058378?needAccess=true (accessed 22 September 2016).

Bullock, K., Erol, R. and Tilley, N. (2006) *Problem-oriented Policing and Partnerships: Implementing an evidence-based approach to crime reduction*. Abingdon: Taylor and Francis.

College of Policing (2015) *College of Policing Analysis: Estimating demand on the Police Service*. Available at: www.college.police.uk/News/College-news/Documents/Demand%20Report%2023_1_15_noBleed.pdf (accessed 1 September 2016).

Cooke, C.A. (2005) 'Issues concerning visibility and reassurance provided by the new "policing family"', *Journal of Community and Applied Social Psychology*, 15 (3): 229–40.

Ericson, R. and Haggerty, K. (1997) *Policing the Risk Society*. Oxford: Oxford University Press.

Goldstein, H. (1990) *Problem Orientated Policing*. New York: McGraw-Hill.

Hall, N., Grieve, J. and Savage, S. (2009) 'Introduction: The legacies of Lawrence', in N. Hall, J. Grieve and P. Savage (eds), *Policing and the Legacy of Lawrence*. Cullompton: Willan. pp. 1–21.

Innes, M. (2004) 'Reinventing tradition? Reassurance, neighbourhood security and policing', *Criminal Justice*, 4 (2): 151–71.

Jackson, J., Bradford, B., Hough, M., Myhill, A., Quinton, P. and Tyler, T.R. (2012) 'Why do people comply with the law? Legitimacy and the influence of legal institutions', *British Journal of Criminology*, 52 (6): 1051–71.

Jones, T. (2003) 'Police accountability', in Newburn, T.(ed.) *Handbook of Policing*. Cullompton: Willan.

Jones, T. and Newburn, T. (1998) *Private Security and Public Policing*. Oxford: Clarendon Press.

Lipsky, M. (1980) *Street-level Bureaucracy: Dilemmas of the individual in public services*. New York: Russell Sage Foundation.

Lister, S. (2013) 'The new politics of the police: Police and Crime Commissioners and the "operational independence" of the police', *Policing*, 7 (3): 239–47.

Loftus, B. (2009) *Police Culture in a Changing World*. Oxford: Oxford University Press.

Macpherson, Sir W. (1999) *Steven Lawrence Inquiry, Report of an Inquiry by Sir William Macpherson of Cluny*. London: HMSO.

May, T. (2011) *Theresa May Speech in Full,* 4 October. Available at: www.politics.co.uk/comment-analysis/2011/10/04/theresa-may-speech-in-full

McLaughlin, E. (2007) *The New Policing.* London: Sage.

Reiner, R. (2010) *The Politics of the Police*. 4th edn. Oxford: Oxford University Press.

Reith, C. (1956) *A New Study of Police History*. Edinburgh: Oliver and Boyd.

Scarman, L.J. (1981) *The Brixton Disorders, 10–12 April, 1981: Report of the inquiry by the Rt. Hon., The Lord Scarman, OBE*. London: HMSO.

SIA (2016) *Security Industry Licensing Authority: Licensing statistics*. Available at: www.sia.homeoffice.gov.uk/Pages/licensing-stats.aspx

Skogan, W.G. (2008) 'Why reforms fail', *Policing and Society*, 18 (1): 23–34.

Stenning, P. (2009) 'Governance and accountability in a plural policing environment – The story so far', *Policing*, 3 (1): 22–33.

Thurman, Q., Zhao, J. and Giacomazzi, A.L. (2001) *Community Policing in a Community Era: An introduction and exploration*. Los Angeles: Roxbury Publishing Company.

Tilley, N. (2003) 'Community policing, problem-oriented policing and intelligence-led policing', in Newburn, T. (ed.), *Handbook of Policing*. Cullompton: Willan. pp. 311–39.

Trojanowicz, R.C. and Bucqueroux, B. (1990) *Community Policing: A contemporary perspective*. Cincinnati: Anderson.

Tyler, T.R. (2004) 'Enhancing police legitimacy', *The Annals of the American Academy of Political and Social Science*, 593 (1): 84–99.

Waddington, P.A. (1999) *Policing Citizens: Authority and rights*. Abingdon: Psychology Press.

Woods, E. (2015) *Police Service Strength, England and Wales, 31 March 2015*. London: Home Office. Available at: www.gov.uk/government/uploads/system/uploads/attachment_data/file/445013/hosb0215.pdf

Young, M. (1999) 'Dressed to commune, dressed to kill: Changing police imagery in England and Wales', in K.K.P. Johnson and S.J. Lennon (eds), *Appearance and Power*. New York: Berg. pp. 37–57.

Check out the Companion Website

Want to know more about this chapter? Review what you have been learning by visiting: **https://study.sagepub.com/harding**

- Practice with essay questions
- Test yourself with multiple-choice questions
- Listen to a series of podcasts featuring Neil of Northumbria Police and London's Metropolitan Police Service
- Watch videos selected from the SAGE Video collection

12 Policing as Part of a Multi-agency Approach

Tanya Wyatt and Mary Laing

Introduction

Tackling crime is commonly thought to be the sole remit of the police, but increasingly, a range of actors are working to assist the police with this role. This chapter explores the shift over the past 40 years or so, away from a 'one size fits all' police-dominated mode of governance, enforcement and assistance to a more pluralised 'multi-agency' or 'partnership' regulatory approach. The terms 'multi-agency' and 'partnership' will be used interchangeably in this chapter. Police services are positioned, and work alongside, other actors reactively and proactively to respond to criminal and other socio-legal issues. The chapter will first offer an overview of the multi-agency approach to policing, documenting its histories and the context from which it came. Following this, two case studies will be offered; the first exploring multi-agency responses to violence against sex workers, and the second considering the multi-agency approach taken to policing wildlife crime. Both case studies are UK based. The case studies will provide detailed descriptions of how multi-agency policing can work in practice, and will highlight benefits of the approach. Finally the chapter will end with a discussion of the possible future of such partnerships.

This chapter is slightly different from the others in this section of the book, as it discusses one very specific element of an agency's work. This reflects the importance attached to multi-agency working to prevent and tackle crime, as discussed in Chapter 10, and the fragmentation of responsibility for policing, as discussed in Chapter 11. The case studies use specific examples to demonstrate the practical outcomes of these two key trends.

Historical Context

Since the Metropolitan Police was formed in 1829 and over ensuing decades and centuries, responding to and preventing crime was solely a police responsibility. From truanting school children, to murder investigations and responding to sexual violence, the police were positioned as experts, as they responded to and sought to prevent crime, whilst supporting victims. However, the past three decades have seen academics and practitioners questioning the capacity and ability of the police to react to *all* forms of criminality and deviance. As Walklate (2002: 305) states, there are inherent difficulties 'in expecting the police to respond to the crime problem proactively, reactively and in the preventative capacity all at the same time'.

Since the 1980s, there has been a fundamental shift, with some, but not all, policing tasks taking on a partnership approach. The key developments in this area – e.g. the creation of Neighbourhood Watch schemes, the Five Towns Initiative, the Safer Cities Programme and the Morgan Report – were discussed in Chapter 10. These developments have resulted in a range of organisations – statutory, private and third sector – taking up roles within criminal justice processes. How these partnerships operate locally is negotiated between the police and other key actors, which might include local Councils, third and public sector organisations, private sector organisations, other criminal justice agencies (probation for example), public health bodies and social services.

The 1998 Crime and Disorder Act gave legal responsibility for crime prevention and community safety to local authorities working through Crime and Disorder Reduction Partnerships. So, from 1998, a whole host of agencies not traditionally concerned with policing and regulation came to play a role in local governance and the development of multi-agency working. Following this in 2002, the implementation of the Police Reform Act made local authorities, police authorities, fire authorities and primary health care services the organisations with statutory responsibilities within Crime and Disorder Reduction Partnerships.

As Rowe (2008: 180) subsequently argues, policing has become more 'hybrid' in nature and now involves a plethora of private, public and third sector agencies at a range of scales; it can be (re)conceptualised as a 'complex network of relations that exist between agencies'. Of particular significance is that policing through partnership models now incorporates actors whose original remit was previously not remotely police-focused, as will be evidenced in the case studies below. However, the dual focus on crime prevention and the community safety concerns of all partners has been central to the development of more pluralised policing models (Crawford, 2008).

In addition to crime prevention, another key area for inter-agency working has been the management of violent and sexual offenders in the community, as was noted in Chapter 8. The Criminal Justice Act (2003) provided for the establishment of Multi-Agency Public Protection Arrangements (MAPPA) to protect the public, including previous victims of crime, from such offenders. The police, prisons and probation services are required to work together to assess and manage risk, with other agencies having a duty to cooperate as necessary (Ministry of Justice, 2012).

However, despite this fracturing of responsibility, the police often remain the dominant actor in such arrangements, both in terms of the coordination and the navigation of multi-agency work. Newburn and Jones (2002) note that although groups of actors may claim to work through a partnership approach, actually the distribution of power within such partnerships could be unequal. So the police may be the lead agency where the decision-making resides, which may prove problematic if there are trust and rapport issues with victims and the public. When things do go badly or outcomes are not as expected, the police are often the focus of criticism, but in multi-agency operations this may not be warranted. Indeed, the literature highlights a number of problems with the multi-agency approach, especially in relation to accountability. The Independent Police Complaints Commission (IPCC) is the key mechanism that seeks to hold the police service to account, as discussed in Chapter 19, but how are other agencies working within multi-agency partnerships then held responsible? For individual agencies within multi-agency groups, it is with those individual agencies where accountability for actions ultimately rests, but the IPCC has no oversight regarding partners' actions. Noteworthy is how traditional multi-agency working partnerships have mostly been amongst public sector organisations. However, more recently there has been an increase in private security and other commercial multi-agency partnerships – perhaps then the term 'multi-stakeholder' would better fit this method of regulation. With private companies now part of the multi-agency approach, this potentially expands the range of stakeholders involved to shareholders and company board members. All these agencies taken together can ultimately make accountability fairly complex within this type of regulatory setting.

There are always concerns with agencies' ability to communicate readily and effectively across multiple partners. This becomes particularly tricky in relation to crime prevention where much of the information that should be shared is of a sensitive nature or may actually require special permission to access. Police culture related to suspicion and trust can also hinder more open lines of communication (O'Neill and McCartney, 2014). With the right frame of mind though and with clear procedures for sharing information, agencies can work together with good communication and the potential for good outcomes.

Despite these issues, working in partnership is seen as particularly important at a time of austerity, when police and other agencies are under substantial pressure to ensure that their resources are used efficiently. The link between better use of resources and multi-agency working was asserted by Mike Penning, the Minister of State for Policing, Criminal Justice and Victims, when discussing the level of police grant for 2015–16:

> Police forces are working more closely than ever before to reduce costs and duplication, and have started to work more closely with other emergency services through co-location and collaboration in areas such as mental health. (Home Office, 2014: 1)

This link also appears to be accepted by professionals: Turley et al. (2012: 10) found that the benefits of neighbourhood policing, as perceived by some partners, included improved efficiency and avoiding duplication of effort. However, it should be noted that austerity was not a major factor linked to the creation of multi-agency partnerships in either of the case studies discussed in this chapter.

The pluralisation of policing will be evidenced through the subsequent case study discussion, highlighting that for multi-agency policing to be successful a whole range of agencies need to be involved. In addition, because of the range of partners contributing to policing, it has been argued that there has been a fundamental shift in how governance is performed. Shearing and Wood (2003) argue that governance can now be defined as 'nodal' meaning that commercial and third sector organisations play a role in shaping the processes and actions of criminal justice agencies and vice versa. Reconceptualising what we mean by policing, governance and regulation is therefore central to the literature on multi-agency working. Indeed, Johnston and Shearing (2003) suggest that policing more broadly should be re-imagined as the governance of security. They argue that through processes such as partnership work, policing becomes increasingly 'distanciated' with regulatory practice no longer only embodied and performed by police services, but by a variety of actors within the community.

Case Study: Policing, Multi-agency Interventions and Sex Work

The policing of sex work has changed considerably in the UK since the introduction of vice squads in the 1950s and 1960s, which were commissioned because of growing concerns about street prostitution and its associated 'nuisance' impacting on residents, businesses and communities (Matthews, 2005). Although vice teams were largely disbanded after the 1980s, police forces across the UK have used numerous tactics to stop sex work including: anti-kerb crawling campaigns, shutting down brothels, issuing anti-social behaviour orders (ASBOs), acceptable behaviour contracts (ABCs) and engagement and support orders (ESOs), zero tolerance policing and tolerance zones (Hubbard, 2006; Sanders, 2008; Scoular and Carline, 2014).

Despite these interventions, street sex work continues to exist in city spaces, and commonly reported is the ability of sex workers to exercise geographical mobility, agency and even bargaining skills to resist police tactics and maintain a space in which to work (Hubbard and Sanders, 2003)

However, because of historical and contemporary poor relationships between sex workers and the police as well as budget constraints on law enforcement, alternative modes of regulation have had to be implemented and multi-agency approaches to regulating sex work have become an increasingly favoured mechanism in this context (Cook, 2008). The police, specialist sex work support services, drugs teams, sexual health services, accommodation providers and other key services constitute a number of multi-agency boards and advisory committees across England and Wales tasked with the job of managing sex work in local areas. The make-up of such boards reflects the multi-agency support commonly available to sex workers in towns and cities; service providers have increased in number since the 1980s (Pitcher, 2006). The first agencies were set up following the onset of the HIV/AIDS epidemic, but the original remit of harm minimisation and sexual health has significantly expanded to encompass a broader range of services as it was recognised that sex workers can experience a host of service needs (Pitcher, 2006). Such needs may include (and often differ by sector of work, e.g. street work v. brothel work): sexual health services, welfare and legal advice, drug and alcohol services, assistance with reporting violence, advice around safer sex working, advice on housing and homelessness, police liaison, exiting strategies and mediation with local communities.

The range of services supporting sex workers demonstrates the scope of multi-agency intervention in the context of sex work. Matthews (2005) has argued that police forces are generally supportive of such multi-agency working as it essentially makes their job easier. They have to dedicate less time to policing sex work as outreach workers and service providers who have daily or weekly contact with sex workers are able to informally regulate spaces and practices of work. In relation to community mediation in the context of street work, outreach workers have been known to respond to issues raised by concerned residents and deal with them without the requirement for police intervention (Pitcher et al., 2006). Communities can also benefit from contact with outreach teams; for example, O'Neill and Campbell (2006) undertook a project in Walsall, UK, which involved local residents living in areas of street sex work and female sex workers. The consultation for the project served as a mechanism for each group to learn about the other's concerns about sex work in the local area. As a result, more resources were allocated to schools to work with young people, and to the health authority to work with sex workers, widening the multi-agency approach to managing sex work locally. Pitcher et al. (2006) have demonstrated through research into six spaces of street sex work across the UK that cohesive living and working in spaces of sex work is possible, but that those communities who consulted with multi-agency boards, outreach projects and sex workers were the most successful at this.

Multi-agency intervention is especially important in the context of sex work, as sex workers operating in different parts of the sex industry could be considered marginalised in different ways. Indeed it is evidenced in the literature that those individuals involved in street-based sex work, or opportunistic/survival sex work, commonly experience multiple types of chronic social exclusion (Laing and Irving, 2013). In this area of the sex industry (which commonly makes up one of the smaller percentages of the overall sex industry in country contexts) individuals often experience multiple and reinforcing aspects of social exclusion, including but not limited to:

(Continued)

(Continued)

homelessness, addiction, engagement with the Criminal Justice System, and health and well-being issues. Selling sex for this group may be one economic survival strategy amongst others, and some within this group may not self-define as sex workers (Laing and Irving, 2013). In other parts of the sex industry – for example those working off-street as escorts or in brothels – individuals could also be considered marginalised, but in different ways. For example, many sex workers feel stigma because of their quasi-criminalised status, but also because the work they engage in is considered to challenge normative sexual–social values. Many may also experience loneliness in the course of their work, with some feeling they cannot be 'out' about their sex-working status without suffering discrimination. Migrant sex workers may feel unsure about what access they have to the Criminal Justice System and other services including health services. The quasi-criminalisation of sex work in the UK places sex workers in a marginalised position in terms of their access to the police in the context of reporting violence; but as we shall see, a multi-agency approach is one way of overcoming some of these issues.

Reporting Violence Against Sex Workers: A Multi-agency Approach

One area where a multi-agency approach has had a particularly significant impact is in the reporting of violence and criminality committed against sex workers. As noted above, sex workers historically and contemporarily have had poor relationships with the police, and although levels of violence perpetrated against sex workers in the course of their work can be significant, levels of reporting to the police are low.

'Ugly Mug' or 'Dodgy Punter' schemes provide an example of a multi-agency intervention for preventing violence against sex workers, but more importantly, they enabled violence and victimisation to be reported, and other sex workers to be alerted about potentially dangerous individuals. Local schemes operate whereby if a sex worker is victimised they, or a practitioner, could report the incident to a specialist local sex work support project, who would then distribute information about the incident and the alleged offender to other sex workers. They may also report the incident to the police if consent is given. Some sex workers also share Ugly Mug information online and peer-to-peer. Such schemes have been in operation in the UK for over 20 years. Never before however have they been 'joined up' so that sex workers could access information about incidents anywhere in the country – which is especially important for sex workers who tour or work in various areas.

Since July 2012 however, a scheme has been in operation in the UK, a system called 'National Ugly Mugs' (NUM), which is the first national reporting system of its kind in the world. The aims of NUM are to encourage the reporting of violent incidents, improve personal safety of sex workers by providing information about alleged dangerous individuals, bring offenders to justice by working with the police, and deliver a strong message that violence against sex workers is neither acceptable nor inevitable. NUM operates through a web-based hub and is run by the NUM team in association with the UK Network of Sex Work Projects (UKNSWP). Sex workers and practitioners who are members submit reports of incidents online; the reports are then turned into alerts and are disseminated to members nationally via text and email. Where consent is given, information captured in the alerts is shared anonymously or with full disclosure with police services and those incidents involving serious crime – for example, rape, sexual assault and murder – are shared with the Serious Crime Analysis Section, which is part of the National Crime Agency (Laing and Pitcher, 2013). Therefore an escort working across multiple cities could access Ugly Mug reports for every city s/he works in. NUM also has the potential to capture reports about offenders who travel.

Box 12.1

A Successful, Multi-agency NUM Outcome (adapted from Feis-Bryce, 2015)

In April 2013, an escort in London was taken by her driver to an appointment at a client's house. On arrival, the client took her into his home, locked her in his bedroom, brandished a knife and threatened to kill her if she did not have sex with him. He raped her, took nude photographs and said he would 'cut her beautiful face'. The ordeal lasted more than two hours.

Following the incident, she attended a specialist sex work project appointment at a hospital, during which she disclosed to the nurse that she had been raped. She was adamant that she did not want to report it to the police, but the nurse helped her to submit a report to NUM with consent to share the intelligence anonymously with the police. The escort wanted to warn other sex workers via NUM by alerting them not to take appointments with the man, but then move on with her life. However, she suffered from nightmares and flashbacks.

The intelligence she provided was submitted to an intelligence unit at the Metropolitan Police with whom NUM has a formal intelligence-sharing partnership. The police used the anonymous intelligence to identify the alleged offender. They contacted NUM and the specialist sex work project asking them to act as an intermediary to speak to the victim and to clarify some details. She was at this stage happy to assist anonymously, so provided the requested information. Throughout this process however, her confidence in the police increased. She saw they were taking the incident seriously and were not interested in pursuing charges around sex work. She was also supported through the process by an Independent Sexual Violence Advisor (ISVA) through the sex work project. As a result of this multi-agency intervention and approach, she decided to make a full report to the police, which resulted in the arrest of the man.

When he was interviewed by the police, he stated that he had hired an escort, had sex, but refused payment. He denied threatening her with a knife and keeping her locked in his room. Later when the police searched his property they found the knife, as described by the escort in her initial report to NUM. He was charged with rape and held on remand despite applying for bail. NUM and the specialist sex work project worked closely with the police in preparing for the trial, and the nurse was called as a first disclosure witness. The escort, whose first language is not English, had an experienced court interpreter work alongside her whilst she was giving evidence, which, she said, was extremely valuable.

It took the jury just over an hour to find the man guilty; he was sentenced to 10 years in prison for rape. The escort was very happy with the outcome and thankful for the support of multiple agencies involved.

The case study demonstrates the importance of multi-agency intervention in the context of reporting violence against sex workers and the important role specialist sex work services can play in bringing violent offenders to justice. Although the police played a central role, they would not have been alerted to the offender had the escort not been supported by a nurse, an ISVA, the specialist sex work project and NUM. In addition, the decision to make a full report to the police came after working with these agencies for some time to build confidence. Key to the escort getting to the point of full disclosure to the police was the non-judgemental approach of the agencies, as well as their specialist knowledge about sex work. Evidently, specialist organisations such as NUM are well placed to manage processes of reporting violence against sex workers, especially since it is well documented that sex workers will rarely report to the police themselves. When they do the outcome is often negative and victims feel humiliated and undeserving of victim status (Laing and Irving, 2013; although there are some notable exceptions to this, see Campbell, 2014). Reflecting earlier discussions of Shearing and Wood (2003) of a move to 'nodal governance', this is an example of how organisations outside of criminal justice settings can work alongside criminal justice agencies to produce results.

Case Study: Wildlife Crime

The policing of wildlife crime is undertaken by a variety of organisations, both governmental and third sector. Wildlife crime is defined by numerous Acts some with centuries of history (Vincent, 2014). Predominantly, the legislation, like the Wildlife and Countryside Act 1981, the Deer Act 1991, the Protection of Badgers Act 1992 and the Hunting Act 2004 – to name only a few – aims to address the decline in species (Vincent, 2014) as well as prevent cruelty. Badger baiting (dogs chasing badgers from their sett and then killing them), hare coursing (the same with hares), poaching of mammals, fish and birds, poisoning of raptors, disturbing protected species and trafficking of endangered species and their products are examples of wildlife crimes prohibited by UK law (Northumbria Police, 2015a). The actors committing these offences are equally as varied; they range from individuals taking advantage of an opportunity to large-scale sophisticated serious organised crime (Wyatt, 2013; Vincent, 2014). The motivation behind wildlife crime is also diverse (Nurse, 2011). As Nurse (2013) proposes, there are four categories of drivers for wildlife crime. There are profit-driven offenders; those who are pressured by their employer as part of a legitimate business; offenders who commit wildlife crime for status or power; and those who do so as a sport or pastime. As is evident, the offences, offenders and motivations are complex and wide ranging and therefore a challenge for police.

Although the police themselves have jurisdiction over wildlife crime, there is no requirement for them to have dedicated officers to handle wildlife offences. This means some constabularies have no specific wildlife crime experts. Others, like Northumbria Police (2015b) for instance, have several wildlife crime officers. Presumably this high number, relative to other constabularies, is a reflection of the more rural setting of the region and therefore the possibility for more wildlife to be victimised. Even with specialist wildlife crime officers, the wildlife-related investigations are in addition to the officer's normal duties (Northumbria Police, 2015b). Therefore, overall there are very few officers specialising in wildlife offences, so only a small number of officers are trying to prevent and investigate the varied and complicated realm of wildlife crime. This can be seen as one of the inequalities inherent in wildlife crime in that wildlife killed and abused by humans are silent and hidden victims who are not deemed to warrant the attention of the Criminal Justice System. Another inequality that is evident is that not all species are treated equally (Wyatt, 2013). So-called charismatic mega-fauna and mammals are the species that are of the most concern to humans. When wildlife does receive attention, a multi-agency policing approach to wildlife crime helps to remedy the shortfalls. One of the main benefits of multi-agency policing is that partners (third sector organisations) can fill the gaps, such as lack of staff to combat wildlife crime, that police forces are unable to adequately address.

It is recognised by the police and charities that the lack of attention paid to wildlife crime is a cause for concern because of the negative impact on the environment and wildlife and because of the links to other forms of criminality such as gambling, robbery and vandalism. This concern is reflected in the creation of the National Wildlife Crime Unit (NWCU) and the Partnership for Action Against Wildlife Crime in the UK (PAW UK). The NWCU consists of 11 staff who support police officers and partners anywhere in the UK (NWCU, n.d.). These staff are investigative analysts and intelligence officers. Similarly, PAW UK is a supportive structure for police and their partners. They help 'statutory and non-government organisations to work together to combat wildlife crime. Its objectives are to reduce wildlife crime through effective and targeted enforcement, better regulation and improved awareness' (PAW UK, n.d.). The multi-agency approach has been fully embraced as there are dozens of non-governmental organisations that are members of PAW UK (as well as PAW Scotland, Northern Ireland and Cymru). As one example, World Animal Protection – formerly the World Society for the Protection of Animals (WSPA) – is predominantly a campaigning and lobbying charity trying to prevent the cruelty and suffering of animals worldwide (World Animal Protection, n.d.). Their role in the multi-agency policing of wildlife crime in the UK is one of aware-ness-raising and public engagement. They are currently campaigning to raise awareness around the illegal trade in wildlife and have produced a summary report of the nature and scope of wildlife crime in the UK (World Animal Protection, 2014). Other partner organisations take on functions that are more clearly law enforcement. In order to more fully explore how multi-agency policing works in practice, just two of the many partners – the League Against Cruel Sports (LACS) and the Royal Society for the Protection of Birds (RSPB) – will be discussed further.

League Against Cruel Sports (LACS)

LACS is a charity organisation with a long history of battling against the suffering of animals in the name of sport. For over 90 years, staff and volunteers of LACS have, like World Animal Protection, lobbied the government. Their aim has been to ban hunting and campaign to raise public awareness of animal cruelty. Additionally, they take a much more active role in the policing of wildlife crime. There are four main activities that LACS engage in: first, they expose the cruelty of animal sports and the people who are involved. This is accomplished by undertaking investiga-tions and gathering evidence, which is then given to the police for use in further investigations and prosecutions. Exposure is also achieved through report writing and research as well as obtaining media coverage (LACS, 2015). Clearly, LACS take a very active role in wildlife crime policing as they effectively perform police duties by investigating illegal sport and collecting the evidence to then arrest and prosecute the offenders. For example in October 2014, *The Telegraph* reported three men had been found guilty of illegal fox hunting because of secret filming undertaken by LACS investigators (Watson and Perry, 2014). Presumably, LACS had received intelligence that the hunt was going to be taking place and then managed to film the trio using their hounds to chase the fox. Their footage resulted in the arrest and conviction of the three men.

Second, LACS lobbies and raises awareness through meetings with businesses, politicians and government agencies as well as appearing on television, such as *Sky News*, to promote the enforcement of existing laws and the change of laws to better protect animals (LACS, 2015). Third, people seek assistance from LACS to help stop wildlife crime in their neighbourhoods, so LACS provides support and advice to citizens and acts as a liaison between the public and government agencies, including law enforcement (LACS, 2015). This has meant contacting Local Authorities to ensure they are enforcing the laws and helping landowners to keep poach-ers off their property (LACS, 2015). Finally, in a proactive approach to prevent hunting, LACS

(Continued)

(Continued)

buys land in hunting areas to disrupt and monitor hunting on adjacent properties. They also continue to hold the 'sporting rights' of land they have sold to ensure hunting does not reappear in those areas (LACS, 2015).

LACS takes a multifaceted approach to policing illegal hunting. A core aspect of thwarting this hunting is the investigation of illegal hunts and hunters and the gathering of evidence, often video footage, of these crimes. LACS investigators are often retired police officers, so have the skills to investigate such incidents. The investigations and gathering of evidence could well be undertaken by wildlife crime police officers, but as indicated there are very few of them and wildlife violations are not a priority, so are side-lined compared to other crimes. The actions of LACS are then critical to there being (any) prosecutions of illegal hunting and to the success of the investigations and criminal cases. The RSPB undertakes a similar partnership role.

Royal Society for the Protection of Birds (RSPB)

The RSPB is even older than LACS. It was started in the late 1800s by a women's only group in protest to a devastating fashion trend – plumed hats – that was causing the extinction of numerous species of birds around the world (RSPB, n.d.a). Their mission to protect bird life and their environments has continued to the present day, where the RSPB play an integral role in protecting birds and their habitats. Not only does this role involve conservation, reintroduction and education projects, but it also involves aspects of policing. RSPB staff and volunteers actively guard and watch over nests of the most vulnerable species of birds in order to prevent the illegal capturing of endangered and protected birds and their eggs (RSPB, 2013). Specific protection measures for criminal targets are one of the techniques used in situational crime prevention. By developing and then employing tactics that make it more difficult to steal something or vandalise a property, potential targets are more protected from both opportunistic and planned crimes. In this case, the tactic used is the surveillance of nests. This 'target hardening' approach (Nurse, 2011) has helped hen harriers, white-tailed eagles, red kites and buzzards to make nests, though all bird of prey species in the UK continue to be persecuted to some degree through collection or by poisoning because they are viewed as competing with human hunters of bird species like grouse (RSPB, n.d.b). Records of such persecution are collected and compiled into an annual report by the RSPB to assist police as well as to lobby the government for policy changes. Collection and reporting of such data is another aspect of multi-agency policing that in other contexts (street crime for example) would be undertaken by support staff of law enforcement agencies in order to assist with intelligence and strategic planning.

Several of the recommendations made in the annual bird crime report by the RSPB (2013) are to increase the multi-agency nature of policing wildlife crime. The organisation advises that Natural England, the advisor to the government regarding environmental protection, should be given the authority to protect wildlife and their habitats. Presumably, this would entail giving some enforcement power to Natural England to combat wildlife offences. Another recommendation is to improve the coordination between statutory agencies. As discussed below, one of the key criticisms of multi-agency policing is the lack of communication and cooperation amongst the partners involved.

Clearly, there are benefits to having NGOs as partners in policing wildlife crime. Namely, much of the policing is done by these organisations as it is not a priority for constabularies who devote few staff and resources to wildlife offences. NGOs are essential to lobby for policy changes in this area and are the main way in which the public are made aware of wildlife crime. Undoubtedly because of these benefits, in the realm of wildlife crime, partnership policing will continue and most likely expand.

Discussion

The role of multi-agency working in the current climate of austerity and police cuts is an important one as police are increasingly forced to make decisions about what they are able and not able to respond to. The multi-agency model facilitates the movement of some of these responsibilities onto other actors freeing up police time, capacity and resources. The two case studies presented in this chapter highlight the benefits of multi-agency policing. Regarding the partnerships surrounding sex work, it is evident that the other agencies provide invaluable intelligence about crimes that the police would in all likelihood otherwise never receive. Thus, these partnerships are crucial in bringing offenders to justice. Furthermore, the partners supporting the police are approachable and trusted by sex workers. With time, this trust and rapport may also be shared between police officers and sex workers. Possibly, this connects to O'Neill and McCarthy's (2014) work that argues police officers often gain a lot from engaging in partnership work, and this has contributed to the fracturing or dilution of negative expressions of the traditional police canteen/occupational culture. In the case study about sex work, the improved reputation of the police made it possible to bring a perpetrator to justice, but possibly has more far-reaching impacts by improving the relationship between (some) police and sex workers. The wildlife crime case study demonstrated that charity organisations can fill the shortfall in staffing and resources by actively helping law enforcement to prevent, respond to and collect evidence about wildlife crimes as well as collect crime statistics to support the police.

The case studies also highlight some of the difficulties and issues associated with multi-agency working, most notably the questioning of the role of non-police actors by the public. As mentioned above, research has found wildlife offenders do not recognise the authority of NGOs to stop the offending behaviour. NGOs then are viewed as lacking the legitimacy to police wildlife (and other) offences (Nurse, 2011; Wyatt, 2016). Presumably, such perceptions can potentially lead to hostile, antagonistic exchanges between offenders and NGO staff. This leads to another limitation of multi-agency policing, which is the potential danger of charity or volunteer workers policing possibly violent and possibly armed offenders. Whereas in the above example with LACS, one of the investigators was a retired police officer, this may not be the case for every NGO investigator or volunteer who may be faced with a person committing a crime. The concern then is to ensure that NGO staff are properly trained to handle hostile situations so that they and the public are safe.

Summary

In the last 40 years duties that were once thought to be the responsibility of the police have been undertaken by other organisations. These organisations come from the third and private sectors and from other government agencies. The

(Continued)

(Continued)

resulting multi-agency approach to policing can be applied to many different situations. This is evident by the two case studies presented in this chapter – sex work and wildlife crime. In regards to the former, specialist sex work support services, drugs teams, sexual health services, accommodation providers and other key services all contribute to the well-being of sex workers and play a role in reporting the violence against them. For wildlife crime, NGOs are crucial in sharing intelligence, collecting evidence and gathering crime data for understaffed and under-resourced police constabularies.

The multi-agency approach has been criticised for having poor communication between organisations, the lack of accountability of partner agencies and the potential danger to the staff of the partner organisation. Despite these drawbacks, multi-agency policing is a beneficial approach to responding to, and preventing, crime. It provides more staffing, resources and information to the police as well as improving their reputation and trustworthiness to victims and the public, which ultimately makes them more successful in solving and preventing crimes. With continued cutbacks and outsourcing of what was once only within the government's remit, multi-agency policing – particularly involving private commercialised partners – is undoubtedly an approach that will continue and most likely expand. The aim should be to sign agreements and put in place mechanisms of accountability for all multi-agency operations. The successes documented in this chapter show that cooperation between these partners can lead to improved care of and justice for victims.

Acknowledgements

Thanks to Matthew Jones (Northumbria University) for his comments and suggestions on the chapter and also to Sarah Soppitt (Northumbria University) for guidance and resources on the history of multi-agency working.

Discussion Questions

1. In what ways might multi-agency policing be of particular benefit to marginalised groups?

2. Do you think multi-agency policing is useful for all types of criminality? What might be the exceptions?

3. What are the similarities and differences in regards to inequalities in the two case studies?

4. How can partners be held accountable in multi-agency policing?

——————— **Further Reading** ———————————————————

Sanders and colleagues' (2009) textbook is an excellent introductory source for beginning to learn about the sex industry, the actors involved and how it is regulated and shaped in various ways. The various actors and agencies involved in regulating the industry at various scales are explored in some detail.

Sanders, T., O'Neill, M. and Pitcher, J. (2009) *Prostitution: Sex work, policy and politics*. London: Sage.

For more about the policing of wildlife crime, Nurse's (2015) latest book details the multi-agency approach involving NGOs not just in the UK, but also on a global scale.

Nurse, A. (2015) *Policing Wildlife: Perspectives on the enforcement of wildlife legislation*. London: Palgrave Macmillan.

For more about multi-agency policing in general and more practically, see Bryant and Bryant's edited handbook outlining the history and philosophy of British policing as well as the steps to applying to be a police officer.

Bryant, R. and Bryant, S. (2015) *Blackstone's Handbook for Policing Students*. Oxford: Oxford University Press.

Also for a more general discussion of the multi-agency approach, the chapter 'Policing in a multi-agency context', in Paterson and Pollock's (2011) book provides good background information.

Paterson, C. and Pollock, E. (2011) *Policing and Criminology*. Exeter: Learning Matters.

——————— **References** ———————————————————

Campbell, R. (2014) 'Not getting away with it: Linking sex work and hate crime in Merseyside', in N. Chakroborti and J. Garland (eds), *Responding to Hate Crime: The case for connecting policy and research*. Bristol: Policy Press.

Cook, I.R. (2008) 'Mobilising urban policies: The policy transfer of US business improvement districts to England and Wales', *Urban Studies*, 45 (4): 773–95.

Crawford, A. (2008) 'Plural policing the UK: Policing beyond the police', in T. Newburn (ed.), *Handbook of Policing*. 2nd edn. London: Routledge. pp. 147–81.

Feis-Bryce, A. (2015) *A NUM Outcome – Sex worker raped at knife point*. Provided via personal correspondence.

Home Office (2014) House of Commons Written Statement (HCWS129) *Police Grant Report England and Wales 2015/16*. Available at: www.parliament.uk/documents/ commons-vote-office/December%202014/17%20December/12-Home-PoliceGrant.pdf. Accessed 5 September 2016.

Hubbard, P. (2006) 'Out of touch and out of time? The contemporary policing of sex work', in R. Campbell and M. O'Neill (eds), *Sex Work Now*. Cullompton: Willan. pp. 1–32.

Hubbard, P. and Sanders, T. (2003) 'Making space for sex work: Female street prostitution and the production of urban space', *International Journal of Urban and Regional Research*, 27 (1): 75–89.

Johnston, L. and Shearing, C. (2003) *Governing Security: Explorations in policing and justice*. London: Routledge.

Laing, M. and Irving, A. (2013) *PEER: Exploring the lives of sex workers in Tyne and Wear*. Newcastle: The Cyrenians.

Laing, M., Pitcher, J. with Irving, A. (2013) *National Ugly Mugs Pilot Scheme: Evaluation report*. Manchester: NUM.

League Against Cruel Sport (LACS) (2015) *What We Do*. Available at: www.league.org.uk/who-we-are/what-we-do. Accessed 5 September 2016.

Matthews, R. (2005) 'Policing prostitution ten years on', *British Journal of Criminology*, 45 (6): 877–95.

Ministry of Justice (2012) *MAPPA Guidance 2012, Version 4*. Available at: www.gov.uk/government/uploads/system/uploads/attachment_data/file/406117/MAPPA_guidance_2012_part1_v4_Feb_2015.pdf. Accessed 5 September 2016.

National Wildlife Crime Unit (NWCU) (n.d.) *Structure of the Unit*. Available at: http://www.nwcu.police.uk/about/structure-of-the-unit/. Accessed 5 September 2016.

Newburn, T. and Jones, T. (2002) *Consultation by Crime and Disorder Partnerships*. London: Home Office.

Northumbria Police (2015a) *What is Wildlife Crime?* Available at: www.northumbria.police.uk/about_us/wildlife/whatiswildlifecrime/. Accessed 5 September 2016.

Northumbria Police (2015b) *Wildlife Crime Officer*. Available at: www.northumbria.police.uk/about_us/wildlife/wildlifecrimeofficer/. Accessed 5 September 2016.

Nurse, A. (2011) 'Policing wildlife: Perspectives on criminality in wildlife crime', *Papers from the British Criminology Conference*, 11: 38–53.

Nurse, A. (2013) 'They shoot horses don't they? Policing wildlife, perspectives on criminality in wildlife crime', in D. Westerhuis, R. Walters and T. Wyatt (eds), *Emerging Issues in Green Criminology: Power, justice and harm*. Basingstoke, UK: Palgrave Macmillan. pp. 127–44.

O'Neill, M. and Campbell, R. (2006) 'Street sex work and local communities: Creating discursive spaces for genuine consultation and inclusion', in R. Campbell and M. O'Neill (eds), *Sex Work Now*. Cullompton: Willan. pp. 33–61.

O'Neill, M. and McCarthy, D. (2014) '(Re)negotiating police culture through partnership working: Trust, compromise and the "new" pragmatism', *Criminology and Criminal Justice* 14 (2): 143–59.

Partnership for Action Against Wildlife Crime UK (PAW UK) (n.d.) *Partnership for Action Against Wildlife Crime UK*. Available at: www.gov.uk/government/groups/partnership-for-action-against-wildlife-crime. Accessed 5 September 2016.

Pitcher, J. (2006) 'Support services for women working in the sex industry', in R. Campbell and M. O'Neill (eds), *Sex Work Now*. Cullompton: Willan.

Pitcher, J., Campbell, R., Hubbard, P., O'Neill, M. and Scoular, J. (2006) *Living and Working in Areas of Street Sex Work*. Bristol: The Policy Press. pp. 235–62.

Rowe, M. (2008) *Introduction to Policing*. London: Sage.

Royal Society for the Protection of Birds (2013) *Bird Crime Report*. Available at: www.rspb.org.uk/Images/birdcrime_2013_tcm9-384665.pdf. Accessed 5 September 2016.

Royal Society for the Protection of Birds (n.d.a) *History of the RSPB*. Available at: www.rspb.org.uk/whatwedo/history/index.aspx. Accessed 5 September 2016.

Royal Society for the Protection of Birds (n.d.b) *White-tailed Eagle*. Available at: www.rspb.org.uk/whatwedo/species/casestudies/whitetailedeagle.aspx. Accessed 5 September 2016.

Sanders, T. (2008) *Paying for Pleasure, Men Who Buy Sex*. Cullompton: Willan Publishing.

Scoular, J. and Carline, A. (2014) 'A critical account of a "creeping neo-abolitionism": Regulating prostitution in England and Wales', *Criminology and Criminal Justice*, 15 (5): 608–26.

Shearing, C. and Wood, J. (2003) 'Nodal governance, democracy, and the new "denizens"', *Journal of Law and Society*, 30 (3): 400–19.

Turley, C., Ranns, H., Callanan, M., Blackwell, A. and Newburn, T. (2012) *Delivering Policing in Partnership*, Home Office Research Report 61 Summary. Available at: www.gov.uk/government/uploads/system/uploads/attachment_data/file/116524/horr61.pdf. Accessed 5 September 2016.

Vincent, K. (2014) 'Reforming wildlife law: The Law Commission proposals for wildlife law and wildlife sanctions', *International Journal of Crime, Justice and Social Democracy*, 3 (2): 67–80.

Walklate, S. (2002) 'Community and crime prevention', in E. McLaughlin and J. Muncie (eds), *Controlling Crime*. 2nd edn. London: Sage.

Watson, L. and Perry, K. (2014) 'Three hunt leaders guilty of illegal fox-hunting'. Available at: www.telegraph.co.uk/news/uknews/law-and-order/11160851/Three-hunt-leaders-accused-of-illegal-fox-hunting.html. Accessed 5 September 2016.

World Animal Protection (2014) *Wildlife Crime Report 2014*. Available at: crimestoppers-uk.org/media/281484/wildlife_crime_report_aug14.pdf

World Animal Protection (n.d.) *About Us*. Available at: www.worldanimalprotection.org.uk/campaigns/wildlife/wildlife-crime. Accessed 5 September 2016.

Wyatt, T. (2013) *Wildlife Trafficking: A deconstruction of the crime, the victims and the offenders*. Basingstoke, UK: Palgrave Macmillan.

Wyatt, T. (2016) 'Victimless venison? Deer poaching and black market meat in the UK', *Contemporary Justice Review*, 19 (2): 188–200.

Check out the Companion Website

Want to know more about this chapter? Review what you have been learning by visiting: **https://study.sagepub.com/harding**

- Practice with essay questions
- Test yourself with multiple-choice questions
- Listen to a series of podcasts featuring Neil of Northumbria Police and London's Metropolitan Police Service
- Watch videos selected from the SAGE Video collection

13   Prosecution and the Alternatives

Alison Howey

Introduction

This chapter will explain why the Crown Prosecution Service (CPS) was formed, and will analyse the relationship between the CPS and the police. It will provide an overview of the functions of the CPS and the development of its role since inception. Specific issues such as the alternatives to prosecution (out of court disposals), the CPS role in assisting and supporting vulnerable and intimidated victims and witnesses, and the checks in place to ensure that they are fulfilling their role correctly (such as the Judicial Review Process), will also be considered.

Timeline

1829   Police took on the role of prosecuting offenders

1880   First Director of Public Prosecutions (DPP) appointed

1962   Royal Commission argued it was inappropriate for police officers to investigate and prosecute cases

1981   Philips Inquiry argued that police officers could not be relied on to make fair decisions as to whether to prosecute

1986   Crown Prosecution Service (CPS) became operational

1998   Glidewell Report recommended changes to the work and structure of the CPS

2003   Criminal Justice Act introduced conditional cautions

2013   Chair of Magistrates' Association warned that cautioning had 'got out of hand'

2014   Pilot launched of scrutiny panel for cautions

Formation of the Crown Prosecution Service

Historically, the only route to prosecution in England was via a private prosecution, brought at the expense of the aggrieved person. From 1829 onwards, after the formation of the Metropolitan Police Force, the police took on the role of prosecuting suspected criminals. The Criminal Law Commission reported in 1845 that prosecutions were conducted in a 'loose and unsatisfactory manner' and that the 'duty is frequently performed unwillingly and carelessly' (Grieve, 2013). The report recommended the appointment of public prosecutors. In 1879 the Prosecution of Offences Act came into force, and in 1880 the Home Office appointed the first Director of Public Prosecutions (DPP) to deal with important or complex cases. Once the decision to prosecute had been made, the conduct of the prosecution was then taken over by the Treasury Solicitor. However, until 1986, most criminal prosecutions remained the responsibility of the police.

In 1962 a Royal Commission decided that it was not appropriate for the same officers to both investigate and prosecute cases, and recommended that all police forces should have separate prosecuting solicitors' departments. The system was described as 'haphazard, inefficient and often arbitrary and unfair' (Grieve, 2013: 3). In 1978, after an inquiry (The Fisher Inquiry)

into the Maxwell Confait murder case (http://www.richardwebster.net/then
ewinjustices.html), a wider review was commissioned. The Royal Commission
on Criminal Procedure (The Philips Inquiry) reported in 1981 that the police
officers who investigated alleged offences could not necessarily be relied
upon to make fair decisions as to whether to prosecute them, there was a
lack of consistency between the different police forces concerning decisions
to prosecute, and too many inherently weak cases were proceeding to court in
circumstances where there was little prospect of convictions being achieved.
Consequently the Commission recommended that police forces should no
longer both investigate offences and make the decision over whether to bring
prosecutions, save for minor crimes such as traffic and regulatory offences
(National Archives, n.d.).

A White Paper 'An Independent Prosecution Service for England and Wales'
published in 1983 led to the Prosecution of Offences Act 1985 (the Act) which
created an independent prosecuting service for England and Wales, the CPS.
The intention in forming the CPS was to ensure that the functions of investigating crime and prosecuting crime were to be kept separate, with the aim
that the prosecuting service would be independent from the police. The CPS
became operational in 1986, although private prosecutions are still possible
(see Box 13.1).

Box 13.1

Private Prosecutions

There are still several private prosecutions in the criminal courts, for example the Royal
Society for the Prevention of Cruelty to Animals (RSPCA) prosecute animal welfare offences;
the police prosecute minor road traffic offences, apply for Domestic Violence Protection Orders
(DVPO) and make Proceeds of Crime Applications (POCA); the Local Authorities prosecute
such matters as truancy, fly tipping, and dog fouling; the Driver and Vehicle Licensing Agency
(DVLA) prosecute driving licence offences; and the Probation Service bring prosecutions for
breaches of their Orders.

The Act provided that the CPS was to be headed by the Director of Public
Prosecutions (DPP) who was appointed by the Attorney General (AG) who, in turn,
was answerable to parliament for the actions and conduct of the CPS. The AG has
the role of superintendent and is required to safeguard the independence of prosecutors but has limited practical involvement in cases that effect national security.
The DPP, through the CPS, has responsibility for the conduct of criminal proceedings instituted by the police force, Her Majesty's Revenue & Customs (HMRC) and
other investigative agencies (see Box 13.2).

Box 13.2

Other Investigative Agencies

Other investigative agencies include the National Crime Agency, UK Border Agency, HM Revenue & Customs (HMRC), Department for Work and Pensions (DWP), Department for Environment, Food and Rural Affairs (DEFRA), Department of Health (DoH), and Medicines and Healthcare Products Regulatory Agency.

A review of the CPS, chaired by Rt Hon. Sir Iain Glidewell, was presented in 1998 (The Glidewell Report). The report concluded that the CPS 'has the potential to become a lively, successful and esteemed part of the Criminal Justice System, but that, none of these adjectives applies to the Service as a whole at present' (Glidewell, 1998: 7). The report recommended that the CPS must give greater priority to the more serious cases, it must establish a new organisation, structure and style of management (division into 42 geographical areas was recommended) and it must establish its position more clearly as an integral part of the criminal justice process (Glidewell, 1998: 16–20).

There were originally 31 geographical areas, reduced in 1993 to 13 areas, but increased after the Glidewell Report to 42 as recommended. However, after a spending review in 2010, the number of areas was reduced again to 13. Each CPS area has a Chief Crown Prosecutor and a team of prosecutors, case workers and administrative staff. Crown Prosecutors are predominantly legally qualified solicitors or barristers who undertake the day-to-day conduct of prosecutions including their presentation in court. There are also some Associate Prosecutors who are not legally qualified but have limited rights of audience in the Magistrates' Courts (CPS, n.d.a).

Function of the Crown Prosecution Service

The CPS is the principal prosecuting authority for England and Wales, acting independently in criminal cases investigated by the police and other investigators. It works closely with the police and other investigators to advise upon lines of inquiry, and decide upon appropriate charges or other outcomes, in accordance with the Code for Crown Prosecutors. It keeps all charges under continuous review, prepares the cases and presents them in court and provides information, assistance and support to victims and prosecution witnesses.

The core responsibilities of the CPS are threefold:

1. To provide legal advice to the police and other investigative agencies,

2. To decide whether a suspect should be charged with a criminal offence and prosecuted for it,

3. To conduct prosecutions in court. (CPS, 2015: 4)

The Provision of Legal Advice

Prior to a decision as to whether to charge a suspect, the CPS provides advice to the police, and other investigative agencies, about the applicable legal tests and evidential requirements. This enables the police and other investigators to appreciate what must be proved in a given case, and what further evidence needs to be obtained before a suspect can be charged (CPS, n.d.b).

Criticisms raised by the police, surrounding delays in obtaining advice from the prosecutor prior to charging (House of Commons, 2009: para. 20), have been addressed by the introduction of CPS Direct who offer a virtual (or online) prosecutor on a 24/7 basis.

Decisions to Charge and Prosecute

The role of the CPS in decisions to charge and prosecute is affected by the nature of the offence. Offences are categorised as summary only, either-way, or indictable only offences. Summary offences are less serious matters that are heard in the magistrates' court, by a single District Judge or lay magistrates without a jury, although there are some limited exceptions where such offences can be sent to the Crown Court. Either-way offences are those offences that can be heard in either the magistrates' court or the Crown Court. There will be an allocation, or mode of trial hearing, in the magistrates' court, that will decide whether or not the magistrates' powers will be sufficient to sentence, if convicted. Where the sentencing powers are not considered to be sufficient, the matter will be sent to the Crown Court, for trial and/or sentence. Indictable only offences are the most serious crimes and whilst all charges begin in the magistrates' court, such cases will be sent to the Crown Court after the initial hearing (for examples of offences in each category, see Chapter 14).

For most either-way offences, and all serious and indictable only offences, the police need to seek authorisation from the CPS in relation to (a) whether to charge a suspect and (b) the correct offence to charge the suspect with. Offences where the police can charge without seeking advice from the CPS include any summary only offences, including criminal damage cases where the damage is below £5,000; any offence of retail theft or attempted retail theft, regardless of anticipated plea, as long as the offence is suitable for disposal in the magistrates' court; and any either-way offence where the anticipated plea is one of guilty, and the matter is suitable for sentencing in the magistrates' court. (Case files are now categorised as being Not Guilty Anticipated Pleas (NGAP) or Guilty Anticipated Pleas (GAP) (CPS, 2013a).) However, the greater volume of more minor offences means that, according to the Association of Chief Police Officers (ACPO), 60 per cent of charging decisions remain with the Police (House of Commons, 2009: Part 2, para. 15).

The 1985 Prosecution of Offences Act provides that guidelines be issued to Crown Prosecutors. These guidelines are contained in the Code for Crown Prosecutors (the Code) and the Director's Guidance on Charging, and set out the general principles to be applied in determining whether proceedings should be commenced against a suspect, and which charge should be brought. Although each prospective case must be considered upon its own merits, Crown Prosecutors are obliged to apply the principles contained in the code, and a failure to do so could result in a high court action to Judicially Review the CPS, particularly in circumstances where the CPS have declined to prosecute (see below section on Judicial Review).

There is now also a victim's right to review the decision not to charge. After the case of R v. Christopher Killick [2011] EWCA Crim 1608, the Court of Appeal held that victims also have the right to seek a review of the CPS decision not to prosecute, without having to seek Judicial Review, and there should be a clear procedure regarding how to do so. The CPS now publishes a Victims' Code, which sets out the procedure to seek a review of decisions not to charge, to discontinue, or to otherwise terminate proceedings.

The CPS is under a duty to continually review cases and can overturn an original decision not to prosecute in certain circumstances. For example, where new evidence comes to light, where a different jurisdiction such as an inquest concludes that a prosecution should be brought, or where a review of the decision shows that it was wrong and therefore a prosecution should be brought to maintain confidence in the system. The police may disagree with the CPS decision and there are local systems in place, set out in the Director's Guidance on Charging, to resolve such matters.

It should also be borne in mind that, where the CPS reverses a decision not to prosecute, the defendant may, in certain circumstances, have grounds to pursue an abuse of process argument. Where the CPS decide to reverse a decision in the opposite direction – i.e. reverse a decision to prosecute – they can leave a matter to lie on file, withdraw proceedings prior to a plea being entered, discontinue proceedings prior to trial, or offer no evidence at trial stage if the case cannot be proved for various reasons.

The Code for Crown Prosecutors sets out the duties of the prosecutor and aims to ensure that they operate fairly, independently and objectively, and always act in the interests of justice rather than only for the purposes of obtaining a conviction. Once the police have investigated an alleged offence, they provide the CPS with a file of evidence. The CPS will then conduct a review of the evidence against the suspect in accordance with the Code and the Director's Guidance on Charging. Thereafter a decision will be made on whether to charge the suspect with an offence. That decision will be made in accordance with two questions, which together are called the Full Code Test (CPS, n.d.c):

1. Is there sufficient evidence to provide a realistic prospect of a conviction?

This relates to both the sufficiency of the evidence and the quality of it. The prosecutor needs to decide if the evidence is admissible in court, reliable and credible and that each element of the offence can be proved.

Subject to one exception, called the Threshold Test (see below), if the first question is answered in the negative then the suspect should not be prosecuted, and it is unnecessary to move on to the second question. Where the Crown Prosecutor is of the view that it is more likely than not (balance of probabilities test) that the court would convict the accused person, then the first question will be answered in the affirmative, and in that eventuality the Crown Prosecutor will move on to consider the second question.

2. Is the prosecution required in the public interest?

It does not follow that, simply because there is a realistic prospect of a conviction, the suspect must be charged with a criminal offence. A Crown Prosecutor will consider all aspects of the case when deciding whether it is in the public interest for a prosecution to be brought. Examples of when it might not be in the public interest are: (i) where an accused person caused no harm by their actions; (ii) where any penalty imposed by a court would be minimal; (iii) where an accused person is terminally ill; or (iv) where an out of court disposal is used as an alternative to criminal proceedings.

Box 13.3

Alternatives to prosecution

Out of court disposals (OOCD) include: cannabis warnings, fixed penalty notices (FPN), penalty notices for disorder (PND), speed awareness courses, triage, simple cautions, conditional cautions and community resolution.

Examples of when a Crown Prosecutor might consider it to be in the public interest to charge and prosecute an accused person might be where: (i) the case is serious and significant harm was caused; (ii) the accused person has a substantial criminal record; or (iii) the case involves multiple incidents. In making the decision regarding public interest the Crown Prosecutor should consider the views of the victim, although they are not determinative, and the decision remains one for the Crown Prosecutor.

The Threshold Test is utilised on occasions where, although the Crown Prosecutor recognises that there is a deficiency in the evidence, they have reasonable grounds to believe that the evidence is available, and will be received in the near future. In such circumstances, a decision on the sufficiency of the evidence can be based on the entirety of the evidence (i.e. both on the evidence they have and that which they expect to receive). An example of such a circumstance might be where the case involves a serious assault such as grievous bodily harm and a medical report from the doctor, to confirm the severity of the injuries, has not been received but the police assure the Crown Prosecutor that the medical evidence will be delivered imminently (CPS, n.d.c).

Judicial review of CPS decisions

If an application for Judicial Review of a CPS decision is successful, the court will direct the CPS to reconsider its position. However, the final decision remains with the CPS. Case law highlights the type of decisions that the courts are likely to refer back to the CPS to reconsider. Applications for Judicial Review where the CPS have decided not to prosecute have been successful in several cases: examples are provided below.

> R v. DPP, ex parte C [1995] 1 Cr App R 136
>
> The Divisional Court held that it had the power to interfere with a decision not to prosecute where the prosecutor had failed to follow the policy contained in the Code for Crown Prosecutors. The court did expressly state that this power should only be used sparingly, in cases where the CPS arrived at their decision by using some unlawful policy, they did not follow the settled policy, or their decision was perverse. In this case the prosecutor had sought to convict on a less serious charge and did not question whether or not the evidence satisfied the criteria for a more serious charge.
>
> R v. DPP, ex parte Treadaway, *The Times*, 31 October 1997
>
> The DPP decided not to prosecute five police officers for an assault upon a male, despite him being awarded damages for that assault in the High Court. The Divisional Court held that, whilst the civil court's determination was not binding upon the DPP, it had set out detailed findings and firm conclusions that required further detailed analysis by the CPS.
>
> R v. DPP, ex parte Manning [2001] QB 330
>
> The Divisional Court held that whilst the DPP was under no duty to provide reasons for a decision not to prosecute, it was reasonable to do so in circumstances where a person had died in custody and an inquest had reached a verdict of unlawful killing. In this case the court found that the prosecutor had failed to take into account certain evidence and had applied the incorrect test in considering the prospect of success.
>
> (CPS, 2009)

Conducting Prosecutions in Court

The majority of prosecutions are conducted by CPS-employed barristers and solicitors, although they also instruct self-employed counsel, and also employ non-legally qualified associate prosecutors who have some limited rights of audience in the magistrates' court (under the Prosecution of Offences Act 1985). The Courts and Legal Services Act 1990, as amended by the 1999 Access to Justice Act, established a scheme for CPS-employed solicitors and barristers to appear in the Crown Court as Higher Court Advocates (or Crown Advocates) (CPS, n.d.c).

CPS role re witnesses

A fundamental part of the CPS's role is to protect the public; provide information, support and assistance to victims and prosecution witnesses; and to deliver justice.

The Victims' Code highlights the enhanced entitlements of certain groups such as victims of serious crime, those persistently targeted, vulnerable or intimidated victims, and those who are victims of 'hate crime' (see below) (CPS, n.d.d).

The Prosecutors' Pledge (which has much in common with the Victims' Charter, discussed in Chapter 20) states 'Wherever there is an identifiable victim, the CPS will follow the commitment given in the Prosecutors' Pledge'. The Pledge undertakes to:

- Take into account the impact upon the victim when making a charging decision;
- Inform the victim where the charge is withdrawn, discontinued or substantially altered;
- When practical, seek the victim's view, or that of the family, when considering the acceptability of a plea;
- Address the specific needs of a victim and, where justified, seek to protect their identity by making an appropriate application to the Court;
- Assist victims at Court to refresh their memory from their written or video statement and answer their questions on Court procedure and processes;
- Promote and encourage two way communication between victim and Prosecutor at Court;
- Protect victims from unwarranted or irrelevant attacks on their character and seek the Court's intervention where cross-examination is considered inappropriate or oppressive;
- Upon conviction, robustly challenge defence mitigation which is derogatory to a victim's character;
- Upon conviction, apply for appropriate Orders for compensation, restitution or future protection of the victim;
- Keep victims informed of the progress of any appeal, and explain the effect of the Court's Judgment.

(CPS, n.d.e)

The CPS states that it is fully committed to taking all practical steps to help victims and witnesses through the ordeal of being involved in the Criminal Justice System and they publish guidance to prosecutors about their role in relation to witnesses (Speaking to Witnesses at Court, CPS Guidance – to be fully implemented in 2016).

The CPS publishes a large range of specialist guidance and information documents relating to the prosecution of certain types of crimes including: domestic abuse, rape, cases involving children as victims and witnesses, crimes against older persons, crimes against those with a physical and/or learning disability, and/or mental health issues, hate crimes (discussed in more detail below), forced marriage and honour-based crime, and sexual abuse.

The Youth Justice and Criminal Evidence Act 1999 (YJCEA) introduced a range of special measures designed to assist vulnerable or intimidated witnesses to give their best evidence.

Special Measures

Not all witnesses are eligible for special measures, the YJCEA provides for special measures for those who are vulnerable or may be intimidated. The YJCEA defines vulnerable witnesses as all child witnesses (under 18 years), and any witness whose quality of evidence is likely to be diminished because they:

- Are suffering from a mental disorder;
- Have a significant impairment of intelligence and social functioning;
- Have a physical disability or are suffering from a physical disorder.

Intimidated witnesses are defined as those suffering from fear or distress in relation to testifying in the case:

- Victims of sexual offences are automatically eligible for special measures, as are victims of certain gun and knife crimes. Victims of serious crimes such as domestic violence, hate crimes, kidnap, attempted murder and arson with the intent to endanger life may be regarded as being intimidated witnesses.

The actual measures available to assist such witnesses comprise of screens to shield the witness from the defendant in court, live links where the witness gives their evidence via a camera from another room, the facility to give evidence in private whereby some people will be excluded from the court room, the removal of the judges' and barristers' wigs and gowns, video recorded evidence such as an Achieving Best Evidence (ABE) interview, use of an intermediary in the giving of evidence, and aids to communication such as an interpreter or a hearing device connection. Courts can also use a combination of any of the relevant measures available, such as giving evidence via a live link but using the physical screens in court to hide the TV screen, so that the accused cannot identify the witness. Where a witness requires an intermediary there will usually be a 'ground rules hearing' to establish how to best facilitate that witness. This will involve a discussion between the legal representatives and the court as to the style of questioning, the use of plain language, the requirements of regular breaks, etc., and may involve the rearrangement of the court room and positioning of the parties.

The YJCEA prohibits the cross-examination of certain witnesses, such as children, victims in sexual cases, and certain other protected witnesses, by an unrepresented defendant. In such cases, the courts have a duty to appoint, and pay for, a legal representative to conduct the cross-examination, but that representative will not represent the defendant other than at that stage, and will take no further part in the proceedings. These provisions are to protect vulnerable or intimidated witnesses from a defendant without legal representation. There are now specific Domestic Violence (DV) courts in each area that deal only with such cases, and they will be attended by an Independent Domestic Violence Advisor (IDVA) to assist the victims and provide relevant information to the prosecutor and the court regarding such issues as the requirement of a Restraining Order.

The police should speak to each witness at the earliest opportunity, preferably when their statement is taken, and should enquire if that witness requires any special measures and the reasons for their need, before communicating this information to the prosecutor. This is important as there are strict time scales for notification to the defence and the making of the formal application to the Court (CPS, n.d.f).

Formal Application for Special Measures

Applications are made under the provisions of Part 29 of the Criminal Procedure Rules and should ideally be made with the supporting information identifying the needs of the witness, and the stipulation of which measure is required. In the magistrates' court the application must be made within 14 days of a not guilty plea being entered for adults, and within 28 days of the first hearing of a youth. In the Crown Court the application must be made within 28 days of the accused being sent, or committed to, the Crown Court.

The defence must have an opportunity to object to such an application. Applications can be made at a later stage in the proceedings, with the leave of the court, provided there is an explanation for any delay (CPS, n.d.f).

The CPS Role in Prosecuting Hate Crimes

The CPS and Association of Chief Police Officers (ACPO) define a hate crime as:

> any criminal offence which is perceived by the victim, or any other person, to be motivated by hostility or prejudice based on a person's race or perceived race, religion or perceived religion, sexual orientation or perceived sexual orientation, disability or perceived disability, and any crime motivated by hostility or prejudice against a person who is transgender or perceived to be transgender. (CPS, n.d.g)

Special measures are particularly helpful in these types of cases, where the victim feels intimidated and vulnerable and the Witness Care Unit (WCU) can arrange for pre-court visits to show the witness the facilities available, prior to the trial date.

Where a person is convicted of such a crime, the prosecutor will notify the sentencing judge or bench that the offence is deemed to be a hate crime and seek an uplifted sentence. The case of Regina v. Kelly and Donnelly [2001] EWCA Crim 170, and Section 146 of the Criminal Justice Act 2003, provides for an increase in sentences for these types of crimes. The CPS procedure is that the prosecutor invites the sentencing tribunal (that is the judge or magistrates hearing the case) to state in open court what the sentence would be without the appropriate uplift, and to state what the actual uplifted sentence is, taking into account the aggravating factor.

Alternatives to Prosecution – Out of Court Disposals – Adults

Out of court disposals have been described as 'simple, swift and proportionate responses to low-risk offending' (House of Commons, 2015a: 3) and 'the most important change in criminal procedure … in the past 100 years' (House of Commons, 2015b: 5). The number of out of court disposals administered in the year ending March 2014 was 318,500 (House of Commons, 2015b). However, there have been several criticisms of the process, particularly over the use of cautions. A caution is a formal warning, administered by the police, to a person who has committed an offence. In January 2013 the Chairman of the Magistrates' Association wrote to the Justice Secretary, Right Honourable C. Grayling MP, calling for an inquiry, and described the practice of cautioning as having 'got out of hand' (House of Commons, 2015a: 10). Criticisms included the use of cautions for serious offences, repeated use for persistent offenders, and a significant variation between criminal justice areas. Figures revealed that in the 12-month-period ending June 2014, there were 86,000 cautions administered for indictable and either-way offences, including just over 500 for indictable only offences. The caution process was said to have been 'used inappropriately in up to 30% of cases' (House of Commons, 2015a). The conclusion of the report was that a scrutiny panel should be established in all police force areas to provide consistency, and feedback for training and guidance. The new system was piloted in three police forces from November 2014.

The Criminal Justice Act 2003 introduced conditional cautions for adults, and the Director's Guidance on Adult Conditional Cautions provides supporting guidance as to which offences are suitable. Where there is sufficient evidence to charge an offender and the public interest can be met by the imposition of conditions that suitably address the behaviour, and can provide reparation or redress to the victim or the community, then it may be appropriate to issue such a caution. Offences classified as hate crimes or domestic violence will not be considered as appropriate to be dealt with in this way. Indictable only offences may only be considered for a conditional caution in exceptional circumstances and must be referred to the CPS for a decision. The Legal Aid, Sentencing and Punishment of Offenders Act 2012 (LASPO) introduced changes to the scheme and dispensed with the need for the police to seek authorisation from the prosecutor in all but indictable only offences.

The Crime and Courts Act 2013 provides courts with the power to defer passing a sentence while restorative justice is undertaken, if both victim and offender agree to this course of action. (Restorative justice is defined in the Introduction to Part Two of this book.) There is also the facility for pre-sentence restorative justice to take place, or 'on the street' restorative justice implemented by the police as an alternative to court proceedings and/or part of the cautions and conditional cautions programme. Several areas have now established effective, women specific, triage programmes, working with the CPS, police, and other associated groups (such as drugs services) and women's projects (Hull and Greater Manchester). Triage programmes are discussed further below.

Alternatives to Prosecution – Out of Court Disposals – Youths

(See also Chapter 18.)

For the purposes of the Criminal Justice System, youths are young persons aged from 10 to 17 years at the time of their initial arrest.

In dealing with offences committed by youths the police can consider taking no further action, community resolution or triage, youth cautions, youth conditional cautions or proceeding to charge. Police services and Youth Offending Services (often referred to as Youth Offending Teams (YOTs), Youth Engagement Services (YES) or Youth Justice Services (YJS)) should have a local joint working protocol established to administer their out of court disposal process. The Youth Offending Services should undertake a full assessment of the youth to assess the reoffending risk factors, to determine the nature and content of the appropriate intervention package, to explore the offender's attitude to such an intervention and assess the likelihood of them engaging with the process, and to discuss the possibility of them complying with any restorative justice elements of the intervention (Youth Justice Board, 2014).

Triage

The triage system was introduced in certain areas, as an additional tool for Youth Offending Services, to target young offenders of low-level crimes and prevent their introduction into the Criminal Justice System. Triage offers an informal pre-court option that seeks to engage with young people who accept responsibility for their criminal behaviour and agree to engage with a programme of requirements devised to address their risks and vulnerabilities. Successful completion of the programme will result in there being no prosecution against the offender.

The police will refer the relevant young offender to the Youth Offending Services where their needs and behaviour will be assessed, and a programme of intervention will be agreed with the youth and their families. Triage is envisaged as a brief intervention to challenge offending behaviour, by engaging the youth in reparative, restorative and rehabilitative activities that address the needs of both the victim and the offender, and the factors contributing to the offending. The system also builds in activities to engage the young offender in constructive main-stream leisure activities and can offer referrals to necessary support services such as substance misuse services, education and training, pregnancy and associated advi-sory services, housing support services and Child and Adolescent Mental Health Services (CAMHS).

On completion of the triage programme the Youth Offending Services manager will report back to the police upon the work undertaken, the levels of engagement, and the feedback from the offender and their parent or carer regarding the experi-ence. Where the offender fails to engage they may be offered a further opportunity to comply or the police can take alternative appropriate action to address the offending in question.

The process is typically expected to be completed within a maximum of 28 days with the offender being on police bail throughout that period. At the end of this process, a robust exit plan is envisaged and arrangements can be made to refer the young person to relevant intervention or ongoing support services as required.

The Ministry of Justice describe this programme as 'a brief intervention to chal-lenge their offending behaviour' (Youth Justice Board, 2014).

Testimonial

In Blackpool, an inspector responsible for Community Safety and Partnerships reports that:

> The Child Action North West's Youth Triage project has made a tremendous difference. It has provided young people with the opportunity to reflect, consider their attitude and behaviour and perform various forms of restorative work both to individual victims and the wider community. The police in Blackpool fully support this project and actively seek to embrace any opportunity that will prevent young people from being criminal-ised; they also see it as a truly effective way to prevent children and young people from reoffending. The success of this programme over the last 18 months is clear. The trust that the police have in the project is evidenced by the increasing numbers of young people who are diverted into this community resolution/restorative justice approach rather than being reprimanded (or as of now cautioned). The police see this project as one of the lynchpins in terms of early action and achieving better outcomes for both the young people involved and the wider community across Blackpool. (Child Action North West, n.d.)

Analysis of the Changing Role of the CPS, and the Relationship Between the Police and the CPS

The CPS was formed in 1986 due to concerns regarding the unfairness, ineffi-ciency, and lack of accountability of the previous system (Grieve, 2013), whereby the police carried out the dual roles of investigation and prosecution. The 1983

White Paper entitled 'An Independent Prosecution Service for England and Wales' envisaged that the CPS would take the charge and the evidence from the police, process it and parcel it out to independent lawyers. Over the years, as the CPS settled into its new role within the Criminal Justice System, its role and functions have changed dramatically. This has led to criticism from many interested parties, and several governmental reviews of the service.

The working relationship between the police and the CPS has been described as 'a significant, unparalleled, collaborative project' (House of Commons, 2009: para. 16). However, there have been difficulties in the development of this project. The Glidewell Review (1998) referred to concerns raised by the police regarding delays in obtaining the requisite advice from the prosecutor, and to their perceived view that the CPS had developed a practice of 'safe-charging' or 'under-charging' to manipulate statistics, and increase the rate of convictions. There certainly appears to be an indication of resentment by the police, in the early days, relating to the transfer of power regarding the charging of offences. However, the contrary argument has to be taken into account, which is that the CPS was formed, and the role of charging was transferred, due to an abundance of acquittals, and cases being discontinued, as a result of the police over-charging, or charging where the requisite elements could not be proved (House of Commons, 2009: para. 17). In relation to charging, the Attorney General has noted that 'what we are getting is a greater degree of acuity, judgement, sharpness about what is necessary, and what is possible ...' (House of Commons, 2009: para. 25) and that the CPS has a role to play in demanding more and better evidence from the police at the charging stage. A sign of how far the relationship between the police and the CPS has now improved is that the House of Commons (2009: para. 26) has expressed concern that the two organisations may be so close that there is a perception of a lack of independence.

It has been said that the introduction of conditional cautions, which are decided by the CPS without any reference to the courts, represents a 'blurring of the boundary between the role of the Courts and the role of the Prosecutor' (House of Commons, 2009: para. 13). This is due to the perception that the CPS is playing the role of investigator, prosecutor and judge when they decide to administer such alternatives. However, in reality, the majority of cautions and conditional cautions are administered by the police and not the CPS (House of Commons, 2009: Part 2, para. 15), who only need to authorise exceptional cases.

The CPS role in assisting victims and witnesses, in the presentation of their best evidence, has also been criticised, as has the provision of advice to the sentencing tribunal regarding the uplift of sentences for certain crimes. There is a key question around motivation: when the CPS provides this assistance to vulnerable and intimidated witnesses are they doing so because they have decided that these witnesses are telling the truth, and thereby taking on the role of the tribunal, or are they merely providing a service to assist these persons when accessing the court system? The CPS has the responsibility for conducting the prosecution of offences in the Criminal Justice System and consequently acquires the role of assisting witnesses involved in that process. The court still retains the power to ultimately decide upon the quality of any evidence presented.

Digitalisation of cases has been introduced to attempt to streamline the delivery of documents between the police and the CPS. This has caused its own difficulties, not least where systems have been incompatible, and has created extra work in the short term (House of Commons, 2009: para. 23). The digital system is currently expanding to include the court, the defence and the Probation/Youth Offending Services (HMIC and HMCPS, 2013: 40).

The introduction of Higher Court Advocates (HCA or Crown Advocates) has caused concern for independent lawyers who have seen work that has historically been sent out to them increasingly being undertaken by CPS in-house advocates. In addition to the loss of work, some have expressed fears that standards of advocacy have dropped. In practice however, it appears that the HCAs tend to do most of the preliminary Crown Court hearings and continue to instruct independent lawyers to conduct the trials (House of Commons, 2009: paras 60–78).

The CPS has come under specific media criticism in relation to recent prosecutions and acquittals for historic sexual allegations (CPS, 2013b). The CPS guidance refers to a delay in reporting a sexual offence not being indicative of a false allegation, and states that prosecutors should be proactive in encouraging the police to investigate thoroughly to uncover any available supporting evidence. In 2014 the National Police Chief's Council (NPCC) set up a coordination hub to oversee the investigation of allegations of historic child sex abuse. At the time of writing, there are several ongoing investigations of such abuse (BBC, 2015).

The Chief Prosecutor in England and Wales, DPP Alison Saunders, has robustly defended the CPS decision to prosecute historic sex abuse cases, despite recent high-profile acquittals, and stated that the CPS would continue to attempt to prosecute persons suspected of sexual abuse:

> Justice can only be done if prosecutors remain independent and fair, regardless of who a defendant might be ... Should these prosecutions have taken place? Of course, parliament agrees, as it has set no time limit on bringing rape and sexual offence cases, as it has for other offences. The public would be horrified if we did not prosecute because a complaint came many years after the event. (*Guardian*, 20 February 2014)

It is important that all criticisms are carefully considered as the prosecution of offenders is a major financial burden on the government and the taxpayer; the CPS spent £572.4 million in the year ending March 2015 (CPS, 2015: 15). However, the service is subject to inspection, various audits, reviews and recommendations in the interests of transparency.

HM Crown Prosecution Service Inspectorate (HMCPSI) is the independent statutory body that reports annually to the Attorney General upon the effectiveness and efficiency of the CPS. The CPS has to take account of any findings, and implement any recommendations made. The DPP is the Accounting Officer and has responsibility for reviewing the effectiveness of the CPS, and there is also the Internal Audit and Executive Group who have the responsibility for the development and maintenance of the internal framework, as well as other external audits.

Current Direction

In the 2014–15 Annual Report and Accounts of the CPS, Alison Saunders DPP reported on the four strategic objectives that the CPS set out to achieve in that year, which were to make their service to victims and witnesses central to everything they did, to ensure the highest standard of casework quality, to provide their people with the tools and skills for the job, and to maximise efficiency. In the period covered by the report, the CPS secured 554,784 convictions, which was an 83.5 per cent conviction rate. Whilst there has been a decline in the number of cases prosecuted, there has been an 'exceptional and unexpected' growth in cases involving rape, child sex abuse, and domestic violence (CPS, 2015: 6). The report highlighted the commitment of CPS to improving the 'at court' experience for victims. After a national survey of victims and witnesses, there were plans to implement a revised and improved system in relation to speaking to witnesses. The prosecution of violence against women and girls also continues to be a focus for the CPS (CPS, 2015: 8).

Summary

The CPS was created largely as a response to concerns over the police being responsible for both investigations into crime and the prosecution of offenders. It exists to provide advice to the police and other investigative agencies, to make decisions about charging and prosecution, and to conduct prosecutions in court.

In deciding whether to charge and prosecute, the CPS will consider whether there is sufficient evidence to provide a realistic prospect of conviction and whether a prosecution is in the public interest. Victims have a right to review of a CPS decision not to charge and its decisions can also be challenged via judicial review. The Prosecutors' Pledge sets out the obligations of the CPS towards victims and there are special measures that can be put into place for vulnerable witnesses. The most notable alternatives to prosecution for adults are the issuing of cautions and conditional cautions, while for young people there are other options such as triage. The CPS is rarely involved in the decisions to use these options rather than to prosecute the offender.

While there have been many (and, at times, contradictory) criticisms of the CPS during its lifetime, the evidence presented in this chapter suggests that it is demonstrably moving towards the potential envisaged in the Glidewell Report (1998: para. 26) to become a lively, successful and esteemed part of the criminal justice process.

Discussion Questions

1. Is it appropriate that individuals and other organisations can still bring private prosecutions or should all prosecutions be the responsibility of the Crown Prosecution Service?

2. Should victims have a role in the decision whether or not to charge a suspect? Or will their input undermine careful legal judgment about the likelihood of securing a conviction?

3. Does the public interest test carry a risk of bias? Should whether there is sufficient evidence be the only test applied to decide whether a prosecution should be brought?

4. Do some special measures bias the trial towards the prosecution, by preventing the effective cross-examination of victims or witnesses?

5. Are out of court disposals an effective method of saving costs and preventing people from becoming involved in more formal criminal justice procedures? Or do they represent an easy option for offenders?

6. Does the prosecution of historic sexual abuse cases mean that huge time and energy are wasted on people who no longer present a danger of reoffending?

Further Reading

To read more about the Philips Inquiry and the manner in which its findings were implemented, see:

White, R.M. (2006) 'Investigators and prosecutors or, desperately seeking Scotland: Re-formulation of the "Philips Principle"', *Modern Law Review*, 69 (2): 143–82.

For a critical view of CPS guidance on the treatment of witnesses, see:

Baki, N. and Agate, J. (2015) 'Too much too little too late? Draft CPS guidance on speaking to witnesses', *Entertainment Law Review*, 26 (5): 155–9.

For an insight into some of the procedures involved in tackling historic child sex abuse, see:

Crown Prosecution Service (2013) *Child Sex Abuse Review Panel*. Available at: www.cps.gov.uk/victims_witnesses/child_sexual_abuse_review_panel/index. html. Accessed 6 September 2016.

References

BBC (2015) *Historical Child Abuse: Key investigations*. Available at: www.bbc.co.uk/news/uk-28194271. Accessed 6 September 2016.

Child Action North West (n.d.) *Testimonials – Youth triage*. Available at: www.justice.gov.uk/downloads/youth-justice/effective-practice-library/child-action-north-west-youth-triage-testimonials.pdf. Accessed 6 September 2016.

Crown Prosecution Service (2009) *Appeals: Judicial review of prosecutorial decisions: Legal guidance*. Available at: www.cps.gov.uk/legal/a_to_c/appeals_judicial_review_of_ prosecution_decisions/#content. Accessed 6 September 2016.

Crown Prosecution Service (2013a) *The Decision to Prosecute*. Available at: www.cps.gov. uk/victims_witnesses/resources/prosecution.html. Accessed 6 September 2016.

Crown Prosecution Service (2013b) *Guidelines on Prosecuting Cases of Child Sex Abuse*. Available at: www.cps.gov.uk/legal/a_to_c/child_sexual_abuse/. Accessed 6 September 2016.

Crown Prosecution Service (2015) *Annual Report and Accounts*. Available at: www.gov. uk/government/uploads/system/uploads/attachment_data/file/438548/49940_CPS_ Annual_Report_2015_print.pdf. Accessed 6 September 2016.

Crown Prosecution Service (n.d.a) *Introduction: Facts about the CPS*. Available at: www. cps.gov.uk/about/facts.html. Accessed 6 September 2016.

Crown Prosecution Service (n.d.b) *CPS Relations with the Police*. Available at: www.cps. gov.uk/legal/a_to_c/cps_relations_with_the_police. Accessed 6 September 2016.

Crown Prosecution Service (n.d.c) *Prosecution Policy and* Guidance. Available at: www. cps.gov.uk/prosecution_policy_and_guidance.html. Accessed 6 September 2016.

Crown Prosecution Service (n.d.d) *Victims and Witnesses*. Available at: www.cps.gov.uk/ victims_witnesses/index.html. Accessed 6 September 2016.

Crown Prosecution Service (n.d.e) *The Prosecutors' Pledge*. Available at: www.cps.gov.uk/ publications/prosecution/prosecutor_pledge.html. Accessed 6 September 2016.

Crown Prosecution Service (n.d.f) *CPS Commitments to Support Victims and Witnesses: Legal guidance*. Available at: www.cps.gov.uk/legal/v_to_z/cps_commitments_to_ victim_and_witnesses/. Accessed 6 September 2016.

Crown Prosecution Service (n.d.g) *Hate Crimes and Crimes against Older People*. Available at: www.cps.gov.uk/publications/equality/hate_crime/index.html. Accessed 6 September 2016.

Glidewell, I. (1998) *The Review of the Crown Prosecution Service: Summary of the main report with the conclusions and recommendations*. Chairman Rt Hon. Sir Iain Glidewell. Presented to Parliament by the Attorney General by Command of Her Majesty, June 1998, Cm 3960 (The Glidewell Report). Available at: www.gov.uk/government/uploads/ system/uploads/attachment_data/file/259808/3972.pdf. Accessed 6 September 2016.

Grieve, D. Rt Hon. (2013) *The Case for the Prosecution: Independence and the public interest*. Available at: www.gov.uk/government/speeches/the-case-for-the-prosecution- independence-and-the-public-interest. Accessed 6 September 2016.

Her Majesty's Inspectorate of Constabulary and Her Majesty's Crown Prosecution Service Inspectorate (2013) *Getting Cases Ready for Court: A joint review of the quality of prosecution case files*. Available at: www.justiceinspectorates.gov.uk/hmic/publications/ getting-cases-ready-for-court/. Accessed 6 September 2016.

House of Commons (2009) *The Crown Prosecution Service: Gatekeeper of the criminal justice system – Justice Committee, Section 2 Defining the role of the prosecutor*. Available at: www.publications.parliament.uk/pa/cm200809/cmselect/cmjust/186/18605. htm. Accessed 6 September 2016.

House of Commons (2015a) *Out-of-Court Disposals, Home Affairs*. Available at: www. publications.parliament.uk/pa/cm201415/cmselect/cmhaff/799/79904.htm. Accessed 6 September 2016.

House of Commons (2015b) *Home Affairs – Fourteenth Report, out of court disposals*. Available at: www.publications.parliament.uk/pa/cm201415/cmselect/cmhaff/799/79902. htm. Accessed 6 September 2016.

National Archives (n.d.) *Royal Commission on Criminal Procedure (Philips Commission): Records.* Available at: http://discovery.nationalarchives.gov.uk/details/r/C3028. Accessed 6 September 2016.

Youth Justice Board (2014) *Use Out-of-court Disposals: Section 1 Case Management Guidance.* Available at: www.gov.uk/government/publications/use-out-of-court-disposals/use-out-of-court-disposals-section-1-case-management-guidance. Accessed 6 September 2016.

Check out the Companion Website

Want to know more about this chapter? Review what you have been learning by visiting: **https://study.sagepub.com/harding**

- Practice with essay questions
- Test yourself with multiple-choice questions
- Listen to a series of podcasts featuring Neil of Northumbria Police and London's Metropolitan Police Service
- Watch videos selected from the SAGE Video collection

14 Criminal Courts

Bankole Cole and Timi Osidipe

Introduction

Criminal courts are very important institutions in the criminal justice process in England and Wales. Whereas the police and the Crown Prosecution Service may have ascertained that a crime has been committed and evidence has been prepared and brought to court in order to prove the guilt of the accused, the final decision as to whether a crime has, indeed, been committed and the appropriate punishment for the crime, lies with the criminal courts. Thus, whether justice has been achieved or not is often linked with the decisions of the courts. Justice by courts has two meanings; namely first that an appropriate and fair sentence has been passed and second that each party to the case (defence and prosecution) has been given equal opportunities to exercise their legal rights and present their cases before the court without fear of intimidation or discrimination and that the defendant had been presumed innocent until proven otherwise.

This chapter examines the role and functions of criminal courts in England and Wales. A brief history of criminal trials is provided together with a description of the structures, jurisdictions and sentencing powers of the different courts that try criminal cases in England and Wales. The chapter focuses specifically on magistrates' courts and the Crown Court as they are the two main criminal courts wherein most criminal cases are tried. The chapter will show how the court experience can be disadvantageous to certain defendants because of their social class, gender and ethnicity and how this is further compounded by the tightening of the rules on legal-aid support for poor people appearing in court on serious charges. The challenges imposed by the increasing use of scientific testimony in complex cases and the various factors that often impact on the sentence will be discussed as well as various goals that court sentences are supposed to serve both for the offender and society. In addition, the growth of specialist courts will be discussed in the light of criticisms that courts are not suitable for particular offenders and victims. The chapter concludes with a discussion of the main points raised.

History

In the medieval period crime was not a legally defined concept but 'a violation of specific localised norms of blood, kinship and personal obligation between specific groups of individuals' (Lea, 2006: 1). These wrongs were dealt with in different ways, the most prominent being trials by ordeal. Trial by ordeal was a judicial process whereby the guilt or innocence of the accused was proven by subjecting them to a dangerous experience that might lead to their death. The trial methods were numerous, ranging from ordeal by combat to trial by fire, water or hot iron (see Kerr et al., 1992). The apparent biblical support for this practice is based on the premise that God would always intervene to save the innocent but the guilty would die in the process. Because of the belief in divine intervention, it was thought that only the innocent would choose to endure a trial by ordeal. The guilty were more likely to avoid the ordeal and confess or choose a different form of settlement. This approach was far from being fair or foolproof. Allegations were common of the judges, who were mainly priests, manipulating the process in favour of pre-determined verdicts (see Leeson, 2012).

Although trial by ordeal was forbidden by Pope Innocent III in 1215, this medieval trial method continued well into the seventeenth century, when it was used predominantly against women accused of witchcraft (Goss, 2008). The modern-day criminal court system had its origins in the eighteenth century, during the historical period of the Age of Enlightenment. The modern criminal courts only try offences committed against established state laws and those who dispense justice (judges and magistrates) are guided by clearly defined rules of procedure and legal principles.

Structure, Organisation and Functions of Criminal Courts

Criminal courts in England and Wales are structured in a hierarchical way that signifies the types of cases that they try and their sentencing powers. Often referred to as the lower courts, magistrates' courts try the least serious offences. More serious offences are tried by judges who sit in the Crown Court. Criminal cases can proceed beyond the Crown Court only where a defendant has appealed against a sentence passed by a magistrate or the Crown Court. Appeals are heard at the Queen's Bench Division of the High Court of Justice and further, if there are disputes on points of law, at the Criminal Division of the Court of Appeal. The highest court for criminal cases in the UK is the Supreme Court. The Supreme Court was established by the Constitutional Reform Act of 2005 but came into existence in 2009, replacing the Appellate Committee of the House of Lords, which ceased to exist in July 2009 (Slapper and Kelly, 2015). (See www.judiciary.gov.uk/wp-content/uploads/2012/08/courts-structure-0715.pdf for a full diagram of the structure of the courts in England and Wales.)

The Supreme Court hears appeals from all courts (both civil and criminal) and the decisions made by the Supreme Court are final, unchangeable and binding on all courts in the UK. For example, in a judgment given on 18 February 2016, the Supreme Court of the United Kingdom ruled against a 30-year rule whereby an accused person who was present at the scene of a serious crime, for example murder, but did not strike the blow that caused death is also found guilty of murder on the grounds of foresight alone (see Box 14.1 for excerpts from this case).

Box 14.1

Supreme Court Judgment R v. Jogee (Appellant)

Ruddock (Appellant) v. The Queen (Respondent) (Jamaica)

Judgment Given on 18 February 2016

This ruling was in reaction to a doctrine that had been laid down by the Privy Council in Chan Wing-Siu v. The Queen [1985] AC 168. In Chan Wing-Siu it was held that if two people set out to commit an offence (crime A), and in the course of that joint enterprise one of them (D1) commits another offence (crime B), the second person (D2) is guilty as an accessory to crime B if he had foreseen the possibility that D1 might act as he did. D2's foresight of that possibility plus his continuation in the enterprise to commit crime A were held sufficient in law to bring crime B within the scope of the conduct for which he is criminally liable, whether or not he intended it.

According to the Supreme Court:

Paragraph 77: The rule in Chan Wing-Siu is often described as 'joint enterprise liability'. However, the expression 'joint enterprise' is not a legal term of art. [...] As applied to the rule in Chan Wing-Siu, [...] it is understood (erroneously) by some to be a form of guilt by association or of guilt by simple presence without more. It is important to emphasise that guilt of crime by mere association has no proper part in the common law.

Paragraph 79: It will be apparent from what we have said that we do not consider that the Chan Wing-Siu principle can be supported [...] In plain terms, our analysis leads us to the conclusion that the introduction of the principle was based on an incomplete, and in some respects erroneous, reading of the previous case law.

Paragraph 87: [...] The error was to equate foresight with intent to assist, as a matter of law; the correct approach is to treat it as evidence of intent; [...] what was illegitimate was to treat foresight as an inevitable yardstick of common purpose.

(*Source*: www.supremecourt.uk/cases/docs/uksc-2015-0015-judgment.pdf)

The above case shows how court practices and sentencing options can change significantly as a result of new rules set by the Supreme Court. However, Supreme Court judgments do not override the laws in the books although they can have a strong persuasive effect and can be used by the defence in favour of their clients in similar cases tried in the other courts.

The Judiciary

The judiciary in England and Wales is made up of magistrates and judges.

Magistrates

There are two types of magistrates in the English judicial system, namely: lay magistrates (or justices of the peace) and district judges (Smith, 2013). Lay magistrates are ordinary members of their communities who have volunteered for the job. They are appointed by the Lord Chief Justice following a selection process by local advisory committees made up of serving magistrates and local non-magistrates (https://magistrates-association.org.uk/about-magistrates/history-magistrates). Lay magistrates are not required to have legal qualification or training but, once appointed, they must undergo mandatory training at the Judicial College in order to equip them for the job. A person aspiring to be magistrate must demonstrate six 'key qualities' that were set out in 1998 by the Lord Chancellor – good character; commitment and reliability; social awareness; sound judgement; understanding and communication; and maturity and sound temperament (Huxley-Binns and Martin, 2014; Judicial College, 2014).

Lay magistrates usually sit in twos or threes in what is often referred to as 'the bench'. Efforts are usually made to ensure a gender balance on the bench and, where possible, the bench must attempt to reflect the geographical area and ethnic composition of the community it serves (Huxley-Binns and Martin, 2014). In court, lay magistrates (JPs) are advised on some points of law and procedure by legally qualified justices' clerks.

In contrast, district judges (magistrates' courts) are legally qualified magistrates. Previously known as 'stipendiary' magistrates, district judges are empowered to deal with the more complex cases coming before the magistrates' courts (see section 22(1) of the Courts Act 2003).[i] District judges often sit alone but they may sit with two other justices of the peace in what is commonly known as a 'mixed bench'. Currently there are 23,000 lay magistrates, 140 district judges and 170 deputy district judges operating in England and Wales (www.judiciary.gov.uk/you-and-the-judiciary/going-to-court/magistrates-court/).

Judges

With the exception of the district judges who sit in magistrates' courts, all judges in England and Wales sit in the higher courts, namely the Crown Court, the High Courts of Justice, the Court of Appeal and the Supreme Court. All judges in England and Wales (including district judges sitting at magistrates' courts) are appointed by the monarchy on the recommendation of the Lord Chancellor, after a fair and open competition administered by the Judicial Appointments Commission (JAC) (see the Constitutional Reform Act 2005; Crime and Courts Act 2013). This replaced the old system commonly referred to as the 'tap on the shoulder by the Lord Chancellor' or the 'old boys' network' (Huxley-Binns and Martin, 2014). There is also a hierarchy in the judiciary depending on the courts where they sit and the seriousness of the crimes that they may try.

Circuit judges

Circuit judges are the main judges who preside over criminal trials at the Crown Court. Circuit judges must be lawyers with at least 10 years' practice experience and should generally also have served either as part-time recorders on criminal cases or full-time as district judges (www.judiciary.gov.uk/about-the-judiciary/who-are-the-judiciary/judicial-roles/judges/circuit-judge/).

Recorders

The first step to becoming a circuit judge is via appointment to the post of recorder. Sometimes referred to as part-time judges, recorders are barristers or solicitors of at least seven years standing (www.judiciary.gov.uk/about-the-judiciary/who-are-the-judiciary/judicial-roles/judges/recorder/). Although their jurisdiction is similar to that of a circuit judge, recorders will normally handle the less complex or least serious criminal cases appearing before the Crown Court.

High Court judges

High Court judges in England and Wales are appointed to deal with the more complex and difficult cases. The High Court consists of three divisions, namely: The Queen's Bench which deals with both criminal and civil cases; the Family Division which deals with family law and probate cases; and the Chancery Division which deals with civil and commercial cases. In order to be eligible to be appointed as a High Court judge, it is necessary either to have been qualified as a barrister or solicitor and have gained experience in law for at least seven years or to have been a circuit judge for at least two years. In the past, appointments were predominantly made from the ranks of Queen's Counsels (QCs), particularly from QCs who had sat as deputy High Court judges or recorders. However, this exclusive privilege no longer exists as progression is now available for solicitors to rise to the position of a solicitor-advocate and then aspire to become a High Court judge. High Court judges usually sit in London, but they also travel to major Crown Court centres around England and Wales and may also sit at the Court of Appeal where they assist the Lord Justices in the hearing of criminal appeals (Slapper and Kelly, 2015).

Criminal Trials

Criminal cases in England and Wales are tried in two main courts: magistrates' courts and the Crown Court. Almost all criminal cases start in a magistrates' court but the final venue of trial of a case will depend on the seriousness of the charge and the sentencing powers of the trial court. Crimes in England and Wales are divided into three broad categories namely:

1. Indictable only offences: These are serious crimes for which heavy penalties are prescribed by law. Examples of indictable only offences include murder, manslaughter, robbery, rape and serious offences against the person, for example, causing grievous bodily harm with intent and aggravated burglary. These crimes are tried mainly in the Crown Court, with the option of a jury being present.

2. Summary offences: These are less serious offences, including most motoring offences, alcohol-related incidents, disorderly behaviour and minor criminal damage cases. These crimes are tried mainly by magistrates, without a jury.

3. Offences triable 'either-way': These are crimes that fall within the sentencing powers of both magistrates and the Crown Court. Often referred to as hybrid offences, they include less serious assaults and criminal damage in excess of £5,000; offences of deception or fraud, bigamy, and sexual activity with a child under the age of 16; certain drug offences and serious fraud offences. (See www.judiciary.gov.uk/you-and-the-judiciary/going-to-court/magistrates-court/)

Magistrates' Courts

A defendant will be tried and sentenced in a magistrates' court only if the sentence for the offence falls within the sentencing power of magistrates. A magistrate can impose a variety of sentences including a community sentence, a fine of up to £5,000, a prison sentence up to six months or a combination of these penalties. A magistrate may impose up to 12 months' imprisonment in total on a conviction for more than one offence and a fine in excess of £5,000 if allowed by specific laws.

Indictable (more serious) offences often carry penalties that are beyond the sentencing powers of magistrates. In such cases, a magistrate will have no option but to refer the defendants, on indictment, for trial at the Crown Court. In 'either-way' cases, the Sentencing Council has issued new allocation guidelines that came into effect in 2016 and which require that all either-way offences should be tried by magistrates. (See www.sentencingcouncil.org.uk/wp-content/uploads/Allocation_Guideline_2015.pdf)

However, where a magistrates' court has chosen to try an either-way offence and the sentence to be imposed on the offender exceeds that allowed to magistrates, the magistrates' court will be required to commit the offender to the Crown Court for sentence (see www.gov.uk/courts). Official statistics indicate that more than 97 per cent of criminal cases are tried by magistrates (Lord Chancellor's Department, 2003; Ministry of Justice, 2014b). On average, about 1.5 million to 2 million criminal cases go through the magistrates' courts each year. (See www.cps.gov.uk/legal/s_to_u/summary_offences_and_the_crown_court/)

The Crown Court

The Crown Court is a single court that sits in 76 Crown Court locations in six circuits, namely: the Midland and Oxford; North Eastern; Northern; South Eastern;

Western; and Wales and Chester (Slapper and Kelly, 2015). The criminal justice functions of the Crown Court are mainly five-fold:

1. To try serious criminal cases passed to them, on indictment, by magistrates.

2. To try either-way criminal cases received directly from magistrates' courts.

3. To pass sentence on either-way criminal cases tried by magistrates but referred to them for sentencing.

4. To pass sentence on any summary offence committed to them for sentence by magistrates under section 6 of the Power of Criminal Courts (Sentencing) Act 2000. This will usually apply where a defendant is committed for sentence at a Crown Court for a number of offences made up of both either-way and summary offences. The Crown Court, in passing sentence on the either-way offence, will also have to pass sentence on the summary offence but the sentence that can be imposed by the Crown Court on the summary offence cannot be higher than that which a magistrates' court is allowed to give for that offence. A Crown Court cannot impose a higher sentence for a summary offence simply because the defendant was sentenced for that offence at a Crown Court. (www.cps.gov.uk/legal/s_to_u/summary_offences_and_the_crown_court/)

5. To hear appeals against a magistrates' court's conviction or sentence. (www.gov.uk/courts/crown-court)

Criminal trials at the Crown Court are tried by judges, but there is a hierarchy of judges in the court depending on the seriousness of the case to be heard. Recorders and circuit judges try the least serious (class three) offences, which include offences such as kidnapping, burglary, grievous bodily harm and robbery. Class two offences, which include rape and manslaughter, are usually heard by a circuit judge, under the authority of a presiding High Court judge, while class one offences, which include the most serious offences such as treason and murder, are usually heard by a High Court judge sitting alone.

It is estimated that about 100,000 cases per year are passed on by magistrates, to be tried at the Crown Court. A further 40,000 either-way cases tried by magistrates are also passed on to the Crown Court for higher sentences (Ministry of Justice, 2014b).

The Trial

The main business of the criminal court is the trial. This is essentially the process whereby a defendant's guilt or innocence is tested against facts and evidence presented before the court by the Crown Prosecution Service (CPS, discussed in Chapter 13) on behalf of the police. In court, the suspect becomes the accused or defendant and the charges are contained in an indictment. The task before the defendant-accused is simple: to accept the charges and allow sentence to be passed or refute some or all of the charges and allow the prosecution to prove guilt beyond any reasonable doubt.

The Court Experience

Criminological studies on courts have shown that court trials can be a daunting experience for defendants, especially those who are from poor economic backgrounds. Pat Carlen's classic study of summary proceedings in London's magistrates' courts (1976) shows how the structural arrangements inside the courtrooms can be intimidating to defendants, and how poor defendants who are not legally represented can feel lost and bewildered by the court process (see also Dell, 1971). Carlen likened the court to a 'theatre of the absurd'; one in which the defendant's participation is minimal in a theatrical display of justice that is dominated by the court officials. Doreen McBarnet's (1984) study in Scotland's Sherriff's Courts also showed how the language of the court can be mystifying to working-class defendants and limit their ability to participate effectively in their own trials. (See also Jacobson et al. (2015) on similar experiences among poor defendants tried at the Crown Court and Cole (1990) on the experiences of similar defendants in Nigerian magistrates' courts.)

Criminological writers on courts have also expressed concerns about the treatment of victims and witnesses in court. Although many changes have been made to allow the courts to respect the rights of victims and witnesses attending court (see Chapters 13 and 20), the law still allows the cross-examination of victims and witnesses in a manner that might be perceived as intrusive and intimidatory (see example in Box 14.2).

Box 14.2

Cross-examination

Defence: If this is what in fact happened, what you said about being dragged by the hair, did you attempt to do anything about it? Did you not attempt to retaliate?

Complainant: Yes, I did.

Defence: What did you do?

Complainant: I struggled with him to get away.

Defence: Such as?

Complainant: I was trying really hard to get away, but he just kept pushing.

Defence: Did you have a handbag with you?

Complainant: Yes.

Defence: Why did you not try to strike him with your handbag at that stage?

Complainant: It was up my shoulder. I didn't manage to get it down off my shoulder.

Defence: Did you not try to punch him or strike him in any way?

Complainant: Yes, I did.

Defence: Did you not try to get up when you were pushed down?

Complainant: Yes, I did.

Defence: Did you not think of poking him in the eyes?

Complainant: No, I didn't think of that.

Defence: Did you not think that might have been a good way of repelling an attack by any man?

Complainant: I didn't think of that.

Source: Chambers and Millar (1987) 'Proving sexual assaults: Prosecuting the offender and persecuting the victim', in P. Carlen (ed.) *Crime, Gender and Justice*. Milton Keynes: Open University Press..

Legal Aid

Criminal trials can be very costly, especially where serious allegations are made that the defendant feels must be challenged in court. Criminal trials can also require knowledge of laws and procedures that ordinary defendants may not have. Hence, the advice or support of a legal practitioner is a crucial legal right of defendants, especially poor and uneducated defendants, appearing in court.

In England and Wales, legal aid is a post-Second World War invention, introduced by The Legal Aid and Advice Act 1949 (Ling et al., 2015). This provision was established to support people who could not afford legal services for their trials, in line with the post-war welfare ideology of state welfare support in almost all aspects of life. At inception the focus was on civil cases, but in 1964, this was extended to criminal cases (Huxley-Binns and Martin, 2014). However, recent public debates on legal aid have centred on the increasing costs to the state of providing legal aid almost blindly to the presumed poor. Between 1997 and 2007 the cost of legal aid increased from £1.5 billion to £2.1 billion (Scott, 2015: 1). This led to stringent measures being imposed in the form of means testing before legal aid is approved for a case (Huxley-Binns and Martin, 2014).

The need to further reduce the cost of legal aid was paramount in the policies of the Coalition government (2010–15) and the following Conservative government (2015 to date). This was manifested in a series of consultative documents on legal aid reforms that culminated in even more stringent restrictions being imposed on legal aid (Ministry of Justice, 2010, 2011, 2013a, 2013b, 2014a; McGuiness and Grimwood, 2015). For a person in England and Wales to be eligible for legal aid (sometimes referred to as a representation order), they must:

a) have a case that is eligible for legal aid;

b) be able to prove that the problem is serious; and

c) be able to prove that they are unable to pay for legal costs. (Scott, 2015)

Criminal legal aid is divided into two sections: 'crime lower' workload which covers work in police stations, magistrates' court and prisons, and 'crime higher' workload which is for legal representation in the Crown Court (Scott, 2015). Those who fail to meet the criteria for legal aid, however poor, will have to fund their own defence in court (Legal Aid Agency, 2015). However, due to protests by a variety of civil and legal groups, including the Law Society, the Lord Chancellor and Secretary of Justice initiated further reforms to the legal aid system in 2016 in order to address some of the issues raised by the protesters (see www.parliament.uk/business/publications/written-questions-answers-statements/written-statement/Commons/2016-01-28/HCWS499).

Determining Guilt

Finding a defendant guilty or not guilty may be a long process depending on the elements of the offence that need to be proven and the complexity of the charges. In complex cases, where the court needs to understand complex financial, scientific or medical evidence – for example in cases of complex fraud, cybercrime or an unusual cause of death – the court may call upon experts to examine the evidence and present their findings before the court and jury. Experts could be forensic scientists, psychologists, firearms experts, psychiatrists, computer experts or medical practitioners. Experts have featured in several high-profile cases, for example the use of forensic experts was central to securing the eventual convictions of David Norris and Gary Dobson for the murder of Stephen Lawrence (see http://www.bbc.co.uk/news/uk-16402466).

Experts do not have to appear in court and the court does not have to rely exclusively on expert evidence unless it is overwhelming and convincing in the context of other facts and evidence before the court. An example of a case where erroneous and inadequate expert evidence led to a wrongful conviction was that of Sally Clark, where the expert evidence of a paediatrician, Professor Sir Roy Meadow, and the failure of the prosecution forensic pathologist to disclose important microbiological reports led to her conviction for the murder of two of her sons who died suddenly within two weeks of their births. Sally Clark's conviction was overturned but only after a second appeal in January 2003 (http://news.bbc.co.uk/1/hi/uk/6460669.stm).

Sentencing

Once the guilt of the accused is proven, the court will have to proceed to sentence but this does not usually happen immediately after the case is concluded. The judge or magistrate may need time to decide on the appropriate sentence. The defendant will either be released on bail or remanded in prison while awaiting sentence.

The time awaiting sentence will depend on the number of issues to be considered before a final judgment is given and the appropriate sentence imposed.

The sentence is the most significant activity in a criminal court. For the public, the sentence is often equated with the notion that justice has been done. Sentencing is not simply a decision that is based on the whims and caprices of judges or magistrates. A sentence is the outcome of a systematic and careful consideration of several factors, both legal and non-legal, in an effort to determine the most appropriate sentence that fits the crime and the offender. These factors include:

- the nature and gravity of the offence, as defined by current law;

- age of the offender, for example, whether the offender is a juvenile or an adult;

- past criminal record (previous convictions imply a criminal history which may demand that the offender be punished more harshly than a person in court for the first time for the same offence);

- the type of victim (offences against small children and vulnerable people often incur heavy sentences);

- the degree of responsibility for the crime; for example, whether the offender was the main actor or an accomplice;

- the state of mind of the accused during the commission of the offence; for example, evidence of an impairment of the mind (mental illness) or other defences like provocation might be significant factors in determining the extent of guilt of the accused;

- whether the law has recently changed; an offender may receive a higher or lower sentence because a new law has come into force that sets a new sentence tariff for the offence;

- whether the accused pleaded guilty early in which case they are entitled to take advantage of the sentence discount (reduction) set down by the Sentencing Guidelines Council, which is currently no greater than one third of the maximum sentence prescribed for the offence (Sentencing Guidelines Council, 2007; Criminal Justice Act 2003, s. 144);

- any other information about the accused or the offence in the form of expert or scientific evidence or reports by public bodies such as the probation service that throw more light onto the personality of the offender and the circumstances under which the offence was committed.

What is the Purpose of a Court Sentence?

David Garland argued that 'the various sanctions available to the court are not merely a repertoire of techniques for handling offenders; they are also a system of signs which are used to convey specific meanings' (Garland, 1990: 256). For a punishment to be meaningful or justifiable it must convey a specific message to the public as to why, for example, one offender received a fine and another was sent to prison. However, as there are sentencing tariffs set for most crimes, including the maximum and minimum sentences that the courts are allowed to impose for offences within a crime category, it is not uncommon that an offender who has committed a crime with a tariff ranging from imprisonment to a community rehabilitation order may, after consideration of all the factors, get the latter whilst another offender is sent to prison for the same offence. This raises the question of whether in sentencing the offender is more important than the crime. Whereas a popular perception of sentencing is that the punishment should fit the crime, in reality, the court strives to fit the punishment to both the crime and the offender. The offender must deserve the punishment. In other words, a sentence may be appropriate to a crime but too harsh for a particular offender. Courts are more likely to treat first offenders as less blameworthy and therefore deserving of lesser punishment than offenders with a criminal history. Although not specifically stated in law, a sentence is often an attempt by the court to achieve one or a number of goals either for the offender or society. Common goals of sentencing include the following:

- Individual deterrence: to deter the offender from committing the crime again.

- General deterrence: to deter potential offenders in society from committing the crime because they know what the consequences might be.

- Incapacitation: to protect society from the offender by making sure that they are unable to commit further crimes for as long as possible, either by means of imprisonment or electronic tagging.

- Restoration: to repair the harm done to the victim (this may include making the offender apologise or make amends for their crimes to the victims or the community).

- Rehabilitation: to offer the offender an opportunity to address their offending behaviour, for example through treatment programmes, so that they desist from future offending and live a law-abiding life.

- Retribution: to deliver the appropriate punishment that the offender deserves by virtue of their guilt and culpability. In this case, the punishment is an end in itself; it is given for no reason other than the fact that the offender deserves to be punished.

(these purposes are discussed further in Chapter 4 and in Ashworth et al., 2009; see also Walker, 1991; Duff and Garland, 1994).

Dangerous Offenders

In exceptional circumstances, the courts are allowed to pass a sentence that is longer than that prescribed by law for an offence, where the offender is deemed to be dangerous (see Criminal Justice Act, 2003, s. 229; Criminal Justice and Immigration Act, 2008 s. 17). A dangerous offender is someone who has committed a dangerous offence (see Schedule 15 of the Criminal Justice Act, 2003; see also the Modern Slavery Act, 2015, s. 6 where human trafficking, slavery, servitude and forced or compulsory labour are regarded as dangerous offences); has a criminal record for previous serious crimes, and whose pattern of behaviour, character or mental condition gives a reasonable cause for concern that he or she is likely to offend again in the foreseeable future, if not punished more severely for the current offence (see Floud and Young, 1981; Bottoms and Brownsword, 1982). The extended sentence, however, is not necessarily spent in custody but could involve intensive supervision in the community (see Powers of Criminal Courts (Sentencing) Act, 2000, s. 85; Criminal Justice Act, 2003, s. 227–228; Criminal Justice and Immigration Act, 2008 s.15; Legal Aid, Sentencing and Punishment of Offenders Act, 2012, s. 122). It has been argued that the imposition of an extended sentence amounts to disproportionate sentencing that, according to international laws and conventions, is a form of arbitrary punishment and therefore a violation of human rights (see Van Zyl Smit and Ashworth, 2004). However, these debates have not led to any changes in judicial practice. Instead, under the Criminal Justice Act, 2003 s. 226, British judges can impose life sentences with whole-life tariffs in the most heinous cases of murder. Such sentences mean that a prisoner will never be released. Current recipients of this sentence include Michael Adebolajo and Michael Adebowale, who were convicted of killing Fusilier Lee Rigby in Woolwich, south-east London, in May 2013 (www.theguardian.com/law/2014/feb/18/whole-life-sentences-can-continue-appeal-court-rules).

'Race' and Sentencing

Since their first publication in 1997, the Section 95 (Race and the Criminal Justice System) statistics (based on section 95 of the 1991 Criminal Justice Act) have persistently shown black and minority ethnic people (BMEs) to be disproportionately represented as defendants in the courts. Various explanations have been offered for ethnic disproportionality in criminal justice more generally; these are discussed in Chapters 5 and 6. However, a body of literature exists that appears to indicate that black and minority ethnic offenders are not fairly treated in court and that the sentences that they receive are sometimes disproportionately heavier when compared with sentences given to white offenders for the same crimes. For example: studies have shown that black and minority ethnic defendants are more likely to be tried in higher courts where they stood to receive heavier sentences (Walker, 1989; Brown and Hullin, 1992; Hood, 1992). Hood (1992) further argued from his study in the West Midlands that black offenders were more likely to receive longer custodial sentences than their white counterparts charged with similar offences (comparing like with like) and were even likely to receive more punitive sentences when they had committed less serious crimes than their white counterparts. Hood

(1992) claimed that even where defendants had received non-custodial sentences, black offenders were more likely to be placed at the upper end of the tariff than whites. In addition, in their study at Leeds magistrates' courts, Brown and Hullin (1992) found that where defendants had similar criminal records, minority ethnic defendants received more severe sentences than whites and that, where defendants did not have criminal records, minority ethnic defendants were still given more severe sentences. In her study in London, Walker (1989) found that minority ethnic men were more likely to be denied bail (and remanded in custody) before and during their trials so that those found 'not guilty' were more likely to have spent some time in prison before their acquittal. Moxon (1988) added from his study at the Crown Court that black defendants were more likely to be sent to prison for offences for which imprisonment was just an option. Although no clear conclusion of direct racism in the courts can be deduced from these studies, there is substantial evidence of discriminatory practices again minority ethnic offenders appearing in the courts (see Hudson, 1989). This has led to claims that the courts might be institutionally racist as defined by Macpherson (1999) (see www.independent.co.uk/news/uk/crime/courts-are-biased-against-blacks-with-white-offenders-less-likely-to-be-jailed-for-similar-crimes-8959804.html) (see also Chapter 5 in this volume).

Specialist Courts

Some of the criticisms that have been levelled against the court system in England and Wales include that they are far too formal, that they do not adequately involve the defendants and victims in the proceedings, and that the procedures and outcomes are not suitable for some types of offenders and victims. In the classic article 'Conflicts as property', Nils Christie (1977) described formal court proceedings as 'non-happenings'. As he puts it 'conflicts have been taken away from the parties directly involved and have become other people's property' (Christie, 1977: 1). This has led to the growth of alternative forms of dispute resolution, including restorative justice, and specialist courts that deal with specific types of offenders and victims. Examples include: community justice courts, specialist mental health courts (MHC), dedicated drugs courts (DDC) and specialist domestic violence courts (SDVC). Often referred to as 'problem solving' courts, a key feature of these courts is the involvement of other agencies and service providers, alongside court officials, in the operation of the courts and the delivery of court sentences.

The specialist mental health courts and dedicated drugs courts were set up to address the needs of offenders whose offending behaviours are believed to emanate from mental illness or drug misuse. Their aim is to reduce reoffending by offering credible alternatives to custodial sentences, enhanced psychiatric services or regular and mandatory drug testing and treatment while at court, and to signpost offenders to mental health or drug treatment and rehabilitation services that could appropriately address their needs (see McIvor et al., 2006; Pakes et al., 2010)

In contrast, the specialist domestic violence court is a victim-focused court. The key aim of these courts is to provide an environment in which female victims of violence in relationships are enabled, through support in court, to give evidence against their perpetrators without fear of intimidation and for this support to exist during the trials and after sentence. Thus, the features of these courts include separate entrances, exits and waiting areas for men and women so that victims do not have to face the risk of being confronted or intimidated by their attackers while attending court. In addition, the court business is handled by people who are trained and equipped to handle domestic violence cases, including accredited independent domestic violence advocates (IDVAs) and specially trained judiciary, prosecutors and police officers. Like the other problem-solving courts, support is provided for the victims and perpetrators by agencies and service providers who work in court alongside criminal justice court officials (Home Office, 2006).

Specialist courts are an idea that emanates from the USA where they are known to be quite successful. However, in the UK, evaluations of the specialist mental health courts pilots (Pakes et al., 2010; Winstone and Pakes, 2010), the dedicated drugs courts (McSweeney et al., 2010; Kerr et al., 2011) and the specialist domestic violence courts (Cook et al., 2004; Robinson, 2008) have all shown that these courts are in need of further reforms in order for them to be able to adequately meet the needs of the offenders and victims for whom they have been set up.

Summary

In this chapter it has been shown that the criminal courts occupy a significant and strategic place within the Criminal Justice System in England and Wales and that the business of the courts is complex. It has been shown that the venue for the trial of a crime will depend on the type of crime committed and the sentencing powers of the trial court. There is a hierarchy of courts ranging from magistrates' courts to the Supreme Court, which is the highest court of justice in the UK. Magistrates try more than 90 per cent of criminal cases but the most serious offences are tried at the Crown Court by recorders, circuit judges and High Court judges. Sociological studies of the courts, for example by Pat Carlen, have shown that the court experience can be intimidating and bewildering to both defendants and victims, especially those from poor economic backgrounds whose predicaments have been made even worse by the most recent cuts in legal aid. However, the courts' main function is to determine whether a defendant is guilty and to provide sentences that are appropriate to the crime and suitable for the offender. It has been shown that sentencing can be an intricate process which often involves the consideration of a range of factors. Judges and magistrates must consult the current sentencing guidelines before a final decision is reached. Discretion in sentencing is allowed, for example, where a defendant is considered to be a dangerous offender in which case the law permits the court to give an

(Continued)

(Continued)

extended sentence beyond that which is stipulated for the offence. Research findings have indicated that black and minority ethnic people are discriminated against in court, especially in sentencing.

However, the criminal court is not a static and reactionary institution. From a barbaric era of trial by ordeals in the medieval period, the criminal courts in England and Wales have developed into a sophisticated institution that is bound by the rule of law. But criticisms have been raised by those who believe that the courts is far too formal and does not cater well for particular victims and offenders. These criticisms have led to the emergence of different 'problem solving' courts, such as the dedicated drugs court, specialist mental health courts and specialist domestic violence courts. Findings from evaluations of these courts have shown that much more is needed in order for them to be as effective as expected. Nevertheless, constant review of procedures, for example by the Sentencing Guidelines Council, and training by the Judicial College has meant that the British judicial system remains modern and current and is committed to the dispensation of fair justice.

Discussion Questions

1. Does the Supreme Court have too many powers?

2. What should be the most important factor in sentencing – the offence, the offender or the victim? Give reasons for your answer.

3. What are the likely impacts of the proposed legal aid reforms?

4. Are the courts racist, sexist and anti-working class?

5. Are specialist courts soft options?

Note

i. There are district judges who sit in the County Court. Because they hear only civil and family cases, they are not discussed in this chapter.

Further Reading

Fitz-Gibbon, K. (2016) 'Minimum sentencing for murder in England and Wales: A critical examination 10 years after the Criminal Justice Act 2003', *Punishment and Society*, 18 (1): 47–67.

Hemmens, C., Brody, D.C. and Spohn, C. (2016) *Criminal Courts: A contemporary perspective.* 3rd edn. London: Sage Publications Ltd.

Lippmann, M. (2015) *Criminal Evidence*. London: Sage Publications Ltd.

Kautt, P. and Tankebe, J. (2011) 'Confidence in the criminal justice system in England and Wales: A test of ethnic effects', *International Criminal Justice Review*, 21 (2): 93–117

Smartt, U. (2006) *Criminal Justice*. London: Sage Publications Ltd.

Smartt, U. (2009) *Law for Criminologists: A practical guide*. London: Sage Publications Ltd.

Spohn, C. and Hemmens, C. (2012) *Courts: A text/reader*. 2nd edn. London: Sage Publications Ltd.

References

Ashworth, A. (2007) 'Sentencing', in M. Maguire et al. (eds), *The Oxford Handbook of Criminology*. 4th edn. Oxford: Oxford University Press. pp. 990–1023.

Ashworth, A. (2015) *Sentencing and Criminal Justice*. Cambridge: Cambridge University Press.

Ashworth, A., von Hirsch, A. and Roberts, J. (2009) (eds) *Principled Sentencing*. Portland, OR: Hart Publishing.

Bottoms, A.E. and Brownsword, R. (1982) 'The dangerousness debate after the Floud Report', *British Journal of Criminology*, 22 (3): 229–54.

Brown, I. and Hullin, R. (1992) 'A study of sentencing in the Leeds magistrates' courts: The treatment of ethnic minority and white offenders', *British Journal of Criminology*, 32 (1): 41–53.

Carlen, P. (1976) *Magistrates' Justice*. London: Martin Robertson.

Christie, N. (1977) 'Conflicts as property', *British Journal of Criminology*, 17 (1): 1–15.

Cole, B. (1990) 'Rough justice: Criminal proceedings in Nigerian magistrates' courts', *International Journal of the Sociology of Law*, 18 (3): 299–316.

Cook, D., Burton, M., Robinson, A. and Valley, C. (2004) *Evaluation of Specialist Domestic Violence Courts/Fast Track Systems*. London: Crown Prosecution Service and Department of Constitutional Affairs.

Dell, S. (1971) *Silent in Court: The legal representation of women who went to prison*. London: Social Administration Research Trust.

Duff, A. and Garland, D. (eds) (1994) *A Reader on Punishment*. Oxford: Oxford University Press.

Floud, J.E. and Young, W.A. (1981) 'Dangerousness and Criminal Justice', *Cambridge Studies in Criminology*, 47, London: Heinemann.

Garland, D. (1990) *Punishment and Modern Society: A study in social theory*. Oxford: Oxford University Press.

Goss, K.D. (2008) *The Salem Witch Trials: A reference guide*. Westport, CT: Greenwood Press.

Home Office (2006) *Specialist Domestic Violence Court Programme Resource Manual*. London: Home Office.

Hood, R. (1992) *Race and Sentencing*. London: Clarendon Press.

Hudson, B. (1989), 'Discrimination and disparity: The influence of race on sentencing', *New Community*, 16 (1): 23–34.

Huxley-Binns, R. and Martin, J. (2014) *Unlocking the English Legal System*. 4th edn. London: Routledge.

Jacobson, J., Hunter, G. and Kirby, A. (2015) *Inside Crown Court: Personal experiences and questions of legitimacy*. Bristol: Polity Press.

Judicial College (2014) *Prospectus – April 2014–March 2015*. London: Judicial College.

Kerr, H.M., Forsyth, R.D. and Plyley, M.J. (1992) 'Cold water and hot iron: Trial by ordeal in England', *The Journal of Interdisciplinary History*, 22 (4): 573–95.

Kerr, J., Tompkins, C., Tomaszewski, W., Dickens, S., Grimshaw, R., Wright, N. and Barnard, M. (2011) *The Dedicated Drug Courts Pilot Evaluation Process Study*. Ministry of Justice Research Series 1/11 January. London: HMSO.

Lea, J. (2006) *Crime and Punishment in Early Britain*. Available at: www.bunker8.pwp. blueyonder.co.uk/history/36802.htm [accessed 14 January 2016].

Leeson, P.T. (2012) 'Ordeals', *Journal of Law and Economics*, 55 (3): 691–714.

Legal Aid Agency (2015) *Criminal Legal Aid Manual. Applying for aid in criminal cases in magistrates' court and Crown Court*. London: Legal Aid Agency.

Ling, V., Pugh, S. and Edwards, A. (eds) (2015*) LAG Legal Aid Handbook 2015/16*. London: Legal Aid Group.

Lord Chancellor's Department (2003) *National Strategy for the Recruitment of Lay Magistrates*. London: LCD. Available at: http://webarchive.nationalarchives.gov.uk/+/ http:/www.dca.gov.uk/magist/recruit/natstrat_magrecruit_full.pdf. [Accessed 20 January 2011].

Macpherson, W. (1999) *The Stephen Lawrence Inquiry: Report of an inquiry by Sir William Macpherson*. London: HMSO.

McBarnet, D. (1984) *Conviction: Law, the state and the construction of justice*. Basingstoke: Macmillan.

McGuiness, T. and Grimwood, G.G. (2015) *Changes to Criminal Legal Aid*. Briefing Paper: No. 6628. London: House of Commons Library.

McIvor, G., Barnsdale, L., Eley, S., Malloch, M., Yates, R. and Brown, A. (2006) *The Operation and Effectiveness of the Scottish Drug Court Pilots*. University of Stirling: Department of Applied Social Science.

McSweeney, T., Meadows, P., Metcalf, H., Turnbull, P. and Stanley, C. (2010) *The Feasibility of Conducting an Impact Evaluation of the Dedicated Drugs Court Pilot*. Research Summary 2/10. London: Ministry of Justice.

Ministry of Justice (2010) *The Proposals for the Reform of Legal Aid in England and Wales*. Consultation Paper CP 12/10. London: The Stationery Office Limited.

Ministry of Justice (2011) *Reform of Legal Aid in England and Wales: The government response*. Cm8027. London: The Stationery Office Limited.

Ministry of Justice (2013a) *Transforming Legal Aid: Delivering a more credible and efficient system, Consultation Paper*. CP 14/2013. London: Ministry of Justice.

Ministry of Justice (2013b) *Transforming Legal Aid: Next steps*. London: Ministry of Justice.

Ministry of Justice (2014a) *Transforming Legal Aid – Next Steps: Government response*. London: Ministry of Justice.

Ministry of Justice (2014b) *Court Statistics Quarterly, January to March 2014*. London: Ministry of Justice.

Moxon, D. (1988) *Sentencing Practice in the Crown Court*. Home Office Research Study 103. London: HMSO.

Pakes, F., Winstone, J., Haskins, J. and Guest, J. (2010) *Mental Health Court Pilot: Feasibility of an impact evaluation*. Research Summary 7/1. London: Ministry of Justice.

Robinson, A. (2008) *Measuring What Matters in Specialist Domestic Violence Courts*. Paper 102. Cardiff: Cardiff School of Social Sciences.

Scott, E. (2015) *Future of Legal Aid – Library notes*. London: House of Lords.

Sentencing Guidelines Council (2007) Reduction in Sentence for a Guilty Plea: Definitive Guideline. Available at: www.sentencingcouncil.org.uk/publications/item/reduction-in-sentence-for-a-guilty-plea-definitive-guideline. [accessed 2 September 2016].

Slapper, G. and Kelly, D. (2015) *The English Legal System*, 16th edn. London: Routledge.

Smith, A.T.H. (2013) *Glanville Williams: Learning the law*. 15th edn. London: Sweet & Maxwell.

Van Zyl Smit, D. and Ashworth, A. (2004) 'Disproportionate sentences as human rights violations', *Modern Law Review*, 67 (4) July: 541–60.

Walker, M. (1989) 'The court disposals and remand of white, Afro-Caribbean and Asian men (London 1983)', *British Journal of Criminology*, 29 (4): 353–67.

Walker, N. (1991) *Why Punish?* Oxford: Oxford University Press.

Winstone, J. and Pakes, F. (2010) *Process Evaluation of the Mental Health Court Pilot*. Research Series 18/10. London: Ministry of Justice.

Check out the Companion Website

Want to know more about this chapter? Review what you have been learning by visiting: **https://study.sagepub.com/harding**

- Practice with essay questions
- Test yourself with multiple-choice questions
- Listen to a series of podcasts featuring Neil of Northumbria Police and London's Metropolitan Police Service
- Watch videos selected from the SAGE Video collection

15 Community Sentences

George Mair

Please note that all sentencing statistics used in this chapter have been taken from Ministry of Justice figures available from the MoJ website.

Introduction

Because imprisonment is the most serious court sentence that is available in England and Wales, it is easy to understand why the prison dominates the sentencing landscape. However, without community sentences the way in which the courts currently deal with offenders would be – quite literally – inconceivable. At the most fundamental level, community sentences deal with far more offenders than prisons and for this reason alone they are a vital part of the sentencing process. Without them, we would require either a huge increase in the number of prisons (and the financial costs of this alone would be prohibitive) or the invention of a number of new ways of dealing with offenders (and innovation in this area is not common).

What do we mean by the term 'community sentences'? This is not an easy question to answer definitively. Some would define them as only those court sentences organised and operated by the probation service; for others, the definition would be any non-custodial sentence made by the courts (this chapter will not discuss out-of-court disposals such as cautions, fixed penalty notices, etc.). Even if we could decide conclusively on one of these two definitions, there would be problems with terminological shifts over time, e.g. in the Criminal Justice and Court Services Act 2000, the probation order was renamed as the community rehabilitation order, the community service order became the community punishment order, and the combination order – with great imagination and ingenuity – became the community punishment and rehabilitation order. Yet a further level of complication is ensured by the fact that – however, we decide to define them – there have been additions (and, less often, subtractions) over time. Taking only the main sentences that apply to those aged 18 and over (this chapter does not discuss the community sentences available for those under 18 – see Chapter 18), the following have been the principal changes during the last 70 years.

- 1948 – absolute discharge; conditional discharge; fine; attendance centre order; probation order (plus a handful of conditions).

- 1973 – absolute discharge; conditional discharge; compensation order; fine; attendance centre order; probation order (plus a handful of conditions); community service order; suspended sentence.

- 1991 – absolute discharge; conditional discharge; compensation order; fine; attendance centre order; probation order (plus conditions); community service order; combination order (plus conditions); suspended sentence; curfew order.

- 2001 – absolute discharge; conditional discharge; compensation order; fine; attendance centre order; community rehabilitation order (plus conditions); community punishment order; community punishment and rehabilitation order (plus conditions); drug treatment and testing order; curfew order.

- 2005 – absolute discharge; conditional discharge; compensation order; fine; community order; suspended sentence order.

Clearly, sentences have been added, some have been withdrawn, and some names have been changed. It is important to be clear about we mean when we discuss community sentences and for the purpose of this chapter they will be taken to be all those court sentences that do not involve custody and, more specifically, those sentences which have been available since 2005. This immediately introduces a problem. The suspended sentence order (SSO) is – legally – a custodial sentence even though, as long as its conditions are fulfilled, it will be served in the community and it is operated by probation staff. I would, therefore, argue that it is – for my purposes – a community sentence.

This chapter will be organised in two parts. First, a description of community sentences, how they have developed over time and how they are used by the courts; and second, a discussion of their significance and some of the key issues and challenges facing them. All data are taken from the Ministry of Justice website (www.justice.gov.uk/) unless stated otherwise.

The Development of Community Sentences

It is clear from the changes discussed above that the tendency for community sentences was to grow in number and scope from the end of the Second World War until a retrenchment following the Criminal Justice Act 2003. This was only partly a result of a belief that such sentences were a good thing; it was much more to do with a growing prison population and the need to try to resolve this. Both the suspended sentence – introduced in the 1967 Criminal Justice Act – and the community service order which was introduced in the 1972 Criminal Justice Act, were aimed at offering alternatives to custody. The growth in the number and type of conditions that could be added to a probation order (and later a combination order) was aimed at making probation more rigorous and demanding, and thereby encouraging its use as an alternative to custody. Despite the fact that the 1991 Criminal Justice Act officially did away with the rhetoric of 'alternatives to custody', the combination order and the curfew order were both aimed squarely at the diversion from custody market.

By the beginning of the twenty-first century there were 10 main community sentences (not counting the suspended sentence, which was still in existence but only used in exceptional circumstances) and more than a dozen conditions which could be added to a probation order or a combination order – but only as an individual requirement. This rather messy and fragmented situation had grown over time without any rational planning and raised more questions than it answered (e.g. Why are several 'alternatives to custody' needed?; Why are so many conditions available for a probation or combination order?; What is the effect of adding new sentences to the tariff?). The Halliday review of the sentencing framework (2001) argued that the situation was unsatisfactory, muddled, overly rigid, inconsistent and lacking in transparency and made recommendations that would lead to a more coherent structure. As a result, the Criminal Justice Act 2003 scrapped the existing sentences that were based on some form of supervision (the community rehabilitation order, the community punishment order, the community punishment and rehabilitation order, the drug treatment and testing order, the curfew order and the attendance centre order) and replaced these by two 'generic' orders – the community order and the suspended sentence order. The two new sentences became available to the courts in April 2005.

What do each of the current community sentences offer?

Absolute Discharge

This is the least punitive sentence that a court can pass insofar as it involves no restrictions on the offender and does not require him/her to do anything whatsoever. It is, therefore, a nominal sentence. In 2014 a total of 5,785 absolute discharges were made by the courts. Focusing only on adults aged 18 and older, 4,889 absolute discharges were made on this age group (0.4 per cent of all sentences for this age range). However, as a result of the complete lack of punitive bite of the absolute discharge, one might expect its use to be limited in certain ways – and this is indeed the case. Only 1.5 per cent (74 in total) of all absolute discharges were made in the Crown Court and this is because the Crown Court only deals with the most serious offences where, if the defendant is found guilty, a much more serious sentence than an absolute discharge is likely to apply. Following on from this, only 20 per cent of absolute discharges were made on those aged 18 and older in respect of indictable offences; the remaining 80 per cent were made for summary offences, which are, by definition, less serious. Thus, the absolute discharge is only rarely used in the Crown Court and is mostly used for summary offences. Its use has decreased considerably over recent years: in 1999 a total of 15,584 were passed (1.1 per cent of all sentences) compared to 14,938 (1 per cent of all sentences) in 2004 and 5,785 in 2014 (0.5 per cent).

Box 15.1

Types of Offence

As discussed in Chapter 13, there are three kinds of offences:

- summary offences are those which can *only* be tried in the magistrates' courts;
- either-way offences are those which can be tried in *either* the magistrates' courts *or* the Crown Court
- indictable offences can be tried in the Crown Court.

For the purposes of this chapter, the term indictable offences is used to include *both* either-way *and* indictable offences.

Conditional Discharge

This is a warning penalty; it carries the threat of punishment. Like the absolute discharge, the conditional discharge carries no immediate punishment, but the offender remains liable to punishment if he/she is convicted of a further offence during a period specified by the court (which can be up to three years). If this happens then the individual will be sentenced for the original offence as well as for the new one. In 2014 a total of 72,470 conditional discharges were passed by the courts, 68,587 of these were on offenders aged 18 and over (5.8 per cent of all sentences for this age group). It is, therefore, a much more common sentence than the absolute discharge. But its use is still limited; only 1,636 conditional discharges were made in the Crown Court (2.3 per cent of all such sentences). However, unlike the absolute discharge, almost half (49 per cent) of all conditional discharges made on those aged 18 and above are for indictable offences; the remainder are used for summary offences. So while – as we might expect given the nature of Crown Court cases – conditional discharges are rarely used there, they are used equally for indictable and summary offences. This sentence, too, has been decreasing in use over the past decade: 114,010 in 1999 (8.1 per cent of all sentences), 98,312 in 2004 (6.3 per cent of all sentences) and 72,470 in 2014 (5.9 per cent).

Table 15.1 shows the offences for which both kinds of discharge were used in 2004 and 2014. Although they are being used less often by the courts, they are being used more often for indictable offences – particularly theft and drugs offences. This may be due to a reluctance to use police cautions to deal with what are minor examples of these offences, thereby leading to 'up-tariffing' and 'net-widening'. It could also be that sentencers are resorting to fines less often to deal with such offences, but Table 15.2 suggests otherwise.

Table 15.1 Absolute discharge and conditional discharge by offence group, 2004 and 2014 (%)

Offence	Absolute discharge		Conditional discharge	
	2004	2014	2004	2014
Violence	1.1	1.2	3.6	1.2
Sexual	0.1	0.1	0.2	0.1
Robbery	–	–	–	–
Theft	4.9	9.0	23.7	29.3
Criminal damage and arson	0.5	0.3	2.3	0.5
Drugs	3.0	5.5	6.8	11.3
Possession of a weapon	0.5	0.6	0.2	0.7
Public order	0.2	1.9	0.3	1.5
Fraud	0.3	0.3	3.0	2.0
Miscellaneous	7.3	5.1	3.9	2.5
Summary offences	82.4	75.7	56.0	50.8
Total No.	14,938	5,785	98,312	72,470

(Ministry of Justice, 2015)

The Fine

The fine is the backbone of the sentencing system. If, as I argued at the start of this chapter, sentencing would be impossible without community sentences, then the fine lies at the heart of this. The majority of sentences passed by the courts are fines. According to Bottoms (1983: 186) 'The fine … accords with some of the central features of classical jurisprudence, being calculable, unarbitrary and public'. Ashworth (2015: 346), too, sees the fine in very positive terms:

> The fine is often presented as the ideal penal measure. It is easily calibrated, so that courts can reflect differing degrees of gravity and culpability. It involves no physical coercion and is non-intrusive, since it does not involve supervision or the loss of one's time. It is largely reversible, in the event of injustice. Indeed, it is straightforwardly puni-tive, 'uncontaminated by other values'.

Fines can be imposed for almost any offence. In the Crown Court, the maximum fine is unlimited; in magistrates' courts there was, until recently, a maximum of £5,000 but this was abolished under the Legal Aid, Sentencing and Punishment of Offenders Act 2012. In the case of *summary* offences, there are five levels of fine depending upon the seriousness of the offence:

Level 1	£200
Level 2	£500
Level 3	£1,000
Level 4	£2,500
Level 5	unlimited.

In 2014, a total of 853,335 fines were made by the courts with 844,568 of these in respect of offenders aged 18 and above (71.7 per cent of all sentences passed on this age group). The vast majority of fines (99.8 per cent) are made in the magistrates' courts and, as might be expected from this, 93.7 per cent are made in respect of summary offences. Despite its current dominance in sentencing, the fine was even more dominant in the past, and one of the key developments in sentencing in the last 50 years has been the declining use of the fine. This is especially the case for indictable offences. In 1980, almost half (48 per cent) of all sentences passed by the courts for indictable offences were fines; 10 years later this figure had dropped to 35 per cent and a further 10 years on (2001) it was 24 per cent. Today only 20 per cent of sentences for indictable offences are fines. When we discuss the increasingly punitive society we live in, we usually think of imprisonment and its growth over the past 20 years, but the decreasing use of the fine is another key indicator of this punitive trend.

The use of the fine may have declined, but the average amount imposed has increased. The amount of a fine depends upon the seriousness of the offence; thus the average fine for offences of criminal damage and arson was £163 in 2014, while the average fine for a violent offence was £535. In 2000, the average fine imposed by the courts was £137; in 2014 it had risen to £241. There is, of course, a consid-erable difference between the average fine imposed at the Crown Court and that imposed at magistrates' courts – £7,718 and £225 respectively. This is only partly due to the fact that the Crown Court deals with more serious cases, which will for the most part receive more serious sentences than a fine, but also because organisations are more likely to be fined at the Crown Court and the amount of fines levied on organisations will be higher than that on individuals.

What kind of offences is the fine used for? Table 15.2 provides the answer to this over the last decade. As mentioned earlier, the fine is overwhelmingly used for summary offences; where it is used for indictable offences these tend to be theft and drugs, but these cases will be very minor examples of such crimes. It is notable that over the past decade, fines have decreased by almost 220,000 although there has been a slight increase between 2012 and 2014.

Table 15.2   Use of fines by offence group, 2004–14 (%)

Offence	2004	2007	2010	2012	2014
Violence	0.1	0.1	0.1	0.2	0.2
Sexual	–	–	–	–	–
Robbery	–	–	–	–	–
Theft	1.7	1.5	1.9	1.9	2.1
Criminal damage and arson	0.1	0.1	0.1	0.1	–
Drugs	1.3	1.5	2.6	2.6	2.3
Possession of a weapon	0.2	0.1	0.1	0.1	0.1
Public order	0.1	–	0.2	0.3	0.4
Fraud	0.2	0.2	0.2	0.1	0.2
Miscellaneous	2.2	1.6	1.4	1.2	0.9
Summary offences	94.0	94.8	93.3	93.4	93.7
Total No.	1,072,502	933,817	893,931	823,288	853,335

(Ministry of Justice, 2015)

The Community Order and the Suspended Order

The biggest changes to community sentences in general were implemented in 2005 (following the Criminal Justice Act 2003) when all of the existing sentences operated by the National Probation Service were abolished and two new generic sentences were introduced. The community order (CO) and the suspended sentence order (SSO) look very similar, but there are three significant differences. First, the SSO is legally a custodial sentence (which, if there are no compliance problems, will be served in the community). Symbolically, this is an important development for probation as staff are now dealing with those who have been sentenced to imprisonment (albeit suspended). Second, the CO can be made for up to 36 months, whereas the maximum length of the SSO is 24 months. And third, both sentences are made up of a number of requirements that the court imposes and there are minor differences between these depending upon whether the sentence is a CO or SSO, but crucially – following the Legal Aid, Sentencing and Punishment of Offenders Act 2012 – a court may now make a SSO without any requirements at all. When the orders were introduced there were 12 requirements available, but there have been changes since then and the current requirements for both orders are set out in Box 15.2. The differences are minimal; essentially they are governed by the maximum length of each sentence. Since December 2013, there has to be a punitive requirement (or a fine) in all COs.

> **Box 15.2**
>
> ## Requirements Available for the CO and SSO
>
> Unpaid work (40–300 hours to be carried out within 12 months)
>
> Rehabilitation activity (up to 36 months; *maximum of 24 months for the SSO*; replacing the supervision and the specified activity requirements)
>
> Programme requirement
>
> Prohibited activity requirement (36 months maximum; *24 months for the SSO*)
>
> Electronic monitoring requirement (2–16 hours per day, maximum of 12 months)
>
> Exclusion requirement (up to 24 months)
>
> Residence requirement (36 months maximum; *24 months for the SSO*)
>
> Mental health treatment requirement (up to 36 months; *maximum of 24 months for the SSO*; consent required)
>
> Drug rehabilitation requirement (6–36 months; *6–24 months for the SSO*; consent required)
>
> Alcohol treatment requirement (6–36 months; *6–24 months for the SSO*; consent required)
>
> Alcohol abstinence and monitoring requirement (120 days maximum)
>
> Foreign travel requirement (maximum 12 months)
>
> Attendance centre requirement (12–36 hours, only for those aged 18–25)

In 2014, a total of 98,905 offenders commenced a community order and 45,238 commenced a suspended sentence order. Although the Sentencing Guidelines Council (2004) made it clear that they saw both sentences as offering an alternative to a short custodial sentence, almost half of COs (49.1 per cent) were made for summary offences, and this was the case for almost one-third (31.4 per cent) of SSOs (and it is worth recalling that the SSO is, technically, a custodial sentence). Table 15.3 shows the offences for which each order is used.

Table 15.3 Offenders starting the CO and SSO by offence group, 2008–14 (%)

Offence	Community order				Suspended sentence order			
	2008	2010	2012	2014	2008	2010	2012	2014
Violence	8.9	9.7	8.1	7.8	17	19.6	6.8	15.8
Sexual	0.7	0.8	1.0	1.1	1	1.0	1.0	1.3
Robbery	0.2	0.2	0.2	0.1	1	1.0	1.2	1.0
Burglary	4.1	3.9	3.8	2.9	6	5.8	6.2	5.8
Theft/ handling	19.4	21.6	22.9	22.4	15	14.5	16.9	16.1
Fraud/ forgery	4.6	5.3	5.8	5.4	6	6.9	7.6	7.2
Criminal damage	3.1	3.0	2.7	0.6	2	1.4	1.3	0.6
Motoring	0.7	0.6	0.6	0.5		1.9	1.7	1.9
Other indictable	10.3	11.1	10.6	10.0	17	16.5	16.8	18.9
Summary offences	48.0	43.8	44.3	49.1	34	31.4	30.2	31.4
Total No.	120,743	132,470	115,115	98,905	45,502	48,872	46,146	45,238

(Ministry of Justice, 2015)

Since 2010, the number of both orders has been decreasing. The SSO, as befits its status as a custodial sentence, deals with more serious offences than the CO – it is twice as likely to be used for violent offences and for burglary and less likely to be used for summary offences.

The vast majority of orders only have one or two requirements, and since their introduction six requirements (supervision – now replaced by the rehabilitation requirement – unpaid work, programme, drug treatment, curfew and specified activity) have made up more than nine out of ten COs and SSOs. Mair (2011: 228) argues that despite being targeted as alternatives to custody, 'the new orders have made no contribution to diversion from custody'.

The Compensation Order

The compensation order was introduced in the Criminal Justice Act 1972 and so has been around for more than 40 years. Its use has been repeatedly encouraged, e.g. the 1982 Criminal Justice Act gave the compensation order priority over a fine if the offender had a low income, and in 1988 the Powers of the Criminal Courts (Sentencing) Act required courts to consider a compensation order in all cases where there was death, injury, loss or damage and to give reasons if an order was not made. There is no limit to the amount of compensation that can be ordered. In 2014, a total of 6,230 compensation orders were made – a considerable decrease from the total of 10,333 made in 2004; the drop has been in the order's use for summary offences. In 2014, 54 per cent of compensation orders were made for summary offences; the great majority of those made for indictable offences (87 per cent) were made for theft. The Legal Aid, Sentencing and Punishment of Offenders Act 2012 made yet another effort at encouraging compensation, but there is little reason to be optimistic about the outcome.

The Significance of Community Sentences and Key Challenges

Perhaps the most significant point to make about community sentences is simply to reiterate what was noted in the opening paragraph of this chapter. Community sentences deal with far more offenders than prison does; of 1,215,695 sentences passed by the courts in 2014, only 7.5 per cent were immediate custody. In other words, more than nine out of ten sentences passed by the courts are community sentences. Our love affair with prison tends to have blinded us to just how important community sentences are in this respect. Without them, what would we do with offenders?

Further, they do their work much more cheaply than prison. The cost of a prisoner for 12 months is £34,766, while the cost of a community order/suspended sentence order is £4,305 (2012/13 figures; National Offender Management Service, 2014). And the costs associated with the other community sentences are minimal; fines pay for themselves, compensation orders require only basic administration, and absolute and conditional discharges require little in the way of resources.

And thirdly, they are at least as effective – if not more so – than prison in terms of the reconviction rates associated with them. Measuring reconviction rates is problematic and complicated (see Lloyd et al., 1994; Mair et al., 1997) but their message is unequivocal with regard to community sentences. While it is not legitimate simply to compare the reconviction rates for different sentences (as different types of offenders get different sentences), the latest 12 month reconviction rates are: absolute/conditional discharges 34 per cent; fines 29 per cent; community order 36 per cent; suspended sentence order with requirements 30 per cent; custody 45 per cent (Ministry of Justice, 2015).

One major issue with regard to the use of community sentences (indeed, any sentence) is gender distribution. There are far more male offenders dealt with by the courts than females; in 2014 there were 1,153,059 offenders sentenced where gender was known. Of these, 73 per cent were male and 27 per cent female. Table 15.4 shows the gender distribution of the sentences we have been discussing. On the face of it, this suggests that women are more likely to be fined and less likely to receive a community sentence, a SSO or a compensation order.

Table 15.5 sets out the proportionate use of sentences in the Crown Court and the magistrates' courts for men and women. Although the table does not take into account the different offences for which male and female offenders are convicted – and we do know that offending patterns are different between men and women and therefore sentences will be different – it does seem women are less likely to receive a custodial sentence than men; they are much more likely in the Crown

Table 15.4 Gender distribution of community sentences 2014 (%)

Community sentence	Male	Female
Absolute discharge	77	23
Conditional discharge	75	25
Fine	69	31
Community sentences	83	17
Suspended sentence order	84	16
Compensation order	81	19

Court to receive a SSO; they are more likely to receive a community sentence in the Crown Court but less likely in the magistrates' courts; they are more likely to be fined than men in the magistrates' courts; and they are twice as likely as men to receive a conditional discharge in the Crown Court. As mentioned earlier, these different uses of community sentences for men and women may reflect different offences or less serious examples of the same offence types. It may be that there is a reluctance to pass custodial sentences on women in the Crown Court and this is why the SSO is used so often for women in that venue (indeed it is the most common sentence for women in the Crown Court). In the magistrates' courts this same process may be at work but takes place down the tariff, so that women are less likely to receive a community sentence but more likely to be fined. Whatever the reasons, there are clearly gender differences in the use of community sentences that require further exploration.

Table 15.5 Distribution of sentences by gender and court type 2014 (%)

Sentence	Crown Court		Magistrates' courts	
	Male	Female	Male	Female
Custody	57	33	5	2
SSO	25	40	3	2
Community sentences	12	19	11	6
Fine	2	2	71	83
Absolute discharge	–	–	–	–
Conditional discharge	2	4	7	6
Compensation order	–	–	1	–
Other	2	2	2	1
Total No.	77,425	8,675	769,284	297,675

(Ministry of Justice, 2015)

The lack of research into discharges is worrying. Admittedly, there were fewer than 6,000 absolute discharges made in 2014, but who exactly are they being used for and why do magistrates use them? If the offence is so minor as to merit an absolute discharge, then one might ask why an out-of-court penalty such as a caution is not applied, which would save the costs and stress of a court appearance. The decreasing use of the absolute discharge should be explored; if it continues to decline it might well simply disappear. Is this desirable? Why are magistrates becoming more reluctant to use it? Can its decline be reversed? Given its lack of punitive bite is it worth trying to rejuvenate this most lightweight sentence?

And what about conditional discharges, of which almost 72,500 were made in 2014? Again, we know little about why sentencers use this as opposed to a penalty such as a fine. Research carried out almost 20 years ago suggested that magistrates found it difficult at times to choose between a fine and a conditional discharge (Flood-Page and Mackie, 1998). The same study found that female offenders were twice as likely to receive a conditional discharge as males which, as Gelsthorpe and Loucks (1997) argue, may be due to a reluctance to fine women who do not have paid employment, and who have responsibility for children. As Table 15.5 shows, however, this disparity in use of the conditional discharge no longer applies, and women are more likely than men to be fined in the magistrates' courts.

How does the threat that is contained in the conditional discharge operate for offenders? Do they think about that when they are tempted to offend, or is it quickly forgotten? Given that conditional cautions are now available that can impose requirements on offenders but do not need a court appearance, is there a need to consider imposing some real requirements with a conditional discharge? Such a development would, of course, move the sentence up-tariff and make it more punitive, but is it competing with conditional cautions? There is clear evidence of decline in use and it would be interesting to explore why this is occurring.

The fine remains the foundation of sentencing, despite – again – showing clear signs of long-term decline in use. There may be a number of reasons for this decline, which began in the 1980s. First, as courts have become more punitive, then fines may be seen as too soft a sentence. Second, there are problems with the enforcement of fines and if sentencers consider that a fine may be unpaid they will tend to opt for another sentence (which is likely to be more punitive rather than less). Third, courts worry about using the fine on the unemployed – an issue which began to become significant in the 1980s, which saw an increase in unemployment levels. Fourth, there have always been problems about how to assess disposable income, upon which a fine is based. Offenders have a vested interest in trying to minimise their income in the hope that a fine will be low. Fifth, and closely related to the issue of how to assess income accurately, is the question of equity and fairness. If one offender earning £50,000 a year and another earning £20,000 a year are fined £500 for the same offence, the impact of this will be much greater on the low earner, which goes against the basic principles of justice.

One way of dealing with this fundamental problem and an approach to the fine which is followed in many European countries is the unit or day fine. This is described by those who evaluated the trials of the scheme in this country as follows:

> The problem of imposing fines which are appropriate both to the offence and the offender is one which is faced by all jurisdictions, and a growing number of countries have adopted day fines as the solution. The schemes vary, but all follow the same basic pattern in that the fine is based on multiples of a day's disposable income. There is nothing sacrosanct about 'days' in terms of assessing disposable income. The essential characteristic of this approach is simply that punishment is expressed in terms of a *number* of units, which is determined according to the seriousness of the offence, having regard to all the facts of the case. The *amount* of each unit is governed by the court's assessment of disposable income, and by that alone. (Moxon et al., 1990: 2)

The trials demonstrated that unit fines were viable and likely to lead to improved enforcement and this approach was adopted in the magistrates' courts in the 1991 Criminal Justice Act, coming into operation on 1 October 1992. By summer 1993, unit fines had been abolished by the Criminal Justice Act 1993. Ashworth (2015: 349) lists a number of reasons why this reversal occurred, but the main one was: 'The system resulted in particularly high fines for offenders who might previously have received relatively low fines, especially middle-class motoring offenders with moderately or well-paid jobs.' Although this was one of the objectives of the introduction of the unit fine, there were a number of media stories of wide variations in fines for similar offences and the government decided to call a halt to the initiative. Despite continuing support for the principle of unit fines from the Halliday report (2001) and the first Carter Review (2003), the unit fine has not been reintroduced. The government has encouraged the use of fines (Ministry of Justice, 2011) but so far there is little evidence of any marked upswing in their use. It will be interesting to monitor whether the increase in use between 2012 and 2014 shown in Table 15.2 continues.

The problems associated with the fine also haunt the compensation order. Reparation, however, is one of the aims of sentencing and the compensation order would seem ideally placed to achieve this. If used more would this lead to a reduction in the use of fines? And would this be desirable given that the state profits from fines? It would seem that sentencers have routinely ignored the need to give primacy to compensation and more effort needs to be put into changing this mindset. Cavadino et al. (2013: 125) suggest a state-driven compensation scheme:

> We would therefore favour a scheme in which the revenue from fines is used to fund a reformed criminal compensation scheme that would not be subject to the vagaries of offenders' financial circumstances and willingness to pay up. Indeed, this could form an important part of a more radical reformulation of our existing system of punishments in which the elements of reparation for victims and the reintegration of offenders are given far greater prominence.

The community sentences that have undergone the most significant changes have been those run by the probation service. On the whole, the new sentences are seen fairly positively:

There is no doubt that both orders are considered an improvement on what was previously available for sentencers and probation officers; their versatility and flexibility are particularly appreciated. (Mair and Mills, 2009: 48)

But there are key challenges that need to be addressed. The first of these is perhaps the fragmentation of the community order and the suspended sentence order. Both orders are made up of one or several requirements (unless a SSO with no requirements is passed), and these requirements may be operated by a number of providers. Thus, a CO with a curfew requirement, a programme requirement and a drug rehabilitation requirement is likely to be seen by at least four different agencies: the private company that runs electronic monitoring, the agency that operates the programme requirement, the drugs agency that is used to deliver drug rehabilitation, and the offender manager who oversees the order as a whole. Trying to coordinate these different providers may prove problematic, which could have consequences for the effectiveness of the sentence. Having to see a number of different agencies may lead offenders to perceive not a coherent sentence but a number of sentences that have no obvious relationship with each other. To make matters worse, it is quite possible that the agencies involved in the delivery of requirements are a mix of public, private and voluntary with very different working methods, cultures, types of staff and so on.

These, however, are examples of potential fragmentation at the micro- or meso-level. At the macro level there is the issue of probation now being split between a National Probation Service (NPS – a public service) which provides pre-sentence reports (PSRs), carries out risk assessments and deals with high-risk offenders sentenced to COs and SSOs, and Community Rehabilitation Companies (CRCs – private companies) which deal with low- and medium-risk offenders. This structure is a result of the increasing privatisation of criminal justice as a whole, which began in earnest when Wolds prison was privatised in 1992. Government pushed probation services to increase partnership working in the early 1990s (seen by many as a possible precursor to privatisation), curfew orders enforced by electronic monitoring – which was run by private companies – began to be used on a trial basis in 1995, the first Carter Review (2003) proposed introducing contestability into the provision of probation services in 2003, and in February 2015 the NPS was dismantled so that 21 CRCs now run the bulk of probation-based work in England and Wales, while what is left of the NPS deals with around 25 per cent of the work.

Box 15.3

The Probation Service

There was a probation service for only a very brief period (2001–15). From its beginnings in 1907, it developed as a number of separate local services, and at the start of the twenty-first century there were more than 50 probation services in England and Wales. In 2001, with the

(Continued)

(Continued)

creation of the National Probation Service, 42 probation areas were created. At this time, probation ran several sentences, as noted above, prepared court reports (pre-sentence reports), which assessed the risk posed by offenders and suggested the most appropriate sentence, and worked with prisoners both pre- and post-release. It has traditionally been associated – not always accurately – with a 'soft' approach towards offenders. In the last 30 years, probation has been subjected to a great deal of policy interest; indeed, some might argue, persistent government attack. This has led to a number of significant developments (e.g. the introduction of National Standards and performance indicators, greater central control over how to work with offenders, resource constraints, major structural change) which overall may impact negatively upon the morale of probation staff, and therefore upon the effectiveness of their work (for a recent history of probation see Mair and Burke, 2011).

Whatever one might think about the principle and practice of privatisation (and there are certainly arguments on both sides), what has been done to the proba-tion service does not look particularly efficient in organisational terms. One arm (the NPS) carries out risk assessment and prepares PSRs, the bulk of which is done for private companies who take over the management of the offender if he /she receives a CO or SSO and has been assessed as being low or medium risk. Except, of course, where the only requirement is a curfew order when the CRC or NPS will not be involved at all, only Capita who run electronic monitoring in England and Wales. This does not, on the face of it, look especially efficient – and it gets worse. There are eight different CRCs covering the country; Sodexo is the largest provider with six areas, followed by Purple Futures with five; six other companies cover between three and one area. This is fragmentation on a large scale. It is much too early in this brave new world of mixed provision to tell whether the various agencies are working smoothly together but it is essential that they do.

For example, if a medium-risk offender is reassessed as becoming high risk, then the management of the offender moves from the CRC to the NPS. It is vital for public safety and the effective management of the sentence that this process is carried out smoothly. Even if it is, however, there is the issue of the offender having got used to his original offender manager and now having to build some kind of relationship with a new and unknown offender manager. It would be much simpler to deal with changing levels of risk if these could be contained within the same organisation.

At present, risk assessment and the preparation of PSRs rest with the NPS and there is a strong case that this should remain so. If CRCs were to take over this responsibility there would be a very clear conflict of interest: if CRCs wanted more offenders (which would mean more money and probably more profit) then they could write PSRs that tended to rate the risk as low or medium and made strong arguments for a CO or SSO which they would then provide. And it is worth noting that PSRs are no longer four-to-six-page documents which have taken up to several weeks to prepare, with meetings with the offender, perhaps also his/her family, employer, conversations with his/her GP, and so on. More and more, courts are relying on written Fast Delivery Reports (FDRs) which can be delivered in a matter of days, or oral FDRs which are done on the same day following a short adjournment by the court for the assessment to take place. In 2011 the total number of FDRs was 126,423, more than double since 2006 and making up more than six out of every ten (62 per cent) of all court reports. By 2014 the total number of court reports had dropped to 141,932 from 204,631 in 2011, but 108,179 of these were FDRs – more than three-quarters (76 per cent) of all reports. Indeed, oral reports made up more than one-third more (36 per cent) of all FDRs, and more than a quarter (28 per cent) of all reports. Given the significance for effectiveness of fitting the appropriate programme to the right offender, and the number of combinations of requirements possible with COs and SSOs, the increasing reliance on oral FDRs is rather worrying.

Another challenge facing those who provide the CO and SSO is the implementation of payment by results. It would be difficult to argue against the principle of paying those who provide effective sentences, but the principle raises a number of important questions that have yet to be answered satisfactorily. First, effectiveness is to be measured by a simple binary measure of whether or not an offender has been reconvicted, which is a crude and somewhat limited approach (see Lloyd et al., 1994; Mair et al., 1997). Second, as a CO or SSO is likely to involve several providers of services, how is the payment divided up if there is a positive result? Third, in the desire to earn money it would not be surprising if CRCs were keen to ensure that they only dealt with those cases where there was a high possibility of success, so there would be cherry-picking (and, incidentally, the NPS would be left to deal with those offenders who are least likely to have successful outcomes). Fourth, in the wish to maximise payments, if a CRC discovered a consistently highly effective way of working with offenders (admittedly unlikely) and thereby ensured full payments, could the effective programme be rolled out (sold?) to other CRCs given commercial pressures? Would the successful CRC not wish to retain its successful programme for its own use? The potential for serious disagreements and over-complicated procedures in payment by results is considerable (for a useful discussion of the payment by results model see Fox and Albertson, 2011, 2012).

One clear trend in the use of probation-based sentences over the past 20 years or more has been that they have become increasingly punitive and they have been used more often for summary offences. As Table 15.3 shows, around half of COs and almost one-third of SSOs (technically a custodial sentence) were made for summary offences. Rod Morgan (2003) has discussed the 'silting-up' of probation-based sentences by low-risk offenders which means that these sentences are not dealing with the kind of offenders they should be, but with those who could be fined or even conditionally discharged. As Ashworth (2015: 373) rightly argues, sentencing has become more punitive across the whole range of penalties:

There is broad agreement about what happened in English sentencing in the ten years prior to the 2003 Act: the use of imprisonment has increased sharply, many of those who would previously have received a community sentence or a suspended sentence were sent to custody, and many of those who would previously have been fined (and latterly, some of those who would have received a conditional discharge) were given community sentences. There was, in other words, a ratcheting-up of sentence severity, a gradual up-tariffing of offenders with increases in the use of both custody and community sentences.

The Crime and Courts Act 2013 made it mandatory for community orders to include at least one punitive requirement or a fine or both, unless there were exceptional circumstances that would make this unjust. This is a very clear move to make the community order more punitive and one might pose the question of just how punitive community sentences should be. The more they are forced in this direction, then the more they will lose the particular advantages that they offer. They cannot compete directly with prison in punitive terms, yet it sometimes feels as if this is precisely what governments wish they would do. If pushing them to become more punitive meant that they were more likely to be used to divert offenders from custody, then toughening-up the CO might be justified, but there is very little evidence to support this argument.

Since the introduction of the CO and the SSO, six requirements have accounted for more than nine out of ten of all those used (Mair, 2011). The supervision, unpaid work, curfew, specified activity, accredited programme, and drug treatment requirements are by far the main building blocks of the orders. There may be a number of reasons for the lack of use of the remaining requirements (see Mair, 2011) but one of them may be a lack of imagination and creativity on the part of probation staff. It is possible that with the introduction of CRCs, the relative use of requirements may begin to change, but as – for the present – the staff of CRCs are ex-NPS staff, this is unlikely. Given the range of requirements available, greater use of those rarely used might be a welcome development. Interestingly, given the new requirement for all COs to have a punitive requirement, there has been an increase of more than 400 per cent in the use of the prohibited activity requirement for both the CO and the SSO during 2014 (there have also been significant increases in curfew and exclusion requirements – both punitive).

Conclusions

It would be difficult to over-state the importance of community sentences, yet – apart from a recent upsurge in probation-based research (Mair and Burke, 2011), there has been a surprising lack of academic interest. Given the size of the prison population (currently around 86,000) and little sign that this will decrease in future (see Ministry of Justice projections of the prison population), a concerted effort to rejuvenate community sentences so that they can divert more offenders from custody would seem wise. The usual approach has been to put together some form of intensive probation (for example, see Folkard et al., 1974; Mair et al., 1994) and leave it to the courts to make use of this as they see fit. Political will has been conspicuously lacking in all these efforts, yet is a vital ingredient for successful diversion from custody. But so too is the need to divert low-risk offenders from the CO and SSO to the fine, and to make more use of the conditional discharge – perhaps introducing some relevant conditions to the latter to make it more demanding than at present.

A window of opportunity may have opened up following Michael Gove's announcement in December 2015 of the abolition of the Criminal Courts Charge, which may have been having an adverse impact upon fines and compensation orders, and a major review of financial penalties:

> the Ministry of Justice will be reviewing the entire structure and purpose of court-oriented financial impositions for offenders, with a view to considering options for simplification and improvement. The current array of sanctions and penalties is complex and confusing. I would, therefore, like to bring greater simplicity and clarity and I would like to achieve three other goals. Firstly, I would like to give the judiciary ... greater discretion in setting financial orders. Second, I would like to explore how we can make financial penalties a more effective tool in helping to deliver improved non-custodial sentences. And, my third hope is that we can properly – and fairly – ensure that money raised through financial penalties plays an appropriate – and sustainable – role in supporting taxpayers to meet the costs of running the courts. (Gove, 2015)

Just how far this review will have a positive impact upon financial penalties remains to be seen, but it does at least offer a good opportunity to think carefully about such sentences and it is to be hoped that the opportunity will not be wasted. Community sentences as a whole are far too important to be left to fragmented and incoherent development. A wide-ranging examination of all of them, how they relate to each other, and their role in sentencing would be a major step forward. Just over a decade ago, the Coulsfield inquiry looked into community sentences (Coulsfield, 2004; Bottoms et al., 2004) but this had two limitations: first, it was an unofficial inquiry without government backing; and second its main interest was in alternatives to prison. Community sentences – or at least some of them – can certainly provide a direct alternative to prison, but they also offer much more than that, and this chapter has tried to show their significance and to point to their potential.

Discussion Questions

1. What is the point of absolute and conditional discharges?

2. Should the fine be used more often?

3. Are both the community order and the suspended sentence order needed?

4. Is it possible to use community sentences as feasible alternatives to custody?

———————— **Further Reading** ————————

Ashworth, A. (2015) *Sentencing and Criminal Justice*. 6th edn. Cambridge: Cambridge University Press. Chapter 10 of this book discusses 'Non-custodial sentencing' from a more legal point of view, examining principles and practice.

Cavadino, M., Dignan, J. and Mair, G. (2013) *The Penal System: An introduction*. 5th edn. London: Sage. This is one of the key texts on sentences and how they work; it also contextualises them theoretically and politically.

O'Malley, P. (2009) 'Theorizing fines', *Punishment and Society*, 11 (1): 67–83. An excellent article that attempts to reclaim the fine as a serious sanction.

The Probation Journal. Sage. This peer-reviewed journal is published four times a year and is focused on articles about the work of probation. It is an invaluable source for keeping up-to-date with research into community penalties.

———————— **References** ————————

Ashworth, A. (2015) *Sentencing and Criminal Justice*. 6th edn. Cambridge: Cambridge University Press.

Bottoms, A.E. (1983) 'Neglected features of contemporary penal systems', in D. Garland and P. Young (eds), *The Power to Punish: Contemporary penality and social analysis*. London: Heinemann.

Bottoms, A., Rex, S. and Robinson, G. (2004) *Alternatives to Prison: Options for an insecure society*. Cullompton: Willan.

Carter, P. (2003) *Managing Offenders, Reducing Crime*. London: Strategy Unit.

Cavadino, M., Dignan, J. and Mair, G. (2013) *The Penal System: An introduction*. 5th edn. London: Sage.

Coulsfield, Lord (2004) *Crime, Courts and Confidence: Report of an independent inquiry into alternatives to prison*. London: The Stationery Office.

Flood-Page, C. and Mackie, A. (1998) *Sentencing Practice: An examination of decisions in magistrates' courts and the Crown Court in the mid-1990s*. Home Office Research Study 180. London: Home Office.

Folkard, M.S., Fowles, A.J., McWilliams, B.C., McWilliams, W., Smith, D.D., Smith, D.E. and Walmsley, G.R. (1974) *IMPACT: Intensive Matched Probation and After-Care Treatment*. Home Office Research Study 24. London: HMSO.

Fox, C. and Albertson, K. (2011) 'Payment by results and social impact bonds in the criminal justice sector: New challenges for the concept of evidence-based policy?', *Criminology and Criminal Justice*, 11: 395–413.

Fox, C. and Albertson, K. (2012) 'Is payment by results the most efficient way to address the challenges faced by the criminal justice sector?', *Probation Journal*, 59: 355–73.

Gelsthorpe, L. and Loucks, N. (1997) 'Magistrates' explanations of sentencing decisions', in C. Hedderman and L. Gelsthorpe (eds), *Understanding the Sentencing of Women*. Home Office Research Study 170. London: Home Office.

Gove, M. (2015) Speech to the Magistrates' Association National Council on 3 December 2015. Available at: www.gov.uk/government/speeches/speech-to-the-magistrates-association [accessed 12 January 2016].

Halliday, J. (2001) *Making Punishments Work: Report of a review of the sentencing framework for England and Wales*. London: Home Office.

Lloyd, C., Mair, G. and Hough, M. (1994) *Explaining Reconviction Rates: A critical analysis*. Home Office Research Study 136. London: HMSO.

Mair, G. (2011) 'The community order in England and Wales: Policy and practice', *Probation Journal*, 58: 215–32.

Mair, G. and Burke, L. (2011) *Redemption, Rehabilitation and Risk Management: A history of probation*. London: Routledge.

Mair, G. and Mills, H. (2009) *The Community Order and the Suspended Sentence Order Three Years On: The views and experiences of probation officers and offenders*. London: Centre for Crime and Justice Studies.

Mair, G., Lloyd, C. and Hough, M. (1997) 'The limitations of reconviction rates', in G. Mair (ed.), *Evaluating the Effectiveness of Community Penalties*. Aldershot: Avebury.

Mair, G., Lloyd, C., Nee, C. and Sibbitt, R. (1994) *Intensive Probation in England and Wales: An evaluation*. Home Office Research Study 133. London: HMSO.

Ministry of Justice (2011) *Breaking the Cycle: Government response*. London: Ministry of Justice.

Ministry of Justice (2015) *Proven Re-offending Statistics Quarterly Bulletin: January to December 2013, England and Wales*. London: Ministry of Justice.

Morgan, R. (2003) 'Thinking about the demand for probation services', *Probation Journal*, 50: 7–19.

Moxon, D., Sutton, M. and Hedderman, C. (1990) *Unit Fines: Experiments in four courts*. Research and Planning Unit Paper 59. London: Home Office.

National Offender Management Service (2014) *National Offender Management Service: Business Plan 2014–2015*. London: Ministry of Justice.

Sentencing Guidelines Council (2004) *New Sentences: Criminal Justice Act 2003 guideline*. London: Sentencing Guidelines Council.

Check out the Companion Website

Want to know more about this chapter? Review what you have been learning by visiting: **https://study.sagepub.com/harding**

- Practice with essay questions
- Test yourself with multiple-choice questions
- Listen to a series of podcasts featuring Neil of Northumbria Police and London's Metropolitan Police Service
- Watch videos selected from the SAGE Video collection

16 Imprisonment

Charlotte Bilby

Introduction

When breaking the law is discussed, it is not unusual for the conversation to quickly turn to imprisonment. As seen in the last chapter on community sentences, the vast majority of people convicted of an offence never see the inside of a prison cell. In the year leading up to September 2015, of the 1.22 million people who were found guilty of an offence and sentenced only 88,500 were given immediate custody (Ministry of Justice, 2016a). So, why is it the case that there is a disproportionate amount of criminological interest in prisons, and why are they so emotive to many outside the criminological community?

We are told that prisons in England and Wales are in a state of crisis, with the prison population set to reach 90,000 by 2020 (Ministry of Justice, 2013). This could be seen as being nothing new; the history of imprisonment shows us that prisons have almost always been in crisis. Questionable prison hygiene, sanitation, conditions and overcrowding – catalysts for John Howard and Elizabeth Fry's work in the late 18th and early 19th centuries – are issues often reflected in research since the prison population's rapid growth in the last 20 years. Recent inspection reports talk of low staff numbers, bullying and violence by prisoners, lack of rehabilitative opportunities, and filthy prison kitchens and washing facilities. In 1895, the Gladstone Report considered the importance of separating different types of prisoners, and noted that prisons should reform as well as punish people. This can be compared with the recent history of psychological treatment programmes to address offending behaviour, and the role of prisoner employment, vocational training and education to prepare people for work outside prison.

This chapter will explore imprisonment in England and Wales today, and will do this by explaining how history, politics and theoretical understanding of justice have shaped prison regimes. As well as considering how we punish and rehabilitate adults, it will look at why male prisoners are categorised into four risk levels, and the impact that this has on the different types of prisons and the way they are run. Prisons in England and Wales are not just under government control; about 10 per cent are run by private sector companies, some of which also have Community Rehabilitation Company contracts (see Chapter 15). The impact of private and not for profit organisations taking part in punishment and rehabilitation will be discussed. The chapter will also look at whether decent support is given to the different groups within prison; for example are the health and social care needs of male prisoners over the age of 55, or vulnerable women prisoners, being met? With the growing length of prison sentences, you will be asked to consider whether people who pose little risk of harm to society might be better punished and rehabilitated in places other than prison.

Since the eighteenth century punishment of people who break the law has become increasingly private and secret (Garland, 1990). It happens out of the sight of the general population, behind high fences and with seemingly impenetrable rules. This chapter will investigate behind the prison walls, and unpick the questions of how and why we deprive people of their liberty.

Timeline

1777   John Howard's report into prison conditions

1877   Prisons Commission took over the administration of prisons and their inspection

1895	Gladstone Report recommended substantial changes to imprisonment
1898	Prison Act arising from the Gladstone Report
1948	Criminal Justice Act ended penal servitude and corporal punishment in prisons
1973	Community service introduced
1995	Incentives and Earned Privileges scheme introduced
2007	Corston Report examined the needs of women in the prison estate
2013	House of Commons Justice Select Committee inquiry into the needs of older prisoners

The History of Prisons

The History after the Bloody Code and Transportation of Offenders

Until the late 18th and early 19th centuries, the state publicly punished poor people for breaking the law by putting them in the village stocks, or executing them at town gallows. Often the public humiliation of punishment did not end there, with offenders' bodies being left on gibbets or in metal cages, where they would rot as a sign to all people who might be thinking about breaking the law. These public punishments, very crude attempts at what might be called general deterrence, became a more and more usual sight, with lower level offences being punished more harshly – something that we could term up-tariffing. This collection of offences for which execution and corporal punishment became the norm was known as the Bloody Code (Scott and Flynn, 2014), and were increasingly questioned by those who were interested in the reform of punishment. But the question then arose as to what should be done with people who had broken the law if they were not executed. Some courts were so reluctant to sentence people to death that they deliberately started to find people not guilty so that their lives could be saved.

This criminal justice crisis came at the same time as the numbers of people being transported to the USA and Australia started to decline. From about 1850 there were almost no offenders leaving the UK to serve sentences abroad. This meant that the government needed to start to look at how it was to punish those who had broken the law (Johnston, 2010). The result of these combined pressures was the building of new prisons, mainly on what were the outskirts of towns and cities. These large Georgian and Victorian prisons are still in use, for example HMPs Durham, Leicester and Manchester all still house prisoners in their original buildings. These buildings were not just a place to hold the numbers of offenders who would not now be either executed or transported, but they were also a symbol of state power. They were often built to look like fortified castles, with crenellations around the top of the walls, or larger and more looming imitations of the Victorian workhouses. Just like the public gallows and gibbets of the previous century, they were an attempt at general deterrence, with the imposing nature of the buildings seeking to ensure that people did not commit crime (Jewkes and Johnston, 2007; Moran, 2015). The tough regimes, with their hard labour, were intended both to instil a Christian moral sense in the offenders, and to act as a specific deterrence to those who experienced the regimes.

The first inspections of prisons were undertaken by John Howard, the High Sherriff of Bedfordshire, who began by inspecting the prisons in his own county but then expanded this role to the rest of the country. As a result of this tour he both gave evidence to a House of Commons select committee in 1774 and wrote a report in 1777 that outlined the appalling conditions in which people were held. The prisons were insanitary, unhygienic and, according to Howard, supported prisoners', and often prison officers', drunkenness. The impact of Howard's work had a sustained impact on the way in which prisoners are held today. For example the idea of cellular confinement, rather than holding people together in a group, comes from Howard's work (Johnston, 2010). He was also one of the first to argue that the purpose of imprisonment was not solely punishment and that consideration should also be given to ideas of rehabilitation. This was to be achieved through hard labour and Christian instruction, and might not be considered as rehabilitative in its nature now.

Elizabeth Fry continued the work of Howard in her work with women prisoners. She visited Newgate prison in London in the early nineteenth century, and like Howard, was appalled at the squalor in which prisoners were held. Children were held with their imprisoned mothers, and some women were held without trial. As well as being the first woman to give evidence to a parliamentary select committee, Fry set up prison schools and systems to help women learn to read and stitch, which would help them in finding work after release. Her work influenced the Home Secretary Sir Robert Peel's 1832 Gaols Act, which included measures such as payment to prison officers, the right of magistrates to inspect local prisons and the provision of female guards for women prisoners. Although it took time for these elements to be enacted, Fry's role in these reforms should not be forgotten (Carlen and Worrall, 2004).

The Separate and Silent System and Its Critics and the Impact of the Gladstone Committee Report

In 1877 the Prisons Commission, an organisation under the control of the Home Office, was created and took over the administration of prisons in England and Wales and their inspection. By 1881 all prison staff had been brought under its regulation, meaning that prisons were now essentially under the control of the national government, rather than being run locally by each county. But prison reform was not consistent or carried out effectively enough. Herbert Gladstone, who was an MP and an Under Secretary in the Home Office, chaired a committee that considered the ways in which prison should be run (information taken from the websites of the National Archives: www.nationalarchives.gov.uk/). The investigation took place at a time when there was a seeming reduction in the rate of serious and violent crime, but a concern about the impact that imprisonment was having on those who were deemed 'habitual criminals'; that is repeat offenders. The harsh regimes of the separate and silent systems, and the requirement that prisoners do hard labour for no apparent reason, was considered to be having little effect on a good proportion of the 'criminal classes' (Johnston, 2016). The separate and silent systems required prisoners to be kept apart from each other at all times and to stop them from speaking to each other. Prisoners were made to wear masks and were separated both in cells and individual stalls while in chapel. An example of this can be seen in Lincoln castle, which used to house the city's prison.

The Gladstone Report, which was presented in 1895 and led to the Prisons Act of 1898, is considered to be the signal of the start of the modern prison system, and with it, 'the perpetual state of crisis' (Fitzgerald and Sim, 1982 as cited in Cavadino et al., 2013: 9) that the system finds itself in. The report stated that the separate and silent systems should be abolished and prison should be considered not simply a place of punishment, but a place where people would be rehabilitated and reformed. This 'ameliorative creed' (Radinowiscz and Hood as cited in Harding, 1988) was accepted by government officials, and not just the well-to-do Victorians who had prospered during the industrial revolution. This acceptance seemed to be based on a movement towards paternalism and philanthropism, which meant that the wealthy felt it was part of their duty to help those poorer than themselves.

Prisons in the Post-war Period and the Impact of the Criminal Justice Act 1948

After the Second World War there was a wholesale change to the way in which politics and the approach to meeting the needs of all communities were thought of in the UK. The National Health Service was created, support and benefit for those who were unemployed was altered, and many industries were nationalised. Among these changes were some fundamental alterations to the Criminal Justice System, including embryonic discussions about the abolition of the death penalty. The Criminal Justice Act 1948 was groundbreaking in that it removed the sentence of penal servitude (Johnston, 2016). This meant that people could no longer be sentenced to carry out hard labour for no wages. The act also outlawed corporal punishments in prison, such as whipping. Despite it being over 60 years since the piece of legislation was passed, many herald this, rather than the Gladstone Report, as the start of the modern prison system.

The Act also started to consider how prisoners were housed, and proposed different types of punishment according to the prisoner's age, seriousness of offence and criminal history. While prisons were still central to the Criminal Justice System, there was a belief that the system had to rehabilitate those who had broken the law; a welfare approach to offending behaviour. The Act saw other forms of punishment and rehabilitation being used:

- Corrective training meant release of the prisoner on condition that further offence would result in sentencing.

- Detention centres were residential institutions for young offenders (under the age of 21).

- Attendance centres were aimed at young offenders who had committed minor crimes. The young offender was required to attend the centres at weekends, and undertake rehabilitation activities.

(Information taken from the websites of the National Archives (www.national archives.gov.uk/) and the Howard League for Penal Reform (www.howardleague. org/about-us/).

Prisons in the Recent Past

Since the end of the Second World War, society has dramatically changed. These societal changes, unsurprisingly, have had an influence on the ways in which we punish and rehabilitate offenders. Change did not happen all at once, and the change might not always be considered to be progressive.

The 1960s saw the abolition of the death penalty in England and Wales, the creation of the parole board and the introduction of suspended sentences. These last two elements were designed to reduce the prison population, as there were concerns that it was growing too quickly. The parole board (which is discussed further in Chapter 17) enabled prisoners to apply for early release from prison, and the suspended sentence meant that not all those sentenced to custody would immediately be sent to prison. Coupled with changes to the ways in which community sentences operated in the early 1970s, a move away from the use of imprisonment could be detected.

From the early 1970s onwards, there was a political resurgence of ideas of liberalism. In the UK and in the USA, these ideas were developed by political figures such as Margaret Thatcher and Ronald Regan. Simplistically, they were concerned about the interference that the state had in people's lives. They believed that people needed to have the social agency to get up and change their lives, and that this would not be achieved through state intervention. This change involved ensuring that tax payers did not have to support people who were unemployed or sick to any great extent. In some respects, the same was true of the Criminal Justice System. While people should be punished for their offences, the state should not have to pay for the costs of transgression. In England and Wales, it was identified that prison was expensive and that a form of punishment in the community would be preferable in many cases. In 1973 community service was created and was used as both a punishment in itself and as a way of trying to divert people away from the prison system. At the same time, Robert Martinson and his colleagues published a highly influential piece of research saying that there was not enough evidence to demonstrate that rehabilitative approaches worked in changing offenders' behaviour (Hollin and Bilby, 2007).

The Role of Prison in an Era of 'What Works'

During the 1990s there was a resurgence in the use of offending behaviour programmes, which had fallen out of favour in the 1970s after Martinson's suggestion that 'nothing works'. As part of their re-introduction, a great deal of government money was put aside for research looking at how able they were in reducing reoffending rates. Comparisons between different programmes were made, and comparisons were made between programmes run in prison and those in the community (see for example Friendship et al., 2003). What these pieces of research showed was that sending people to prison for a short time was less likely to reduce reoffending than being sentenced to a community order with a requirement to take part in an offending behaviour programme. However, despite these findings, the numbers of people in prison rose dramatically throughout the 1990s, and into the start of the twenty-first century, as governments felt the need to demonstrate that they were being 'tough' in the area of crime.

Types of Prison

In England and Wales men over the age of 21 are held in prisons, and young men between the ages of 15 and 21 are placed in Young Offender Institutions (YOI). The situation for women offenders is different. Women over the age of 17 go into the main prison estate, where there is special provision for them. Younger children are held in secure training centres (see Chapter 18). With the number of young people being sentenced to prison going down, some YOIs have been closed or reclassified as adult prisons. This means that young prisoners' family and friends often have to travel very long distances to see them, causing problems and potentially having a negative impact on rehabilitation.

After a series of breakouts in the 1960s, adult male prisoners were categorised, based on their likelihood of escape. This categorisation then mapped onto the prison regime, with prisons usually housing one or two categories of prisoner:

Category A Prisoners whose escape would be highly dangerous to the public, the police or the security of the state, for whom the aim must be to make escape impossible.

Category B Prisoners for whom the very highest conditions of security are not necessary but for whom escape must be made very difficult.

Category C Prisoners who cannot be trusted in open conditions but who do not have the resources and will to make a determined escape attempt.

Category D Prisoners who present a low risk; can reasonably be trusted in open conditions and for whom open conditions are appropriate.

Categorisation is not always as simple as this. For women there is no categorisation, and prisons are either *open*, for less serious offences, or *closed*. There are only 13 prisons for women, and half have mother and baby units, where applications can be made for children to stay with their mothers until they are 18 months old.

Prisons are also designated as *resettlement* or *training* prisons. These are for prisoners who have less than 12 months of their sentence remaining, and where the focus is on helping prisoners learn vocational skills that may help them find employment after release. *Local* prisons are where prisoners are sent from the courts, after sentence. Sometimes a prisoner might serve their whole sentence in a local prison, but if their sentence is over four years they may be sent to a *dispersal* prison that is more appropriate to their security categorisation.

In prisons there are also specialised units where some prisoners gain additional support. For example some high security prisons (category A) have units for prisoners with a personality disorder (PD) and who are considered to be particularly dangerous. They may also have PIPE (psychologically informed planned environments) that aims to help PD prisoners to adapt to life in a mainstream prison setting (Turley et al., 2013).

The aim is to ensure that prisoners move through the risk categories. This is especially true of category A prisoners, whose risk of causing harm to the public needs to be addressed before they are released. A prisoner who has committed a category A offence, typically one that results in a life sentence, should move towards category D prisons before they can be released. This means that prisoners have to acknowledge their guilt and address their offending behaviour before they can be granted parole or released.

Prisons Now

The Role of Prison in the Twenty-first Century

The role of the prison in the twenty-first century could be said to be both similar to and utterly different from prisons of the past. Theoretically imprisonment still includes ideas of retributive justice, that is punishing people for law breaking. However, ideas of rehabilitation are much more prominent, and are much less based on religious notions of redemption. Ideas of philanthropic paternalism, most notable in the Victorian period, where those who have the means and the capacity to help should do their utmost to support people who have offended or are in need, are still evident (see for example Pratt, 2002; Daems, 2008; and Garland, 2012). Yet, there has been a movement away from paternalistic ideas, to a popular punitivism, meaning that offenders are seen as being rational actors, who need to be dealt with strictly and with certainty so that they are deterred from offending again. Prison continues to 'communicate', or tell us stories, about how punishment functions as part of a country's political process and theoretical outlook (Rex, 2004).

From the mid-1990s the prison population began to grow at a faster rate than previously; in 1993 the population was just under 42,000, it is now around 86,000

(Ministry of Justice, 2013, 2016a). In just over 20 years the prison population has almost doubled, despite the recorded crime rate going down for almost all of this period. In England and Wales we lock up the largest proportion of our population in Western Europe, with 147 people per 100,000 in the population in prison (Institute for Criminal Policy Research, undated). There are a number of explanations as to why this is the case. The number of people who are sentenced to immediate custody has increased; people are being sentenced to longer spells in prison and the recall rate for people who are released on licence has also increased. The average prison sentence is 16.4 months, a figure that continues to rise (Ministry of Justice, 2016a). One reason for the number of people being sentenced to immediate custody increasing is that the types of offence that they are tried for are becoming more serious. Despite the reduction in the crime rate from the mid-1990s onwards, the figure of people who are being tried for offences related to drugs, violence and sexual offences has increased. This may be in part due to people feeling more likely to trust the police and courts in getting them 'justice', particularly in the case of historic sexual offences.

Prisons are expensive to run – it costs, on average, £33,330 to keep a prisoner locked up for a year (Ministry of Justice, 2015). At a time when public sector organisations are stretching their resources to cover working with more people, and private sector companies need to ensure that they are profitable, this means that, once again, the prison system is in crisis. The crisis has had an impact in a number of ways including overcrowding and prisoners being locked in their cells for longer periods. The knock-on effects are prisoners not being able to attend education or work regularly, or being unable to access services that they need in a timely fashion.

Overcrowding

The overcrowding noted by John Howard and Elizabeth Fry in the eighteenth and nineteenth centuries remains a major problem today. The Certified Normal Accommodation (CNA) is the number of bed-spaces that a prison was originally meant to hold. This number is used to identify whether, and to what extent, a prison is full or overcrowded. Every month the Ministry of Justice produces information showing the numbers in each prison, and the extent to which they exceed their CNA. The prisons also have an operational capacity, which is the number of spaces currently available to house prisoners. The operational capacity is much larger than the CNA, as cells that were originally meant for one person now hold two.

Overcrowding is a significant problem. Only 30 per cent of the prisons and YOIs in England and Wales are operating within their CNA, and the most overcrowded prison holds almost twice as many people as it should (Ministry of Justice, 2016a).

The top five currently most overcrowded prisons are listed in Table 16.1.

Overcrowding in prisons has an impact on the welfare of prisoners and prison officers. As discussed in Chapter 9, Her Majesty's Inspectorate of Prisons regularly reports on the outcome of inspections of prisons. These reports often highlight very poor conditions, with overcrowding being a key aggravating factor.

Table 16.1 Most overcrowded prisons in England and Wales

Prison name	CNA	Prison population	Number over CNA	% of CNA in use
Kennet (HMPS)	175	338	163	193
Leeds (HMPS)	669	1129	460	169
Swansea (HMPS)	268	444	176	166
Wandsworth (HMPS)	943	1568	625	166
Exeter (HMPS)	318	521	203	164

(Ministry of Justice, 2016b)

Mental Health in Prisons

Mental health issues are a significant problem within prisons around the world (Scott and Codd, 2010). They affect all sections of the prison population: men, women and children. Each year there are thousands of incidents of self-harm and the numbers of those managing to take their own lives has recently started to increase again. The Ministry of Justice's safe custody statistics (2016a) on deaths in prison showed that in 2004 the number of self-inflicted deaths was 96. This number dropped to 58 in both 2010 and 2011, but increased again to 89 in 2014. Part of the reduction was due to action that was taken after the Corston report (2007). This report investigated the needs of women in the prison estate. While women make up around 4 per cent of the prison population in England and Wales, they are disproportionately represented in the numbers of self-inflicted deaths. In the community men are more likely than women to commit suicide, but the reverse is true in prison (Corston, 2007).

Prison reform organisations suggest that the recent increase in the number of prisoners committing suicide is simply down to the reduction in the numbers of prison staff available, arising from cuts in public sector funding and the reduction in numbers of staff in privatised prisons, so that they can be as economically efficient as possible. The reduced number of prison officers means less time spent on the wing, checking on prisoners' safety and security. The cuts to classes, the restrictions on access to books and materials sent from home, the longer time locked in cells and the restrictions on time spent associating with others all have an impact on mental health (see also Chapter 5 in this volume).

Ageing Prison Population

Prisons are built for fit young men. The Victorian and Georgian buildings still in use have narrow landings, lots of stairs and spaces that are difficult to manoeuvre in. The money a prisoner is allowed to spend each week is related to their ability to work or take part in education and training. If a prisoner does not do what they are told by a prison officer or staff member, they may be punished. Although over two-thirds of the prison population in England and Wales is under the age of 39, the fastest growing group in prison is the over 50 year olds (Omolade, 2014). This is due to lengthening prison sentences over the past 20 years, the greater likelihood of parole being denied, the return of people who break their licence conditions, and the rise in the imprisonment of older people for historic offences.

Prison is not good for your health. As noted above, we see people in prison with serious mental ill health, and sometimes undiagnosed physical health problems. Prison ages you, and it is recognised that prisoners generally have the health of someone 10 years their senior (Crawley and Sparks, 2006). This means that prisoners are considered to be 'older' when they reach the age of 55 – certainly not old by usual standards in the UK. In 2013 the House of Commons Justice Select Committee opened an inquiry into older prisoners, and gathered evidence from academics, practitioners and campaigners. Although the committee understood that older prisoners might face difficulties in prison – e.g. having mobility problems, not being able to work because of poor eyesight, or deteriorating hearing meaning that requests and instructions are sometimes missed – it was noted that these problems were not uniform, and a national strategy for older prisoners was deemed unnecessary (Justice Select Committee, 2013). It is certainly true that not all older prisoners are the same, but they are a group of people whose needs are not always addressed in an appropriate way. To take an example, a group of older men in one high-security prison were confined to a few cells in a vulnerable prisoner unit, with their access to other parts of the wing restricted. This essentially meant that they were doubly incarcerated, or kept with offenders that they would not normally associate with. In other prisons in the UK and the USA, buddy systems are in place to support prisoners who may need help, not just older prisoners, with everyday activities such as collecting meals or medication, or being moved around the prison. This type of relationship is often beneficial for all involved – prisoners who have helped others explain the sense of satisfaction – however, there are questions about whether this relationship is always free from exploitation, and whether prisoners are trained by staff for a caring role (see, for example, Crawley 2007).

Box 16.1

What's it Like to be in Prison? A Prisoner's View

Erwin James is a former prisoner. During his time in prison he wrote a regular column for *The Guardian* newspaper, which is still available on the website. Now he is a journalist, author and the editor in chief of *Inside Time*, the national newspaper for prisoners. Below are two extracts from his work.

On cells and the cleanliness of prisons

A 'good' cell has a premium. People wait weeks and often months to get one. Some people pay. When I was in prison the going rate to get somebody to move out of a yearned-for cell was ten £2 phone cards. Most of the cells I inhabited in my early years were damp and infested to different degrees with cockroaches. It often took me up to a year or more to secure a decent cell. When in-cell sanitation began to be installed in the 90s, cells effectively became toilets. The 'stainless' steel lavatory units would corrode from the urine and excrement and unless they were cleaned thoroughly every day they created a potent odour and veritable health hazard. Later, when the units were decommissioned and replaced with porcelain, it was still hard to go into a cell where a previous occupant had made no attempt to keep the toilet clean.

www.theguardian.com/society/2008/jan/11/prisonsandprobation.comment

On mental health

The Gambler's visit got off to a bit of a morose start – as he walked through the gate he passed a police incident van going out. He learned from Rinty that a fellow lifer, someone with mental health problems, had committed suicide earlier in the day. The man had been sectioned before and sent to special hospital for 'treatment'. Eventually a man in a white coat had decided he was well enough to be sent back to jail – he didn't last long. A number of times during my own twenty years of incarceration I saw exactly the same thing happen. Men breaking down, being sent to hospital only to be returned later and breaking down a second time only more severely. Prison you see is not a place for the mentally unwell – yet so many people there are quite obviously suffering from mental problems.

www.erwinjames.co.uk/blog/?p=229

Incentives and Earned Privileges Scheme

One of the elements that rules the way in which prisoners live in prison is the Incentives and Earned Privileges (IEP) scheme, which was set up in 1995. The scheme was set up to incentivise 'responsible behaviour' (Cavadino et al., 2013). Initially this meant getting a job, and taking part in other purposeful activity, now prisoners 'have to work towards their own rehabilitation, behave well and help others. The absence of bad behaviour alone will no longer be sufficient to progress through the scheme' (National Offender Management Service, 2013: 40). There are four levels of the IEP scheme, and each reflects, amongst other things, the amount of money that prisoners can earn, whether they can wear their own clothes, the number of visits they can receive, and if they are allowed to rent a TV set from the prison.

Since November 2013 there are four levels of the IEP scheme.

- Basic – this level is for prisoners who have not 'engaged sufficiently' with the regime. They have not taken part in activities that will help with their rehabilitation or behaved well while in prison. Prisoners on this level must wear prison-issued clothing and do not have the opportunity to rent a TV set.

- Entry – all new prisoners, either convicted or on remand, start on this level. They are allowed to rent TV sets from the prison, but all convicted male prisoners have to wear prison-issued clothing (remand and women prisoners are allowed to wear their own clothing). Prisoners on this level have to show that they are behaving well and taking an active part in the requirements of them in the early stages of their sentence in order to move on to the next level.

- Standard – on this level prisoners can spend more of their own money (either sent in from outside or earned while in prison), and can have more visits, as well as being entitled to rent a TV set. Prisoners get to this level by showing that they are engaged in their sentence plan, including actively seeking to take part in treatment programmes.

- Enhanced – This is the highest level of the scheme. Prisoners are allowed more visits, can spend more money each week, and can have access to hobby materials and gym time. In order to reach it prisoners must show that they have a commitment to change their offending behaviour, and that they proactively make changes. This level also requires prisoners to help out in the prison, by becoming Wing representatives or taking part in a Buddy or Listener scheme. If prisoners do not keep taking part in these types of activities, or are seen to carry out an act of misconduct, then the prison can revoke their IEP status.

The introduction of the new system in November 2013 (Ministry of Justice, 2013) was controversial, still relying on prison officer discretion, and seen as unduly harsh in a number of respects. For example, it set out a list of clothing that prisoners could have, re-emphasised the amount of personal possessions a prisoner could have in their cell, and restricted the hours some prisoners could spend in the gym. The most controversial aspect was that it set out the number of books that a prisoner could hold in their cell, and stopped friends and family from sending books into prisons. The reasoning behind this decision focused on the space in prisons for personal belongings, and worries about the type of reading materials that were being sent in. However, many prison reform, human rights and literacy campaigners, as well as prominent authors, disagreed strongly with this stance (Crook, 2014; Howard League, undated). Their argument was that restricting the number of books negatively affected prisoners' rehabilitation, both through their ability to study and to help maintain positive mental health. After a number of months of campaigning, which included people posting 'shelfies' (pictures of their book shelves) on social media and copying in the Ministry of Justice, and national newspapers taking up the argument, the ban was reversed. Prisoners may order books from designated suppliers, and families and friends may send books in. However, the books are still subject to volumetric control.

Transforming Rehabilitation?

It is unsurprising that there is almost constant change in the prison system. Just as society changes, so too does the way in which people are sanctioned for breaking

=== **Box 16.2** ===

What is it Like to be in Prison? A View from the Outside

At Northumbria University, some final-year undergraduate students spend one day per week in a prison. This experience is excellent in a number of ways, including helping challenge or support previously held views about prisons and prisoners. One student's views were:

> From inside the prison it is easy to see the different dynamics at work: the complex world of incarceration becomes clearer. Articles and books that I have read about the prison make more sense now.

> Working in this environment has also helped me understand about how the prison service as a whole works and enables me to appreciate the many things that occur 'behind the scenes', which never seem to be mentioned by the media.

> My views have changed towards prisoners and prison in general. Even as a criminology student, my opinions on what prison was like were highly influenced by TV programmes and stories in the media. (Quoted in Ridley, 2014: 24)

the law. The question still remains whether prisons manage to address the needs of prisoners in the twenty-first century, or indeed help them to fit back into a twenty-first-century society. For example, for reasons of security there is no internet access allowed in any prison: how might this hinder the rehabilitation of people who are already marginalised?

Since the election of the Coalition government in 2010 and the Conservative government in 2015, there have been some significant changes to the way in which offenders are punished and rehabilitated. These changes, part of the Transforming Rehabilitation agenda (discussed in detail in Chapter 17), have had an impact on the way in which people with less than 12 months to serve on their sentences spend their time in prison. These last 12 months are a time in which prisoners are made ready for employment after release. This means that they spend their time primarily on gaining skills and experience that should help in finding a job.

Rather than the traditional patterns of employment and skills, such as construction, prisons have started to work with private companies and third-sector organisations to provide opportunities that mirror work outside. Timpson's and Max Spielmann, both private companies, support the employment of prisoners and former prisoners inside and outside prison. Other prisons have created their own social enterprises, for example, HMP Durham has a woodwork shop that sells planters, benches and Christmas decorations, and HMP Kirklevington Grange has a café and sells eggs, plants and hanging baskets to the public. Both of these prisons are designated resettlement prisons. The Clink restaurants in Cardiff, Brixton, High Down and Styal prisons are further examples of enterprises that support work undertaken by prisoners.

Summary

This chapter has shown that there has been constant change in the way in which prisons are run and managed in England and Wales since they were first created as sites of punishment. There has been a move away from corporal and capital punishment, where a person's body is punished for wrongdoing, to ideas of punishing a person as a whole entity. The ideas of reform have changed as well, from trying to get people to adhere to a Christian way of life, to addressing their offending behaviour through education, working on their triggers for offending through psychologically informed programmes. These changes in practice have been based on changes in the political views of the time, not only about how we should manage Criminal Justice Systems, but also about how central government should work.

Since the eighteenth century there have been reports into the state of prisons; how clean or overcrowded they are, and what type of punishment and rehabilitation are offered. It appears that prisons have always been in a state of crisis, not an enviable place to be; suggesting governments have not learned how to make punishment and rehabilitation effective.

Prisoners are held differently from how they were in the middle of the last century. Now adult male prisoners are categorised based on their likelihood of escape and the seriousness of their offence, which crudely maps on to the type of prison that they will be in. While there are some good examples of prisons offering support, work, education and the chance of employment to prisoners, HMIP continues to report on prisons where many aspects of positively run prisons are lacking. This may have an impact on a prisoner's likelihood of reoffending after release, or on their physical and mental wellbeing while in prison. However prisons have changed, it is clear that prisoners in England and Wales are still trying to manage what Sykes (1958) termed the pains of imprisonment.

—————— Discussion Questions ——————

1. Do you think that it is fair that prisoners should be paid for their work in prison? Prisoners' wages are not comparable with the national living wage – with some prisoners only being paid £4 per week. Would your answer be different if a private company was profiting from having work carried out by prisoners, rather than people outside prison? In 2015 the government made over £5 million from winning work contracts, possibly due in part to the labour costs being low. How do you feel about this? If a prisoner has a job in the community (they are released on a temporary licence towards the end of their sentence to help them fit back in) and earns more than £20 per week, part of their earnings is paid to charities that support victims. Do you think that this is the right thing to do?

2. Look at the HMIP report on HMP Pentonville in 2015 (www.justiceinspectorates. gov.uk/hmiprisons/wp-content/uploads/sites/4/2015/06/Pentonville-print-2015. pdf). This report is unusual as photographs of the conditions in the prison are included. They show filthy toilets, unclean and uncared for washing areas, piles of rubbish, clothing and bed linen. The report's introduction notes that the challenges the prison faced at the time of the previous inspection had not been addressed, conditions for prisoners were unacceptable, and staff sickness rates were high. With staff on sick leave, how might the prison punish and rehabilitate prisoners with humanity? How are living conditions in the prison to be improved? How can prisoners routinely take part in education, training and employment opportunities?

3. What do you think would be the public and media's reaction if the government were to announce a major programme of public spending to provide new prisons where all prisoners had cells with sufficient space for their needs, access to high-quality education and training, and (subject to good behaviour) frequent visits from their family?

Further Reading

Crewe, B., Warr, J., Bennett, P. and Smith, A. (2014) 'The emotional geography of prison life', *Theoretical Criminology*, 18 (1): 56–74. This article looks at how prisoners negotiate being in prison. It talks about how some spaces might feel 'safer' than others.

Hedderman, C. (2010) 'Government policy on women offenders: Labour's legacy and the coalition's challenge', *Punishment and Society*, 12 (4): 485–500. This article, written just at the end of the Labour governments, considered how women offenders have been managed in the early part of the 21st century.

Liebling, A. (2011) 'Moral performance, inhuman and degrading treatment and prison pain', *Punishment and Society*, 13 (5): 530–50. This article talks about the nature of 'humanity' and 'dignity' and the way in which they are demonstrated in prison.

Millie, A. Jacobsen, J. and Hough, M. (2003) 'Understanding the growth in the prison population in England and Wales', *Criminal Justice*, 3 (4): 369–87. This article looks at the reasons for the growth in the prison population at the beginning of the 21st century.

References

Carlen, P. and Worrall, A. (2004) *Analysing Women's Imprisonment*. Cullompton: Willan.

Cavadino, M., Dignan, J. and Mair, G. (2013) *The Penal System*. 5th edn. London: Sage.

Corston, J. (2007) *A Report by Baroness Jean Corston of a Review of Women with Particular Vulnerabilities in the Criminal Justice System*. London: Home Office. Available at: www. justice.gov.uk/publications/docs/corston-report-march-2007.pdf (accessed October 2015).

Crawley, E. (2007) 'Imprisonment in old age', in Y. Jewkes (ed.), *Handbook on Prisons*. Cullompton: Willan. pp. 224–44.

Crawley, E. and Sparks, R. (2006) 'Is there life after imprisonment? How elderly men talk about imprisonment and release', *Criminology and Criminal Justice*, 6 (1): 63–82.

Crook, F. (2014) 'Comment: Why has Grayling banned prisoners being sent books?' Available at: www.politics.co.uk/comment-analysis/2014/03/23/comment-why-has-grayling-banned-prisoners-being-sent-books (accessed February 2016).

Daems, T. (2008) *Making Sense of Penal Change*. Oxford: Oxford University Press.

Friendship, C., Blud, L., Erikson, M., Travers, R. and Thornton, D. (2003) 'Cognitive-behavioural treatment for imprisoned offenders: An evaluation of HM Prison Service's cognitive skills programmes', *Legal and Criminological Psychology*, 8 (1): 103–14.

Garland, D. (1990) *Punishment and Modern Society: A study in social theory*. Chicago: University of Chicago Press.

Garland, D. (2012) 'Punishment and social solidarity', in J. Simon and R. Sparks (eds), *The Sage Handbook of Punishment and Society*. London: Sage. pp. 23–39.

Harding, C. (1988) '"The inevitable end of a discredited system"? The origins of the Gladstone Committee Report on Prisons, 1895', *The Historical Journal*, 31 (3): 591–608.

HMIP (2015) *Report on an Unannounced Inspection of HMP Pentonville 2–13 February 2015* Available at: www.justiceinspectorates.gov.uk/hmiprisons/wp-content/uploads/sites/4/2015/06/Pentonville-print-2015.pdf (accessed February 2016).

Hollin, C. and Bilby, C. (2007) 'Addressing offending behaviour: "What works" and beyond', in Y. Jewkes (ed.), *Handbook on Prisons*. Cullompton: Willan. pp. 608–28.

Howard League for Penal Reform (undated) *Books for Prisoners*. Available at: http://howardleague.org/what-you-can-do/our-achievements/books-for-prisoners/ (accessed September 2016).

Institute for Criminal Policy Research (undated) *World Prison Brief*. Available at: www.prisonstudies.org/highest-to-lowest/prison_population_rate?field_region_taxonomy_tid=14&=Apply (accessed January 2016).

Jewkes, Y. and Johnston, H. (2007) 'The evolution of prison architecture', in Y. Jewkes (ed.), *Handbook on Prisons*. Cullompton: Willan. pp.174–98.

Johnston, H. (2010) 'The cell: Separation, isolation and space in the architecture of the birth of the prison', *Prison Service Journal*, 187: 9–14.

Johnston, H. (2016) 'Prison histories, 1770s–1950s: Continuities and contradictions', in Y. Jewkes, B. Crewe and J. Bennett (eds), *Handbook on Prisons*. 2nd edn. Abingdon: Routledge. pp. 24–38.

Justice Select Committee (2013) *Fifth Report: Older prisoners*. Available at: www.publications.parliament.uk/pa/cm201314/cmselect/cmjust/89/8902.htm (accessed February 2016).

Ministry of Justice (2013) *Story of the Prison Population: 1993 – 2012 England and Wales*. Available at: www.gov.uk/government/uploads/system/uploads/attachment_data/file/218185/story-prison-population.pdf (accessed February 2016).

Ministry of Justice (2015) *National Offender Management Service Annual Report and Accounts 2014–15 Management Information Addendum*. London: Ministry of Justice. Available at: www.gov.uk/government/uploads/system/uploads/attachment_data/file/471625/costs-per-place.pdf (accessed February 2016).

Ministry of Justice (2016a) *Criminal Justice Statistics Quarterly Update to September 2015 England and Wales*. London: Ministry of Justice. Available at: www.gov.uk/government/uploads/system/uploads/attachment_data/file/501181/quaterly-update.pdf (accessed February 2016).

Ministry of Justice (2016b) *Safety in Custody Statistics England and Wales Deaths in Prison Custody to March 2016 Assaults and Self-harm to December 2015*. London: Ministry of Justice. Available at: www.gov.uk/government/uploads/system/uploads/attachment_data/file/519425/safety-in-custody-march-2016.pdf (accessed September 2016).

Moran, D. (2015) *Carceral Geography: Spaces and practices of incarceration*. Farnham: Ashgate.

National Offender Management Service (2013) *Prison Service Instruction 30/2013 Incentives and Earned Privileges.* Available at: www.justice.gov.uk/offenders/psis/prison-service-instructions-2013 (accessed December 2015).

Omolade, S. (2014) *The Needs and Characteristics of Older Prisoners: Results from the Surveying Prisoner Crime Reduction (SPCR) survey. Analytical summary.* London: Ministry of Justice. Available at: www.gov.uk/government/uploads/system/uploads/attachment_data/file/368177/needs-older-prisoners-spcr-survey.pdf (accessed February 2016).

Pratt, J. (2002) *Punishment and Civilization. Penal tolerance and intolerance in modern society*. London: Sage

Rex, S. (2004) 'Punishment as communication', in A. Bottoms, S. Rex and G. Robinson (eds), *Alternatives to Prison: Options for an insecure society*. Cullompton: Willan. pp. 113–34.

Ridley, L. (2014) 'No substitute for the real thing: The impact of prison-based work experience on students' thinking about imprisonment', *The Howard Journal*, 53 (1): 16–30.

Scott, D. and Codd, H. (2010) *Controversial Issues in Prisons*. London: Sage.

Scott, D. and Flynn, N. (2014) *Prisons and Punishment: The essentials*. London: Sage.

Sykes, G. (1958) *The Society of Captives*. Princeton: Princeton University Press.

Turley, C., Payne, C. and Webster, S. (2013) *Enabling Features of Psychologically Informed Planned Environments.* London: Ministry of Justice. Available at: www.gov.uk/government/uploads/system/uploads/attachment_data/file/211730/enabling-pipe-research-report.pdf

Check out the Companion Website

Want to know more about this chapter? Review what you have been learning by visiting: **https://study.sagepub.com/harding**

- Practice with essay questions
- Test yourself with multiple-choice questions
- Listen to a series of podcasts featuring Neil of Northumbria Police and London's Metropolitan Police Service
- Watch videos selected from the SAGE Video collection

17 Parole and Release from Prison

Harriet Pierpoint[i]

Introduction

Nearly all prisoners are released at some point. Most countries have some system of early release with post-release supervision (Padfield et al., 2010). This serves a number of purposes: to motivate good behaviour in prison; to protect the public; to reduce the risk of reoffending; and to manage prison overcrowding.

In England and Wales, the date on which a prisoner is released, with or without supervision, and how long that post-release supervision goes on for, depends on a number of factors. Moreover, the rules and procedures governing early release have changed considerably over the years. This chapter will outline the historical background of these release mechanisms right up to the present day, including the introduction of 'parole' in 1968, following the Criminal Justice Act 1967, and the changes that accompanied the 'Transforming Rehabilitation' (TR) initiative in February 2015. It will also discuss, with reference to a recent research summary some of what is in place in terms of 'resettlement'. This is the work done with ex-prisoners to help them 'resettle' when returning to the community after release from prison, such as help with housing or education, training and employment, and the current challenges in this field.

Historical Background of Early Release, Parole and Post-release Supervision

This section will consider the historical background of early release, parole and post-release supervision, pointing out some of the key changes that have occurred in this field. The history of the probation service and prisons has been discussed in Chapters 15 and 16. The origins of early release and post-release supervision are closely linked to these histories.

For many years before parole, prisoners could earn early release by, for example, good behaviour or with prison governor approval. As shown in Figure 17.1, 1968 saw the introduction of a more formal and more independent system with rules and criteria as to who could be released and at what point. This was known as 'parole'.

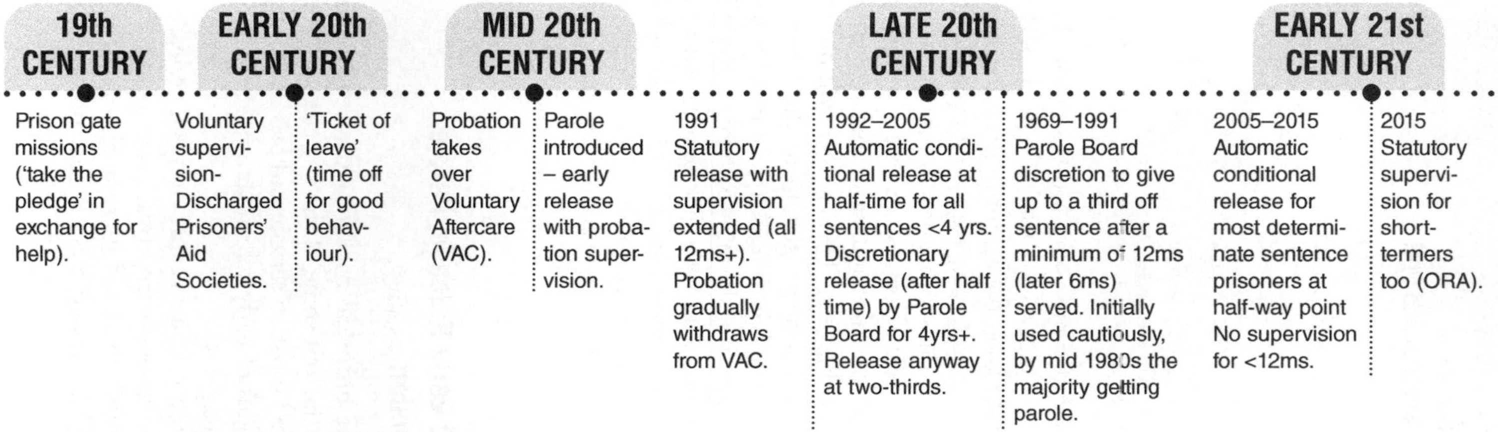

19th CENTURY

Prison gate missions ('take the pledge' in exchange for help).

EARLY 20th CENTURY

Voluntary supervision– Discharged Prisoners' Aid Societies.

'Ticket of leave' (time off for good behaviour).

MID 20th CENTURY

Probation takes over Voluntary Aftercare (VAC).

Parole introduced – early release with probation supervision.

1991 Statutory release with supervision extended (all 12ms+). Probation gradually withdraws from VAC.

LATE 20th CENTURY

1992–2005 Automatic conditional release at half-time for all sentences <4 yrs. Discretionary release (after half time) by Parole Board for 4yrs+. Release anyway at two-thirds.

1969–1991 Parole Board discretion to give up to a third off sentence after a minimum of 12ms (later 6ms) served. Initially used cautiously, by mid 1980s the majority getting parole.

EARLY 21st CENTURY

2005–2015 Automatic conditional release for most determinate sentence prisoners at half-way point No supervision for <12ms.

2015 Statutory supervision for short-termers too (ORA).

Figure 17.1 Timeline of the history of early release, parole and post-release supervision in England and Wales

In terms of what happens after release, the roots of post-release supervision are in the voluntary as opposed to the statutory sector. As shown in Figure 17.1, from the 1870s, prison-gate missions and then Discharged Prisoners' Aid Societies offered assistance to released prisoners on a voluntary basis. By the 1960s, probation took over Voluntary Aftercare (VAC) and, for many years after, the Probation Service included 'After-Care' in its title.

Parole Board

The Parole Board was established in 1968 following the Criminal Justice Act 1967. Its purpose was to 'advise' the Home Secretary in the exercise of the powers to release prisoners on licence and to recall prisoners to custody.

The Parole Board is an independent body that risk assesses prisoners to primarily decide whether they can be safely released into the community (see the Parole Board webpages at www.gov.uk/government/organisations/parole-board). Since its creation, the Parole Board has undergone a number of changes including its sponsorship, function and remit, which will now be considered.

The home of the Parole Board within the Criminal Justice System and its sponsorship has changed over the years. The Board was first constituted in November 1967 with administrative arrangements handled, first, by a Parole Unit set up in the Home Office, and then, from 1983, by the Prison Service (later to be absorbed into the National Offender Management Service (NOMS) in 2004). Since 1996, the Board has had the status of an executive non-departmental public body (NDPB). It is now sponsored by the Ministry of Justice (MoJ) – the ministerial department with NOMS in its remit. This means that, while it receives its funding from central government (the MoJ), its day-to-day operations are independent from the Ministry. That said, the Secretary of State for Justice (who has oversight of all of MoJ business) appoints members of the Parole Board and is able to issue guidance to the Board about how it should make its decisions. This is considered in more detail below in the section on the decision-making process.

From an Administrative to a Judicial Function and Human Rights

Since the creation of the Parole Board, its function has shifted from an advisory body to serving more of a judicial role. The Board's original function was to use its discretion to decide whether a prisoner could be given the 'privilege' of serving the remainder of his or her sentence out of custody. This recommendation was normally made 'on papers' and the Board did not have the final say. Nowadays the Board adjudicates on whether a prisoner is 'entitled' to be released based on specific risk criteria often at 'oral hearings' where the prisoner is present and legally represented. There have been a number of reasons for this change. The first reason was the introduction in 2005 of indeterminate sentences of Imprisonment for Public Protection (IPP). In brief, the length of these sentences, which were abolished in 2012 (although many prisoners who received them are still in custody and subject to their rules), was indefinite. After the minimum custodial term or 'tariff' set by the judge during sentencing has expired, the prisoner can only be released if the Parole Board determines that the risk they pose to the public has been sufficiently reduced to do so. Therefore, prisoners are 'entitled' to regular reviews by the Parole Board of their case. Given the Parole Board's decisions determine the liberty or continued incarceration of the individual, they directly engage the right to liberty under Article 5 European Convention on Human Rights (ECHR). Article 5 includes certain procedural rights in Article 5(4) and states that:

> Everyone who is deprived of his liberty by arrest or detention shall be entitled to take proceedings by which the lawfulness of his detention shall be decided speedily by a court and his release ordered if the detention is not lawful.

The Human Rights Act 1998 incorporated the ECHR into domestic law (see Chapter 22). Case law from the domestic courts (particularly the Supreme Court judgment in the case of Osborn, Booth and Reilly handed down on 9 October 2013) and the European Court of Human Rights has brought around changes to the parole system in three main areas: the need for prisoners to be afforded procedural rights, including oral hearings; the need to avoid excessive delay in considering cases; and the need for the Parole Board to be independent. Although groups like JUSTICE consider this shift from an administrative towards a judicial function to be 'a positive change in the constitutional status of the parole system', they remain concerned about its continued lack of independence and think it should become an independent judicial body making independent decisions about the release of prisoners without any government influence (see below and JUSTICE (2009) for further details).

Remit of the Parole Board

The remit of the Parole Board in terms of which prisoners it can consider for parole has also changed significantly over time. Initially, parole was applied to prisoners with both determinate and indeterminate sentences (see Chapter 15 for an explanation of different types of sentence). However, determinate-sentence prisoners were taken out of the parole system in 2005. The present-day arrangements will now be considered in more detail.

Determining the Date of Release

The date on which a prisoner is released, with or without supervision, and how long that supervision goes on for, depends on:

- the type/length of his/her sentence;

- when the prisoner was convicted;

- the prisoner's behaviour in prison (extra days can be imposed by adjudications or 'nickings');

- any time spent on remand (waiting for trial or sentencing).

The different systems for determining release will now be considered.

Short-term Determinate Sentences

If the prisoner has a determinate (fixed term) sentence (see Chapter 15 for an explanation of different types of sentence), he or she will normally be released automatically halfway through their sentence. Until 2015, anyone sentenced to 12 months or less was released at this point without supervision or licence requirements imposed upon them. However, since February 2015 and the Offender Rehabilitation Act 2014, part of the 'Transforming Rehabilitation' (TR) changes, no matter how short the sentence, the prisoner will be released (at the half-way point of their sentence) 'on licence[ii]' and this licence period will be followed by a post-release supervision period. Table 17.1 gives examples of the rules before and after the changes.

Table 17.1 Release dates and arrangements on release for determinate sentences

| Sentence imposed by court | Offences committed before 1 February 2015 | | Offences committed on or after 1 February 2015 | |
	Period in custody before release	Arrangements on release	Period in custody before release	Arrangements on release
6 month sentence	3 months	3 months in community, but with no licence conditions or supervision	3 months	3 months' licence and 9 months' post-sentence supervision. Total supervision 12 months
10 month sentence	5 months	5 months in community, but with no licence conditions or supervision	5 months	5 months' licence and 7 months' post-sentence supervision. Total supervision 12 months
18 month sentence	9 months	9 months' licence	9 months	9 months' licence and 3 months' post-sentence supervision. Total supervision 12 months

Source: www.sentencingcouncil.org.uk/about-sentencing/types-of-sentence/determinate-prison-sentences/

Being 'on licence' means that the ex-prisoners must adhere to certain conditions like restriction of movement and not committing any offences (see www.justice.

gov.uk/downloads/offenders/psipso/psi-2015/psi-12-2015-licences-conditions-supervision.pdf for a list of conditions). If an offender breaches the terms of their supervision they may be returned to custody.

Long-term Determinate Sentences

Offenders given determinate imprisonment sentences of two years or more now serve half their sentence in prison and serve the rest of the sentence in the community on licence (e.g. those given an eight-year sentence will automatically be released after four years) under the Criminal Justice and Immigration Act 2008. Again the licence will include conditions and, while on licence, an offender will be subject to supervision. If an offender breaches their conditions, they may be recalled to prison.

The Parole Board (discussed below) is not involved in this system for determinate sentences; they only now deal with indeterminate sentences and 'legacy' long sentences discussed below.

Indeterminate Sentences (IPPs and Lifers)

If the prisoner has an indeterminate (non-fixed term/IPP) or life sentence[iii], he or she can only be released on the recommendation of the Parole Board (the government will apply to the Board for parole on the prisoner's behalf). It is also worth noting that the Parole Board deals with the small remaining number of prisoners who were sentenced to lengthy fixed terms of imprisonment for offences committed before 4 April 2005, as well as with (again, small numbers of) prisoners serving an extended sentence for the public protection (EPP) for offences committed on or after 4 April 2005; in such cases, the prisoner may apply for 'parole' and will only be released subject to approval by the Parole Board. Generally though, the work of the modern Parole Board is taken up with considering release for offenders sentenced to indeterminate periods of custody – i.e. IPPs and lifers.

The Parole Board considers the level of risk the prisoner would pose to the general public, if released into the community, once they have completed the minimum time they must spend in prison. Tariff is the term used to describe the mandatory period of time a prisoner, serving a life or indeterminate sentence, must serve in custody prior to being considered for release. A prisoner will only be released after this period if the Parole Board thinks it safe to do so. Once released, the offender will be 'on licence' and supervised by a probation officer. If, however, the Parole Board considers that the prisoner continues to pose a risk to the community, he or she will continue to be detained. Cases are reviewed within two years if parole is declined. The current decision-making process of the Parole Board will now be considered in more depth.

Decision-making Process

As explained above, the Parole Board is an independent body that carries out risk assessments on certain prisoners to determine whether they can be safely released into the community. The Parole Board has 204 members who make the assessments and decisions. The vast majority of Board members are part-time. They include judges, psychiatrists, psychologists, probation officers and independent lay members.

They can decide whether a prisoner should be released or recommend that they be moved to an open prison. A new Member Case Assessment (MCA) system was implemented in March 2015. This means that now every case which is referred to the Parole Board is dealt with in the same way, whatever the type of sentence. The main steps in the process are summarised below:

1. A single member reads the parole 'dossier' and any representations from the prisoner or his or her legal representative.

2. The dossier includes details of the original offence, any previous convictions, behaviour in prison, details of any courses undertaken during the sentence, and details of the proposed release plan. It also includes reports from those who have come into close contact with the offender, such as psychologists, probation staff and prison officers and medical, psychiatric and psychological evidence. It may also include the victim statement and the offender's case for release.

3. The decision will then either be made by that member based on the information provided on the papers or the member will decide that the case must be considered at a face-to-face oral hearing. An offender or his or her legal representative can also write within 28 days to explain why they believe an oral hearing should be held. As discussed above, most cases will need an oral hearing.

4. There are up to three members on an oral panel. In addition to the prisoner and the panel, others who may be present include the legal representative, the victim, and witnesses such as the prison psychologist.

5. The Parole Board writes to the offender with their decision. The hearing and full decision is kept private.

6. A prisoner may be able challenge the Parole Board's decision. He or she cannot appeal against the decision, it is possible to apply for judicial review if important information was not given to the Parole Board or the application was not dealt with appropriately, e.g. the decision was unlawful or unreasonable.

The Test

The Board's powers and duties when making decisions arise from three primary sources: its statutory framework, including the Parole Board Rules 2011 (see www.legislation.gov.uk/uksi/2011/2947/contents/made) as amended in 2014 (www.legislation.gov.uk/uksi/2014/240/contents/made); the common law requirements of fairness; and requirements that arise from the ECHR. The procedures and tests for release that it must apply in indeterminate sentence cases are contained in the Crime (Sentences) Act (C(S)A) 1997, and in determinate sentence cases, including extended sentences, in the Criminal Justice Act (CJA) 2003. The Justice Secretary has a statutory power to give the Parole Board 'directions as to the matters to be taken into account by it' when considering referrals to it.

The test to be applied by the Parole Board in satisfying itself that it is no longer necessary for the protection of the public that the prisoner should be confined, is whether the lifer's level of risk to the life and limb of others is considered to be more than minimal. It is not a requirement to balance the risk against the benefits to the public or the prisoner of release. There are two aspects to this test: the type of risk and the level of that risk that will justify the Board deciding that the prisoner should not be released (Legal Action Group, 2016). The Parole Board is ultimately looking at whether or not the prisoner has reduced his/her risk throughout his/her time in custody. Hence, the following will provide guidance to the Board when making this decision:

- The prisoner's background;

- The nature and circumstances of previous offending;

- The nature and circumstances of the index offence[iv];

- The impact the index offending has had on the victim, or the victim's family;

- The judge's sentencing remarks;

- Opinions of medical professionals, if relevant;

- Indications as to whether the prisoner has made positive efforts to address the factors that led to his/her offending behaviour;

- Records of any disciplinary offences;

- The prisoner's behaviour to staff and other prisoners;

- The security category the prisoner resides in;

- Representations made by, or on behalf of, the victim or the victim's family.

Criticisms of and Alternatives to Parole

As well as continuing to be criticised for lacking sufficient independence from the executive as discussed above, the Parole Board has been criticised on a number of other levels discussed in this section. The alternatives to parole that have been suggested in the literature will also be summarised.

The Risk Assessment: Attributes and Risk of Criminality

The test to be applied by the Parole Board puts risk to the public at the forefront of the Parole Board's considerations, but there is no systematic scheme for assessing that risk. This raises the question of what factors does the Parole Board consider in practice? Moreover, the Parole Board is free to consider the factors listed under the previous section, but there is no indication of the relationship between these attributes and criminal risk. For many of these factors, and many others widely assumed to be risk indicators, no relationship with risk has ever been demonstrated. This raises the second question of what relationship, if any, is there between the factors considered in practice and risk?

There have not been many empirical studies of the Parole Board's decision-making in practice in England and Wales (although there is a more extensive literature from the US and elsewhere). The most recent study of risk decisions in parole was by Forde in 2014. He reviewed 29 international papers involving 20,568 participants. Although Forde (2014) questioned the quality of the studies reviewed, he firmly concluded that, whatever the jurisdiction and whatever the precise details of the measurements used, most parole decisions are relatively predictable on the basis of only a few variables, although these are not always the same and any causal relationship is often unclear.

Forde (2014) also reported on his own study of how parole decisions related to three widely used risk assessment instruments (the PCL-R, the HCR-20, and the SVR-20), and recommendations of professionals (psychologists and probation officers) on 100 life sentence prisoners in England and Wales, 84 of whom were eligible for parole. The study found that parole decisions were related to the recommendations of professionals, especially that of the offender manager. Bradford and Cowell (2012) also found that the decisions in England and Wales generally followed offender managers' recommendations, but simultaneously complained that their reports relied too much on second-hand information. Relying on a report, which one complains is insufficiently evidence-based, suggests considerable confusion.

Padfield and Liebling (2000) reported a study of the Parole Board of England and Wales relating to their decisions on discretionary lifers.[iii] The study involved direct observation of discussions by parole panels and found that there was very little systematic risk assessment and indeed that risk was rarely discussed. Bradford and Cowell (2012) reported similar findings from a study of prisoners given indeterminate sentences for public protection. There was no correlation between the statistical risk measure and likelihood of parole, and the bulk of those retained in closed prison conditions had low risk scores.

One final question is what measures are used of these factors? Are they appropriate indicators? A previous head of the Parole Board, Sir David Latham, was reported in the press as saying that he was concerned that the official statistics showing how likely previous similar criminals were to reoffend, and on which panels rely in making their decision, were not 'robust' and underplay the extent of reoffending by life sentence prisoners who are released from prison (*Daily Mail*, 2011).

The research tends to support the conclusion that the present system of risk assessment for parole in England and Wales is not evidence-based, the measures may be flawed and that as a result many low-risk prisoners are likely to undergo prolonged detention unnecessarily (e.g. Forde, 2014). It has been found that, when Parole Board members have estimated risk, they have overestimated the actual degree of risk posed by many prisoners (as indicated by the actuarially-calculated risk of reconviction score) and hence denied parole to low-risk prisoners (Hood and Shute, 2000). However, a couple of high-profile inquiries into serious further offences on parole (see Fitzgibbon, 2008) and the revelations in press tend to fuel concern that 'too many dangerous offenders are walking the streets when they should be behind bars' (e.g. *Daily Mail*, 2011).

Cautionary Decision-making

As well as the Parole Board being criticised in the press for releasing high-risk offenders as mentioned above (e.g. *Daily Mail*, 2011), at the same time, conversely, the Parole Board has been criticised in the past for being too cautious in its decision-making (e.g. McMurran et al., 2013).

Table 17.2   Release rates of completed paper and oral parole hearings 2010–16

Financial year	Overall release rate (%)
2010/11	13
2011/12	13
2012/13	21
2013/14	20
2014/15	18
2015/16	17

Source: FOI request to Parole Board, provided 16 May 2016

As shown in Table 17.2 above, release rates, in the last couple of years, show a slight decline in the number of prisoners being granted parole. However, this decline is not substantial. That said, research in the past has shown that many offenders who are denied parole could be freed without any risk to the public (Hood and Shute, 2000). Indeed, one small-scale study by Fitzgibbon (2008) found that probation parole reports, which we know from above are more influential in the decision-making process, assess risk higher than OASys (a risk measurement tool) in terms of harm to others.[v] This tendency has sometimes been attributed to panel members unconsciously reflecting increasingly risk-averse public attitudes (Hill, 2010) and public reactions to high-profile cases like the Biggs and Venables cases (see www.bbc.co.uk/news/uk-24052192 on the latter case).

Ineffective Case Management

A further criticism that has been levied at the Parole Board is that it has been ineffective in managing its caseload. One such report, dealing with life- and indeterminate-sentence prisoners, details the problems caused by the lack of compliance with time-tabling (JUSTICE, 2009). Related to this, in a separate report, the National Audit Office estimated that delays in releasing prisoners cost an estimated £2m in 1998–9 (National Audit Office, 2000). The Parole Board for England and Wales Annual Report and Accounts 2014/15 (see https://www.gov.uk/government/uploads/system/uploads/attachment_data/file/446277/Parole_Board_for_England_and_Wales_Annual_Report_2014.15.pdf) details the Parole Board's latest attainments against certain key performance indicators (KPIs) or case management targets. For example, offenders should be provided with an oral hearing date within 90 days of becoming ready to list. In the first half of the year, over 80 per cent of all cases were provided with an oral hearing date, but it dropped to an average of 74 per cent towards the end of the year. The Parole Board attribute this to the Osborn decision cited above. The decision sets out that, to comply with common law standards and respect the right to privacy under article 5(4) of the ECHR, the Board should hold an oral hearing whenever fairness to the prisoner requires one. Prior to the Osborn decision, the demand for oral hearings averaged 335 cases being referred for an oral hearing per month, whereas, during 2014/15, this increased to 570 per month resulting in a backlog of cases. They intend to reduce this backlog by introducing a number of measures including the increased use of video for remote hearings.

Alternatives to Parole

In response to these criticisms, a number of alternatives to parole and the Parole Board have been suggested in the literature. These have included:

- Replacing the Parole Board with a Parole Tribunal. This would be part of the Tribunals Service, whereby the Secretary of State would not issue guidance to the new tribunal nor appoint its members – they should be appointed by an independent body such as the Judicial Appointments Commission (see JUSTICE, 2009).

- Putting the boot on other foot whereby the presumption would be that the prisoner 'would' get parole at the end of serving his or her tariff. This could then be challenged if there was a risk-related reason.

- Abolishing the Parole Board by only having determinate sentences (as in Norway).

Supervision and Resettlement

Once an offender has been released, he or she will be subject to licence and supervision requirements as discussed above. This section will briefly discuss some of what is in place in terms of 'supervision' and 'resettlement', but with an emphasis on the latter. Resettlement is the work done with ex-prisoners to help them 'resettle' when returning to the community after release from prison, such as help with housing or education, training and employment. Broadly speaking, supervision has traditionally been focused on ex-prisoners who pose a high 'risk of harm' (e.g. MAPPA for high risk sexual/violent offenders – see www.gov.uk/government/publications/multi-agency-public-protection-arrangements-mappa--2 and see also Chapter 8). Ex-prisoners with a low risk of harm, but often a high risk of (minor) reoffending and high needs, have until of late been largely neglected. However, as discussed above, the TR Programme makes provision for all short prison terms to be followed by 12 months of supervision on licence. It is the resettlement work involved with these ex-prisoners that is the focus of this section. However, by way of setting the scene, it is firstly useful to summarise some of the problems that prisoners face when they are released from prison.

Problems Facing Prisoners upon Release

MoJ statistics show that the proven reoffending rate for adult offenders released from custody in 2013 was 46 per cent (which means that 46 per cent of offenders were reconvicted of an offence committed in a one year follow-up period following their release). Since 2004, the overall rate for those released from custody has remained relatively stable at around 45 per cent to 49 per cent. The rate for those released from short sentences has been consistently higher compared to those released from longer sentences. Adults who served sentences of less than 12 months reoffended at a rate of 59.3 per cent, compared to 34.7 per cent for those who served determinate sentences of 12 months or more (MoJ, 2013b). There are problems with using reconviction data to measure reoffending (see Chapter 21), but these statistics do highlight that nearly half of offenders released from prison reoffend, and can often find themselves back in prison, particularly short-term prisoners. This phenomenon is known as the 'revolving doors' problem and was in part the reason for the government's TR changes.

The transition from prison to the community can be very difficult. Offenders can face many problems (see Hagell et al., 1995; Maguire and Nolan, 2007), in addition to avoiding reoffending. These include issues relating to:

- accommodation;
- employment;
- poverty and debt;
- substance abuse;
- social isolation/family breakdown;
- mental health.

Prisoners often lose their accommodation, employment and family ties upon entry into prison. Among other reasons, the mere fact of being an ex-prisoner and others' perceptions of this makes it more difficult to re-establish these things. Labelling theory even proposes that how an individual is categorised and described by others in their society can shape that individual's behaviour, that is that others' stereotypes of ex-offenders can make them more likely to reoffend (see Becker, 1963), regardless of the other pressures listed here.

Table 17.3 Social Exclusion Unit data (2002) on male short-term prisoners

	Male short-term prisoners (%)	General population (%)
2+ mental disorders	72	5
Unemployed	67	5
No qualifications	52	15
Homeless	32	1
Receiving benefits	72	14
Drug use in previous year	63	38

The Social Exclusion Unit data (2002), given in Table 17.3, shows the extent to which these problems have been over-represented in the population of male short-term prisoners compared to the general population. Such problems can be so acute that the disproportionate numbers of drug overdoses, drug-related deaths and suicides among recently released prisoners are well documented in the literature (e.g. Pratt et al., 2006).

Resettlement Work

The 2010 Coalition government's TR programme purportedly aimed to reduce the high rates of reoffending discussed above through a number of measures:

- Setting up 21 privatised Community Rehabilitation Companies (CRCs) to work with low- and medium-risk offenders.

- Introducing an element of payment-by-results (PbR) to CRC contracts.

- Establishing a new National Probation Service (NPS) to take responsibility for assessing the risks offenders pose, producing pre-sentence reports and managing high-risk offenders.

- Providing rehabilitative support to prisoners on sentences of less than 12 months (under the mechanisms described under the section above on the systems of determining the date of release).

- Restructuring the prison estate to facilitate 'through-the-gate' resettlement support through a network of resettlement prisons. (MoJ, 2013a)

The theoretical basis of the TR changes is unclear. One motivation of privatisation and PbR is to save money, but the government also argued that their approach would be rehabilitative and it is certainly true that short-termers, even with their acute needs, had been neglected before.

The 'through the gates' resettlement support, mentioned above, includes someone meeting the released offender at the prison gates to provide continuous support from custody to community and the use of mentors for short-term prisoners being released in the community. It has been widely recognised that rehabilitative interventions in prison are more likely to be effective if followed up systematically after release (Hudson et al., 2007). Moreover, the current reforms were preceded by several pathfinder projects financed under the government's Crime Reduction Programme and designed to test new approaches to the provision of resettlement services for short-term prisoners. Evaluations of these projects (Lewis et al., 2003; Clancy et al., 2006) demonstrated the importance of 'continuity' between work in prison and after release, including efforts by professional staff or mentors to develop relationships with prisoners that will be continued 'through the gate' (Hudson et al., 2007). Since then, some organisations or charities have already been providing a mentoring scheme for prisoners when they are released from prison. Sometimes these schemes include access to peer mentors or advisors inside and/or outside of prison. The term peer is used to denote that the mentor/advisor is an ex-offender him- or herself. I recently evaluated one such service. Some of the findings are included in the research summary below.

Summary of recent research: Evaluation of the St Giles Trust Cymru Through the Gates Resettlement Service

This was an evaluation of a 'through the gates' resettlement service whereby caseworkers, sometimes with the assistance of a volunteer or a peer advisor, offered practical help and signposting to other support services both before release in prison and following release in the community for as long as required by the client. The peer advisors in prison were a group of current prisoners and the peer advisors in the community were ex-prisoners. The evaluation included:

• A reconviction study and a study of financial impact

• Analysis of outcome data including attitudes to offending

• Interviews with service providers, peer advisors and service users (n=60).

At the time of writing results of the interviews are available to report on. The respondents are shown in Table 17.4.

Table 17.4 Respondents

Category of respondent	No of respondents interviewed
Total service providers (SP)	**22**
Caseworker/Special interest worker	6
Project manager	4
Volunteer	2
Trainer	3
Steering group member (SGM)	6
Representative from partner organisation	1
Total peer advisors (PA)	**28**
In the community	3
In prison	25
Total service users (SU)	**10**
In the community	7
In prison	2
Refuser (RF)	1
OVERALL TOTAL OF RESPONDENTS	**60**

Peer advisor scheme in prison

- All interviewees felt that there is value in using prisoners (and ex-prisoners) as peer advisors:

  o Because it's better to speak to somebody who has been in the same situation sometimes as well, because they understand. Because speaking to somebody on the street, or somebody who has not been in trouble, you can't give a full explanation, and they don't understand where you are coming from sometimes. Whereas if you have been in trouble before and they've been in trouble, they've got more of an understanding of how everything works you see.' (SU8)

- Peer advisors often reported of themselves: improved feelings of self-worth; self-confidence; and listening and communication skills:

  o 'and I have grown as a person. My confidence has grown, I am a better person, I look at things differently now … If I didn't get that chance I would probably be in the same situation, taking drugs, but now I am different … I am a different guy now.' (PA9)

- That said, often, while peer advisors wanted to encourage clients not to reoffend, they felt that their role was limited to being 'middle men'. There were also some difficulties in recruiting peer advisors and clients.

Post-release service in the community

- All bar one of the service users were very positive about the service:

  o 'They're doing absolutely everything. It's the best – I've got to say this – it's the best place that has ever helped me. Because at other agencies I've been, I won't mention any names, I haven't seemed to get help, you know, that's needed. (SU5)

- Most interviewees understood the main aim of the project to be to reduce reoffending, although most of the service's work focused on securing housing for clients. However, the service did provide support/referrals to other organisations in many other areas.

- Some considered the service involved 'supporting clients in doing things for themselves', whereas for others it concerned 'doing everything for them'.

- The main barriers/challenges were:

  o Delays at housing offices and the unavailability of accommodation for clients upon release

  o Lack of funding for client training courses.

Release, Supervision and Resettlement: Challenges

Some of the practical challenges for resettlement and peer advice schemes were highlighted in the above research. A small body of literature has raised other concerns over resettlement under the TR programme.

Absence of Evidence Base

A number of commentators have warned that, with the TR agenda, the government has moved from a position of relative stability in an area not recently attracting significant public concern towards a policy that has little evidence base and was not based on an assessment of current strengths or performance (Gavrielides, 2013; Harper, 2013; Broad and Spencer, 2015; Hall, 2015). In other words, the probation service, before it was fragmented into the NPS and CRCs, managed to sustain and sometimes reduce reoffending, but little account was taken of this in the recent redesign. International examples also show the negative impact of privatisation if values are secondary (Hall, 2015).

Net-widening and Up Tariffing

Net-widening is the process of using a new measure, not (or not only) to encompass the target group of offenders but also to drag into the net people who might otherwise have benefited from a lesser response (see, for example, Morgan, 2008). In this context, the fear is that magistrates will up tariff to a custodial sentence to ensure that the offender receives a degree of supervision where they previously would have imposed a lesser, community one that may not have included any supervision.

Offender Engagement

Another early evaluation of TR identified the fragmentation of contact with offenders going through the court process. The increasing use of group induction meant that many offenders had contact with numerous probation staff before meeting the offender manager who would be working with them and that delays in starting to form the crucial working relationship with their supervisor might well reduce the likelihood of effective work being undertaken (HM Inspectorate of Probation, 2014). This is worrying given, as mentioned above, it is important that there is 'continuity' for the offender throughout the process in terms of the work undertaken with the prisoner and with professional staff or mentors from the prison setting to after release (Hudson et al., 2007). Regardless of changes in staff, it could be unrealistic to expect this category of offender to engage with staff anyway. Many of these 'clients' will have received a prison sentence as they have been unsuccessful in completing a community sentence previously, including that they have failed to engage with an offender manager previously. Therefore, there could be little reason to think that they will now engage. Moreover, in the past, large numbers of ex-prisoners have been returned to prison for technical failures in compliance with licence requirements (Solomon, 2005). In combination, this could lead to multiple prison returns and contribute to the 'revolving door' revolving faster, which this policy was aiming to slow down.

Marketisation and Quality of Service

Partly related to the issue of engagement is the fear that an emphasis on marketisation and open competition will lead to a 'race to the bottom', where private companies try to undercut each other in order to win TR contracts (Harper, 2013) and that smaller services will be excluded from the supply chain (Marples, 2013). It could be that smaller services, which are sometimes thought to be the ones that engage best with offenders and ex-offenders, will be excluded because (1) they do not have sufficient income to provide a service prior to their PbR (PbR) (see the section on PbR below) and (2) they do not have the workforce to cover the geographical area required. The Centre for Social Justice (2013 as cited by Marples, 2013) estimates that there are 1,475 voluntary, community and social enterprise (VCSE) organisations whose service users are offenders, ex-offenders and their families. Of these 3 per cent have an income greater than £5 million (e.g. Turning Point (£80 million) and Nacro (£71 million)), 23 per cent have an income greater than £500,000, 51 per cent have an annual turnover or income of £150,000 or less and 4.8 per cent had no income at all. Hence, Bastow (2014) predicted an oligopoly comprising capital-intensive contracts with large services, which could stifle innovation. Moreover, larger private companies may have undercut themselves by too great a margin to be able to deliver high quality services. Although it is suggested that each Tier 1 contractor (the main contractor for the CRC) will need to have some diversity in their supply chain, that is that they will sub-contract to other smaller contractors to provide some of their services, it has been suggested that complex supply chains are more expensive to manage and Tier 1 will have to compete on price (Association of Chief Executives of Voluntary Organisations, 2013 as cited in Marples, 2013). In other words, smaller services could still be excluded as sub-contractors. If this proves to be correct it has wide implications for VCSE, in that smaller services would need funding in order to stay afloat and maintain service provision in the meantime (Marples, 2013)

Reoffending as a Measure of Success and PbR

The critique that reoffending, or more accurately reconviction rates, is a too simplistic measure to be used to define success is well documented (see, for example, Copas and Marshall, 1998). In brief, reconviction is a measure of the process of an individual being (re)detected and (re)convicted of an offence within a particular time frame. Of course, it may under-estimate reoffending by, for example, not capturing undetected offending or focusing on a short time frame. However, the concerns here are, firstly, reconviction rates may reflect the practice of targeting the 'usual suspects' characterised by their powerlessness, who perpetrate generally low level/less serious crimes (see Clarke (2014) and Chapters 5 and 6). The second concern here is that it does not capture successes or progress, which may be very important in working towards reducing reoffending (such as in accommodation or employment) or at least reducing the frequency or severity of offending behaviour. Therefore, the valuable work carried out, often by the smaller, creative services, which focuses on facilitating this progress is not recognised. However, despite that, reoffending is the measure that the government selected to underpin its PbR (PbR) for CRC contracts under the TR reforms. Clarke (2014: 21) argues that what this 'does not offer is any incentive to improve the circumstances or experiences of individuals or communities affected by the problem of "crime" or wider social harms'.

Summary

The systems of release and parole have undergone some major changes over the years. The Parole Board has moved from an administrative body providing recommendations on whether prisoners should have the privilege of serving out their sentences in more congenial circumstances to more of a judicial body providing decisions on whether prisoners should continue to be incarcerated or should be given their liberty. Questions still remain over its independence. Moreover, there are a number of factors related to decision-making which could mean that many prisoners may be undergoing prolonged detention unnecessarily, which include: the lack of consideration of evidence-based risk; the influence of public attitudes to risk; and delays in oral hearings.

Parole is only one mechanism by which prisoners are released, normally the most serious offenders. The TR reforms include changes to the release and resettlement of short-term prisoners. Once released, these ex-prisoners are often confronted with a range of problems from accommodation to health issues. The TR reforms have also expanded the 'through the gates' arrangements to try to help this category of ex-prisoner, as well as extending supervision to this group. However, there will be challenges in the implementation of these changes in terms of, for example, dealing with up tariffing and non-engagement, risking increased prisoner returns and pressure on prisons. Some maintain that the changes were ill thought through and not based on a body of evidence. However, it does seem that there are benefits to the mentors themselves – with ex-offenders often reporting improved feelings of self-worth, self-confidence and listening and communication skills from being involved in this role.[vi]

More broadly, the current reforms seem to reflect ongoing, dual (but possibly not compatible) concerns. The first concern is to control ex-prisoners through post-sentence supervision to respond to continuing demands to manage 'risk' (Maguire and Kemshall, 2004) and to counter heightened fear of crime and improve greater community safety (Garland, 2001), and the second concern is try to meet their needs by systematically following up rehabilitative interventions in prison after release (Hudson et al., 2007) to reduce reoffending. The waters are further muddied in terms of the types of services (large, private companies) contracted with these tasks and how their success is being measured (PbR based on reoffending rates).

Discussion Questions

1. What is parole?

2. What are the main differences that the 'Transforming Rehabilitation' changes made to the release of prisoners?

3. What criticisms have been made of the Parole Board and what alternatives have been suggested?

4. What is resettlement and why is it so important?

5. What are the main differences that the 'Transforming Rehabilitation' changes made to the resettlement of prisoners?

———— **Notes** ————

i. I would like to thank Professor Mike Maguire for his comments on a draft of this chapter. I would also like to thank him for allowing me to attend a number of his presentations on this topic which were very helpful. In addition, I would like to thank St Giles Trust Cymru and HMP Cardiff and their staff, clients and inmates for participating in my research cited in this chapter, and NOMs in Wales for allowing the results to be published.

ii. As well as serving a community sentence (discussed in Chapter 15), someone being 'on probation' also refers to someone who has been released from prison on licence or on parole.

iii. There are two types of life sentence. Mandatory life sentences are imposed on those convicted of murder and there are three variants depending on the offender's age. Discretionary life sentences are the maximum sentences for those convicted of a serious offence, e.g. manslaughter, attempted murder, rape, armed robbery, arson. Again, there are three variants depending on the offender's age.

iv. The most serious offence if the prisoner is serving a sentence for a number of offences.

v. Alternatively, it could indicate more in-depth knowledge informing the parole report's assessment than in the OASys assessment or that inaccuracy in completing OASys alters risk levels, missing important information regarding past and present histories/situations (Prins, 1999).

vi. There could be further changes in store for the released prisoners. For example, it has been suggested by Michael Gove that prisoners who gain qualifications while in prison could be allowed to leave prison early under an 'earned release' scheme (see www.theguardian.com/society/2015/jul/17/earnged-release-prisoners-michael-gove-education-learning).

———— **Further reading** ————

This article provides a useful overview of the background to TR:

Annison, A., Burke, L. and Senior, P. (2014) 'Transforming Rehabilitation: Another example of English 'exceptionalism' or a blueprint for the rest of Europe?' *European Journal of Probation*, 6 (1): 6–23.

This book provides a discussion of the dilemmas currently confronting the Parole Board:

Padfield, N. (2007) *Who to Release? Parole, fairness and criminal justice*. Cullompton: Willan Publishing.

This book provides an overview of the different policies and practices for dealing with releasing ex-offenders from prison within Europe:

Padfield, P., Van Zyl Smit, D. and Dünkel, F. (eds) (2010) *Release from Prison: European policy and practice*. Cullompton: Willan Publishing.

These pieces provide useful background reading on resettlement:

Maguire, M. (2007) 'The resettlement of ex-prisoners', in L. Gelsthorpe and R.N. Morgan (eds), *Handbook of Probation Studies*. Devon: Willan. pp. 398–424.

Maguire, M. and Raynor, P. (2006) 'How the resettlement of prisoners promotes desistance from crime: Or does it?' *Criminology and Criminal Justice*, 6 (1): 17–36.

References

Bastow, S. (2014) 'Transforming rehabilitation: Evolution not revolution', *Criminal Justice Matters*, 97 (1): 10–11.

Becker, H. (1963) *Outsiders*. New York: Free Press.

Bradford, S. and Cowell, P. (2012) 'The decision making process at parole interviews (indeterminate imprisonment for public protection sentences)'. Research summary 1/12. Available at: www.justice.gov.uk/downloads/publications/research-and-analysis/moj-research/decision-making-process-parole-reviews-ipp.pdf [accessed 3 May 2016].

Broad, R. and Spencer, J. (2015) 'Understanding the marketisation of the probation service through an interpretative policy framework', in M. Wasik and S. Santatzoglou (eds), *The Management of Change in Criminal Justice*. London: Palgrave Macmillan. pp. 64–79.

Clancy, A., Hudson, K., Maguire, M., Peake, R., Raynor, P., Vanstone, M. and Kynch, J. (2006) *Getting Out and Staying Out: Results of the prisoner resettlement pathfinders*. Bristol: Policy Press.

Clarke, B. (2014) 'Chasing the "reoffending" rainbow', *Criminal Justice Matters*, 97 (1): 20–1.

Copas, J. and Marshall, P. (1998) 'The offender group reconviction scale: A statistical reconviction score for use by probation officers', *Journal of the Royal Statistical Society*, Series C (Applied Statistics), 47, (1): 159–71.

Daily Mail (2011) Available at: www.dailymail.co.uk/news/article-1345078/Number-prisoners-offend-released-licence-far-higher-know-admits-parole-board-boss.html#ixzz43YA7JUU4 [accessed 3 May 2016].

Fitzgibbon, W.D. (2008) 'Fit for purpose? OASys assessments and parole decisions', *Probation Journal*, 55 (1): 55–69.

Forde, R.A. (2014) 'Risk assessment in parole decisions: A study of life sentence prisoners in England'. Thesis: University of Birmingham.

Garland, D. (2001) *The Culture of Control*, Oxford: Oxford University Press.

Gavrielides, T. (2013) 'Mind the gap: Quality without equality in transforming rehabilitation', *British Journal of Community Justice*, 11 (2–3): 135–47.

Hagell, A., Newburn, T. and Rowlingson, K. (1995) *Financial Difficulties on Release from Prison*. London: Policy Studies Institute.

Hall, S. (2015) 'Why probation matters', *Howard Journal of Criminal Justice*, 54 (4): 321–35.

Harper, C. (2013) 'Transforming rehabilitation and the creeping marketisation of British public services', *British Journal of Community Justice*, 11 (2–3): 37–41.

Hill, A. (2010) 'Many offenders in jail too long, says parole chief', *The Guardian*. Available at: www.guardian.co.uk/society/2010/jul/19/offenders-jail-too-long-parole-chief [accessed 22 March 2016].

HM Inspectorate of Probation (2014) 'Transforming Rehabilitation – Early implementation'. Available at: www.justiceinspectorates.gov.uk/hmiprobation [accessed: 22 March 2016].

Hood, R. and Shute, S. (2000) *Parole System at Work: A study of risk based decision-making*. London: Home Office Research Development and Statistics Directorate. Available at: http://webarchive.nationalarchives.gov.uk/20110218135832/rds.homeoffice.gov.uk/rds/pdfs/hors202.pdf [accessed 18 April 2016].

Hudson, K., Maguire, M. and Raynor, P. (2007) 'Through the prison gate: Resettlement, offender management and the birth of the "seamless sentence"' in Jewkes, Y. (Ed.) *Handbook of Prisons*. Devon: Willan, pp. 629–659.

JUSTICE (2009) *A New Parole System for England and Wales*. London: JUSTICE. Available at www.nuffieldfoundation.org/sites/default/files/A%20New%20Parole%20System%20for%20England%20and%20Wales.pdf [accessed 13 September 2016].

Legal Action Group (2016) *Parole Board Decision Making*. Available at www.lag.org.uk/media/143635/chapter_3_-_parole_board_decision_making.pdf [accessed 22 March 2016].

Lewis, S., Vennard, J., Maguire, M., Raynor, P., Vanstone, M., Raybould, S., and Rix, A. (2003) *Resettlement of Short-Term Prisoners: An evaluation of seven pathfinders*. London: Research, Development, and Statistics Directorate, Home Office. Available at: www.homeoffice.gov.uk/rds/pdfs2/occ83pathfinders.pdf [accessed 13 September 2016].

McMurran, M., Khalifa, N. and Gibbon, S. (2013) *Forensic Mental Health*. London: Routledge.

Maguire, M. (2007) 'The resettlement of ex-prisoners', in L. Gelsthorpe and R.N. Morgan (eds), *Handbook of Probation Studies*. Devon: Willan. pp. 398–424.

Maguire, M. and Kemshall, H. (2004) 'Multi-agency public protection arrangements: Key issues' in H. Kemshall and G. McIvor (eds) *Managing Sex Offender Risk*. London: Jessica Kingsley, pp. 209–24.

Maguire, M. and Nolan, J. (2007) 'Accommodation and related services for ex-prisoners', in A. Hucklesby (ed.), *The Resettlement of Ex-Prisoners*. Devon: Willan. pp. 144–73.

Maguire, M. and Raynor, P. (2006) 'How the resettlement of prisoners promotes desistance from crime: Or does it?' *Criminology and Criminal Justice*, 6 (1): 17–36.

Marples, R. (2013) 'Transforming rehabilitation – The risks for the voluntary, community and social enterprise sector in engaging in commercial contracts with Tier 1 providers', *British Journal of Community Justice*, 11 (2–3): 21–32.

Ministry of Justice (2013a) *Transforming Rehabilitation: A Strategy for Reform*. London: Ministry of Justice.

Ministry of Justice (2013b) *Proven Re-offending Statistics Quarterly Bulletin January to December 2013, England and Wales*. Available at: www.gov.uk/government/uploads/system/uploads/attachment_data/file/472524/proven-reoffending-2013.pdf [accessed 3 May 2016].

Morgan, R. (2008) *Summary Justice: Fast – but fair?* London: Centre for Crime and Justice Studies. Available at: www.crimeandjustice.org.uk/sites/crimeandjustice.org.uk/files/Summary-justice.pdf [accessed 24 May 2016].

National Audit Office (2000) *Report by the Comptroller and Auditor General: Parole (HC 456 Session 1999-2000)*. London: The Stationery Office. Available at: www.nao.org.uk/wp-content/uploads/2000/05/9900456es.pdf [accessed 3 May 2016].

Padfield, N. and Liebling, A. (2000) *An Exploration of Decision-Making at Discretionary Lifer Panels*, Home Office Research Study No. 213. London: Home Office Research, Development and Statistics Directorate.

Padfield, P., Van Zyl Smit, D. and Dünkel, F. (eds) (2010) *Release from Prison: European policy and practice*. Cullompton: Willan Publishing.

Pratt, D., Piper, M., Appleby, L., Webb, R. and Shaw, J. (2006) Suicide in recently released prisoners: A population-based cohort study', *The Lancet*, 368 (9530): 119–23.

Prins, H. (1999) *Will They Do It Again? Risk assessment and management in criminal justice and psychiatry*. London: Routledge.

Social Exclusion Unit (2002) *Reducing Re-offending by Ex-Prisoners*. Office of the Deputy Prime Minister.

Solomon, E. (2005) 'Returning to punishment: Prison recalls', *Criminal Justice Matters,* 60, 24–5.

Check out the Companion Website

Want to know more about this chapter? Review what you have been learning by visiting: **https://study.sagepub.com/harding**

- Practice with essay questions
- Test yourself with multiple-choice questions
- Listen to a series of podcasts featuring Neil of Northumbria Police and London's Metropolitan Police Service
- Watch videos selected from the SAGE Video collection

18 Youth Justice

Tim Bateman

Introduction

The term 'youth justice' is generally understood to refer to the set of arrangements pertaining to children below 18 years of age in conflict with the law. On this account, youth justice constitutes the state's response to youth crime and to children in trouble.

In one sense, such an articulation is uncontroversial and, at this level, the youth justice landscape is readily delineated. Accordingly, this chapter commences with an overview of the distinct organs of youth justice provision in England and Wales and describes the range of criminal sanctions available to children. It also explores the extent to which the treatment of children diverges from, or replicates, that for adult offenders.

However, a simplistic identification of youth justice with process implies a non-ideological reaction to children's challenging behaviour and, thereby, obscures an array of questionable assumptions about the nature of youth crime and the deeply political determination of responses to it. One way of illuminating such assumptions is to ask why a distinct system of justice for children is necessary.

Answers to that question typically draw on a binary distinction between welfare and justice models (Hazel, 2008). The former highlights similar characteristics of children who transgress the law and those in need of care and protection. It understands youth crime as symptomatic of underlying need and, correspondingly, endorses treatment to address the causes of delinquency rather than punishment focused on the symptoms. Justice, by contrast, emphasises that what distinguishes youth offending from other forms of problematic behaviour (and 'young offenders' from other children in need) is precisely its criminality. But since children are less accountable for their actions than their adult counterparts, a distinct response – that systemically mitigates for age – is required. Transgressions of the law should thus be met by punishment that is proportionate, in accordance with clearly delineated safeguards, and appropriately tempered to allow for reduced culpability. Welfare need, according to justice tenets, should be addressed outside the criminal arena (Smith, 2005).

The highly politicised nature of youth justice discourse is evidenced by the impact of key moments on the development of policy. For instance the murder of two-year-old James Bulger in 1993 by two boys, themselves barely over the age of criminal responsibility, acted as a catalyst for a 'punitive turn' (Muncie, 2008). This was patently not an evidence-based response to shifts in the volume or nature of young people's behaviour but had, nonetheless, profound implications for the treatment of some of society's most deprived children. More recent developments in youth justice are similarly more fruitfully explained by swings in political mood than patterns of youth crime or demonstrable effectiveness.

Timeline

1907   Probation of Offenders Act introduced statutory probation and supervision for those below the age of 16

1908   The Children Act established the juvenile court for children aged 7–16 years with jurisdiction over criminal and care matters

1933   Children and Young Persons Act (CYPA) – the minimum age of criminal responsibility was raised to 8 years

1963   Children and Young Persons Act (CYPA) – the minimum age of criminal responsibility in England and Wales was raised to 10 years

1964   The Longford report 'Crime: A challenge to us all' was published and in Scotland the Kilbrandon report was published

1969   Children and Young Persons Act introduced supervision orders and care orders as sentences for children's offending

1989   Children Act abolished the care order as a criminal sanction and created a new family proceedings court, separating for the first time care matters from crime, which continues to be dealt with in the juvenile court

1991   The UK became a signatory to the UN Convention on the Rights of the Child (UNCRC)

1991   Criminal Justice Act replaced the juvenile court with the youth court, extending the age range of the youth justice system to include 17-year-olds

1993   James Bulger murdered. The case prompted a 'moral panic' about youth crime and led to a 'punitive turn'

1997   New Labour's White Paper 'No More Excuses'

1998   Crime and Disorder Act (CDA) created youth offending teams and the Youth Justice Board for England and Wales, as well as introducing a statutory aim for the youth justice system of preventing offending by children and young people

1999   Youth Justice and Criminal Evidence Act introduced referral orders as a near mandatory sentence for children appearing in court for the first time who admit the offence

2008   Youth Crime Action Plan introduced a target to reduce the number of 'first time entrants' to the youth justice system

2008   Criminal Justice and Immigration Act replaced all existing community sentences for children by the youth rehabilitation order with an extensive range of requirements

The 'Creation' of Youth Justice

Reference to a youth justice system implies that arrangements for dealing with children in trouble are sufficiently distinct from those for adult offenders to warrant separate appellation. That level of distinction is a recent phenomenon. Until the mid-nineteenth century, the legal framework and sentencing powers for dealing with adults and children over the age of criminal responsibility were identical. Indeed Arthur (2010) argues that prior to the establishment of separate custodial provision for children in the 1850s, the category 'young offenders' had no precise denotation. The creation of alternative sanctions in the form of reformatories and industrial schools – children's prisons, despite the benevolent tone of the titles – allowed 'juvenile delinquency ... gradually to take on [its] modern meaning as a ... distinctive social problem' (Arthur, 2010: 7).

The gradual accumulation of provisions specifically applicable to children continued throughout the century but most commentators point to later developments as constituting the defining moment at which talk of a separate system became legitimate (Pitts, 2005). The Children Act 1908 established the juvenile court as a discrete venue for proceedings – criminal and care – involving children aged 7–16 years. The previous year, the Probation of Offenders Act had introduced statutory probation as an alternative to punishment and created designated probation officers for supervisees below the age of 16, heralding the development of a specialist workforce for children subject to penal measures (Arthur, 2010).

The principal characteristics of a youth justice system were consequently in place, in incipient form, by the first decade of the twentieth century: distinct institutional arrangements; a discrete youth justice profession focused on rehabilitation as well as punishment; and a separate framework of sanctions.

The Youth Justice Apparatus

The minimum age of criminal responsibility in England and Wales, as established by the Children and Young Persons Act (CYPA) 1963, is 10 years (Bateman, 2012a); young people aged 18 years or over are considered adults for criminal justice purposes. The juvenile court was renamed the youth court in 1992, with the amendment marking an extension of jurisdiction to encompass 17-year-olds (Watkins and Johnson, 2009). The Children Act 1989 had already separated care and crime matters through the establishment of the family proceedings court; the youth court's sole focus is thus children in trouble (Stanley, 2005).

Youth proceedings resemble those in the adult magistrates' court. They are presided over by a bench of three lay magistrates or, less frequently, a professionally qualified district judge who may sit alone. Cases are tried on an adversarial basis and defendants are deemed innocent unless the case is proved 'beyond all reasonable doubt' (Chapter 14 this volume).

There are, however, differences. Magistrates appointed to the youth panel must already have substantial experience in the adult court and receive specialist training (Stanley, 2005). Proceedings are less formal, defendants are addressed by first name, and magistrates are encouraged to engage with children, albeit with variable success (Allen et al., 2000). The principle of 'open justice' pertains in the adult system reflecting an assumption that the operation of justice should be transparent and that the public has a right to know what punishments have been inflicted upon whom. This principle is heavily circumscribed in the youth court, which is closed to the public. The CYPA 1933 also provides for a presumption of reporting restrictions, although this can be waived in particular circumstances, affording a limited right to privacy (Hart, 2014a).

The Agencies of Youth Justice

For much of the last century, rehabilitation of children in trouble was regarded as a social work function; although 'juvenile justice' became a distinct specialism from the early 1980s, that specialism remained firmly located within the broader discipline (Haines and Drakeford, 1998). In many areas, probation took responsibility for older children, blurring boundaries between child and adult provision, but this was at a time when probation officers were social-work trained (Mair and Burke, 2011).

A complete separation was effected through the 1998 Crime and Disorder Act (CDA), which established youth offending teams (YOTs) as the primary agency responsible for the delivery of youth justice services (Burnett, 2005). It also delineated, for the first time, the statutory remit of those services, as shown in Box 18.1.

Box 18.1

Youth Justice Services Defined in s38 of the 1998 Crime and Disorder Act

- provision of appropriate adults for children in police custody;
- assessment of, and interventions with, children subject to pre-court disposals;
- support for children on remand;
- placement of children remanded to local authority accommodation;
- provision of court reports;
- supervision of children subject to court orders in custody and the community.

YOTs are multi-disciplinary bodies, reflecting a (contested) reading of the evidence that effective intervention should address a range of 'criminogenic' risk factors (Home Office, 1997). The legislation obliges local authorities, with other partners, to establish a YOT consisting of a:

- social worker
- probation officer
- police officer
- education worker and
- health worker. (Great Britain, 1998)

In practice, YOTs are significantly larger than the statutory minimum membership implies: in 2015, despite a national fall in staffing of more than a quarter between 2009/10 and 2013/14, 35 per cent of YOTs had a workforce exceeding

50 (Deloitte, 2015). More concerning, it is doubtful whether the vision of a highly skilled, multi-disciplinary, workforce was ever realised in many areas. Some agencies – health in particular – have faltered in their required contribution to the partnership (Currie, 2009). Moreover, the majority of YOT workers (one recent estimate suggests three-quarters) are not professionally qualified (Deloitte, 2015). This picture has prompted suggestions that the introduction of YOTs represented a dilution of professionalism (Pitts, 2001).

If YOTs provide the mechanism for local delivery, the CDA also attempted to ensure central coordination through the creation of the Youth Justice Board (YJB), with a statutory remit to monitor the operation of the youth justice system, advise government and promote good practice. The Board also acts as the conduit for central funding to YOTs and commissions youth custodial provision (Allen, 2005). Its role is discussed further in Chapter 8.

Contemporarily, political commitment to localism has encouraged increasing variety, with the 'pure' YOT as a stand-alone entity something of an endangered species, accounting for just 15 per cent of youth justice provision (Deloitte, 2015). YOTs have become increasingly integrated with other local services in response to falling caseloads, financial contraction and a greater focus on prevention (Youth Justice Board, 2015a), prompting suggestions of a tendency towards a 'post-YOT youth justice' (Byrne and Brookes, 2015).

Youth Justice Sanctions

Formal sanctions for children who offend are distinct from those for adults, although the differences are sometimes semantic rather than of substance.

Pre-court measures, for instance, closely mirror adult provision. Where a child admits an offence and the public interest does not require prosecution, available formal sanctions consist of a youth caution or youth conditional caution. The main difference between these disposals and their adult counterparts is the obligation on the YOT to undertake assessments of and, where appropriate, offer interventions to, children given a second caution (Hart, 2014b).

Like that for adults, the sentencing framework for children is predicated on the notion of proportionality, wherein the restriction of liberty imposed by the court must be commensurate with the gravity of the offence (Sentencing Guidelines Council, 2009). Statutory thresholds, which must be crossed before certain disposals are deployed, create three sentencing bands: custodial orders; community sentences (in practice, the youth rehabilitation order); and first-tier disposals. A custodial sentence cannot be made unless the court determines that the offending is 'so serious that neither a fine alone nor a community sentence can be justified'. Equally, the court cannot pass a community sentence unless it deems the offending 'serious enough to warrant it' (Great Britain, 2003: ss52 and 148). If neither threshold is met, the court must impose a first-tier disposal.

This generic framework is modified considerably in the case of a child through a range of competing principles, introduced at different times and reflecting the 'multiple discourses' that constitute the youth justice 'melting pot' (Fergusson, 2007: 179). Courts are also required to have regard to the welfare of the child (Great Britain, 1933). The CDA 1998 provides that the principal aim of the youth justice system is the prevention of offending and reoffending of children, and mandates: 'all persons and bodies carrying out functions in relation to the youth justice system to have regard to that aim' (Great Britain, 1998: s37). Less frequently recognised is the court's obligation to take account of relevant international instruments, in particular the UN Convention on the Rights of the Child (UNCRC) to which the UK became a signatory in 1991 (Goldson and Muncie, 2015). The Convention requires that the best interests of the child 'shall be a primary consideration' (United Nations, 1989: article 3(1)), arguably a stronger obligation than having regard to welfare. It also precludes the use of detention for children except as 'a measure of last resort' (United Nations, 1989: article 37(c)), which might be thought more restrictive than the domestic custody threshold.

This assortment of principles potentially pulls in different directions. For example, the child's best interests may not always accord with what the court considers will prevent offending. Conversely, where the offence is relatively minor but welfare concerns significant, the principle of proportionality might be in tension with attending to the child's needs. Such complexity no doubt contributes to the phenomenon of 'justice by geography' whereby outcomes for similar offending diverge dramatically between areas (Bateman and Stanley, 2002).

The range of court orders available to children who offend – detailed in Table 18.1 – have, with notable exceptions, functional adult equivalents.

Table 18.1 Court orders for children and their adult equivalents

Level of sanction	Orders for children	Adult equivalent order
First-tier penalties	Fine	Fine
	Absolute/conditional discharge	Absolute/conditional discharge
	Compensation	Compensation
	Reparation order	No equivalent
	Referral order	No equivalent
Community sentences	Youth rehabilitation order	Community order
Custodial sentences	Detention and training order (up to 2 years)	Imprisonment
	Detention at HM Pleasure	Mandatory life sentence
	Extended sentence for dangerousness	Extended sentence for dangerousness
	Long-term detention for grave crimes (more than 2 years)	Imprisonment

The reparation order, as the name implies, requires the child to undertake a specified number of hours of direct or indirect reparation. It has no adult counterpart but is used rarely. In 2013/14, the order made up less than one per cent of all youth sentences (Ministry of Justice/Youth Justice Board, 2015a). By contrast, the referral order is widely used, accounting for nearly 40 per cent of youth penalties, and represents a genuinely distinctive sanction that has no corresponding adult penalty. The extensive use is explained by the fact that, where a child appearing in court for the first time pleads guilty, a referral order is mandatory unless the court discharges or imprisons them, or makes a hospital order (Ministry of Justice/Youth Justice Board, 2015b).

On implementation, the referral order was only available on a single occasion for a first offence, but subsequent legislation has extended the circumstances in which it can be made. Currently an order can be imposed in any case where the child admits the offence, irrespective of antecedent history. The loosening of the criteria has been accompanied by a corresponding rise in the proportion of sentences that result in a referral order, from 27 per cent in 2002/03 to 37 per cent in 2013/14 (Ministry of Justice/Youth Justice Board, 2015a).

The distinctive quality of the referral order resides in the fact that its effect is to refer the child to a meeting of a youth offender panel (YOP) whose purpose is to agree a 'contract' that lays out expectations for the duration (3 to 12 months) of the order. The length alone is determined by the court, which has no further influence. The panel comprises two community volunteers and a member of the YOT acting in an advisory capacity. The process purports to be restorative (see Chapter 20), enabling victims, should they wish to participate:

> to say how they have been affected by the offence, ask questions, receive an explanation and/or an apology and discuss how the offender can make practical reparation for the harm that has been caused. (Ministry of Justice/Youth Justice Board, 2015b: 10)

The panel also aims to provide the child with the opportunity to take responsibility for harm caused and make amends directly to the victim or indirectly to the community.

The referral order has attracted considerable approbation. Crawford and Newburn (2003: 242), for instance, suggest that it 'intimates that it may just be possible to do youth justice differently'. Certainly, where victims attend panel meetings, they express a high degree of satisfaction; children also indicate that they are treated with more respect than in court (Crawford and Newburn, 2003). Nonetheless, the extent to which the process is fully restorative is questionable.

Victim involvement is the exception rather than rule: one study found victims were present at just five per cent of panels. Child participants, while preferring the panel to court, view the primary purpose to be punishment (Crawford and Newburn, 2003) and many are 'mystified rather than reformed or restored by the process' (Newbury, 2011: 104).

The detention and training order (DTO) is the sole youth court custodial sentence. It is available for up to two years on a child aged 12 years or older where the standard custodial threshold applies, but the court must also determine that the defendant is a 'persistent offender' where they are under 15. By default, half of the order is served within custody with the remainder completed under YOT supervision in the community; there is, however, provision for early or late release for sentences of eight months or longer depending on the child's progress (Nacro, 2007).

Youth court custodial powers are considerably greater than those in the adult magistrates' court where the maximum term for a single offence is six months. Conversely, the circumstances in which jurisdiction may be refused by the youth court are more circumscribed. Longer custodial sentences are, nonetheless, available for children convicted of 'grave crimes'[i] or who commit violent or sexual offences and are deemed 'dangerous'. Cases of homicide are automatically heard in the Crown Court and children convicted of murder are subject to detention at Her Majesty's pleasure, the equivalent of an adult mandatory life sentence. Otherwise jurisdiction may be refused where the grave crimes or dangerousness criteria apply; the sentence then available in the Crown Court is the same as the adult maximum (Stone, 2010).

Incarcerated children are detained in a discrete secure estate for under 18s consisting of three types of establishment:

- Young offender institutions (YOIs), the largest by some margin, accommodate boys aged 15–17 years and closely resemble adult prisons;
- Secure training centres (STCs) are smaller, privately managed, custodial institutions that hold boys and girls aged 12–17 years;
- Secure children's homes (SCHs) are childcare establishments that may also accommodate children deprived of their liberty on welfare grounds. They are the smallest of the three forms of custodial provision and accommodate children from age 10, assessed as particularly vulnerable. (Gyateng et al., 2013)

Staffing ratios vary considerably between establishments, corresponding to their respective size: YOIs have an average of one member of staff to every ten children; the equivalent ratios in STCs and SCHs are two to six and two to three respectively (Gyateng et al., 2013). Differences in staffing levels are in turn mirrored in unit costs: in 2012, placement in a YOI cost £65,000 per annum compared with £178,000 in an STC and £212,000 in an SCH (Justice Committee, 2013).

Placements are determined by the YJB in consultation with YOTs. Decisions are influenced by:

- gender (girls cannot be placed in YOIs);
- age (10–11-year-olds can only be placed in SCHs);
- vulnerability (boys aged 15 years and above are placed in YOIs unless deemed vulnerable); and
- availability.

In practice, as shown in Table 18.2, the large majority of incarcerated children, 68 per cent in August 2015, are detained in YOIs (Youth Justice Board, 2015b). It is difficult to avoid the conclusion that the secure estate is configured largely to accommodate financial considerations.

Table 18.2 Configuration of the secure estate for children and young people, August 2015

Establishment type	Staff to child ratio	Unit cost per annum	Percentage of total custodial population
Young offender institution	1:10	£65,000	68.5
Secure training centre	2:6	£178,000	21.1
Secure children's home	2:3	£212,000	10.4

While youth justice thus differs in important respects from the adult system, significant overlap between the two remains. Indeed the youth justice system has attracted criticism precisely because it is insufficiently distinct, in contravention of the requirements of the UNCRC (National Association for Youth Justice, 2015).

The existence of YOTs and the specialist training undertaken by the youth court judiciary notwithstanding, other agencies dealing with children in trouble, including police, defence lawyers, and Crown Court judges, have no specialist practitioners (Carlile, 2014). Sanctions available for children, with the notable exception of the referral order, replicate those for adults in all but name and the framework, within which they are embedded, derives from the adult justice system with modifications to formalise mitigation for youth. Indeed, the connection between the adult and youth justice systems is such that criminal legislation applies automatically to children unless they are explicitly excluded from its remit.

The grave crime provisions entail that, despite a presumption of trial in the youth court, children are routinely exposed to adult terms of incarceration in the Crown Court, a venue designed to deal with serious adult offending. During 2013/14, through this mechanism, 279 children were subjected to sentences of imprisonment longer than the two-year maximum permitted in the youth court (Ministry of Justice/Youth Justice Board, 2015a).

Models of Youth Justice

Descriptions of process are in themselves an inadequate articulation of the dynamics of youth justice: responses to children who offend embody tacit assumptions about youth crime and are determined, partly, by political imperatives. The standard classificatory approach that characterises a system according to how closely it exemplifies tenets of welfare or justice, while offering a useful starting point, also fails to capture the complexity of policy and practice. In any given period, the treatment of children in trouble might manifest a range of contradictory features. Moreover, regimes that appear to accord with the same model can generate markedly different outcomes. For instance, a falling custodial population in the 1980s is often attributed to the impact of a 'back to justice' movement (Haines and Drakeford, 1998). Yet a rapidly escalating reliance on incarceration in the next decade is also frequently characterised as a retreat from welfare (Hopkins Burke, 2008).

For such reasons, McAra and McVie (2015) suggest that a dichotomous model is inadequate, arguing that it is possible to discern five 'modes' of youth justice that dominate contemporary discourse: just deserts (or justice), welfare, restorative, actuarial and diversionary whose defining features are described schematically in Table 18.3. Even this more sophisticated taxonomy may be insufficiently nuanced. Kelly and Armitage (2015:117) have, for instance, convincingly proposed that there are 'diverse diversions'.

Table 18.3 'Modes' of youth justice

Paradigm	Understanding of the offending child	Aim/purpose	Extent/nature of intervention
Just deserts (justice)	Rational and responsible	Deter and punish	Proportionate to offending
Welfare	Non-rational, victim of circumstance	Diagnose and treat need	Proportionate and appropriate to needs
Restorative	Rational and responsible, needing to make amends	Make amends, support victim and reintegrate the child into the community	Proportionate to the harm caused and appropriate to making amends to victim
Actuarial	Dangerous, the bearer of risks	Reduce current and future risk and protect victims and the public	Proportionate to assessed risk
Diversionary	Adapted to ascribed identities; bearer of deviant status	Diminish negative effects of system intervention and avoid labelling	Minimum necessary

Adapted from McAra and McVie (2015)

From Welfarist Ambition to Popular Punitivism: Youth Justice in the Second Half of the Twentieth Century

The creation of the juvenile court in 1908 represented an uneasy compromise between welfarism and justice. In dealing with matters relating to care as well as crime, it acknowledged the common origin of childhood difficulties, but retribution remained a dominant rationale. The court was thus an agency 'for the rescue as well as the punishment of juveniles' (cited in Gelsthorpe and Morris, 1994: 951). For more than half a century thereafter, youth justice in England and Wales assumed an increasingly welfarist hue, in step with an emerging 'rehabilitative ideal' (Allen, 1981). The principle that courts were obliged to have regard to the welfare of the child was introduced by the CYPA 1933 (Arthur, 2010). The age of criminal responsibility was raised successively, to 8 in 1933 and 10 in 1963, intimating that younger children's delinquency should, where intervention was necessary, be dealt with through social welfare provision (Bateman, 2012a).

In retrospect, the 1960s represents the pinnacle of welfarist pretentions. The 1964 Longford report developed a far-reaching argument for the abolition of the juvenile court and its replacement by family councils comprised of social workers and others 'selected for their understanding ... of children' (Bottoms, 2002: 221). Predictably, the proposals drew a welter of antagonism from a broad constituency (Thorpe et al., 1980). While Scotland, endorsing the Kilbrandon report published at the same time, did proceed to replace the court with a welfare-based children's hearing system (Whyte, 2005), the ensuing CYPA 1969 in England and Wales was considerably less radical and was in any event selectively implemented.

For instance, a provision to raise the age of criminal responsibility to 14 years remained unimplemented until removed from the statute book in 1991 (Bateman, 2012a). The CYPA 1969 also proposed to replace child custody with care and supervision orders but, while the latter were introduced, imprisonment remained available. The grafting of welfare disposals onto the existing panoply of sanctions led to an increased use of both with the former functioning as 'complementary' rather than as an alternative to the latter (Rutherford, 1992: 60), affording a 'net-widening' mechanism that criminalised younger children for lesser offending. Between 1973 and 1978, youth cautions and convictions rose by 20 per cent (Home Office, 1984). The expansion in custody was sharper: between the passage of the Act and 1977, there was a 158 per cent increase in children consigned to detention centres (Thorpe et al., 1980).

This experience sparked a powerful backlash against the welfarist impulses identified as responsible. If focusing on children's needs implied levels of intervention not warranted by the offending, then, the proponents of a 'new orthodoxy' reasoned, such needs should be addressed outside the justice system (Haines and Drakeford, 1998: 50). The logic of that critique, outlined in Box 18.2, challenged a number of assumptions implicit in the welfare model.

Box 18.2

The 'New Orthodoxy' Critique

- Most youth crime is trivial and transitory; left to their own devices children grow out of crime; intervention is frequently unnecessary;
- Contact with the justice system is criminogenic; welfarist responses that net-widen are counterproductive;
- Intervention within that system should be limited by considerations of proportionality; outstanding welfare need should be addressed outside it by mainstream services.

Ostensibly a call for a return to justice, this was justice with a light touch whose philosophical underpinnings leaned heavily on a labelling perspective (Becker, 1963) and were influenced by Schur's (1973: 155) injunction to 'leave the kids alone'. These premises determined that the role of youth justice intervention was to promote decarceration, diversion, and decriminalisation (Goldson, 2005) through a practice of 'necessary minimum intervention', a paradigm more in keeping with McAra and McVie's (2015) diversionary mode than a straightforward justice model.

The practitioner and academic lobby found an unlikely ally in the Conservative administration, headed by Margaret Thatcher. Despite coming to power on a law and order agenda, the government encouraged increased cautioning and funded alternatives to custody (Bateman, 2012b). Pitts' (2003) credible explanation of this conundrum points to a tension at the heart of the Thatcherite project: a government committed to being tough on crime was also politically wedded to a reduction in expenditure. Minimum intervention was in part an expression of crude economic calculation. The practical impact was remarkable: between 1980 and 1990, the number of children sentenced to custody declined by 80 per cent (Bateman, 2014). Criminal care orders, which had increasingly come to be understood as an additional form of custody, were abolished by the Children Act 1989.

But the new orthodoxy unravelled as rapidly as it formed. James Bulger's murder transformed a growing political unease with non-intervention into a 'popular punitivism' (Bottoms, 1995) that, from 1993, discarded diversionary principles, and saw a corresponding explosion, approaching 90 per cent over the next decade, in child imprisonment (Bateman, 2012b). The 'punitive imperatives' (Goldson, 2002: 386) that drove this turn derived from a fervent attempt by mainstream parties to harness perceived public concerns over youth crime – exemplified by the Bulger case – thereby generating a penal 'arms race' (Centre for Social Justice, 2012: 26) in which assuaging public sentiment took priority over evidence. Harsher legislative provisions and tougher judicial decisions ensued. The antipathy towards welfare that had developed during the 1980s became firmly entrenched, exemplified in the title of New Labour's White Paper 'No More Excuses' (Home Office, 1997). In the less tolerant climate, proportionality took on a different complexion as cases that would not previously have been considered 'so serious' as to warrant imprisonment now became so. The light touch of the previous decade was eschewed as justice revealed its hard face.

New Labour, Managerialism and Risk

Labour's eager participation in the arms race signalled a departure from the party's previous understanding of offending as a social problem. Under Blair's leadership that understanding was replaced by a populist commitment to being tough on crime, particularly focused on the wrongdoings of the young (Matthews and Young, 2003).

Following the party's 1997 electoral success, any expectations that punitivism had run its course were quickly rebuffed. The 1998 Crime and Disorder Act, the administration's flagship legislation, was animated by a commitment to early formal intervention, to 'nip offending in the bud' (Home Office, 1997) and rapid escalation thereafter if offending continued. The Act:

- introduced a 'three-strikes' pre-court 'final warning' scheme, accelerating the decline in diversion from court;

- abolished the principle of *doli incapax* which had precluded prosecution of children under 14 unless it could be shown that they knew their actions were 'seriously wrong'; and

- loosened the criteria for child imprisonment, encouraging continued growth in the incarcerated population.

Dubbing it 'old hat', Fionda (1999) intimates that the legislation simply repackaged existing youth justice policies. However, contending that Labour's reform package lacked distinctive qualities would be unfair. While innovation often did, as Fionda suggests, consist in a more rigorous application of existing trends, on occasion, it went beyond simple reinforcement in a number of ways, summarised in Table 18.4, generating a complex interplay of competing philosophies rather than espousing any single model of youth justice.

First, New Labour insisted that children should be held accountable for their behaviour. In language redolent of, then prime minister, John Major's assessment that the Bulger murder demonstrated the need to 'condemn a little more and understand a little less' (Haydon and Scraton, 2002), 'No More Excuses' announced that the function of youth justice should be to 'confront ... [children] with their behaviour and help ... [them] take more personal responsibility for their actions' (Home Office, 1997: preface). This constituted a challenge to the idea that the treatment of children in trouble should reflect their reduced culpability, assuming a level of rationality that had previously been ascribed to adults alone.

Second, the government promoted restorative justice, particularly through the establishment of the referral order, but also introducing a presumption that any penalty would incorporate an element of reparation. While this development met with general approval, critics have argued that it can also be seen as reflecting the influence of accountability already described: on this view restoration is consistently coupled with 'responsibilisation' (Cunneen and Goldson, 2015: 146).

Third, the creation of the YJB heralded an increasingly managerialist approach, prioritising process, targets, and centralised oversight. Public sector governance had previously adopted elements of managerialism, but it was now taken to new heights. The government imposed a myriad of performance indicators that required YOTs to report on more than 3,000 data items (National Audit Office, 2010), leading to complaints that youth justice was increasingly measured in terms of 'what's counted' rather than what counts (Pitts and Bateman, 2010) and that practitioner discretion and innovation was fettered by the requirement to complete reams of paperwork and tick boxes (Pitts, 2001).

Finally, Labour championed a concentration on risk. Feeley and Simon (1992) had already drawn attention to a tendency for justice systems to adopt a risk management rather than transformative rationale that aimed to manage dangerous individuals rather than reform them. The tendency matured under New Labour. *Asset*, the YJB's standardised assessment, required practitioners to score children against 12 'risk' domains and the scoring determined what was to be addressed in supervision (Baker, 2005). Where risk to the public was identified as a feature of the case, the supervision plan was also expected to outline how the public would be protected. New Labour thus introduced core elements of McAra and McVie's (2015) actuarial mode.

This actuarial stance reached its logical culmination with the implementation of the 'scaled approach' in 2009. Hitherto risk assessment had determined the *nature* of intervention, but the new approach also aligned the *intensity* of compulsory intervention to the total *Asset* score rather than offence seriousness or court order. Children assessed as being in the highest category of risk bracket were required to attend four times as many appointments as lower risk children, irrespective of the gravity of their offending. The approach thus represents a partial abandonment of proportionality, prioritising risk factors, or 'criminogenic' needs as they are also known, over considerations of justice. Since indicators of need, whether criminogenic or welfare, are proxies for disadvantage, the scaled approach has attracted criticism for 'punishing poverty' (Bateman, 2011).

Table 18.4 The constituents of youth justice under New Labour

Themes	How manifested	Implications
Making children accountable	'No more excuses' Rejection of welfare 'Nipping offending in the bud' Confronting children with their behaviour	Harsher punishment Early formal intervention Net-widening Children treated more like adults (adultification)
Restoration	Focus on restorative justice The referral order Presumption of reparation in all cases	An alternative discourse to punishment Reparation/unpaid work as a form of 'adultification'
Managerialism	Creation of YJB Targets, standards and prescribed processes	A standardised approach rather than meeting individual need Practice driven by targets Undermining of practitioner discretion
Actuarialism/ Risk management	*Asset* assessment framework The 'scaled approach' Linking content and intensity of intervention to risk scores	Neglect of welfare need in favour of addressing 'criminogenic' factors Disadvantage attracts higher levels of punishment

Analysing the Present: Austere or Tolerant Youth Justice?

If the onset of the punitive turn can be traced to the early 1990s, a more recent, but equally fundamental, policy about-face can also be dated with some precision. On attaining power in 2010, the Coalition government established three high-level indicators for youth justice whose logic would appear consistent with a diversionary paradigm and contrary to the punitive dynamic of the prior period. The targets, retained by the subsequent Conservative administration elected in 2015, require reductions in:

- the number of first-time entrants (FTEs)[ii]

- reoffending; and

- the child custodial population. (Bateman, 2014)

In truth the important shift had occurred some years earlier with the adoption of the FTE target in New Labour's 'Youth Crime Action Plan' (Home Office, 2008). The profound influence of such political intercession is clear in the data. Table 18.5 indicates that FTEs and the custodial population both began to fall sharply in that year in a dramatic reversal of previous trends: between 2008 and 2014/15, the former declined by 78 per cent, the latter by two-thirds.

Table 18.5 Trends in first time entrants to the youth justice system and child custodial population

Year	First time entrants	Year (August)	Custodial population
2003/04	88,403	2004	2,785
2004/05	96,147	2005	2,930
2005/06	107,623	2006	3,067
2006/07	110,757	2007	2,991
2007/08	100,380	2008	3,019
2008/09	80,352	2009	2,504
2009/10	62,563	2010	2,099
2010/11	45,968	2011	2,066
2011/12	36,922	2012	1,622
2012/13	28,059	2013	1,232
2013/14	22,393	2014	1,068
		2015	971

Derived from Ministry of Justice/Youth Justice Board (2015a) and Youth Justice Board (2015b)

Such large-scale reductions were achieved through a 'reinvention of diversion' that both relaxed the operation of the final warning scheme (abolished under the Coalition in favour of a return to cautioning) and promoted a range of informal responses to minor offending at the local level that led to a corresponding reduction in formal sanctions (Smith, 2014). Such developments were facilitated by, and were a reflection of, a relegation of youth crime from the political foreground it had previously occupied and a move towards increased local and practitioner autonomy, resulting in a substantial decline in centralised performance monitoring (Bateman, 2014).

The contemporary youth justice landscape thus has important affinities with the earlier diversionary era of the1980s, exemplifying Bernard's (1992) thesis of a 'cycle of juvenile justice' whereby periodic backlashes give rise to an alternation of tolerance and toughness. Interestingly, the similarities between the two periods are not restricted to trends in diversion and decarceration: both were distinguished by political regimes that were ostensibly tough on law and order but nonetheless delivered a more tolerant youth justice. Governments at both times were also pledged to austerity. It is arguably no coincidence that the FTE target was adopted at the height of the financial crisis in 2008 (Bateman, 2014).

It is important, however, not to overstate the parallels. Diversion and decarceration were spearheaded in the 1980s by a vibrant practitioner lobby, with endorsement from government (Allen, 1991); the present dynamic is arguably reversed, driven by centrally imposed targets, with tacit support at local level (Bateman, 2012b). The risk-management edifice erected by New Labour remains in place and exerts a powerful influence over practice, even if the development of a new assessment framework, in the form of AssetPlus, dulls some of its sharper edges (Baker, 2012). Kelly and Armitage (2015: 128) observe that the continued sway of 'risk thinking' inculcates much diversionary activity, imbuing it with an interventionist tone that distinguishes it from the minimalism of the Thatcher era. Consequently, many children are diverted *into* programmes that look, and are experienced as being, similar to those that previously accompanied formal sanctions, a tendency encouraged no doubt by the high thresholds for services in the social care sector which often precludes referral to more mainstream provision. If current youth justice is most accurately described as diversionary in McAra and McVie's (2015) terms, it is a variant of its precursor that prevailed during the 1980s.

Summary

This chapter has offered an overview of the creation of youth justice as a separate system that offers a distinct approach to children in trouble albeit with substantial similarities to that for adult offenders. It has summarised the current framework that governs the treatment of children who offend and described the agencies that operate within that framework.

However, the chapter has also shown, through historical exploration, that youth justice is more than process and apparatus. The philosophical assumptions underpinning intervention change – sometimes rapidly – over time and these shifts are frequently a response to political or economic considerations or trigger events such as the Bulger murder, rather than changes in children's behaviour or the development of the evidence-base. The welfare–justice dichotomy that often frames youth justice discourse cannot capture that complexity.

Currently youth justice displays largely diversionary impulses, but these are tinged with punitive undercurrents and bounded by an adherence to risk management and early intervention. This amalgam is a fragile one with austerity favouring increased diversion and the enduring need for neoliberal administrations not to appear soft on crime pulling in an opposite direction.

How these tensions play out is hard to predict. In September 2015, Michael Gove, then Minister of Justice, announced a review of youth justice to report in the summer of 2016 to consider whether the 'current arrangements are fit for purpose' (Gove, 2015). The outcome is presently unknown, but arguments adduced in this chapter suggest that a conceptually consistent, evidence-based, approach to children in trouble is not guaranteed.

Discussion Questions

1. To what extent are arrangements for dealing with children in trouble different from those for adults?

2. What does it mean to say that the murder of James Bulger was a 'trigger event'? In what ways did it impact on the treatment of children in trouble?

3. Why do discussions of youth justice frequently start with welfare and justice?

4. If welfare is in the best interests of the child, why did a welfarist approach fall out of favour during the 1980s?

5. How might one best characterise contemporary youth justice? To what extent is it similar to youth justice in the 1980s?

Notes

i. Generally speaking, grave crimes are those which can attract 14 years or more imprisonment in the case of an adult, but they include a small number of sexual and firearms offences with shorter maximum terms.

ii. An FTE is a child who receives a formal youth justice disposal for the first time.

Further Reading

For a comprehensive overview of youth justice, within the context of wider criminological theory, see:

Muncie, J. (2013) *Youth and Crime*. 4th edn. London: Sage.

A thoughtful account of the development of policy and practice in youth justice in England and Wales from the 1980s onwards, and a critical exploration of the ideas underlying those developments, can be found in:

Smith, R. (2014) *Youth Justice: Ideas, policy, practice*. 3rd edn. London: Routledge.

For a useful collection that addresses a spectrum of contemporary youth justice debates, see:

Goldson, B. and Muncie, J. (eds) (2015) *Youth Crime and Justice.* 2nd edn. London: Sage.

The following provides an analysis of the most recent trends in the treatment of children in trouble in England and Wales:

Bateman, T. (2015) *The State of Youth Justice: An overview of trends and developments.* London: NAYJ.

——— **References** ———

Allen, C., Crow, I. and Cavadino, M. (2000) *Evaluation of the Youth Court Demonstration Project*. London: Home Office.

Allen, F. (1981) *Decline of the Rehabilitative Ideal: Penal policy and social purpose*. New Haven: Yale University Press.

Allen, R. (1991) 'Out of jail: The reduction in the use of penal custody for male juveniles 1981–1988', *Howard Journal*, 30 (1): 30–52.

Allen, R. (2005) 'The role of central government and the Youth Justice Board', in T. Bateman and J. Pitts (eds), *The RHP Companion to Youth Justice*. Lyme Regis: Russell House. pp. 26–31.

Arthur, R. (2010) *Young Offenders and the Law*. London: Routledge.

Baker, K. (2005) 'Assessment in youth justice: Professional discretion and the use of Asset', *Youth Justice*, 5 (2): 106–22.

Baker, K. (2012) *AssetPlus Rationale*. London: YJB.

Bateman, T. (2011) 'Punishing poverty: The 'scaled approach' and youth justice practice', *Howard Journal*, 50 (2): 171–83.

Bateman, T. (2012a) *Criminalising Children for no Good Purpose: The age of criminal responsibility in England and Wales*. London: NAYJ Justice.

Bateman, T. (2012b) 'Who pulled the plug? Towards an explanation of the fall in child imprisonment in England and Wales', *Youth Justice*, 12 (1): 36–52.

Bateman, T. (2014) 'Where has all the youth crime gone? Youth justice in an age of austerity', *Children and Society*, 28 (5): 416–24.

Bateman, T. and Stanley, C. (2002) *Patterns of Sentencing: Differential sentencing across England and Wales*. London: YJB.

Becker, H. (1963) *Outsiders: Studies in the sociology of deviance*. New York: NY Free Press.

Bernard, T.J. (1992) *The Cycle of Juvenile Justice*. Oxford: Oxford University Press.

Bottoms, A. (1995) 'The philosophy and politics of punishment and sentencing', in C. Clarkson and R. Morgan (eds), *The Politics of Sentencing Reform*. Oxford: Clarendon Press.

Bottoms, A. (2002) 'On the decriminalisation of the English juvenile courts', in J. Muncie, G. Hughes and E. McLaughlin (eds), *Youth Justice: Critical readings*. London: Sage. pp. 216–27.

Burnett, R. (2005) 'Youth offending teams', in T. Bateman and J. Pitts (eds), *The RHP Companion to Youth Justice*. Lyme Regis: Russell House. pp. 106–12.

Byrne, B. and Brookes, K. (2015) *Post-YOT Youth Justice*. Howard League What is Justice Working Paper 19/2015. London: Howard League.

Carlile, Lord (2014) *Independent Parliamentarians' Inquiry into the Operation and Effectiveness of the Youth Court*. London: NCB.

Centre for Social Justice (2012) *Rules of Engagement: Changing the heart of youth justice*. London: CSJ.

Crawford, A. and Newburn, T. (2003) *Youth Offending and Restorative Justice: Implementing reform in youth justice*. Cullompton: Willan.

Cunneen, C. and Goldson, B. (2015) 'Restorative justice? A critical analysis', in B. Goldson and J. Muncie (eds), *Youth Crime and Justice*. 2nd edn. London: Sage. pp. 137–56.

Currie, F. (2009) *Actions Speak Louder – A second review of healthcare in the community for young people who offend*. London: Healthcare Commission and HMI Probation.

Deloitte (2015) *Youth Offending Team Stocktake*. London: Deloitte.

Feeley, M. and Simon, J. (1992) 'The new penology: Notes of the emerging strategy of corrections and its implications', *Criminology*, 30 (4): 449–74.

Fergusson, R. (2007) 'Making sense of the melting pot: Multiple discourses in youth justice policy', *Youth Justice*, 7 (3): 179–94.

Fionda, J. (1999) 'New Labour, old hat: Youth justice and the Crime and Disorder Act 1998', *Criminal Law Review*, January, 36–47.

Gelsthorpe, L. and Morris, A. (1994) 'Juvenile justice 1945–1992', in M. Maguire, R. Morgan and R. Reiner (eds), *The Oxford Handbook of Criminology*. Oxford: OUP.

Goldson, B. (2002) 'New punitiveness: The politics of child incarceration', in J. Muncie, G. Hughes and E. McLaughlin (eds), *Youth Justice: Critical readings*. London: Sage. pp. 386–99.

Goldson, B. (2005) 'Beyond formalism: Towards "informal" approaches to youth crime and youth justice' in T. Bateman and J. Pitts (eds), *The RHP Companion to Youth Justice*. Lyme Regis: Russell House. pp. 236–41.

Goldson, B. and Muncie, J. (2015) 'Children's human rights and youth justice with integrity', in B. Goldson and J. Muncie (eds), *Youth Crime and Justice*. 2nd edn. London: Sage. pp. 227–57.

Gove, M. (2015) *Announcement of a Review into Youth Justice*. Available at: www.gov.uk/government/speeches/youth-justice [accessed 17 May 2015].

Great Britain (1933) *Children and Young Persons Act 1933*. Chapters 12, 23 and 24, George V. London: HMSO.

Great Britain (1998) *Crime and Disorder Act 1998*. Chapter 37, Elizabeth II. London: TSO.

Great Britain (2003) *Criminal Justice Act 2003*. Chapter 44, Elizabeth II. London: TSO.

Gyateng, T., Moretti, A., May, T. and Turnbull, P. (2013) *Young People and the Secure Estate: Needs and interventions*. London: YJB.

Haines, K. and Drakeford, M. (1998) *Young People and Youth Justice*. London: Palgrave MacMillan.

Hart, D. (2014a) *What's in a Name? The identification of children in trouble with the law*. London: Standing Committee for Youth Justice.

Hart, D. (2014b) *Pre-court Arrangements for Children who Offend*. London: NAYJ.

Haydon, D. and Scraton, P. (2002) 'Condemn a little more; understand a little less: The political context and rights implications of the domestic and European rulings in the Venables–Thompson case', *Journal of Law and Society*, 27 (3): 416–48.

Hazel, N. (2008) *Cross-national Comparison of Youth Justice*. London: YJB.

Home Office (1984) *Criminal Statistics for England and Wales 1983*. Cmnd 9349. London: HMSO.

Home Office (1997) *No More Excuses: A new approach to tackling youth crime in England and Wales*. London: Home Office.

Home Office (2008) *Youth Crime Action Plan*. London: Home Office.

Hopkins Burke, R. (2008) *Young People, Crime and Justice*. Cullompton: Willan.

Justice Committee (2013) *Youth Justice*. London: The Stationery Office.

Kelly, L. and Armitage, V. (2015) 'Diverse diversions: Youth justice reform, localized practices and a "new interventionist diversion"', *Youth Justice*, 15 (2): 117–33.

Mair, G. and Burke, L. (2011) *Redemption, Rehabilitation and Risk Management: A history of probation*. Abingdon: Routledge.

Matthews, R. and Young, J. (2003) 'New Labour, crime control and social exclusion', in R. Matthews and J. Young (eds), *The New Politics of Crime and Punishment*. Cullompton: Willan. pp. 1–32.

McAra, L. and McVie, S. (2015) 'The case for diversion and minimum necessary intervention', in B. Goldson and J. Muncie (eds), *Youth Crime and Justice*. 2nd edn. London: Sage. pp. 119–36.

Ministry of Justice/Youth Justice Board (2015a) *Youth Justice Statistics 2013/14: England and Wales*. London: Ministry of Justice.

Ministry of Justice/Youth Justice Board (2015b) *Referral Orders and Youth Offender Panels: Guidance for the courts, youth offending teams and youth offender panels*. London: Ministry of Justice.

Muncie, J. (2008) 'The "punitive" turn in juvenile justice: Cultures of control and rights compliance in western Europe and the USA', *Youth Justice*, 8 (2): 107–21.

Nacro (2007) *The Detention and Training Order: Current position and future developments*. London: Nacro.

National Association for Youth Justice (2015) *Manifesto 2015*. London: NAYJ.

National Audit Office (2010) *The Youth Justice System in England and Wales: Reducing offending by young people*. London: NAO.

Newbury, A. (2011) 'Very young offenders and the criminal justice system: Are we asking the right questions?', *Child and Family Law Quarterly*, 23 (1): 94–114.

Pitts, J. (2001) 'Correctional karaoke: New Labour and the zombification of youth justice', *Youth Justice*, 1 (2): 3–16.

Pitts, J. (2003) *The New Politics of Youth Crime: Discipline or solidarity*. Lyme Regis: Russell House.

Pitts, J. (2005) 'The recent history of youth justice in England and Wales', in T. Bateman and J. Pitts (eds), *The RHP Companion to Youth Justice*. Lyme Regis: Russell House. pp. 2–11.

Pitts, J. and Bateman, T. (2010) 'New Labour and youth justice: What works or what's counted?', in P. Ayre and M. Preston-Shoot (eds), *Children's Services at the Crossroads*. Lyme Regis: Russell House. pp. 52–63.

Rutherford, A. (1992) *Growing Out of Crime*. 2nd edn. Winchester: Waterside Press.

Schur, E. (1973) *Radical Non-intervention: Rethinking the delinquency problem*. Englewood Cliffs: Prentice Hall.

Sentencing Guidelines Council (2009) *Overarching Principles – Sentencing youths*. London: Sentencing Guidelines Council.

Smith, R. (2005) 'Welfare versus justice – Again?', *Youth Justice*, 5 (2): 3–16.

Smith, R. (2014) 'Reinventing diversion', *Youth Justice*, 14 (2): 109–21.

Stanley, C. (2005) 'The role of the courts', in T. Bateman and J. Pitts (eds), *The RHP Companion to Youth Justice*. Lyme Regis: Russell House. pp. 83–9.

Stone, N. (2010) 'Developments in determining mode of trial for grave allegations', *Youth Justice*, 10 (1): 73–83.

Thorpe, D.H., Smith, D., Green, C.J. and Paley, J.H. (1980) *Out of Care: The community support of juvenile offenders*. London: George Allen and Unwin.

United Nations (1989) *United Nations Convention on the Rights of the Child*. Geneva: UN.

Watkins, M. and Johnson, D. (2009) *Youth Justice and the Youth Court: An introduction*. Hook: Waterside Press.

Whyte, B. (2005) 'Youth justice in other UK jurisdictions: Scotland and Northern Ireland', in T. Bateman and J. Pitts (eds), *The RHP Companion to Youth Justice*. Lyme Regis: Russell House. pp. 19–25.

Youth Justice Board (2015a) *Youth Offending Teams: Making the difference for children and young people, victims and communities*. London: YJB.

Youth Justice Board (2015b) *Monthly Youth Custody Report August 2015*. London: YJB.

Check out the Companion Website

Want to know more about this chapter? Review what you have been learning by visiting: **https://study.sagepub.com/harding**

- Practice with essay questions
- Test yourself with multiple-choice questions
- Listen to a series of podcasts featuring Neil of Northumbria Police and London's Metropolitan Police Service
- Watch videos selected from the SAGE Video collection

19 Dealing with Complaints and Misconduct

Jamie Harding

Introduction

Within criminal justice the inequalities in power between 'service providers' and 'service users' are obvious. The quotation marks are used because many who use the services would prefer not to – criminal justice agencies are among the relatively small number of organisations that, on occasions, force their services on unwilling recipients. Given the power imbalance, it is particularly important that there are effective mechanisms in place to investigate allegations of wrongdoing on the part of the agencies of criminal justice and, where appropriate, to take action to remedy the injustice.

It was noted in Chapter 8 that a number of inspectorates, such as Her Majesty's Inspectorate of Constabulary (HMIC) and Her Majesty's Inspectorate of Prisons (HMIP), have the role of regulating criminal justice agencies and maintaining standards. Their role is different from the one of dealing with complaints by people who feel that they have been badly and/or unjustly treated. Complaints are dealt with by a number of agencies, according to which part of the criminal justice process the complainant feels aggrieved by:

- Complaints against the police can be made at the local police station or to the Independent Police Complaints Commission (IPCC).

- Complaints against the Crown Prosecution Service (CPS) should be made initially to the local branch, then (if still dissatisfied) to the Chief Crown Prosecutor within the area and finally in writing to the CPS Correspondence Unit.

- Complaints about treatment by the court (rather than its decision) should be made initially where the problem arose, then to a senior manager at the office and finally to the complaints, correspondence and litigation team.

- Complaints against a probation service should be made initially through the internal complaints system and then to the Prisons and Probation Ombudsman (PPO).

- Complaints against a prison, immigration removal centre or Young Offender Institution (YOI) should again initially be made internally before being taken to the PPO.

- Complaints against a Youth Offending Team should be made to the local government ombudsman.

- Complaints against a verdict, finding or sentence of the court should be made by appeal to the court first, then to the Criminal Cases Review Commission (CCRC), who may refer the case back to the relevant Court of Appeal.

So there is an untidy mix of internal complaints procedures, specialist agencies and one agency (the local government ombudsman) whose primary focus is not criminal justice. It is the three specialist agencies for dealing with complaints – the

IPCC, the PPO and the CCRC – that will be covered in detail in this chapter. The Court of Appeal (Criminal Division) is also discussed because its role is closely tied to that of the CCRC.

Timeline

1907   Court of Criminal Appeal established

1964   Police Act clarified the legal right of citizens to make complaints and led to Complaints and Discipline departments being created within police forces

1977   Police Complaints Board (PCB) created

1985   Police Complaints Authority (PCA) replaced the Police Complaints Board

1990   Riots at Strangeways and other prisons

1991   Woolf Report published

1993   Royal Commission on Criminal Justice established

1994   First Prisons Ombudsman appointed

1995   Criminal Cases Review Commission created

2004   Independent Police Complaints Commission (IPCC) replaced the PCA

2013   Home Secretary announced transfer of resources from police forces to IPCC

2016   Government announced renaming of IPCC as the Office for Police Conduct and proposed new powers through the Police and Crime Bill

Police Complaints

Issues and Difficulties in Dealing with Police Complaints

The Independent Police Complaints Commission (IPCC) is the latest of a number of agencies that have sought to deal with the complex issues associated with complaints against the police. As McLaughlin (2007: 173) notes, such complaints are almost inevitable, given the unique powers that police officers have – to intervene in the life of citizens, to coerce and to use lethal force.

Smith (2005: 123) suggests that an effective and fair system for dealing with complaints against the police is essential if policing by consent (discussed in Chapter 11) is to be a reality. Similarly, confidence in the system of complaints against the police, particularly among some minority ethnic communities, has been argued to be central to relationships between the police and the public by both Lord Scarman (1981) in his report into the disturbances in Brixton and elsewhere in 1981 and by Sir William Macpherson (1999) in his report into the investigation of the murder of Stephen Lawrence. The IPCC (2014a: 6) has argued that its work, for example over deaths in custody, is essential to prevent a breakdown of trust.

Despite the assumption that public confidence in the police and in the complaints system are closely linked, the empirical evidence is not available in the UK to link these two factors in the way that has been attempted in the USA (see Sindall et al., 2012: 748). However, establishing public confidence in the complaints system has been an aim of policy in many societies. A central concern is often that there should be 'independent' investigation of complaints, although this term can be interpreted in different ways. Savage (2013: 100–1) reports that workers in the IPCC and similar bodies operating elsewhere found that there were three elements to their understanding of independence: impartiality, 'separateness' from the police, and objectivity.

The question of 'separateness' is related to a difficult one of who should conduct investigations. Systems where the police are solely responsible for investigating complaints have been widely criticised (Waters and Brown, 2000: 617); in particular, the number of substantiated complaints is often so low as to create suspicion (Thomassen, 2002: 202). However, civilians investigating complaints can also be problematic because they may lack investigatory skills and 'cultural knowledge': civilian involvement does not necessarily lead to more complaints being substantiated (Thomassen, 2002: 201–2). In the UK, there has been historic opposition to civilian involvement in investigations arising from the doctrine of constabulary independence (Smith, 2009: 424–5) and a number of practical arguments: for example, civilian investigation would damage self-esteem, imply a lack of trust and increase police deviance because officers would refuse to cooperate with civilian investigators (McLaughlin, 2007: 174).

So, to summarise, it is difficult to establish what the impact is of the public feeling more or less confident in the complaints system, there are difficulties with both civilians and police officers being involved in investigating complaints, and – even when civilians are involved – there is no universally agreed definition of what it means for an investigation to be 'independent'. Nonetheless, attempts to design the most appropriate possible complaints system have been going on for several decades: the next section discusses the different historical stages of the process in England and Wales.

The First Statutory Complaints System and the First Independent Body

Following a number of scandals that involved convictions and dismissals of senior police officers, a Royal Commission on Policing reported in 1962; it recommended some amendments to the method of dealing with complaints, but that this should remain solely the responsibility of police officers (Glass, 2014: 3). The 1964 Police Act codified the legal right of citizens to make complaints and led to the establishment of Complaints and Discipline departments (McLaughlin, 2007: 174–5), but there was no independent element to this system (Waters and Brown, 2000: 619–20).

The Metropolitan Police Scandal of the 1970s (see Chapter 7 and http://www.telegraph.co.uk/news/obituaries/politics-obituaries/8037604/Sir-Robert-Mark.html) led to the creation of a civilian-led body, the Police Complaints Board, in 1977, although opposition from within the police ensured that its powers were limited to scrutinising reports and deciding whether to refer cases to disciplinary panels (Glass, 2014: 4–5).

The Police Complaints Authority (PCA)

The creation of the Police Complaints Authority (PCA) in 1985 arose partly from concerns over corruption in the Metropolitan Police Service and partly from Lord Scarman's report into the 1981 Brixton disorders (discussed above). The PCA provided more independent oversight, managing the investigation of the most serious complaints, although these investigations continued to be conducted by police officers themselves (Rowe, 2014: 75). McLaughlin (2007: 176–7) notes that the law, and the structure and powers of the PCA, presented difficulties such as police officers exercising their right to silence when being questioned over alleged misconduct and internal disciplinary procedures requiring the same standard of evidence as a criminal trial.

The difficulty of making a successful complaint meant that many who felt wronged instead launched civil actions: McLaughlin (2007: 177–8) argues that the police losing a number of high-profile civil cases was one of a number of factors that contributed to pressure for change in the late 1990s. Internally, chief constables became concerned that networks of corrupt officers were avoiding punishment from the discipline and complaints system. Externally, pressure from Europe led to a wider recognition of the role of human rights in police work; Professional Standards Departments began to be created partly to ensure that rights were respected. In addition, the Good Friday agreement (www.bbc.co.uk/history/events/good_friday_agreement) created an independent ombudsman for dealing with complaints in Northern Ireland and a series of reports (including the MacPherson report) were critical of the existing system.

The Independent Police Complaints Commission (IPCC)

The IPCC replaced the PCA and is the body that currently deals with complaints against the police. It was created by the 2002 Police Reform Act and became operational in 2004. Its primary purpose was identified in law as increasing public confidence in the complaints system. In addition to complaints, it can also investigate potential misconduct when no complaint has been made (Savage, 2013: 98) and considers all cases of deaths after recent contact with the police, including those that occur in police pursuits or police custody.

The IPCC has a number of options for dealing with complaints:

- Independent investigations, conducted by IPCC investigators, are undertaken in the most high-profile cases such as those involving death after police contact.

- Managed investigations are conducted by the Professional Standards Department (PSD) of the force concerned under the direction and control of an IPCC investigator.

- Supervised investigations involve the IPCC setting terms of reference for an investigation by the PSD of the force complained against. The outcome can be appealed to the IPCC.

- Local investigations are carried out entirely by the PSD and also carry the right of appeal to the IPCC. With the agreement of the complainant, there can be 'local resolution' where the matter is dealt with by an inspector of the police force concerned. (House of Commons Home Affairs Committe, 2010: 4)

The ability to conduct investigations is one of the key differences between the IPCC and the PCA (Savage, 2013: 97). IPCC investigators are granted most of the powers of police officers, e.g. they can make arrests and search premises. Some investigators are former police officers, others have experience of undertaking investigations into benefits fraud and health and safety, while some have no experience and need full training into the role (Savage, 2013: 99).

Criticisms and Calls for Reform

As the Home Affairs Committee (2012–13, cited in Home Office, 2013: 6) noted, confidence in the police had been shaken by a number of recent high-profile cases, many of them relating to historic failings, such as Operation Yewtree (www.nspcc.org.uk/globalassets/documents/research-reports/yewtree-report-giving-victims-voice-jimmy-savile.pdf) and the Hillsborough Inquiry (www.ipcc.gov.uk/hillsborough). Inevitably, this has led to questions about the regulation of the police, linked to a number of criticisms of the IPCC.

Few Independent Investigations

Throughout the lifetime of the IPCC, concerns have been expressed about the level of resources with which it has been provided and the impact that this has had on its ability to conduct independent investigations (e.g. House of Commons Home Affairs Committee, 2010). On its creation the IPCC was funded to carry out only 30 independent investigations a year, most of which involved deaths rather than complaints (Glass, 2014: 6). The IPCC's main role remains dealing with appeals against the manner in which complaints have been dealt with by police forces: in 2012, it determined 4,965 appeals, arising from 30,143 complaints made against the police in England and Wales (Glass, 2014: 6). Where the IPCC does not conduct investigations itself, there are concerns over the extent of influence that it has: for example the Home Affairs Committee of 2012–13 argued that:

> 'Supervised Investigations' do not offer rigorous oversight of a police investigation, nor do they necessarily give the public a convincing assurance that the investigation will be conducted objectively. (quoted in Home Office, 2013: 11)

Relationship with Complainants

Former IPCC commissioner Deborah Glass (2014: 9) has noted that the complaints system is complicated and may prove very difficult to understand for the complainant. Concerns about the IPCC's relationship with complainants have been raised by a *Guardian* investigation (reported on 25 February 2008, www.theguardian.com/politics/2008/feb/25/police.law), the BBC Radio Four *File on Four* programme of 19 January 2010 (House of Commons Home Affairs Committe, 2010: 3) and the IPCC's own (2014a: 12) review of its treatment of deaths after contact with the police.

Perceived Bias Towards Police Officers

Regular surveys have shown a high level of confidence among the public in the impartiality of the complaints process, albeit with lower levels of confidence among those who classified their ethnic origin as 'Black' (IPSOS MORI and the IPCC, 2014: 41–2). However, concerns have been expressed by the pressure group Inquest (House of Commons Home Affairs Committe, 2010: 14) and the IPCC's own investigation of deaths after contact with the police (IPCC, 2014a: 9) as to the extent to which it is, and is seen to be, independently investigating cases involving deaths of members of the public. The employment of ex-police officers by the IPCC also creates concerns over impartiality, particularly if they are investigating ex-colleagues (House of Commons Home Affairs Committe, 2010: 15).

Perceptions of bias among complainants are perhaps unsurprising given that, historically, 5 per cent of complaints against the police are upheld in England and Wales (Glass, 2014: 12), with large regional differences (House of Commons Home Affairs Committe, 2010: 5–6). Former IPCC commissioner John Crawley has expressed concern that, of all the complaints investigated in 2007–8, only 15 officers lost their jobs, one was demoted, and 24 were fined a few days' pay – a total of 0.028 per cent of the national workforce (*Guardian*, 7 April 2009, www.theguardian.com/society/2009/apr/08/police-complaints-commission). Glass (2014: 11) notes that when police officers are dismissed, this tends to happen in closed misconduct proceedings where the outcomes are not usually publicised, so the public may be unaware that decisive action has been taken.

The IPCC can point to a number of factors in defence of its independence: new guidance issued in 2010 raised the percentage of upheld complaints to 12 per cent

(Glass, 2014: 12), better safety guidelines are claimed to have halved the number of deaths in police custody since 2004 (IPCC, 2014a: 6) and there are examples of both thematic reports (IPCC, 2014b) and individual cases (IPCC, 2014c) where the IPCC has been highly critical of the police. However, these developments may count for little when compared to high-profile cases such as the shooting of Mark Duggan (see Box 19.1).

Box 19.1

Mark Duggan Case Study

The shooting of Mark Duggan by the Metropolitan Police was the trigger for the Tottenham riots of 2011. After the shooting, the IPCC wrongly reported that Duggan had fired on police officers, failing to attribute this comment to the Metropolitan Police. There was also a delay in informing Duggan's family of the shooting and the minicab in which Duggan had been travelling was removed from the scene and then returned before forensic examination could take place. The officers involved wrote statements together and refused to be interviewed by the IPCC, which only added to public disquiet at the manner in which the matter had been handled (*Guardian*, 8 January 2014). The IPCC subsequently accepted that there were failings by both itself and the Metropolitan Police Service in the liaison with Duggan's family (IPCC, 2012).

The IPCC's subsequent report into the shooting exonerated the police officers at the scene, but also called for improved accountability, suggesting that the lack of an audio or video record made it impossible to be certain what had happened (IPCC, 2015). These findings were meticulously argued but caused further anger among Duggan's family and the wider community (*Guardian*, 25 March 2015), with his mother calling for a judge-led public inquiry on the fourth anniversary of the shooting (*Guardian*, 4 August 2015).

Current Policy on Police Complaints

The Conservative-led administration of 2010–15 was broadly supportive of the IPCC: a position that may have been influenced by its tense relationship with police forces, most notably over the 'Plebgate' incident (www.theguardian.com/politics/2014/sep/01/plebgate-report-key-points-andrew-mitchell-met-police). Key measures taken by this administration were:

1. The 2014 Anti-Social Behaviour Crime and Policing Act increased the powers of the IPCC and required police forces to publish responses to its recommendations.

2. The Home Secretary announced to Parliament on 12 February 2013 that the IPCC would be expanded by transferring resources from Professional Standards Departments to enable it to undertake more independent investigations (Home Office, 2013: 1).

3. The volume of complex and high-profile cases involving possible police misconduct that arose during this period, together with the still limited resources available to the

IPCC, meant that it became part of a very complex mix of investigations. Historic enquiries into Hillsborough and Jimmy Savile were dealt with by a combination of the National Crime Agency, a chief-constable-led review with some IPCC oversight, the HMIC and enquiries led by police forces. In addition, a historic investigation into alleged police corruption linked to the murder of a private detective in London in 1987 was conducted by a judge-led enquiry (Stevens, 2013: 129–30).

In 2016, the Conservative government announced that the Independent Police Complaints Commission was to be renamed the Office for Police Conduct, to reflect broader powers that it was to be given, and that the renamed, reformed organisation would be headed by a director general rather than a number of com-missioners (Home Office, 2016a). The 2016 Police and Crime Bill proposed to introduce measures that would strengthen Police and Crime Commissioners' (see Chapter 11) oversight of the local complaints system, broaden the definition of a complaint, simplify the appeals procedure, extend the police discipline system to retired or resigned police officers and introduce a system of super-complaints against broad national or local trends in policing (Home Office, 2016b). At the time of writing, it is not clear whether these proposals will pass into law without major changes or whether they will be sufficient to address some of the historic difficulties discussed above.

The Prisons and Probation Ombudsman

The method of dealing with complaints against the action of prison staff (and more recently others, such as probation officers) has not been as controversial as the method of dealing with complaints against police officers, although one common factor is that the current system for dealing with complaints arose from a crisis, namely the disturbances at Strangeways and other prisons in 1990 (discussed in more detail in Chapter 16). At this point there was a complex system of unsatis-factory options for prisoners to make complaints. The internal complaints system was widely perceived to be unfair – prisoners could face disciplinary action if they made a complaint against an officer that was judged to be false – and included no independent element. Externally, prisoners could complain to a range of people or seek a judicial review through the courts, but these options were time-consuming and expensive (Cavadino and Dignan, 2007: 233).

The Woolf Report of 1991 identified the need for prisons to provide security, control and justice. Woolf insisted that prisoners should not leave prison embittered or disaffected as a result of an unjust experience (Scott, 2007: 58). Specifically, Woolf recommended that the complaints system within prisons must include an independent element and recommended the creation of a post that he described as an Independent Complaints Adjudicator. This proposal was accepted by the government and the first Prisons Ombudsman was appointed in 1994. In 2001 the ombudsman's remit was extended to cover the National Probation Service and in 2004 the investigation of all deaths in prison was added to the role (Cavadino and Dignan, 2007: 234). Immigration detainees have been able to complain to the ombudsman since 2006 (PPO, undated).

Complaints received by the PPO that have not been internally investigated by the agency concerned, or where the internal investigation has been poor, are referred back to the original agency. Complaints are also not investigated if there is no substantial issue or no positive outcome that can arise from an investigation.

The PPO investigated 192 deaths in prison during 2012–13, with the majority found to be from natural causes. During the year 5,374 complaints were received, of which:

- 91% were about the prison service;

- 7% were about the probation service;

- 2% were about immigration detention; and

- 31% of complaints were upheld. (Newcomen, 2013: 9–15)

Shaw (2009) notes that, with time, the balance of complaints that the ombudsman's office has dealt with has moved away from simple grievances such as lost property and towards issues that are more closely aligned with the aims of criminal justice processes, e.g. sentence planning and access to programmes. The role of the PPO has developed to try to identify themes across a number of cases, with 'learning lessons' reports being published on the website (PPO, undated). Thematic analysis in the PPO's 2012–13 annual report led to suggestions for improvements in areas such as the prison disciplinary system, end-of-life care for older prisoners, the internal complaints system of probation trusts, the prevention of suicide among children in custody, responding to religious issues and dealing with sexual abuse (Newcomen, 2013: 10–11). The annual report praised prisons and probation services for continuing to accept almost all of the ombudsman's recommendations, to put in place improvement plans and to learn lessons in most cases (Newcomen, 2013: 7).

Agencies that Deal with Wrongful Convictions

Whereas the Independent Police Complaints Commission and the Prisons and Probation Ombudsman deal specifically with alleged wrongdoing on behalf of staff of criminal justice agencies, this is not necessarily the case with the two final agencies to be considered in this chapter – the Court of Appeal (Criminal Division) or CACD, and the Criminal Cases Review Commission (CCRC). These agencies deal with what are popularly known as 'miscarriages of justice' although the term 'wrongful conviction' is more accurate because miscarriages can take other forms, such as people falling foul of laws that are inherently unjust (Walker, 1999: 33–7). Naughton (2013: 32) makes a distinction between those wrongful convictions brought about by unintentional acts (e.g. an honest mistake on the part of a jury) and those which arise when criminal justice is deliberately subverted, either by employees of criminal justice agencies or by external agents – for example, witnesses who deliberately give false testimony (Naughton, 2013: 35). This section will discuss wrongful convictions more broadly, while recognising that the cases causing greatest concern have often been those that appear to involve deliberate subversion by staff of criminal justice agencies.

Convictions that are now seen as obviously wrong have a long history (see, for example, the Pendle Witch Trials of 1612, www.pendlewitches.co.uk/). Where such cases have raised public concern, there have sometimes been major implications for criminal justice: for example, the abolition of the death penalty was linked to the wrongful conviction and execution of Timothy Evans for the murder of his daughter (http://innocent.org.uk/cases/timothyevans/index.html). Similarly, the introduction of new procedures for police investigations under the 1984 Police and Criminal Evidence Act (PACE) was prompted partly by the wrongful conviction of three youths for the murder of Maxwell Confait (Naughton, 2013: 1–2; and see www.richardwebster.net/thenewinjustices.html). The creation of the CACD and the CCRC both followed high-profile cases where wrongful conviction appeared to have taken place.

The Court of Appeal (Criminal Division) (CACD)

Prior to 1907 methods of questioning decisions of the courts were extremely limited, based on very specific criteria and infrequently used (Nobles and Schiff, 2000: 41–2). The Home Office could exercise the Royal Prerogative of Mercy by issuing a free pardon, a conditional pardon (involving commutation of the death sentence) or remission of sentence (Nobles and Schiff, 2000: 42–3). However, exercise of the prerogative often depended on an influential person taking up the case (Naughton, 2013: 3).

The creation of the Court of Criminal Appeal in 1907 followed high-profile campaigns against apparent wrongful convictions such as those of Florence Maybrook and Adolf Beck; Beck was twice convicted of larceny on the basis of mistaken eyewitness evidence (Naughton, 2013: 1). Following an Inquiry into Beck's case, the 1907 Criminal Appeal Act gave powers for the Court of Criminal Appeal to hear appeals on three grounds:

1. If the verdict of the jury was unreasonable or could not be supported by the evidence;

2. If there had been a 'wrong decision on any question of law'; or

3. If 'on any ground there was a miscarriage of justice'. (Naughton, 2013: 144)

However, in practice the Court of Criminal Appeal was unwilling to oppose the original verdict of juries or to accept fresh evidence in cases referred directly to it, although more willing to consider this new evidence in cases referred by the Home Secretary (Nobles and Schiff, 2000: 60–1). Public pressure eventually led to reforms in the 1960s, including the merger of the Court of Criminal Appeal and the Court of Appeal, which was then divided between the Civil Division and the Criminal Division. The Court of Appeal (Criminal Division) (CACD) was given powers to order a retrial, rather than having to choose only between quashing or upholding a conviction (Nobles and Schiff, 2000: 62). The standard for the CACD quashing a conviction or ordering a re-trial was that the conviction was 'unsafe' (Naughton, 2013, 148–9).

Naughton (2013: 153–4) highlights a number of cases that suggest that, when considering whether a conviction is 'unsafe', the CACD has been more concerned with correct procedure than in the factual guilt or innocence of the person convicted. Possibly because of its narrow legal focus, the CACD used its new power to order retrials very sparingly: only 14 retrials occurred between 1981 and 1986 (Nobles and Schiff, 2000: 79). These figures were to increase dramatically after developments in the late 1980s and early 1990s, which are discussed in the next section.

The Criminal Cases Review Commission (CCRC)

Creation of the CCRC

The Criminal Cases Review Commission (CCRC) was established by the 1995 Criminal Appeal Act, as recommended by a Royal Commission on Criminal Justice. The Royal Commission was established in 1993 after a number of high-profile miscarriages of justice, which damaged public confidence and made clear that Home Secretaries had sometimes refused to refer cases to the CACD for political rather than legal reasons (Naughton, 2010a: 1). Among these cases was that of the Cardiff Three (see Box 19.2).

Some of the highest profile cases where convictions were finally overturned, despite substantial resistance to their referral to the CACD, reflected wider inequalities within society and criminal justice. The Guildford Four and the Birmingham Six were Irish republicans whose convictions were eventually quashed when, among other matters, it emerged that police officers had fabricated statements. Mental health problems played a part in the conviction of another suspected IRA member, Judith Ward, whose confession for delivering bombs was eventually discounted by the CACD on the basis of mental instability (Walker, 1999: 46–8). Another case with racial overtones was that of the Tottenham three – young African Caribbean men who were convicted of the brutal murder of PC Keith Blakelock during the Broadwater Farm riot of 1985. The CACD quashed the convictions in 1991 on the basis of the mental state of one defendant at the time of his confession, the undue denial of a lawyer to another and evidence that police had altered statements in the case of the third (Walker, 1999: 50).

The 1993 Royal Commission criticised the division of the Home Office that dealt with alleged miscarriages of justice, C3, for being insufficiently independent of the government, slow, inefficient, reactive and deferring too much to the courts. The CCRC received approximately nine times the resources that had been allocated to C3 (Nobles and Schiff, 2010: 151).

Work of the CCRC

The CCRC states its purpose as 'to review possible miscarriages of justice in the criminal courts of England, Wales and Northern Ireland and refer appropriate cases to the appeal courts' (CCRC, 2014: 3). For a case to be accepted it must already have been appealed or leave to appeal must have been refused. There has to be new evidence, or a new line of argument, not advanced in previous proceedings (O'Brian, 2011: 1).

Until 2012, the CCRC had operated with a typical caseload of less than 1,000 per year. Following the introduction of a simplified 'easy read' application form, this caseload increased substantially – to 1,625 in 2012–13 and 1,470 in 2013–14. However, in 2013–14 48 per cent of applications were 'No Appeal' cases, where there had been no previous appeal or request of leave to appeal. In 2013–14 72.5 per cent of applications were from people in custody and 27.5 per cent from people who were at liberty. The CCRC prioritises cases for people who are currently in custody (CCRC, 2014: 13–15). Of those cases that are referred and eligible for consideration by the CCRC, the long-term rate of appeal to the CACD has been approximately 7.5 per cent (CCRC, 2014: 15–16); the appeal has been allowed in approximately 70 per cent of cases (CCRC, 2014: 20–21).

The Chair of the CCRC, in its 2013–14 annual report, commented that police misconduct and non-disclosure of information to the defence remained key themes of cases investigated by the CCRC. In addition, questions of discrimination continued to be raised by cases of asylum seekers whose 'offence' had involved their entry to the United Kingdom and by the prosecutions of victims of human trafficking who had been compelled to undertake criminal activities (CCRC, 2014: 7–8).

Criticisms of the CCRC: The basis of referral

The CCRC has been criticised for being insufficiently concerned with whether a person is 'factually innocent', i.e. did not commit the crime of which they have been convicted. The purpose of investigations by the CCRC is defined by the 1995 Criminal Appeal Act as determining whether there is a 'real possibility that the conviction, verdict, finding or sentence would not be upheld were the reference to be made' (to the CACD). This means that the CCRC is subject to the legal criteria applied by the CACD; likely factual innocence is not specified as the reason for referring a case (Naughton, 2010a: 2). The CCRC itself has stated that 'We do not consider innocence or guilt, but whether there is new evidence or argument that may cast doubt on the safety of an original decision' (CCRC, 2008, cited in Naughton, 2010b: 22). In addition, the CCRC reviews only the part of the evidence that might meet the 'real possibility' criteria, rather than the entire case (Naughton, 2010b: 25–6). The 'success rate' of applicants compares unfavourably to the 10 per cent of cases that were referred by C3 to the CACD before the CCRC was created (Nobles and Schiff, 2010: 151).

Criticisms of the CCRC: Fresh evidence

The close alignment of the standards of the CACD and the CCRC in determining whether fresh evidence should be considered means that it is difficult to discuss the two bodies separately when considering this key criterion for defining a conviction as unsafe. In deciding where to consider fresh evidence the CACD considers:

> whether the evidence appears capable of belief;
>
> whether it offers grounds for allowing an appeal;
>
> whether the evidence could have been produced at the original legal proceedings; and
>
> whether there is a reasonable explanation for the failure to produce it at the original proceedings. (Naughton, 2010b: 21)

The CCRC's close adherence to these principles in deciding whether to accept or refer cases has been criticised by Naughton (2010a: 4), who argues that it is unlikely that the case of the Birmingham Six would have been referred back to the CACD by the CCRC because evidence of police misconduct and inaccurate forensic testimony was available at the time of the original trial (Naughton, 2010a: 4). Malone (2010: 107–9) criticises the CCRC for being unwilling to consider 'fresh' evidence in the form of new expert opinion (e.g. of forensic evidence). The CCRC has drawn too heavily, in Malone's opinion, on two Court of Appeal judgments – one that ruled that expert evidence that could have been put before the original jury should not be considered to be 'fresh' and another that indicated that evidence from a new expert witness should not be considered if it is the same or similar in content to that which was advanced by another witness at the original trial.

Evaluation and future prospects

Reflecting some of the above criticisms, Duff (2009) contrasts the more flexible approach of the Scottish Criminal Cases Review Commission with the position in England and Wales where, as one of the first commissioners put it: 'we can't refer a case simply because it stinks' (quoted in Duff, 2009: 701). However, the CCRC has been widely acclaimed internationally (Naughton, 2010a: 3–4) and its supporters argue that there is nothing to be gained by it referring convictions to the CACD when there is little or no prospect of them being overturned (Robins, 2014: 218).

In July 2015, the House of Commons Justice Select Committee made a number of recommendations to the government in relation to the CCRC and the

CACD – most notably that the CCRC should be less cautious in its application of the 'real possibility' test and that the CACD should consider quashing convictions where it had serious doubts about the verdict, even when there was no fresh evidence or legal argument. The government's response to these recommendations was cautious (Ministry of Justice, 2015: 4) but it is possible that they could eventually lead to significant changes.

Box 19.2

Cardiff Three Case Study

The case of the Cardiff Three was one that caused huge public concern due to the brutality of the original crime, the imprisonment of three innocent men and the collapse of the trial of the police officers who were suspected of intimidating suspects and witnesses.

On Valentine's Day 1988, sex worker Lynette White was found murdered, with more than 50 stab wounds. Five men were arrested and charged with her murder and three of them – Tony Paris, Yusef Abdullahi and Stephen Miller (White's boyfriend) – were convicted and jailed for life in 1990. They were released on appeal in 1992, when it was shown that Miller's interview had breached PACE guidelines (Naughton, 2013: 30). A painstaking reinvestigation of the case, which began in 1999, produced DNA evidence leading detectives to another man, Jeffrey Gafoor, who confessed to the crime in 2003 (*Guardian* 17 September 2012, www.theguardian.com/uk/2012/sep/17/cardiff-three-five-wait-justice).

The CACD accepted that the three wrongly convicted men had been subjected to the most hostile and intimidating approach by police officers that was possible without actually using physical violence. Three witnesses whose testimony had been central to their conviction – Mark Grommek, Leanne Vilday and Angela Psaila – were imprisoned for 18 months each for perjury in 2008. The prosecution accepted that the 'witnesses' had been subjected to the same type of intimidation as the accused. In passing the sentence for perjury the judge noted that the behaviour of the police had been 'unacceptable in a civilised society' but that there had been opportunities for the witnesses to tell the truth, if not to the police then to the court (Naughton, 2013: 63–5).

Following an IPCC-supervised investigation by South Wales Police (SWP), eight police officers and two civilians were subsequently charged with perjury. However, the trial ended on 1 December 2011 after prosecuting counsel formally offered no evidence because it appeared that the SWP senior investigating officer had given an instruction to shred four files of documents. It subsequently emerged that the documents had not been shredded; a further investigation by the IPCC found that, on the balance of probabilities, no instructions had been given to destroy the documents but that mistakes had been made in their receipt, recording and storage, making them difficult to locate. The IPCC recommended that three officers should receive management action over disclosure processes but that their errors, particularly in view of the 800,000 pages of documents to be processed, were not sufficient to warrant formal misconduct proceedings (IPCC, 2013).

A report by Her Majesty's Crown Prosecution Service Inspectorate similarly concluded that police and prosecutors had been overwhelmed by the scale of the disclosure exercise, but that there was no reason to believe that any actions had been taken from an improper motive. The Crown Prosecution Service (CPS) accepted the findings of the report and implemented changes such as appointing suitably experienced prosecuting lawyers and ensuring clearer communications between them and the CPS (Crown Prosecution Service, 2013).

However, it seems highly unlikely that those wrongly imprisoned, or those witnesses who experienced intimidation, would feel that three police officers being subject to management action and changes to CPS procedures was a sufficient response to the injustice that they had experienced. Home Secretary Theresa May was also dissatisfied with the outcome, announcing, in February 2015, that there would be a QC-led investigation examining why the prosecution of the former police officers was abandoned, whether boxes of documents were overlooked by the prosecution and what lessons had been learned from the collapse of the trial (Home Office, 2015).

Summary

The agencies discussed in this chapter were all created to tackle perceptions that there was injustice within criminal justice processes and that existing mechanisms for dealing with this injustice were inadequate. The Prisons and Probation Ombudsman – the least controversial of the organisations – was created in response to Lord Woolf's concerns that justice was not being seen to be done within prisons and that an independent element was needed to any complaints system. The steady expansion of the ombudsman's role, and the acceptance of almost all recommendations made, suggest a widespread acceptance of its value.

How to include an effective independent element (however defined) in the system of police complaints is a question that has been frequently debated since the 1960s, with the Independent Police Complaints Commission (IPCC) being the latest of a number of bodies that have sought to increase public confidence in the complaints system. However, the IPCC has been the subject of much criticism, with its role assumed to be linked to falling confidence in the police: it has been variously suggested that it is under-resourced, unsympathetic to complainants and biased towards police officers. The coalition government of 2010–15 took various measures to try to tackle these criticisms, most notably by allocating more resources in order to facilitate more independent investigations, and further changes are expected in the current parliament.

Misconduct among police officers is one of a number of reasons that people may be wrongfully convicted. While the Court of Appeal has existed for over a century, high-profile cases of the late 1980s and early 1990s suggested that the system by which the Home Secretary decided which cases to refer to it was flawed. The Criminal Cases Review Commission, which took over this role, is a body that is admired elsewhere in the world, but one which has been criticised for being too concerned with legal definitions rather than the layperson's view that people should not be convicted of crimes that they did not commit.

Given the huge changes that have come about in the manner of dealing with complaints against criminal justice agencies in the last 30 years, it seems reasonable to assume that the process will continue to evolve, with police complaints (as has often been the case) being the focus of continuing controversy and change.

——————— ## Discussion Questions ———————

1. Can the public ever trust the police if they feel that the complaints system is unfair?

2. Are police officers (or ex-police officers) the only people with the skills to investigate allegations of crimes committed by other police officers?

3. Does taking all complaints against police officers seriously undermine their authority and mean that they spend too much time justifying themselves rather than serving and protecting the public?

4. Have failings in the system of dealing with complaints against the police led some officers on some occasions to believe that they are beyond the law?

5. Should prisoners and other offenders have to go through internal complaints systems before their case can be considered by the Prisons and Probation Ombudsman? Does this rule mean that some will be discouraged from making a complaint and harbour a grievance instead?

6. Is the Court of Appeal (Criminal Division) too reluctant to admit that the courts have made a mistake?

7. If the Criminal Cases Review Commission were to give more weight to 'factual innocence', would this undermine the role of juries?

8. If there were less strict rules about the admission of fresh evidence, would the Criminal Cases Review Commission face an unmanageable number of applications involving new expert witnesses?

——————— ## Further Reading ———————

Graham Smith has written a number of helpful journal articles about the issues surrounding complaints against the police. In addition to those referenced above, it would also be helpful to read:

Smith, G. (2004) 'Rethinking police complaints', *British Journal of Criminology*, 44: 15–33.

For a radical view of police complaints, see:

Williams, R. (2015) *Rough Justice: Citizens' experience of mistreatment and injustice in the early stages of law enforcement.* Sherfield-on-Loddon: Waterside Press.

For more about the murder of PC Keith Blakelock and its aftermath, including the convictions that were quashed, see:

Moore, T. (2015) *The Killing of Constable Keith Blakelock: The Broadwater Farm riot.* Sherfield-on-Loddon: Waterside Press.

There is very little written about the Prisons and Probation Ombudsman, although the organisation's website is one very useful source of information. Similarly, the websites of the Independent Police Complaints Commission and Criminal Cases Review Commission also have helpful, up-to-date information.

References

Cavadino, M. and Dignan, J. (2007) *The Penal System: An introduction*. 4th edn. London: Sage.

Criminal Cases Review Commission (2014) *Annual Report and Accounts 2013/14*. Available at: http://ccrc.wpengine.com/wp-content/uploads/2015/03/ccrc-annual-report-accounts-2013-14.pdf (accessed 4 September 2016).

Crown Prosecution Service (2013) *CPS Response to HMCPSI Review into the Disclosure Handling in the Case of R v Mouncher and others*. Available at: www.cps.gov.uk/news/articles/cps_response_to_hmcpsi_review_of_lynette_white_case/ (accessed 4 September 2016).

Duff, P. (2009) 'Straddling two worlds: Reflections of a retired Criminal Cases Review Commissioner', *The Modern Law Review*, 72 (5): 693–722.

Glass, D. (2014) *Towards Greater Public Confidence: A personal review of the current police complaints system in England and Wales*. Available at: www.ipcc.gov.uk/sites/default/files/Documents/speeches/A-review-of-the-complaints-system-by-Deborah-Glass-March-2014.pdf (accessed 4 September 2016).

Home Office (2013) *Independent Police Complaints Commission*. Available at: www.gov.uk/government/uploads/system/uploads/attachment_data/file/228950/8598.pdf (accessed 4 September 2016).

Home Office (2015) *Home Secretary Announces Investigation into Collapsed Police Trial*. Available at: www.gov.uk/government/news/home-secretary-announces-investigation-into-collapsed-police-trial (accessed 4 September 2016).

Home Office (2016a) *Home Secretary Announces Reforms to IPCC*. News Story, 7 March.

Home Office (2016b) *Police and Crime Bill, Factsheet: Overview of the Bill*. Available at: www.gov.uk/government/uploads/system/uploads/attachment_data/file/499172/Factsheet_Overview.pdf (accessed 4 September 2016).

House of Commons Home Affairs Committee (2010) *The Work of the Independent Police Complaints Commission, Eleventh Report of Session 2009–10*. Available at: www.publications.parliament.uk/pa/cm200910/cmselect/cmhaff/366/366.pdf (accessed 4 September 2016).

Independent Police Complaints Commission (2012) *Report of the Investigation into a Complaint Made by the Family of Mark Duggan about Contact with Them Immediately After His Death*. Available at: www.ipcc.gov.uk/sites/default/files/Documents/investigation_commissioner_reports/Duggan_Final_Report_Foreword_29_Feb_2012.pdf (accessed 4 September 2016).

Independent Police Complaints Commission (2013) *IPCC Publishes Report of its Lynette White 'Missing' Documents Investigation*. Available at: www.ipcc.gov.uk/news/ipcc-publishes-report-its-lynette-white-%E2%80%98missing%E2%80%99-documents-investigation (accessed 4 September 2016).

Independent Police Complaints Commission (2014a) *Review of the IPCC's Work Involving Deaths*. Available at: www.ipcc.gov.uk/page/review-ipccs-work-relation-cases-involving-death (accessed 4 September 2016).

Independent Police Complaints Commission (2014b) *Police Handling of Allegations of Discrimination*. Available at: www.ipcc.gov.uk/sites/default/files/Documents/guidelines_reports/IPCC_report_police_handling_of_allegations_of_discrimination_June2014.pdf (accessed 4 September 2016).

Independent Police Complaints Commission (2014c) *IPCC outlines criminal and misconduct proceedings over Avon & Somerset police treatment of Bijan Ebrahimi*. Available at: www.ipcc.gov.uk/news/ipcc-outlines-criminal-and-misconduct-proceedings-over-avon-somerset-police-treatment-bijan (accessed 4 September 2016).

Independent Police Complaints Commission (2015) *The Fatal Police Shooting of Mr Mark Duggan on 4 August 2011*. Available at: www.ipcc.gov.uk/sites/default/files/Documents/investigation_commissioner_reports/IPCC-investigation-report-fatal-shooting-of-MD.pdf (accessed 4 September 2016).

IPSOS MORI and the IPCC (2014) *Public Confidence in the Police Complaints System*. Available at: www.ipcc.gov.uk/sites/default/files/Documents/guidelines_reports/IPCC_Public_confidence_survey_2014.pdf (accessed 4 September 2016).

Macpherson, Sir W. (1999) *The Stephen Lawrence Inquiry – Report of an inquiry by Sir William Macpherson of Cluny*. CM 4262-1. London: HMSO.

Malone, C. (2010) 'Only the freshest will do', in M. Naughton (ed.), *The Criminal Cases Review Commission: Hope for the innocent?* Basingstoke: Palgrave Macmillan. pp. 107–17.

McLaughlin, E. (2007) *The New Policing*. London: Sage.

Ministry of Justice (2015) *Government Response to the Justice Select Committee's Twelfth Report of Session 2014–15 Criminal Cases Review Commission*. Available at: www.gov.uk/government/uploads/system/uploads/attachment_data/file/445037/ccrc-response.pdf (accessed 4 September 2016).

Naughton, M. (2010a) 'Introduction', in M. Naughton (ed.), *The Criminal Cases Review Commission: Hope for the innocent?* Basingstoke: Palgrave Macmillan. pp. 1–16.

Naughton, M. (2010b) 'The importance of innocence for the criminal justice system', in M. Naughton (ed.), *The Criminal Cases Review Commission: Hope for the innocent?* Basingstoke: Palgrave Macmillan. pp. 17–40.

Naughton, M. (2013) *The Innocent and the Criminal Justice System*. Basingstoke: Palgrave MacMillan.

Newcomen, N. (2013) *Prisons and Probation Ombudsman for England and Wales, 2012–13 Annual Report*. Available at: www.gov.uk/government/uploads/system/uploads/attachment_data/file/264062/8702.pdf (accessed 4 September 2016).

Nobles, R. and Schiff, D. (2000) *Understanding Miscarriages of Justice*. Oxford: Oxford University Press.

Nobles, R. and Schiff, D. (2010) 'After ten years: An investment in justice?', in M. Naughton (ed.), *The Criminal Cases Review Commission: Hope for the innocent?* Basingstoke: Palgrave Macmillan.

O'Brian, W.E. Jr (2011) 'Fresh expert evidence in CCRC cases', *King's Law Journal*, 22 (1): 1–26.

Prisons and Probation Ombudsman (undated) *Brief History*. Available at: www.ppo.gov.uk/about/vision-and-values/brief-history/ (accessed 4 September 2016).

Robins, J. (2014) *The First Miscarriage of Justice: The 'unreported and amazing' case of Tony Stock*. Sherfield-on-Loddon: Waterside Press.

Rowe, M. (2014) *Introduction to Policing*. 2nd edn. London: Sage.

Savage, S. (2013) 'Thinking independence: Calling the police to account through the independent investigation of police complaints', *British Journal of Criminology*, 53: 94–112.

Scarman, Lord (1981) *The Brixton Disorders 10–12 April 1981 – Report of an inquiry by the Rt Hon Lord Scarman OBE*. London: HMSO.

Scott, D. (2007) 'The changing face of the English prison: A critical review of the aims of imprisonment', in Y. Jewkes (ed.), *Handbook on Prisons*. Cullompton: Willan Publishing. pp. 447–66.

Shaw, S. (2009) 'Two hundred years of Ombudsman history', *Inside Time Magazine*, August. Available at: http://www.insidetime.org/two-hundred-years-of-ombudsman-history/ (accessed 4 September 2016).

Sindall, K., Sturgis, P. and Jennings, W. (2012) 'Public confidence in the police: A time-series analysis', *British Journal of Criminology*, 52: 744–64.

Smith, G. (2005) 'A most enduring problem: Police complaints reform in England and Wales', *Journal of Social Policy*, 35 (1): 121–41.

Smith, G. (2009) 'Citizen oversight of independent police services: Bifurcated accountability, regulation creep, and lesson learning', *Regulation and Governance*, 3: 421–41.

Stevens, J. (2013) *Policing for a Better Britain: Report of the Independent Police Commission*. Available at: www.lse.ac.uk/socialPolicy/Researchcentresandgroups/mannheim/pdf/PolicingforaBetterBritain.pdf (accessed 4 September 2016).

Thomassen, G. (2002) 'Investigating complaints against the police in Norway: An empirical investigation', *Policing and Society: An International Journal of Research and Policy*, 12 (3): 201–10.

Walker, C. (1999) 'Miscarriages of justice in principle and practice', in C. Walker and K. Starmer (eds), *Miscarriages of Justice: A review of justice in error*. Oxford: Oxford University Press. pp. 31–64

Waters, I. and Brown, K. (2000) 'Police complaints and the complainants' experience', *British Journal of Criminology*, 40: 617–38.

Check out the Companion Website

Want to know more about this chapter? Review what you have been learning by visiting: **https://study.sagepub.com/harding**

- Practice with essay questions
- Test yourself with multiple-choice questions
- Listen to a series of podcasts featuring Neil of Northumbria Police and London's Metropolitan Police Service
- Watch videos selected from the SAGE Video collection

20   Supporting Victims and Witnesses

Ian R. Cook and Pamela Davies

Introduction

Since coming into government, we have modernised and rebalanced the Criminal Justice System in order to place victims and witnesses at its centre. Victims and their families have for too long felt far from being fully included in the criminal justice process ... But giving victims a voice is vital. Vital for justice, vital for crime fighting – but most of all, vital for the victims themselves. We are determined as a [New Labour] Government to make sure that their voice is heard. (Falconer, in Home Office, 2005: 2)

The [Coalition] Government is committed to ensuring that the justice system is fair, accessible, and delivers the justice victims and witnesses need, deserve and demand. (Blunt et al., in Ministry of Justice, 2011: 1)

Both quotations above are taken from forewords (guest introductions) to governmental documents on aspects of the Criminal Justice System. The first is written by Lord Falconer, then Secretary of State for Constitutional Affairs, and the second, written six years later, by senior politicians at Westminster and the Welsh Assembly. Published before and after a change of government in 2010 – from New Labour to a Conservative–Liberal Democrat Coalition – the two forewords are similar, talking of a need to place the needs and voices of victims and witnesses at the centre of the Criminal Justice System. This stance was echoed in the subsequent 2015 electioneering, with both Labour and the Conservatives promoting the establishment of a new Victims' Law. Victims and witnesses, it would seem, have become increasingly important when politicians develop criminal justice policy and engage in political campaigning.

In this chapter we will go beyond the political rhetoric to explore two important themes. Under the first, we explore the evolving role and position of victims and witnesses in the Criminal Justice System in England and Wales. Under the second we review public and voluntary sector support and assistance for victims and witnesses. The chapter will draw upon the plethora of research and policy developments that have focused on the needs of, and service provision for, victims and witnesses. It will also draw on a wider body of knowledge emanating from two movements: the victim movement and the feminist movement (the latter having had a huge impact in the development of support for women victims of violence in the home).

Following a timeline of key developments, the structure of the remainder of the chapter is as follows. It begins by considering the terms 'victim' and 'witness' and how these terms are defined. The implications of these 'labels' or 'statuses' are considered throughout. We then examine the evolving role of victims and witnesses in the Criminal Justice System in England and Wales and further afield. Following this we critically consider the journey of victims and witnesses through the Criminal Justice System, looking at three issues in particular: attrition (i.e. cases dropping out); secondary victimisation; and, through a case study of Victim Support, the provision of services by voluntary organisations.

Timeline

1964   Criminal Injuries Compensation Board (CICB) set up to administer the Criminal Injuries Compensation Scheme (CICS) for victims of violent crime

1972   First UK Women's Aid refuge set up in Chiswick, London

1974   First Victim Support project set up in Bristol

1976   First UK Rape Crisis Centre opened in London

1982   First British Crime Survey

1986   Childline established

1986   The Islington Crime Survey

1987   First Home Office funding for Victim Support

1989	Victim Support launched the first victim/witness in court project
1990	Home Office *Victim's Charter* published
1991	The Home Office fund Victim Support's Crown Court Witness Service
1995	Victim Support UK publishes *The Rights of Victims of Crime*
	Criminal Injuries Compensation Act (sets out statutory tariff of injuries)
1996	*Victim's Charter* (revised 2nd edn) published
1996	'One Stop Shops' and 'Victim Statements' piloted
1996	National network of Victim Support's Victim/Witness Support schemes in Crown Courts
1999	Home Office funding to establish the Witness Service in Magistrates' Courts
2000	Criminal and Court Services Act (imposed duties on Probation Service to inform victims about serious and violent and sexual offenders)
2001	Victim Personal Statements (VPS) introduced
2002	Home Office *Victim's Charter* (revised 3rd edn) published
2003	Victim Support provides a Witness Service in all criminal courts
2004	Domestic Violence, Crime and Victims Act
2005	*The Code of Practice for Victims of Crime* published
2007	The *Witness Charter* published
2009	Sarah Payne appointed first Victims' Champion
2010	Louise Casey appointed as first Victims' Commissioner (followed by Baroness Newlove in 2012)
2010	Jonathan Djanogly MP appointed Victims Minister (followed by Helen Grant MP in 2012 and Mike Penning MP in 2014)
2011	Victims' Services Alliance formed
2012	41 Police and Crime Commissioners elected
2013	A revised *Code of Practice for Victims of Crime* published
2013	*The Witness Charter: Standards of care for witnesses in the Criminal Justice System published*
2013	Victims' Right to Review introduced
2015	Revised *Code of Practice for Victims of Crime* published

Conceptualising Victims and Witnesses

Defining and identifying victims of crime is not straightforward. Indeed, definitions of the term victim are controversial and range from a narrowly defined victim *of crime* to more expansive conceptualisations that are inclusive of those who have suffered harm and injustice. Both Walklate (2007) and Rock (2002, see Box 20.1) promote an expansive definition, with Walklate defining a victim as 'an individual who has suffered some kind of misfortune' (2007: 27). Misfortune might encompass those experiencing physical, financial, emotional or psychological harm.

Box 20.1

Victim

Rock (2002: 13–14) suggests 'victim' is an identity and a social artefact that is constructed by different actors in different contexts. It is usually now associated with crime but also relates to someone suffering some kind of misfortune.

Divided opinions on definitions provoke debate about who *qualifies* as a victim. Can, for instance, someone be culpable in their own misfortune and, if so, do they qualify as a victim? Should we consider those close to the direct victim also as victims, such as the non-abusing family members of child sexual abuse? Many agree with the Norwegian criminologist Nils Christie (1986) who reasoned that the subsequent treatment of victims by the Criminal Justice System is often linked to whether they are deemed to be 'ideal victims' or not. 'Ideal victims' are those who are most readily given the complete and legitimate status of being a victim. Such victims attract this status because they are perceived as vulnerable, defenceless and clearly innocent. They are therefore worthy of a sympathetic and compassionate response including support and compensation (Meyer, 2016: 2–3; see Box 20.2).

Box 20.2

Holly Wells and Jessica Chapman as archetypal ideal victims

In the summer of 2002, 10-year-old girls Holly and Jessica went missing from their home in the quiet market village of Soham. Their disappearance, accompanied by photographs of the two girls, was a constant presence in the British media for almost two weeks before their bodies were discovered in a shallow grave. Local school caretaker Ian Huntley was then arrested and charged with their abduction and murder. During the search for the two girls, the media visually represented the two girls as 'young bright, photogenic girls from stable loving families, middle-class family backgrounds, and each had an exemplary school record' (Greer, 2007: 23). This according to Greer (ibid.: 23) made them 'archetypal "ideal victims".

Societal expectations about who qualifies as a victim, as well as how a victim should behave, can have very real consequences for those called upon as witnesses. Christie's ideal victim tries to encapsulate this, as does Cole's (2007) notion of the 'true victim'. Cole argues that a true victim is a 'noble' victim who suffers in silence; they refrain from gaining sympathy or publicly displaying weakness. They command their own fate and do not exploit their injuries and their victimisation must be immediate and concrete and without any doubt. Taking the definitional and labelling controversy further, feminists prefer to use the term *survivor* rather than victim (see Box 20.3). From a feminist perspective 'survivor' denotes a more active and positive image of women who overcome particular experiences. This concept challenges perceptions of the female victim as passive, helpless, powerless, blameworthy or victim-prone and signifies the negotiating and coping strategies women employ to live their daily lives (Stanko, 1990).

Box 20.3

Victim→Survivor

Not everyone who suffers victimisation likes to think of themselves as, or to be called, a victim. Feminists including those involved with Rape Crisis centres prefer to speak of survivors, for a number of reasons. First, using the term 'survivor' makes clear the seriousness of rape as, often, a life-threatening attack. Second, public perceptions are shaped by terminology and the word 'victim' has connotations of passivity, even of helplessness. In the context of a movement that aims to empower people who have been victimised, this is clearly inappropriate: 'using the word "victim" to describe women takes away our power and contributes to the idea that it is right and natural for men to "prey" on us' (London Rape Crisis Centre, 1984: iv).

While criminologists have spent time thinking about the identity of a victim, witnesses have largely been ignored. The *Oxford Dictionary of English*, however, defines witness as a *noun* – 'a person who sees an event, typically a crime or an accident, take place' – but also as a *verb* – to 'see (an event, typically a crime or accident) happen'. The emphasis is on sight, hence the synonym eyewitness. As with a victim, a witness is usually understood *relationally* – that is, in relation to the other people and things involved in the event(s). Box 20.4 outlines the definition of witness in section 52 of the Domestic Violence, Crime and Victims Act 2004. Central to this definition is the idea that witnesses are those who are able to assist in criminal proceedings.

Box 20.4

Definition of a Witness in Section 52 of the Domestic Violence, Crime and Victims Act 2004

(4) 'Witness' means a person (other than a defendant) —

(a) who has witnessed conduct in relation to which he may be or has been called to give evidence in relevant proceedings;

(b) who is able to provide or has provided anything which might be used or has been used as evidence in relevant proceedings; or

(c) who is able to provide or has provided anything mentioned in subsection (5) (whether or not admissible in evidence in relevant proceedings).

(5) The things referred to in subsection (4)(c) are —

(a) anything which might tend to confirm, has tended to confirm or might have tended to confirm evidence which may be, has been or could have been admitted in relevant proceedings;

(b) anything which might be, has been or might have been referred to in evidence given in relevant proceedings by another person;

(c) anything which might be, has been or might have been used as the basis for any cross examination in the course of relevant proceedings.

There has been a particular emphasis in England and Wales since the late 1990s on identifying, and service provision for, a particular group of witnesses: Vulnerable and Intimidated Witnesses. Following the Youth Justice and Criminal Evidence Act 1999, these two groups are eligible for 'special measures'. These allowances can include screens in the courtroom to prevent the defendant and the witness seeing each other, and allowing the defendant to give evidence via a live video link from somewhere outside the court room. Special measures are discussed in detail in Chapter 13.

The Criminal Justice System relies on victims and witnesses in a number of ways, including reporting crimes and furnishing the police – often gatekeepers to the Criminal Justice System – with information to aid in building evidence for a court case. However, not all victims and witnesses report incidents to the police for a variety of reasons as we know from successive sweeps of the British Crime Survey (now the Crime Survey England and Wales) since the early 1980s. Thus, those 'on record' as victims and witnesses within the Criminal Justice System are only a small and distorted proportion of those suffering misfortune.

The Role of Victims and Witnesses in the Criminal Justice System

A commonplace critique of the Criminal Justice System in England and Wales is that it has marginalised victims and witnesses, taken them for granted and given little attention to any rights or needs that they may have (Victim Support, 2010). This is not a new criticism. Indeed, Kearon and Godfrey (2007: 30) argue that victims of crime in the UK were disempowered in the 1840s, becoming 'less able to initiate prosecutions, or control the court process' with their role in court reduced to 'witnesses to a case brought in the *public interest*'. Rock (2007: 38) elaborates further on these ideas when he portrays the victim of crime as:

the 'forgotten person' who appeared only as a witness, an applicant for compensation or a complainant or *alleged* victim until the conclusion of a trial. The prime conflict at law did not touch significantly on the victim: it was deemed to be between two parties only, the prosecution and the defendant, and the individual victim merely provided evidence of an offence that, for all practical purposes, was committed not so much against him or her but against the collectivity in the form of the Crown, the State or the community. Private wrongs were a matter for tort and civil procedure.

Given the functional importance of crime victims to the operation of the Criminal Justice System in England and Wales, and their crucial role in providing evidence, it is perhaps surprising that it was not until the post-war period that the first significant mechanisms were introduced to support the direct victim. This began with the introduction of criminal injuries compensation in 1964 whereby victims of reported violent crime could claim financial compensation from the state. Since this time there have been a number of developments and alterations in the provisions of support and assistance for victims of crime. Some of these are listed in the Timeline at the start of this chapter.

At this point, it is important to position the increased centrality of the victim within the Criminal Justice System in its broader historical and geographical context. A key consideration is the emergence of a victims' movement in the UK and other parts of the world during the latter part of the twentieth century. This movement was in reaction to the marginalisation of victims in the Criminal Justice System and in recognition of the under-reporting of victimisation. The victims' movement also corresponded with, and blurred with, the 'second wave' feminist movement. The latter raised awareness of the victimisation of women in the home and of women's experiences of sexual violence and campaigned for such violence to be recognised by the Criminal Justice System and society more widely (Davies, 2011). England and Wales has not been alone as these movements also gathered pace elsewhere. As Sebba (2001: 36) notes, lobbying by feminists and organisations devoted to victim assistance was:

> instrumental in the intensive barrage of victim-related legislation and policy reform which were instigated in the 1980s and 1990s ... and included the granting of procedural rights to victims in the course of the trial process (and subsequent proceedings), victim-oriented sentencing dispositions such as restitution, the introduction of state compensation boards and victim assistance programmes.

A range of supportive provisions and victim assistance schemes can now be identified in most jurisdictions across the world, all of which have differing relationships to their respective Criminal Justice Systems. Some victim services are at arm's length or fully independent of the government, some are provided under statute, others by voluntary groups and charities. How victims access and experience these supportive provisions is explored in the next section. Focusing predominately on the UK, both Kearon and Godfrey (2007) and Rock (2007) demonstrate that the victim was in effect reinvented as a witness or, worse still, a tool of the Criminal Justice System. That being said, Fyfe (2005: 514) reminds us that victims rather than witnesses became the primary focus of the early reforms:

[D]espite the incontrovertible importance of witnesses, their role in the criminal justice system has, until recently, largely been taken for granted. Witnesses were rarely given any preparation or assistance in relation to their appearance at court, despite the fact that giving evidence in court and being cross-examined can be intimidating and distressing experiences. Moreover, they frequently had to endure long waiting periods in court buildings where they risked encounters with the accused and their supporters. Nevertheless, the concerns of witnesses were largely invisible to policy-makers. Unlike victims, who were gradually becoming recognised as needing and deserving government assistance, witnesses had not achieved the same status.

In bringing this section on the role of victims and witnesses in the Criminal Justice System to a close we introduce the concept of 'procedural justice'. We do so in order to consider whose interests are being served and supported as the role of victims and witnesses changes and as support and assistance has evolved. Simply put, procedural justice equates to fair treatment. Procedural justice emphasises the fairness of the process by which decisions are made (Elliott et al., 2014). In the following sections we review the extent to which evolving support and provisions are introduced to meet the wants and needs of victims and witnesses. We also consider how these same developments can be seen rather differently, not as primarily in the interests of victims and witnesses but as efficiency measures designed to improve the smooth running of the Criminal Justice System and to please the voting public.

Evolving Support and Assistance for Victims and Witnesses of Crime

As noted above, the Criminal Justice System in England and Wales – echoing most of its counterparts in other parts of the world – has traditionally had scant regard for the needs of victims and witnesses of crime. However, many changes have been introduced, particularly since the early 1990s, aimed at 're-balancing' the system in favour of victims and witnesses (and, by implication, at the expense of offenders). Criminal justice policies in different countries have been mobilised to bring the victim and witness (more) centre stage with new policies introduced and old ones repackaged claiming to meet their needs and rights. Victims' 'rights' debates are increasingly central to developments in different criminal justice systems. However, the 'rights' of the victim in penal procedure in common law countries such as England and Wales, Australia, Canada, New Zealand and most of the USA are largely limited to that of witness for the prosecution, though changes have recently seen the granting of participatory rights for crime victims as part of a concerted endeavour to bring the victim to the forefront. Some of the changes made in recent years, such as the measures to protect witnesses in court, seem to have improved the victims' position yet victimological commentators continue to be sceptical about the extent to which policies advocated in the name of the victim are a good thing (Davies, 2015).

As the timeline at the start of this chapter shows, a series of changes in the Criminal Justice System have taken place in England and Wales repositioning the victim and the witness in recent decades. A key development, and a catalyst for further changes, was the publication of the *Victims' Charter: A statement of the rights of victims of crime* (Home Office, 1990). It claimed to set out for the first time the rights and entitlements of victims of crime. The revised version, published by the Home Office six years later in 1996, tellingly had a different sub-title *Victims' Charter: A statement of service standards for victims of crime* – a more realistic reflection of the actual contents. The vocabulary used had shifted from 'rights' to 'service standards'. Nevertheless the introduction of the *Victims' Charter* was a key landmark development that acknowledged the importance of the victim in securing justice.

The *Victims' Charter* was revised again in 2005 under the New Labour government (Office for Criminal Justice Reform, 2005) again in 2013 under the Coalition government (Ministry of Justice, 2013a), and once more by the Conservative government (Ministry of Justice, 2015). The latest document, the *Code of Practice for Victims of Crime*, takes the form of a 104-page document comprising 20 entitlements for victims of crime (a selection of these are summarised in Box 20.5). Related to this, the document also lists minimum standards for 14 different service providers. The language of the document is also revealing: the words 'entitled' and 'entitlements' appear continually throughout the document, with far less references to duties and duty. Common phrases in the document are 'putting victims first' and 'vulnerable victims'. If we take the Victims' Code as approximately indicative of the current state of victim-oriented policy, rights-based vocabularies remain noticeably absent.

Service provision for witnesses in England and Wales has lagged behind that for victims. This is best illustrated by the development of the *Witness Charter* 17 years after the original *Victims' Charter*. The New Labour government introduced the *Witness Charter* in 2007 (Office for Criminal Justice Reform, 2007). It outlined 34 'standards of care', informing both defence and prosecution witnesses of what they should expect from the different criminal justice agencies and from lawyers involved in the case. These were reduced and revised into 21 standards of care in the updated 2013 *Witness Charter* (Ministry of Justice, 2013b).

Box 20.5

A Selection of the Key Entitlements for Victims in the Victims' Code 2015 (Ministry of Justice, 2015: 5)

- A written acknowledgement that you have reported a crime, including the basic details of the offence;
- A needs assessment to help work out what support you need;
- Be informed about the police investigation, such as if a suspect is arrested and charged and any bail conditions imposed;
- Make a Victim Personal Statement (VPS) to explain how the crime affected you;

- Read your VPS aloud or have it read aloud on your behalf, subject to the views of the court, if a defendant is found guilty;

- Be informed if the suspect is to be prosecuted or not or given an out of court disposal;

- Be informed of the time, date and location and outcome of any court hearings;

- Be informed if you need to give evidence in court, what to expect and discuss what help and support you need with the Witness Care Unit;

- Arrange a court familiarisation visit and enter the court through a different entrance from the suspect and sit in a separate waiting area where possible;

- Apply for compensation under the Criminal Injuries Compensation Scheme;

- Receive information about Restorative Justice and how you can take part;

- Make a complaint if you do not receive the information and services you are entitled to, and receive a full response from the relevant service provider.

The 2005, 2013 and 2015 versions of the Victims' Code have all highlighted the availability of restorative justice to victims of crime. In contrast, the two incarnations of the Witness Charter have not mentioned restorative justice. Although restorative justice is notoriously difficult to define, it can be seen as a process of dialogue between victim and offender in which the victim describes their feelings about the crime and the harm caused as a result and, from this, they both develop a plan to repair the harm done. A commonly used phrase by advocates of restorative justice is, unlike other criminal justice mechanisms, it 'gives victims a voice'. It is a process that is increasingly used within the Criminal Justice System in England and Wales. As the 2015 Victims' Code outlines, all victims are entitled to receive information on restorative justice and it is potentially available to all victims of crime at all stages of the criminal justice process, although there are local differences in service provision. While it is technically available for all victims, there is controversy around its use for certain offences including domestic violence, sexual assault and hate crime (Cuneen, 2010).

Despite progressive moves such as the introduction of restorative justice, it would seem that victims and witnesses of crime in England and Wales continue to occupy a position defined by their perceived need rather than by any notion of rights (Goodey, 2005; Rock, 2014). Significantly, the various incarnations of the Witness Charter and the Victims' Code cement procedural justice. They give neither witnesses nor victims 'enforceable rights, but merely permit them to complain if the service obligations are not met' (Wolhuter et al., 2009: 5). Thus, in bringing this section on evolving support and assistance for victims and witnesses of crime to a close we return to the concept of procedural justice to summarise how the provisions that have emerged over the last 20 to 30 years or so might be interpreted from a victim/witness perspective. The rhetoric and language of 'entitlements', the concerns with giving victims a voice and treating victims and witnesses with respect and dignity would seem to amount to what Elliott and colleagues (2014: 590) term the 'relational criteria' of procedural justice, that is:

> politeness, concern for rights, treatment with dignity and respect, expression and consideration of views, neutrality of decision-making process, addressing needs and concerns, doing the right thing by the victim, explanation of reasons for police actions, and police trustworthiness.

Such justice is not rights-based justice as such but one conceived in terms of a more limited *procedural* fairness.

Experiencing the Criminal Justice System

With the developments above in mind, how do victims and witnesses experience the Criminal Justice System in England and Wales? There is no homogenous experience. Every victim and witness is different as are their interactions and perceptions of the Criminal Justice System. That being said, both the Victims' Code and Witness Charter highlight a typical 'journey' through the Criminal Justice System in an attempt to provide clarity to victims and witnesses. The Victims' Code (Ministry of Justice, 2015) suggests there are five stages that victims will encounter if their case goes to court: reporting the crime; police investigation; charge and pre-trial hearings; trial; and after the trial. In a similar fashion, the Witness Charter (Ministry of Justice, 2013a) is structured according to a journey a witness might take through the Criminal Justice System, focusing on the police investigation, pre-trial arrangements, arriving at courtroom, speaking in court, and post-trial. Both documents represent these in flow chart form. There are multiple routes on both charts – the victim's flow chart, for instance, has a number of 'exit points' for victims while the witness's flow chart begins to take two possible paths depending on whether the witness is required to give evidence in court or not. The text of the Witness Charter and the Victims' Code also reveal that the journeys through the Criminal Justice System are not uniform as particular groups – such as Vulnerable and Intimidated Witnesses in the Witness Charter – have special entitlements at different points in their journey.

At this point, it is worth exploring three issues that affect the journeys of many victims and witnesses through the Criminal Justice System that are often overlooked in discussions of victims and witnesses. They are the processes of attrition and secondary victimisation and the provision of services by voluntary organisations.

Attrition

Attrition in criminal justice refers to the 'drop out' of cases. In rape cases attrition is stubbornly problematic (Daly and Bouhours, 2010). Hester (2013) notes that rape cases can drop out at any one of three stages: at police involvement and investigation, during CPS involvement, or at court. Her recent research into rape cases and the Criminal Justice System in the North East of England found that three quarters of the cases dropped out at the police stage with many of these involving very vulnerable victims such as those with extensive mental health problems (Hester,

2013). Measures to protect rape victims in court (who fall into the 'vulnerable victim' category) seem to be having little impact on the attrition rate for rape victims. Perceptions of the 'credible' ideal victim on the one hand and 'non-credible' culpable victims who 'precipitated' their rape on the other appear firmly entrenched. Special measures have yet to impact on the attrition rate and 'victim blaming' attitudes continue to thrive in the Criminal Justice System in England Wales.

Secondary Victimisation

Secondary victimisation refers to the further harm caused to victims of crime as a direct result of their participation in the Criminal Justice System. It is often emotional or psychological, and is not necessarily a deliberate act. As noted by Wolhuter et al. (2009: 47), it can take a number of forms:

> Insensitive questioning by the police, the failure to communicate information about what is happening in the victim's case, delays, unexplained decisions by the prosecution to drop a case ... and aggressive cross-examination in the court process have been recognised as causing the victim further suffering which amounts to secondary victimisation.

Secondary victimisation is related to, and indeed a form of, repeat victimisation in which individuals suffer more than one incident of victimisation. On the one hand, it is clear that the Witness Charter and the Victims' Code try to encourage practices by criminal justice practitioners and agencies that limit secondary victimisation for victim-witnesses, even if they do not use the phrase secondary victimisation. On the other hand, scholars have argued that there are systematic faults with the Criminal Justice System that create the conditions for secondary victimisation to take place. Wolhuter et al. (2009), for example, point to two systemic problems. The first is the 'institutional culture' of criminal justice agencies that combine a 'crime-control focus on "catching criminals" or obtaining convictions' with some prejudices and stereotypes towards marginalised groups in society, meaning that the needs of victims and witnesses are sidelined, especially those from certain parts of society (ibid.: 48). The second is the common law adversarial system that repositions the victim as a witness and views the crime as a crime against the state rather than against the victim. This system uses the principle of orality whereby all evidence must be produced in court and it must be orally introduced (Goodey, 2005). Under this system, the courtroom can be particularly difficult for victims and witnesses:

> During the trial itself the English adversarial process involves a contest between the prosecution and the defence in which cross-examination is the primary weapon. Defence counsel resort to tactics under cross-examination designed to undermine the prosecution or attack the credibility of the witness. This experience of cross-examination has been regarded as one of the more traumatic forms of secondary victimisation, particularly in rape trials. (Wolhuter et al., 2009: 48)

The example of cross-examination in Chapter 14 illustrates this point further.

Taking the example of rape, victims and witnesses are often known to one another and their status as victim/witness/perpetrator becomes indistinct and blurred to bystanders, potential witnesses, magistrates, jury and judge in a court of law rendering victimhood difficult to prove. Often the victim is also the sole witness. Scholars have highlighted how defence lawyers in the adversarial system use aggressive questioning in order to expose 'untruths' in a victim's testimony, and often call into question the victim's lack of consent to sex by reference to past sexual behaviours (Lees, 1997; see also Rock, 1991). In England and Wales, the witness is entitled to be treated with dignity and respect under the Victims' Code and the Witness Charter, but the system also acknowledges the rights of the defendant to a fair trial. This is sometimes represented as a balancing act between the rights of the victim and those of the accused (Goodey, 2005). In these scenarios victims may fail to meet the ideal victim criteria and risk being discredited as non-credible witnesses and undeserving victims. The common law adversarial approach to criminal justice has tended to adopt the 'ideal victim' and a similarly 'ideal witness' approach to testimony in court.

Service Provision by the Voluntary Sector

As part of a wider shift in *what* services are provided for victims and witnesses and *who* delivers these services in England and Wales, recent decades have witnessed a range of voluntary organisations becoming increasingly involved in the provision of services and support for victims and witnesses of crime (Williams and Goodman, 2007). Organisations such as Victim Support, Childline and Rape Crisis, among many others, have become important bodies in this, operating not-for-profit, staffed predominately with volunteers and with varying degrees of support and funding from state bodies. In the case study box below, we will explore the work of victim support and how it has changed over the years.

Case Study: Victim Support

Victim Support was initially set up in Bristol in 1974 and by the early 1980s it had become an extensive network of local schemes across England and Wales with a central headquarters in London (Simmonds, 2013). Reacting against a void in dedicated victim services, Victim Support focused their energies on using volunteers to visit victims of crime. 'Their role', as Simmonds (2013: 203) notes, 'was to offer emotional support and practical assistance within a few days of the crime occurring – in other words they provided an outreach service offering crisis intervention.'

Though a charity, Victim Support is primarily funded through government grants. In the financial year 2013/14 its income was £50.2 million of which £39.4 million was from the Ministry of Justice (Victim Support, 2014). It was in 1987 under the Conservative administration that significant funding for Victim Support was forthcoming from the government, reflecting their ease with both the politically neutral stance of Victim Support (compared to the critical stance of other charities such as Rape Crisis) as well as their shared belief in creating 'active citizens' who help each other (Mawby and Walklate, 1994; Wolhuter et al., 2009).

Four significant changes have taken place within Victim Support. The first is the shift away from the focus on victims of burglaries in the early stages – due in part to the police's reluctance to refer more serious crimes to a volunteer-dominated organisation (Simmonds, 2013) – to 2014 where approximately 1,110 staff and 3,000 volunteers delivered a range of services to victims and witnesses of all types of crime (www.victimsupport.org.uk). With regards to victim services, empha-sis has remained on providing emotional support and practical help for victims of crime, irrespective of their age or whether the crime has been reported or not. They continue to provide 'the sticking plaster for many victims in the aftermath of crime' (Goodey, 2005: 104). Victim Support's (2014) annual report, for instance, notes that they gave practical and emotional help to 152,726 victims and took part in 59,927 face-to-face meetings with victims between April 2013 and March 2014.

A second key change was the incorporation of services for witnesses of crime. Between 1989 and 2015 Victim Support delivered a Witness Service, piloted first in selected Crown Courts then extended to all criminal courts in England and Wales by 2003. It provided emotional support and practical help for prosecution and defence witnesses as well as their family and friends (Wolhuter et al., 2009), with the aim of making the experience of being in court less daunting and confusing. As part of this, they arranged pre-trial courtroom tours, supported witnesses during the trial, and provided witnesses with private waiting areas in court. The third change is the increased politicisa-tion of Victim Support. From the mid 1990s onwards they have been vocal in advocating changes to the current provisions for victims and witnesses of crime (Wolhuter et al., 2009: 146–8).

The fourth change is more recent and involves changes to the awarding of government grants for services for victims and witnesses of crime that have had significant repercussions for Victim Support. The recently introduced Police and Crime Commissioners (PCCs) were given the responsibility for awarding contracts for services for victims of crime (with an empha-sis here on services being both decided locally and economically competitive). In 2014, Victim Support had to bid against other tenders to be awarded the contracts. As a result, most PCCs have awarded Victim Support with a contract to provide core witness services (e.g. in Surrey and Lancashire) with some awarding contracts to other organisations (e.g. in Staffordshire to a partnership led by Citizens Advice). In Northumbria the grant allocation was awarded to an agency created by the PCC Vera Baird QC – 'Victims First'. In 2014, the contract for the Witness Service was also put out to tender by the Ministry of Justice and unlike victims' services this was not divided up into local contracts. Victim Support bid against, and lost to, Citizens Advice for this contract. As of April 2015, Citizens Advice is now running the Witness Service. In sum-mary, voluntary organisations have played an increasingly important role in delivering services for victims and witnesses, but as we can see with the example of Victim Support their services, funding and relationship with government is subject to change.

Summary

There have been a number of positive developments within the English and Welsh Criminal Justice System regarding victims and witnesses of crime. Yet as we have discussed in this chapter there remain a number of deep-rooted problems, most notice-ably the prevalence of secondary victimisation and high attrition rates. We have argued that these issues have not been addressed adequately and the changes made to the Criminal Justice System are somewhat cosmetic, the result of politicians' attempts to please the voting public or trying to cut costs – rather than to make real improvements to the way victims are treated. Measures that are introduced without due regard to the wants and needs of victims and witnesses can have unintended but harmful conse-quences where they are victimised by the system itself. The developments pioneered

(Continued)

(Continued)

by senior politicians arguably take the form of procedural justice for victims and witnesses of crime where politeness, dignity, respect and explanatory communication are all that victims and witnesses can expect.

Finally, the question of entitlement or 'right' to support remains controversial. Governmental attention to victims and witnesses has seen them chartered, codified, politicised and homogenised. Establishing what the needs of victims and witnesses are and matching these needs with effective support is difficult enough. It is perhaps even harder without legal rights (Davies, 2015). At the time of writing there is a proposed new Victims' Law. Readers are encouraged to think about whose interests are being served in this endeavour as the shape and content of this legislation is consulted about, debated and formulated.

Discussion Questions

1. Beyond their rhetoric of bringing victims to the 'centre' or 'heart' of the Criminal Justice System, have policy makers in England and Wales done enough to meet the needs of victims and witnesses of crime?

2. Discuss the following statement: Victims' primary role in the modern Criminal Justice System in England and Wales is to act as 'evidentiary cannon fodder' (Braithwaite and Daly, 1998: 154).

3. Why has the development of services and support for witnesses seemingly lagged behind those for victims in England and Wales?

Further Reading

Academic reading for this topic tends to be split into those on victims and those on witnesses. Three particularly useful books on victims, victimology and the Criminal Justice System are highly recommended:

Davies, P., Francis, P. and Greer, C. (2017) (eds) *Victims, Crime and Society: An introduction*. 2nd edn. London: Sage.
Walklate, S.L. (2017) (ed.) *Handbook of Victims and Victimology*. London: Routledge.
Wolhuter, L., Olley, N. and Denham, D. (2009) *Victimology: Victimisation and victims' rights*. London: Routledge-Cavendish.

There is comparatively less literature on witnesses and the Criminal Justice System. Paul Rock, however, provides a compelling account of the position of witnesses in the courtroom:

Rock, P. (1991) 'Witnesses and space in a Crown Court', *British Journal of Criminology*, 31 (3): 266–79.

Nick Fyfe also provides a fascinating analysis of the experiences of intimidated witnesses and the measures designed to reduce their vulnerability:

Fyfe, N. (2005) 'Space, time and the vulnerable witness: Exploring the tensions between policy and personal perspectives on witness intimidation', *Population, Space and Place*, 11 (6): 513–23.

References

Braithwaite, J. and Daly, K. (1998) 'Masculinities, violence, and communitarian control', in S.L. Miller (ed.), *Crime Control and Women: Feminist implications of criminal justice policy*. Newbury Park, CA: Sage. pp. 151–72.

Cole, A. (2007) *The Cult of True Victimhood*. Stanford, CA: Stanford University Press.

Christie, N. (1986) 'The ideal victim', in E.A. Fattah (ed.), *From Crime Policy to Victim Policy*. London: Macmillan. pp. 17–30.

Cuneen, C. (2010) 'The limitations of restorative justice', in C. Cuneen and C. Hoyle (eds), *Debating Restorative Justice*. Oxford: Hart. pp. 101–31.

Daly, K. and Bouhours, B. (2010) 'Rape and attrition in the legal process: A comparative analysis of five countries', *Crime and Justice*, 39: 565–650.

Davies, P. (2011) *Gender, Crime and Victimisation*. London: Sage.

Davies, P. (2015) 'Victims: Continuing to carry the burden of justice', *British Society of Criminology Newsletter*, 76: 16–17.

Elliot, I., Thomas, S. and Ogloff, J. (2014) 'Procedural justice in victim–police interactions and victims' recovery from victimisation experiences', *Policing and Society*, 24 (5): 588–601.

Fyfe, N. (2005) 'Space, time and the vulnerable witness: Exploring the tensions between policy and personal perspectives on witness intimidation', *Population, Space and Place*, 11 (6): 513–23.

Goodey, J. (2005) *Victims and Victimology: Research, policy and practice*. Harlow: Pearson.

Greer, C. (2007) 'News media, victims and crime', in P. Davies, P. Francis and C. Greer (eds), *Victims, Crime and Society*. London: Sage. pp. 20–49.

Hester, M. (2013) *From Report to Court: Rape cases and the Criminal Justice System in the North East Executive Summary*. Bristol: University of Bristol in association with the Northern Rock Foundation.

Home Office (1990) *The Victims' Charter: A statement of the rights for victims of crime*. London: Home Office.

Home Office (1996) *Victims' Charter: A statement of service standards for victims of crime*. London: Home Office.

Home Office (2005) *Hearing the Relatives of Murder and Manslaughter Victims: Consultation*. London: Home Office.

Kearon, T. and Godfrey, B.S. (2007) 'Setting the scene: a question of history,' in S. Walklate (ed.), *Handbook of Victims and Victimology*. Cullompton: Willan. pp. 17–36.

Lees, S. (1997) *Ruling Passions: Sexual violence, reputation and the law*. Buckingham: Open University Press.

London Rape Crisis Centre (1984) *Sexual Violence: The reality for women*. London: London Rape Crisis Centre.

Mawby, R. and Walklate, S.L. (1994) *Critical Victimology*. London: Sage.

Meyer, S. (2016) 'Still blaming the victim of intimate partner violence? Women's narratives of victim desistance and redemption when seeking support', *Theoretical Criminology*, 20 (1): 175–90.

Ministry of Justice (2011) *Achieving Best Evidence in Criminal Proceedings: Guidance on interviewing victims and witnesses, and guidance on using special measures.* London: Ministry of Justice.

Ministry of Justice (2013a) *Code of Practice for Victims of Crime.* London: Ministry of Justice.

Ministry of Justice (2013b) *The Witness Charter: Standards of care for witnesses in the criminal justice system.* London: Ministry of Justice.

Ministry of Justice (2015) *Code of Practice for Victims of Crime.* London: Ministry of Justice.

Office for Criminal Justice Reform (2005) *The Code of Practice for Victims of Crime.* London: Office of Criminal Justice Reform.

Office for Criminal Justice Reform (2007) *The Witness Charter: Our promise to you.* London: Office of Criminal Justice Reform.

Rock, P. (1991) 'Witnesses and space in a Crown Court', *British Journal of Criminology*, 31 (3): 266–79.

Rock, P. (2002) 'On becoming a victim', in C. Hoyle and R. Young (eds), *New Visions of Crime Victims*. Oxford: Hart Publishing. pp. 1–22.

Rock, P. (2007) 'Theoretical perspectives on victimisation', in S. Walklate (ed.), *Handbook of Victims and Victimology*. Cullompton: Willan. pp. 37–61.

Rock, P. (2014) 'Victims' rights', in I. Vanfraechem, A. Pemberton and F. Mukwiza Ndahinda (eds), *Justice for Victims: Perspectives on rights, transition and reconciliation*. Abingdon: Routledge. pp. 11–31.

Sebba, L. (2001) 'On the relationship between criminological research and policy: The case of crime victims', *Criminal Justice*, 1 (1): 27–58.

Simmonds, L. (2013) 'Lost in transition? The changing face of victim support', *International Review of Victimology*, 19 (2): 201–17.

Stanko, E. (1990) 'When precaution is normal: A feminist critique of crime prevention', in L. Gelsthorpe and A. Morris (eds), *Feminist Perspectives in Criminology*. Milton Keynes: Open University Press. pp. 171–83.

Victim Support (2010) *Victims' Justice? What victims and witnesses really want from sentencing.* London: Victim Support.

Victim Support (2014) *Trustees' Annual Report 2013/14*. London: Victim Support.

Walklate, S.L. (2007) *Imagining the Victims of Crime*. Maidenhead: Open University Press.

Williams, B. and Goodman, H. (2007) 'The role of the voluntary sector', in S. Walklate (ed.), *Handbook of Victims and Victimology*. Cullompton: Willan. pp. 240–55.

Wolhuter, L., Olley, N. and Denham, D. (2009) *Victimology: Victimisation and victims' rights*. London: Routledge-Cavendish.

Check out the Companion Website

Want to know more about this chapter? Review what you have been learning by visiting: **https://study.sagepub.com/harding**

- Practice with essay questions
- Test yourself with multiple-choice questions
- Listen to a series of podcasts featuring Neil of Northumbria Police and London's Metropolitan Police Service
- Watch videos selected from the SAGE Video collection

Part Three

Key Issues in Criminal Justice

Pamela Davies, George Mair, Jamie Harding

As noted in Part One, the criminal justice process does not exist in a vacuum and in that part of the book we provided a context for criminal justice that is specific to England and Wales. In this, the third and final part of the book, a different yet increasingly significant context for criminal justice is contemplated. We have called this part of the book *Key Issues in Criminal Justice*. This concluding part comprises of three chapters. We do not claim that the key issues we have selected are comprehensive in terms of issues that have impacted upon, or are likely to impact upon, criminal justice in the future. Indeed, many of these 'key issues' are precisely what all the contributors have been asked to write substantive chapters on. We have chosen to focus on what we feel are, overall, the most pertinent with respect to criminal justice in the present and into the future. Each of these contributions is important for students of criminal justice and criminology to consider in their own right.

Part Three opens with Chapter 21 where Mike Rowe considers the all-important question: Does the criminal justice process work? This chapter necessitates a discussion of how best to understand the concept of 'effectiveness' and the various ways in which this can be measured and assessed. Thus the first task the author tackles is to clarify the benchmark against which any judgement can be made about effectiveness. The chapter then goes on to consider each component part of the criminal justice process in turn, analysed according to the key question of the effectiveness of current operations. In the final part of the chapter a broader review examines social, economic, political and cultural factors that shape the wider context in which criminal justice operates.

Globalisation and international criminal justice is the focus of Chapter 22 where Matthew Hall explores globalisation and its impact over recent years on both policy and practice in criminal justice across multiple jurisdictions. His discussion outlines the broad contours of interconnected processes occurring at the global level and he emphasises how the English and Welsh criminal justice process has been heavily influenced in its operation by such global processes, as has the approach to crime and justice policy adopted by the succession of governments responsible for it. In this chapter, the author illustrates how international influences are most overtly felt through the work of transnational organisations like the European Union and the United Nations – as well as the operation of institutions like the International Criminal Court and the European Court of Justice. However, he also shows how the more profound influences are in fact less overt: constituting macro-legal, -social, -political and -economic trends. The chapter outlines what is meant by 'globalisation' and highlights the indeterminate nature of the concept. It discusses some of the key features of globalisation as it relates to the operation of criminal justice both in England and Wales and further afield. Moreover, Hall demonstrates how, in recent years, these processes appear to have driven criminal justice towards an increasingly law and order orientated, punitive ideology. An aspect of this process is the rechristening of traditional social problems as threats to security. Four key features of globalisation are focused upon: crime control, popular punitiveness and international terrorism; securitisation and risk management; victimisation; and human rights.

Reading this part of the book should provide a clear understanding of how what works in matters of criminal justice is a problematic and often controversial methodological and research issue. This is also complicated by historical, sociological and shifting paradigmatic and theoretical positions about the purpose and aims of a justice system and process. The reader will also be sensitised to the global and international dimensions to the governance of crime and justice as we stride towards the third decade of the twenty-first century. As editors of the book we have authored the 'Introduction' and the shorter introductions to the three 'Parts' of the book: Part One *The Criminal Justice Process in Context*, Part Two *The Criminal Justice Process* and Part Three *Key Issues in Criminal Justice*.

We are also the authors of Chapter 23, the final chapter of the book entitled Criminal Justice Futures. In this concluding chapter we have speculated about a number of what we see as the main macro- and meso-level issues that will – probably – go to shape criminal justice in the next 5–10 years. Our thinking on these issues is entirely grounded in what has been examined in the preceding chapters of the volume. We are guided also by the historical timeline as presented in Chapter 1, and discussed more fully in Chapter 2, in terms of historical trajectories that are likely to inform the future of crime control and criminal justice more broadly. While we note that the predictive power of criminology has been weak in the past, we are confident that discussion of these issues will provide plenty of food for thought as criminal justice continues to develop, for better or worse, in the future.

Check out the Companion Website

Want to know more about this chapter? Review what you have been learning by visiting: **https://study.sagepub.com/harding**

- Practice with essay questions
- Test yourself with multiple-choice questions
- Listen to a series of podcasts featuring Neil of Northumbria Police and London's Metropolitan Police Service
- Watch videos selected from the SAGE Video collection

21   Does the Criminal Justice Process Work?

Mike Rowe

Introduction

Directly or indirectly citizens are made aware of the inadequacies of the criminal justice process on a daily basis. Either as victims, witnesses or offenders we might experience crimes that go undetected or do not end in a conviction. The media frequently report cases in which the court system is held to have failed to deliver justice: either through passing sentences perceived to be unduly lenient or through prosecuting cases that should not properly have been the business of the police or the courts. In June 2015, for example, the British media reported the case of a motorist prosecuted and fined for driving in the middle lane of the motorway; one example of a wider tendency of the media to downplay the significance of driving offences (Corbett, 2000). Such cases are often contrasted with examples of 'real' offenders being given 'soft' community sentences, or restorative justice orders regarded by many media commentators as lacking in deterrent or retributive capacity. A key narrative of 'popular punitiveness' is that the Criminal Justice System has become ineffective, overly bureaucratic, and inappropriately prioritises the rights of offenders above the claims of victims and the public at large (Pratt, 2007). Such questions are explored throughout the rest of this chapter. Following this introduction is a discussion of how best to understand the concept of 'effectiveness' and the various ways in which this can be measured and assessed. After that, each component part of the criminal justice process is addressed in turn to consider key questions relating to the effectiveness of current operations. In the final part of the chapter a broader review examines social, economic, political and cultural factors that shape the wider context in which criminal justice operates.

What Makes Criminal Justice 'Effective'?

Individual instances of the criminal justice process failing to result in a just or appropriate outcome do not, in and of themselves, demonstrate that the process does not work in wider terms. The size, scale and scope of the criminal justice process mean that there will be outcomes that appear not to 'work' in various ways. The business of criminal justice (more of which below) is huge in terms of volume. In 2014 there were 127,000 police officers in England and Wales, who implement approximately 1,000,000 arrests each year (Home Office, 2015). Some of these arrests result in defendants appearing before a magistrates' court; in the first quarter of 2015 the 240 magistrates' courts in England and Wales received 403,000 cases. The 80 Crown Courts in England and Wales received more than 33,000 cases during the same period (Ministry of Justice, 2015a). A proportion of these cases resulted in prison sentences: the population of prisons in England and Wales has tended to rise over recent decades. As of June 2015 the prison population was 86,028. The National Offender Management Service (NOMS) employed 32,560 staff in prisons and 8,730 staff in the probation service (Ministry of Justice, 2015b). Unsurprisingly this volume of criminal justice work requires significant public spending. A study by the Centre for Crime and Justice Studies found that 'public order and safety' spending (a category including police, courts, prisons, offender programmes and immigration) totalled £32.3 billion in 2011/12, a reduction from a peak of £36 billion in 2009/10 (Garside and Silvestri, 2013).

The cost, scale and size of the Criminal Justice System are considerable but the number of arrests, court cases, and custodial sentences passed each year might be regarded as insubstantial in the face of the volume of crime committed. Police services in England and Wales recorded more than 3.8 million offences in the year to 31 March 2015 (an increase of 3 per cent on the previous year, but a reduction of 32 per cent on the figure a decade earlier) (Office of National Statistics [ONS], 2015a). A broader measure of crime, the Crime Survey for England and Wales, calculated from household surveys rather than police-recorded offences, found the number of offences to be nearly 6.8 million (a reduction of 7 per cent from the previous year and a reduction of 36 per cent from a decade earlier) (ONS 2015a); these statistics are discussed further in Chapter 3.

In the face of this volume of activity establishing whether the Criminal Justice System is effective is not an easy task. It requires addressing some preliminary questions. First, the word 'effective' has to be considered. Clearly no human organisation is likely to be wholly effective, operating perfectly without error. A lower standard has to apply, therefore, but at what point it is established that the Criminal Justice System is 'good enough' to be considered effective inevitably is a somewhat subjective decision. Perhaps a comparative analysis might help reach a judgement, such that the Criminal Justice System of England and Wales is considered effective, or otherwise, in relation to arrangements operating in similar late-modern, western liberal democracies. Similar comparison might be made with earlier periods in the same society so that consideration of current effectiveness is made in relation to preceding times. Some of these measures will be used in the discussion below. As well as deciding what should be the acceptable threshold of effectiveness – 'better than before', 'worse than in other societies', and so on – the discussion below reflects on different dimensions inherent in the question. As is considered in other contributions to this collection, there is a fundamental question of whether the broad amalgamation of agencies involved in the delivery of criminal justice can be considered a 'system' in any meaningful sense. In this chapter the Criminal Justice System is considered in terms of how individual offenders, victims or witnesses experience it and so the processes that engage them are those that inform judgements about effectiveness. Certainly, the research and policy literature, and political and media debate, routinely demonstrate a lack of effective communication, unhelpful rivalry, and fundamental tension between police, courts, prosecutors, offender managers and so forth. Frequent complaints include that there is a lack of 'joined-up' thinking or 'silo mentalities' such that agencies maximise their perceived self-interest above those of the broader sector. These concerns have underpinned much policy reform in criminal justice during recent decades. The promotion of multi-agency working was a hallmark of New Labour criminal justice policy in the late 1990s (Hughes, 2007), and more recently the promotion of 'total place' or 'community budgeting' approaches have sought to encourage greater collaboration between local agencies (Joyce, 2006). Despite extended efforts, a common finding of research into multi-agency working in criminal justice is that competition, rivalry, and poor communication characterise many instances of apparent collaboration, despite the examples of success noted in Chapter 12. In that context, to talk of a criminal justice 'system' ascribes too much coordination and intelligent design to a confused, complex and multi-layered set of relationships. For the purposes of the discussion that follows, it is assumed that it is feasible to consider the Criminal Justice System although it is acknowledged that in organisational and structural terms it is likely that the dysfunctionality of inter-agency operation might be an important obstacle to effective service delivery.

The central theme of the discussion also requires consideration of the purposes of the Criminal Justice System, a question that has already been considered in Chapter 4. It needs to be established not just how effectiveness can be measured but also what are the primary outcomes: what is the Criminal Justice System for?

An immediate answer might be that it is to enforce the law and to administer justice, but such a response raises a range of sub-questions. Recent debates relating to the development of a more effective police service, capable of responding to increasing and developing public demand in a period of reduced resources, have often focused on defining the mandate of the service. Since the early 19th century this has generally been expressed in terms of preventing and detecting crime and preserving public tranquillity (Emsley, 1996). In practice it is widely understood that only a minority of police-officer time is spent directly responding to victims, investigating offences or pursuing criminals. Added to this is a wide programme of crime prevention work that can extend from providing architectural advice to town planners to drug education among young people or distributing security hardware to vulnerable groups. All of that might fall within the remit of crime prevention and detection but to those tasks must be added a plethora of activity including traffic patrol, assisting other emergency services, communicating information to insurance companies, crowd control, ceremonial duties, surveillance, and responding to neighbourhood incivilities and disputes. The breadth of the police role was identified by Egon Bittner who argued that perhaps the only core characteristic was that they were tasks that no other agency could be expected to provide. He expressed the view that 'no human problem exists, or is imaginable, about which it could be said with finality that this certainly could not become the proper business of the police' (Bittner, 1974: 30). The breadth, complexity and open-ended nature of the police mandate suggests that determining if they are effective is a far from easy task.

Similar problems apply to the prosecution and court systems. The administration of justice is beset with competing demands and tensions between the legitimate claims of victims, witnesses, offenders and wider society. Although successive governments (at least as far back as John Major's administration, which published the Victims Charter in the early 1990s) have pledged to put victims of crime at the heart of the Criminal Justice System, in practice the fundamental adversarial court system means that interests of victims are weighed in the balance with the rights of offenders and the 'public interest' more widely. For this reason, assessing whether prosecution and court systems 'work' requires consideration of which interests the agencies should be pursuing. The prosecution of offenders might work in terms of meeting the broad requirements of the law and established policy but not be seen to work in the interests of offenders, who might claim at an individual level that no prosecution 'works' to their advantage. Equally, courts could conceivably pass sentences that satisfy victims but are considered draconian in terms of established legal and social norms.

In the section below the three broad component parts of the Criminal Justice System are reviewed in more detail to consider their effectiveness. While the preceding review of the various mandates of the component parts of the system need to be kept in mind, the discussion below is based around whether the police, prosecution and courts, and the prison and probation services work effectively in terms of delivering the core activities each is tasked with. Towards the end of this chapter the focus turns to an increasingly important facet of the core question by considering developing ways in which the private sector delivers criminal justice in England and Wales and the extent to which this 'works' in business terms.

Police

As has been outlined above the mandate of the police is broad, even to the extent that some have argued it is almost without limit. This is a significant challenge, but the discussion below focuses on the narrower question of whether policing is effective in terms of the part of the police role that is concerned with the prevention and detection of crime. One measure of police effectiveness might be the level of recorded offences. Table 21.1 indicates that across many categories the number of crimes recorded by the police in England and Wales has declined in recent years, a trend that continues a crime reduction that goes back to the mid 1990s (Tonry, 2014). There has been a reduction in all crime from 68.9 per 1,000 of the population in 2011 to 60.8 per 1,000 in 2014. Most other acquisitive crimes listed in the table have also reduced over the same time period: vehicle offences have dropped from 7.5 to 6.3 per 1,000 of population, for example. Some other categories have increased: notably sexual offences and violence against the person.

Table 21.1 Crime per 1,000 population, 2014 and 2011, by selected crime type

Crime type[1]	2014[2]	2011[2]
All crimes	60.8	68.9
Victim-based crime	54.0	61.0
Violence against the person	12.2	11.1
Homicide	0.0089	0.0107
Sexual offences	1.3	0.9
Robbery	0.9	1.4
Theft	30.9	36.2
Vehicle offences	6.3	7.5
Shoplifting	5.6	5.3
Drug offences	3.2	4.0

[1] per 1,000 population;   [2] 12 months to September

Source: HMIC (undated)

On face value, if the role of the police is to reduce crime, it seems that this data indicates some success, but in practice recorded crime figures such as this are a hugely problematic measure of police performance. As many have argued (see for example Reiner (2007) for a summary), incidents of crime have to negotiate a series of hurdles before they come to be recorded by the police. On some occasions police might record more incidents of a crime as a result of policy or other changes that make such offences more likely to be reported in the first instance and may also make it more likely that officers will record them. Furthermore it might be that wider social changes influence the extent to which crimes are reported to and recorded by the police. One of the challenges police services have faced in recent years is an increase in reports of historical sex offences, some of which seem likely to have followed in the wake of high-profile cases and widespread media attention these have attracted. An increase in such reports might well help explain the rise in the number of sexual offences evident in Table 21.1 but it would make little sense to suggest that this reflects a failure on the part of the police. Indeed, for many forms of crime that have traditionally been under-reported and under-recorded by the police, for example, domestic violence and hate crimes, an increase in reporting is often seen as a positive indicator in that it suggests greater trust in the police on the part of victims.

If recorded offences are a problematic guide to police effectiveness – since they do not reflect overall crime patterns in a reliable way – then an alternative measure might be detection rates: the proportion of offences that are 'cleared up' by the police, either resulting in a sanction (which includes a criminal conviction, or some other formal sanction from the Criminal Justice System) or a non-sanction (for example, in cases where the identified offender has died). Detection rates vary considerably depending upon the offence type, as Table 21.2 demonstrates.

Table 21.2   Percentage of crimes 'cleared-up', by offence type, 2012–13

Offence type	Percentage cleared-up
Violence against the person	41
Sexual offences	29
Robbery	21
Theft	18
Criminal damage and arson	16
Drug offences	94
Possession of weapons offences	88
Public order offences	62
Miscellaneous crimes against society	69
Total	29

Source: Smith et al. (2013: 25)

In overall terms the clear-up rate of 29 per cent had increased by 0.3 per cent since the previous year and was the highest rate since the national crime recording standard was introduced in 2003. In these terms it might be argued that policing is 'working' better in terms of the threshold discussed earlier in the chapter: that it compares favourably with previous periods. Nonetheless, as Table 21.2 indicates, the rate varies hugely with considerable variation between offence categories. While 94 per cent of drug offences are cleared-up, this outcome is only achieved in

16 per cent of cases of criminal damage and arson. Moreover, while only 41 per cent of recorded cases of violence against the person are cleared-up, the figure for the sub-set of homicide (not shown in this table) was 90 per cent. Similarly, within the theft category, which shows an overall clear-up rate of 18 per cent, only 4 per cent of recorded thefts against the person resulted in a clear-up while the comparable figure for shoplifting was 59 per cent.

One challenge in using clear-up rates as a basis to decide if the police are effective is the more general problem of attrition. Just as it might be argued that changes in recorded crime rates can be explained by a host of wider social, legal and institutional factors that might have little to do with the police service. High clear-up rates for shoplifting and drug offences are likely to reflect that there is a high correlation between reporting and recording and the apprehension of an offender. Unless and until the offender is identified it is unlikely that a crime would be noted or recorded; thus the clear-up rate is relatively high compared to other categories of offence (such as criminal damage) where the distance between offence and offender might be greater.

Another perspective on the effectiveness of police can be gained by considering the extent to which the public are satisfied with police and have confidence in their ability to respond to crime. While public perceptions are inherently a subjective measure, providing visible reassurance to the public has come to be regarded as an important element of the policing mission (Innes, 2004). The Crime Survey for England and Wales found that 63 per cent of respondents in 2013–14 gave a positive rating for local police, a figure broadly comparable with recent years (ONS, 2015b). Ratings of satisfaction appear to vary according to police visibility such that those who perceived the police to be highly visible in their locality were more likely to report high levels of satisfaction, and vice versa. Victims of crime were more positive in terms of satisfaction with the service they had received from the police: with 74 per cent reporting they were 'very' or 'fairly' satisfied. Confidence that the police are effective at catching criminals has increased in recent years: in 2007–8 53 per cent of respondents said the police were 'very' or 'fairly' effective, a proportion that rose to 68 per cent by 2013–14 (ONS, 2015b).

Prosecution and Courts

One element of the prosecuting and court systems that makes judgements about effectiveness difficult is the use of exemplary sentences. In the aftermath of the summer riots of 2011 the capacity of the court system was extended through late-night and weekend sessions such that cases could be heard quickly and the justice system could be seen to be working against the maxim that 'justice delayed is justice denied'. Not only were prosecutions rapid, sentences were sometimes considerably harsher than might have been passed in other circumstances. Lightowlers and Quirk's (2015) analysis of court sentencing in response to the disorders found that there was an apparent increase in the severity of sentences passed but, most significantly, this was only one component of a more general 'uplift' in criminal justice outcomes. Thus, Crown Prosecution Service decisions to prosecute were taken on a lower threshold than usual such that, for example, young people were more likely to be charged than would be the case in other circumstances. Moreover, the nature of the charges laid was more serious and there was greater use of remand into custody than would usually be expected. At many stages, they argued, the Criminal Justice System responded with greater severity in response to the disorders. It could be that exemplary sentences such as these serve to deter other potential offenders and this might be legitimate. Prosecutorial guidelines suggest that more serious charges be applied for some crimes that occur during public disorder, notably that charges of burglary be laid rather than the less serious charge of theft. In other terms, though, Lightowlers and Quirk (2015) argue that the legality of some of the 'uplift' in criminal justice decisions might be questionable.

The effectiveness of exemplary court sentences can be considered from two perspectives. First, is the Kantian formalist position that suggests that the court system, which is mandated to apply laws created through the democratic process, is inherently ineffective in circumstances where those laws are breached. Second, is a consequentialist test of effectiveness that considers the impact of exemplary sentences in preventing further crime or disorder. From this perspective the use of relatively tough sentences is to be evaluated in terms of whether it has a deterrent effect, either specifically in terms of deterring the individual person sentenced from committing further offences or more generally in the sense that the wider community is dissuaded from crime. One difficulty in relation to the wider general deterrent effect is that of the hypothetical counterfactual such that it is not possible to know what the crime trend or rate might have been had the exemplary sentence not been passed. In the context of the 2011 disorders, for example, the impact of sentences on subsequent unrest cannot be measured, and any decline in unrest might be attributable to a whole host of other factors. A significant problem with the general deterrent effect is that any impact of tough sentencing needs to be considered alongside the perceived risk of apprehension. A lengthy prison sentence or hefty fine will not deter an individual who perceives that there is little risk of being apprehended (Ashworth, 2015). Moreover, the general deterrent effect of punishment is tempered also by public knowledge about the severity of punishments, which tends to be variable in terms of accuracy and is influenced by social factors (Apel, 2013). Ashworth (2015: 84) summed up the challenges of understanding the effectives of deterrence in the following terms:

> Deterrence must operate (if at all) through the potential offenders' minds, so it is essential that they know about the severity of the probable sentence, take this into account when deciding whether to offend, believe that there is a non-negligible risk of being caught, believe that the penalty will be applied to them if caught and sentenced, and refrain from offending for these reasons. These subjective beliefs are vital components in the operation of deterrent policies, and all must therefore be *investigated* if research is to be reliable. Few studies satisfy these criteria, and they provide no basis for sentencing policies that simply involve increasing severity in the hope of reducing offending levels.

Prisons and Probation

As with the other component elements of the criminal justice 'system', addressing the extent to which prisons and probation 'works', requires consideration of the functions of these sets of institutions. Two broad areas are considered below: first, the extent to which these services manage offenders in a way that protects public safety, and, second, the extent to which they enable the rehabilitation of offenders.

In very simplistic terms, the prison service is effective in ensuring that prisoners are held securely. The rate at which prisoners escape or abscond while on license is very low. During 2013–14 the average prison population was around 85,300 and over that period one escape from a prison escort and 12 from prison contractors were recorded (Ministry of Justice, 2015c). There were no escapes from prisons themselves. Within prisons, however, research evidence suggests considerable levels of suicide and self-harm, especially among females. Ministry of Justice (2015d) data shows that the suicide rate (self-inflicted deaths per 1,000 in prison population) has risen in recent years to 0.98 in 2014, when 84 prisoners committed suicide. The figure had fallen for several years and the peak since 1978 had been 1999 when the rate was 1.40. (These figures are discussed further in Chapters 5 and 16.) A study of measures to detect and prevent self-harm among prisoners reflected on the difficulties of defining how 'self-harm' might be operationalised and that this makes it difficult to find comparable data between countries and over time (Horton et al., 2014). Nonetheless, the study suggested that over 2011 the incidence of self-harm in prisons is 8 per cent, with a rate of 6.9 per cent for males and 29.4 per cent for females. Large-scale studies suggest that the rate within the overall community is likely to be around 4 per cent. While the rate within prisons is clearly higher, this might reflect the socio-economic, mental health status and demographic profile of prisoners (Horton et al., 2014).

Beyond the fundamental test of keeping prisoners secure a more significant outcome of the prison and probation system is to prevent future offending. Testing effectiveness in these terms is hugely challenging, as the increasing literature around the concept and practice of desistance from crime illustrates (Maruna, 2001). As a measure of effectiveness the output of the probation service suggests that a majority of community orders are completed successfully. Between April and June 2015, 22,424 orders were terminated and 67 per cent of those were either completed or were finished early for 'good progress' (Ministry of Justice, 2015e).

Completing the orders in the sense of coming to the end of a programme of therapy, training, restitution work and so on is a measure of successful throughput but reveals little about the longer term impact on offenders. One of the challenges of establishing that an offender has ceased to commit crime is the timeframe over which desistance is measured. As Maruna (2001) pithily observed it is ultimately only at the point of death that it is possible to state with certainty that an individual has stopped committing crime. As is outlined below, recidivism often is measured in terms of subsequent court conviction, caution, reprimand or warning, which raises the possibility of 'false desistance' such that an offender appears to have stopped committing crime but, in practice, continues offending but without being caught (Carlsson and Sarnecki, 2016). Although the term implies total cessation, desistance is often considered in more nuanced ways such that an offender who commits crime less frequently, or commits less serious offences, might also be regarded as being on a desistance pathway. From that perspective a successful outcome for prisons and probation services might be one where reoffending is more intermittent or crimes are committed with lower scores on the gravity scales used in offender management to track individual behaviour patterns.

In overall terms, the rate of proven reoffending – recidivism – has been relatively stable in England and Wales in recent years. Ministry of Justice (2015f) data shows that 514,000 adult and juvenile offenders were cautioned, received a non-custodial conviction at court or released from custody in 2013 and so became the cohort of ex-offenders at that point. Over the following 12 months (plus a further six months to incorporate any court proceedings) approximately 136,000 committed a proven reoffence. On this basis the proven reoffending rate was 26.5 per cent. There were considerable differences in terms of gender and age:

- Male offenders had a reoffending rate of 28.0%

- Female offenders had a reoffending rate of 19.6%

- 15–17 year olds had a reoffending rate of 37.8%

- Those over 50 had a reoffending rate of 13.1%.

The data also suggests, though, that offence category, length and type of sentence and the number of prior convictions also have a bearing on reoffending:

- Those who committed theft had the highest proven reoffending rate at 42.9%

- Those who committed fraud had the lowest rate at 11.3%

- Those who served sentences of less than 12 months had a reconviction rate of 59.3%

- Those who served more than 12 months had a reconviction rate of 34.7%

- Those who served over 10 years had a reconviction rate of 18.3%

- Those with no other convictions had a reoffending rate of 8.1%

- Those with 11 or more prior convictions had a rate of 47.0%.

Using reoffending rates to test the effectiveness of the prison and probation system requires caution in that the prospects of offender desistance are influenced by a host of factors beyond the remit of the Criminal Justice System. Housing, employment, substance abuse, and social relationships are among the criminogenic risk factors that shape offending and clearly agencies within criminal justice have limited capacity in many of these domains (McNeil et al., 2010). Just as it is important to recognise that medical practitioners might not be able to prevent the recurrence of illness or disease so too that reconviction rates cannot simply be read as evidence of the failure of prisons or offender management agencies.

Analysing the Present: An Efficient Criminal Justice Process?

Much of the analysis and discussion developed above indicates that, first, assessing whether the Criminal Justice System is effective depends largely upon the yardstick against which it is measured. As was noted in the section following the introduction to this chapter, traditional measures tend to be in terms of crimes committed, clear-up rates, the productivity of the court system, reconviction rates and so on. The second general conclusion is that the Criminal Justice System works to the extent that it produces reasonable outcomes and is judged relatively favourably by the public (in England and Wales, at least). The third main theme is that the successes and failures identified in terms of crimes prevented, detected, and prosecuted and the offenders incarcerated and rehabilitated can only loosely be attributed back to the agencies of the Criminal Justice System. The incidence, quality and nature of crime are shaped by demographic, social, biological, cultural, political, architectural, technological (and many other) factors that are only partially, if at all, within the purview of the police, the courts, prisons, or probation services. The challenge of attributing changes in crime to the effectiveness of the criminal justice process is a methodological problem frequently faced by those conducting evaluations. In their celebrated Realist Evaluation model, Pawson and Tilley (1997) suggest that to be convincing any study needs to understand the context in which practice occurs and the outcomes that follow from it. To ensure that the latter are related to the practice itself, and not to some extraneous factor, it is also necessary (they argued) to identify the mechanism by which the practice produced a particular set of outcomes – only once that is done can it be said with confidence that the intervention was responsible for the result.

This task is more pressing in an environment whereby criminal justice policy is influenced increasingly in England and Wales by models of payment by results, as has been the case over the last 15 years or so. Private companies, public sector agencies, and third-sector organisations are contracted to deliver policing, prosecution and courts, prisons and probation on the basis that their funding is determined, at least in part, by demonstrable success in terms of outcomes. An early example of this approach in England and Wales is the project at HMP Peterborough starting in 2010 whereby private finance was used to build the jail, which is run by Sodexo and supported by third-sector organisations providing post-release assistance for prisoners and their families. Part of the arrangement is that funding from the government is based upon achievement of a 7.5 per cent (or greater) reduction in offending (Whitehead, 2015). For these funding arrangements to work it needs to be established that the intervention delivered by, for example, a Community

Rehabilitation Company (CRC), is properly linked to an ex-offender's continuing desistance. As has been noted, a host of extraneous factors might explain desistance and it could be that an impact results from a combination of influences delivered by various agencies as well as wider social networks. Coupled with these influences, offender's own self-identity, reflexivity and personal relations also shape their desistance (Vaughan, 2007; Rowe and Soppitt, 2014). Much of the research work into desistance from crime talks of ex-offenders undertaking a journey from crime to 'lifestyle normalisation', and that the journey is long, meandering and often is characterised by diversions back into harmful or criminal activity (Sampson and Laub, 1993; Maruna, 2001). Given the messy reality and fuzzy boundaries of desistance it becomes extraordinarily difficult to decide which agencies or programmes are credited with delivering change. This is the problem of attribution.

Beyond the important debate about payment by results (PbR) is the underlying shift towards a privatised criminal justice system whereby investment in facilities and the provision of services are contracted to private companies. The question of whether criminal justice 'works' can increasingly be answered in terms of profit-generation. The morality of criminal justice delivered on a for-profit basis has been widely discussed (Reiner, 2007) but the economic basis of policing, prisons and offender management becomes increasingly important in England and Wales. Whether for reasons of austerity or ideology, governments have sought to develop new models whereby public organisations are forced to join with private- and third-sector agencies to deliver services. The Peterborough prison example stands out, but the wider Transforming Rehabilitation (TR) agenda applied to offender management and a number of initiatives relating to policing illustrate the ambition of private corporations (including large multinational corporations) to make criminal justice 'work' as a means of generating profit. Following the government's 2010 Comprehensive Spending Review, two police services (Surrey and West Midlands) announced plans to put all activity out to tender, raising the prospect that core activities such as street patrol and arrest would be run by private contractors. Although these plans were withdrawn, there has been considerable 'outsourcing' of back-office police functions and in some cases the provision of security patrols by private companies (Crawford and Lister, 2006). Crawford (2013) argued that policing is an area identified by private security companies as an opportunity for growth. While the political and symbolic capital, and the authority and legitimacy to which these give rise, are qualities of the public police that the private sector might find difficult to emulate, it is clear that private companies are set to make policing a profit-generating activity.

Similarly, developments around offender management in England and Wales, in the guise of the Transforming Rehabilitation agenda, have opened the way for considerable private-sector involvement. Essentially the management of 'medium-' and 'low-'risk offenders has been made the business of Community Rehabilitation Companies contracted to the Ministry of Justice. Many of those are operated by private companies and critics have argued that they are likely to operate a series of strategies (such as relying on electronic monitoring and cherry-picking low-risk clients) that will reduce costs, and so work from a profit-maximisation perspective but might be less effective in terms of reducing offending in wider terms (Clare, 2015). Critics of US penal policy since the 1980s have argued that the increasing use of incarceration owed more to socio-ideological concerns about a growing underclass and the political imperative of successive administrations towards punitivism (Simon, 2008; Wacquant, 2009). The extent to which criminal justice has expanded in the USA is evident by the extent to which prisons are an important component of local economies. In some states, governments provide fiscal incentives to encourage private companies to locate correctional facilities in their districts as a form of inward investment that will provide employment opportunities for the local population and help sustain the tax base (Williams, 2011). In this way, criminal justice works in broad economic terms, generating profit, creating employment and sustaining secondary services among subcontractors and suppliers.

The Criminal Justice System in England and Wales has not yet been privatised to the extent evident elsewhere. On the horizon, though, is the risk that the pursuit of profit and the ideological imperative towards privatisation and the valorisation of free-market service delivery threaten to transform not just the way that criminal justice operates but also debate about what constitutes an effective system. Returning to the question of whether the Criminal Justice System 'works', and recalling the earlier discussion of the various approaches to understanding what makes for an effective system, there is a danger that a retreat from public social democratic values, and the need to ensure justice and equity, will lead to a scenario in which cost-benefit analysis and the primacy of risk management of crime triumphs. Not only will such a society prove more dangerous and crime-ridden, so too will there be a reduction in the capacity of criminal justice agencies to work in the wider public interest.

Summary

Understanding whether the criminal justice process works requires, first, clarification of the benchmark against which any judgement can be made. Clearly the huge volume of activity surrounding agencies and processes of criminal justice means that some outcomes will occur that are undesirable and there will be occasions when the process does not work according to the norms and regulations that frame criminal justice. The fundamental goals of criminal justice are contested, different interests and priorities apply and this lack of consensus also means that deciding whether the process works remains a matter of subjective interpretation. The chapter moved on to consider how the three broad component parts of the criminal justice process – police; prosecution and courts; prisons and offender management – operate and how effective is their performance.

(Continued)

(Continued)

It was noted that police services have experienced a decrease in recorded crime in recent years, measured as per 1,000 of the population. While this might be indicative of effectiveness, it must be remembered that recorded crime rates are greatly influenced by administrative and other factors which mean that they do not accurately reflect real trends and patterns. An alternative measure is the clear-up rate, which varies considerably across crime type. It might be a measure of effectiveness that the police clear-up 94 per cent of drug offences, for example, but this is off-set by a comparable rate of just 16 per cent in terms of criminal damage and arson. Public satisfaction with the police has been relatively stable in recent years (overall 63 per cent were satisfied with local policing in 2013–14), with higher rates for those who regard the police as highly visible in local communities.

Understanding whether prosecution and courts 'work' is also complex, partly because it is difficult to determine what deterrent impact (if any) sentences have upon offending. The use of exemplary sentences (heavier punishments passed to deter would-be offenders) is often cited as a means of making the courts system more effective but it is not easy to test the extent to which there is any impact of this kind. Moreover, research evidence suggests that the weight of a sentence needs to be considered alongside the perceived risk of apprehension. If individuals are unaware of the length or impact of court sentences it seems illogical to argue that they can influence behaviour.

Prison and offender management might be considered effective against two criteria. First the extent to which offenders are held securely. It has been shown that security is effective in terms of keeping individuals incarcerated but that levels of death and self-harm are cause for concern. The second broad set of criteria relate to recidivism – the extent to which offenders desist from or continue to commit crime. The official measure of reoffending stands at 26.5 per cent (i.e. 26.5 per cent of those completing a sentence are reconvicted within 18 months), a rate which has remained relatively stable. However, this overall rate differs considerably in terms of gender, age, offence type, and the number of previous convictions. This variation underscores wider research findings that show that desistance from crime depends significantly on wider social, economic and cultural factors that are beyond the remit of the criminal justice process. This represents further reason to note that judging the effectiveness of criminal justice is a fraught and complex matter.

The changing landscape of criminal justice in England and Wales is such that private sector companies and practices are increasingly contracted to deliver processes described in this chapter. A key feature of this has been the development of payment by results such that contractors are recompensed on the basis of the extent to which they meet key performance targets. The inherent problem of attributing outcomes to criminal justice interventions reflects a broader conceptual problem of deciding if policing, prosecution and courts, prisons and offender management work effectively.

Discussion Questions

1. Can criminal justice processes be expected to have a strong impact on the nature or extent of crime?

2. Against what criteria should we judge whether criminal justice processes are effective?

3. What impact might privatisation have on consideration of the effectiveness of criminal justice?

Further Reading

Reiner's (2007) *Law and Order: An honest citizen's guide* provides an engaging review of the politics and practice of criminal justice. He critically reviews the processes by which crime figures are collated and the politics of law and order in Britain and the USA.

Carlsson and Sarnecki's (2016) *An Introduction to Life-course Criminology* provides an up-to-date review of international research findings exploring the complex factors that shape the onset, sustenance of and desistance from offending behaviour. The book provides a strong foundation from which to consider the extent that criminal justice agencies can have any input into any stage of a criminal career.

Bittner's classic 1974 article 'Florence Nightingale in pursuit of Willie Sutton: A theory of the police' continues to provide an excellent analysis of the breadth, complexity and contradictory nature of the police role. To determine the extent to which the police are effective it is first necessary to decide what their key task ought to be: this article provides an excellent introduction to that important debate.

Williams's (2011) *The Big House in a Small Town: Prisons, communities and economies in rural America* provides a (sometimes alarming) account of the economic and political impact of private prisons in the USA. Consideration of the extent to which prisons work will increasingly be done from the perspective of multinational corporations that have a different perspective on this question from those rooted in notions of public provision and social justice.

References

Apel, R. (2013) 'Sanctions, perceptions, and crime: Implications for criminal deterrence', *Journal of Quantitative Criminology*, 29: 67–101.

Ashworth, A. (2015) *Sentencing and Criminal Justice*. 6th edn. Cambridge: Cambridge University Press.

Bittner, E. (1974) 'Florence Nightingale in pursuit of Willie Sutton: A theory of the police', in H. Jacob (ed.), *The Potential for Reform of Criminal Justice*. Beverly Hills: Sage Publications. pp. 17–40.

Carlsson, C. and Sarnecki, J. (2016) *An Introduction to Life-Course Criminology*. London: Sage.

Clare, R. (2015) 'Maintaining professional practice: The role of the probation officer in community rehabilitation companies', *Probation Journal*, 62: 49–61.

Corbett, C. (2000) 'The social construction of speeding as not "real" crime', *Crime Prevention and Community Safety – An International Journal*, 2 (4): 33–46.

Crawford, A. (2013) 'The police, policing and the future of the "extended policing family"', in J. Brown (ed.), *The Future of Policing*. London: Routledge.

Crawford, A. and Lister, S. (2006) 'Additional security patrols in residential areas: Notes from the marketplace', *Policing and Society*, 16: 164–88.

Emsley, C. (1996) *The English Police: A political and social history*. London: Longman.

Garside, R. and Silvestri, A. (2013) *UK Justice Policy Review: Volume 2*. London: Centre for Crime and Justice Studies/Hadley Trust.

HMIC (undated) *Crime and Policing Comparator Data*. Available at: www.justiceinspec torates.gov.uk/hmic/crime-and-policing-comparator [accessed 9 December 2015].

Home Office (2015) *Police Workforce, England and Wales, 30 September 2014*. London: Home Office.

Horton, M., Wright, N., Dyer, W., Wright-Hughes, A., Farrin, A., Mohammed, Z., Smith, J., Heyes, T., Gilbody, S. and Tennant, A. (2014) 'Assessing the risk of self-harm in an adult offender population: An incidence cohort study', *Health Technology Assessment*, 18 (64): 1–151.

Hughes, G. (2007) *The Politics of Crime and Community*. London: Palgrave.

Innes, M. (2004) 'Reinventing tradition? Reassurance, neighbourhood security and policing', *Criminal Justice*, 4 (2): 151–71.

Joyce, P. (2006) *Criminal Justice: An introduction to crime and the criminal justice system*. Cullompton: Willan.

Lightowlers, C. and Quirk, H. (2015) 'The 2011 English "riots": Prosecutorial zeal and judicial abandon', *British Journal of Criminology*, 55: 65–85.

Maruna, S. (2001) *Making Good: How ex-convicts reform and rebuild their lives*. Washington: American Psychological Association.

McNeill, F., Raynor, P. and Trotter, C. (eds) (2010) *Offender Supervision: New directions in theory, research and practice*. Cullompton: Willan.

Ministry of Justice (2015a) *Criminal Court Statistics Quarterly, England and Wales, January to March 2015*. London: Ministry of Justice.

Ministry of Justice (2015b) *National Offender Management Service Workforce Statistics Bulletin, 31st March 2015*. London: Ministry of Justice.

Ministry of Justice (2015c) *Prison and Probation Performance Statistics 2014 to 2015*. London: Ministry of Justice.

Ministry of Justice (2015d) *Safety in Custody Quarterly Bulletin: June 2015*. London: Ministry of Justice.

Ministry of Justice (2015e) *Offender Management Statistics Quarterly: April to June 2015*. London: Ministry of Justice.

Ministry of Justice (2015f) *Proven Re-offending Statistics, Quarterly Bulletin, January to December 2013, England and Wales*. London: Ministry of Justice.

Office of National Statistics (2015a) *Crime in England and Wales, Year Ending March 2015*. London: ONS.

Office of National Statistics (2015b) *Chapter 1: Perceptions of the Police*. London: ONS.

Pawson, R. and Tilley, N. (1997) *Realist Evaluation*. London: Sage.

Pratt, J. (2007) *Penal Populism*. London: Routledge.

Reiner, R. (2007) *Law and Order: An honest citizen's guide*. Bristol: Polity Press.

Rowe, M. and Soppitt, S. (2014) '"Who you gonna call?" The role of trust and relationships in desistance from crime', *Probation Journal*, DOI: 10.1177/0264550514548252.

Sampson, R.J. and Laub, J.H. (1993) *Crime in the Making: Pathways and turning points through life*. Cambridge, MA: Harvard University Press.

Simon, J. (2008) *Governing Through Crime: How the war on crime transformed American democracy and created a culture of fear*. New York: Oxford University Press.

Smith, K., Taylor, P. and Elkin, M. (2013) *Crimes Detected in England and Wales 2012/13, Home Office Statistical Bulletin, 02/13*. London: Home Office.

Tonry, M. (2014) 'Why crime rates are falling throughout the western world', *Crime and Justice*, 43: 1–63. Chicago: University of Chicago Press.

Vaughan, B. (2007) 'The internal narrative of desistance', *British Journal of Criminology*, 47: 390–404.

Wacquant, L. (2009) *Prisons of Poverty*. Minneapolis: University of Minnesota Press.

Whitehead, P. (2015) 'Payment by results: The materialist reconstruction of criminal justice', *International Journal of Sociology and Social Policy*, 35: 290–305.

Williams, E. (2011) *The Big House in a Small Town: Prisons, communities and economies in rural America*. Santa Barbara: Praeger.

Check out the Companion Website

Want to know more about this chapter? Review what you have been learning by visiting: **https://study.sagepub.com/harding**

- Practice with essay questions
- Test yourself with multiple-choice questions
- Listen to a series of podcasts featuring Neil of Northumbria Police and London's Metropolitan Police Service
- Watch videos selected from the SAGE Video collection

22 Globalisation and International Criminal Justice

Matthew Hall

Introduction

This chapter is concerned with globalisation and its impact over recent years on both policy and practice in criminal justice across multiple jurisdictions. The following discussion outlines the broad contours of what is increasingly understood as a network of interconnected processes occurring at the global level. What is clear is that notwithstanding the apparent distinctiveness of the English and Welsh Criminal Justice System (characterised by its strict adherence to court procedure and evidential rules) this system has been heavily influenced in its operation by such global processes, as has the approach to crime and justice policy adopted by the succession of governments responsible for it. We will see below that while such international influence is most overtly felt through the work of transnational organisations such as the European Union and the United Nations – as well as the operation of institutions like the International Criminal Court and the European

Court of Justice – the more profound influences are in fact less overt: constituting macro-legal, -social, -political and -economic trends. In any case, globalisation implies it now makes less sense to demarcate strictly between 'British' and other criminal justice systems. As Roux (2002: 430) argues:

> In this day and age, no country can view itself as an island. All countries, great and small, developed or developing, experience the effects of globalisation.

This chapter begins by outlining what is meant by 'globalisation' and highlights the indeterminate nature of the concept. The chapter then discusses some of the key features of globalisation as it relates to the operation of criminal justice both in England and Wales and further afield. These will be categorised into four groupings:

- crime control, popular punitiveness and international terrorism;
- securitisation and risk management;
- victimisation;
- human rights.

These are broad combinations of features that cannot convey the full intricacies of globalisation in all its complexity, but will serve to highlight its key dimensions in relation to crime and criminal justice. Throughout, this chapter will draw particular attention to the impact of international organisations and institutions on the development of the criminal law in England and Wales. In so doing, the discussion will also examine how the effect of globalisation has frequently been one of extending neo-liberal, punitive ideologies which has increasingly brought states in direct conflict with conceptions of due process and human rights.

Conceptualising 'Globalisation'

Until quite recently, systematic comparison of the approaches taken by different states to crime and criminal justice was relatively uncommon in mainstream criminological literature (Nelken, 2007). When such comparison did take place, it often involved separating different criminal justice systems around the world in to one of two models – 'adversarial' or 'inquisitorial'. Other scholars have adopted a more sophisticated approach, including Cavadino and Dignan's (2007) categorisation of countries according to dominant political ideologies.

The above notwithstanding, the notion of globalisation, as introduced above, implies from the outset that such stark categorisations of different approaches to criminal justice may be becoming less relevant in late modernity. Despite broad agreement over the existence and impacts of globalisation, however, the concept itself remains loose: a rhetorical shorthand for a whole collection of macro-social phenomena. Reinicke (1997) for example criticises the fact that the term 'globalisation' is often used interchangeably with 'interdependence'. Most commonly, the term has been used to convey a sense of transnational interconnectedness between processes previously isolated within individual states. In the criminal justice sphere, the influence of globalisation tends to be illustrated by reference to a recent emphasis in multiple jurisdictions on the management of risk, a rise in what Bottoms (1995) labelled 'punitive populism' (now more often referred to as 'popular punitiveness') and the general swing towards crime control at the expense (it is argued) of due process (see Chapter 4). This is especially so in relation to certain forms of major transnational crime, which are often conceptualised as a threat to *security* (to be discussed below). Examples of such threats include issues of migration, environmental harm, human trafficking, tax evasion and, significantly, international terrorism.

Several commentators have attempted to be more specific about the meaning of globalisation. For Giddens (1990), for example, the key characteristic of globalisation is the decoupling of time and space. Scholte (2000) prefers to think of globalisation as 'deterritorialisation' (p. 46) whilst also emphasising that 'the only consensus about globalisation is that it is contested' (p. 41). Indeed, such is the conceptual confusion surrounding globalisation that Wallerstein (2000: 28) expresses doubts as to the overall utility of the term:

> Personally I think it [globalisation] is meaningless as an analytical concept and serves primarily as a term of political exhortation.

Clearly, it is a vast oversimplification to approach the globalisation of crime and criminal justice simply as 'all' jurisdictions producing identical solutions to given problems. On this point, Nelken (1997) and Muncie (2005) have emphasised that while 'blueprint' solutions to the problems presented by crime and disorder are being proliferated internationally 'the argument that criminal justice is becoming a standardised global product can only be sustained at the very highest level of generality' (Nelken, 1997: 252). As a consequence, such blueprints become adapted to the more local context.

Nevertheless, it is evident that the forces of globalisation have created great synergies between traditionally disparate criminal justice systems. We can also see that criminal justice policy in many different countries has coalesced around common issues, driven by both formal international institutions and broader macro-sociological processes. In the latter case, Boutellier (2000) argues that, in our post-modern society the perspective of *victims* of *suffering* has become the focal point for gauging the moral legitimacy of criminal law. Boutellier calls this the 'victimalization of morality' and it might be taken to explain one of the globalised themes discussed below, the greater attention paid to victims of crime.

Garland (2001) similarly explains the emergence of parallel criminal justice policies in different countries as one aspect of a change in mood concerning criminal justice, reflecting broader social changes witnessed across western jurisdictions. For Garland, this development is grounded in the collapse of support for penal-welfarism in the 1970s, constituted by a loss of faith in the rehabilitative ideal (see Chapter 2). This heralded a 'fundamental disenchantment' with the criminal justice system and a loss of faith in its ability to control crime. Consequently, we have seen a shift in focus away from the causes of crime onto its consequences, including victimisation. Governments faced with such problems redefine what it means to have a successful criminal justice system, by portraying crime as something the state has little control over. The government therefore focuses on the *management* of criminal justice. In the face of growing concern that little can be done about crime, Garland argues that governments deny their failure by turning to ever more punitive policies.

Having examined some of the broad theoretical approaches and explanations applied to 'globalisation', this chapter now examines some of the common features characterising this process that have emerged across jurisdictions.

Crime Control, Popular Punitiveness and International Terrorism

Recent debates on criminal justice matters at both a domestic and international level have become dominated by reference to punitive rhetoric, the 'politicisation' of crime and 'punitive populism' (Bottoms, 1995). These perspectives reflect Garland's (2001) wider notion of an increasingly globalised 'culture of control' and view criminal justice as one of the means by which this control is achieved. As such, several commentators have emphasised the increasingly retributive character of criminal justice policy across many jurisdictions in late modernity and how this seems to betray a prioritisation of the goal of crime (and disorder) control over the requirements of due process (see Downes and Morgan, 2002). Muncie (2005: 36), for example, notes:

> There has been a remarkable correspondence in the nature of juvenile/youth justice reform particularly across many western societies in the past 40 years ... collectively these processes suggest an acceleration of the governance of young people through crime and disorder.

Although in more recent years mainstream political parties in most developed states have established a form of middle ground 'second order consensus' on law and order issues (Downes and Morgan, 2002) it seems that this punitive impetus remains. Many examples can be drawn to illustrate the apparently globalised criminal justice blueprints adopted in England and Wales to punitive ends. These include the introduction (in the Crime (Sentences) Act 1997) of mandatory life sentences for offenders who commit a serious violent or sexual offence for a second time. The inspiration for this measure was the US 'three strikes and you're out' model and its adoption in England and Wales reflected what Cavadino and Dignan (2007: 115) call 'a conscious political decision to "play the law and order card" for all it was worth'. Another telling milestone in the prioritisation of law and order philosophy in England and Wales came with the introduction of a whole raft of measures in the Criminal Justice Act 2003, which challenged traditional due process ideals. These included the admission of hearsay evidence in criminal trials (s.114) and also (in some circumstances) disclosure of previous convictions and other examples of 'misconduct' (s.98) by defendants, even when such misconduct did not amount to criminal activity.

Walklate (2007) has drawn links between the economic aspects of globalisation and the development of such retributive criminal justice policies. In particular, this author notes how globalisation opened criminal justice systems in many countries to economic demands like efficiency, effectiveness, and value for money. Drawing once again on Garland's (2001) discussion, Walklate argues that in response the UK government looked towards the USA for guidance, which has led to the proliferation of popular punitiveness.

The late 1990s to early 2000s has also witnessed what has been described as a 'widening of the net' (see McMahon, 1990) of penal control: whereby an increase in alternative or non-criminal justice solutions to given social problems has arguably brought more individuals under the control of the state. As noted by Muncie (2005), this is particularly apparent in relation to young people and is highlighted by the development in England and Wales of 'Anti-Social Behaviour Orders' (ASBOs) under the Crime and Disorder Act 1998. Although these orders are officially classed as civil actions intended to prevent behaviour that falls below the threshold of criminal activity, breach of these orders is a criminal offence. Consequently, it has been argued that ASBOs effectively impose criminal liability 'through the back door' and in so doing bypass traditional procedural safeguards (Muncie, 2005) (see Chapter 18 for further discussion).

In a similar vein we might also highlight the proliferation of fixed penalty notices under the Criminal Justice and Police Act 2001 which can be issued summarily by officers in cases of *alleged* 'low-level, anti-social and nuisance offending' (Ministry of Justice, 2014; Grace, 2014).

International Terrorism

To illustrate the globalisation process and its impact on how states have embraced crime control ideology, state responses to terrorism are now considered. As noted by Newburn (2007: 921):

> If any one thing captures the way in which issues associated with globalisation have affected the territory in which criminologists have an interest, it is surely the emergence of international terrorism as a key issue of our times.

Terrorism as an international concept exemplifies the notion of transnational (as well as domestic) security – discussed in more detail below. It is therefore not surprising that responses to terrorism, certainly in the global north, appear to follow a particularly globalised blueprint characterised by pro-active policing and an extension of police powers.

In England and Wales we see this development most palpably in the Terrorism Acts of 2000 and 2006. This legislation contains a suite of measures including:

- the proscription of organisations 'concerned in terrorism' (2000, s.3(5)(d));

- crimes and powers of forfeiture in response to the financial support of terrorism (2000, ss.15, 17 and 18);

- offences concerned with preparing to commit acts of terrorism or encouragement of terrorism (2006. s.5);

- other notable adaptations of more standard powers of the police include provision to detain terrorist suspects for up to 14 days (2000, s.41).

Perhaps most significantly, the Acts also contain numerous extensions of standard police powers for use in suspected terrorist cases. Initially, such modifications included, in s.44 of the 2000 Act, provision to stop and search a person without the need to demonstrate a reasonable suspicion that that person was involved in terrorism. This could occur provided a time-limited authorisation had been put in place by a senior officer for a given area. Ultimately, the tensions between crime control and due process requirements engendered by this reform saw the UK taken to the European Court of Human Rights, discussed in Box 22.1.

Box 22.1

In Gillick v. United Kingdom (2010) 50 EHRR 45 the European Court of Human rights ruled that s.44 of the Terrorism Act of 2000 breached Article 8 (and possibly Article 5) of the Convention. Specifically, this was because neither the officer conducting the stop and search nor the authorising officer needed to give any thought under the legislation to whether such searches were 'reasonable', 'necessary' or 'proportional', merely that they were 'expedient' to prevent acts of terrorism.

The s.44 power was reformed in 2011 such that the authorisation to make an order must now be based on 'a reasonable suspicion that an act of terrorism will take place'. The new provisions continue to allow individual officers working under such an authorisation to stop and search without any reasonable suspicion.

Even more controversial was the later introduction of Control Orders under the Prevention of Terrorism Act 2005. The orders themselves were put in place to replace a power of indefinite detention without trial for certain terrorist suspects under the Anti-Terrorism, Crime and Security Act 2001. This power, like that in s.44 above, was deemed incompatible with the ECHR by the UK's own House of Lords in Secretary of State for the Home Department v. AF [2009] UKHL 28. As a replacement, Control Orders sought to place restrictions on the activities of suspected terrorists: over their movements, communications, associations and possession/use of certain items. Effectively the orders also allowed for a form of indefinite house arrest. Significantly for the present discussion, these measures were again based on a US model under the US Patriot Act 2001. Control Orders too received considerable criticism by both the Strasbourg Court (A v. United Kingdom

(2009) 49 EHRR 29) and the House of Lords (Secretary of State for the Home Department v. JJ [2007] UKHL 45) and were replaced in 2011 with a new system of 'Terrorism Prevention and Investigation Measures' notices under the Act of the same name. Although more limited than the old Control Orders, such notices still have significant impacts on those to whom they are issued including restrictions on their residence, travel, electronic communications, associations and place of work.

The above, necessarily brief, overview of the response to terrorism in England and Wales encapsulates a trend seen more broadly in recent years of states finding themselves increasingly in conflict with human rights principles in pursuit of law and order or, as discussed below, increased security. In England and Wales, this conflict has again been exemplified recently by the issuing to universities in March 2015 of government statutory guidance under s.29 of the Counter-Terrorism and Security Act 2015. These indicate that such institutions are now under a statutory duty to have 'due regard to the need to prevent people from being drawn into terrorism' (HM Government, 2015). The extent to which this duty will conflict with the separate requirement of universities to promote freedom of speech has already been a topic of heated debate (Morgan, 2015).

In relation to terrorism, similar packages of reforms have built up in most western jurisdictions over the last 20 years: accelerating dramatically in the wake of large terrorist events such as 9/11 and the London bombings of July 2005. Indeed, it is notable that, up until these events, terrorism itself was not a topic often discussed by criminologists. Increasingly, however, responses to terrorism as an international crime are being held up as the archetypical example of the extremes of popular punitive ideology. Indeed, these policies abound despite considerable evidence and reservations from researchers concerning whether many of these freedom-limiting measures in fact work to prevent terrorist atrocities (Green and Ward, 2004). Globally, this can be viewed as just one aspect of the securitisation of criminal justice matters, to which this chapter will next turn.

Securitisation and the Management of Risk

Underlying the shift in approach towards crime control and popular punitiveness has been a global change in the mindset of states away from merely *responding* to crime and towards the assessment, management and risk of *future* crime and disorder. Loader and Sparks (2007) identify this move to crime *prevention* as an 'anxiety' encountered in the criminological literature:

> The concern here is that, far fr°m rebuilding the capacity of states to deal in effective *and* accountable ways with transnational organised crime, the fears of such crimes are, instead, being 'exploited with a view to cutting normative corners and eroding civil rights'. (p. 90)

'Crime' here is but one part of a wider emphasis on preserving 'security' at the international level. Goodey (2005) describes this trend in terms of 'a continuum of insecurities' in which people conflate fear of crime at the local, neighbourhood level with much wider fears about the supposed global criminal threat of 'outsiders'. This again reflects how globalisation creates an environment in which governments feel obliged to restore falling confidence in the ability of their criminal justice systems to reduce risk. It also helps to explain why 'terrorists', and especially 'international terrorists' serve as the definitive threat to security to be combated by any means necessary. Security is increasingly applied to a diverse range of concerns including environmental and water security (Odorico et al., 2013), data and information security as well as more traditional concepts of economic and territorial security.

As an aspect of this process, much has also been written about the *commodification* of security and its development into a large multinational business. This effectively sees corporations taking on many of the responsibilities traditionally carried out by states in relation to criminal justice. Most obvious of these is the expansion of private prison models, run by global security companies such as G4S and Blackwater, as part of what Lilly and Knepper (1993) term an 'international corrections-commercial complex'. For example, it has been argued that South Africa's 2001 adoption of private prisons was heavily influenced by the lobbying of such corporations, coupled with the wholesale export of Britain's 'Private Finance Initiative' (PFI) model of privatisation (Prison Reform Trust, 1997).

Along with terrorism, the new focus on transnational security has directed attention towards an array of other *transnational* crime problems, including human trafficking and – more controversially – the criminalisation of migration. Indeed, the recognition that such problems to some extent can only be addressed at a level above the nation state has facilitated the creation of international crime-prevention bodies, the most well known of which are INTERPOL and Europol.

The issue of human trafficking in particular highlights the international influence on domestic crime prevention methods across jurisdictions (see Case Study below). On this point, Segrave et al. (2009) note:

> [T]he re-emergence of trafficking in persons on the international agenda coincided with the fall of the Berlin Wall and a period of increased mobility from the Global South to the Global North. (p. 16)

Case Study: Human Trafficking in the Netherlands

Human trafficking, and specifically sex trafficking, has been a particular concern for the government of the Netherlands, where the recent relaxing of laws pertaining to prostitution and brothels has sparked some criticism both within and outside that jurisdiction (US Department of State, 2008). This being the case, the government has been keen to demonstrate its

(Continued)

(Continued)

serious response to human trafficking, and has publicised its prosecutorial successes in the area on a global scale (Associated Press, 2006). In the year 2000, the Netherlands also became the first country in the world to establish an independent National Rapporteur on Human Trafficking. The Netherlands later named human trafficking as one of its main priorities during its Chairmanship of the Organization for Security and Co-operation in Europe (OSCE) in 2003 and also proposed making the subject a major theme at the Economic Forum of the OSCE of the same year (see Everts, 2003).

The UK has been instrumental in promoting the issue of human trafficking in Europe. The year 2002 saw the publication of the EU Proposal for a Council Directive on Short-term Residence Permit Issues in Relation to Victims of Action to Facilitate Illegal Immigration or Trafficking in Human Beings. The following year, the UK Home Office funded the pilot 'Poppy' projects to provide shelter and basic services to its victims. The international chain of causation actually becomes cyclical at this point as following this the UK made human trafficking a priority during its tenure as president of the G8 and the Council of the European Union. This facilitated the adoption of an EU action plan on this issue in December 2005 and the launch of a consultation on a domestic action plan, covering England and Wales and Scotland, in early 2006 (Home Office and Scottish Executive, 2006).

The impetus of governments from all jurisdictions to take action on human trafficking has been very much galvanised by transnational pressures, not least because the US Department of State produces a yearly Trafficking in Persons (TIP) Report in which jurisdictions are rated according to their adherence with US recommendations on the issue. The report is mandated under the key US legislation on human trafficking, the Trafficking Victims' Protection Act of 2000, the stated aim of which is to:

> [R]aise global awareness, to highlight efforts of the international community, and to encourage foreign governments to take effective actions to counter all forms of trafficking in persons (US Department of State, 2008).

Lee (2007) explains that a poor rating in the report can lead to a withdrawal of all non-humanitarian aid from the USA and the denial of funding for anti-trafficking initiatives from international donors and NGOs. Both the Netherlands and New Zealand, along with several Australian jurisdictions, have received criticism in the TIP for their partial decriminalisation of prostitution: which is viewed in the reports as incompatible with a robust policy to fight trafficking. Such criticisms are in fact obligatory for the compilers of the TIP following a US policy decision taken in December 2002 that the US government opposes prostitution and any related activities, including pimping, pandering or maintaining brothels as contributing to the phenomenon of trafficking in persons.

It is clear that human trafficking is an area of policy that has been greatly spurred on by transnational and international pressures. Following the UN protocol, it is also an issue where most jurisdictions have adopted a very similar (globalised) model of legislation to address the problem. Of course, initiatives to fight human trafficking also constitute part of most governments' wider crime prevention strategy: as the links between this activity and other criminal networks (drugs; weapons profits funnelled into other criminal activities; car theft rings; terrorist groups) is well documented (Delport et al., 2007). In these ways, trafficking is construed as an issue of security as well as a humanitarian issue.

Human trafficking is of course a form of forced migration, or at least migration procured through deception. In recent years concern about migration itself has been expressed by many governments and has led to an increasingly punitive stance being taken towards the issue. This is exemplified by the rhetorical reclassification of 'asylum seekers' as 'economic migrants'. Concerns abound on illegal immigrants 'disappearing' within western countries and, as such, most jurisdictions have taken the step of detaining asylum seekers and other 'irregular migrants' in secure facilities pending the outcome of their applications for leave to remain within the country. Reflecting themes already discussed in this chapter, it is notable that many countries have looked to the private sector to provide such facilities. For some humanitarian commentators the consequences of this policy have been profoundly worrying:

> Those persons who are looking for protection or for ways of trying to survive by undeclared work are literally locked up and guarded as if they were criminal prisoners, and very often their living conditions in detention are even worse than living conditions in criminal prisons (Jesuit Refugee Service, 2015).

Such measures have led commentators in the criminological field to criticise what they see as the effective criminalisation of migration in many jurisdictions making up the global north (Zamora-Kapoor and Verea, 2014). Punitive rhetoric concerning so-called 'economic migrants' reached a peak in the UK in the summer of 2015 when (allegedly) large numbers of refugees attempted to enter the UK through the Channel Tunnel from an unofficial camp in Calais. The camp itself – branded 'the Jungle' by the media – was widely portrayed by both media and government sources as a lawless ghetto and a genuine threat to British security. The government's punitive approach towards ('economic') migrants was clear in its statements on the matter:

> Just as we are generous to those who need our help, the UK will be tough on those who flout our immigration rules or abuse our hospitality as a nation (Home Office, 2015).

In response to these concerns, the government introduced the Immigration Bill, which at the time of writing is still working its way through the parliamentary system. In its present form the Bill includes numerous extensions on regulatory and police powers with regard to immigrants including: powers to collect and check fingerprints; powers to search for passports; powers to implement embarkation controls; and powers to examine the status and credibility of migrants seeking to marry or enter into civil partnership. The Bill will also cut the availability of appeal mechanisms for immigrants denied leave to remain and creates a new crime of 'illegal working'.

Recent responses to migration therefore exhibit many of the same features of neo-liberal agendas. These include a move to more punitive measures, a withdrawal from due process and – perhaps more so than any other area – a sense of scapegoating for the failings of the criminal justice process. Clearly, the 'threat' of what David Cameron described in August 2015 as a 'swarm' of migrants entering the UK illegally exhibits classic signs of 'othering' described in the criminological literature (as indeed does the characterisation of the migrant camp as a 'jungle').

The Globalisation of Victim Reform: Tools of Popular Punitiveness?

This chapter has already made mention of 'criminal victimisation' at a number of points in its discussion of globalisation. In particular, we have seen how both Boutellier (2000) and Garland (2001) observe how the neo-liberal trends discussed in the previous sections pre-empt a greater focus on *victims of crime* by all the jurisdictions affected. What I seek to emphasise in this section is how, although well intentioned, much of the attention paid to victims by states in recent years has in fact reinforced and supported the globalised crime control neo-liberal agenda outlined above.

From the outset, the kindling of *policy* interest in victims towards the end of the 1980s was heavily influenced by international institutions. The United Nations was drawing attention to victims (Joutsen, 1989), and various international meetings were hosted on the topic by the Council of Europe and The European Institute for Crime Prevention and Control throughout the 1970s and 1980s (Mawby and Walklate, 1994). A landmark development for all jurisdictions was the introduction of the UN's 1985 Declaration of Basic Principles of Justice for Victims of Crime and Abuse of Power followed, in Europe, by the Council of Europe's Recommendation on the position of the victim in the framework of criminal law and procedure. The 1985 UN Declaration requires victims to be treated with compassion and respect for their dignity. It also requires that crime victims be given access to compensation mechanisms, information about the criminal process, and that the inconvenience caused by this process is kept to a minimum.

Robert Elias argues that victim policies in the USA have from the beginning been used as a tool to facilitate state control:

> [V]ictims may function to bolster state legitimacy, to gain political mileage, and to enhance social control (Elias, 1986: 231).

The argument is that politicians use victims as political ammunition in elections, and as a means of legitimising increasingly punitive measures. Hence, Fattah (1992) characterises the ostensibly pro-victims reform agendas witnessed in most western jurisdictions as 'political and judicial placebos' (p. xii). Garland's (2001) view that victims and the treatment of victims is now the yardstick by which a criminal justice system is legitimised helps explain why governments across multiple jurisdictions appear to be seeking out new kinds of victim to support. In a sense, criminal justice systems now need victims as much as they need convictions and, as such, new types of victim and new types of harm are identified to fill the void left by dropping public confidence in those systems. New victims are also created by statutory changes such as the introduction of crimes of witness intimidation and the expansion of the (legal) concept of rape. The increased attention paid to non-criminal anti-social behaviour (noted above) is another prime example, where the ASBO scheme in England and Wales sets out to support not only the direct victims of said (already non-criminal) acts, but also the *witnesses* of those acts. From the defence perspective this has worrying implications; generally speaking, to expand the concept of victimhood is also to widen the category of 'deviant' acts attracting the attention of the Criminal Justice System. This raises the important concern that expanding the notion of victimhood can serve the ends of retribution and is therefore more properly thought of as part of the growth in popular punitiveness.

South Africa is a stark example of this overlap between victim and crime prevention priorities, principally because the crime rate in that jurisdiction reached crisis point after democratisation (Hall, 2010). Similar examples can be drawn from England and Wales, where in 2002 the Home Office set out its reform agenda in the following terms:

> Our programme of reform is guided by a single clear priority: to rebalance the criminal justice system in favour of the victim and the community so as to reduce crime and bring more offenders to justice (Home Office, 2002: para. 0.3).

In this construction, it would appear that reforms in favour of victims are grounded in the higher set of priorities to reduce crime and prosecute more offenders (see Box 22.2).

In the USA too the need to tackle high crime levels has frequently been cited as one of the driving influences behind the victims' movement (Young, 1997). Indeed, the development of government interest in victims in many western jurisdictions seems to coincide with findings from the first victimisation surveys that crime was more widespread than had previously been thought (David et al., 1990).

Box 22.2

'Rights' for Victims of Crime?

Ashworth (2000) is also concerned with the use of victim policies to further the ends of popular punitiveness. For Ashworth, allowing victims the right to participate in the criminal process presents an unacceptable risk of interfering with the rights of defendants. In particular, Ashworth (2000) argues forcefully that the involvement of victims in sentencing through victim impact statements has been used as a means of legitimising a punitive stance against offenders. Many other examples, common to most western jurisdictions, can be drawn in this regard. These include: limitations on defendant's questioning of (rape) victims; mandatory arrest policies in cases of domestic violence and the anonymisation of witnesses giving evidence in court.

Victim policy in many jurisdictions has also included a strong emphasis on reducing waiting times, delays in court procedure and provision of information. Such goals are often backed by the proliferation of strict targets. In individual jurisdictions, victims have often been presented as the ultimate beneficiaries of these targets although many governments have been similarly upfront in admitting that, to some extent, by helping victims they are helping themselves. The point is made succinctly in the 2002 report of the Victim Services division of the Newfoundland and Labrador Department of Justice (2002: 2):

> While such services assist victims, they also promote greater efficiency and effectiveness in criminal justice system operations.

Similarly, a report from a survey of witness satisfaction carried out in Gauteng, South Africa, notes:

> Underpinning this concern is a belief that witnesses [including victims who are witnesses] should be supported in participating in the criminal justice system, not only because they have needs and concerns, but because this will serve the cause of improving the effectiveness and efficiency of the criminal justice system in its task of bringing offenders to justice (Bruce and Isserow, 2005: 45).

Returning for a moment to the issue of popular punitiveness and its role in shaping victim policies, it is telling that this extract cites increased convictions as the ultimate aim of the exercise. This notwithstanding, the quotation demonstrates the equally important point that the goals of reducing delays and time wastage themselves bring benefit to victims, especially when waiting around to give evidence in court. Indeed, the efficient handling of cases is a pledge made to victims themselves in most of the victims' charters introduced across jurisdictions.

To some extent then, victims have much to gain from increased criminal justice efficiency. Nevertheless, we can express concern that policies claiming to assist victims are in fact not designed around these purposes: not least because, under this construction, efficiency goals often trump the meeting of victims' needs. A clear example came in England and Wales in October 2003 with the introduction of a consultation paper *Securing the Attendance of Witnesses in Court* (Home Office, 2003). This document invited consultation on the proposed resurrection of witness orders to compel witnesses' attendance at Crown Court and summary trials. These proposals illustrate the fact that, although improving victim and witness satisfaction and making them feel more at ease with their role in the Criminal Justice System is presented as the headline policy, these aims are still connected with the less personal goal of getting witnesses (not victims) to come to court and thus improving the operation of the system. This indicates a very different set of priorities from those implied by the pledge made by many governments to put victims and witnesses at the heart of the Criminal Justice System, or the apparent moves from an institutional-based to a citizen-based Criminal Justice System (Tapley, 2002). Instead, it reminds us that governments are still very concerned with efficiency and the associated low public confidence (and escalating costs) in the Criminal Justice System, and that these concerns have a large influence on measures incidentally benefiting victims and witnesses. In this respect, victim policies become another aspect of the globalised move towards a prioritisation of crime control over due process and a dedication to neo-liberal notions of cost-effectiveness witnessed above.

Human Rights, Globalisation and Criminal Justice

It has been demonstrated above that globalised shifts towards law and order policies have frequently come into conflict with the parallel development in late modernity of 'human rights'. This section seeks to emphasise the more general growth of 'rights-language' across jurisdictions and how the proponents of such rights play a large role in the transnational policy networks we have seen drive domestic criminal justice reforms.

Tracing back to the UN's 1948 Universal Declaration of Human Rights, the modern development of 'rights' has been an international and globalised movement for the last 50 years. As a consequence, the 'rights' label has been attached to a diverse range of groups defined in terms of gender, disability, age, cultural origin and sexuality amongst many others. This is mirrored by a growing consensus in the criminological literature that:

> The legitimacy of a justice system lies in its ability to protect human rights. This is typically interpreted as the duty of the justice system to protect the rights (Wemmers, 1998: 73).

This view once again relates the issue to concerns about the perceived legitimacy of criminal justice systems, in accordance with Garland (2001) and Boutellier's (2000) constructions.

As might be expected, the influence of such rights discourse has been longest felt in those countries with a firm history of granting enforceable 'rights' to their citizens. Hence, the first US Victims' Rights Week was organised by the Philadelphia District Attorney in 1975. The notion of victims having 'rights' was also a founding concept for the 1982 Presidential Taskforce on victims, which would go on to recommend an amendment to the US constitution guaranteeing victims' rights. At the state level, Rhode Island became the first state to amend its constitution to guarantee victims' rights in 1986. Similarly, Rock (1990) discusses how the human rights agenda played a key role in the development of victim policies in the Attorney General's Office of Canada in the 1970s and 1980s. In 1988, prompted by the 1985 UN Declaration, all Canadian Ministers of Justice agreed to adopt a uniform policy statement of victims' rights that would be used to guide their legislative and administrative initiatives in the criminal justice sphere.

In Europe, the notion of rights is traditionally a less engrained concept in many jurisdictions (Merrills and Robertson, 2001). This is especially the case in the UK, where there is no written constitution. Consequently, European nations were slower to refer to victims having rights in official policy documents than was generally the case in North America. Indeed this is a relatively recent development, following the proliferation of rights language in a 2001 EU Framework Decision on the standing of victims in criminal proceedings (2001/220) and, before that, the introduction of the European Convention on Human Rights in 1950. Nor was this always a steady development in European jurisdictions. For example, government policy in England and Wales fluctuated from the language of 'rights' in their first Victims' Charter (Home Office, 1990), following the UN in its preamble to the 1985 Declaration, to that of 'service standards' in the second Charter of 1996. Subsequently the rhetoric reverted back to 'rights' after the 2001 EU Framework Decision: by which time Rock (2004) confirms the prevailing influence of the human rights agenda on British victim politics. In the Netherlands too, whilst this jurisdiction (like England and Wales) has a relatively long history of affording services to victims and even procedural involvement in the Criminal Justice System, legislation that expressly referred to the rights of victims was only passed in 2005. The extent to which utilising the *language* of rights is commensurate to the actual *granting* of genuine rights is a question to be left for another forum although the example of the Netherlands clearly demonstrates that the 'rights issue' was influencing domestic policies well before the language was directly applied to victims in government circles.

The creation of globalised victim policies has therefore been intertwined with the development of rights in a broader sense across jurisdictions. We have noted already that to some this is a controversial development, bringing concerns that to afford rights to victims of crime may reduce the rights of defendants (Ashworth, 2000). In another sense however, this can be viewed as one aspect of a general social phenomenon of modernity: whereby rights are being applied to traditionally marginalised or vulnerable groups.

Summary

This chapter has discussed the concept of globalisation and its impact on criminal justice mechanisms in England and Wales, as well as drawing examples from further afield. We have seen how the macro-social, -political, -economic and -legal drivers that make up globalisation have had a definitive effect on domestic justice systems. In recent years, these processes appear to have driven these systems towards an increasingly law and order orientated, punitive ideology. An aspect of this process is the rechristening of traditional social problems as threats to security. We have seen how government responses in England and Wales to issues such as terrorism, migration and anti-social behaviour all reflect these perspectives. Such underlying goals are also evident on closer inspection of many of the policies ostensibly directed at helping victims of crime in their interaction with criminal justice processes. Ultimately for some of the most marginalised or 'othered' groups within society these goals appears to be trumping human rights and due process concerns. This state of affairs points to the continued, and indeed growing, need for criminologists to approach the issues of crime, disorder and justice mechanisms from a critical perspective.

Discussion Questions

1. In what ways has globalisation highlighted (and reinforced) the traditional distinction drawn between crime control and due process in criminal justice systems?

2. Is 'terrorism' a special problem that requires special criminal justice solutions?

3. Which international bodies have had most influence on domestic criminal justice processes in England and Wales and beyond?

4. Are victims of crime being used as tools of popular punitiveness?

5. What is the role of the private sector in the globalisation of criminal justice and security concerns?

Further reading

Bottoms, A. (1995) 'The philosophy and politics of punishment and sentencing', in C. Clark and R. Morgan (eds), *The Politics of Sentencing Reform*. Oxford: Clarendon Press. pp. 17–50.

Bottoms' conceptualisation of criminal justice in late modernity as being dominated by a quest for popular punitiveness has become a core reference for those seeking to understand the development of criminal justice at a wide socio-political level.

Garland, D. (2001) *The Culture of Control: Crime and social order in contemporary society*. Oxford: Oxford University Press.

Similarly, Garland's wide-ranging thesis is considered by many the definitive starting point for understanding the role of globalisation in the development of criminal justice across the developed world (especially in the UK and USA).

Green, P. and Ward, T. (2004) *State Crime*. London: Pluto Press.

Green and Ward offer a clear introduction to the role of the nation state in the committing or facilitation of 'crimes' and 'abuses of power' in the late-modern era.

Lilly, J. and Knepper, P. (1993) 'The corrections-commercial complex', *Crime & Delinquency*, 39: 150–66.

This piece offers a concise discussion of the nature of international security corporations and their role in and influence on domestic policy making across many western jurisdictions.

References

Ashworth, A. (2000) 'Victims' rights, defendants' rights and criminal procedure', in A. Crawford and J. Goodey (eds), *Integrating a Victim Perspective within Criminal Justice: International debates*. Aldershot: Ashgate Dartmouth. pp. 185–204.

Associated Press (2006) 'Six get heavy sentences in Dutch human trafficking trial', *USA Today*, 7 November: 12.

Bottoms, A. (1995) 'The philosophy and politics of punishment and sentencing', in C. Clark and R. Morgan (eds) *The Politics of Sentencing Reform*. Oxford: Clarendon Press. pp. 17–50.

Boutellier, H. (2000) *Crime and Morality: The significance of criminal justice in post-modern culture*. Dordrecht: Kluwer.

Bruce, D. and Isserow, M. (2005) *Putting People First? A survey of witness satisfaction in three gauteng magistrates' Courts*. Johannesburg: Centre for the Study of Violence and Reconciliation.

Cavadino, M. and Dignan, J. (2007) *The Penal System: An introduction*. 4th edn. London: Sage Publications.

David, J., Stubbs, J. and Pegrum, F. (1990) *Services for Victims of Crime in Australia*. Griffith: Criminological Research Council.

Delport, E., Koen, K. and Songololo, M. (2007) *Human Trafficking in South Africa: Root causes and recommendations*. Paris: United Nations Educational, Scientific and Cultural Organisation.

Downes, D. and Morgan, R. (2002) '"The skeletons in the cupboard": The politics of law and order at the turn of the millennium', in M. Maguire, R. Morgan and R. Reiner (eds), *The Oxford Handbook of Criminology*. 3rd edn. Oxford: Oxford University Press. pp. 286–321.

Elias, R. (1986) *The Politics Of Victimization: Victims, victimology and human rights*. New York: Oxford University Press.

Everts, D. (2003) 'Human trafficking: The ruthless trade in human misery', *Brown Journal of World Affairs*, 10: 149–58.

Fattah, E. (1992) 'Victims and victimology: The facts and the rhetoric', in E. Fattah (ed.), *Towards a Critical Victimology*. New York: Macmillan. pp. 29–56.

Garland, D. (2001) *The Culture of Control: Crime and social order in contemporary society*. Oxford: Oxford University Press.

Giddens, A. (1990) *The Consequences of Modernity*. Cambridge: Polity.

Goodey, J. (2005) *Victims and Victimology: Research, policy and practice*. Edinburgh: Pearson.

Grace, S. (2014) 'Swift, simple, effective justice? Identifying the aims of penalty notices for disorder and whether these have been realised in practice', *Howard Journal of Criminal Justice*, 53 (1): 69–82.

Green, P. and Ward, T. (2004) *State Crime*. London: Pluto Press.

Hall, M. (2010) *Victims and Policy Making: A comparative perspective*. Cullompton: Willan Publishing.

HM Government (2015) *Revised Prevent Duty Guidance for England and Wales: Guidance for specified authorities in England and Wales on the duty in the Counter-Terrorism and Security Act 2015 to have due regard to the need to prevent people from being drawn into terrorism*. London: HM Government.

Home Office (1990) *Victims' Charter: A statement of the rights of victims*. London: UK Home Office.

Home Office (2002) *Justice for All*, Cm 5563. London: The Stationery Office.

Home Office (2003) *Securing the Attendance of Victims in Court: A consultation paper*. London: HMSO.

Home Office (2015) *Home Secretary Statement on Illegal Immigration in Calais* [online]. Available at: www.gov.uk/government/speeches/home-secretary-statement-on-illegal-immigration-in-calais [accessed 27 October 2015].

Home Office and Scottish Executive (2006) *Tackling Human Trafficking – Consultation on Proposals for a UK Action Plan*. London: HMSO.

Jesuit Refugee Service (2015) *Detention in Europe* [online]. Available at: www.detention-in-europe.org/ [accessed 27 October 2015].

Joutsen, M. (1989) 'Foreword', in HEUNI, *The Role of the Victim of Crime in European Criminal Justice System*. Helsinki: HEUNI.

Lee, M. (2007) *Human Trafficking*. Cullompton: Willan Publishing.

Lilly, J. and Knepper, P. (1993) 'The corrections-commercial complex', *Crime & Delinquency*, 39: 150–66.

Loader, I. and Sparks, R. (2007) 'Contemporary landscapes of crime, order and control: Governance, risk and globalization', in M. Maguire, R. Morgan and R. Reiner (eds), *The Oxford Handbook of Criminology*. 3rd edn. Oxford: Oxford University Press. pp. 78–101.

Mawby, R. and Walklate, S. (1994) *Critical Victimology*, Thousand Oaks: Sage Publications.

McMahon, M. (1990) '"Net-widening": Vagaries in the use of the concept', *British Journal of Criminology*, 30 (2): 121–49.

Merrills, J. and Robertson, A. (2001) *Human Rights in Europe*. Manchester: Manchester University Press.

Ministry of Justice (2014) *Penalty Notices for Disorder (PNDs)*. London: Ministry of Justice.

Morgan, J. (2015) *Universities Must Assess Risk of Students Becoming Terrorists, Says Home Office* [online]. Available at: www.timeshighereducation.com/news/universities-must-assess-risk-of-students-becoming-terrorists-says-home-office/2019067.article [accessed 27 October 2015].

Muncie, J. (2005) 'The globalization of crime control – The case of youth and juvenile justice neo-liberalism, policy convergence and international conventions', *Theoretical Criminology*, 9 (1): 35–64.

Nelken, D. (1997) 'The globalization of crime and criminal justice: Prospects and problems', *Current Legal Problems*, 50: 251–77.

Nelken, D. (2007) 'Comparing criminal justice', in M. Maguire, R. Morgan and R. Reiner (eds), *The Oxford Handbook of Criminology*. 4th edn. Oxford: Oxford University Press. pp. 139–58.

Newburn, T. (2007) *Criminology*. 2nd edn. Abingdon: Routledge.

Newfoundland and Labrador Department of Justice (2002) *Annual Report of Victims Services for the Period April 1, 2001–March 31, 2002*. St John's: Newfoundland Department of Justice.

Odorico, P., Bhattachan, A., Davis, K., Ravi, S. and Runyan, C. (2013) 'Global desertification: Drivers and feedbacks', *Advances in Water Resources*, 51: 326–44.

Prison Reform Trust (1997) 'Privatisation under way in South Africa', *Prison Privatisation Report International*, 10: 1.

Reinicke, W. (1997) 'Global public policy', *Foreign Affairs*, 76: 127–51.

Rock, P. (1990) *Helping Victims of Crime: The Home Office and the rise of victim support in England and Wales*. Oxford: Oxford University Press.

Rock, P. (2004) *Constructing Victims' Rights: The Home Office, New Labour and victims*. Oxford: Clarendon Press.

Roux, N. (2002) 'Public policy-making and policy analysis in South Africa amidst transformation, change and globalisation: Views on participants and role players in the policy analytic procedure', *Journal of Public Administration*, 37: 418–37.

Scholte, J. (2000) *Globalization: A critical introduction*. London: Macmillan.

Segrave, M., Milivojevic, S. and Pickering, S. (2009) *Sex Trafficking: International context and response*. Cullompton: Willan Publishing.

Tapley, J. (2002) *From Good Citizen to Deserving Client. Relationships between victims and the state using citizenship as the conceptualizing tool*. Southampton: University of Southampton.

US Department of State (2008) *Trafficking in Persons Report 2008*. Washington: Department of State.

Walklate, S. (2007) *Imagining the Victim of Crime*. Maidenhead: Open University Press.

Wallerstein, I. (2000) 'From sociology to historical social science: Prospects and obstacles', *British Journal of Sociology*, 51: 25–35.

Wemmers, J.-A. (1998) 'Procedural justice and Dutch victim policy', *Law & Policy*, 20: 57–76.

Young, M. (1997) 'Victim rights and services: A modern saga', in R. Davis, A. Lurigio and W. Skogan (eds), *Victims of Crime*. 2nd edn. Thousand Oaks: Sage Publications. pp. 194–210.

Zamora-Kapoor, A. and Verea, M. (2014) 'Public attitudes toward immigration in turbulent times', *Migration Studies*, 2 (2): 131–4.

Check out the Companion Website

Want to know more about this chapter? Review what you have been learning by visiting: **https://study.sagepub.com/harding**

- Practice with essay questions
- Test yourself with multiple-choice questions
- Listen to a series of podcasts featuring Neil of Northumbria Police and London's Metropolitan Police Service
- Watch videos selected from the SAGE Video collection

23   Criminal Justice Futures

George Mair, Jamie Harding, Pamela Davies

Seeking to predict the future of criminal justice is, of course, a task that is full of uncertainties and one where criminology has a poor track record, as noted by Mike Hough in Chapter 9. Sparks (2013: 149) notes that the interest of politicians and the public in penal policy 'comes in flurries as major stories break and scandals and cause celebres are played out'. History is littered with incidents – for example, high-profile prison escapes of the 1960s, the murder of James Bulger in 1993, the riots of 2011 – that have shocked the public and that governments have felt obliged to respond to, sometimes with measures that have a long term impact (e.g. the creation of four categories of prisoner) and sometimes with those that appear to have little impact beyond the immediate crisis (e.g. harsh sentences for those involved in the riots).

A second factor that makes prediction difficult is the impact of personalities: Chapter 2 highlighted the change to the direction of prisons policy that appeared to arise from Chris Grayling's replacement as Justice Secretary by Michael Gove; a change of direction that was supported in a major speech by David Cameron. Since that time, as a result of the referendum vote in favour of leaving the European Union, David Cameron has resigned as Prime Minister, to be replaced by Theresa May. Michael Gove is no longer Justice Secretary; his replacement is Elizabeth Truss. And Mrs May has been replaced as Home Secretary by Amber Rudd. So far, the government has been busy with the issues associated with Brexit and there has been little movement on the criminal justice front. However, leaving the EU is likely to have consequences for criminal justice; will we be involved in Europol or the European Arrest Warrant, for example (see below).

A great deal of government policy is reactive rather than proactive and this also makes prediction difficult. It is worth noting that no criminologists predicted the sustained drop in crime that has been a marked feature of the penal landscape for around 20 years, and there is little agreement about the reasons that lie behind this. Indeed, it is likely that there will be new debates about whether there really has been a decrease in crime given the recent CSEW data on cybercrime (see Chapter 3).

Although Cavadino and Dignan (2006: 62) correctly warn that criminal justice policy can change direction very quickly and quite irrationally, for the most part change is gradual and incremental and sudden u-turns are the exception. In what follows we note the main issues that will – probably – go to shape criminal justice in the next 5 to 10 years. It should be emphasised that many of these issues – which we discuss separately – are, in fact, linked closely with each other. They are in no particular order except that the more macro issues are considered first.

- Given what we know about the present government's economic policy, which is its overriding concern, we can be fairly certain that austerity will be the most significant factor for criminal justice (as it will be for many other policy areas), despite some speculation that the worst of austerity is behind us. The various criminal justice agencies have already been hit hard by cost-cutting initiatives and it is likely that demands for savings will continue. Thus criminal justice agencies will be under pressure to make savings and to provide ever increasing evidence of value for money. Economy, efficiency and effectiveness (the three Es) was a mantra of the Thatcher administrations in the 1980s; this morphed into what became known under the Labour governments of 1997–2010 as 'New Public Management' (Martin, 2002) and has continued with the Coalition and now the Conservative governments' commitment to reducing public expenditure. The continuing fall in crime rates is currently a useful justification for reduced expenditure on criminal justice, although it is interesting to speculate what would happen if crime were to start to rise – would this lead to increased expenditure or would it be seen as a sign of inefficiency? Austerity is related directly or indirectly to each of the issues below.

- Competition, marketisation and privatisation all arise from the same underlying belief – that private sector provision is more efficient, effective and economic than a state monopoly. This belief has been a driver in criminal justice since the first prison was privatised in 1992 and it has been influential since. The fragmentation of policing and the introduction of private sector provision in prisons and offender management are measures that are unlikely to be reversed: while Labour were critical of the creation of Community Rehabilitation Companies while in opposition, history would suggest that they are unlikely to reverse this measure if/when they return to power. As Tim Newburn notes in Chapter 8, youth justice has been identified as another area where the government wishes to spread competitive principles.

- The globalisation of criminal justice is likely to continue as the risks presented by terrorism and cybercrime increase. At the time of writing, the importance of international cooperation to tackle terrorism has been highlighted by the close links between terrorist attacks in Paris (in November 2015) and in Brussels (in March 2016). The frustrations expressed by police forces at their ability to effectively tackle cybercrime, where the perpetrator and victim are often in different continents, were recently reflected by Metropolitan Police Commissioner Sir Bernard Hogan-Howe, who suggested that banks should not refund customers for online fraud arising from inadequate online security (*Guardian*, 24 March 2016).

- Intimately related to globalisation are the themes of immigration and asylum seekers and how these different issues are regularly conflated and are increasingly perceived as criminal justice problems. At the time of writing immigrants are being increasingly labelled as criminals as they are implicated in debates about the UK's membership of the EU. Simply ensuring that immigrants are treated fairly by the criminal justice agencies and that adequate translation services are available to them are significant problems, and if numbers grow and/or perceptions of their criminality develop, such problems will be exacerbated.

- Although it is difficult to disentangle what might be 'true' from the claims and counter-claims being bandied around by both sides in the arguments about continued membership of the EU, there is little doubt that the decision that has been made following the 23 June 2016 referendum will have an impact upon criminal justice. How far judicial cooperation in criminal matters, the European arrest warrant, Eurojust and Europol might continue if the UK left the EU, or is a significant question that will only become clear over time.

- Will crime continue to fall, will it stabilise, or will it begin to rise? As crime is the immediate driver for criminal justice this question is critical. If it continues to fall (despite the sudden introduction of cybercrime to the crime figures) then we could see fewer magistrates' courts, with the ideal of local justice becoming less significant, and police numbers could be cut further, with potential implications for public confidence. If crime starts to rise then there will be demands for increased spending and greater effectiveness, and the increasingly punitive sentencing that has been seen for at least 20 years may become even harsher.

- Technology is likely to impact further on all of the traditional criminal justice agencies. The police are moving towards using hand-held tablets to record stops and they are also developing an interest in body-cameras, which could have a major effect upon interactions with the public and make the resolution of most complaints easier. Courts are already making use of CCTV to avoid a prisoner having to travel from his/her cell to court for a continued remand in custody; and the Civil Justice Council has recently floated an internet-based dispute resolution system for claims up to £25,000, based upon eBay's online dispute resolution model. This approach could spread to the working of the criminal courts for less serious cases. Prisons making use of electronic locking systems to reduce the number of frontline staff, low-level offenders reporting virtually to probation services or Community Rehabilitation Companies, the extension of electronic monitoring via tags and the national roll out of sobriety tags (after a successful pilot in some London boroughs, *Guardian*, 27 July 2015) are all measures that are easy to envisage developing further, which would increase the move towards a surveillance society.

- The long struggle to achieve greater equality and a greater recognition of diversity issues within criminal justice agencies is set to continue. In the year to the writing of this chapter, Her Majesty's Inspectorate of Constabulary have published a report criticising police forces for continuing difficulties associated with the stopping and searching of men from minority ethnic groups (HMIC, 2015), a review of custody policy for transgender prisoners has been announced (*Guardian*, 1 December 2015) and the Prime Minister asked David Lammy MP to investigate evidence of possible bias against defendants from minority ethnic groups in the areas of charges, courts, prisons and rehabilitation (Prime Minister's Office, 2016). So agencies will need to continue to seek to address the diversity issues that were all but invisible in criminal justice until the Scarman report of 1981, including the class bias that Chapter 6 indicated was increasingly evident.

- An area that has been shamefully neglected in the past, but which criminal justice agencies are likely to have to pay increasing attention to, is the needs of victims, particularly women and children. The Home Secretary made Violence Against Women and Girls a policy priority (HM Government, 2016) and reports by Inspectorates have increased pressure on both the Crown Prosecution Service (HM Crown Prosecution Service, 2016) and police forces (*Guardian*, 8 October 2014) to improve their services to victims of rape. Although, of course, women are not exclusively the victims of domestic violence or rape, these policy developments suggest that the importance of crimes against them will continue to increase within criminal justice. Similarly crimes against children have taken on a high profile within criminal justice following the death of Jimmy Savile, the resulting Operation Yewtree – which is the highest profile of a number of investigations into child sexual abuse (*Guardian*, 4 August 2015) – and revelations about historic sex abuse in institutions such as churches (Church of England, 2016). Findings of the inadequate response of agencies to Savile's victims (Gray and Watt, 2013) have been supplemented by criticisms in other cases involving children: in February 2016 the Independent Police Complaints Commission reported that it was involved in no fewer than 55 investigations connected to child sexual abuse in Rotherham, from a failure to act on reported child sexual exploitation to corruption by police officers (IPCC, 2016). A recent report for the Office of the Children's Commissioner (OCC, 2015: 4) suggested that only one in eight children who are victims of sexual abuse come to the attention of statutory agencies and that, even when children tell someone about the abuse, this often does not lead to it stopping (OCC, 2015: 11). The weight of evidence in this area, together with extensive media coverage, suggests that agency responses to the sexual abuse of children will be a focus of attention for some time. One likely impact is that prosecutions for historic sex offences are likely to continue at their current level, meaning that the number of older men who are imprisoned will continue to increase.

- Structural change may be inevitable. Unlike probation services, the 21 Community Rehabilitation Companies do not share boundaries with police forces and it is likely that police forces themselves will face pressure to re-organise into large units to save money. Instead of allowing this to happen piecemeal and without any central planning, the government may step in to direct the process – or indeed move to a regional model. It may even be possible to think about a National Police Service, given the existence of the National Crime Agency and the College of Policing, and the creation of one police force for all of Scotland.

- Finally, there are a number of other issues that will impact to some extent upon criminal justice in the future but where the specific impact is open to question. (1) Will payment by results (PbR) change the way work with offenders is carried out? PbR is now enshrined as a model for prison and probation work; although only a small proportion of the total payment is currently dependent upon results, this could change with time. Possible consequences are agencies becoming more risk averse, some providers being forced out and an effective monopoly being created or (as the government hopes) increased competition and greater effectiveness. (2) What will be the impact of the aging prison population? There are around 12,000 inmates aged 50 and over (14 per cent of the prison population); more than 2,000 in this age group are serving life sentences. Those aged 60 and above are the fastest growing age group in prisons and prisons will need to respond to their needs – healthcare alone will be a significant issue. (3) How are Community Rehabilitation Companies going to work? Within weeks of them starting work on 1 February 2015, Sodexo – the largest provider with six CRCs – was planning to make redundancies and introduce biometric reporting using cash-machine-style kiosks (*Guardian*, 3 March 2015). At least one other CRC provider (Working Links) has also been reported as planning job cuts (*Independent*, 1 April 2016). This does not bode well barely a year into the new arrangements. (4) What changes will be made to non-custodial disposals for offenders? A new system of out-of-court disposals for adults has recently completed a 12-month trial in three police forces (the results are awaited) but, if this is rolled out nationally, there will be an end to the present system of six alternatives, with the proposed new approach of community resolution and suspended prosecution being rather more punitive (House of Commons, 2015). There may also be changes in financial penalties as the Justice Secretary announced a wide-ranging review of court-ordered financial impositions on offenders in December 2015. (5) Will the court system become more flexible and more responsive to specific needs? Despite closing the North Liverpool Community Justice Centre a few years ago, the Justice Secretary expressed interest in community justice and it is possible that a new generation of community justice courts will emerge – although how much funding might be available for such an initiative is another matter. Indeed, there is potential for more specialist courts to emerge; there are already a handful of domestic violence courts and drug courts. If there are enough offences to support their existence and certain magistrates become highly experienced in these specific types of crime, this could be a very positive step. (6) Will Police and Crime Commissioners (PCCs) be accepted as a permanent part of criminal justice? Low turnout was a major feature of the first set of elections of PCCs; it remains to be seen whether interest in their role will increase, whether this role will expand and whether measures will be taken to ensure greater consistency of practice. The potential for PCCs to play a significant role in holding the police to account and in the provision of prison and probation services is considerable. Their role could also widen to take on the commissioning of services for victims and this too would be a significant development.

Although it might be pleasing from a narrative point of view to end this book with a neat summation of the future direction of criminal justice, this would be a foolish undertaking. The factors that we have outlined are all likely – in one way or another – to have an impact upon criminal justice agencies and how justice is delivered, but just how that impact works in practice is impossible to predict. Criminal justice will continue to be caught in the tension between fragmentation and centralisation, it is likely to carry on with its punitive trajectory, and demands for (cost-)effective work will not diminish. Even if crime were to continue to fall (and just how far could it fall?), the future is unlikely to bring any easing of the pressures faced by those who work to bring about criminal justice.

——————— **References** ———————

Cavadino, M. and Dignan, J. (2006) *Penal Systems: A comparative approach*. London: Sage.

Church of England (2016) *Elliott Review Findings, News Release, 15.3.2016*. Available at: www.churchofengland.org/media-centre/news/2016/03/digest-reports-on-elliott-review-findings.aspx (accessed 2 September 2016).

Gray, D. and Watt, P. (2013) *Giving Victims a Voice*. London: National Society for the Prevention of Cruelty to Children and Metropolitan Police. Available at: www.nspcc.org.uk/globalassets/documents/research-reports/yewtree-report-giving-victims-voice-jimmy-savile.pdf (accessed 2 September 2016).

HM Crown Prosecution Service Inspectorate (2016) *Thematic Review of the CPS Rape and Serious Sexual Offences Units*. Available at: www.justiceinspectorates.gov.uk/hmcpsi/inspections/thematic-review-of-the-cps-rape-and-serious-sexual-offences-units/ (accessed 2 September 2016).

HM Government (2016) *Ending Violence against Women and Girls Strategy 2016–2020*. Available at: www.gov.uk/government/uploads/system/uploads/attachment_data/file/505961/VAWG_Strategy_2016-2020.pdf (accessed 2 September 2016).

HM Inspectorate of Constabulary (2015) *Stop and Search Powers 2: Are the police using them effectively and fairly?* Available at: www.justiceinspectorates.gov.uk/hmic/publications/stop-and-search-powers-2-are-the-police-using-them-effectively-and-fairly/ (accessed 2 September 2016).

House of Commons (2015) *Home Affairs – Fourteenth report out of court disposals*. Available at: www.publications.parliament.uk/pa/cm201415/cmselect/cmhaff/799/79902.htm (accessed 2 September 2016).

Independent Police Complaints Commission (2016) *IPCC Update on Investigations into How South Yorkshire Police Handled Reported Child Sexual Exploitation in Rotherham*. Available at: www.ipcc.gov.uk/news/ipcc-update-investigations-how-south-yorkshire-police-handled-reported-child-sexual (accessed 2 September 2016).

Martin, S. (2002) 'Best value: New public management or new direction?' in S.P. Osborne and K. McLaughlin (eds), *New Public Management: Current trends and future prospects*. London: Routledge. pp. 129–40.

Office of the Children's Commissioner (2015) *Protecting Children from Harm: Summary*. Available at: www.childrenscommissioner.gov.uk/sites/default/files/publications/ Protecting%20children%20from%20harm%20-%20executive%20summary_0.pdf (accessed 2 September 2016).

Prime Minister's Office (2016) *Review of Racial Bias and BAME Representation in Criminal Justice System Announced, Press Release*. Available at: www.gov.uk/government/news/ review-of-racial-bias-and-bame-representation-in-criminal-justice-system-announced (accessed 2 September 2016).

Sparks, R. (2013) 'States of insecurity: Punishment, populism and contemporary political culture' in S. McConville (ed.), *The Use of Punishment*. Abingdon: Taylor & Francis, pp. 149–74.

Check out the Companion Website

Want to know more about this chapter? Review what you have been learning by visiting: **https://study.sagepub.com/harding**

- Practice with essay questions
- Test yourself with multiple-choice questions
- Listen to a series of podcasts featuring Neil of Northumbria Police and London's Metropolitan Police Service
- Watch videos selected from the SAGE Video collection

Glossary

Adversarial an adversarial system of justice refers to a legal system characterised by a trial where the prosecution and defence are in opposition to one another in the search for justice. An adversarial system is a feature of countries that follow the common law. See **Inquisitorial**.

Attrition refers to the 'drop out' of cases from the Criminal Justice System.

Austerity and 'austerity measures' are not new terms but have recently entered the criminal justice vocabulary because of the impacts on crime, its control and support for victims. Following the global recession and the European sovereign debt crisis, and with debt levels unacceptably high, dramatic budget cuts have been imposed in the public, voluntary and private sectors cutting and reducing spending.

College of Policing the professional body for policing.

Community safety any action taken by an individual or agency to reduce the likelihood of a wide range of harms occurring; this term is associated with multi-agency partnerships.

Community sentence in this book, any non-custodial sentence passed by the courts; can also be used to refer to a sentence of the courts that combines punishment with activities carried out in the community.

Complainant the person or institution making a formal accusation. The prosecuting witness sometimes referred to in legal terms as the plaintiff.

Crime and Disorder Reduction Partnerships the previous name for what are now known as Community Safety Partnerships, consisting of key agencies (police, local authorities, fire authorities and clinical commissioning groups) with the responsibility to tackle local crime and disorder by working with other organisations.

Crime prevention any action taken by an individual or agency to reduce the likelihood of crime occurring.

Criminogenic leading to crime or criminality. For offenders, a distinction is often made between criminogenic needs (which increase the risk of crime if they remain unmet) and other needs.

Crown Court the criminal court that deals with serious offences and appeals referred from the magistrates' courts.

Cybercrime crimes committed with the assistance of, or by means of, a range of digital technologies.

Decarceration is the opposite of incarceration and refers to a policy of reducing either the number of persons imprisoned or the rate of imprisonment in a given jurisdiction. It may also be described as the process of removing people from institutions such as prisons or mental hospitals.

Desistance a term used to measure the effectiveness of criminal justice interventions. Desistance as applied to prison and probation service outcomes implies total cessation; however, if an offender commits crime less frequently, or commits less serious offences, they might also be regarded as being on a desistance pathway.

Detection rate the proportion of offences that are 'cleared up' by the police, either resulting in a sanction or a non-sanction.

Determinate sentence a determinate sentence is a sentence with a fixed term to its length. This is in contrast to a non-determinate or indeterminate sentence. See **Indeterminate sentence**.

Deterrence the use of punishment as a threat to discourage – or deter – people from offending or from reoffending.

District judges full time, salaried members of the judiciary who work in the magistrates' court, mainly hearing criminal cases, youth cases and some civil proceedings.

Diversion channelling offenders away from formal legal proceedings. This term is most often used in relation to young people, where contact with formal criminal justice processes is considered to carry the risk of embedding them into an offending lifestyle.

Divisional court a High Court, sitting with at least two judges, that hears some criminal cases and some judicial review cases.

Doli incapax means someone is incapable of criminal intention or malice and in England and Wales a child under 10 is said to be *doli incapax*, that is, incapable of crime.

Due process a system of checks and balances and a principle which ensures fairness and justice by balancing different parties' rights.

Either-way offence a case that can be tried in either the magistrates' courts or the Crown Court. A magistrates' court will refer such an offence to be tried in the Crown Court if it believes its own powers may be insufficient to impose an appropriate sentence.

False testimony giving a false oath in judicial proceedings. A witness is guilty of perjury if they knowingly give false testimony. See **Perjury**.

Fine a monetary charge imposed on individuals who have been convicted of a crime or lesser offence.

First time entrant (FTE) an FTE is a child who receives a formal youth justice disposal for the first time.

Hate crime a crime, typically involving violence, where the perpetrator's hostility is based on hostility or prejudice to an identifiable group of people, e.g. gay people or members of specific ethnic groups.

Home Office the government department responsible for immigration and passports, drugs policy, crime policy, counter-terrorism and policing.

Human rights basic, universal, moral and sometimes legal rights that denote how you can be expected to be treated as a person.

Ideal victim a term coined by Christie (1986 – see Chapter 20 References) to denote the major attributes belonging to a model crime victim. It is a contentious term suggesting an 'innocent', victim where the victim has played no part in their own victimisation and fits the stereotyped view of a victim who deserves help. Such victims need to be vulnerable, innocent, incapable of fighting back against an assailant, previously unacquainted with the offender, with no offending history of their own.

Indeterminate sentence an indeterminate sentence is a sentence with no fixed term where imprisonment is for reasons of public protection (IPP) or is a life sentence. See **Determinate sentence**.

Indictable only offence a serious offence that can only be tried in the Crown Court.

Inquisitorial an inquisitorial system of justice refers to a legal system characterised by a trial where the method for exposing evidence in court is to discover the facts in the search for justice. An inquisitorial system is typical feature in countries that base their legal systems on civil or Roman law.

Judicial review a procedure by which a court can review an action taken by a public body and secure a declaration, order, or award.

Lay magistrate a volunteer judicial office holder, not necessarily with legal training or qualifications, who serves in the magistrates' courts.

Legal rights rights that are enshrined within the rules of a legal system and that are bestowed onto a person, and are guaranteed by, a legal system.

MacPherson Report the report, published in 1999, into the investigation of the murder of Stephen Lawrence, which argued that the Metropolitan Police Service was institutionally racist.

Magistrates' courts these deal with civil matters and less serious criminal offences, where the maximum penalty that can be imposed is six months' imprisonment.

Multi-agency working different services, agencies and teams of professionals and other practitioners working together to provide services.

Neighbourhood policing the police working with local residents and other agencies to tackle issues that are of concern locally.

Neo-liberal a concept drawn from political-economic thinking which, used in the context of criminal justice, is used to be critical about the market-based philosophies and influences over crime control. Neo-liberalism focuses on the customers of justice.

Net-widening a term often used in analyses of the unintended effects of providing alternatives to imprisonment such as community corrections or diversion programmes to direct offenders away from court.

Out of court disposal methods of dealing with less serious offences that can be administered locally without the need to go to court.

Parole is the term used to refer to the status whereby a prisoner is released from prison on licence by the Parole Board while his or her sentence is still ongoing.

Partnership working see **Multi-agency working**.

Perjury giving false oath in judicial proceedings. A witness is guilty of perjury if they knowingly give false testimony. See **False testimony**.

Policing by consent an approach to policing that draws its power from the common consent of the public, although not all individuals, ensuring public approval and cooperation.

Primary crime prevention any action that has the aim of preventing crime by making it more difficult or less rewarding to commit, e.g. fitting window locks or removing valuables from cars.

Prison estate the collective term for all prison buildings in England and Wales.

Prison regime the phrase usually means how a prison operates. The timetable for the day, and the way the officers manage people and procedures could all come under the phrase prison regime.

Prosecutor a lawyer who, in a court case, accuses a person of a crime and tries to prove that they are guilty.

Punitive ideologies ideologies that show a leaning towards retribution and incarceration as opposed to reform and rehabilitation in conceptualisations and practical applications of punishment.

Recidivism the term often used instead of reoffending. Recidivism is the proven rate of reoffending.

Reconviction reconvictions are used to determine reconviction rates, which are often used synonymously with reoffending rates, although they are (theoretically at least) different. Such measures help us to know how effective we are in reducing criminal reoffending and how well we are managing and supporting those that enter the Criminal Justice System.

Reoffending rate this is a measure used to gauge the effectiveness of criminal justice interventions. Reoffending is often used interchangeably with the term recidivism.

Resettlement this term is used to capture the transition prisoners endure on release from prison and in their status passage from prisoner to ex-prisoner. Resettlement work helps them 'resettle' when returning to the community after release from prison. Such activities can involve help with housing or education, training and employment.

Responsibilisation a term that refers to the process where we are rendered individually responsible for a task that previously would have been the duty of another or would not have been recognised as a responsibility at all. Usually refers to the avoidance or displacing of a duty or responsibility – such as the responsibility for crime, disorder and victimisation – from a state agency on to other parties.

Restitution used in connection with community sanctions and refers to the notion of paying something back to the victim or the community.

Restorative justice a form of justice that concentrates on repairing the harm caused by criminal behaviour.

Retributive justice a form of justice that is wedded to the principle that people are deserving of proportionate punishment.

Scarman Report the report into the Brixton disorders of 1981 that highlighted the breakdown of relationships between the police and the African-Caribbean community as a key cause.

Secondary crime prevention working with individuals who are believed to be 'at risk' of committing crime to seek to prevent this from happening.

Secondary victimisation this can occur as part of the criminal justice experience. Secondary victimisation exacerbates feelings of victimisation and results from the insensitive treatment of victims of crime – often inadvertently – by the Criminal Justice System (or by friends and acquaintances). Barristers, jurors, police officers may be a cause of secondary victimisation.

Secure Children's Home (SCH) childcare establishments that may also accommodate children from the age of 10, deprived of their liberty on welfare grounds and assessed as particularly vulnerable.

Secure Training Centre (STC) secure, privately managed, custodial institutions that hold boys and girls aged 12–17 years.

Sentence plan the document agreed between an offender and their offender manager about what needs to be done during a sentence. This might include taking part in offending behaviour or drug rehabilitation programmes

Situational crime prevention measures that seek to influence an offender's decision or ability to commit crimes at specific times and places.

Slop out Before there was in-cell sanitation – that is a toilet – each prisoner had to remove the bucket of human waste from their cell in a process called slopping out. It was outlawed in 1996, and all cells now have to have their own toilets.

Social crime prevention measure that seeks to influence the social causes of crime rather than reducing the opportunities for crime.

Social exclusion a process by which individuals and groups are denied access to rights, opportunities and resources that are normally available to other individuals and groups.

Stakeholder an individual or organisation affected by an organisation, strategy or project.

Summary-only offence an offence that is tried only in the magistrates' courts, where the maximum sentence is six-months' imprisonment.

Supervision in criminal justice terms, supervision is related to the role of the probation service or to Community Rehabilitation Companies. Supervision is one of a range of options open to courts when sentencing individuals found guilty of criminal behaviour. Such supervision can also take place when an offender leaves prison.

Survivor this term, as opposed to that of victim, acknowledges victims' agency, and active resistance. This label challenges the notion of victim passivity, and in particular it is often used by feminists in connection with women's resistance to their apparent structural powerlessness and potential victimisation.

Tariff is the term used to describe the mandatory period of time a prisoner, serving a life or indeterminate sentence, must serve in custody prior to being considered for release.

Tertiary crime prevention measures targeted at those who have committed crime with the aim of preventing further offending.

Third sector the part of society consisting of organisations that are not part of government and not run for profit, including charities, voluntary and community groups, and cooperatives.

Treatment programmes usually a term to mean psychologically informed programmes to address offending behaviour, but it can also mean programmes to deal with drug or alcohol use, or mental ill health.

Victim in the most generalised sense this term is used to refer to people who may have suffered misfortune. A victim of crime refers to someone having been criminally victimised (see also discussion in Chapter 20).

Volumetric control the volume of personal belongings a prisoner can hold in their cell. The volume is equivalent to just under a cubic meter.

Welfarist variously refers to attitudes, practices and policies that have a social welfare orientation to them. In the criminal justice context 'welfarist' refers to a range of responsibilities that belong, or belonged, to the state.

Witness someone who has personal knowledge through having seen, heard, or experienced an accident, event or crime.

Young Offender Institution (YOI) secure accommodation for the incarceration of boys aged 15–17 years.

Youth justice the approach to policies and systems of justice that deals with those between the ages of 12 and 17 who get into trouble with the law.

Index